STUDIES IN PUBLIC COMMUNICATION

A. WILLIAM BLUEM, GENERAL EDITOR

CONGRESS
AND THE
NEWS MEDIA

STUDIES IN PUBLIC COMMUNICATION

MASS MEDIA AND COMMUNICATION
Edited by Charles S. Steinberg

THE LANGUAGES OF COMMUNICATION
A Logical and Psychological Examination
by George N. Gordon

TO KILL A MESSENGER
Television News and the Real World
by William Small

INTERNATIONAL COMMUNICATION
Media—Channels—Functions
Edited by Heinz-Dietrich Fischer and John Calhoun Merrill

THE COMMUNICATIVE ARTS
An Introduction to Mass Media
by Charles S. Steinberg

PERSUASION
The Theory and Practice of Manipulative Communication
by George N. Gordon

MASS MEDIA AND THE SUPREME COURT
The Legacy of the Warren Years
Edited by Kenneth S. Devol

THE PEOPLE'S FILMS
A Political History of U.S. Government Motion Pictures
by Richard Dyer MacCann

THE IMPERATIVE OF FREEDOM
A Philosophy of Journalistic Autonomy
by John Calhoun Merrill

CONGRESS AND THE NEWS MEDIA
Edited by Robert O. Blanchard

AMERICAN BROADCASTING
A Source Book on the Development of
Radio and Television to the 1970s
by Lawrence W. Lichty and Malachi C. Topping

STUDIES IN PUBLIC COMMUNICATION

CONGRESS
AND THE
NEWS MEDIA

EDITED, WITH COMMENTARIES
AND CONTRIBUTIONS BY

ROBERT O. BLANCHARD

COMMUNICATION ARTS BOOKS

HASTINGS HOUSE, PUBLISHERS, NEW YORK

For Lydia,

Bobby and Timmy

Library of Congress Cataloging in Publication Data

Blanchard, Robert O   comp.
    Congress and the news media.

    (Studies in public communication) (Communication
arts books)
    Bibliography: p.
    1. Government and the press—United States.   2. United
States.   Congress.   I. Title.
PN4738.B5   323.44'5   74–1091
ISBN 0–8038–1192–6 Cloth Edition
ISBN 0–8038–1194–2 Paper (text) Edition

Published simultaneously in Canada by
Saunders of Toronto, Ltd., Don Mills, Ontario

Printed in the United States of America
Designed by Al Lichtenberg

CONTENTS

Preface   ix

Introduction by A. William Bluem   xiii

Part One   ACCESS AND ACCOMMODATION

1 **Establishing New Traditions**   7

The Reporter's Place in the House: A Debate, 1789–90   8
Annals of Congress

Access for the Official Press: A Debate, 1800   15
Annals of Congress

The Letter-Writers in the Senate   28
Frederick B. Marbut

2 **Accommodation and Regulation of the Corps**   40

The Standing Committee of Correspondents   40
Frederick B. Marbut

Access for the Underground Press   49
Luther A. Huston

Modern Accommodation: The New Patronage?   50
James White

3 **Modern Access Issues**   58

Emigration of Power to the Little Legislatures   58
J. Russell Wiggins

Equality of Access for Broadcast Journalism   66
William Small

Modern Access for Broadcast: Congressional Hearings, 1969   70
Special Subcommittee on Legislative Reorganization

Part Two   INTERDEPENDENCE AND INTERACTION   91

4 The Balance of Publicity Powers   99

   The Executive Dominates the News   100
   Thomas Curtis

   Equal Time for Congress: Congressional Hearings, 1970   103
   Communications Subcommittee, Senate Commerce Committee

   Congressional Use of Publicity   128
   Francis E. Rourke

   Congress, Publicity and Public Policy   131
   Nelson W. Polsby

5 Congressional Perspectives on the News Media   135

   The Value of Publicity   136
   Charles L. Clapp

   Mr. Agnew, You Are Wrong About the Press   139
   Bob Eckhardt

   Member Attitudes on News Media Role   146
   William L. Hungate

   Guess Who's Not Coming to the Gridiron Club Dinner?   149
   Shirley Chisholm

   An Oldtimer's View of the Press   153
   Richard Bolling

   A Newcomer's View of the Press   160
   Clem Miller

6 The Congressional Correspondents and Their World   165

   The Variety of Correspondents   168
   Robert O. Blanchard

   The Correspondents Describe Their Work   180
   Robert O. Blanchard

7 Solons and Scribes   239

   Symbiosis: Congress and the Press   240
   Delmer Dunn

The Stuff of Which Good Reporting is Made   250
Douglass Cater

'Covering' The Senate   253
Donald R. Matthews

A View from the President's Room   269
Richard L. Riedel

Senator Lyndon Johnson: A Correspondent's View   283
Stewart Alsop

Senator Wayne Morse: A Correspondent's View   288
A. Robert Smith

Correspondents as Participants: Case I   300
Bert Andrews

Correspondents as Participants: Case II   309
Noel Epstein

The News Media and the Bobby Baker Case   315
Laurence Stern and Erwin Knoll

Nobody Covers the House   322
Michael Green

The Press and Washington's Own Suburban Five   331
Lewis W. Wolfson

8   **Congressional Publicity in Action**   345

The Congressional Hearing as Publicity Vehicle   346
Douglass Cater

Congress, Television and War Protests   352
William Small

The Sam Ervin Show   356
Laurence Leamer

TV Lights, Invitations, Kisses and Phone Calls   367
Jeannette Smyth

Keeping in Touch with the People, Getting Along
           with the Press . . .   370
Donald G. Tacheron and Morris Udall

. . . And, Frankly, Getting Reelected   384
Mark J. Green, James M. Fallows and David R. Zwick

Congress and the Media: Partners in Propaganda   388
Ben H. Bagdikian

Part Three   CONFLICT AND COOPERATION   399

 9 **Broadcast Journalism Rights: First Amendment Conflict**   405

'The Selling of the Pentagon': Partisan Involvements
    and Antagonisms   406
Jerome Barron

The First Amendment and Broadcast Journalism:
    A Debate, 1971   410
Congressional Record

10 **Freedom of Information and Shield Legislation**   439

A New FoI Watchdog Needs Watching   440
Robert O. Blanchard

The Federal Shield Law We Need   447
Fred P. Graham and Jack C. Landau

The Potential Dangers of Shield Legislation   455
Charles L. Bennett

11 **Fair Trial Vs. Free Press**   458

The Battle of Watergate TV   460
George Lardner, Jr.

Fair Trial and the Watergate Hearings   464
John J. Sirica

Due Process of Law   468
The Times

TV's Incandescent and Damaging Presence in the
    Hearing Room   472
Spiro Agnew

Due Process and the President   479
Washington Post

Trial by Publicity?   482
Jules Witcover

Nixon and His Aides Believe Hearing is a Witchhunt   486
Bob Woodward and Carl Bernstein

BIBLIOGRAPHY   488

INDEX   492

PREFACE

THE ROLE OF THE NEWS MEDIA in our political processes today is both newsworthy and political. It is a major topic of national debate. It also is a subject receiving increasing academic consideration. The role of the news media in both uncovering the Watergate scandals and spotlighting its congressional and executive investigations has only served to intensify public and academic interest in the subject.

However, public and academic interest is dominated by the relations between the President and the news media. There has been a relative lack of attention and understanding of relations between Congress and the news media. Even the relations between the highly secretive U.S. Supreme Court and the news media have received more systematic analysis.*

This book attempts to redress this imbalance by bringing together for the first time much that has been written about relations between Congress and the news media. In addition, it includes some original research and transcripts of congressional proceedings which have not been widely available. It represents a broad approach to Congress-media relations. It considers more than current issues. It includes, but looks beyond, relationships between members of Congress and correspondents. It presents an historical dimension and a context in which Congress is viewed as a political communicator. It describes Congress as an important molder and reflector of the public's attitude toward the news media—through congressional hearings and debates as well as in its legislation.

The juxtaposition of scholarly, journalistic, eye-witness and verbatim accounts suggest perhaps more strongly than before that Congress and the news media have important independent powers in our pluralistic

---

* See Grey, David L., *The Supreme Court and the News Media*. Northwestern University Press, 1968 and Devol, Kenneth S., *Mass Media and the Supreme Court*. Hastings House, 1971.

political system. It more clearly illustrates that Congress and the news media have always needed one another, and still do.

Selections in this book describe how news correspondents become both the sources and channels of information among members of Congress and among Congress and the public and other agencies of government. Correspondents have "map making" or "agenda setting" power, as Bernard Cohen has said, to focus and comment on issues and officials of their choosing. Some selections describe the extent to which Congress can influence freedom of the news media. Others suggest that correspondents and members of Congress have always recognized the powers they have over one another.

Do scholars and students recognize or understand the role of news media in the federal legislative process? Do representatives of the news media recognize or understand the role of Congress in defining and determining their freedoms? The major purpose of this book is to facilitate the raising of these and similar questions more often, more forcefully and more systematically than before.

In Part One, Access and Accommodation, attention is given to the history of relations between Congress and the media. This is—in part—an attempt to bring to the study of government-media relations some balance between the study of the executive and legislative branches. The historical cases used can be contrasted and compared with modern proceedings, debates and accounts which are included in other parts of the book.

Part Two, Interaction and Independence, presents a broader picture of the more contemporary complexity of relationships between Congress and the news media. It suggests that the nature and extent of Congress-media interaction are influenced by the White House. Congressional attitudes toward the news media, for instance, seem to be influenced in part by congressional anxiety over the growing power of the executive branch over the legislative branch. Before Watergate, many members of Congress perceived that this power was enhanced or even created by the President's ability to dominate national news. It remains to be seen what effect Watergate will have on the legislative-executive balance. In any case, the news media's role in the system of checks and balances is an important consideration in Congress-media relations. Washington correspondents' attitudes and their social, professional, political and economic environments are additional elements in the chemistry of Congress-media relationships. These elements influence what is "news" since "news" usually is what journalists decide it is.

Part Two deals also with alternative channels of communication developed by Congress and its members. Both the opportunities provided by technology and the need created by complexity and size have resulted in newsletters, film production capacity and other information-propaganda channels for Congress. These are devices which Congress and its members have developed to reach far-flung, diverse and mobile mass constituencies —to get around the mass media channels controlled by a series of "gate-keeper" correspondents and editors. The ultimate in this congressional drive both to reach constituencies directly and to compete with the President's command of the national news is represented by proposals for public service television time for Congress.

As this book goes to print, more comprehensive and ambitious congressional efforts are underway for Congress, as an institution, to achieve greater access to the news media. Sen. Lee Metcalf (D.-Mont.) and Rep. Jack Brooks (D.-Tex.) have scheduled hearings for late February, 1974 for their Joint Committee on Congressional Operations. They will consider proposals, including those in a committee report to be released at that time, "Congress and Mass Communication: An Institutional Perspective." One proposal will include continuous televising of congressional proceedings (chamber and committee) for the use of the media, similar to the services provided the media by the United Nations. The committee study and the hearings represent the first comprehensive effort by Congress to systematically analyze its institutional relationship with the mass media, particularly with the newer electronic media of communication.

Part Three, Conflict and Cooperation, presents some major contemporary news media freedom conflicts between the federal government and the news media which have been or still are being fought on the congressional battleground. It is often in these conflicts that Congress demonstrates its considerable powers of defining the extent of news media freedoms. Although the powers of the executive and judicial branches, especially the U.S. Supreme Court, are not to be underrated, Congress at times has overshadowed the other branches as an adversary or friend of the news media. This influence does not exist alone in legislation. Congressional investigations, hearings and debates have been providing effective forums for both attacking and protecting the news media. More recent examples of major news media freedom issues aired in Congress include the freedom of information investigations and legislation, congressional investigation and criticism of network news documentaries, proposed federal laws protecting the right of journalists to maintain the confidentiality of their sources, and the free press vs. fair trial debate surrounding the Watergate hearings.

An attempt has been made to include a variety of primary material— congressional proceedings published in the *Annals of Congress, Congressional Globe* and *Congressional Record,* published congressional hearing transcripts, articles in scholarly journals, personal histories, newspaper and magazine articles, and articles in professional publications.

I am indebted to those authors and publishing houses which allowed the use of copyright material, and to Washington correspondents who replied to questionnaires and consented to interviews. Contributors and publishers are listed in footnotes which accompany each article.

Valuable support and encouragement were given the editor by Curtis MacDougall of Northwestern University; Samuel J. Archibald and D. B. Hardeman of Washington, D.C.; Julius Duscha of the Washington Journalism Center; Robert Peabody and Francis Rourke of Johns Hopkins University; Donald Matthews of the Brookings Institution; John Stewart and Donald Tacheron of the Joint Committee on Congressional Operations; Vic Reinemar and Brit Englund of the office of Senator Lee Metcalf; Walter Oleszek, of the Library of Congress; congressional press gallery staff members Benjamin C. West, Thayer V. Illsley, Joseph E. Wills and Robert M. Menaugh; William Shannon and Marjorie Hunter of the *New York Times*; Spencer Rich and Richard Lyons of the *Washington Post*; Vincent Burke of the *Los Angeles Times*; Paul Wieck of the *Albuquerque Journal*; Edmond LeBreton of the Associated Press; Daniel Rapoport formerly of United Press International, and W. Donald Bowles and Robert P. Boynton of the American University.

I am indebted to Dr. Charles Steinberg of Hunter College and to my colleagues, Edward Bliss, Jr., Jerry Hendrix, Jack Orwant and Lewis Wolfson, for their assistance and comments and, particularly, to students in the Public Affairs Graduate Journalism program at The American University who are identified elsewhere in the book.

Finally, I am grateful to Helen Paravati, Marian Putnam and Nancy Pane of the staff of the Department of Communication, and to The American University and its Office of Graduate Studies and Research for their support and assistance.

March 1, 1974   ROBERT O. BLANCHARD
                                                The American University
                                                Washington, D.C.

INTRODUCTION

Congress and the News Media is the tenth volume to be published in our *Studies in Public Communications*. Initiated with publication of Charles S. Steinberg's *Mass Media and Communication* in February of 1966, it is gratifying to note that the series has been able to attract so many worthy and able scholars in eight brief years.

It was our hope that the series would attract thinkers and scholars who were interested not only in the historical mass media context but also had vital interest in some of the direct contemporary problems confronting the media and their relationship to our society. Again, our hopes were answered. In the course of these eight years we have heard not only from those with broad academic interests in communication like Charles Steinberg, George Gordon and John Merrill, but we have also been fortunate in being able to publish thoughtful analyses of the operational realities of the contemporary media practice in "the real world." William Small has created an important work in his *To Kill A Messenger*. Richard Dyer MacCann has given us a scholarly history of U.S. Government motion pictures which moves up through the entire decade of the 60's. And Kenneth Devol has preceded Robert Blanchard in producing an excellent analysis of how the contemporary media interact and relate to our major political institutions.

As one considers the realities of American political communication—set forth in rich detail in Dr. Blanchard's account of the news media *vis-a-vis* the Congress of the United States, it is useful to review the achievements of the true master of political image-making—the hero of Frank Baum's immortal children's classic, *The Wizard of Oz*. After all, was it not the great Oz who convinced a bumbling tin man that "testimonials to good deeds" were an adequate substitute for a genuine heart? Did not Oz himself persuade a cowardly lion that a medal was the equivalent of genuine courage? And did not the genius from the Emerald City lead a stuffed straw man to believe that a diploma was a worthy substitute for brains?

As one reads Dr. Blanchard's fascinating collection of historical and contemporary accounts of battles between politicians and journalists, it becomes clear that at one time or another each have also had visions of perpetrating such political myths upon an unsuspecting public. At one time not too long ago, it was thought that only the politician was regarded as a wizard of political myth-making, but it soon became apparent that members of the journalistic profession—whether out of ideological concern or simple economic necessity—were giving lessons to politicians.

Once both parties began to present a world without fear, disorder or confusion most of us could only begin to react like Dorothy—the little heroine of Baum's story—who was pretty certain that the Wizard would not get her back to Kansas with a bag of hot air. She was wise enough to let him go by himself while she relied upon more traditional modes of transport like magic slippers and fairy godmothers.

Perhaps the most any of us can rely upon during the political bombardments of the 70's are magic charms—but Dr. Blanchard's work offers more considered paths for us to pursue. His analysis is long overdue. He is a most welcome contributor to this series.

A. WILLIAM BLUEM, PH.D.
Professor of Media Studies
S. I. Newhouse Communication Center
Syracuse University

Part One

ACCESS AND ACCOMMODATION

During any day that Congress is in session, he drives on to the Capitol grounds where parking space is at a premium. But he possesses a parking permit. He is entitled to take a reserved spot near the East Front of the Capitol.

After parking, he walks over to a congressional office building to attend a committee hearing. No matter how many people are waiting in line outside the hearing room, he is permitted to enter and sits at a special table near the front. There, he is supplied with a list of witnesses scheduled to give testimony and prepared copies of their statements. If the hearing is delayed, he can adjourn to a private room and wait to be notified that the hearing is about to begin.

Following the hearing (he may or may not stay for all of it), he takes a subway to the Capitol where a special elevator is waiting to take him to the third floor. Entering an area designated for his use, he picks up his mail and any phone messages received while he was away. He also is informed, by an alert and congenial gallery staff, of any congressional activity that might interest him and supplied with pertinent written material.

Then, if he wishes, he can do some office work using the facilities available to him such as typewriters, phones and stationery. Or, he may enter a special gallery above the floor of the Senate or the House of Representatives where he may take notes or read, activity not permitted by those in other galleries.

If he has any questions regarding the activities of Congress, he can ask one of the several congressional employees assigned to assist him, or he might look for the answer himself by going to the Senate library. The library is not open to the public, but he generally has free access to it.

If he is hungry by this time, he may again take a special elevator to the Senate restaurant where he bypasses long lines by entering a private dining room. After lunch, he returns to the third floor where again he is brought up to date on the latest congressional activity. Then, he can relax in a large leather easy chair, read a newspaper or chat with friends.

The person is not a congressman or senator. Nor is he on the staff of a congressman or senator although many of his privileges are similar to theirs. He is not even an employee of the federal government. He is a news reporter, one of almost 2,400 men and women accredited to cover the activities of Congress on a regular basis.

In some respects, the amount of accommodation given to members of the press by Congress is staggering. In addition to various courtesies accorded them, such as private elevators, dining rooms and parking permits (over 100 spaces are reserved for the press), newsmen have full access to the press galleries.

The term press gallery at one time referred only to the areas above the rostrums on the House and Senate floors. Today its meaning has grown to include some 15 rooms, most adjacent to the galleries themselves, which serve as message and information centers, work areas and lounges for use by reporters covering Congress.

To maintain the operation of the galleries, Congress has provided a staff of 24 superintendents and assistants, whose annual salaries total close to half a million dollars. In terms of space, a priceless commodity within the Capitol, the press galleries occupy an estimated 9,000 square feet.

The galleries are equipped with nearly 200 typewriters, 12 radio studios, five film studios and countless telephones, file cabinets, tables, chairs and other pieces of office furniture and equipment. In each of the five congressional office buildings, the press galleries also have rooms set aside for use by newspeople, as well as six radio and three film studios, and three darkrooms. Each of the studios is equipped with special wiring and lighting necessary for television and the darkrooms are fitted with everything necessary for the de-

velopment of film except chemicals and paper. An additional film studio is located in the basement of the Capitol.

Accredited members of the press may make almost unlimited use of gallery facilities and equipment. Except for special items which may be requested, all the facilities and equipment are available to the press free of charge. . . .

—JAMES WHITE

THESE PRIVILEGES of access and accommodation, generously accorded by the U.S. Congress to the news media at the taxpayer's expense, appear to represent a dramatic improvement from the First Congress. There representatives of the press were driven from the foot of the House Speaker's chair to the public gallery. The Senate was not even open to the public or press until five years after it was first convened.

To be sure, Part One presents a picture of increasing access to the congressional chambers and galleries for reporters, increasing accommodation to a growing number of Washington correspondents and the addition of new channels of information from Congress to the public. Congress granted access to only a few local representatives of the highly partisan press of the early 19th Century. During this period the Washington-based press depended largely on government printing or other political patronage. Congress conducted most of its business in the chambers and, other than its own terse journal entries required by the Constitution, used the local press to record these proceedings.

By the 1970's there were hundreds of professional reporters in Washington, representing or serving financially-independent national news media. For nearly 100 years Congress has been recording and publishing its own proceedings and it has developed other independent publishing and information-dispensing facilities.

Yet, it has been argued that Congress is less accessible in the last third of the 20th Century than it was 180 years ago. Much important business of Congress is conducted in closed committee rooms. The "proceedings" of Congress, as miraculously published daily in the *Congressional Record*, are notoriously unrepresentative of what actually takes place and thus serve as one of the many modern public propaganda outlets for members of Congress. In spite of generous accommodations and privileges, the visual and audio channels of the broadcast media—which most Americans use as their major sources of news—are still banned from the chambers when Congress is in regular session. And they have access only to the largely staged proceedings of the little legislatures—the committees and subcommittees.

Perhaps both views—more access and less access—of the 180-year history of Congress-media relationships are valid. On one hand, there has been dramatic change. Congress has become more than a legislature. It has become an umbrella for many little legislatures, a forum for presidential aspirants, an incubator for minority causes waiting for their time to come, a watchdog of the executive, and, for some, a retirement home and social club. The press, in the meantime, has become the news media. The two institutions, like the American government and the nation's capital, have changed dramatically. As the changes have taken place necessary adjustments have been made.

But the changes have been more in form than in substance. For instance, the early reporters of Congress functioned also as stenographers of the proceedings, publishers of congressional proceedings, government printers, publisher-editors of local newspapers, press secretaries to Presidents and members of Congress, major national news services to newspapers in distant cities, and propagandists for political parties and special interests. Many of these familiar modern terms were unheard of in the 18th and 19th Centuries, but the functions they represent were being performed until the mid-19th century, nonetheless, by a handful of journalists in Washington.

In these forerunners, we can look for the roots of the present more specialized and complex patterns of relations between Congress and the news media. Although the emphasis in Part One is on the issue of access and the development of accommodation, we can see the interdependence of the Congress and the news media and the increasing specialization and complexity in their interaction which will be examined in Part Two. From the first session of the First Congress in which there was debate over the coverage by a local newspaper, to the present, we see also the parallel and alternating relationships of conflict and cooperation, subjects examined in Part Three.

In short, the rites and rules governing news media access and accommodation in Congress are the unique result of 180 years of still-unresolved conflict between the ancient privilege of legislative secrecy and the more recent principles of a free press brought about by the practical needs of a new democratic republic.

Establishing New Traditions

THE NEW CONGRESS of the United States was hesitant about granting reporters access or special accommodation to its proceedings. English and colonial legislative precedent, including the Constitutional Convention, was one of secrecy.

Working against this ancient tradition, however, were partisan politics and the housekeeping and communication imperatives of Congress in a new democratic republic. The press, it seems, nearly always was able to count on a faction in Congress which either needed its presence or feared its wrath—or both. During the nearly 100 years before Congress agreed to record and publish its own proceedings, it depended on the press to perform the function of keeping a record of the proceedings for its own members' use and for distribution to their constituencies.

The earliest confrontation between tradition and newer realities took place in the House of Representatives in 1789 in a debate which was reported by the press of the time and reprinted in the *Annals of Congress*, the only record of the congressional debates for many years.

Two years later anti-Federalist Philip Freneau began a crusade which led to the opening of the U.S. Senate to the press in 1793. His ardor for freedom of the press was spurred on by some political and personal financial considerations since he was the publisher of the *National Gazette*. It was established after Secretary of State Thomas Jefferson subsidized Freneau with a $250-a-year position as a translator in the State Department to counter the influence of John Fenno's *Gazette of the United States*, the Federalist organ.

When Congress moved to Washington, the problem of where to place the Philadelphia newspaper reporters was replaced by a new problem: where to find any recorders or printers at all. But soon the lure of printing contracts from Congress and other printing patronage from the federal government attracted some enterprising editor-printers.

First among these official journalists was Samuel Harrison Smith, founder of the *National Intelligencer*, a newspaper which was to dominate

Washington journalism and congressional reporting for a half-century. His attempts to gain access to Congress have been recorded by William E. Ames, a major historian of early Washington journalism. (See Bibliography.)

Smith's successors were Joseph Gales and William W. Seaton who later played a major role in collecting, recording and publishing the proceedings of Congress known as the *Annals of Congress* and later the *Register of Debates*, the most complete records of the proceedings of Congress until the establishment of the rival *Congressional Globe* in 1834.

The *Annals of Congress* provide the excerpts from the congressional debate over the admission of Smith and Thomas Carpenter to the House. Their successful access to and accommodation by Congress marked the beginning of official Washington journalism which reached its zenith in the Washington *Globe*, successor to the *Intelligencer*.

By the 1830's Congress and the press achieved some rapport, with Congress having the upper hand over the press through printing patronage and special access powers. Although partisan politics inhibited total control, the patronage system dictated that the editors enjoy support of a majority of the members of Congress.

However, a new era of relations between Congress and the news media had begun by 1840 as the emerging Washington corps of correspondents challenged the favored access provided the Washington newspapers.

Frederick Marbut focuses on the role of James Gordon Bennett and his *New York Herald* in moving Congress to accommodate the expanding corps of correspondents. Bennett was a worthy representative of the new journalism of that time which was less dependent on political or government support for funds and audience and was based on larger circulation, more general audiences and commercial advertising. The expanding channels of political communication created greater problems for members of Congress desiring to control the flow and content of reporting about their words and deeds.

THE REPORTER'S PLACE IN THE HOUSE
A DEBATE, 1789–90
Annals of Congress

(Rep. Aedanus Burke of South Carolina introduced a resolution nearly six months after the organization of the House, charging that inaccurate reporting in the *Congressional Register*, a privately-owned

Reprinted from the *Annals of Congress*, 1st Cong., 1st Sess. (Philadelphia, Pa., 1789-90), Vol. I, pp. 952-956, 1095-1098.

newspaper, violated the privileges of the House. The reporters fled
from their privileged position "at the very foot of the Speaker's chair."
From their exiled position in the public galleries, the reporters [then
also referred to as printers, stenographers or short-hand writers] apparently were selective about whom they recorded in the debate from
that great distance. Following is their account of the debate, written
in the third person stenography common at that time.—Ed.)

Debates of the House

(September 26, 1789)

Mr. Burke called up the following resolution, which he had laid on
the table the 21st of this month:

Resolved, That the several persons who have published the debates
of this House, in the Congressional Register, and in the newspapers of
this city, have misrepresented these debates in the most glaring deviations
from truth; often distorting the arguments of the members from the true
meaning; imputing to some gentlemen arguments contradictory and
foreign to the subject, and which were never advanced; to others, remarks
and observations never made; and, in a great many instances, mutilating,
and, not unfrequently, suppressing whole arguments upon subjects of the
greatest moment; thus throwing over the whole proceedings a thick veil
of misrepresentation and error; which being done within the House, at
the very foot of the Speaker's chair, gives a sanction and authenticity to
those publications, that reflects upon the House a ridicule and absurdity
highly injurious to its privileges and dignity.

Resolved, That to misrepresent the debates of the House, whether it
arises from incapacity, inattention, or partiality, has a mischievous tendency
to infringe the freedom of debate, and that this House should no longer
give sanction to it.

After the resolution was read, Mr. Burke supported it by a reference
to the misconceptions and blunders which had been printed. Mr. Bland
and Mr. White made some observations on the subject, none of which,
however, the editor had an opportunity of taking down.

Mr. Stone said, that there were undoubtedly inaccuracies published;
but he was far from supposing this a solid reason for prohibiting the
printing of their debates. He had the misfortune, he believed, not to be
understood by some of those who attempted to detail what he said;
because they had put into his mouth sentiments which his heart never
felt, nor his head comprehended; but he should never think of suppressing
what the world thought valuable information on this account. Speaking
from his memory, and his own observations on the publications alluded to
in the resolution, he was induced to say, that one of them was condemned
in a degree beyond what he thought justice required. What he had mentioned of inaccuracies applied to the newspapers. The Congressional

Register, he believed, was free from misrepresentations, other than sometimes changing the mode of expression or emphasis of language, which, he
presumed, was unavoidable, or necessary, when gentlemen delivered their
sentiments on the floor without system or grammatical precision. He did
not pretend to assert further than for what he had spoken himself, that
this work had some merit on account of its accuracy. He hoped, therefore,
the motion would not be agreed to.

Mr. Gerry said, these publications had a tendency to exalt some
members and to depress others. Whence it arose that this was the case
he did not pretend to say. He would exercise charity in this regard, and
suppose it arose from inability or inadvertency in the reporters. But there
was one thing very remarkable, that all the arguments on one side were
fully stated, and generally took up some columns in the newspapers; while
the arguments of the other side were partially stated, and condensed to a
few solitary lines. Now, this circumstance could not proceed from the
arguments not being heard, because gentlemen on the one side generally
spoke as low as the gentlemen on the other; but, from whatever cause it
proceeded, it had a tendency to hold one part up in a ridiculous point of
view. If it was necessary to amuse the public in this way, to be sure they
must submit to it; but he could not believe it necessary. He thought some
regard ought to be paid to the reputation of the speakers, as it might
influence that quality abroad; for he believed the debates of the House
were neither confined to this city nor the United States.

He had made an observation, that the printers had it in their power,
by misrepresentation, to make whom they pleased ridiculous in the eyes
of the world, or to exalt those whose sentiments they favored. Viewing
the publications in this point of light, they were matters of serious
reflection; and, if they were conducted on principles of party, they might
be one of the most dangerous engines in the hands of faction, and have
a malignant and mischievous tendency upon the public voice of America.
The debates of the British Parliament are published, it is true; but they
never permit them to be taken down, they never give them the least
sanction; because they know the serious consequences resulting from an
improper use of such a liberty. But, notwithstanding all this, he was in
favor of disseminating useful information, by a correct and impartial
publication of the speeches.

Mr. Page moved to let the motion lie on the table. He should object
to driving the gentlemen who were at the foot of the Speaker's chair into
the gallery. He looked upon such a measure as the first step towards
driving them and all their hearers out of the House. It was well known to
gentlemen, that they were admitted by the tacit consent of the members,
and he would not acquiesce in a violent removal. He thought those
gentlemen, who had reason to complain that they were held up in a
ridiculous light by the printers, had now sufficient revenge by the severity

of the motion, and he hoped it might induce more accurate and impartial sketches of the debates in future, to the full satisfaction of those gentlemen. But he would rather submit to all the inconveniences of ridicule than sacrifice what he thought a valuable publication of useful and interesting information to his constituents.

Mr. Burke did not wish to draw the House into a tedious debate; sooner than be the occasion of it at this time, he would withdraw the motion. But he did not approve of sacrificing the honor and dignity of the House, by putting it into the power of the printers, as it were, by their sanction. The publication of the debates of the British Parliament was not authorized by that body; they were published by men who got access to their galleries. So here, he would be content if they were taken in the same way; but he did not like that the world should suppose these publications were authorized by the House. In truth, the misrepresentation he complained of was principally occasioned by the partiality of the printer who sat at the foot of the chair, in his publications on the most important questions that had been brought forward. He did not see him there now; but if he saw him there again, and he continued to print falsely what was said by gentlemen on this floor, he would renew the motion which he now withdrew.

Mr. Hartley wished a decision on the motion. He contemplated the question as involving in it an attack upon the liberty of the press.

Mr. Sumter.—As the motion was withdrawn, he would not speak upon it; but if a motion were made to authorize the publication of the debates, in an able and impartial manner, by a gentleman who was thought qualified for the purpose, he would give it his support.

Mr. Gerry held a wish of the same nature; for he was a friend to a fair and impartial publication.

Mr. Tucker said, that he thought a motion of the following import might be adopted:—That every person who was permitted to take down the debates ought to do it, to the best of his ability, in an accurate and impartial manner.

Mr. Bland held a similar sentiment.

Mr. Lee thought there was an impropriety in admitting short-hand writers to publish the debates, by the declared authority of the House; but he was far from objecting to their publishing, as they had heretofore done, by their tacit consent.

Mr. Madison thought it improper to throw impediments in the way of such information as the House had hitherto permitted from the purest motives; but he believed it equally improper to give the publication of their debates a legislative sanction, because it would be making the speakers, in some instances where they were misunderstood, answerable for the sentiments they never entertained. He had seen in the newspapers very great misconceptions of what fell from him; but he had no reason to

believe it was done in order to cast a veil over his declarations, or to
pervert them, with an intention of rendering him ridiculous. He believed
the same was just as it applied to the speeches of other gentlemen. But,
be this as it might, it gave him no concern, because he was not responsible
for what was published, as it was done without his interference. If any
thing was done in this matter, which tended to give a sanction to any
publication, he presumed the members must be, individually, at the
trouble of correcting and revising their speeches. This was an inconvenience he did not wish to encounter: he therefore concluded it best to
leave it on its present footing.

Mr. WHITE disapproved the idea of giving a sanction to the publications by any vote whatever; but he was friendly to the practice of publishing the debates, because it conveyed useful information, and gave
much satisfaction to those citizens who cannot attend in the gallery, to
hear the sentiments of those who represent them.

Mr. TUCKER withdrew the motion he had suggested, with a hope that
the printers would be more cautious in future in their publications, and
study a greater degree of accuracy and impartiality. . . .

[Nearly four months later, on January 15, 1790, the issue is brought up
again.   —Ed.]

Mr. HARTLEY moved an adjournment, when Mr. PAGE rose and said,
he wished to call the attention of the House, before they adjourned, to a
subject which he thought of importance, and which ought no longer to
be in the undecided state it had been in since the last session; it was this,
whether the persons who had taken down and published the debates of
the House, by the tacit consent of the members during the last session,
and who had withdrawn from the seats they then held in the House, to
the gallery, during this session, might not return to the same seats. He
supposed that they had modestly withdrawn, on the supposition that the
debate which took place just before the adjournment, showed that the
sense of the members was against their sitting in the House; but the
contrary was the case; that he knew their publications had given great
satisfaction to many of the constituents of that House: that the House
was applauded for its conduct on that occasion, both at home and abroad,
and had been highly commended for it in some British publications; that
he was anxious that the short-hand writers should resume their seats in
the House, lest it might be insinuated by the jealous enemies of our
Government, that the House of Representatives were more republican
and indulgent the last session than this; that removing those writers to
the gallery, was but a step towards removing them from the House, and
that this suspicion would be increased by circumstances which, however
innocent, nay proper in themselves, might be misunderstood and excite
uneasiness. The doors of the gallery had been two days shut, the House
had made a parade through the streets, and had displayed their eagle in

their hall; that these circumstances, if followed by the exclusion of the short-hand writers, might spread an alarm which ought to be avoided; he therefore hoped that those gentlemen who had retired to the gallery might be informed that they might return to the seats they occupied in the last session—that he avoided making a regular motion to this effect, because he knew that some worthy members who wished to admit those writers, or any others, did not think their admission ought to be sanctioned by vote, and appear on the journals, lest that might sanction and authenticate erroneous publications; but that if he should not discover that the sense of the members present was in favor of the ideas he had expressed, that to-morrow he would bring forward a motion made by a member from South Carolina, (Mr. TUCKER) last session, for that purpose, for he had no fears that a vote of the House to authorize the admission of such writers, would make the House answerable for their publications.

Mr. HARTLEY withdrew his motion for adjournment, in order that the subject alluded to by the gentleman from Virginia (Mr. PAGE) might be understood.

Mr. WHITE said, he felt averse to enter into a positive resolution for the admission of any person to take down the debates, but wished them permitted to a convenient seat within the bar for the purpose of hearing with greater accuracy. But he feared that a vote of the House would give a sanction to the details, which the publications ought not to have. Not that he thought them worse than similar publications in other countries, on the contrary, he thought them better, if he judged from what had fallen under his particular observation, and what he recollected to have from others. He did not wish a positive motion for the admission of short-hand writers, because gentlemen might object to a vote of the kind, and he should be very loath to discourage publications of the advantages of which he was well convinced; he knew they had given great satisfaction to the people of America, and it was a satisfaction of which he would not deprive them. Although these publications had not given an exact and accurate detail of all that passed in Congress, yet their information had been pretty full, and he believed the errors not very many; those that were made, he supposed to arise rather from haste or inadvertence, than from design. He was convinced of this, from the disposition the publishers had manifested to correct any errors that were pointed out, and the pains they sometimes took to ask gentlemen what were their particular expressions, when they either did not hear distinctly, or did not comprehend the speaker's meaning. He wished, therefore, the business might go on; but silently, as it had heretofore done, without the express approbation of the House. He was fully convinced, that neither the editor of the Register, nor any other man, but the members of the House, had a right to a seat within those walls, without the consent of every member; but he thought this consent would be tacitly given if no gentleman opposed their introduction, and in this way he most heartily concurred with his colleague in agreeing to the admission of such persons as thought themselves qualified, and were inclined to take down and publish their debates and proceedings; he should be glad to see them in the seats they had last session, but he should object to the vote being entered on the journals of the House.

Mr. BOUDINOT thought the mode proper to be pursued on this occasion, would be to give a discretionary power to the Speaker to admit such persons as he thought proper. Under such a regulation, short-hand writers might be admitted, without giving to their publications any degree of legislative authority.

Mr. THATCHER hoped that it was not the intention of gentlemen to confine the business to one person only, because others might appear of equal capacity, and equally deserving of encouragement.

Mr. PAGE said, he did not wish to confine the vote to any two or three writers, he cared not how many were admitted. It ought to be remembered, that he said, when this subject was before the House at the last session, that he saw no reason why Mr. FENNO should not be within the house as well as Mr. LLOYD, instead of being in the gallery. He had no objection to admitting any number of short-hand writers, provided they did not incommode the members.

Mr. SMITH, (of South Carolina.)—I do not wish, Mr. Speaker, to exclude others from a convenient seat; but at the same time, I think those who were here before, have a pre-emption right to the best. I assure you, sir, I am sorry for the loss of them off the floor, because I think their publications had a salutary tendency. It has been said, that it was the design of the shorthand writers to give a partial representation of our proceedings. I believe, if they are not correctly given, it is owing to the hurry in which business of this kind is conducted, and I am confirmed in this opinion, by some errors which I have discovered in the publication of our proceedings. It was said that a committee was appointed to bring in a bill for the preservation and safe-keeping of the *accounts* of the United States. I thought within myself that we were not so tenacious on this head, therefore suspected some mistake, and on consulting the journals I found that a committee had been appointed to bring in a bill for the safe-keeping and preservation of the *acts* of the United States: The similarity of the letters in these two words, and the great abridgment short-hand writers are obliged to make for the sake of expedition, may have caused him to substitute the one for the other; in another place, I found a greater blunder still: it was said, that the House had appointed a committee for the regulation of the *barbers* of the United States; this struck me as a very gross misrepresentation, for I could hardly believe, that the Legislature of the Union, would, at so early a day, attempt to usurp an authority not vested in them by the Constitution, and that, too, over a body of men, who could at any time put an end to the tyranny with the edge of the razor; but on searching the minutes of this case, I found that a bill was brought in for the regulation of the *harbors* of the United States. Upon the whole, I believe, inaccurate as this work is, it has given to our constituents great satisfaction, and I should be glad to see our *Argus* restored to his former situation behind the Speaker's chair, from whence he could both see and hear distinctly everything that passed in the House.

ACCESS FOR THE OFFICIAL PRESS:
A DEBATE, 1800

Annals of Congress

(When Congress moved to Washington, the question of access also became one of accommodation. Since no facilities existed in the new House chamber for reporters or stenographers, as they were sometimes known, Samuel Harrison Smith requested permission to place a desk inside the rail in order to better hear the debates. The following is the debate over Smith's and Thomas Carpenter's memorial to the House for admission within the bar—Ed.)

REPORTING THE DEBATES

(December 4, 1800)

Mr. HILL presented a memorial from Samuel Harrison Smith and Thomas Carpenter, representing that they had undertaken to report the debates of the House; that, contrary to their expectation—on the suggestion of inconvenience to the members—they had not received permission to occupy a situation within the bar, without which they were unable to state with fidelity the proceedings and debates; and praying the permission of the House to be admitted within the bar.

As soon as the memorial was read, the SPEAKER rose and observed, that feeling himself responsible to the House for the faithful discharge of the duties attached to his situation, he thought it proper to state the line of conduct he had pursued in this business. He stated that he was applied to by letter on the first day of the session, by Mr. Stewart, requesting permission to occupy a place within the bar; that he immediately took the request into consideration; that, in the mean time, similar requests were made by other individuals; that, on observing the structure of the room and the arrangement of the furniture, it at once appeared to

Reprinted from the *Annals of Congress*, 6th Cong., 2d Sess. (Washington, D.C., 1800), Vol. 10, pp. 797-99, 806-16.

him inconsistent with the dignity of the House or the convenience of
the members to grant the permission asked; that the area was too small
to afford the necessary accommodation; that the position considered as the
least inconvenient to the House was within the window-frames; that, in
his opinion, this position would not be agreeable to the stenographers,
as the view of the members on the opposite side of the House from either
window would be obstructed; that, if a position was assigned in any other
part of the House, the stenographers would be between the Chair and
some of the members, which would render the preservation of order
impossible; that he had stated these reasons, and informed the applicants
that, if agreeable to them, he would assign a place in the gallery, which
should be set apart for their exclusive use; and that he considered that to
be the most eligible position. He concluded by repeating, that it was, in
his opinion, absolutely impossible to preserve the dignity of the House,
and to maintain the convenience of the members, if the requested permission were given. Such was his first, his invariable opinion—it was
unaltered—it was still the same.

Mr. NICHOLS said, that the members of the House must feel a common interest in having the debates taken with fidelity. If the debates were
taken, they ought to be taken with precision. Those who took them should
not be debarred from the best means of hearing with accuracy. For his
part he could not discern the inconvenience alleged to exist. The desk,
which it was necessary to admit within the bar, would not project beyond
the window-frame; and as to the remark of the Speaker respecting the
inconvenience of such a position to the stenographers, it was easily
obviated by the consideration, that any innaccuracy which might occur
in the report of the individual who took them on one side of the Chair,
would be checked by the reporter situated on the other side.

He thought the desire of the memorialists ought not to be passed
over lightly. They had a right to the best place the House could assign.
He moved the reference of the memorial to a select committee.

Mr. HILL observed that as the memorial contained no facts that
required the investigation of a committee, and as the House possessed all
the information that could guide their decision, he did not discern the
propriety of the proposed reference. He had prepared a resolution, which,
if the motion for a reference were withdrawn, he would offer.

Mr. NICHOLAS immediately withdrew his motion. Mr. HILL then
proposed a resolution substantially to this effect: that Mr. Speaker be
requested to assign places within the bar for the stenographers.

Mr. OTIS was sorry the gentleman from Virginia had withdrawn his
motion to refer the memorial to a select committee, as he thought the
subject required examination before a decision was made. There appeared
to him much weight in the ideas of the Speaker. Grant, for the sake of
argument, that four persons may be accommodated at the windows. Might
there not be other applications? Was any gentleman prepared to say how

many would be made? If the permission were once granted to one, would it not be necessary to extend it to all? Would the House suffer any individual to have an exclusive benefit whereby a stamp of authenticity would be fixed on his statements.

This business, in one shape or other, had often been before the House, and all conversation respecting it had always issued in leaving it to the regulation of the Speaker. This appeared to him the best termination it could receive.

From the attention he had paid to the debates reported this session, he believed them to be better and more accurately taken, than they had been on former occasions. This to him was a proof that the present situation of the stenographers was a good one. He acknowledged, at the same time, that the ability with which the debates were taken entitled those who took them to the best accommodation the House could afford. He concluded with renewing the motion for a reference to a select committee.

Mr. NICHOLAS replied, that no debate had taken place which could test the accuracy of the stenographers. From his own experience he pronounced the situation at present occupied utterly inconvenient. What he had some days since remarked had been misstated. He well knew that this did not arise from the inability of the reporter to state correctly what occurred. He knew him to be intelligent, and finally capable of conceiving and conveying the meaning of any remarks which could be made in that House. But it arose from his situation, from which it was impossible to hear distinctly.

He declared the objections of Mr. OTIS, in relation to the number of applicants, perfectly chimerical. Did the gentleman suppose that the number would be so great as to make a demand on their seats? As well might he imagine this, as that they would swell to the ideal compass he had given them. It was known to the House, that at Philadelphia the number was small; seldom more than two, and often not more than one persevered during the session, though a greater number appeared on its earliest days. Fact and experience, therefore, demonstrated the fallacy of the danger apprehended from this source.

The question was then taken on the reference to a select committee, and carried, ayes 42, noes 34.

And a committee of five, viz: Messrs. OTIS, NICHOLAS, PLATT, MORRIS, and HILL, was appointed. . . .

REPORTING THE DEBATES

(Tuesday, December 9, 1800)

The House proceeded to consider the report of the committee to whom was referred the memorial of Samuel Harrison Smith and Thomas

Carpenter, made yesterday, and which lay on the table; and, the same being again read, in the words following, to wit:

"The committee to whom was referred the memorial of Samuel Harrison Smith and Thomas Carpenter, report the following resolution, which they recommend to the House:

"*Resolved,* That it is not expedient for this House to make any order upon the subject of the memorial of Samuel Harrison Smith and Thomas Carpenter, presented on the fourth day of December instant."

Mr. CHRISTIE moved the reference of the report to a Committee of the Whole.

Mr. GRISWOLD opposed the reference.

The House divided—for the reference 43 against it 46.

Mr. JACKSON made several remarks, and concluded by calling for the yeas and nays, which were ordered.

Mr. NICHOLS said, in a Government like ours, the theory of which is republican, and the practice of which he hoped would always continue to be republican, he considered the representatives of the people responsible to the people, by whom they were created. It was necessary, to give efficacy to this responsibility, that the people, who were to judge, should possess the purest information, as to not only the acts, but the motives of the public agents. It was of little consequence to them to know what laws are enacted, compared with a knowledge of projects that were attempted or prevented, and the grounds on which they were supported or opposed. Nor could the merits of the acts themselves be understood, unless the reasons for them were stated. It was, therefore, of the highest consequence that the reasons for our conduct should be clearly understood, that our measures may be comprehended, and our motives also known, that our constituents may judge whether we have faithfully discharged our duty.

Under this view of the subject, he thought it extremely indelicate to resist the admission within the bar of those persons who thought themselves qualified to take the debates and proceedings of the House. But what rendered the attempt still more improper, was, its being an innovation on the practice of the House. For, since he had been a member of the Legislature, individuals of this description had been placed by the House at their ease, in a situation convenient for hearing what passed. Why is this practice, hitherto unopposed, now to be broken in upon? For such an innovation and departure from the established practice of the House, there ought to be the strongest reasons; particularly when the attempted innovation respected, and was made by, those whose conduct was to be scrutinized.

It was not without deliberation that the practice of the House had been instituted and adhered to. Some gentlemen had, some time since, contemplated the employment of a particular individual, whose services were to be paid for by the House. But the idea was abandoned, from the supposed sanction given by such an act to his statements; whereby the House might be made responsible for his accuracy and talents.

The difficulty attending the business he acknowledged to be great. But, for the reasons he had assigned, he thought the House had acted right in forbearing to interfere, further than by merely assigning a convenient place to the stenographers. It was deemed safest to confide the business to persons not known officially to the House, whose own individual interest would constitute the best pledge for their fidelity. Though no precise resolve had been passed to this effect, it was well understood that this was the course the House meant to pursue, after having given the subject a deliberate and solemn consideration.

Shall we now, said Mr. N., after this mature consideration, on the mere suggestion of personal inconvenience, on a subject of such importance as to invite a gentleman from a considerable distance, [referring to some old plan,] shall we, after the sanction of an uniform practice, fortified by the long period for which it has been observed, on the suggestion of a trifling inconvenience, which, he believed, on examination, would not be found to exist at all, adopt the innovation proposed by the report of the committee? For his part, he thought they were all deeply interested in having the debates well taken, as it was not in their power altogether to prohibit their being taken.

He had heard but two objections made to the old plan. The first was, that by passing a resolve admitting stenographers within the bar, the House gave a sanction to the reports published by them. The second was, that, as the Speaker had heretofore had the management of the business, it would be wrong to take it out of his hands.

As to the first objection, he thought it altogether incorrect. The resolution, submitted by the gentleman from North Carolina, (Mr. HILL,) which he wished the House to adopt, does not propose the selection of any particular person. It admits, generally, those individuals who wish to take the debates. Can this admission make us responsible for the conduct of men we do not know, and over whom we have no control? Have we heretofore been considered as responsible? And wherein consists the difference between our past situation and the situation we shall be in, if the motion of the gentleman from North Carolina be adopted? We shall then only have done that which before had been done by the Speaker. Governed by a sense of duty, the Speaker had refused admission within the bar. It became, therefore, necessary, in order to admit it, for the House to pass a resolution. But it did not follow that the least responsibility would arise from such an act.

Indeed, by admitting the stenographers within the bar, the responsibility of the House would be diminished; for, if the House admitted them, no one could then say that it had done anything that interfered with a faithful report of the debates; whereas, by excluding the stenographers, the unavoidable inaccuracies committed, might be charged to the House.

The second objection made to the resolution of the gentleman from North Carolina, was that, as the Speaker had heretofore had the management of the business, it would be wrong to take it out of his hands.

Mr. N. in reply to this objection, that the power, heretofore exercised by the Speaker on this subject, had not been expressly delegated to him by the House. It had often been thought of, but no decision had heretofore been made. As the object asked related to the convenience of the members, he thought they were the best judges of the propriety of granting it. The inconvenience alleged to exist was entirely a matter of opinion. He thought it either had no existence or a very limited one. As he had remarked before, the subject was extremely delicate. He would not consent to furnish room for being charged with a wish to suppress the means of making an inquiry into his conduct. He believed that the innovation contended for, would be so viewed; so far, therefore, from considering it as innocent, he viewed it as wrong in itself, and likely to be mischievous in its effects.

Mr. Otis was one of those who was not disposed to make a strong stand against the resolution offered by the gentleman from North Carolina. He did not view the point in so interesting a light as did the gentleman who had preceded him. It appeared to him in the shape of a question of convenience; and as to his own situation, it could not be affected by any permission given to stenographers to come within the bar. Many of the arguments he had heard, implied that the situation at present occupied by the stenographers was exclusive of all others; whereas if that were inconvenient they might take any other, so that they did not come within the bar.

It is true that the stenographers have hitherto been admitted within the bar. They were admitted because there was room. But, in our present chamber, the room was less; nor could they occupy a part of that little, without materially interfering with the convenience of the members.

In his opinion, the proper question for the House to consider was, whether an admission should take place independent of the Speaker, or whether he should decide its propriety. It did not follow, if the Speaker retained the management, that the exclusion would apply to all occasions. It was true, that the places desired by the stenographers were generally assigned to the high Executive officers of the Government, and the foreign Ministers. But if, in consistence with their accommodation, the indulgence could be granted, during any important debate, he had no doubt of the Speaker's readiness to admit them, and they might thus obtain a temporary place within the bar.

Mr. O. thought the remarks of the gentleman from Virginia covered too much ground. They ascribed to the friends of the report an attempt to preclude the people from obtaining all information of what passed in the House. No such design existed. For his part, he wished the people to know everything that occurred within these walls. There was no doubt of the debates, as heretofore given, being an inadequate organ of the ideas of the members; they had been taken for nearly twelve years, and sometimes they had been accurate, and at other times very inaccurate; and so complete had the distortion of sentiments often been, that had it not been for the name that was attached to a particular speech, the member, to whom it was ascribed, would not have known it to be his. Mr. O. would, notwithstanding, not deny the ability of a person who read the debates, to form a tolerable idea of the arguments used on a particular subject.

The charge of innovation. Mr. O. thought unjust. He proposed to leave the business as it had heretofore been left, free from any resolve of the House, to the control of the Speaker. By this conduct, no sanction would be given to the performances of any reporter; but, on the other hand, if the House passed a resolve, divesting the Speaker of his previous power, they would render themselves responsible, and would virtually give a sanction.

If it were resolved that the House should interfere, he would much rather select and pay an individual competent to the business, and appeal, for the faithful discharge of his trust, to his candor and impartiality.

If the House passed the resolution admitting the stenographers within the bar, Mr. O. asked whether they would not in fact be officers of the House. The only difference between them and the other officers would be that one would be paid and the others would not.

Mr. O. said that, in his opinion, the most inconvenient position in the House had been taken by the stenographers. It was near the Clerk's office, between which and the bar there was a perpetual passage of the members. If an experiment were made of a position on the other side, or in the upper gallery, he was persuaded it would be found very convenient. Are not, said Mr. O., the galleries constructed for the express purpose of hearing? Are they not intended for the good people of the United States? And if they can hear in them cannot the stenographers also?

Mr. O. concluded by stating the extreme inconvenience that would arise from admitting the stenographers; the interference it would produce with the assignation of seats to the Secretaries of our Government and the foreign Ministers; and with declaring his opinion that it was most expedient to adopt the report of the committee.

Mr. NICHOLSON said, that if he understood the objections made by the gentleman from Massachusetts to granting an admission of the stenographers within the bar, they might be classed under three heads: 1. It will be against precedent; 2. It would prevent the members from having elbow-room; 3. There is a possibility that the Speaker may indulge the stenographers.

As to the first objection, he would ask whether the House had not a right to exercise any power themselves that was exercised by the Speaker. Hitherto the Speaker has exercised the power, and admitted the stenographers within the bar; he now refuses to do it, and we are called upon to perform what he refuses. If we think it proper to admit them, we have a right to do it. The power heretofore exercised by the Speaker was derived from us, according to the well known maxim. *Qui facit per alium, facit per se.*

But we are told that the admission would interfere with the accommodation of the four Secretaries and the foreign Ministers. Suppose it should, said Mr. N.; I ask whether the convenience and the interest of the people of the United States are to be prostrated by our complaisance to the Secretaries and foreign agents? It is our duty to enable the people to obtain the best information of what is doing here that we can supply. Shall we abandon our duty? Shall we sacrifice the interest of our constituents to a sense of politeness to these gentlemen? It would be much better to submit to the inconvenience experienced by the Secretaries and the foreign Ministers, if there is not room for them within the bar, than to conceal from the people the knowledge they have a right to possess. Let, then, the foreign Ministers, if there be such a competition, retire into the galleries.

He considered the subject as of high importance both to the country and the members themselves. They all ought to desire their conduct to be rigidly inspected.

Gentlemen say that the debates have been heretofore imperfectly taken. Will they remedy the evil by excluding the stenographers from places within the bar? If, heretofore, notwithstanding the favorableness of their position, when stillness and silence reigned, they have been unable to take the debates with precision, can it be expected that, driven to a distance from most of the members, surrounded by a crowd in perpetual motion, they will be able more successfully to accomplish their object? Sir, said Mr. N., the expectation is absurd. It cannot be done. I have placed myself without the bar, and I declare it impossible to hear correctly. If, then, you are determined to exclude them from their usual places, you had infinitely better turn them out of the House altogether.

As to the convenience of the galleries for hearing, Mr. N. was not able, from a trial made by himself, to decide upon it. But he had heard but one uniform opinion, which was, that owing to the constant passage of persons, and the frequent crowd it would contain, it was impossible to hear there with any distinctness. With respect to the remarks made by the gentleman from Massachusetts on this point, he thought them altogether inapposite. The gallery was not constructed by us, and if it were a bad place for hearing it arose not from any fault to be ascribed to us.

All that we did was to open our doors to all citizens who conducted themselves with decorum.

The personal inconvenience to members alleged, did not, in the opinion of Mr. N., exist. He thought there was ample room. The chamber they occupied was similar to that in Philadelphia, and the positions desired by the stenographers were relatively the same as those in Philadelphia. By advancing the Clerk's table three feet, every difficulty would be removed.

Mr. RUTLEDGE said, that the members who had preceded him had talked much about the necessity of giving the people correct information of the transactions of that House. He believed there was not a single member who did not wish to impart to the people all the knowledge they could receive, and who did not highly prize the means of information furnished by the proceedings of that House. On this point there was no division. No one was desirous of excluding the stenographers, or prohibiting the publication of debates. The only question really before the House was, whether they should confide in the integrity and the talents of the Speaker, who had hitherto merited their confidence, or whether, divesting him of his power, they should exercise a right themselves hitherto attached to his office.

Such a mode of procedure as had been pursued on this occasion was not conformable to that heretofore practised. An application somewhat similar had been, some time since, made to the Speaker. The Speaker decided, and the House, without debate, acquiesced in his decision. A stenographer had grossly misrepresented a member, and when required to correct his false statement, had insolently refused to do it, and added to the previous injury of misstatement insult of the most contumelious kind. The Speaker dismissed him from his place for this barefaced misconduct. Some of his friends made an appeal to the House. The House acted wisely, and, with becoming dignity, refused to interpose.

Now, said Mr. R., if any other stenographer, like the one I have alluded to, shall make it his systematic practice to misrepresent, and he continue as heretofore to hold his place at the tenure of the Speaker's permission, he may be dismissed by the Speaker without troubling the House. But should the motion made by the gentleman from North Carolina prevail, we shall be perpetually appealed to, and occupied in debate. For these reasons he trusted the report would be agreed to.

Mr. HILL said he considered the subject as simply involving an address to the sentiments of the members on the ground of personal convenience, and that on that ground he was ready to sacrifice any little inconvenience to the accommodations of the stenographers; stating at the same time his entire reliance upon the integrity and talents of the Speaker.

Mr. GRISWOLD said, this is nothing less than an appeal from the Chair. To the Speaker has heretofore been committed the regulation of the admission of all persons whatever within the bar. This is the only correct mode in which such an object can be accomplished. The Speaker must exercise the discretion hitherto vested in him, otherwise the order of the House cannot be preserved. The object now is to take this power from the Speaker, and to open the area of the House to the stenographers, without the Speaker's approbation. It is said that only two persons at present apply. But if the door be once opened to admission in this way, there may be no end to intrusion. The Speaker being divested of power to act, and the necessity of acting being evident, the House will be perpetually troubled with appeals.

In his opinion, the power confided to the Speaker had been exercised in this case with great propriety. It must be apparent to everybody that the area was too small to justify the admission of the stenographers. He believed it to be an idle pretence that the stenographers could not hear. He believed it to be a mere matter of pride, which would be gratified by an appeal from the Chair, and a reversal of the decision of the Speaker by the House.

Mr. THATCHER, persuaded that all the information derived from the debates of this House was of little comparative importance when viewed in relation to the general mass of information possessed by the people, cared but little for the event of the resolution before the House. Upon this ground he felt no anxiety whatever. As a matter of order, it might perhaps be of some importance. As to the convenience of position, he doubted whether a more correct account of the debates could not be given from a situation from without the bar than within it. His reasons were these: It was well known that for four or five sessions after the organization of the Federal Government stenographers never came within the bar, and their positions during that period were as remote from the members as at present. Yet if any man would appeal to the debates then taken, he would find them as correctly taken as they have been at any time since. It is true, there were complaints of inaccuracy, but the debate takers never assigned, as a justification of their errors, the inconvenience of their situations; on the contrary, they declared that they did as well as they could, and contended that their reports were as correct as the nature of the case permitted.

When the seat of Government was transferred to Philadelphia, and the stenographers occupied places within the bar, complaints increased, the debates were taken more incorrectly, and two or three of the stenographers were actually turned out of the area within the bar; one of whom, he believed, was sent into the upper gallery.

The incorrectness of the published debates did not arise so much from an inability to hear as from an inability to take down a rapid speech.

Mr. T. said he believed the debates as taken down by Mr. Lloyd, were as accurately taken as any taken before or since. The conclusion he drew from these facts was, that if the stenographers were admitted by the

House within the bar, the public would gain nothing by it. He had, however, no objection to their admission, if the Speaker approved it. They might, as far as he cared, take any place in the House; even seats along side of the Speaker.

Mr. Davis had expected to hear substantial reasons in support of the report of the committee. None such had been offered. It was said that the stenographers could hear very well from their present positions. He denied it. The reporter could not possibly hear. Though himself nearer the gentleman, he had not heard a word that fell from the gentleman from North Carolina.

He trusted the House would admit the stenographers within the bar. If not admitted, the conversation and passage of the members around them will at once prevent the debates from being well taken, and be a perpetual excuse for their errors. But if admitted, they will have no such apology, and they will be within the power of the House.

The great mass of our citizens are too remote to attend your debates. They rely on those who report them. Not more than forty or fifty persons transiently appear in the galleries, who are not equal to diffusing a knowledge of your proceedings. Exclude the stenographers, and you may as well shut your doors. It may be said that you print your Journals; but who reads them? They are scarcely read by the members themselves. On great national questions the people ought to know, not only what you do, but also the principles that guide you.

The gentleman from South Carolina was willing to place the stenographers under the coercion of the Speaker, but was unwilling to place them under the coercion of the House. For this part, he thought differently. He did not wish to see them at the mercy of the Speaker.

Several allusions had been made to the treatment of a reporter at Philadelphia, who had been driven from the House by the Speaker. He recollected the affair, and, in his opinion, the Speaker had in this case been actuated more by personal enmity than by any other motive.

Mr. H. Lee next rose. He said he put it upon the candor of his colleague from Virginia to declare whether, in his opinion, any gentleman in that House wished to suppress his sentiments, or was disposed to shrink from an avowal of them. If an individual were to judge from the debate of to-day, he would infer that it was the desire of some members on that floor to conceal their sentiments from the people. No such thing was the case. We are as anxious as those who differ with us that the people should know what we think, say, and do.

The only question was, whether the Speaker shall exercise a certain power which he can conveniently, and which he has hitherto honorably exercised, or whether we shall assume it with all its inconveniences. He hoped we should not. He feared no inaccuracy so long as the debates published received no sanction from the House.

Have you, said Mr. L., no greater objects to engage your attention than whether this man or that man shall go out of your bar or remain within it? He thought the House might be better employed.

Mr. MACON understood the subject before the House very much as his colleague did. The question was simply whether we will take upon ourselves inconveniences alleged to exist, or keep the stenographers without the bar. He was convinced that the situations occupied by the stenographers were badly calculated for hearing, as even within the bar the members could scarcely hear each other.

One reason had great weight with him. It was, that if the House made a rule in relation to the admission of the stenographers, it would be placing law in the room of discretion. He preferred a certain rule to a vague discretion.

The danger apprehended from a crowd of stenographers was farcical. Since he had been in Congress he had never seen more than three or four. And if the number admitted should prove inconvenient, it would be time enough, when the inconvenience was experienced, to remedy it.

Mr. S. SMITH said the question was entirely one of convenience. He would not ascribe to any member a desire to suppress his sentiments. The speeches never went forth as delivered. Yet it was desirable to assign to the stenographers the most convenient places. He had heard gentlemen on both sides of the Chair declare they would experience no inconvenience from the admission of the stenographers. For himself, from his situation, he could experience none. He believed, indeed, that the members could be heard from any part of the House, and nearly as well in one place as in another. But as other gentlemen hold a different opinion, and the stenographers had hitherto been admitted within the bar, he had not the least objection, and would vote for their admission.

In this stage of the debate, the SPEAKER arose, not, he said, to inquire into the consequences of the House acting in the business, but again to repeat the line of conduct he had pursued, and the motives which had influenced his conduct; he did this for the information of members not in the House at the time he had before addressed the House. The SPEAKER then repeated what he had before stated, viz: that on being appealed to by Mr. STEWART, he had declared to him his decision before any other application had been made; that he had spoken to many members, all of whom, without a single exception, had approved his ideas, and concluded with again declaring, as he had before declared, that the stenographers could not be admitted within the bar without violating the order of the House and the convenience of the members. It was, he said, for the House to decide—to them only was he responsible.

Mr. NICHOLAS understood it to be the object of those who supported the admission of the stenographers within the bar to place them upon the same footing they had heretofore held. This was his object. All the remarks, therefore, made respecting their independence of the Chair, were inapplicable. They would still be subject to his control, except as to the single point of situation. In short, the business would be restored to its old form.

His colleague had made an appeal to his candor. He wished to know whether he (Mr. N.) thought that he or any other gentleman in that House wished to suppress his sentiments, or was disposed to shrink from an avowal of them? He would answer the appeal made by his colleague, and would tell him that he did not feel himself at liberty to form conjectures respecting the opinions of others, but decided from facts. If he heard gentlemen make use of arguments so weak as those he had heard that day in defence of their sentiments, he would say that their feelings differed essentially from his. He would say that, judging them by their arguments, they do not wish publicity to be given to the debates of this House.

What do the gentlemen tell us? Does it not amount to this: that their complaisance for the Speaker suffers him to judge for them in a case where they are the best judges; and would not this complaisance go to this length, that if the Speaker should judge wrong, they will not interfere to correct his error?

We are told by a gentleman just up that the application made proceeds from pride, and that it can proceed from nothing else. But the gentleman has not assigned his reasons for this extraordinary charge.

It is contended that any place without the bar will be convenient for the stenographers. Let the place be pointed out. Let the gentlemen who urged this show us a place without the bar inaccessible to the whispers of the members and the pressure of a crowd. Do they imagine that any particular place can be assigned to which they can insure a profound silence, and from which every person can be withheld? Do they not know, have they not experienced, that when business presses, when subjects of importance are discussed, a crowd is produced, noise ensues, and interposing obstacles render it impossible either to hear or see the members? In such cases, by far the most interesting that can occur, a recess within the bar can be their only protection.

The gentleman from Massachusetts had put the business upon a very extraordinary footing—a footing that he did not expect from him. He represented that it would be safe to trust the reporters to the Speaker's indulgence. For his part, he did not think it would be safe in such hands. Shall the Speaker have the discretion of saying what debates shall be taken and what shall not? Shall he, and he only, have the public ear? Could the Speaker desire this? Surely he could not. He ought rather to desire the House to decide generally than thus impose upon him such an invidious task.

Mr. N. said, he considered those who report the debates as appearing in this House on behalf of the people of the United States, to whom they communicated what passed here. The people were entitled to this information; and if, as observed by the gentleman from Massachusetts, either foreign Ministers or Secretaries, or any other gentleman in long robes, interfered with such an object, they ought to give way. He knew not wherein consisted the propriety of assigning them particular seats. What right had they to exclusive seats? He knew no connexion that subsisted between them and this House. Be the right as it may, he was not for sacrificing a solid benefit to mere complaisance.

But a gentleman has told us that one stenographer, for his misrepresentation and insolence, had been discharged by the Speaker. In the course of debate, Mr. N. said, he had studiously avoided any allusion to this circumstance. Nor would he now say anything about it, as he thought it altogether foreign from the present question.

The respect which gentlemen expressed for the Speaker appeared to him to lead them from the object they professed to have in view. For, at present, the stenographers are not under the control of the Speaker. But admit them within the bar, and if they are guilty of misconduct, if they infringe any of the rules of the House, the Speaker has them within his power.

Some gentlemen apprehend the admission of a crowd of stenographers. The thing is morally impossible. When Congress met in a large populous city, where several daily papers were printed, we saw but two reporters. Here, removed from the busy world, where the demand for that description of labor which arose from publishing the debates was not nearly so great, and, of consequence, the profit less, it could not be expected that there could be more.

Mr. N. concluded by declaring that, in his opinion, it was the duty of the House to decide in this case. The Speaker had changed the established practice of the House. It became, therefore, the House to inquire whether he had done what he ought to have done; which, if he had omitted to do, if devolved on them to see effected.

Mr. WALN spoke in favor of the adoption of the report.

The question was then taken by yeas and nays, on agreeing to the report of the select committee, and carried by the casting vote of the Speaker. There being yeas 45, nays 45. . . .

THE LETTER-WRITERS IN THE SENATE

By Frederick B. Marbut

The sharp editorials and Washington letters of June 1841, berating the United States Senate with the sarcastic harshness at which James Gordon Bennett and his New York *Herald* staff excelled, have been noted

Reprinted from *Journalism Quarterly*, Volume 28, Number 3 (1951), pp. 342-50, by permission of the editor and author.

by several journalism historians and students of the relations between the press and Congress.[1] The *Herald* attacked the Senate for limiting admission to its press privileges to the reporters for the Washington papers. None of the writers, however, points out the background of the quarrel, nor do any give its conclusion. None shows that when the Senate adopted the rule three years earlier, the New York *Express* fought it unsuccessfully almost as vigorously as did Bennett in 1841, with no support at that time from the aggressive Scotch editor.

The Senate first opened its doors to the public, although providing no special facilities to the press, in 1795. On January 5, 1801, for the first time the Upper House, acting on a petition from Samuel Harrison Smith of the *National Intelligencer*, adopted a resolution but made no provision in its Standing Rules, admitting "any stenographer, or note-taker" to "such place, within the area of the Senate Chamber, as the President shall allot." [2] A debate on December 17, 1827 resulted in another resolution instructing the Secretary, under the direction of the President of the Senate, to "cause seats to be prepared for the accommodation of the Reporters of the proceedings of the Senate." [3] The discussion showed that the action was intended to direct the body's officers to provide facilities for the reporters at such points on the floor or in the gallery where they could best hear.

This and other moves in either house of Congress in these years applied not only to the "letter-writers" or correspondents, who wrote comment or explanatory articles for the distant papers and are paralleled by today's occupants of the press gallery. They applied also to the reporters or stenographers—and the two words were sometimes used synonymously in Congressional debate—who tried to take fairly complete verbatim notes of speeches and print them in their respective journals. These latter were the direct ancestors of today's skilled stenographers for the *Congressional Record* who move about the floor following the speakers and taking care to note their exact words. These press accounts were the only record of speeches, for the *Journals* gave, and give today, bare statements of official action. These minute-to-minute stenographic accounts, widely printed in the country's newspapers, were marked by incompleteness and inaccuracy, intentional or unintentional, that brought from the lawmakers either condemnation or efforts to provide facilities by which the stenographers could hear better.[4]

At some time during the next few years, the secretary apparently placed the reporters in the eastern gallery. The Senate then met in the old chamber that was later occupied by the Supreme Court and is now a pausing place of only a moment as Capitol guides conduct their tourist charges through the historic old building. On February 27, 1835 Senator Alexander Porter of Louisiana got the Upper House to adopt a motion that a committee of three "be appointed to examine the report into the expediency of so arranging the seats in the Senate Chamber as will promote the convenience of members, and facilitate the despatch of public business." On March 3 he reported from the committee a motion for a series of rules governing the galleries and limiting those who had access to the floor. The proposals included the following:

> 2. That the Reporters be removed from the eastern gallery, and placed on the floor of the Senate, under the direction of the Secretary.

No action was taken before that session closed, but on December 7, as the 24th Congress convened, the proposal was approved. Thus for the first time specific provision was made for the press in the Senate's Standing Rules.[5]

This was the stage-setting when the Senate eyed the press in 1838. Through actions on March 24 and 26 and April 24, the Senate considered a special committee's proposal that the 47th rule, which listed the persons who might be admitted to the Senate floor, be amended. Most of the rule, under the proposed change, was the same as that adopted in 1838, although buried in its text, among the list of those having the floor privilege, was the following, all of which was new: [6]

> . . . two reporters for each of the daily papers, and one reporter for each tri-weekly paper published in the City of Washington, whose names shall be communicated in writing by the editors of those papers to the Secretary of the Senate, and who shall confine themselves to the seats now provided for them.

The committee report was printed, but it gave only the text of the proposed new rule, without discussing its cause.[7] The *Congressional Globe* failed even to say that the committee reported. The press both of Washington and the rest of the country ignored the matter. The committee report lay without action until the last night, July 9, when it was adopted in the usual close-of-the-session rush on motion of Senator Ambrose H. Sevier of Arkansas.[8]

The press still failed to note it. On January 31, 1840, however, a Baltimore *Republican* editorial, apparently written by its Washington correspondent, said the rule had been adopted at the insistence of Senator John M. Niles, a Connecticut Democrat, "for the express purpose of turning a class of libellers into the galleries, who were in the daily habit of defaming him and the Vice President of the United States, Col. Johnson."

Reporters felt the rule's force, of course, when Congress reconvened in December. The *Congressional Globe* reports that on the 22nd: [9]

> Mr. NORVELL presented the memorial of William Hunt, James F. Otis, Erastus Brooks, William Elwyn Moore, E. Kingman, and William H. Witman stating that they are severally reporters of

Congressional proceedings for the Baltimore American, New York Express, Ohio Statesman, Georgia Journal, Southern Patriot, Charleston Courier, Mobile Register, Lancaster Intelligencer, and that by the rule of the Senate they are deprived of the opportunity and privilege of obtaining information of Congressional proceedings for their respective papers; that the provision of the Senate exclusively furnishing the facilities they ask to city reporters, does not furnish the people of the country with full reports of what takes place until several days after the date of such transactions, where it is the duty and purpose of the above named reporters to transmit such intelligence by each day's mail; and praying that the Senate may assign them such seats on the floor, or in the galleries, as may enable them to discharge their duties to those whose agents they are. The memorial was referred to the Committee on the Contingent Fund.

On January 5, 1839 the committee proposed that the front seats of the eastern gallery to the right of the Chair be set apart for the reporters.[10] The report precipitated a debate that runs through almost four pages of the *Congressional Globe* and found the Democrats, in general, opposing the plan and the Whigs supporting it. Some of the remarks of Senator Niles, while perhaps more violent than was typical, nevertheless show the attitude of many of his colleagues towards the reporters. He said, in part, as quoted in the partially first-person and partially third-person style characteristic of 1839 Congressional reporting:

> He was somewhat surprised at a proposition that the body should sanction, and in some manner endorse, the vile slanders that issue daily from these letter writers by assigning them seats within the chamber. Who were these persons who styled themselves reporters. Why miserable slanderers, hirelings hanging on to the skirts of literature, earning a miserable subsistence from their vile and dirty misrepresentations of the proceedings here, and many of them writing for both sides. . . . Perhaps no member of that body had been more misrepresented and caricatured than himself by those venal and profligate scribblers, who were sent here to earn a disreputable living by catering to the depraved appetite of the papers they work for. . . . Was he not unwilling to do any act that might be supposed to interfere in the slightest degree with the freedom of the press, he would move some resolution to prevent their coming within the walls of that body at all. As it was, let them take their seats in the galleries and write what they pleased, without asking for the sanction of the Senate; for he would not consent for their accommodation, to exclude the honest and respectable citizens who came there as spectators.

Those senators who supported the committee's proposal agreed that much of the letter-writers' work was vicious but, as Senator John Norvell, the Michigan Democrat who sponsored the petition, put it: "It would enable them to perform, with greater facility and accuracy, their engagements to the newspaper press and the reading public." Niles's motion to table finally passed 20 to 17.[11]

No representative of the New York *Herald, Courier and Enquirer,* or *Journal of Commerce* signed the petition as such, although all of these papers had Washington correspondents. Kingman, during much of his Washington career, wrote for the last-named paper, although perhaps he signed this petition as representative of the Charleston *Courier*.[12] Erastus Brooks was the younger brother of James Brooks, editor and publisher of the Whig New York *Express,* and corresponded for that paper.[13] A William Hunt was listed as a claim agent in the 1846 Washington city directory (doubling as claim agents was a practice of several Washington correspondents), but no other record appears of any one by that name who might have been the signer of the Senate petition. The other three appear only this once in the records of capital journalism, and cannot be further identified.

The *Express,* for Erastus Brooks seems to have been the spark-plug of the movement and perhaps was the principal target of Niles in getting the rule through, reacted violently. On January 8 it ran an editorial, part of which follows:

RIGHTS OF REPORTERS

We see that a majority of the members of the United States Senate, 20 ayes and 17 nays, have shut out the Newspaper Reporters (for Newspapers out of the City of Washington) from the Senate, by indefinitely postponing a Resolution that seats be provided for their accommodation in the gallery. We also learn that Senators Niles, Strange and Buchanan accompanied their votes, particularly the two first, with very abusive remarks of the Reporters and the Press in General.

The bitter hostility of such men as Niles to a Free Press is easily accounted for as it tears the Lion's Skin from the Jackass, and distinguishes the braying of that stupid beast from the roar of the Noble Monarch of the Wood. Nor is it remarkable, perhaps, that such a man as Strange, the cockloft hero, perhaps of some social circle, six feet by eight feet in length and breadth, should be chagrined that the Press does not discover him to be so great a man as he fancied he should be, before he trod the arena of the United States Senate. Mr. Buchanan's hostility, however, we cannot account for, as he really is a man of talent, unless he be what the Democracy of the days of Madison charged him with being—an enemy of a Free Press. . . .

After another long paragraph, the editorial was followed by a Washington letter signed by "E.B." and dated "Washington, Jan. 5—Saturday Evening." It said, in part:

Editors, Publishers and Readers you should have been in the Senate-Chamber to-day between the hours of twelve and two. You would have seen in that legislative hall, where meet a part of the assembled wisdom of the land, a sight which perhaps you have imagined although you may never have laid eyes upon the reality of the picture. You would have seen the manner of conducting a trial by some of our "most potent, grave and reverened seignoirs—our very noble and approved good masters," you would have been subdued by their arguments and have been charmed by their eloquence. . . .

The article gave the history of the exclusive rule, which, it said, "was smuggled through the United States Senate in the absence, I believe, of a quorum," and described the reporters' petition. It continued:

> You have the story, and now for the actors who upon one side— favoring the report of the committee,—were Messrs. Preston and Knight. Upon the other side, the speaking characters were Messrs. Niles, Buchanan, King and Strange. Let me introduce to you the characters *propria persona.* First then for Doctor NILES of Connecticut. Nature made him an ostler. Chance, and his own roguery made him an United States Senator. The worst part of nature, therefore, has been despoiled of some of her best proportions. Never was fellow meaner than this same Niles who with the fancies of a dolt makes pretensions to the intellect of the most talented man in the country. His manners are bad, and his breeding worse. . . .

The letter similarly raked some of the other opponents, although none so harshly as Niles.

The *Journal of Commerce*, which was not represented by the petitioners, in a long Washington letter printed on January 8 gave a restrained account of the proceedings, and mildly criticized both the Senate and the correspondents. The Charleston *Courier* limited the debate account to little more than routine treatment in its regular place in Congressional proceedings. While giving Niles's remarks in a few words, it devoted considerable space to South Carolina's Senator William C. Preston, who had supported the correspondents. Among the other papers represented by the petitioners, the *Southern Patriot* of Charleston, the Mobile *Daily Commercial Register and Patriot*, and the *Ohio Statesman* of Columbus ignored the matter.

The *Express* continued for a month to belabor the Senate in editorials and Washington letters before it gave up. The *Herald*, meanwhile, limited itself to a sarcastic Washington letter in the issue of January 12. Signed "Horace," it said, in part:

WASHINGTON, Jan. 7, 1839

On Saturday last the poor reporters who had petitioned for a separate seat in the eastern gallery of the Senate, were rowed up Salt River by the locofoco members, who seemed to be in a terrible fury with the letter writers for not allowing them to have more talent and decency than they possess. Some of these gentlemen were in the

gallery, listening to the debate with anything but a quiet spirit. Old
daddy Niles thought himself, as usual, exceedingly sarcastic and eloquent on the occasion, for having been held up to ridicule by some
of those he had abused in good set terms. . . .

Going finally into a long account of an explanation made to the Senate
by Vice President Richard M. Johnson, written in an exaggerated way to
make the officer look as absurd as possible, it concluded: "But the Vice
President's thoughts, when reflecting on his family, are apt to be *dark* and
gloomy and confused." That Johnson was the father of a Negro girl's
children was a notorious morsel of Washington gossip.[14]

During the next three years, ways were found to get around the
rule. The Baltimore *Republican* editorial of January 31, 1840 and a letter
to President *pro tem.* Samuel Southard of the Senate, printed in the New
York *Herald* of July 2, 1841, said that the *National Intelligencer* claimed
seats both for reporters for its daily and its tri-weekly editions. Inasmuch,
however, as the congressional reports in the tri-weekly were printed from
the type that had been used in the daily editions, one reporter served for
both, and therefore it was able to "farm out" the extra seats. It may have
been imperfect enforcement of the Senate rule that made Bennett think
his men would be admitted if he stepped up his accounts of floor
proceedings.

The Whig party victory of 1840 and President William Henry Harrison's call for a special session to convene at the end of May, 1841
spurred the country's interest in capital proceedings. On Harrison's death,
John Tyler allowed the special session call to stand. Since the Washington
papers had found complete stenographic reports of Congressional proceedings an expensive burden and had, at this time, fallen into the habit
of abbreviating them, often at the expense of accuracy, and since the
Herald had now funds to undertake an expensive enterprise, it prepared
to seize the prestige and circulation to be gained from exhaustive accounts
of the two houses at work. It said on May 24:

> Next Monday, the Extra Session of Congress opens—and one
> of the most important it will be that has been held in many years.
> The tariff, bank, public lands, a bankrupt law, and various other
> financial and commercial measures will be examined and discussed. A
> full, accurate, and comprehensive *daily* report of the debates in both
> houses will, therefore, be one of the most important pieces of enter-
> prise that an independent press, situated in the center of the social,
> financial and political systems of this country, can possibly give. The
> public expect it from some quarter.
>
> To meet this expectation, as far as we can, we have now or-
> ganised, at vast expense, an efficient *corps* of the ablest reporters that
> this country can afford, who will furnish us, at the close of every day's
> proceedings, a report of the debates. This will be transmitted to us

by Express mail, and will invariably appear in the second edition of the Herald on the second day after. . . .

In the execution of this enterprise we anticipate not much difficulty, although we learn that the Washington newspapers are secretly combining, to cause Congress to exclude all reporters for distant cities, from the usual facilities of the two houses. We cannot believe that such short-sighted illiberality can exist a moment. . . .

The House of Representatives admitted correspondents for outside papers and was not involved in the controversy.

This service the *Herald* was preparing to offer was a stenographic account of the minute-to-minute proceedings of a type that is never today attempted by the press. It was to be in addition to the contributions of "correspondents" or "letter-writers" whose comments on the capital background appeared over anonymous signatures. The nearly-verbatim reports were to be supplied by a staff mustered by Robert Sutton who, according to Benjamin Perley Poore, was a "short, stout, pragmatical Englishman, whose desire to obtain extra allowances prompted him to revise, correct, and polish up reports which should have been verbatim." [15]

The *Herald* of June 2 said Bennett's plans had struck a snag. A Washington account dated Monday, May 31 gave a routine report on the opening day of the special session, and added, at the end:

EXCLUSION OF HERALD REPORTERS FROM THE SENATE

At the close of the day's proceedings, the President *pro tem.,* Mr. Southard, Senator from New Jersey, sent the sergeant-at-arms to inform Mr. Sutton, reporter for the Herald, that he wished to see him. The request was instantly attended to, and Mr. Southard then intimated that the Herald reporters could not be permitted to have access to the Reporters' desks in the Senate Chamber in future. . . .

The account, obviously written by Sutton, continued in mild language to discuss the rule. But the mildness dropped from the editorial, presumably Bennett's, in the next day's issue. It said:

We have to record this day one of the most outrageous, highhanded, unconstitutional acts ever perpetrated by any legislative assembly in a free land—an act of depotism, tyranny and usurpation against the liberty of the press which the House of Lords of England, at this day, would not attempt against any newspaper in England.

The reporters of the New York Herald were, on Monday last, excluded from the usual seats and facilities appropriated to such a purpose, by the Hon. SAM. SOUTHARD, President, *pro tem.,* of the U.S. Senate. . . .

The rule, the article continued, limited press accommodations in the upper house to "the pauper and mendicant prints of Washington," and readers were promised that, since the paper had organized a "superb *corps* of Reporters at Washington, at an expense of nearly $200 per week," they would receive complete accounts in spite of the restriction. Post-master General Francis Granger, it intimated, was being influenced to delay the paper's mail.

Nearly every issue of the *Herald*, during the next week, found occa-sion, in commenting on some item or other of Washington news, to bring in another rap at the Senate, and the fact that "enormous expense," nearly $200 per week, was involved, was hammered home repeatedly. An editorial on June 10 included a letter Bennett sent to Senator Henry Clay of Kentucky, saying, among other things, that he intended to give the reports "without asking any of the printing or indirect remuneration of that body," and declaring that he addressed himself to the Kentuckian, the most powerful member of a Whig-dominated body, "as one of the most liberal and enlightened members."

Clay's reply was inserted in an editorial on the 12th. Dated the 7th, the letter promised that "I will see if your Reporter cannot, by some modification of the rule, be admitted, as it would give me pleasure to be instrumental in rendering that accommodation to you." The editorial continued:

> One of our purposes . . . has been to put down the lying, slander-ing, letter-writing systems which is pursued by a set of miserable ad-venturers at Washington. . . .
>
> The principle of our power is our locality in New York, the centre of an immense intellectual empire. The Washington prints are lo-cated in a village, merely, and, therefore, have to resort to the public treasury, and to assume the position of public paupers. . . .

The *Express*, which had unwillingly surrendered three years earlier when the Democrats dominated the Senate, did not now support the *Herald's* fight on a chamber led by its own political patrons. Erastus Brooks was no longer its Washington correspondent, but it had long accounts of the floor proceedings of the two houses. Only on June 23 did it comment on Bennett's dilemma:

> REPORTERS IN THE SENATE CHAMBER—Reporters in the Senate Chamber [sic]—We have heard much said of late in re-gard to the exclusion of the Reporters of a City paper from the Senate chamber at Washington. The language of vituperation has been ex-hausted almost in abuse of the presiding officer of the body for the exclusion, when in fact he had no more control over the admission or rejection of a reporter than the mayor of the city or anybody else who had no power. . . . We do not like the rule, and took ground against it, when it was adopted, as partial, unjust and tyrannical; . . . We have re-ported the proceedings in the Senate for several years at Washington,

and for the majority of the time we were compelled to do so with the crowd in the gallery, remembering what we could, and writing as we could, sometimes upon a hat, sometimes upon the back of a good natured friend who was willing to serve us as a desk for want of a better.

The *Herald's* onslaught ended July 2 with an editorial which repeated much that had been said, but included a long letter which Sutton sent to Southard on June 23. That document protested that an *Express* representative used the third seat claimed by the Washington *National Intelligencer* for its tri-weekly edition, and asked that space be reserved for the press in the "square gallery." That is the gallery which still looks down over that room from the east. The "circular gallery" which was there at that time has been removed.

On the day this article appeared, Senator Richard Henry Bayard, a Delaware Whig, moved that "so much of the 47th rule . . . as respects the admission of reporters on the floor of the Senate be referred to a select committee." With that resolution adopted, Bayard was named chairman.[16] The *Herald's* routine Congressional report quoted Clay as saying during debate on the measure that he had himself intended to offer a similar step. An editorial two days later, the paper's last reference to the controversy, praised the committee's appointment, but rapped the Washington Post Office for delaying its mails as much, it said, as 12 to 20 hours behind the regular time. "We have strong reasons for suspecting," it added, that the delay was brought about by the Washington papers' influence.

On July 8 the committee reported, and the Senate adopted, the following resolution:[17]

> That so much of the 47th rule of the Senate as admits reporters on the floor of the Senate, be rescinded; and that the Secretary cause suitable accommodations to be prepared in the eastern gallery, for such reporters as may be admitted by the rules of the Senate.

On July 24, Senator Southard issued an order which, not being a part of the Standing Rules, was printed neither in the *Journal*, the *Congressional Globe*, nor the official compilations of the Senate's orders. It read:[18]

> The report of the committee having left the arrangement of the Reporters under the superintendence of the Presiding officer of the Senate—
> *Let the following Rules be adopted:*
> 1. None are to be admitted within the Reporters' rail, who are not really and *bona fide* Reporters, to be so certified by the *Editors* of the papers for which they report.

2. The Editors of the daily papers in Washington, are to have two Reporters. If they issue a tri-weekly, this will not entitle them to an additional Reporter.

3. A tri-weekly in Washington is to have one Reporter.

4. No paper out of Washington is to be entitled to more than one Reporter.

5. The desks will be numbered from one to ten.

6. The numbers will be drawn for. And, if the paper is entitled to two Reporters, they will occupy the desk adjoining, in addition to the one they drew.

7. After the numbers are decided, let a certificate signed by the Sergeant-at-Arms of the Senate, be given, thus:—

"No .... Reporter's Desk,

Admit the Reporter for ...."

If any Editors employ more than one Reporter, they can, in this mode, change as often as they see fit.

These regulations have been submitted to, and approved by the committee appointed on the conduct of Reporters. SAM'L. L. SOUTHARD, President &c.

Senate Chamber, 24th July, 1841.

These regulations apparently governed the press in the Upper House until it moved to its present quarters, and assigned the present gallery to the reporters, in January 1859. Thus Bennett won the fight which the *Express* had lost three years earlier.

NOTES

[1] Willard Grosvenor Bleyer, *Main Currents in History of American Journalism* (Boston, Houghton Mifflin Co., 1927), 196, quoting Isaac C. Pray, *Memoirs of James Gordon Bennett and His Times* (New York, 1855), 289-290; Frank Luther Mott, *American Journalism* (Revised Edition, New York, Macmillan, 1950), 309; Frederick Seaton Siebert, *The Rights and Privileges of the Press* (New York, Appleton-Century, 1934), 59.

[2] *Annals of Congress*, 7th Cong., 1st Sess., 22; *Senate Journal*, 38, 41; *National Intelligencer*, Jan. 8, 1802.

[3] *Register of Debates*, 20th Cong., 1st Sess., 8.

[4] Elizabeth Gregory McPherson, *The History of Reporting the Debates and Proceedings of Congress*, unpublished Ph.D. thesis, University of North Carolina, 1941, *passim*.

[5] *Senate Journal*, 23rd Cong., 2nd Sess., 198, 236. The *Register of Debates* shows no discussion of the move; *Senate Journal*, 24th Cong., 1st Sess., 5.

[6] *Senate Journal*, 25th Cong., 2nd Sess., 311, 318, 376.

[7] *Senate Document*, 25th Cong., 2nd Sess., No. 403.

[8] *Congressional Globe*, 25th Cong., 2nd Sess., 506.

[9] *Congressional Globe*, 25th Cong., 2nd Sess., 61.

[10] *Ibid.*, 100.

[11] *Ibid.*, 100-103.

[12] Frederick B. Marbut, "Early Washington Correspondents: Some Neglected Pioneers," JOURNALISM QUARTERLY, XXV (Dec. 1948), 369-374.

[13] *Dictionary of American Biography*, III, 76-77.

14 Arthur M. Schlesinger Jr., *The Age of Jackson* (Boston: Little, Brown and Company, 1945), 141.

15 Benjamin Perley Poore, *Perley's Reminiscences of Sixty Years in the National Metropolis* (2 vols., Tecumseh, Mich. 1889), I, 260.

16 *Senate Journal*, 27th Cong., 1st Sess., 73; *Congressional Globe*, 145.

17 *Senate Journal*, 78.

18 *Manual of Parliamentary Practice, compiled originally for the Senate of the United States by Thomas Jefferson. The Constitution of the United States, and the Rules for Conducting Business in Both Houses of Congress; With all the Amendments, erasures and additions down to the year 1848. . . .* (Columbus, O., 1848), 192-194.

2

Accommodation and Regulation
of the Corps

Frederick Marbut, in *News From the Capital*, (see Bibliography) recounts the major 19th Century conflicts between the emerging news media and Congress as both institutions worked out a new, albeit tenuous, balance in their relationships. The major outcome of this process was the establishment of the Standing Committee of Correspondents.

By the 1870's the Rules Committee of the Senate had initiated the practice of having a group of correspondents, subject to check by the responsible authority in each house, rule on who could be admitted to the galleries. This led to the establishment of the Standing Committee of Correspondents which, since 1916, has been recognized as the governing body of the press galleries. Marbut's history of the Committee is reprinted here.

Since the issue of access seems to have stabilized, the question of gallery access now is one mainly determined by the correspondents themselves. This is illustrated by Luther Huston's account of the 1971 controversy over gallery admission for a representative of the Underground Press Service.

Congress' preoccupation now appears to be the nature and extent of its accommodation of the news media. This is summarized by James White.

THE STANDING COMMITTEE OF CORRESPONDENTS
By Frederick B. Marbut

Every year the 700 * Washington newspapermen who have been admitted to membership in the Press Galleries of Congress elect some of their number to the Standing Committee of Correspondents. In even-

Reprinted from *Journalism Quarterly*, Volume 38, Number 1 (1961), pp. 52-58.
* This figure was about 1,200 in 1973.—Ed.

numbered years they elect two and in odd-numbered years, three. Those named serve two years. Thus the committee consists of five, elected for overlapping terms.

The committee passes on applications for membership in the Press Galleries.* It negotiates with the Architect of the Capitol and appropriate committees for improvements in the press facilities in the Capitol and in the office buildings. It selects the Press Gallery superintendents and their assistants although, once nominated by the committee, those employes are paid from public funds. It arranges for press facilities at committee hearings. It may seek expulsion from the Press Galleries of those who violate its rules or the rules of Congress.

Furthermore, the National Committee of each political party has placed the Standing Committee in charge of press facilities at its national conventions. The Republican party started doing so in 1904 and the Democrats in 1912. And the model for control of press facilities of the national parliamentary body in Washington seems to have been followed in many of the other world capitals and in state capitals.[1]

Since 1943 the committee has kept careful records, which are preserved by Joseph E. Wills, superintendent of the Senate Press Gallery.[2] The files contain an irregular collection of minutes and correspondence, some of which dates from as early as 1911. They contain nothing, however, from the nineteenth century. Those records which would tell of the committee's origin are gone. But a miscellaneous set of records is available which makes it possible to piece together much of the story of how it began.

It was apparently organized about 1877. By that time the Standing Rules in the House of Representatives provided special galleries for the press, ruled that no claim agents might be admitted under pretense of being reporters, ordered seats available on the floor for the Associated Press, and placed the galleries under control of the Speaker. Similar rules had been adopted by the Senate although in 1873 that body placed the Rules Committee rather than the President Pro-Tem. in charge.[3]

There were never-ending efforts by lobbyists and claim agents to pose as correspondents and secure the newspapermen's privileges. Some department clerks engaged in part-time reporting. Some legitimate reporters used their press gallery privileges and congressional contacts to branch out into such profitable sidelines as lobbying, pressing claims and selling tips to lobbyists and speculators. Members of the two houses were annoyed to have the privileges which they extended thus misused. Those correspondents who did not engage in such practices wanted to exclude those who did. The burden on the Speaker and the Rules Committee must have been great. The answer seemed to be to give extensive au-

---

* The Radio-Television, Periodical and Photographers' Galleries elect their own committees.—Ed.

thority to an elected police group among the reputable correspondents but to make their work subject to check by the responsible authority in each house. That happened about 1877.

Readers of the discussion which follows must keep in mind the fact that three different sets of rules or regulations are to be considered. First, the House of Representatives, by resolutions or rules changes in 1802, 1811, 1813, 1815, 1838, 1852, 1857 (the date the present quarters were occupied) and 1866 had directed how the Press Galleries were to be governed. In the second place the Senate had acted in 1802, 1827, 1835, 1838, 1841, 1858 (again, the time of occupancy of the present Senate Chamber) and 1873. Thirdly, acting within the framework of the rules or resolutions acted on on these dates, the Speaker and the Rules Committee, working with the Standing Committee, laid down the regulations which are the subject before us.

Imperfect records show:

1. Washington correspondents met on November 5, 1877, to select a committee to confer with Speaker Samuel J. Randall. The meeting received very sketchy treatment in the Washington press, leaving us today not knowing who the committee members were.[4]

2. There was another meeting in April 1879, this time in the New York *Times* Washington office. Those present adopted rules prepared by the executive committee regulating admission to the reporters' galleries in both houses. The *Evening Star* of April 4 said: "The old executive committee of last year was reelected, consisting of Mr. George W. Adams, Gen. H. V. Boynton, E. B. Wight, L. Q. Washington and William C. MacBride." The papers represented by this group were, respectively, the New York *World*, the Cincinnati *Gazette*, the Chicago *Tribune*, the Louisville *Courier-Journal* and the Baltimore *American*. Boynton had commanded Union regiments in the Tennessee campaigns of 1862 and 1863 and was wounded at Missionary Ridge.

3. Five days later, Adams sent a note to Speaker Randall. Using a plain sheet of paper, he wrote by hand a letterhead: "Press Gallery. H. of R." "Please sign the accompanying tickets for admission to the Reporters Gallery as approved by the Standing Committee of Correspondents on the gallery," he asked.[5] This seems to be the earliest record now to be found which uses the words "Standing Committee of Correspondents." The note shows that the committee was in effective working operation by then.

4. On March 3, 1883, Boynton telegraphed to the Cincinnati *Commercial-Gazette* a story angrily blasting J. Warren Keifer of Ohio, the Speaker. As part of that story, he wrote that James G. Blaine and Randall, during the respective terms in which each presided over the House, had extended special help to the correspondents. "Under Speaker Randall new rules were adopted and better facilities extended than were ever

enjoyed before," he wrote. Blaine, a Maine Republican, wielded the gavel from 1869 to 1875 and Randall, a Democrat from Philadelphia, from 1876 to 1881.

5. Boynton's story arose out of a quarrel which he had with Keifer during which the latter accused him of making a corrupt approach. Keifer said in a speech in the House and later before an investigating committee that Boynton tried to bribe him to put through a private land bill out of which the reporter stood to profit heavily. If it had been true, under the rules Boynton would have been expelled from the Press Galleries. A thorough committee investigation vindicated Boynton and caught Keifer up in a clumsy set of untruths.

The investigating committee, meeting in 1884, introduced into its record a set of regulations governing the Press Gallery which Keifer had signed on becoming Speaker in 1881. They read: [6]

Rules Governing the Press Gallery of the House of Representatives

1. Persons desiring admission to the Press Gallery shall make application to the Speaker, as required by Rule 36 of the House of Representatives; and shall also state, in writing, for which paper or papers they are employed; and shall further state that they are not engaged in the prosecution of claims pending before Congress, and will not become so engaged while allowed admission to the gallery.
2. The applications required by Rule I shall be authenticated in a manner that shall be satisfactory to the standing committee of correspondents, who shall see that the occupation of the gallery is confined to bona fide correspondents for daily newspapers, and not exceeding one seat shall be assigned to each paper.
3. Clerks in the Executive Department of the Government, or persons engaged in other occupations whose chief support is not derived from newspaper correspondence, are not entitled to admission.
4. Wives and families of correspondents are not entitled to admission.
5. The gallery, subject to the approval of the Speaker of the House of Representatives, shall be under the control of the Standing Committee of correspondents.

> H. V. Boynton
> Wm. C. MacBride
> E. B. Wight
> Edwin Fleming
> F. A. G. Handy
> Committee of Correspondents

6. During the session which convened in December 1879, the House rewrote its rules. The meeting described under point No. 2 of this article could have been called as part of the discussion of the rules' revision. The

provision of the new rules governing the press gallery was essentially the rule of 1857, although it was shortened a good deal. A requirement that applicants for admission specify in writing the name of their paper and the part of the gallery they would occupy was removed. So was one forbidding extension of gallery privileges to claim agents. Although these sections were taken out of the House rule, they were present in the regulations drawn by the Standing Committee as given above. The rule of 1879, however, did specifically authorize the Speaker to admit two Associated Press reporters to the floor, as had been done since 1866, and it placed him in control.

The records on these six points make it pretty clear what happened. At some point, Speaker Randall and the newly created Standing Committee worked out between them an agreement as to the extent to which the latter would govern the Press Galleries. Randall no doubt signed an order setting out these regulations, and from that time on the committee passed on applicants for membership and sent the names to the Speaker for him to issue admission cards. When Keifer succeeded to the Speakership, he signed the same regulations, as have all speakers since that time.[7] When the Standing Rules were revised in 1879, it was possible to take certain points out of the rules and include them in the regulations signed by the Speaker.

The Senate moved in the same direction a few years later. That body adopted an extensive revision of its rules on January 16, 1884. Rule XXXIV under this revision reaffirmed the Rules Committee's power to govern the Senate wing of the Capitol. And it directed the committee to "make such regulations respecting the reporters' gallery of the Senate as will confine its occupation to *bona fide* reporters for daily newspapers, assigning not to exceed one seat to each paper." [8]

The committee next drafted new regulations under its authority to govern the north wing of the building and approved them on March 15. Included as "Rule IV" were provisions assigning various parts of the gallery to the public, to the ladies, the President, Senators' families and diplomats. They set aside the gallery behind the Vice President's chair for reporters. That had been the press gallery since the chamber was first occupied in 1859 and is reserved for the press today.

"Rule V" was in language almost identical to that of the regulations which Randall and Keifer had approved in the House except for different paragraphing and the fact that it recognized the Rules Committee, rather than the Speaker, as the governing authority to which the Standing Committee was responsible. From 1884 to the present the rule laid down by the Senate committee in the annually-published compilation of rules for the regulation of the Senate wing of the Capitol has been that agreed to by the Standing Committee, by the Speaker of the House and by the Senate Rules Committee. Since 1888 they have been published in each issue of the *Congressional Directory*.

Those regulations were kept essentially intact until 1947 although they were modified in small details. In 1891, Speaker Thomas B. Reed approved additions which would direct the Standing Committee to report to him violations of the provisions and which also provided that the press list in the *Congressional Directory* be limited to correspondents sending material by telegraph. In 1896 the Senate conformed. At the same time, the latter agreed that "Correspondents entitled to the privileges of the Press Gallery may be admitted to the Marble Room under such regulations as may be prescribed by the Committee on Rules." In 1916 the House wrote into its Standing Rules authority for the Standing Committee to control Press Gallery employees, subject to the Speaker's direction.

As the twentieth century advanced, the Standing Committee faced the problems raised by the fact that media other than newspapers were reporting the news and knocking at the Press Gallery doors. After hearings and discussions between 1933 and 1938 it voted to refuse to admit radio reporters. As a result, both houses of Congress, in 1939, set up separate galleries for radio reporters, allowing them to be governed, as were the Press Galleries, by the Speaker and by the Rules Committee, with immediate control in the hands of the Executive Committee of the Radio Correspondents' Association. Since 1953 it has been the Radio and Television Correspondents' Association. Magazine writers, too, soon gained separate gallery and similar governing arrangements.

After 1947, the problem of the Negro press and government information services created issues that resulted in redrawing the regulations that had stood with minor amendments since 1884.

Minutes of the Standing Committee show that as early as November 18, 1943, it discussed a letter to Speaker Sam Rayburn from the Associated Negro Press in which there was submitted an application for membership in the Press Galleries. At that meeting Merriman Smith, United Press White House correspondent, told the committee that the White House Correspondents' Association had received a similar letter and had referred the matter to Stephen T. Early, the President's press secretary. Discussion showed that the committee members felt that since the Negro journals were weekly papers rather than dailies they did not qualify. The applications were tabled pending further information.

Similar action was taken two years later when another application from a Negro reporter for Negro journals was received. The applicant this time was Louis R. Lautier, who a few years later became the first of his race to be admitted to membership in the National Press Club. When the issue was raised this time, the Rules Committee forced action.

On March 17, 1947, the Standing Committee prepared a statement saying it had refused the Negro's application because he represented weekly papers and the rules limited the Galleries to reporters for dailies.

It asked for a month in which to study possible amendments. The Rules Committee, which had become the Committee on Rules and Administration under the Congressional reorganization of the previous year, called a special meeting for the next day. It failed to act on the proposal for a study but, overriding the Standing Committee, issued a card to Lautier admitting him to the Senate Press Gallery.

The Standing Committee met again the next day. The minutes record that "Members freely expressed their indignation at the arbitrary action of the Senators in ignoring the Standing Committee's recommendation for a one-month study" and referred to "the obvious political motivation behind the Senatorial order." It wrote to Senator Wayland Brooks of Illinois, the committee chairman, that "the unprecedented action of the Senate Rules Committee in overruling the Standing Committee places Mr. Lautier in the incongruous position of being credited to one press gallery and not to the other." Therefore, the letter said, the committee decided to ask the Speaker to issue a card to the House Gallery as well.

Since the Rules and Administration Committee had acted arbitrarily on Lautier's application as an individual instance, in a manner contrary to the regulations as interpreted by the Standing Committee, the latter group decided to revise those regulations to conform. The entire Press Gallery membership was called into a special meeting on May 8 and approved an additional paragraph in the regulations. That paragraph would admit not more than two permanent Washington correspondents for each *bona fide* news association which regularly serviced news of national affairs to a substantial number of weekly newspapers. Those papers must be entitled to second-class mailing privileges, must be sold regularly for profit, and must pay for the service. And the regulations forbade that they be interpreted to admit writers for publications for special economic, labor or business interests. The additional regulation was duly approved by the Senate Rules Committee and by the Speaker of the House.

But the admission of the Negro reporters did not settle the problem of new demands on Press Gallery seats.

Government information agencies started trying in 1943. The Standing Committee minutes for November 18 say that "Mr. Paul Frederickson and Mr. M. F. Stonehouse, O.W.I., appeared before the committee and gave detailed statements concerning the type of news O.W.I. was handling from the hill." (The O.W.I. was the Office of War Information; "hill" is common Washingtonese for the Capitol.) After discussion "it was unanimously agreed that this committee was without jurisdiction in this matter as the rules governing the Congressional Press Galleries clearly prohibit the use of the galleries by Government agencies."

Six years later the State Department applied. In 1949 the Office of International Information, an ancestor of the present United States Information Agency, applied to have its reporters admitted to the Press Galleries. At the same meetings, the Committee considered applicants from the Labor Press Association.

The issue was debated in five meetings between June 27 and October 17. William S. White of the New York *Times*, chairman, felt that both the labor groups and the State Department representative should be admitted, but that they could not be as the regulations stood. He and some other, both on the Committee and among the correspondents outside the membership, felt that the regulations should be amended.

At this point a quarrel developed. Some correspondents who were not members of the Standing Committee determined to oppose any easing of the barriers. Going over the heads of the Standing Committee, they made direct approaches to some members of the Senate Committee on Rules and Administration.[9] The quarrel was reflected in the press committee's minutes. They show motions made, seconded, amended and withdrawn, points of order, appeals to the chair, motions to table and other parliamentary maneuvers among the five members which read like the journal of one of the Houses of Congress itself during the consideration of involved legislation. At one point the Rules and Administration Committee met with the Standing Committee, but the Senators took no action beyond directing the correspondents to settle their own quarrel among themselves. The set of regulations presented below was approved on October 17 and two days later they were accepted by both the Speaker and the Senate Committee.

On the 17th, too, White resigned as chairman of the Standing Committee. In a statement to the Press Gallery membership he said he did so because of the interference of a minority of the accredited correspondents although he found the regulations as finally drafted "did not appear to me to be necessarily objectionable in themselves."

Thus these regulations replaced those which had been originally approved by Speaker Randall, probably in 1879, and had been amended only in minor detail in more than 60 years. Those in force today read:

1. Administration of the press galleries shall be vested in a Standing Committee of Correspondents elected by accredited members of the galleries. The Committee shall consist of five persons elected to serve for terms of 2 years. Provided, however, that at the election in January, 1951, the three candidates receiving the highest number of votes shall serve for 2 years and the remaining two for 1 year. Thereafter, three members shall be elected in odd-numbered years and two in even-numbered years. Elections shall be held in January. The Committee shall elect its own chairman and secretary. Vacancies on the Committee shall be filled by special election to be called by the Standing Committee.

2. Persons desiring admission to the press galleries of Congress shall make application in accordance with Rule 35 of the House of Representatives and Rule 34 of the Senate, which rules shall be interpreted and administered by the Standing Committee of Correspondents.

3. The Standing Committee of Correspondents shall limit membership in the press galleries to bona fide correspondents of repute in their profession, under such rules as the Standing Committee shall prescribe.

4. Provided, however, that the Standing Committee of Correspondents shall admit to the galleries no person who does not establish to the satisfaction of the Standing Committee all of the following:

   (a) That his or her principal income is obtained from news correspondence intended for publication in newspapers entitled to second-class mailing privileges.

   (b) That he or she is not engaged in paid publicity or promotion work or in prosecuting any claim before Congress or before any department of the government, and will not become so engaged while a member of the galleries.

   (c) That he or she is not engaged in any lobbying activity and will not become so engaged while a member of the galleries.

5. The Standing Committee of Correspondents shall propose no changes in these rules except upon petition in writing signed by not less than 100 accredited members of the galleries.

On October 28, the Standing Committee voted to admit two reporters for the Labor Press Association, which its motion carefully pointed out was "an association of newspapers entitled to second class mailing privileges." But it stood firm in its refusal to admit reporters for the State Department information services. On June 1, 1950, it not not only rejected applicants from the Department, but also rejected applications of Gregorii Rassadin and Ivan A. Filippov of *Pravda*. They had given New York addresses on their applications. A motion was adopted that "the State Department and Messrs. Rassadin and Filippov be informed that accreditation by this committee has been and is restricted to resident correspondents in metropolitan Washington."

The minutes of this meeting concluded: "Being informed that the St. Louis Browns had defeated the Nats 5 to 4, the meeting adjourned, subject to call of the Chair, at 11:52 p.m. EDT."

NOTES

[1] I have visited the press galleries in the national parliamentary bodies in Rome, Paris, London, LaPaz, Bogota, Montevideo and Quito, and have discussed the situation in Buenos Aires, Santiago and Caracas, although I did not actually go to the halls of Congress in those cities. I have also visited the press facilities in Boston, Hartford, Harrisburg and Frankfort and the United Nations. While I did not examine the situation in detail in each, it was clear that in many of them arrangements similar to those in

Washington have been worked out and I felt that this country's lead had, in part at least, been followed.

2 My thanks are due to the 1952 Standing Committee which ordered that I have access to the records, and to Wills' predecessor, the late Harold Beckley, for giving them to me and for allowing me to work at his Senate Press Gallery desk to make notes.

3 Part of the prior history of Senate action is described in my own article, "The United States Senate and the Press, 1838-1841," JOURNALISM QUARTERLY, 28:2 (Summer 1951), pp. 342-50.

4 "Use of Reporters' Galleries in the Senate," *Report of the Committee on Rules*, Senate Report No. 317, 76th Congress, 1st Session, April 21, 1939, p. 3.

5 Samuel J. Randall papers, University of Pennsylvania library.

6 "Charges Against H. V. Boynton," *Report of the Select Committee*, House Report No. 1112, 48th Congress, 1st Session, April 1, 1884.

7 Checks in the Library of Congress, the National Archives, the office of Speaker Samuel Rayburn and the clerk of the House failed to produce the original of Randall's order. In 1953 Mrs. Henry Bacon of Goshen, N.Y., Speaker Randall's daughter, turned over her father's personal papers to the University of Pennsylvania library. A search through those papers for 1877, 1879 and 1880 turned up the Adams letter quoted here. There were parts of the vast collection, including correspondence in 1877 and 1878, which I could not take the time to examine. The secret of the Standing Committee's origin may still be in that collection.

8 *Standing Rules for Conducting Business in the Senate of the United States. Reported by the Committee on Rules, January 11, 1884 . . .* (Washington, 1884).

9 I have private, but entirely reliable, information on this point.

ACCESS FOR THE UNDERGROUND PRESS

By Luther A. Huston

By a 3 to 2 vote, after weeks of controversy, the Standing Committee of Correspondents has admitted to membership in the House and Senate press galleries a newsman who once threw a pie in the face of a member of the U.S. Commission on Obscenity and Pornography.

As a result, Thomas King Forcade will be accorded full reportorial privileges on Capitol Hill as Washington correspondent of the Underground Press Service, which provides news reports for underground newspapers throughout the country.

The Standing Committee is a group of five members of the press galleries who are elected annually to oversee press rules for the Capitol. The two members who voted against admission of Forcade are Frank Hewlett, correspondent of the *Salt Lake Tribune* and chairman of the Committee, and Sam Hanna, a reporter for the Timmons News Service which represents papers in Louisiana, Texas, Tennessee, Ohio, and several other states. The three who voted to admit him are Dan K. Thomasson, of the Scripps-Howard Newspaper Alliance, Steven Gerstel of United Press International, and Marjorie Hunter of the *New York Times*.

Reprinted from *Editor and Publisher*, September 18, 1971, by permission of the editor.

Forcade's application had been pending for many weeks. The opposition arose not so much from his qualifications as from his actions. His conduct was angrily denounced by several accredited journalists.

Among his defenders was Fred P. Graham, Supreme Court correspondent of the *New York Times*; Richard Harwood, assistant managing editor of the *Washington Post*, and Nicholas Von Hoffman, a *Post* columnist. Representative Bella Abzug of New York City evidenced interest in the progress of the application.

The pie-throwing incident was the major objection raised by opponents, along with Forcade's testimony before the Obscenity and Pornography Commission. In the spring of 1970 Forcade volunteered to testify at a hearing. He identified himself as a clergyman, sprinkled his testimony with expletives, then pulled a cream pie from a box and hurled it in the face of Commissioner Otto Larsen.

Another incident which figured in the opposition was the time during the Sigma Delta Chi convention in San Diego in 1969 when he heaved a water glass at the press table.

To the opposition, these incidents, and his characterization in a statement put out last July of the standing committee as "a group of puppet journalists," weighed more than complaints of the level of reliable reporting in the underground press.

The attitude of his supporters was expressed by Thomasson, who said "he has never been convicted of anything" and "he meets all the qualifications."

Admission to the Capitol galleries entitles Forcade to apply for membership in the White House Correspondents Association.

The action of the Standing Committee could be overruled by the House or Senate Rules Committees or by the Speaker of the House. None of these, however, has ever overruled an admission. Rejections of admission applications have been overruled.

MODERN ACCOMMODATION: THE NEW PATRONAGE?

By James White

(The nature and extent of modern congressional accommodation of the news media was described by James White in a report written while a graduate student in journalism at The American University in 1972, used here with his permission.—Ed.).

The total expense in terms of real money that the accommodation of the news media by the Congress has cost the taxpayers is virtually impossible to determine. Certain yearly expenditures are on record such as the salaries paid to the superintendents and their assistants. Depending on the longevity of each gallery superintendent (three have worked in the galleries for 40 years), the average superintendent's salary was $22,000 in 1972. Assistant superintendents range in salary from $13,000 to $21,000. Including the salaries on record for secretaries, messengers, doormen, a press liaison, and summer interns, the total cost of personnel for the 1972 fiscal year was about $470,000.

But this figure did not include salaries paid to custodians, electricans, maintenance people and others who regularly service the galleries. Nor are figures available for the cost of heating, cooling and lighting the gallaries.

Some costs have been tabulated in greater detail. In 1971, at the request of the House Subcommittee on Legislative Appropriations, the Clerk of the House supplied the cost of certain items allocated to the House galleries. Furniture expenditures were listed at $16,200. The cost of 92 typewriters in use both in the House galleries and the press rooms in the House office buildings was put at $18,600, with a book value then of $6,900. Supplies for 1970 totaled $1,100 and telephone for the year was $7,500. Using these figures and adding the salaries of House gallery personnel, the total operating expenses for the House galleries for that year would have been $200,000. The capital expenditures for furniture and equipment totaled $34,800.

However, these figures do not reflect the cost of building press facilities such as radio and film studios which require special wiring, soundproofing, glass and lighting fixtures. Nor is the cost of renovating such facilities included. For example, when the House Radio and Television Gallery moved to new quarters in 1966, $130,000 was allocated. In 1970, the gallery requested and received an additional $38,000 for renovation. An extensive renovation of the House Press Gallery was also undertaken in 1965.

On the Senate side, no precise figures are available on the cost of furniture and equipment. Since the Senate galleries have more floor space and a larger staff (salaries totalling $230,600 for 1972), presumably, the cost of establishing and operating the Senate galleries exceeds that of the House.

Despite the large sums of money involved, Congress in recent years has approved allocations for operating expenses of the galleries almost without question. Requests for larger facilities and renovation of present facilities have met with slower approval because of practical limitations within the Capitol. The allocation of space seems to be of greatest concern to members of the Congress who frequently review and sometimes alter space assignments. In recent years, for example, a press room in the Senate Office Building was closed due to lack of use and the House Rules Committee took over occupancy of a press gallery room within the Capitol.

But, for the most part, the members of the press are allowed to run the galleries themselves with little direct supervision by the Congress. Technically, there are four press galleries divided along the lines of the different types of media: daily newspapers, radio and television, periodicals and still photography. However, with the exception of the photographers, each gallery has separate facilities for both houses of Congress, thus creating seven individual units, each with its own superintendent and staff.

The House and Senate side of each gallery act together in important respects. Members of a gallery are permitted to use either the House or Senate facilities and each gallery elects from its membership the Standing or Executive Committee of Correspondents. These committees are the real powers in the galleries, deciding their policies (in accordance with House and Senate rules) and screening applications for gallery membership.

In addition, the Standing Committees have the authority to direct the activities of the congressional employees in the galleries, the superintendents and their assistants. Generally, the day-to-day operation of the galleries is left to the superintendents, but the Standing Committees also have the power to recommend applicants to fill vacant superintendent positions. These recommendations are almost always approved by the Speaker of the House or the Senate Rules and Administration Committee, the theoretical supervisors of the press galleries for each house.

Thus, the principle of accommodation of the press is firmly entrenched in the institutional framework of the Congress. Members of the press are accorded facilities, staffs and special privileges to assist them in the performance of their jobs.

But the principle of accommodation is very much a two-way proposition. While Congress assists the press in reporting its activities, the press assists congressmen and senators in publicizing their individual activities to the voters back home and to the nation as a whole.

Every day, the staffs of dozens of congressmen and senators prepare and distribute press releases to the galleries in the hope that some statement will appear on the evening news broadcasts or in the next day's newspapers. The press galleries regularly receive phone calls from congressional offices informing any reporter interested of stories that might be favorable to the involved congressman or senator. With the easy availability of radio and TV studios, members of Congress also have a greater opportunity to express their views over the airwaves.

In effect, then, making the Congress more accessible to the press has made the press more accessible to the members of the Congress. As one former congressman once said, "If the press did not report Congress, Congress could hardly function. If the sound of congressional voices carried no farther than the bare walls of the chambers, Congress could disband.". . .

The size of gallery membership has grown as well as the number of galleries. From a low point in 1813 when there were only four congressional correspondents, the press gallery had expanded to 91 members in 1881 and to 163 in 1903. By 1960, the number had jumped to 1,326 and 1972 to 2,393, according to the official listing published in the *Congressional Directory*.

The daily Press Gallery has by far the largest membership with 1,178 reporters now accredited who represent 631 separate newspapers and wire services. The Periodical Gallery has 532 members representing 124 publications, many of which are specialized trade journals.

The Radio and Television Gallery lists 504 members representing 115 stations, networks and services. Included in the membership of the Radio and Television Gallery are camera and sound men, who, as part of the TV film crews, need gallery credentials to attend congressional hearings with the TV correspondents.

The smallest gallery consists of the still photographers, 179 in all, representing 41 wire services, magazines and newspapers.

In all, the 1972 figures show that the trend is toward continued growth in the size of all the press galleries. Over 1,000 members have joined the galleries since 1960. Joining a gallery is a relatively simple matter although the rules do vary slightly according to the medium. Generally, reporters and photographers are required to certify that they are bona fide representative of their publication or broadcast station in Washington, that they have no claims before the government, and that they do not represent any lobbying or advertising concerns.

Several galleries issue special or associate memberships to newsmen who do not work in Washington but visit the Capitol at some time during the year and find such credentials useful. The Radio and Television Gallery, for example, had about 100 associate members in 1972 in addition to its regular membership.

But not even counting these special memberships, the newsmen and photographers regularly accredited to the various galleries comprise the largest single press corps in the world. With such numbers, all those accredited to the galleries obviously could not make use of their facilities at the same time. However, large numbers of the correspondents do make frequent use of the galleries in varying degrees.

At many congressional hearings, for example, reporters are assisted by gallery staff members who distribute texts of testimony to be delivered and help arrange equipment for the broadcast media. All the galleries operate information services, including a log of floor votes and committee activities, which are available to reporters by phone.

On days when the amount of congressional activity is minimal, reporters often just stop by their galleries to check for mail and messages, and then leave to pursue stories in other branches of the government.

Some reporters use the galleries only while collecting information and return to their offices to write the story or prepare it for broadcast.

On the other hand, those who use the galleries the most, generally reporters for larger newspapers and broadcast news operations, may spend an entire day in the gallery, listening to floor debate, phoning sources of information, and then writing or broadcasting their stories on the spot.

Although no exact figures are available, Benjamin West, superintendent of the House Press Gallery, estimated that some 600 reporters, about half the total membership of the press gallery, make some use of the press gallery staff or facilities during an average day. Dealing with a different medium and therefore serving different needs, Joseph Darling, assistant superintendent of the Senate Photographers Gallery, said that only 10 to 20 of the almost 200 gallery members use its facilities on an average day.

But while the galleries are able to meet the demands of the newsmen most of the time, "the shortage of space does show up on certain days," according to Joseph Wills, superintendent of the Senate Press Gallery. "The day of the (George) Wallace shooting, for example, you couldn't get a telephone anywhere in the Capitol," he said.

With the exception of the Photographers Gallery, superintendents of six galleries said in recent interviews that the lack of operating space was a major problem, at least to some extent, in each of the galleries. David Secrest, chairman of the Executive Committee of Correspondents for the Periodical Gallery, said that due to the cramped quarters, he never worked in the periodical gallery unless he had to. "Almost everyone in this gallery works out of a briefcase," he said.

In the House Press Gallery, Superintendent West said, "It's not in the foreseeable future, but the day may come when we have to limit the membership for each organization." Major news services such as the Associated Press and United Press International have had as many as 100 representatives in the gallery membership, although only 17 or 18 wire service reporters devote most of their time in the galleries.

To accommodate the growing numbers of newsmen in all the galleries, the superintendents look to a variety of answers less drastic than limiting membership. Several mentioned the hope of gaining additional space if the West Front of the Capitol is extended. Under study for almost 10 years now, the proposal is hotly contested by a number of members of Congress, and the galleries will have to compete with other interests in the Capitol if the space becomes a reality.

The introduction of new technology could also help alleviate the space problem in the Capitol, according to two superintendents. One possibility suggested has been computerizing the *Congressional Record* and other documents, but again such proposals have been under consideration for years and are at best in the distant future.

Jane Ruyle, assistant superintendent in the Senate Radio and Television Gallery, said that the introduction of miniaturized TV camera and recording equipment, already being used by the Columbia Broadcasting System, could result in further space savings.

If the day does ever come when the Capitol Hill press corps has completely outgrown the facilities available, however, it is quite likely that the Congress will come up with additional methods of accommodation. In an age when political successes often weigh in the balance of media coverage, members of Congress have become too dependent on newsmen to ignore their needs.

The press has become as much an institution on Capitol Hill as Congress itself, so much so that Douglass Cater chose to call the Washington reporters "the fourth branch of government." Indeed, the political powers of persuasion common in the chambers and corridors of the Capitol have extended into the routine of the galleries themselves.

The growth of the press gallery facilities, for example, is in large part due to the friendships developed over decades between the gallery superintendents and powerful members of the House and Senate leadership. Several superintendents began their careers at the Capitol in the 1930's as pages or messengers and grew up, in a sense, with the senior members of the Congress.

Consequently, superintendents can lobby for space for their galleries, as was the case of the House Radio and Television Gallery which took over offices formerly occupied by the House Foreign Affairs Committee five years ago. Too, friendships developed with other congressional employees can lead to stationery and books supplied by the Government Printing Office for which two superintendents said they did not have to make an accounting in their budgets.

William Perry, superintendent of the Senate Periodical Gallery for 25 years, said that he supplied the Senate Library with free magazine subscriptions obtained through members of his gallery. This saving allows the Senate librarian to purchase additional books, and cements a relationship which permits reporters access to the library. Theoretically, the library is open only to members of Congress and their staffs.

Perry also distributes complimentary magazines to the offices of the congressional leadership and the cloakrooms as a friendly gesture. The practice has an additional benefit in that members of Congress frequently insert material they read into the *Congressional Record,* a somewhat prestigious tribute to the reporter and publication involved.

Other benefits that Capitol Hill reporters have acquired include parking permits, and a private dining room and elevator. The parking permits (the two daily press galleries have 70 permits alone) represent a substantial amount of congressional accommodation because space outside the Capitol is almost as scarce as that inside. Galleries also issue temporary permits called "hunting licenses" because of the difficulty of finding a free space.

The private press dining room off the Senate restaurant seats only 15 people but enables reporters to avoid long public lines. While newsmen pay the same prices as the public (still a good buy), the mere existence of the private room indicates another measure of accommodation.

Sometimes, accommodation is carried to an extent that exceeds even the limits of congressional hospitality. Superintendent Perry told the story of the chief counsel on the staff of the Senate Rules Committee who, about five years ago, rushed downstairs from a meeting to obtain certain documents for the committee chairman. To return, the counsel hopped on the first available elevator, the press elevator, and asked to be taken upstairs to the waiting chairman.

"Are you a member of the press?" the elevator operator asked. The counsel identified himself and explained the situation, but the operator merely repeated, "This elevator is reserved for members of the press." The next day, the sign above the elevator was changed to read: "Reserved for Press and Senate Staff."

Congressional accommodation of the press takes on an added dimension every four years with the advent of the major political party conventions. Since 1912, the press galleries have been assigned the responsibility for coordinating press coverage for the conventions by the Democratic and Republican National Committees.

Gallery staffs begin preparations more than a year in advance, reviewing applications for credentials, laying out and assigning convention seats to reporters, and arranging for hotel accommodations, typewriters, telephones and television platforms for cameras and lights.

The task was described as immense by all the superintendents involved in preparations for 1972, a task undertaken in addition to maintaining normal gallery functions. Far more newsmen attend the conventions than usually cover Congress as seen in the case of the Senate Photographers Gallery which has accredited almost 400 cameramen for convention coverage, a number double the membership of the gallery.

Most gallery superintendents attend the conventions as well (Congress is in recess during convention periods) and even hire additional staff to assist them. The extra help is paid on a per diem basis by the National Committees, $35 by the Republicans, only $17.50 by the Democrats, and given living quarters.

Superintendents also receive the same allowance in addition to their congressional salaries. Why Congress would permit its employees to coordinate press coverage for the political conventions can only be explained as another example of accommodation, in this case for both the press and the major political parties.

When the conventions were over, the superintendents returned to the galleries to conduct business as usual. One superintendent said he had not had a vacation in 12 years.

Normal work weeks for the gallery staffs usually extend well beyond 40 hours although no overtime salaries are provided. The galleries open around 9 a.m. during the week and remain open until early evening. Galleries are always open when a house of Congress is in session.

When a house meets in an evening session, several galleries pay for the superintendents' meals with funds collected from the membership. Each gallery levies a membership fee ranging from $2 to $6 for use by the Standing or Executive Committees of Correspondents to provide such extras as radio and television receivers, books and incidental items. The profits from vending machines located in the galleries are also given over to the correspondents for use in the galleries.

3

Modern Access Issues

THE FIRST TWO CHAPTERS sketch the evolution of greater, albeit grudging and qualified, access and accommodation of reporters to the proceedings in Congress. It cannot, however, be concluded that the news media of the 1970's have complete or even better access to Congress.

While Congress seems to have adjusted to the changing nature and needs of the news media, it has been changing in other ways. Effective legislative power, as Wiggins points out, has emigrated from the floors of Congress to behind the doors of committee rooms. The news media generally have not had the opportunity to follow Congress into its committee rooms.

A *Congressional Quarterly* survey suggests that the Legislative Reorganization Act of 1970 opened few additional committee doors to the news media, although it did result in the broadcast coverage of House committees for the first time since House Speaker Sam Rayburn prohibited such coverage in 1951.

Meanwhile, in the galleries, William Small describes how the broadcast media have had to struggle for equality of access. He suggests there is a relationship between the extent of media access to government institutions and their relative effectiveness. This will be examined in the next chapter.

The issues of equality of broadcast media access and the closed committees were articulated at hearings in Congress over the proposed Legislative Reorganization Act of 1970. The testimony of Roger Mudd and the network Washington bureau chiefs, and dialogue between them and members of Congress, reflect both their attitudes and the technical complexities involved in the modern access issue.

———

EMIGRATION OF POWER TO THE
LITTLE LEGISLATURES

By J. Russell Wiggins

Only by access to legislative committees can citizens nowadays really know what is going on in Congress and in their state legislatures. There was a time when the country was smaller and when the volume of legislation was not great, in which ordinary citizens by attending the sessions of legislative bodies could get a good notion of the legislative process. This no longer is so. What occurs on the floor often is no more than the formal and final confirmation of decisions really made in the closed sessions of committees.

This emigration of effective legislative power, from the floors of legislative assemblies to committees, began to be noticed with disquiet by students of American government shortly after the turn of the century. . . .

Practical lawmakers in Congress began to worry about the matter, too. Harold L. Ickes, Secretary of the Interior in the Roosevelt administration, recorded in his diary the very strong opinions of Vice President John Nance Garner on the subject of secret committee sessions. Ickes said: 'Vice President Garner remarked that there ought not to be any executive sessions of any congressional committee. He made the point that it was all public business and that reporters should be permitted to attend any committee meeting.' *

This was so much the prevailing view of Congress that when the LaFollette-Monroney Congressional Re-organization Act was passed it provided: 'All hearings conducted by standing committees or their sub-committees shall be open to the public, except executive sessions for marking up bills or for voting or where the committee by a majority vote orders an executive session.' This is Section 133 (f) of the law (Legislative Re-organization Act of 1946).

The committee's understanding of this section, and the public's understanding of it, is plainly stated in the committee report, which says: 'All hearings are required to be open to the public except where executive sessions for marking up bills, or for voting or where the committee by a majority vote orders a secret executive session in the interest of national security.'

This legislation, at the time, seemed a final triumph of the anti-

From *Freedom or Secrecy*, Revised Edition, by James Russell Wiggins. Copyright © 1964 by Oxford University Press, Inc. Reprinted by permission.

* Ickes, Harold L. *The Secret Diary of Harold L. Ickes.* New York: Simon and Schuster, 1953, p. 515.

secrecy philosophy of Wilson and Garner and other practical reformers of our legislative apparatus. It has been no such triumph. . . .

*   *   *

(Since Wiggins wrote these words, Congress enacted a second law aimed at congressional reform, including more open committee meetings. Following is *Congressional Quarterly's** report on committee secrecy a year after the new legislation went into effect, including a nine-year summary of committee secrecy.—Ed.).

Congressional committees conducted 40 percent of their hearings and other meetings behind closed doors in 1972, the year after the Legislative Reorganization Act of 1970—aimed in part at opening such proceedings to the public—took effect.

In 1971, during the first session of the 92nd Congress, 36 percent of all congressional committee meetings were held in secret. But, in recent years, more closed meetings have been held in the second session of a Congress, when the number of mark-up meetings, which are usually closed, increases. (*1972 Weekly Report p. 301*)

The percentage of committee meetings held in secret during second sessions has remained relatively constant over the past seven years. This year's 40 percent figures compares with 42 percent in 1966, 43 percent in 1968 and 41 percent in 1970.

Since 1953, when Congressional Quarterly began its annual study of open and closed committee meetings, 25,368—or 37 percent—of the 68,305 meetings reported have been closed to the public. In the period since 1965, when meetings of the House Appropriations Committee were added to the study, 40 percent of all meetings have been closed. Statistics on committee meetings are given on the following page.

As in the past, the House barred the public from its committee meetings more often than the Senate did. Forty-four percent of all House meetings were closed, more than the 1971 total of 41 percent but less than the 1970 figure of 48 percent.

Senate committees had an over-all secrecy rating of 37 percent—up from 30 percent in 1971 and 33 percent in 1970. Joint committees continued to report a low number of executive (closed) meetings: 13 out of a total of 90.

Reform Legislation

The Legislative Reorganization Act of 1970 contains several provisions intended to bring committee proceedings under public scrutiny. According to the law, Senate committee business meetings must be open except for mark-up (revising, amending and deciding on the final language of a

---

* Reprinted from *Congressional Quarterly*, Volume 30, No. 46 (November 11, 1972) by permission of the publisher.

YEAR	TOTAL MEETINGS	NUMBER CLOSED	PERCENT CLOSED
1953	2,640*	892	35%*
1954	3,002*	1,243	41*
1955	2,940*	1,055	36*
1956	3,120*	1,130	36*
1957	2,517*	854	34*
1958	3,472*	1,167	34*
1959	3,152*	940	30*
1960	2,424*	840	35*
1961	3,159*	1,109	35
1962	2,929*	991	34*
1963	3,868*	1,463	38*
1964	2,393*	763	32*
1965	3,903	1,537	39
1966	3,869	1,626	42
1967	4,412	1,716	39
1968	3,080	1,328	43
1969	4,029	1,470	36
1970	4,506	1,865	41
1971	4,816	1,731	36
1972	4,073	1,648	40
TOTAL*	68,305	25,368	37%

* Meetings of the House Appropriations Committee, all reported closed until 1971, were not included in the study until 1965.

bill) and voting sessions, or when a majority of the committee votes to close them. Committee business meetings in the House must be open unless closed by majority vote. (1970 *Almanac, p. 447*).

House Committees

Excluding the House Appropriations Committee which did not report fully on its sessions, 79 percent of House "business" meetings were closed to the public in 1972. In this tally, business meetings are defined as organizing, discussion, mark-up and voting sessions. The same figure applied to House business meetings held in 1971.

For the second year, the House Appropriations Committee held a selected few of its budget hearings in public. Thirty-three budget hearings —or 8 percent—of a total of 399 meetings were open. No meetings of the committee had been held in public before 1971, when the same percentage of meetings were opened. The Legislative Reorganization Act of 1970 requires that House Appropriations budget hearings be held in open session, except when the committee decides that the testimony may affect national security.

Interstate and Foreign Commerce was the only House committee, besides Appropriations, to meet more than 100 times and close its doors more often than not. It closed 128 of its 231 sessions for a secrecy score of 55 percent—a jump from its 1971 score of 24 percent. Only 15 of its 141 business meetings were open.

The number of closed sessions held by the House Armed Services Committee increased slightly after declining for several years. The committee secluded itself 49 percent of the time, compared to 41 percent in 1971, 57 percent in 1970 and 64 percent in 1969. Fifteen of its 35 business meetings were conducted openly.

Ways and Means continued to hold more than half of its meetings privately; this time 48—or 63 percent—out of 76 were closed. Sixty-two percent of its meetings were closed in 1971 and 70 percent in 1970. All of its 48 executive sessions consisted of business meetings.

The Education and Labor Committee continued its practice of holding open proceedings, closing none of its 141 sessions, which included 25 business meetings. The committee began holding open mark-up sessions in 1967.

Other House committees that met more than 100 times with comparatively few closed sessions were Judiciary, 34 percent closed sessions; Interior and Insular Affairs, 32 percent; Foreign Affairs, 21 percent; and Government Operations, 20 percent.

The Post Office and Civil Service Committee closed only 3 of its 94 meetings. The committee, which voted to mark-up in open session after passage of the 1970 reorganization act, opened 13 of its 16 business sessions.

Senate Committees

Although secret sessions were held less frequently in the Senate, only nine of the 486—or 2 percent—of designated Senate business meetings were open to the public. Three percent of the business sessions were open in 1971.

Of the Senate committees that met more than 100 times, two held the majority of their meetings in executive session. The Finance Committee closed 77 percent of its 110 meetings, an increase over the 47 percent closed in 1971, 42 percent in 1970 and 41 percent in 1969. All of its business sessions were closed.

The Armed Services Committee, which led in Senate secrecy in 1971, closed 72 percent of its 152 meetings, including all business sessions. The committee closed 79 percent of its sessions in 1971 and 78 percent in 1970.

As in 1971, Senate Judiciary led the list of committees that met more than 100 times and often in open session. It closed only 12 percent of its 178 meetings.

Labor and Public Welfare closed 36 percent of its meetings; Commerce, 29 percent, and Interior and Insular Affairs, 25 percent. The Appropriations Committee matched its 1971 secrecy score of 30 percent, closing 98 of its 330 sessions.

Joint Committees

Joint congressional committees held few executive sessions. Of the 90 meetings reported in the Record, only 13—or 14 percent—were closed. The Joint Atomic Energy Committee barred outsiders from 11 of its 25 meetings. The Joint Economic Committee, which met most often, held only open sessions.

New Secrecy Legislation

Government secrecy has become a major political issue, and the practice of holding congressional committee meetings behind closed doors has come under increasing attack from congressional reformers inside and outside Congress.

The 1972 Democratic Platform states that "public business should be transacted publicly, except when the national security might be jeopardized." It calls upon Democratic members of Congress and state legislators to enact laws barring closed committee meetings, including mark-up sessions, unless national security or individual privacy would be jeopardized.

Sen. Lawton Chiles (D Fla.) introduced a bill (S 3881) on Aug. 4, 1972, that meets those qualifications. A similar measure (HR 16450) was introduced in the House by Rep. Dante B. Fascell (D Fla.). The Chiles "Government in the Sunshine" Act would require that all meetings of federal authorities and congressional committees be open to the public—with exceptions for cases that affect national security, individual privacy, internal management of the body or matters required by law to remain confidential.

Introducing his bill, Chiles cited the success of a Florida open meetings law enacted in 1967. "Experience . . . has shown the open meeting principle does not hamper business operations and increases public confidence in government," he said.

No hearings were held on the proposal in either house, but Chiles and Fascell hoped to muster bipartisan support for passage in the 93rd Congress. Sen. Abraham Ribicoff (D Conn.), chairman of the subcommittee on executive reorganization of the Government Operations Committee, promised to push for hearings early in 1973.

In a discussion of the proposal on the Senate floor, Sen. William V. Roth (R Del.) supported it, saying that "the use of secrecy provides an opportunity for the selective and biased release of news on committee business through leaks" by members with axes to grind.

Sen. Robert Packwood (R Ore.), another supporter, declared that he had never seen anything done in executive session "that would not have been done if the doors had been wide open and loudspeakers were blaring the proceedings out into the hallways."

Open, Closed Congressional Committee Meetings 92nd Congress

Senate Committees	1971				1972			
	Open	Closed	Total	Percent Closed	Open	Closed	Total	Percent Closed
Aeronautical and Space Sciences	7	3	10	30%	9	4	13	33%
Agriculture and Forestry	39	19	58	33	15	22	37	59
Appropriations	220	94	314	30	232	98	330	30
Armed Services	32	118	150	79	43	109	152	72
Banking, Housing and Urban Affairs	72	22	94	23	51	27	78	35
Commerce	159	43	202	21	119	48	167	29
District of Columbia	27	5	32	16	23	1	24	4
Finance	35	31	66	47	25	85	110	77
Foreign Relations	72	55	127	43	56	39	95	41
Government Operations	84	9	93	10	22	13	35	37
Interior and Insular Affairs	90	23	113	20	85	29	114	25
Judiciary	142	25	167	15	156	22	178	12
Labor and Public Welfare	171	43	214	20	105	60	165	36
Post Office and Civil Service	16	10	26	38	7	5	12	42
Public Works	52	52	104	50	50	29	79	37
Rules and Administration	8	17	25	68	3	10	13	77
Select Equal Educational Opportunity	30	4	34	12	0	1	1	100
Select Nutrition and Human Needs	18	2	20	10	9	2	11	18
Select Small Business	21	1	22	5	10	0	10	0
Select Standards and Conduct	(Not available)				0	0	0	0
Special Aging	17	0	17	0	8	1	9	11
Veterans' Affairs	13	4	17	24	13	8	21	38
TOTAL	1,325	580	1,905	30%	1,041	613	1,654	37%

House Committees

Agriculture	110	64	174	37%	39	38	77	49%
Appropriations	36	419	455	92	33	366	399	92
Armed Services	110	78	188	41	78	74	152	49
Banking and Currency	52	26	78	33	36	45	81	56
District of Columbia	53	37	90	41	46	22	68	32
Education and Labor	193	6	199	3	141	0	141	0
Foreign Affairs	136	52	188	28	113	30	143	21
Government Operations	131	36	167	22	83	21	104	20
House Administration	9	47	56	84	6	45	51	88
Interior and Insular Affairs	101	26	127	20	104	49	153	32
Internal Security	43	22	65	34	13	9	22	41
Interstate and Foreign Commerce	173	56	229	24	103	128	231	55
Judiciary	80	70	150	47	118	62	180	34
Merchant Marine and Fisheries	84	37	121	31	61	26	87	30
Post Office and Civil Service	88	3	91	3	91	3	94	3
Public Works	74	33	107	31	64	26	90	29
Rules	22	4	26	15	14	0	14	0
Science and Astronautics	47	15	62	24	68	9	77	12
Select Crime Investigation	15	5	20	25	24	5	29	17
Select Small Business	29	1	30	3	32	0	32	0
Standards of Official Conduct	1	13	14	93	0	11	11	100
Veterans' Affairs	25	12	37	32	12	5	17	29
Ways and Means	42	69	111	62	28	48	76	63
TOTAL	1,654	1,131	2,785	41%	1,307	1,022	2,329	44%

Joint Committees

Atomic Energy	22	12	34	35%	14	11	25	44%
Congressional Operations	6	3	9	33	2	1	3	33
Defense Production	3	1	4	25	0	0	0	0
Economic	74	2	76	3	61	0	61	0
Others	1	2	3	67	0	1	1	100
TOTAL	106	20	126	16%	77	13	90	14%
GRAND TOTAL	3,085	1,731	4,816	36%	2,425	1,648	4,073	40%

EQUALITY OF ACCESS FOR BROADCAST JOURNALISM

By William Small

It was 101 years after the printed media did so before electronic newsmen won entrance to the Congressional galleries. The first Press Gallery goes back to 1838 and the 25th Congress when local newspapers were given floor privileges.* A year later, six out-of-town reporters were similarly accommodated. Exactly 100 years later, radio reporters gained access.

A small committee of four organized the effort. Led by the late Fulton Lewis, Jr. (who became first President of the Radio Correspondents Gallery), it included Fred Morrison of the now defunct Transradio Press Service, Albert Warner of CBS (later to go to *U.S. News and World Report*) and Carleton Smith of NBC (later an NBC Vice President). After the gallery committee was formed, Smith was replaced by the late William McAndrew (erroneously listed in one of the early membership lists as "Tom" McAndrew). He became President of NBC News.

This small group prevailed upon Congressman John J. ("Jack") Dempsey of New Mexico to put through an enabling resolution in April of 1939. Five days later, Iowa Senator Guy Gillette offered a similar Senate measure and the Radio Gallery was in business.

Radio was not new to the Congress. The opening of Congress in 1923 was broadcast as was President Coolidge's State of the Union message to that Congress two days later, on December 6. Actually, one month earlier, radio had carried ex-President Woodrow Wilson's Armistice Day message. In February of 1924, Wilson's funeral services were broadcast and in March of the following year, Coolidge's Inauguration. In 1939, however, the broadcaster became a congressionally recognized force. On June 26, 1939, H. R. Baukage of NBC gave the maiden broadcast from a gallery "studio."

The original gallery had twenty-six members (some records say thirty). Today there are almost 450 active members of the Radio and Television Gallery,** and broadcast reports are filed daily by all networks and independents. When the gallery had its formal opening in July of 1939, FDR sent a message hailing its members as "pioneers in a great adventure." With a suspicion shared by political figures ever since, the President added that he urged them to be "fair" in their coverage.

Reprinted from *To Kill a Messenger: Television News and The Real World* by William Small, by permission of Hastings House, Publishers, Inc. Copyright © 1970 by William Small.

* It was earlier than that. See chapter 1—Ed.
** It was about 550 in 1973.—Ed.

Television came later, Harry Truman delivering the first State of the Union telecast in January of 1947. That same year saw the first televised hearing—that of a House (note: *House*) Labor Committee. The main witness was colorful Jimmy Petrillo, grand master of all union musicians.

The real impact of televised hearings, including the great political impact, became evident in 1951 when the late Estes Kefauver held his crime investigation hearings. Early the following year, Speaker Sam Rayburn forbade television from covering Un-American Activities Committee hearings in Detroit. Republicans were upset by the Rayburn ruling, in part because a member of the committee, Rep. Charles E. Potter, was a potential candidate for a Michigan seat. Potter's supporters called it an underhanded means of keeping their man off television in his home state.

In Washington, Minority Leader Joe Martin, Jr. asked for a formal ruling. Speaker Rayburn said the rules of the House are the rules of its committees "and as far as the Chair knows, there is no rule granting the privilege of television."

Since Senate committees establish their own parliamentary procedures, the Senate continued to permit television but the now famous Rayburn Rule became the law of the House. There was exception to come a year later when the GOP won control of the 83rd Congress. Joe Martin became Speaker and without formal ruling, allowed House committees to permit television but in 1954 the Democrats regained control. They reverted to the earlier ban under Rayburn himself and since his death, under Speaker John McCormack.

On the House side, it is still "stake-out" in the hall outside and no television inside.* One can make a case for this contributing to diminishing House influence on the national scene. Not many House members are true national figures. . . . In contrast, many Senate figures are household names. . . .

Without comparable exposure to television, the House is destined to growing obscurity. This is unfortunate. Its work is of equal importance and coverage of the committee, since the floor of the House has limited debate, is all the more vital. One can see the same witnesses say the same things before two committees. On the House side, it is worth a mention; on the Senate side, it can create a national stir. . . .

Television Covers a Filibuster

One of the most interesting examples of television influence on the Congress occurred in 1964 when CBS News arranged to put correspondent Roger Mudd on the steps of the Senate. The idea was to have Mudd report on every single newscast on CBS radio and television, report on the progress of the filibuster over civil rights legislation.

* The House now permits television inside under certain conditions in accordance with the Legislative Reorganization Act of 1970—Ed.

Fred Friendly, then President of CBS News, announced the extraordinary coverage thusly: "The pending civil rights debate and the anticipated filibuster in the Senate give every indication of becoming one of the most important running news stories of the decade. It warrants continuing coverage in the same manner we have dealt with the space shots and with primary elections. The fact that cameras and microphones will not be permitted access to the Senate floor does not affect our responsibility of reporting the debate and filibuster as completely as possible."

The first Mudd report almost aborted. Though CBS News received the necessary permissions, someone forgot to inform the Capitol police and they would not permit the remote truck to park. In a growing snow storm, the mobile unit circled the Capitol parking lot as CBS desperately tried to find someone in authority to get word to the police. Those in authority were fighting the snow on their way to work. Finally, approval came and the technicians raced to set up the cameras.

They would be ready with minutes to spare. Meanwhile, Mudd emerged from the entrance beneath the steps to the Senate with his first interview guest, Senator Hubert Humphrey—Democratic Whip and Floor Leader for the Civil Rights Bill.

Humphrey stepped back immediately—he didn't know about the growing snowfall, he had no coat. "I'll have to get my coat," he said. There was no time. I stepped into the hallway, took off my raincoat and we slipped it on Humphrey. It was several sizes too big, especially as it hung toward his fingertips. We promised to keep a tight shot on him— and did. The Mudd odyssey on the Capitol steps had started.

Actually, before it was over, he had to leave the steps. Growing unhappy with his constant reports, some influential Southerners had prevailed upon the Senate authorities to move Mudd. They said he might attract crowds and obstruct the entrance to the building. We ran a cable underground to the sidewalk across the plaza. Mudd did his reports from there, the steps as a background across the street.

Why were the Southerners unhappy? Some observations by John Horn, then writing for the *New York Herald Tribune*:

It was only several weeks after Mudd took up his vigil that the full significance of his careful TV watch was appreciated. Caught at all hours, on a minimum of four TV programs daily, giving the latest debate report and time count or interviewing Senators on both sides of the argument, Mudd has been as faithful as a postman. Neither snow, nor rain, nor heat, nor gloom of night has stayed this TV courier from the swift completion of his appointed rounds.

His continued presence at the scene of Washington inaction has personalized and dramatized the halting processes of our government to the average viewer in a way no amount of words or secondary reports could have. A viewer could identify with Mudd, stand on the steps with him, and have brought home in a compelling way the Senate stall and sitdown against effective government led by Southern Democrats.

Roger Mudd had been meticulous in seeing that both sides *were* heard. He saw to it that Southerners expressed fully their views as well as Northern Senators who favored the bill and that key to passage, Republican Everett Dirksen, who would ultimately come up with the accepted compromise.

The effect of the coverage was telling, however, with a clock mercilessly superimposed under Mudd as he reported, ticking off the hours, minutes and seconds of the "extended debate" (as Southerners loved to characterize a filibuster). A nation felt that this was not a normal process of government—this was the minority delaying a bill badly needed in a period of growing Negro protest.

A leading and powerful Southern Senator paged me to his office one day and asked me to give reason why the Senate should not stop Mudd's reports. They were, after all, being televised on Senate property.

I answered that the series had gone on too long for that. If banned from Capitol grounds, we would place Mudd on the Mall at the Smithsonian with the Capitol behind him. The publicity would certainly not help the Senate establishment. Furthermore, thanks to Mudd's care, there had been fully as many Southerners interviewed as proponents of the bill.

Luckily, I had checked the list of Mudd's interviews. The one Senator interviewed more than any other was the distinguished gentleman from Georgia, Richard Brevard Russell. Russell was at once the head of the Southern bloc and also the most powerful man in the U.S. Senate.

My Southern friend ended our discussion with a mild plea that "you all continue to be fair to us, you heah?" We were.

Sixty-seven days after it and he started, the filibuster and Mudd came to an end. The Civil Rights Bill was passed.

A good reporter had done a fair and thorough job. He did it under conditions that reached people across the country. The Senate respected him for it. The Senate also sensed that television had been strongly felt.

That influence is now felt daily. When live hearings are telecast, Senators are as conscious of the audience at home as they are of their duty in the room. Often these days, you will hear a Senator tell a witness, "I want that answered while the cameras are on." The business of the U.S. Senate hasn't changed much over the past fifty years but the eyes watching the business have new lenses—and Senators know it.

In a congressional hearing room, late in 1968, Richard Salant of CBS News told a Presidential commission, "If this hearing had been held ten years ago these television cameras couldn't have been in the room and I think that as we learn how to use this medium and by using it, I mean living with it and adjusting to it, I think that the public will be much better served. Television is the first thing, I believe, that has happened in the governmental process that has taken government back to the people because it has been moving further and further away."

MODERN ACCESS FOR BROADCAST:
CONGRESSIONAL HEARINGS, 1969

Special Subcommittee on Legislative Reorganization

Mr. MUDD. I am Roger Mudd and since 1961 have been the Congressional Correspondent for the Columbia Broadcasting System but I am here today as the current chairman of the Executive Committee of the Radio and Television Correspondents Galleries.

I am testifying in behalf of the working reporters and cameramen, regardless of their affiliation, who are members of the Galleries.

Active membership in the two Galleries—House and Senate—now totals about 450 [*]: 175 members from the four major networks—ABC, CBS, Mutual and NBC; 60 members who are independents, group ownership reporters or one-man bureau chiefs who service with local or regional coverage 56 television and 90 radio stations in 64 different cities; the 4-man bureau of UPI Audio, a news service network with about 400 domestic clients; the 11-man bureau of UPI Newsfilm, which supplies 16 domestic clients; the 140 members from the 8 stations in the Washington area and finally the 38 foreign broadcasters representing 38 agencies.

My point in reciting these figures is that the purpose of your rules change—"to educate, enlighten and inform the general public regarding the operations, procedures and practices of the House . . ." would not be fully served, in my opinion, by the present language.

For if you contemplate restricting TV coverage of House hearings to a pool arrangement of either 2 video or electronic cameras or of 2 film cameras, the regional coverage of Capitol Hill—which is truly one of TV news' most encouraging and promising developments of the 1960's—would suffer immeasurably.

I am unable to tell from the present language of the proposed rules change whether you would limit coverage to electronic cameras only. If you would, I have these comments.

Reprinted from *Hearings*, by the Special Subcommittee on Legislative Reorganization, U.S. Congress, House Committee on Rules, 91st Congress, 1st. sess., November 6, 1969, pp. 30-37, 63-75, 79-86.

[*] It was about 550 in 1973.—Ed.

It is a rare hearing, indeed, which would be covered by electronic cameras, because of the extraordinary cost and the logistical barriers to a quick distribution. In 1966, on the Senate side, the networks covered a total of 15 days of hearings—those of Secretaries Rusk and McNamara, George Kennan *et al* before the Foreign Relations Committee; in 1967, the total was 7 days of pick-ups from the Senate TV Gallery during the debate and voting on the censure of Senator Dodd; last year, the total was 2 days—again Secretary Rusk before the Foreign Relations Committee; and in 1969, the total to date is 3 days—the testimony of Secretaries Laird and Rogers before the Foreign Relations and Armed Services Committees on the ABM.

In contrast to these figures, the network *film* camera coverage averages between 10 and 12 hearings a *week*. This is because the film camera and not the cumbersome video camera is TV's indispensable tool for Capitol Hill coverage. It is relatively mobile, comparatively inexpensive to operate and can be turned on and off with the news flow of the hearing.

If you are proposing, however, that pool coverage of House hearings be with film cameras, I would have these comments.

Coverage could theoretically be more frequent, but the delay in and the cost of reproducing the film for as many as 8 members of that day's pool would make the film virtually worthless as fresh news.

Let us assume the House Armed Services Committee has scheduled a series of public hearings on draft reform. It is the turn of CBS to furnish the two film cameras for the hearing. The hearing begins at 10 AM and recesses at 12:15 PM. Two hours and 15 minutes of testimony and interrogation of which the cameras have, at the direction of the news pool producer, recorded 1600 feet of film, which is equivalent to 43 minutes. The film is taken by motorcycle courier to the CBS Bureau on M Street to be processed. It reaches CBS at 12:30 PM and emerges as developed film at 1:15 PM.

CBS must then make enough prints of that film so that each member of the pool has exactly what CBS has. CBS cannot, by pool agreement, begin to edit that film for broadcast until each member of the pool has his print in hand. To make the prints, under foreseeable circumstances, CBS must send the film to the Eastman Kodak laboratories in Gaithersburg, Maryland because the only available, good quality stock for making prints is Kodachrome and Eastman Kodak is the only processor with the necessary machinery to make the prints. This means because of Eastman Kodak's non-news contracts the prints are generally not available for distribution to the pool members until at least 10 o'clock the next morning.

At 10 o'clock the next morning, if any pool member still happens to be interested in the film, the cost of the 1600 foot print would be 25 cents per foot or about $400.

The networks would have no trouble absorbing such a cost. But what about one of our regional gallery members? Take, for instance, the Jack

Williams News Service, which has a client station in Richmond, Virginia. The news director at WWBT–TV wants coverage of the draft hearings with special emphasis on committee member Dan Daniels of Virginia. Williams is forced to pay $400 for 1600 feet of film, which is almost 24 hours behind the news and which probably contains less than 30 seconds of Mr. Daniels.

Were Jack Williams, however, not required to rely on the pool and were permitted to film himself in the Armed Services hearing room, he could concentrate on Mr. Daniels, could have his film on an early afternoon plane to Richmond in time for the early evening local newscast.

There is an alternative way to make film prints but it is not much more satisfactory. CBS could, after the original film emerges at 1:15 PM, make pool copies by transferring it to video tape. Theoretically, the transfer of 43 minutes of film could be made within an hour and the copies distributed to the pool members by about 2:30 PM. But that assumes that CBS could run off all 8 copies at once. No network news bureau in Washington, however, has more than 5 video tape machines and it is an unusual afternoon when even 3 of them are free for copying. The cost would be about half of that for film prints—roughly $210 for 1600 feet but even that is prohibitive for Jack Williams. . . .

As for the effect of your proposal on radio coverage, I have these observations. The language does not specify the restrictions on the number of microphones but I assume your intention is to have a single radio engineer record the hearings and distribute them in the same fashion as the film pool. The problems for such a radio pool would not be much different from a film pool. The original tape would have to be sent to the CBS Bureau for duplicating. With its present facilities, CBS could make up to 7 copies at once. But that also assumes all 8 machines are free. That, too, is rare. The delay in this process would mean that our independent radio reporters, who pride themselves on their speed, would fall behind their present velocity by at least 2 hours.

The system in effect on the Senate side seems to be a good one for radio. A so-called "mult" or "multiple outlet" box, about the size of a small overnight case, is set up in one corner of the hearing room and is patched into the existing audio circuit. The box contains 16 outlets, enabling up to 16 radio reporters—particularly the men who carry those small black shoulder cases—to plug into the mult box and take a feed of the hearing without cluttering either the committee table or the witness table with a gaggle of microphones and wires.

You have gathered by now that the working reporters in the Radio-TV Galleries do not favor a pool system—either video or film—for covering House hearings.

But they are also acutely aware of the problems you gentlemen face in getting any rules change through the House.

It would be their hope and suggestion that instead of the two-camera, one-mike limit on House hearings, the language be amended to delete the restrictions on the number of cameras and that radio coverage be permitted through the "mult box" system.

If this is not possible, given the legislative realities, we would suggest that the number of cameras be raised from 2 to 5—thus paralleling the restrictions on still cameras. It would be understood that 3 of the 5 camera positions would be reserved for the networks, whose presence in itself would reduce regional interest in a given hearing, and that the other 2 positions be a matter of draw or first-come, first-served supervised by the House Gallery staff.

Finally, I express to you the appreciation of the Gallery members for your efforts in recognizing the need and requirement for television and radio coverage of the House. It has been to the detriment of the House and the public that television has gravitated to the Senate side, or other body as you like to say.

Someone once said, "Sure, it's a great body. It's just been in the water too long."

Until you have stood outside a House hearing room and tried to re-create on film what went on inside, you cannot understand the frustration of covering the House with television.

Re-creating is not the function of television journalism. It is unfair to us, unfair to you but most of all unfair to the public.

Mr. [B.F.] Sisk [D.—Calif.]. Assuming you have made some special recommendations, the staff will have that available and then we will go over it.

I appreciate very much your comments with reference to some of these problems. We are really getting down to the nuts and bolts of this situation to some extent, to the mechanics of what we are going to have to do or to provide, if we are going to get the kind of coverage that we are talking about. That is, what we seek to do or else we had just better drop the whole subject.

Now the gentleman from Missouri.

Mr. [Richard] Bolling [D.—Mo.]. Mr. Mudd, the only thing that disturbs me—and it doesn't really disturb me because I have made up my mind that it is fairly clear—it seems to me what we are talking about is full coverage or no coverage, just plain putting it as broadly as that. I don't see how you get away from it.

Mr. Mudd. No, I don't think we are, Mr. Bolling. I think we are taking it upon ourselves to set certain limits. What you have on the Senate side is indeed full coverage, unless John Stennis or the committee chairman rules otherwise; we are free to go into a Senate hearing room, say Foreign Relations or Armed Services or Commerce, with as many cameras as there is room for. We are not told "just three" or "just five or four." That is full coverage. Over here because of the legislative realities that you have mentioned steadily, what we are proposing is, we will hold it down in order to help you get the bill through in order to help us cover the House. If you were to say full coverage you would have no limit at all on the number. A hearing with Secretary Laird and Secretary Rogers on the ABM, a live hearing, my recollection was that there were maybe five of the heavy video tape cameras in the room with platforms, in the big caucus room. Now, they were upon elevated steps so that you can shoot down. Now, that takes over a whole hearing room. That is full, uninhibited coverage. We are not asking for that here because we understand you couldn't get that out of this subcommittee or through your full committee.

Mr. BOLLING. We are actually talking about a partial coverage of the House and House committees as opposed to a full coverage of the Senate and Senate committees?

Mr. MUDD. That is right. Partial restriction on equipment, yes, sir. This would not inhibit the network coverage of it but it would severely limit all our other members, Time, Life, Westinghouse, Capitol Cities, Collingwood, all those independent agencies that I mentioned that like to zero in on one Member and another.

A witness from a hometown, he would be boxed out. We are asking two extra seats to accommodate them.

Mr. BOLLING. I don't ask you to comment on this because it would be unfair. It seems to me my thinking has arrived at the point where if we had to substantially alter our hearing rooms, and so on, to provide facilities for full coverage that that would be the road to take if we are going to get into this. As I say, I don't ask you to comment on it.

Mr. MUDD. That would be another House office building?

Mr. BOLLING. I don't think it would have to be that, but there would probably be a lot of room in a hearing room like this for a small hearing. I am not really in favor of committing myself to another House office building quite yet.

Mr. MUDD. In this hearing room there would be, if you had five machines over there along that line of chairs, that would give the cameras an angle at the committee table and a side angle at the witness. You wouldn't want them up there because they would bother you. You wouldn't put them back here because then you couldn't see the witnesses. There would be lights all over the room.

They wouldn't be bad lights but they would be lights. They would be over in the corner, a box with 16 outlets that the trade independents can plug into, and you would use the existing sound system in the room. There is no getting around it, it is not going to be like it is in here now with the soft light. It will be different.

You probably won't always like the way we cover your hearings. We do the best that we can. To have it any other way, I think, would be more dangerous than the present system.

As someone mentioned, it is a matter of good faith in the Congress and television. We don't always do well, but neither do you, and it is our job to report when you don't.

Mr. [DELBERT L.] LATTA [R.—Ohio]. We have something in common.

Mr. MUDD. Just a brief remark, Mr. Latta. They mentioned 3 days this year on live hearings. You do understand that with the live and the film we are covering an average of 12 hearings a week by film. That is, each network is doing that, but it is just three hearings this year that we have gone out live into everybody's television set. Last year——

Mr. LATTA. Two?

Mr. MUDD. Dean Rusk before the Foreign Relations Committee. The year before, seven. Those were live pickups from the Senate TV gallery during the debate and voting on the Dodd censure. In 1966, 15 days of hearings. That was the Rusk-McNamara-George Kennan Foreign Relations hearings; 15 days.

Remember in the winter of 1966, February and March, I think it was.

Mr. LATTA. If I may——

Mr. MUDD. Those were covered by film, too.

Mr. LATTA. If I may just comment. It seems like in the past all you have been doing is going to Foreign Relations Committee hearings. With the Senate, with the live coverage. Armed Services. I think the people of the country are more interested in what goes on down there——

Mr. MUDD. You understand that the Foreign Relations Committee embarked in that period on a, what they regarded as an educational campaign and asked for live television. They were using the media.

Mr. LATTA. You had the right, as I understand it, under the Senate Rules, to go in other committee hearings to see what is going on, let the people see.

Mr. MUDD. I don't know——

Mr. LATTA. Two days of live coverage in 1968 does not speak well for the industry or the Senate. One of the two fell down. There was not enough interest in the Senate in 1968 to demand more than 2 days. They shouldn't have allowed——

Mr. MUDD. Can you recall some Senate hearings that should have been?

Mr. LATTA. Not offhand.

Mr. MUDD. Where does the blame lie?

Mr. LATTA. Maybe on the Senate. Somebody is to blame.

Mr. MUDD. The point is, citing those statistics on live coverage is not to say that we are not able to do it or interested in doing it, but the cost of it is extraordinary, and because it is, it takes a nationally important hearing to bring in this amount of equipment and this much support from this three-network pool.

Mr. LATTA. Here, as I understand it, you are asking the House to give you that privilege, that right, and then after you get it you are going to spend 2 days or 3 days or 7 days?

Mr. MUDD. No, sir. We are not asking. You are confusing the live——

Mr. LATTA. I am not confusing that. I am talking about live coverage.

Mr. MUDD. We are asking the right for film coverage which is the indispensable television tool on the Hill—not the live camera.

Mr. LATTA. You don't want live coverage in the House, is that what you are saying?

Mr. MUDD. I am not saying that. If it is restricted to live, you will get very little live. If left to the committee chairman for live, that is up to him and we have to respond accordingly. If you permit on a daily basis film coverage with 35 camera positions, you will get, I think, a respectable coverage of the House and we can fulfill our obligations and I think that you will be not displeased.

Mr. LATTA. I am interested in the people of the country and their right to know. If we open up in the House and come up with 2 days' coverage on the Foreign Affairs Committee of the House in 1970, they are going to say there wasn't any other committee down there doing anything.

Mr. MUDD. That situation, Mr. Latta, that——

Mr. LATTA. This is a hypothetical situation?

Mr. MUDD. No; it is not, because it is a statistic. It is 2 days or 3 days this year. That assumes nothing else, no newscast at 6:30 by Brinkley or Cronkite is doing anything else other than the live hearings during the day. It is not that if we go live for 2 days we ignore the rest of the Congress. That is not the limit of television coverage of the Senate. It is 2 days of live hearings.

You have Mansfield here and a press conference there and hearing with film somewhere else and a witness somewhere else. That is not the limit of it.

Mr. LATTA. One further thing while you are here. I listen to your program. I will put that in the record.

Mr. MUDD. Don't delete it from the record.

Mr. LATTA. Let me bring up this thing that I brought up earlier about putting on the chairman of a committee. I think that in the past that we have given a one-sided view too often as the committee feeling. In this country we do have some minorities and we have a minority here in the Congress that perhaps the ranking member ought to be able to go on and tell what his position is.

Mr. MUDD. I heard your comment about that. I take it you mean Senator Fulbright?

Mr. LATTA. Not only him but other people who, say, contacted Chairman Patman for a comment. I believe that I would be the last one here to say that he speaks for all members of his committee. He might give the wrong opinion to the American people of what the position of his committee is.

Mr. MUDD. Of course, in the way of the Senate Foreign Relations Committee, which probably gave rise to your comment, the conservatives on that committee, if I may say so, didn't come to those hearings. Some of them have a very bad attendance record. We filmed and taped and broadcast the comments of those who were there. There were critics there. Fulbright happens to be chairman and Mr. Sisk happens to be chairman here, and any chairman dominates the hearing. That is the way it is, I think.

Maybe I am wrong. I am not sure. Suppose the ranking member of the committee never said anything or made any news?

Mr. LATTA. Still might have the position?

Mr. MUDD. Well, if he didn't enunciate it, we couldn't cover it; could we?

Mr. LATTA. Take these spot announcements or spot time when you put these people on. The chairman will be telling of his position and it might not reflect the feeling of the committee. This is a point that I wish you would think about. Maybe you think that you are doing the right thing, but I do not. As a member of the minority, I think we ought to be heard a little more.

Mr. MUDD. During the Republican Congress the chairman——

Mr. LATTA. That has been a long time.

Mr. MUDD. We are not responsible for that.

Mr. SISK. The gentleman from Missouri, I believe, has a question.

Mr. BOLLING. I feel compelled to make a comment, again not asking for comment.

I think it would be posing an absolutely impossible task on anybody in any media to see to it that all points of view got equal time. For example, I have been in Congress for over 20 years and most of the time that I have been in Congress, although I have been a member of the majority party, I felt very much like a minority. I just think it would be absolutely impossible to expect the media to give equal time to every point of view. I don't see how anybody could judge it.

Mr. MUDD. You try consciously to act for all points of view. It does happen, as you know, that some or all the differing points of view are held by men of unequal stature. What you look for is the significant point of view from the man who has some influence in the House. You are limited as to how much of a hearing you can put on and you are looking for the man on the committee you know to be powerful and know to sway votes, know there is a change in position.

These are the things that you look for. It is impossible if I am assigned three and a half minutes to cover this hearing, really to account for everybody's point of view and each nuance. What you look for——

Mr. Latta. You are not taking my remarks to mean that I suggested that you try to give everybody's point of view time on the air?

Mr. Mudd. No; I was responding to Mr. Bolling.

Mr. Latta. You have a minority and majority opinion usually on these committees. Still it might not divide along party lines. For instance, in Banking and Currency it does not.

Mr. Mudd. The minority and the majority wouldn't be united, either; would they?

Mr. Latta. Right.

Mr. Sisk. If there is nothing else, Roger, we appreciate very much your statement and we appreciate your outlining some of the mechanics and some of the problems. I think it was well brought out.

We will take that into consideration in attempting to see what we can do.

Mr. Mudd. Thank you very much. . . .

[Ed.'s note—Following a statement by John Lynch, network news director of ABC News, accompanied by Frank Jordon of NBC News and William Small of CBS News, this questioning took place:]

Mr. Bolling. Mr. Lynch, I have one question and I am almost sure there is no answer to it, but I would like you to expound on it a little bit.

I have to be somewhat personal about this. Some years ago a very prominent television personality did a program on a person whom I intensely disliked. Ed Murrow did a program on Joe McCarthy. I happen to agree with everything that Mr. Murrow did. I suspect that that program played a major role in the ultimate political destruction of the person in question, Senator McCarthy. I explain my prejudice so that you will see that my sympathy went to the kind of job that was done except for one fact: I thought it represented a rather sharp distortion of the total personality. Now, is what you are saying in effect—from what I have heard of your testimony and what opportunity I have had to read the rest of it—that this kind of thing is inevitable and that if one does not accept that one fails to accept the notion of a free press?

Mr. Lynch. I would say—I would not say that this is inevitable. I would say that that and perhaps other programs as they develop are products of journalistic choice. We cannot delegate the responsibility for a journalistic choice.

Mr. Bolling. In effect, you are saying "yes," that my point is correct, that if we are going to have choice then we must risk a prejudiced view?

Mr. Lynch. I wouldn't say it is risking a prejudiced view. Perhaps you want to say that but I would say it is built into the exercise of journalistic choice, that there should also be the correction of any excesses in that choice.

Mr. Bolling. Now, that is the thing that disturbs me and has disturbed me for years. Some of you may know that a long time ago I opposed any consideration of opening up House committees and, in fact, favored rather a broader approach of opening up the House itself—

Mr. LYNCH. Yes.

Mr. BOLLING (continuing). On what I thought was reasonably sound parliamentary grounds that the committees are only creatures of the institution and the institution itself, while it may sometimes be dull, is the subject that should be covered rather than its creatures.

The problem is, it seems to me, a very serious one because if, for example, a substantial number of people in media work happen to sympathize entirely with my views on a certain subject I might be reported in an extraordinarily favorable light and the people with whom I disagreed would be treated, in a sense, unfairly. Is this an inevitable aspect?

Mr. LYNCH. I don't think it is inevitable at all. I think that many people in our business who have strong personal feelings lean over backwards and are frequently known to over-correct themselves. I would like to give an opportunity to my colleagues to speak to this point.

Mr. JORDAN. If I may, Congressman, the example you used of a television program, while it may have appeared distorted to you might not have appeared distorted to me or to some of your colleagues. I think that is one of the points we are trying to make, that what is one man's meat is another man's poison. What is distortion to one viewer is accuracy to another viewer.

MR. BOLLING. Given my prejudices in this case?

Mr. JORDAN. Yes, even given your prejudices in this case.

Mr. BOLLING. I think we reach a point at which we have two "goods" involved and we have to opt for freedom, the freedom of choice. I am not saying anything against the position you are taking, understand.

Mr. JORDAN. I understand.

Mr. SMALL. Mr. Bolling, you know, to take the matter before us, if you close or continue to close hearings to television you have not changed the opportunity for the excess that you described taking place.

Mr. BOLLING. That is true, but only to a degree. It depends a little bit on how you assess the power of the medium and—with all due respect to my friends in the other media—I think there is sort of a general recognition that television, at least today, is overwhelmingly powerful in the field in which I am engaged on a permanent basis.

Mr. SMALL. I would immodestly agree with you.

Mr. BOLLING. That is all, Mr. Chairman.

Mr. SISK. The gentleman from California, Mr. Smith.

Mr. [H. ALLEN] SMITH [R.—Cal.]. . . . Speaking for myself alone, I am interested in some type of language which would prohibit films for over a year, or some period of time during the 2 years while we are here, being taken by some individual over whom you may not have control but who may be friendly to some opponent, maybe friendly to the sitting Member, and will take good clips and make a good one so that it can be shown Friday, Saturday, and Monday before the election, or could take and cut bad clips and get that to an opponent and Friday night show those, whereas the individual may have asked one question which was sensible and may have laughed at another one, he might just show the laughing part, or reading a newspaper, or tying his shoes, or chewing gum, or smoking cigarettes, indicating that is all that they ever do during the committee hearings. The intent of this is related to that situation.

The stock brokerage firm, where they hire somebody who is out of college, and he comes to one of you gentlemen or a wife or school-teacher and sells you some stock, indicates it is going to go up and that is fine. Suppose it goes down 20 points. So you feel you got cheated. Now, the partners, depending on whether it is a corporation or not, are responsible for every one of their agents in the wrongful acts of their employees. Now, the full purpose of attempting to write the language is to put some stress on you people who are the bosses that you will see that you won't have somebody doing that, that you will have them under control and tied up and won't let somebody sell them for $5,000 and let it go out and be used to absolutely crucify somebody wrongfully, prior to or during the 3 days before election, because obviously every television reporter, every camera, every newspaper reporter is not a close friend of every Member of Congress. There are some differences of opinion with respect to individuals. That can be done. That is what my intent is here.

If you have any suggestion as to how you can rewrite that language to fulfill what I have in mind, I would appreciate your doing it. We have done the best we can without sending you to jail or making it impossible or doing something that we thought you couldn't live with. I don't want you to say "We can't find him. We fired him 6 months ago." What good would that do us then, to try to go out and get some disreputable or unscrupulous individual who would try to peddle that? The ball game is over on Tuesday night, the first Tuesday in November, usually every 2 years.

Mr. SMALL. What we are suggesting here, Mr. Smith, is that what you desire can be accomplished in your existing language which penalizes users of such footage for political purposes.

Mr. SMITH. What do you mean by "user"?

Mr. SMALL. I mean your opponent, the committee supporting him, whoever uses it against you in a campaign.

Mr. SMITH. What good would that do? I am trying to keep you people from letting anybody do an unscrupulous act and then sell it, give it, or turn it over to somebody like that.

Mr. SMALL. You see, our problem is that we don't have control over it once it is on the air. In our home communities the local station can tape the network product.

Mr. SMITH. But you have control over the films from the time they are made until they are gone.

Mr. SMALL. But once it is on the air anyone can record it.

Mr. SMITH. You mean, they are going to record it in their television sets?

Mr. SMALL. It is an accepted practice in all local stations to record news excerpts and use them again later. Now, they, in turn, can sell it locally without our knowledge. It is technically possible for you, sir, to hire a facility here in this city and tape something off the air—it is not legal but you would have that film then in your hands.

Mr. SMITH. That I realize, and that I am not trying to cover. I am trying to cover you people, even as you have someone at the station cut different clips, some employee, and then you may let him go and say that "It is John Jones' fault. Take it up with him."

I want you people to be responsible for John Jones if he does that on a Friday night, Saturday night, Sunday night, or has been working without your knowledge and you didn't approve of it, you are against it; but I want you to take some interest in it and see that it does not happen. Now, if you can write that in, fine, but to shove it off on somebody else, that is not going to accomplish anything as far as I am concerned. This is very important, insofar as the way I vote, on whether or not there would be any coverage whatsoever. So I would suggest that if you can cure that, cure what I have in mind, you might find me somewhat more sympathetic to the situation.

Mr. LYNCH. I think we can say that we will be happy to address ourselves to the language.

Mr. SMITH. I am going to vote against you getting a foot in the door at all, if you are going to want everything controlled, if you are going to want complete control over when you can go in, what you can say, what you can do; we would never get it past a vote. That is my personal opinion for whatever value it is to you.

That is all, Mr. Chairman.

Mr. SISK. The gentleman from Texas, Mr. Young.

Mr. [JOHN] YOUNG [D.-Tex.]. I do have one question. I have an urgent matter that I have to attend to in my office and will ask you to excuse me after I ask this question.

With regard to your statement, Mr. Lynch, as to the technical problems with respect to lighting and so forth, maybe I misunderstood one of the previous witnesses. I had understood him to say that modern technique eliminates the problem of any kind of extra lighting and that sort of thing, so that perhaps maybe pictures were being taken right now here of this gathering.

Mr. LYNCH. He was addressing himself to still photography, not motion picture film or live television. No; the state of the art has not progressed to the point where we can cover you and get a usable picture without bringing in additional lighting.

Mr. YOUNG. Thank you.

If the chairman would excuse me.

Mr. SISK. The gentleman from Ohio.

Mr. LATTA. Just one question. As you indicated in your statement, you want to give an accurate picture and not a distorted one. I agree with you that you do want to do that. I just want to call your attention to something that happens practically all the time in the Senate which does give a distorted picture, in my opinion. You only photograph the chairman of the committee. Maybe you photograph other members of the committee but the fellow that comes out over the news is the chairman of the committee. For instance, Chairman Fulbright leaves the impression that he speaks for every member of that committee. I know that there are other viewpoints there. So it seems to me if you did not want to give a distorted opinion or position, that perhaps it would be a good idea when you put Senator Fulbright on, for example, that you put the ranking Republican member on that committee also, and the same thing would apply if we open this thing up over here, because I might not always agree with our chairman. I think perhaps the minority ought to have some rights, too. Being in the minority for 12 years now, I hope you are sympathetic to my position.

Mr. LYNCH. I concur with you.

Mr. LATTA. That is all, Mr. Chairman.

Mr. SISK. The gentleman from Missouri, I believe, had additional questions.

Mr. BOLLING. What is a kinescope?

Mr. LYNCH. A kinescope is a filmed recording of live television.

Mr. BOLLING. How could you conceivably control kinescope, how could you be expected to?

Mr. LYNCH. I don't believe we could police it.

Mr. BOLLING. In other words, there is no way on earth for you to control your product even though the law says that it is yours? There are disclaimers that come over TV on the things that I watch like sports events, that it cannot be used, but there is no way on earth that you can prevent a thousand or a million people from taking a picture off of the screen?

Mr. LYNCH. Not really, unless it is done under conditions which require it to go over telephone lines or some other means which must be licensed and are subject to some control. But more than kinescoping, the development of home video tape recorders, for instance, is fast approaching the stage where the cost and the availability is going to be within the reach of a lot of homeowners.

Mr. BOLLING. Really, what we are saying about this matter is that you either have freedom to exercise your judgment or you don't, and there really isn't any happy middleground that we can find. That is one of the reasons I have had so much difficulty with this problem. It either has to be a decision that says you have access to this particular material and that you use it within your good judgment, within the restraints of the law, or we can't give you any access.

Mr. LYNCH. Well, greater access, of course, helps us also to develop a better journalistic choice. I would hope we exercise that judgment better now than we did a year ago and that we will next year exercise it better than we do today.

Mr. BOLLING. I am not really being critical; I am just trying to make the point. It seems to me the point is an extraordinarily difficult point when you look at it from all of the aspects that have been raised just in this very brief time by the members of this subcommittee.

I have come to a conclusion which I am prepared to state publicly, that American politicians have to accept the fact that they are constantly in the public eye and that they have to go through this experience. I think it will be rather interesting to see what happens in the House of Representatives for a time after it is first initiated but I think we will probably survive this situation as we have others.

Mr. LYNCH. By the way, on the question of not photographing or televising witnesses who ask not to be, we accept the judgment of the committee on that question.

Mr. BOLLING. That is a constitutional question which I think falls into a different realm. I don't want to pursue it any further. I am convinced this is about as difficult a question as we can face.

Mr. LYNCH. There is precedent for it being followed.

Mr. SISK. I would like to discuss briefly with all three of you gentlemen this problem of pooling. As you recall, we discussed this earlier in a general conference, about the problems we are confronted with.

Mr. LYNCH. Yes.

Mr. SISK. For example, as late as the last day or so, let's say, we had a statement from the chairman and some members of rather important committees with reference to the problems, in their committee rooms, of open hearings, for example, because their hearing rooms were small and it was just the question of open hearings, not of television coverage or radio coverage or still photography, or anything; it was a question of opening those hearings. Now, without calling the name of the committee, you can probably figure out what committee we are talking about. Of course, as Mr. Smith indicates, our own Committee on Rules, there are some questions there. Now, maybe no one would ever want to cover us because I am not sure we are very interesting. But there is this question. I want to get back to the pooling. I am not trying to be insistent because if we are going to open up the Congress, the activities of the House of

Representatives for the benefit of the public—and that is the only purpose, certainly it is the only objective we would have for the benefit of the right of the people to know, and I agree with that right—then there isn't any point in us writing something here that is going to make it impossible for you people in the industry to do a job.

Now, there have been statements made to us by various people in peripheral areas of the industry—speaking now of the manufacturing area and the service area, and so on—with reference to the fact that pooling would not be as difficult as maybe it has been indicated by the industry itself. Now, I do want to discuss this from a purely technical standpoint. I am sure this morning we will hear from some other witnesses at the working level with comments in this area.

What do you gentlemen visualize would be the minimum amount of equipment if we eliminated pooling and said "All right, pooling will not work," as I understand generally you have said again this morning in your statement? Now, with reference to, let's say, general coverage, not talking about live coverage because I recognize there is going to be very little live coverage, what percentage would you say? Put it this way: What percentage of your Senate hearings are live today?

Mr. SMALL. I can't give it to you in percentages, but the total this year was 3 days.

Mr. SISK. Which indicates that it is probably 5 or 10 percent.

Mr. SMALL. No, no, no; it is much less than that. We shoot 10 or 15 hearings per week.

Mr. JORDAN. I would say a tenth of 1 percent.

Mr. SISK. All right. I think it is important, then, for our committee to recognize, then, if pooling, basically, can only be applied in that area— and you correct me if I am wrong, but this is as I understand it—that is the only area in which you might be able to reasonably expect to get by with any kind of pooling, and that would be in live coverage.

Mr. LYNCH. Right.

Mr. SISK. Otherwise it becomes a prohibitive situation with respect to timelag costs, and so forth; isn't that right?

Mr. LYNCH. That is right.

Mr. JORDAN. We are not objecting to electronic coverage pooling.

Mr. SISK. I understand that. That is why I was differentiating between live coverage, as against the general type of coverage you are doing at present and will, of course, I assume, propose to do for the House.

There seems to the committee, as we have discussed this at considerable length, to be some need for some kind of limitation as to the amount of equipment and people that we can permit into a room. We just feel that this is essential, based on the information from the people that we talk to. As I said, for example, as late as yesterday the question was raised with us about the question of inadequacy of hearing room space, even to permit the public to come in to the hearings, which we, hopefully, can bring about, open hearings. Now, would any of you gentlemen outline what would be the minimum? We have to recognize that you three are network people, that you have to have three of them if you all cover it. Now, maybe you all would not cover it, maybe only two of you would cover it. But let's assume it was of some importance, I would assume that ABC, NBC, and CBS would cover it. Now, we have some independents and I see that they are represented here today.

We will be shortly hearing from one of them and maybe others. Now, how do you propose mechanically to set this thing up to make it possible? I have not had an opportunity, maybe as much as I should have, to observe the Senate in action. I would like some information on that. What is the minimum number of cameras, Mr. Lynch, that you feel you could get by with?

Mr. LYNCH. Two of the witnesses who are going to follow I know are very anxious to speak directly to this point. It has been our experience in the Senate, as a rule of thumb—and those witnesses know better than I do—but as a rule of thumb five film cameras generally would be adequate, would meet all the demands for most of them.

Mr. JORDAN. That includes our needs as well as their needs.

Mr. LYNCH. I think the rule of thumb is four or five. In other words, there are not five every time. As you say, sometimes only one network is covering it, sometimes two, sometimes three, but it is a rare occasion when there is ever any request for more than five. They will be able to be more specific on that than I. That is, five film cameras placed side by side.

Mr. SISK. As I understand it, the radio people have no problem because, here again, all of the sound is taken off of one box anyway.

Mr. LYNCH. That is correct.

Mr. SISK. At least for the purposes of the room, it is a pooled sound.

Mr. LYNCH. Yes.

Mr. SISK. So there is no problem there. All we are confronted with here is the matter of the cameras and camera crews, the amount of people involved in actually handling the cameras. Now, this is again strictly my own thinking and not that of the committee, because I am not sure of what we are going to do. I think we have to make a decision in this area because I propose that if we can't do this where it would be beneficial to permit you to cover it, we had better just drop the whole idea. Maybe four, for example, if we permitted four cameras, assuming you are permitted four cameras, and say that you had all three of the networks wanting to cover this, plus one independent, there would have to be some sort of provision for drawing on them, I suppose, would there not? Here again we get down to the mechanics of how this is going to work. Again, to be fair about it, I would assume that the three networks would want equal protection in this area. They would not want to have to draw between themselves as to only two of the three networks being able to cover it. Therefore, they would have to draw if that were so. It is an important hearing that I am talking about.

Mr. SMALL. We are all members of the House Radio-TV Gallery and through that organization this could be worked out to fit such a limitation.

Mr. SISK. Mr. Smith just referred, of course, to educational television, Public Broadcasting Corp. Educational TV coverage, as we already know, are independents in the field. There are those areas in line with Mr. Latta's questions to a witness earlier, for example, from a specific farm area in Ohio, California, or somewhere else where a station more or less independent wishes to come in and televise. Of course, the desire is not to cut off irrevocably these people from having an opportunity. So that there is a question, then, and a real problem without pooling. As I say, if pooling won't work then, as far as I am concerned, I want to consider some other approach. That is what I am trying to say. You gentlemen representing the networks, I feel that if you had some comments that I would ask you to give them. I know there are other people who are going to make comments specifically to this point.

Mr. JORDON. If we thought that film pooling was in any way feasible we would tell you, but as Mr. Lynch said in his statement it simply isn't feasible to do it on a film pool basis. You simply won't get coverage of those hearings on newscasts during the same day.

Mr. LATTA. Mr. Chairman, if I may comment, if we ever had five cameras in the Rules Committee hearing room we would probably have to move out some of the members.

Mr. SISK. As I said, I am not sure they would ever want to cover us, but that is an example.

Mr. JORDAN. These are not five big television cameras that we are talking about; these are five film cameras side by side.

Mr. LYNCH. That is the maximum. We would think that would be the maximum. Might I suggest that if the particular session were that important we might even find a larger committee room.

Mr. SMALL. Mr. Chairman, if I may comment to the point you made a moment ago about the need for individual stations who have special interests, for example in Ohio and elsewhere, our experience has been—and I think you will find this sustained when Mr. Roberts testifies for the Radio, Televison, and News Directors Association—that those individual stations and small group operations on the Hill generally avoid the hearings that the networks cover, not always but frequently, because they feel their stations will be served by their network news coverage and syndication, and they would gravitate toward some of the hearings, Mr. Latta, that you mentioned earlier, that might not be very popular for Walter Cronkite would be big news in Ohio.

So I think that tendency would work against a great proliferation of cameras beyond the figure 5 which was mentioned here.

Mr. Sisk. In just a moment I will yield to the gentleman from Ohio.

We have local stations here which sometimes get very, very interested in certain kinds of hearings, for example, with respect to the District of Columbia, which I suppose might not be of great interest nationally. I have seen that committee literally swamped on what, nationally, you consider a rather insignificant matter. But in the District of Columbia you have WTOP, WMAL, and all the other stations around here that are very much interested.

As you say, the networks probably wouldn't even be covering it.

Mr. Jordan. Thus opening up other positions to those independents.

Mr. Sisk. What I suppose I am getting at is, in order to be orderly on this, it seems like we are going to have to put some kind of limitation. What kind of a limitation can we put, in the way of equipment within a room, that is reasonable, can be lived with, and will not distort, upset, discommode or inconvenience the operation of the committees, but at the same time give the kind of coverage we want to give for information purposes? That is the question I raise.

The gentleman from Ohio.

Mr. Latta. Did I understand you to say that you had only spent about 3 days of filming the Senate this year?

Mr. Small. No, sir. That was live coverage.

Mr. Latta. Live coverage, 3 days?

Mr. Small. Yes, sir.

Mr. Latta. I am amazed at that because here we are talking about fully informing the public. You heard my comments a little earlier about picking out the sensational things, what you think might be sensational, of great public interest. But I am interested in fully informing the public as to what is going on in the Senate and in the House of Representatives. I don't see how you can do that in 3 days with the Senate. I know they haven't done too much over there this year, but——

Mr. Sisk. Will my colleague yield on that to me? On this live coverage, when we talk about live, that means if that committee is in hearing at 10 o'clock in the morning that is going out to Los Angeles at that time in the morning, which is 7 o'clock out there.

Mr. Latta. Sure—you can get up a little earlier.

Mr. Sisk. The point I want to differentiate here is that we are talking about live and other coverage. They cover a lot of hearings over there.

Mr. Smith. And they put them together for their news later on.

Mr. Sisk. Yes; it is rebroadcast on video tape.

Mr. Latta. What you broadcast live today is not news tomorrow.

Mr. Smith. It goes on tonight's news.

Mr. Latta. That is right. You use it today. So you have only had 3 days over there all year?

Mr. Jordan. We have only had 3 days when we have pushed aside our normal programing during the day to run an entire hearing, lasting the morning and perhaps into the afternoon, live.

Mr. LATTA. Would you mind for the record giving us some idea as to the hearings that you covered live over there this year?

Mr. SMALL. I believe one related to Vietnam and the other to the ABM controversy.

Mr. JORDAN. There was the Senate Foreign Relations Committee on the ABM, there was the Armed Services Committee on the ABM, and there was one on Vietnam.

Mr. LATTA. Was there anything on Agriculture?

Mr. SMALL. No, sir.

Mr. JORDAN. No, sir.

Mr. LATTA. That is all.

Mr. SISK. Are there any other questions?

Mr. SMITH. Will you promise the gentleman that you will cover Agriculture for 5 minutes some day?

Mr. JORDAN. We will promise the gentleman that in time we will cover the Agriculture Committee. If we were to put the Agriculture Committee on live over the course of most of the day, I don't know what the effect would be.

Mr. LATTA. I think people would like to see the Senator from Louisiana in action.

Mr. SMALL. Mr. Latta, we have a difference, I think, you and I, on "fully informed." I think of it in terms of more fully informed and I am hoping your actions will permit us to more fully inform your constituents as well as ours. But if we talk about fully informed, in full, you are talking about the Congressional Record and even that really doesn't tell you everything about this Congress.

Mr. LATTA. Let me just comment, if I may. I think the people out in Ohio and in my district are interested in more of what has been going on in the Senate than the ABM and Vietnam this year.

Mr. SMALL. And we have covered a great number of subjects.

Mr. LATTA. You just mentioned that those are the two things you covered there.

Mr. JORDAN. Live.

Mr. LATTA. Live, yes. I think they ought to hear something else live in addition to these two items from the U.S. Senate because these taxpayers out there are paying a lot of money for that performance and I think they ought to see it on television. That is all, Mr. Chairman.

Mr. SISK. The gentleman from Missouri.

Mr. BOLLING. Do you gentlemen have any experience or difficulty with the methodology of the Congressional Record which was mentioned? One of the things that is most peculiar about the Congressional Record is that a great deal that appears in it was never said and a great deal that purports to have been said was never said—speaking of full information. I just add that gratuitously.

Mr. SISK. Do either of you gentlemen want to comment?

Mr. BOLLING. No; I don't even ask them to.

Mr. JORDAN. Thank you.

Mr. SISK. Mr. Lynch, Mr. Jordan, and Mr. Small, we appreciate very much your being before the committee. As I said, I again want to express my appreciation personally to you for your interest over the past months in this particular subject. I think that the committee still has some work to do with reference to the language here and it might be from time to time we may still wish to ask for your advice.

Mr. LYNCH. We would be delighted.

Mr. SMALL. Yes, Mr. Chairman.

Mr. JORDAN. Thank you, Mr. Chairman.

Mr. SISK. Thank you, gentlemen, once again for being here. . . .

Part Two

INTERDEPENDENCE AND INTERACTION

IT WAS INTENDED by the framers of the Constitution that Congress—particularly the House of Representatives—would be the branch most representative of the people. The representatives were to be selected by people in congressional districts of 30,000 people or more. It was assumed, given modest populations and the relatively small number of eligible voters, that the people would know firsthand the character and actions of their representatives. The role of the press in this context was to record, publish and distribute through newspaper exchange in the postal system, the proceedings of Congress to assist members of Congress and their political parties with the necessary task of communication. The role of the press was to supplement the primary sources of information about their congressmen available to constituents—observation, firsthand knowledge and other person-to-person communication.

Since then, the number of congressional districts has grown to 435, the average population of each district has increased to 467,000, and, in order to reach its large and shifting constituents, Congress has developed its own channels of political communication—i.e., the *Congressional Record*, vast printing facilities, newsletter, direct mail and television-film services.

In the meantime, the political press has become the mass media—newspapers, news services, weekly news magazines, radio and television. The news media—those components of the mass media dealing with public affairs—are no longer directly dependent on political or government patronage, although they are increasingly dependent on government regulation of their commercial licenses, business organizations and access to public information.

The overall result of these and other changes, such as the popular election of senators, is not greater power for Congress but greater power for *members* of Congress. In spite of the growth of the corps of Washington correspondents reporting on congressional activities, the net result for the citizen is less personal or firsthand information and observation and greater control by members of Congress over the flow of information to their districts. These changes, aided by committee secrecy at key points of policy-making, increase the ability of members of Congress to secure reelection. This reenforces the development of the seniority system which, in turn, enhances the power, especially in the House, of committee chairmen.

In the meantime, national correspondents devote their time less to covering the House—which has become more specialized, complex, fragmented and secret than the Senate—and more to the President, senators seeking the presidency and national issues which are more dramatically and generously presented (or staged) by both the President and the Senate. Furthermore, the Senate's advising on and consenting to presidential appointments creates frequent opportunities for media attention.

The numerous "locals" (the reporters with small media clients who emphasize the local or regional "angle" of government activity) and the "politicals" (the reporters for journals of opinion, emphasizing the ideological "angles") cover the House more closely than the "nationals." But they specialize and are more dependent on Congress and members of Congress for access and accommodation than are the national media. The "locals" and "politicals" are tied to their geographical or ideological sources of information.

Critically reviewing or thoroughly reporting the performance of these sources, including members of Congress who do not like criticism or who prefer maximum freedom of action, does not make for successful "local" or "political" reporters. Thus, these reporters and their media outlets generally serve to *enhance* the control of members of Congress over the flow of information to their districts and elsewhere.

With part of the news media neutralized or in their service, members of Congress use their own channels to enhance further control over the flow of impersonal information. The development by Congress of its own specialized means of communication and the practice of secrecy and deliberate anonymity outside one's district have made some members of the House extraordinarily powerful. Lack of news media attention to these powerful men in Congress, combined with the development of their own lines of communication with their constituents, gives them a near-monopoly over the content and flow of information which would have astounded the framers of the Constitution or members of the early 19th Century Congresses.

"Aside from issues which arouse strong emotions," Michael Barone said "most Congressmen are relatively free to vote their preferences without hurting their chances for reelection, because to a large extent they control the flow of information to their constituents about their own performance."

Barone has concluded there are winds of change blowing through the House. There has been a decade of decline in liberal and conservative confidence in and reliance on the executive branch. There has been a rising tide of citizen action—ecology groups, peace groups, and lobby and action groups like Common Cause and Ralph Nader's crusade.

The effect on the House, Barone said, has been to break the monopoly of information on the performance of Congress:

> As these groups spread their views and disseminate their data, House members are slowly losing their effective frank-created monopoly over the flow of information about the House's performance. Voters

sharply dissatisfied with current policies now are more willing and more able to make their views known.*

The news media, with their powers as sources and channels of information and with their ability to focus attention and comment on these groups, could play a major role in this change. Yet, it is too early to conclude that the flow of information from and about Congress is going to change significantly.

In the Senate, there appears to be more dependence on the news media than in the House, since a major role of the Senate now seems to be to publicize issues and political personalities. Only a few senators are successful in keeping out of the public spotlight. The growth of the news media has served also to broaden the function of the Senate beyond its chambers, the Capitol and even Washington; to broaden the potential constituencies of the members beyond state lines.

A senator may not appear on the floor of the Senate for a week, while he debates the issues on the "Today Show" on Monday, is interviewed by two dozen newsmen on Tuesday, has his Washington staff produce a press release on Wednesday, inserts a speech in the *Congressional Record* giving the impression that he is in the Senate chambers on Thursday, publicly tours a state where he is running in a presidential primary on Friday, delivers a speech on Saturday which is picked up by a wire service stringer or correspondent, and appears on "Issues and Answers" or "Meet the Press" on Sunday to be reported in the Monday morning papers.

Regardless of the views on the news media held by members of both the Senate and the House, they seem to need and use information *from* the news media. As Delmer Dunn has pointed out, they use the news media by reading and viewing the news, and by talking with correspondents to get intelligence, personal counsel and reactions and opinions from the public.**

At the same time, most members of Congress use the news media as channels for personal publicity, to build program support, to counter the power of the executive branch, to provide neutral information, to test public reaction or otherwise fulfill what they perceive as their responsibilities.

What are the criteria of "news" which the news media apply when they focus attention and comment on issues and officials?

The technology and audience shape correspondents' priorities and determine what they report. Each category of correspondent has his or her peculiar technology and audience—wire service, radio and television service, broadcast network, specialized newsletter, major prestige national daily newspaper, news weekly, small-town daily, syndicated column, etc.

*Barone, Michael, "The Winds of Change in the House," *Washington Post*, Volume 95, Number 256, September 3, 1972, p. C3.
** See Dunn, Delmer, *Public Officials and the Press*, Reading, Mass., Addison-Wesley Publishing Co., 1969.

How these correspondents consciously or subconsciously perceive their function in society influences what and how they report information about Congress. Some view their roles as neutral information transmitters ("just reporting the facts"). Others see themselves as representatives of the public or actual participants in the policy-making processes. These perceptions are made within the more uniformly held norms of "objectivity," accuracy and skepticism—the definitions of which are widely diverse.

The professional definition of "news" also plays a major role in what information is sought and collected about Congress for the mass media. Dunn has identified such criteria as the degree of conflict, controversy, attack, change, uniqueness and personality in events.

Other criteria of "news" include the events of the day—defined by deadline, limited by degree of complexity, and shaped by the ease of coverage and the personal interest of the reporter. A reporter's relations with his professional colleagues, the policy interests of his news organization and his relations with his sources also shape his definition of news.

The methods of gathering news and producing the printed or electronic report impinge on information transmitted about Congress. News-gathering methods include covering meetings and committee hearings, attending press conferences, examining handouts of press releases and talking with sources.

Source-press relationships, including the norms governing these relationships, have played important roles in news about Congress. Some of the customs identified by Dunn include not revealing one's sources, guarding the independence of the reporter, rewarding reporter enterprise and treating the reporter fairly.

Parts One and Two report many changes in relations between the news media and the Congress during the past 180 years. The glitter of the more obvious and dramatic changes in size and technology, however, should not obscure patterns in relations where little change seems to have taken place.

From the beginning, for instance, Congress has alternately closed its doors—chamber and committee—to reporters—partisan and watchdog—while peeking at them through the keyhole to assess their use as channels for favorable mention or publicity; opening the doors a wee bit to leak information to them or entice them with patronage and a little more generous accommodation; or reaching out to slap their wrists with banishment, investigation or even detention by the sergeant-at-arms.

From the beginning, representatives of the press and news media have sought and accepted patronage, access and accommodation from capricious members of Congress. Sometimes they have cooperated with their hosts' desire for uncritical recording or, preferably, unrestrained puffery. Just as frequently, they have bitten the hosts' hands, accepting the hospitality as rights, not privileges, to be exercised as they saw fit—for personal profit, personal glory, partisan politics, hobby horses, noble causes, a drink, the public good, or, whenever possible, all of the above.

From the beginning, members of Congress have confessed their dependence on the press and the news media. The dependence has changed only in form. In the beginning there was the need to have their proceedings recorded, published and distributed through the mails to small and neighborly constituencies. Now many members of Congress seek publicity through the news media to gain the attention of or just recognition from massive and shifting constituencies. They need the cooperation of the news media to compete with the power of the executive branch. Others avoid the news media to maintain control over the flow of information, or misinformation, to their congressional districts.

From the beginning, the press and news media have depended economically on Congress—from patronage for local printers and editors, to privilege and subsidy for news organizations and their reporters from "distant cities."

The Balance of
Publicity Powers

THE GROWTH OF MASS AUDIENCES and communications technology have enhanced the power of the news media to focus and comment on political issues and officials. This growth, many members of Congress have argued, has served to enhance the power of the executive branch at the expense of "other constitutionally co-equal branches of government."

Former Rep. Thomas Curtis (D.-Mo.) expresses the frustrations of many members of Congress, past and present, at the power of the President to influence public opinion by dominating the news. He suggests that this power, which subverts the "deliberative process of the Congress," is increasing now that "quick news has become such an important part of our technologically advanced and busy society."

In testimony Sen. William J. Fulbright (D.-Ark.) presents the congressional view that the executive branch dominates the broadcast media. Fulbright's proposed solution is legislation which would guarantee to Congress public service time on the national television networks. He argues that "the President can command a national television audience to hear his views on controversial matters at prime time, on short notice, at whatever length he chooses, and at no expense to the Federal Government or to his party." He presents evidence of dramatic shifts in public opinion as direct results of such a "near monopoly on effective access to the public attention."

On the other hand, Fulbright argues, members of Congress "are compelled to rely on highly selective newspaper articles and television news slots, which at most will convey bits and snatches of their points of view, usually selected in such a way as to create an impression of cranky carping at an heroic and beleaguered President."

Frances E. Rourke suggests that Congress is not so helpless in its own uses of publicity as Sen. Fulbright seems to argue. He views the use of publicity by Congress as a means by which it vies with the Presidential quest for public attention. As the competition has stiffened, new techniques have been developed, such as public hearings and investigations in Congress. (Techniques of publicity developed by Congress are explored in more detail in Chapters 7 and 8).

Nelson Polsby discusses major differences between the Senate and House which he says patterns of news coverage tend to reenforce. The House, he finds, is more highly specialized in processing legislation. There are more members, many of whom are not reelected enough times to become known. Even senior House members are associated with their committee specialty. In the Senate, there are fewer members and they serve longer terms. Specialization is not as extreme as in the House and a senator is accepted by the news media as an authority on a variety of subjects. As we have seen in previous selections, the Senate is more liberal in allowing news media—especially broadcast—coverage of its committee deliberations. Polsby, like Rourke, suggests that the major public policy roles of the Senate are closely tied to its publicity orientation. The role of publicity is involved in the Senate's roles as an initiator, incubator, modifier and appraiser of policies.

It is too early to assess the long-run effects of the Watergate scandals, the Senate Watergate investigation and the House Judiciary Committee impeachment inquiry on the executive-legislative balance of publicity. It appears, however, that for at least a brief period Congress has begun to redress this imbalance. The Senate, at least, has been demonstrating awesome powers of publicity with the attention and cooperation of the news media. (These and other aspects of the Watergate hearings are considered in Chapters 8 and 11).

THE EXECUTIVE DOMINATES THE NEWS

By Thomas Curtis

. . . In our form of representative government, the President is the Executive to carry out the decisions made by the people's representatives in Congress assembled—although the office has some legislative responsibilities.

In addition, the President has certain powers derived directly from the Constitution and not from the laws enacted by the Congress. Therefore he has a responsibility to report directly to the people on certain matters.

However, the President has a responsibility to report directly to the Congress on these same matters. The Congress in turn has a responsibility

Reprinted from the *Congressional Record*, January 30, 1968, pp. 1483-1484.

and the authority to require the President to report directly to the Congress upon his administration of the laws enacted by Congress, as well as of his direct constitutional powers.

There is an implied constitutional restriction, however, which forbids the President from reporting directly to the people over the heads, as it were, of the people's duly elected representatives on matters which are essentially legislative. Congress, from time to time, has restricted by law the Executive's power to spend money and to use the facilities and the time of executive employees to influence the legislative process. The President and his appointees have the prerogative to present their views in depth to the Congress and congressional committees.

In recent years these restrictive laws have been continuously and openly violated. The greatest lobby in Washington today has become the executive branch of the Federal Government. The techniques employed by it increasingly rely upon misrepresentation rather than appeals to facts and fair arguments. Thinly disguised political blackmail and bribery backstopped by extensive campaigns to propagandize the people have subverted the study and deliberative process of the Congress in all too many instances.

If this process is developed to its ultimate, the Congress will become no more than a sophisticated mechanism to record the effectiveness of the propaganda programs conducted by the Executive financed by tax moneys.

How far we have come in losing sight of the political structure embodied in the Constitution is seen in the format of President Johnson's State of the Union messages. These are no longer messages to the Congress. They are messages to the people over the heads of the Congress with the Congressmen relegated to the position of stage props to enhance the effectiveness of the propaganda extravaganza.

I do not fault the President for this as much as I do the weak leadership of the Congress which permits it. And I fault my own party for not forcefully challenging the President and the Democratic leaders of the Congress on this issue.

It is important not to over-simplify the problem. An important function of executive agencies is to give out factual information to the public from time to time. Many laws require executive agencies to do just that. Some agencies are specifically established for that limited purpose. However, if this function of administrative government is used to propagandizing the people, it not only fails to achieve its proper purpose, it strikes at the heart of the reporting-back function of the Congress so essential to the operation of representative government. . . .

I have sought to point up many other ways in which the President can and does dominate the news daily and insidiously.

Furthermore, the Executive can dominate the quick news which has become such an important part of our technologically advanced and busy society. Actions rather than deliberations are the grist for the 15-second comment in the daily national TV and radio news broadcasts and the 100-word national wire service items printed word for word in the columns of the daily newspapers throughout the country.

The Executive, by definition, acts and so creates news. But not so the Congress which if fulfilling its proper function essentially studies and deliberates. Its only easily reportable actions are the final votes taken at the end of this long drawn out process.

It is difficult to report the study and deliberative process meaningfully and objectively. Certainly it is difficult to report it as "quick" news without over-simplifications. Creating labels and readily recognizable personalities are the techniques of the art.

To the extent that the Congress performs as a study and deliberative body instead of as a super Univac registering the results of the input of the propaganda campaigns, to that extent the ability to "quick" report what Congress is doing is diminished. Conversely, to the extent that the Congress does act as a super Univac, to that extent it lends itself to the "quick" report. The ready quip, the extreme statement, if it can be boiled down to 15 seconds, becomes the basis of the reports of congressional action to the people.

Perhaps if the weekly and the monthly national magazines undertook to report the study and deliberative process in the Congress with more accuracy and less quip and wit, the quick-news media's labels and coined personalities would be less deceiving to the public. Instead of being a guide the weekly and monthly magazines and the documentaries of TV and radio seem to take their guidance from the quickies. Or what is more sinister, they often become the willing accomplices of those, which include the executive, who seek to propagandize the American people rather than to develop a national public dialog by reporting the study and deliberative process.

One eminent reporter, the head of the Washington bureau of a prominent daily newspaper when introduced to a Member of Congress said: "I always enjoy meeting one of my competitors."

This was said partly in jest, but it illustrates an important point. Many reporters seek to make news rather than to report it.

To a reporter seeking to make news, a representative of the people assigned the job of studying and deliberating the social issues to render decisions is indeed a competitor. To such a reporter the manipulation of the news media with its established labels and political dramatis personae is the name of the game. This, however, is the easy game. Reporting the study and deliberative process is an exceedingly difficult game and requires a master's every effort to turn in a creditable performance.

To the historian seeking to write history to manipulate the course of current events instead of grubbing out the truth of past events, the Congressman is also, if not a competitor, at least someone to be manipulated.

The thrust of these perversions of the search for truth is directed not so much to the Executive—who is concerned with action which it is not so easy to misreport as it is to the Congress which is concerned with study and deliberation.

Finally, I would observe that the election process, as well as the legislative process, depends upon accurate reporting to the people. If the issues which face the nation and the positions of the politicians involved are not presented to the people with reasonable accuracy the process of popular election is undermined.

There are two professions which are basically responsible to the people for accurate reporting. First, and primarily responsible are the political representatives themselves and the party leaders. Second, there are the news reporters and the news media. Indeed, if the first group fails to study and deliberate and to make decisions in respect to the issues, or dissembles their individual views on the issues, how indeed, can the news media be faulted?

However, if study and deliberation has gone on, and decisions have been made upon this basis and the quality and quantity of it has not been reported to the people, then indeed the intermediary between the people and their representatives must bear the blame.

I think there is a little question that the weakest link in representative government today is the reporting back to the people of the study and deliberation which goes on on public issues. This weakness is so pronounced today that the blame for it must be widely shared by both professions, that of the politician and that of the reporter as well as by their academic backstoppers, the political scientists and the historians. . . .

EQUAL TIME FOR CONGRESS:
CONGRESSIONAL HEARINGS, 1970

Communications Subcommittee, Senate Commerce Committee

Mr. FULBRIGHT. Within the last year or so Senators have become increasingly concerned with the growth of Presidential power at the expense of the other, constitutionally co-equal branches of our Government.

Reprinted from *Hearings, Public Service Time for the Legislative Branch*, U.S. Congress, Senate, Communications Subcommittee of the Commerce Committee, 91st Cong., 1st Sess., August 4, 1970, pp. 14-21, 71, 77-78.

That concern was expressed in the National Commitments Resolution, adopted by the Senate last year by the vote of 70 to 16. Despite that overwhelming vote and an unassailable constitutional basis, the National Commitments Resolution has had no discernible effect upon the Executive and, as a result, we are compelled to grapple with the issue once again, now under more urgent and agitated circumstances. The initiation of a constitutionally unauthorized, Presidential war in Cambodia has brought the issue to a crisis, compelling the Congress to act in defense of its constitutional war powers. That is the principal significance of the Cooper-Church Amendment and of other pending legislative proposals.

Unfortunately, Congress is at a great disadvantage in the war powers debate, as it is in discussing most issues, because the Executive has a near monopoly on effective access to the public attention. The President can command a national television audience to hear his views on controversial matters at prime time, on short notice, at whatever length he chooses, and at no expense to the Federal Government or to his party. Other constitutional officeholders are compelled to rely on highly selective newspaper articles and television news spots, which at most will convey bits and snatches of their points of view, usually selected in such a way as to create an impression of cranky carping at an heroic and beleaguered President.

The problem for a Senator or Senate Committee is not simply one of being heard. Anything that has the color of scandal, sensation, accusation or prediction will command eager attention from the media. What you cannot easily interest them in is an idea, or a carefully exposited point of view, or an unfamiliar perspective or a reasoned rebuttal to a highly controversial Presidential statement. In recent weeks, for example, the Foreign Relations Committee has heard thoughtful and significant statements on the war by eminent businessmen, political and military leaders, and theologians but, owing to the lack of interest of the media, these proceedings have remained a well-kept secret between the witnesses and the members of the Committee. Why this is so is beyond my understanding. All I do know is that the only reliable way of getting the media to swallow an idea is by candy coating it with a prediction or accusation.

Take for example the issue now under discussion about the war powers of the Congress as against the President's authority as Commander-in-Chief. The whole country heard the President hold forth in his recent press conference about how *he alone* as Commander-in-Chief was responsible for the conduct of the war, the expansion of the war into a neutral country, and the safety of our fighting men. The very words "Commander-in-Chief" are intoned with a reverential awe appropriate to eighteenth century courtiers speaking of "His Most Christian" or "Britannic" or "Imperial and Apostolic Majesty." Millions of people heard the President expound his inflated concept of his role as Commander-in-Chief, but virtually no one outside of this chamber has heard the thoughtful and learned expositions of Senators on constitutional doctrine and the intent of the framers. The result is that the country is suffused with the constitutional theories of Lyndon Johnson and Richard Nixon, while the contrasting views of Jefferson, Hamilton and Madison remain buried in history. As fast as they are called up by members of this body, they are laid again to rest in the pages of the *Congressional Record.*

There is nothing in the Constitution which says that, of all elected officials, the President alone shall have the right to communicate with the American people. That privilege was a gift of modern technology, coming in an age when chronic war and crisis were already inflating the powers of the Presidency. We all remember F.D.R.'s fireside chats on radio and his use of these to win the people to his viewpoints. I am not sure anyone ever did find out whether that battleship really was sent up to Alaska to pick up the President's "little dog Fala." No one cared after the President's skillful use of radio to ridicule the allegation.

Communication is power and exclusive access to it is a dangerous, unchecked power. If Roosevelt had had television, he might have been proclaimed emperor by acclamation. None of F.D.R.'s successors has matched his genius for mass communication, but each one has found television to be a powerful tool in the service of Presidential policies and opinions. Television has done as much to expand the powers of the President as would a constitutional amendment formally abolishing the co-equality of the three branches of Government.

Because the Presidency is institutional and the political parties are not, the networks have not only denied the opposition equal time to reply to Presidential statements, but will not even permit the Democratic National Committee to purchase broadcasting time at commercial rates. CBS has said that it has a general rule against selling time for the presentation of controversial views except during election campaigns. The network of course sets itself up as the sole judge of what is "controversial." In my opinion the moon flights are controversial—I think them an extravagant waste—but the networks provide millions of dollars worth of time to permit us to view every last boring detail of these space flights in living color.

Whatever justification there may be for denying broadcast time to political parties, there can be no justification for denying equal time to the co-equal branches of Government. Under our Constitution there is no paramount branch of the Federal Government; if indeed the framers regarded any branch as *primus inter pares*, it was not the Executive but the Congress, whose powers are spelled out in the Constitution at greatest length and in the greatest detail. If the President is regarded as having the right to communicate with the people through the mass media whenever he wishes, the spirit and intent of our Constitution require that no less a privilege be accorded to the Senate and the House of Representatives, or, if it should claim it, to the judiciary.

With these thoughts in mind, Mr. President, I have recommended to the distinguished Chairman of the Committee on Commerce [Mr. Warren Magnuson] that he and his colleagues consider legislation which would require all television stations licensed by the Federal Communications Commission to provide broadcasting time on demand both to the Congress and the President. The current practice is that the networks provide free time to the President whenever he wishes it, but no statute or FCC regulation requires them to do so. Appropriate legislation might require the networks to provide broadcast time to the President whenever he wishes it and might give the same right to Congress, perhaps to be divided equally between the two Houses and the two parties.

The details of this proposed legislation might best be worked out by the Commerce Committee should they judge that it has merit. My purpose today is to develop and commend the general principle of a Congressional right of access to the mass media. No less than the Executive, the Congress has the right—indeed, one could say the responsibility—to report to the Nation on matters that affect the national interest. The means of exercising that right should exist along with, but entirely independent of, the parallel Presidential right. Broadcast time should be available to the Congress at all times and not simply in order to reply when the President speaks to the nation. The purpose is not to facilitate the expression of partisan views on national issues but to guarantee the right of the people to hear diverse and opposing views regardless of party.

Television is the most potent information medium in our country today. No other medium of communication in history has permitted the transmission of ideas and viewpoints to so many people simultaneously, so graphically and convincingly, whether the idea concerns environmental pollution, the war in Indochina, civil rights, poverty, or student dissent. According to recent surveys, the American public has more faith in the information it gets from television than from any other source and it goes to this source more frequently and for longer periods of time than to any other. By latest count there are nearly 60 million television homes in the United States, and their sets are tuned in for an estimated average of six hours a day—which means approximately 360 million man-hours per day. This is too powerful and dangerous an instrument to be left to the exclusive use of the Executive.

Mr. Chairman, I asked Mr. Lou Harris to give me an analysis of the effect of Presidential speeches, as best he could, on recent important issues. If the chairman would allow me I would like to call attention to a few instances and insert the entire analysis in the record. I think it's quite interesting and it demonstrates, I think, what the chairman has already said about the power of communications through television. These are some examples. I won't read them all. Before the speech by John F. Kennedy on July 26, 1963, announcing the Nuclear Test Ban Treaty, the polls had shown 73 percent favored it. Immediately after his speech on television this jumped to 81 percent. A most dramatic one was in August of 1964. Before the speech of President Johnson with regard to the alleged Tonkin Gulf incident, 42 percent showed a positive position on President Johnson's Vietnam policy. Immediately after that speech on the Gulf of Tonkin it jumped to 72 percent; from 42 to 72 percent, a very dramatic affair. Presenting it on television in that fashion obviously made a tremendous impact.

On the intervention in the Dominican Republic, Mr. Harris did not have a poll immediately prior to the television appearance by President Johnson before the intervention in the Dominican Republic, but immediately after it, 77 percent supported it, although it later became a highly controversial matter.

This is an interesting one: in 1969 President Nixon on May 14 announced on television the policy of phased withdrawals from Vietnam. Prior to that Presidential speech on television 49 percent favored phased withdrawals. Right after it, it jumped to 67 percent.

There are two more.

Senator [HUGH] SCOTT [R.-Pa.]. It was very good news, wasn't it?

Senator FULBRIGHT. Well, it is made to appear so. If you have exclusive access to television time. This is what we're really talking about. You can make anything appear the way you like it if you are the only one who presents the views.

Senator SCOTT. You don't mind if two-thirds of the public were so recorded as favoring a phased withdrawal. You wouldn't quarrel with the right of the public to believe that, would you?

Senator FULBRIGHT. No. I would favor complete withdrawal, phased or otherwise. The difficulty is whether or not it really is designed to achieve its announced purpose.

Two more examples, Mr. Chairman, on April 30, 1970, the President announced on TV the sending of U.S. troops to Cambodia. Before that was announced the poll showed 7 percent favored sending troops into Cambodia, 59 percent favored staying out of Cambodia altogether, 23 percent favored sending advisors only. Remember that, 7 percent favored sending troops in. But after the President's speech on television, 50 percent supported the President sending U.S. troops into Cambodia.

I'm not raising the merits of these issues here. I am only demonstrating the effectiveness of access to the public mind by this medium. That's all. I am not trying to argue about whether he should or should not have gone into Cambodia. But look at the tremendous change from 7 to 50 percent within the course of 8 to 10 days.

On a domestic matter—this is interesting because it still is controversial—President Johnson in 1968 went on television in support of strong gun control legislation. After he made his speech, the percentage went up 10 percent, from 71 to 81 percent, even on an issue like that. This analysis, I might say, shows that the impact on foreign policy measures of various kinds is far greater than on domestic measures. My own view is it is because people feel they are more familiar with the domestic. They are harder to influence directly on particular issues with which they feel they are very familiar. I think you will find it an interesting study and there is a little analysis accompanying the ——

Senator Scott. May I ask one question on that?

Senator, do you have any information from Mr. Harris on the impact of a television appearance by a Senator or Member of the House following a speech by the President? Does it have any impact at all?

Senator Fulbright. I don't have any study of that. We might ask someone. But quite obviously it wouldn't have much because the exposure would be far less, wouldn't it? Does the Senator know of a case where a Senator is given the same exposure in prime time following the President?

Senator Scott. I am curious as to what the Senator thought would be accomplished by having equal time for the Senators? There is no evidence that when this has happened in the past that it has or has not had impact on public opinion.

Senator Fulbright. I have no study of that. I want to reiterate. I don't visualize this simply as an opportunity to contradict or reply to any President, this one or any future President. I think effectiveness of this means of communication has been demonstrated—and I don't by any means wish to denigrate the newspapers. This is no place to argue about it, but Sir William Haley recently had a most interesting article on this subject in the Columbia Journalism Review, on the relative accuracy and effectiveness of television and newspapers—not effectiveness in the sense of influencing the public mind but in seriously explaining news.

I think that the President ought to have the opportunity and be under the responsibility of explaining some of these very important issues. It is not only in foreign relations; just because I happen to be on that committee I tend to talk about it. But take the current issue before the Finance Committee on the family assistance plan. This is a most complicated issue and there ought to be a way, in prime time, to explain this to the American people. There ought to be established ways to do that because it's not only confusing to the members of the committee, I am sure it is to everybody else. It is one of the most complicated proposals I have ever seen.

Senator [John] Pastore [D.-R.I.]. The Senator is not looking for a quarrel, he is just asking for exposure.

Senator Fulbright. That's right.

Senator Pastore. That is all it amounts to.

Senator FULBRIGHT. As Justice Brandeis put it so well, it is out of the friction and conflict—if you want to call it the quarrel—the different views out of which we hope to protect ourselves from autocracy. This is the essence of a democratic system.

And as I said yesterday on the Senate floor, it is very strange that we are tending to use in our system much greater secrecy in some areas than countries like Spain. In the Spanish Parliament they submitted a treaty with the United States. But in our Government, they think that is too sensitive for Congress to deal with; they don't want to submit it at all. This is the kind of issue that demonstrates what I'm talking about, if we intend to preserve our constitutional system.

I think there is no doubt, due largely to television influence, that the Office of the Executive overshadows and in a sense dominates the Legislature. This is not new. I don't want you to take this as a partisan matter. I think it became quite evident with the predecessor of the present President. His predecessor had a most unusual understanding of the Congress and coupling his understanding with his domination of the airways, he did dominate the Congress. He certainly dominated and hoodwinked the Congress at the time of the Tonkin Gulf. This is a most dramatic demonstration of how the public mind was completely taken over, just with a television program. There wasn't anything anybody else could do about it. It was long after that we learned enough even to assert the contrary facts about the case. We didn't know it at the immediate time. But what a tremendous power it gave a man with his understanding of the Congress and the use of television, and he used it to a very great extent.

Mr. Chairman, I assume . . . you [have] the data about the use of the television by Presidents. But President Johnson used it most vigorously.

Senator PASTORE. Do you desire to put any of that in the record?

Senator FULBRIGHT. I don't want to complicate your record.

Senator PASTORE. How long is it?

Senator FULBRIGHT. This is material that I had as background. I don't want to put it in the record. I'll submit it by reference.

Senator PASTORE. We will incorporate it by reference.

Senator FULBRIGHT. You use it for whatever you find use for it.

Senator PASTORE. We will incorporate it by reference.

Senator FULBRIGHT. There is a great deal of data here, how many times it was used and under what circumstances. I don't want to bother you with presenting it.

(The above-mentioned analysis follows:)

IMPACT OF PRESIDENTIAL TELEVISED APPEARANCES

Ever since John F. Kennedy became President of the United States, much has been made of the use of the medium of television as the dominant vehicle through which a president can communicate with the electorate. Back in the early 1960's it was speculated that a youthful, glamorous presidential figure had a substantial advantage over his opposition due to the inbuilt use of the television medium.

However, an examination of the findings of public opinion research surveys before and after major televised presidential speeches since late 1963 seems to indicate that, regardless of the popularity of a president's stand at the time, with rare exceptions, any time the President of the United States makes a televised speech to the American public, his popularity with the electorate and support for his position is almost always enhanced.

This pattern appears to be the case both on domestic and foreign policy issues. In August 1963, before President Kennedy went on television appealing for a Congressional tax cut, 62 percent of the public were in favor of the idea despite the strength of the opposition viewpoint that the nation's budget should be balanced first. After the President's televised speech and, in spite of the increased attention given opposing points of view, 66 percent of the people were in favor of the proposed tax cut.

President Johnson, too, was successful in increasing support for his stands on domestic issues through the use of television. His plea, after Robert Kennedy's assassination, for stronger gun control legislation, met with 81 percent approval by the American public (versus 71 percent approval before his speech). Even in the controversial welfare area, President Nixon was able to gain the support of a plurality of 47 percent of the American public for the new welfare plan he proposed on television in August of 1969—a relatively high figure in view of past public reaction to welfare proposals.

As a matter of fact, the only example of a presidential television speech on domestic affairs that did not successfully bring a substantial rise in public support for a president's point of view, was President Nixon's plea in March 1970 for an end to the postal workers' strike because a national emergency was being created. In spite of his speech, by 61 to 25 percent the public expressed sympathy for the postal workers over the Federal Government, when questioned at the start of the strike.

An examination of readings of presidential popularity before and after major televised speeches on foreign policy issues produces even more evidence of the immense power of televised presidential appearances. Before President Kennedy went on television in July 1963 to announce the start of negotiations with the Soviet Union on the nuclear test ban agreement, 71 percent of the public favored such a treaty. After the president's speech, 81 percent strongly supported the idea.

In August 1964, at a time when President Johnson was vulnerable to Barry Goldwater's charge of a Democratic "no-win" policy in Vietnam and with Johnson's rating on his handling of the Vietnam situation at only 42 percent positive, the President responded on television in the Gulf of Tonkin episode. A high 72 percent of the American people rallied behind him after the TV appearance.

Later, in April of 1965, President Johnson again went on television to explain his sending of U.S. marines into the Dominican Republic. After his third televised speech in defense of his Dominican action, he was able to gain the endorsement of 77 percent of the public.

Public reaction to presidential speeches on the major foreign policy issue of the 1960's, the Vietnam war, shows a clear and distinct pattern of a rise in public support following a presidential TV appearance. Significantly, the positive response to a televised appearance seems to occur irrespective of whether the President wanted to escalate or de-escalate U.S. involvement.

Following the U.S. pause in the bombings of North Vietnam in early 1966, which failed to bring the communists to the negotiating table, 61 percent of the public favored resumption of the bombings. After President Johnson went on TV to announce a resumption of the bombings, support for such raids on North Vietnam rose to 73 percent.

In May of 1969, President Nixon announced on television the pursuit of a different course of action in Vietnam—that of phased withdrawals of American troops from the conflict. Before his appearance, a policy of withdrawal was favored by less than a majority of the public (49 percent). Following his TV speech, a high 67 percent of the public said they supported a plan of phased withdrawals. Again, in October of 1969, less than half of the public (46 percent), gave President Nixon a positive rating on his handling of the Vietnam war, but his televised plea for public support of his Vietnam policies on November 3rd of that year won him the approval of 51 percent of his electorate. Even in late March of this year, when President Nixon's rating on his handling of the war was at one of its lowest points (only 36 percent said he was doing an excellent or a pretty good job), the President's televised April pledge to withdraw another 150,000 U.S. troops from Vietnam boosted his job rating to 40 percent positive, a gain of six points.

The most significant incident of a president's success in enhancing his position with the public through television was President Nixon's speech announcing the sending of U.S. troops into Cambodia. In late April, just prior to the start of the Cambodian mission, only seven percent of the American public favored the sending of U.S. troops into Cambodia (59 percent favored staying out altogether). But within a matter of days after his speech, 50 percent of the people believed the President had done the right thing by sending American troops into Cambodia.

The only two occasions where a major televised presidential speech on foreign policy matters did not serve to enhance a president's popularity rating were President Johnson's announcement on March 31, 1968, of another bombing halt in Vietnam (and also of the fact that he would not seek re-election), and President Nixon's announcement in December of 1969 of a troop withdrawal of 50,000 men. Prior to Mr. Johnson's speech, his rating on his handling of the war was at a low 38 percent positive, and in May that rating remained exactly the same (38 percent). The failure of President Nixon's December speech to move public opinion can be seen by the fact that before the speech, a majority of the public (51 percent) gave him a positive rating on the job he was doing in Vietnam, but after the announced withdrawal, only 48 percent gave him a favorable rating.

Quite obviously there may be other extenuating circumstances surrounding the presidential speeches examined here, and on a number of occasions the mere fact of the President speaking to his electorate, briefing the people, explaining to them what he is doing, whether televised or not, might possibly have been enough to raise his standing in the public's eyes. Clearly the substance of what a president says is important in its own right. But there is evidence here of a correlation between televised presidential speeches and increased public acceptance of the positions expounded by presidents in those appearances.

FOREIGN POLICY

TV APPEARANCE	POLL RESULT
July 26, 1963—JFK announces nuclear test ban treaty on TV.	Before; 73 percent favored. After; 81 percent favored.
Aug. 1, 1964—LBJ on TV on Tonkin Gulf incident.	Before; 42 percent positive on LBJ Vietnam policy. After; 72 percent positive on LBJ Vietnam policy.
May 2, 1965—LBJ on TV to explain Dominican Republic action.	After; 77 percent supported.
Jan. 31, 1966—LBJ on TV to announce resumption of bombing of Vietnam.	Before; 61 percent favored resumption of bombings. After; 73 percent favored resumption of bombings.
Mar. 31, 1968—LBJ announced on TV limited bombing halt and not running for reelection.	Before; 38 percent positive on LBJ on war. After; 38 percent positive on LBJ on war.
May 14, 1969—RMN announced on TV policy of phased withdrawals from Vietnam.	Before; 49 percent favored phased withdrawals. After; 67 percent favored phased withdrawals.
Nov. 3, 1969—RMN plea on TV for support of Vietnam.	Before; 46 percent positive on Nixon on war. After; 51 percent positive on Nixon on war.
Dec. 15, 1969—RMN announces cut of 50,000 troops on TV.	Before; 51 percent positive on Nixon on war. After; 48 percent positive on Nixon on war.
Apr. 20, 1970—RMN pledges on TV to withdraw 150,000 troops from Vietnam.	Before: 36 percent positive on Nixon's handling of war. After; 40 percent positive on Nixon's handling of war.
Apr. 30, 1970—RMN announces on TV the sending of U.S. troops to Cambodia.	Before; 7 percent favored sending U.S. troops. 59 percent favored staying out of Cambodia altogether. 23 percent favored sending advisers only. After; 50 percent supported Nixon's sending U.S. troops into Cambodia.

DOMESTIC AFFAIRS

TV APPEARANCE	POLL RESULT
Aug. 18, 1963—JFK appealed on TV for tax cut from Congress.	Before; 62 percent favored. After; 66 percent favored.
June 7, 1968—LBJ on TV in support of stronger gun control legislation.	Before; 71 percent favored. After; 81 percent favored.
Aug. 8, 1969—RMN on TV urging overhaul of welfare system and his new bill.	After; 47 percent favored.
Mar. 23, 1970—RMN on TV declared national emergency in postal strike.	After; 61–25 percent opposed to government on strike.

Senator PASTORE. Senator Griffin?

Senator [ROBERT P.] GRIFFIN [R.-Mich.]. I don't want to seem impertinent, but since you used the Gulf of Tonkin resolution as an example, let us suppose that your legislation had been in effect at the time the Tonkin resolution was debated and there had been time available for a representative from the Senate to speak to the public, what would they have heard?

Senator FULBRIGHT. I just said, I didn't know enough to give a contrary view at that time. We later did and it would have been most useful after we had the hearings in the committee. We obtained the official documents from the Department of Defense to demonstrate what had happened and what had not happened. It did come later. It would not have been sufficiently timely to offset the effect at the time. But later on I think it would have been most useful. Even today the public and many of the Senators have not found out about what actually happened in the Gulf of Tonkin. A book has been written called, "Truth Is the First Casualty," but very few people have read it. I agree with you, the information was simply not available, no one suspected there had been such deception.

Senator GRIFFIN. Of course we know; and it might be just as well to emphasize, that for a number of years Senate committee hearings have been televised in instances where the networks or others believed there was news value involved. Now, I want to make a rather simple and what I think is a logical alternative suggestion to your legislation and get your comment.

Wouldn't the purpose be served better if the Senate were just to change its rules and to allow the televising and broadcasting of its floor debates? This would be a way, I would think, that the public could be informed of the various points of view without opening up a can of worms in trying to decide who is going to represent the Senate or who is going to represent the various points of view in the Senate. It seems to me that your proposal leads to the committee chairmen having perhaps a preferred status and maybe they should in this kind of situation; or perhaps if party considerations were involved in the selection of the spokesman, concentration would be focused on the attractive Senator to the exclusion of some of the most powerful and effective Senators in our body who I suppose would never have the opportunity to appear on television.

I'm going to use an example of one particular Senator since he is not up for election and because I don't think he would object. Senator John Williams of Delaware, I think we would all agree on both sides of the aisle, is one of the most powerful, effective, influential Senators in the body. I don't see him on television very often. I suppose it is his own choice. He doesn't push himself—I suppose they gave up asking him, after a while, to be on television. And because he is not on television, because the debates of the Senate are not televised, I think the public at large may have a very distorted and warped impression of the Senate. I will not refer to any other Members, although there are others in the same category, who are very effective insofar as their colleagues are concerned, but not very articulate in front of a TV camera. This is a long way of getting back to the question, "Why don't we just televise the debates of the Senate?"

Senator FULBRIGHT. What you say about Senators—Senator [Richard] Russell is even a more obvious example. He has never, even in years past, appeared on television. It is a matter of personal choice. He didn't care to operate that way. He is, as you know, the senior Senator and President pro tem. Senator Williams, to my understanding, doesn't care to use the medium either, and that's his privilege. But, as I said a moment ago, the more I think about it, in nearly every important debate a spokesman develops in nearly every case. Nearly always certain people take the lead. And in some cases, I'm sure if this were done in a serious way, in prime time, my guess is Senator Williams would reconsider. I mean, he doesn't want to go on many of these programs. Many of us have found out they're quite unimportant, really. The exposure is minimal. Usually these panel question programs come on at church time in most of the country, 11 o'clock Sunday morning or Sunday noon. Very few of them are prime time and very few of them are approached with the idea that you're going to really seriously examine important questions. Senator Williams and Senator Russell don't need exposure for more votes at home and they are not interested in that kind of a show. I think that is a matter of personal taste more than anything else.

If you're talking about broadcasting all of the Senate sessions, I think this would be inappropriate. Much of it is routine, much of it is of limited interest. For example, the Senate met this morning at 9:30, and there were a series of speeches. I don't know what they're about, but they enable Members to express themselves primarily on matters of interest to their own constituents. There is nothing wrong with that but I can't imagine it worth being televised.

I do not think that this modification is without merit. Possibly one night a week or two nights a month, we'll say, during a period agreed on by the leadership, perhaps from 8 to 10 or 9 to 10 p.m. TV cameras would be allowed in the Senate. There would be agreement to engage in a particular debate and the purpose here again is not to give advantage to a particular Member. Whichever ones—the leadership usually has no problem about it—are best equipped, based on their involvement in this particular topic, would expound on that particular point of view.

I have already given you one or two examples. There would be no problem in finding others. In most debates there emerges from the exchange of views a couple of fellows who are quite competent to speak for opposing sides. As I said a moment ago, it wouldn't be too difficult. And I won't object if you wish the format of a debate on the Senate floor. To arrange to do that once or twice a month say from 9 to 10 on the Senate floor might be useful, but to do all of a Senate session, I don't think would be at all useful.

Senator GRIFFIN. I don't want to belabor the point, but I don't conceive of the likelihood that all the sessions of the Senate would be televised or broadcast by any means. I think it would be something like the United Nations; it would be available to be televised and broadcast. Obviously when there is something newsworthy going on on the floor the media would carry it just as the media carries the President's news conferences, not because the President demands it, but because they are newsworthy. Or when the President of the United States makes a statement on some subject, it is covered because it is news, and I think if the Senate has got a debate on an issue of public importance that is newsworthy and if it were possible to televise that debate, I think it would be covered.

Senator FULBRIGHT. Of course you say it is news—you are accepting the judgment of the media as to what is news. I think that we should have something to say about what is news. You mentioned a moment ago the broadcasting of committee hearings. Well, the networks just pick and choose. If it is controversial, if you have a highly emotional issue such as crime, for example, or when you had Lucky Luciano—that's very important. But if you have a hearing, a serious hearing——

Senator PASTORE. On the defense budget.

Senator FULBRIGHT. On the defense budget, with three or four of the world's leading physicists, there's nothing to it. They don't consider that news. They may have half a minute, a minute or two. They may have a half a minute of newsreel and all it does is show the man. It means that they are on their toes and they didn't miss the meeting. It is not sufficient to convey any idea at all. We have had Dr. Panofsky, and leading scientific authorities in this field, but the networks wouldn't have any more than a news shot. They don't purport to follow the reasoning and the ideas presented by these men who are of the highest quality in their fields. The public doesn't get it. For the networks it isn't news in their sense. It doesn't have the drama, the excitement and controversy that is transferable into what they call news.

Senator GRIFFIN. A question about your bill, and it is generated I think by this discussion. I think we are getting pretty close now to what is news or what ought to be news. Does your bill require that all the networks carry the program that Congress or representatives of Congress would put on at the same time during prime time so that television viewers would have no choice, that Congressmen would have a captive audience?

Senator FULBRIGHT. It is intended that it be comparable to what the President has, that's the purpose of it. It is to preserve some degree of balance between the Executive and legislative branches of Government, so that the Executive does not overshadow and eventually destroy or dominate the legislature.

When you look around the world, the fact is that most of the people of the world today are ruled by a dominating executive branch. Their legislative bodies have very little to do in determining their future. In other words, it is a form of authoritarianism. I would hope that we can preserve what I conceive to be the basic constitutional system by which the people of this country do preserve an opportunity at least to influence the decisions that affect their lives and fortunes. I think that is what our system was designed to do, and I would like to preserve it. The traditional constitutional balance which we enjoyed up until the last 25 years has been unbalanced.

I think television, because of its peculiar capacity and power, threatens to distort and to destroy that balance. This is all I am trying to get at.

You mention the President. I imagine that executives going back to the caveman days, that is the leader of the tribe and the emperors and the kings through history have a great advantage. And it was a very bold move for our Founding Fathers to try to create a legislative body that could check an executive. Of course they had gone through an experience that led them to try that. Fortunately, it has survived. But even today with the use of television, the Executive will—even if you pass this legislation—retain the glamour of the individual who he represents or the father image, the god king, as they say. I can't do anything about that and I am not trying to destroy the Executive. I am trying to create a balance, a countervailing force. I am not actually trying to create; I am trying to preserve that which was created by the Constitution and I think this medium has unbalanced it.

There was a very interesting article in the Chicago Tribune, which demonstrates the point I make. I will quote one example from the President's recent news conference of how it can be done. I do not use this as any unusual example. I think it is done all the time. The Chicago Tribune, August 3, says this regarding his news conference:

> The final question was not only expected by the President, it was planted by White House aides with a friendly reporter and gave the President a chance to defend himself against critics who have suggested he is spending too much time outside Washington.

Now, it isn't easy for a Congressman to do that. I can't plant a question on "Meet the Press." At least I have never been able to, and I can't plant one on "Face the Nation" or "Issues and Answers," either. I am not given those opportunities, nor is any other Senator in my opinion. So it is in the nature of things. Even if you pass this I don't mean to say it is going to be nice and equal again. But at least there is an opportunity, if we have got enough wisdom to use it, for us to make an effort to enlighten the public on important issues which do not happen to be involved with crime and sex and drugs, that happen to be involved with the security of the country, whether it be the ABM or the Poseidon, or on Vietnam or the Middle East. These are issues which do not have the kind of appeal that incite the news media to broadcast a hearing in a committee.

Senator PASTORE. But the Senator will admit, our real difficulty here, and I think this is a good idea, I don't think anyone can question the fact that the Congress is an equal branch of Government and should be rendered the same courtesy as the judicial or the executive. The Senator will admit that our real problem here, the real complex problem is just how we go about implementing this.

Senator FULBRIGHT. I do. But I don't believe we will grapple with it until you give them the opportunity and time and occasion to do it.

Senator PASTORE. That is why we are interested to hear from all parties to see if we can't come up with ideas.

Senator FULBRIGHT. When I look at how the Senate operates, it really operates by comity except when you get into something controversial, then you decide it by vote. That is what happens.

Senator GRIFFIN. I would like to resume my line of questioning with this observation, Senator:

I think you've made very important points and made some excellent arguments. I do happen to disagree with your approach, though, since, as you referred to our precious freedoms or important freedoms, one of the most important freedoms is freedom of the press. I am concerned that we are moving dangerously close to this legislation to try to legislate what is news or what ought to be the news. I frankly think that despite all the criticism the press receives from those who criticize, Vice President Agnew went about this in the right way. He criticized and asked the media to take a look at itself, but he didn't advocate any legislation that would restrict them or that would require them to determine what is news or what is not news. I think this is a can of worms that we're moving into now. With all due respect to you, I hope that it doesn't get into——

Senator FULBRIGHT. Senator Griffin, you inspire me. I must say, I have to respond in this way: I think Mr. Agnew, representing the executive branch with control over the FCC, doesn't have to propose legislation.

I think by his threats that he has intimidated the media already and I think they already reflect it. I've noticed in many instances they seem to be very restrained in the way they approach these matters. They have certainly felt very shy of anything coming out of the Foreign Relations Committee or any other areas of criticism.

The Vice President, speaking for an executive branch that can do about as it pleases with the regulatory agency, doesn't need legislation. They have all the power they need. You've cited it. You have highlighted exactly the reason why we need the law, to provide some means by which the media can be protected from this kind of attack because if the law requires them to give time, then they have an answer to people like Mr. Agnew who say "You must not do this because it is not in the national interest." They can say the law requires it. They're exposed to this kind of intimidation and being businessmen primarily and not public servants, they do not wish the risk, the loss of their licenses.

I suppose you would say it is a coincidence but let me cite an example. The Washington Post was for a time giving voice to some criticism of the administration, but very shortly after Mr. Agnew's attack a question was raised as to whether or not the Post-Newsweek Co.'s license for a television station in Miami would be renewed, a station estimated to be worth some $20 or $25 million. Being businessmen they can't expose themselves to the loss of that kind of money just for the pleasure of writing an editorial criticizing Mr. Agnew. So they don't write them often anymore, nor does anybody else. So you've demonstrated and given voice to the principle in my view of why the media need this legislation to protect them from that kind of tactic.

Senator SCOTT. Do you think there should be some limit on the number of times during which public interest would have to be provided. Your resolution only provides not less than four times. The media might have to construe that they had to respond every time the Congress wished to speak.

Senator FULBRIGHT. Well, Mr. Leader, maybe I have greater respect for the Congress than you do. I do not think the Senate is made up of a bunch of irresponsible boys who want to go about to speak on every subject.

Senator SCOTT. The Senator hasn't been on the floor recently.

Senator FULBRIGHT. Yes. I was on the floor. In fact, I made a speech yesterday, but I noticed the Senator wasn't there.

Senator SCOTT. The Senator is there so often when the Senator from Arkansas isn't. He should have the opportunity to enjoy his absence when the Senator is speaking.

Senator PASTORE. All right. This is serious now. We've had our fun.

Senator FULBRIGHT. The Senator suggests that the Senate would act irresponsibly in asking for time. I don't believe it would. We thought about this most seriously. It seems to me that four times is a minimum and there would certainly be an opportunity or a need for that many times. Now above that, it is left to the discretion of the leadership, if you like, or a welling up of sentiment which would influence the leadership. I don't think that it is likely that there would be many more than that. If the President continues to use television more and more and makes the kind of impression that he has and precipitates the kind of questions that have been precipitated in recent years, the need might be greater. I think it would be a great mistake to put a limit on it. However, I don't anticipate that the Congress, or certainly the Senate, is going to abuse this privilege. The public would react against them if they do it in a frivolous manner. A Senator may make fun of some Senators and their peculiarities, but on the whole I would say that they act fairly responsibly.

Senator PASTORE. On this point, the President by law does not have any right given to him under the statute——

Senator FULBRIGHT. Correct.

Senator PASTORE (continuing). To have the opportunity of this time that we're talking about. And there's no suggestion here that we should pass such a law. Time is given by the news media or network only because of the prestige of the Office of the Presidency. And no one finds any fault with that. No one finds any fault with that. The President of the United States should speak to his people on the issues he deems necessary, but the Senator from Arkansas is saying that the Congress of the United States, which represents directly the people, should have the same opportunity. Will he be satisfied if this extension of courtesy were given to the Congress by the networks on their own initiative as they do it for the President without statutory findings?

Senator FULBRIGHT. Would the President be satisfied?

Senator PASTORE. No. Would you be satisfied? In other words, if the President asks for the time, the networks don't have to give him the time but realizing the fact he is the prestigious President of the United States, they don't question it. They give him the time at his own choosing, on his own subjects, in his own ways, to discuss whatever he deems necessary.

What if by the same token there was a voluntary agreement in the broadcasting industry to do the same for the Senate of the United States? Would that satisfy the Senator from Arkansas or does he see a flaw in that? In other words, by his bill we would be dictating something for Congress that hasn't been dictated for the Presidency.

Senator FULBRIGHT. As I said a moment ago, this is a complicated question. These networks are basically business organizations. Their stock is sold on public exchanges and they are in it for profit. This custom of allowing the President to use television has grown up. We have inherited the tradition of the divine right of kings, which we are struggling to control through our constitutional processes. This is not new and we have always had the glamorous figure of the leader going back to our caveman days. So I don't criticize them for that, but I can't see them willingly equating a body as diverse as the Congress. The Constitution provides for it, and in our more sober moments most people, I think, certainly do believe that Congress serves a great purpose, a great restraint. But many people harbor a certain kind of contempt for Congress, for all legislative bodies, not just this one and not just these people, I mean as a group. Because even as the Senator from Pennsylvania makes fun of it, about the irresponsible talk——

Senator SCOTT. I picked up the remark of the Senator from Arkansas.

Senator FULBRIGHT. The Senator is not alone. All legislative bodies are a favorite butt for comics. They are always making fun of them. This has happened throughout history. And in other countries they do the same. In many countries they have abolished them as an effective instrumentality. There is no other body in the world comparable to the Congress of the United States. Upper chambers in particular have become ceremonial and we will, too, if we don't perform a function that is worth while, because that's happened in other countries: Canada, England, France, wherever you like. They are ceremonial, honorary bodies with almost no power.

I don't think in all honesty that the networks as business people are going to willingly come along and offer this. It doesn't increase their prestige. This is a public service. I am asking them to do something they don't want to do, something that is not going to enhance their income in any way. It is an educational venture and it is a public service that will probably cost them.

I remember when there was a great flap in 1966 about broadcasting one of the hearings of the Foreign Relations Committee. Mr. Fred Friendly wrote a book about his experience when he wanted CBS to broadcast it. Instead of the hearings, CBS ran "I Love Lucy." It was the fifth rerun, but nevertheless they had a sponsor. They would lose thousands of dollars if they put that aside and broadcast that hearing. They didn't do it. And Mr. Friendly was so furious, as the head of their news division, that he resigned, or perhaps he got fired. One way or another, it was over the controversy of whether they should show "I Love Lucy." That is what happened with an important congressional hearing. That has never happened with the President. No head of CBS or anybody else has ever declined a Presidential—even when the President says the particular appearance—as he did recently—is not newsworthy. They are not going to do that.

Senator PASTORE. But they do have problems, Mr. Fulbright, for this one reason: We are invoking here the fairness doctrine. Now, you'll recall when Mike Mansfield made his speech as a rebuttal to the President's news conference——

Senator FULBRIGHT. Yes.

Senator PASTORE. His opponent requested time and had to be granted time, equivalent time in the State of Montana, only because he was a candidate against Mr. Mansfield. So you run into that problem that has to be considered. And under your plan, any person who is delegated to speak for the Congress under the fairness doctrine, if that particular person is running for office and has an opponent, his opponent is entitled to equal time on the same basis. As a matter of fact, only a few days ago I ran into it myself. I was invited to speak for cystic fibrosis on television, asking for funds to help these unfortunate children that need some help. And I was told categorically that if I did that, my opponent would be entitled to the same amount of time, not on cystic fibrosis but on any political question that he desired to discuss. Now, you see how this gets complicated. We have to look into these matters and we have to unravel the complexities that lead to very serious problems in order to do justice. Otherwise, your opponent is going to say under the guise of him being an incumbent in the Congress of the United States, he is getting an exposure I am not getting and am entitled to it. The reason I raise these points is, somehow in this whole panoramic discussion, we have to look into the details and the preciseness of what we are doing so that we don't get ourselves into a can of worms.

Senator FULBRIGHT. Mr. Chairman, I couldn't agree with you more. That is what I am sure your very efficient staff of your committee can work out, just that sort of thing.

Senator PASTORE. It is not that easy.

Senator FULBRIGHT. I have the greatest confidence that is the sort of thing you can work out.

My purpose is to convince you, if possible, that the Congress needs this if it is to preserve any real function in our system of government. Otherwise, you're more and more cut off from any access to the public mind and we might as well turn it all over to the executive. That is the drift——

Senator PASTORE. We have got to find an answer for it, Mr. Fulbright, and you have been very, very helpful.

Senator SCOTT. Could I ask a couple of questions here?

Senator, the FCC, as you know, is a creature of Congress, not under the control of the executive branch. We can govern whatever legislative changes are pertaining to the FCC and, therefore, it would seem to me that perhaps the fairness doctrine would continue to work. The networks have been willing to give time to matters of great national importance. I wonder why you want to legislate the right of Congress without legislating the right of the President?

Senator FULBRIGHT. They don't need legislation for the President. It is already given to him. You're saying the FCC is under the control of the Congress because it is created by the Congress. I would raise a grave question about this. I guess that Congress created the Defense Department, but if anybody thinks the Defense Department is under the control of Congress, he ought to have his head examined. The Congress is under the control of the Defense Department at the moment. I don't think the Senator is correct in saying that the FCC is under our control. There may be ultimate control if we wish to abolish it by law, but the President appoints these men. The people who are on that body are his appointees and through courtesy, as you have explained, unless a man has committed a crime, Congress doesn't turn him down. I would say the President certainly controls the character and nature of the policies of the FCC. However, if you want to legislate about the President, I have no objection to it. I just assumed that if I proposed that you would take it maybe in the wrong manner. I have no objection—if you're proposing we include the President in giving him only four times, I would support it.

Senator SCOTT. On the contrary, I am proposing we leave well-enough alone.

Senator FULBRIGHT. I know. The Senator likes it the way it is. But I'm trying to preserve it for the future, so that we have a Congress that still functions even after this administration.

Senator SCOTT. I rather think the Senator's pessimism in unwarranted. I don't make the same charges against the Congress or against the Vice President or against the FCC. But suppose we had television during the time of the Founding Fathers. The most garruluous of those Founding Fathers were the Adams brothers and James Madison. How would the Senator have worked out the matter there when one considers if the choice had been between the Adamses and Madison? The names of B. Franklin, T. Jefferson, and G. Washington might have not reached the same proportional importance as history reports. The Senator seems to think television distorts reality. Does he see an analogy here between that situation and the President?

Senator FULBRIGHT. I don't quite know what the point is the Senator is making. It never occurred to me Ben Franklin couldn't hold his own on television or anywhere else, or certainly Jefferson. I don't know what point—are you suggesting George Washington wasn't as articulate and, therefore, would not have survived with television?

Senator SCOTT. I am suggesting the records of these proceedings show who did most of the talking and therefore they would have been the ones most likely to demand equal time.

Senator FULBRIGHT. Well, unfortunately, I am unable to follow what point the Senator is making.

Senator SCOTT. Then we had better leave it alone.

Senator FULBRIGHT. I don't get it.

I didn't say so much that television distorts reality. What I was talking about was the exclusive access of one branch of the Government to the public mind through this capacity, as the Senator from Rhode Island described it very well a moment ago. This is in contrast to the legislative branch, or you might say any conflicting view, the legislature being the coequal branch under the Constitution is the only institution I can think of that would play this role. Now, I think a great country of 200,000,000 should not be subject to—any word I use I suppose you might think is derogatory. I don't mean it that way—to having only one point of view. I mean I don't yet accept the infallibility of any man. It has always seemed odd to me that a man in the Senate is just another Senator, and yet you move him a few blocks away and he becomes infallible. This seems to be an oddity to me. Why is that true? Obviously it is not any doing of his. It is our own creation through the use of such things as television; we create this. No reflection upon him, he is simply a man who is under a system. He didn't create it. I mean no reflection upon this President or any other. He's not responsible for it. I say that technology has created a condition which we need to rectify if we wish to preserve our democratic system. That's really all I am saying. And it is not intended as any reflection upon this President or his predecessor, although his predecessor made great use of it. It happened through technology and it has distorted not reality, but the traditional relationship between the people and their Congress and their Government.

It used to go out in a diverse manner. It was siphoned through many newspapers and you didn't have this single impact at once on all the people. There is nothing comparable to this in history at all. Perhaps you could say in the town meeting, where you maybe have a hundred people, you can in that kind of a system have it. But not on a nationwide scale. That's the distortion, if you want to call it that. It is a new element that has grown up that needs to be taken into account if we really believe in our consitutional system. . . .

Mr. [W. Theodore] Pierson. Mr. Chairman, Senator Scott, it is a pleasure as always to appear here. The position of the Republican National Committee can be summarized briefly as follows: It endorses the concept underlying the Fulbright resolution that the public should have full and continuing access to the views of Members of Congress on the controversial issues of the day.

But we find it difficult to understand how the proposal of Senator Fulbright could be worked out as a practical matter, which has been exemplified many times in the course of the hearing, and how his right of access principle can be limited to the legislative branch of the Federal Government, if adopted as a principle.

These hearings undoubtedly will continue to improve our understanding, but I must confess that up to this point we have the same difficulty in trying to comprehend how the matter would work.

As an alternative to the Fulbright resolution, we suggest that it is within the competence of each House of Congress, without legislation, to gain access to the public via television in a manner that would achieve the objectives of the Fulbright resolution.

Before describing that alternative, I would like to recite the premises that underly our beliefs. We join Senator Fulbright in the view that it is vital to our democratic institutions that the electorate be as fully informed as possible on the crucial issues facing the nation.

Only in this manner can the electorate intelligently exercise its sovereignty. The broadcast media now make extensive efforts to accomplish this through news and interview programs, through panel discussions, through appearance of policymakers in various formats, and through the broadcast of Senate Committee hearings. Except for occasional lapses, we believe that the performance of the broadcast industry in this area has been outstanding.

It seems to be the complaint of Senator Fulbright that such programs by their very format fail to give a Member of the Senate or the House a full opportunity to carefully, thoughtfully, and thoroughly state his position without interruption—an opportunity which the President has when he addresses the Nation. We believe that the Senate and the House without legislation can take internal action which will almost automatically afford the public better access to congressional views via television.

The alternative that we will suggest removes the difficulties that we have in understanding how the rights granted by Senate Joint Resolution 209 could be worked out in actual practice and how the rights established by the amendment could be limited to the two Houses of Congress.

Senator Fulbright in his published statements on the matter has recognized the complexities and difficulties of how to allocate time between the Houses, among its Members, between the parties, among the divisions within each party, and among the controversial issues which are presented to the Nation.

In addition, we do not understand how, conceptually, if a right-of-access to television is established by law for the benefit of the legislative branch of the Federal Government, it could be denied to the executive and judicial branches of the Federal Government or to the legislative, executive, and judicial branches of States and municipalities.

We do not believe that anyone would suggest that the electorate has a vital interest in learning of the views of the Congress on national issues, but no interest in the views of their local and State officials on local and State issues.

If the new and radical doctrine of right-of-access were extended to include the governmental branches of State and local governments, it is not difficult to contemplate that virtually all of the prime time and much of the other time of television stations would be preempted on many broadcast days. In our view this could cannibalize the medium through its failure to serve the other interests and desires of the viewing audience.

We have characterized governmental right-of-access as a new and radical concept—properly, we believe. One of the unique characteristics of our system of broadcast regulation is that the Government except under its war powers, has no right to command licenses to carry Government programs. This uniqueness flows from our singular concepts of press liberty. Certainly, one cannot treat lightly deviations from our basic philosophies of government.

It is because of these misgivings and concerns that we suggest an alternative which we believe will accomplish the goals we have eagerly endorsed.

If the Senate or the House will adapt itself to optimum use of the television media as it has in relation to the printed press and as our last four Chief Executives have done with television, networks and stations undoubtedly would respond just as enthusiastically with the offer of television time for full illumination of important issues as they have responded to presidential addresses and discussions.

Admittedly, this requires quite a radical adaptation on the part of both Houses because, by and large, the Houses of Congress in the past have seemed utterly devoted to excluding television from the coverage of their public debates and discussions. Committee hearings are an exception, but as Senator Fulbright pointed out, they do not permit the complete and thorough exposition of the issues.

It is our view that, if either House would schedule debates in its chambers during prime time on the urgent issues of the day and invited television coverage, such coverage would be forthcoming.

For example, it is inconceivable to us that, if the Senate had called a 2- or 3-hour session in prime time to debate the Cambodian action, the networks could have been kept away—except by barring the doors as you now do.

It is even more unbelievable that any Senator, who could possibly make it, would be absent from the floor. With the powers and skills of both Houses in ordering debates so that all sides are heard, any exhibitionist tendencies to "mug the camera" could be restrained.

In sum, we suggest that each House of Congress without legislation has within its own competence the capacity to obtain access to the public via television. As a bona fide news event, it should be exempt from the equal time provisions of section 315. And as a bona fide news event, it will receive television coverage, the Senate willing.

Our alternative to Senate Joint Resolution 209 we believe offers several advantages over the right-of-access principle the resolution adopts for the Congress, or would adopt for the Congress.

First, it avoids most of the complexities and difficulties presented by Senator Fullbright's means to achieve the goal we all share.

Second, it avoids the necessity of having to embrace new concepts in our constitutional and communications law.

Third, it preserves traditional concepts of journalistic freedom.

Fourth, and I think this is most important, it insures that the television medium will not be used in a manner that goes beyond the tolerance of viewers and thus it will preserve television as a mass medium.

Fifth, it will add to television dramatic new public affairs programs which will enhance its value as an instrument of democracy. . . .

(Later testimony by Julian Goodman, NBC News—Ed.):

Typically, news and discussion programs that deal with controversial issues center on spokesmen, because their views are important and newsworthy. If public understanding, rather than partisan advantage, is the

TODAY—JAN. 1–JUNE 15, 1970

PRO-ADMINISTRATION

Date	By—	Subject
Jan. 22, 1970	U.S. Senator Barry Goldwater (Republican, Arizona)	Supporting Vietnam policy.
Jan. 23, 1970	U.S. Senator Robert P. Griffin (Republican, Michigan)	Do.
Jan. 27, 1970	U.S. Representative John B. Anderson (Republican, Illinois), U.S. Senator William B. Saxbe (Republican, Ohio).	Supporting President's veto of HEW bill.
Feb. 4, 1970	Maurice H. Stans, Secretary of Commerce	Administration's view on black capitalism.
Feb. 5, 1970	Bryce N. Harlow, Counselor to the President	Supporting the President's programs against inflation and pollution.
Feb. 6, 1970	Will R. Wilson, Assistant Attorney General	Administration's fight against organized crime, and for civil liberties.
Feb. 12, 1970	U.S. Senator John Stennis (Democrat, Mississippi)	Uniform policy with respect to desegregation.
Mar. 2, 1970	Gov. Claude Kirk (Republican, Florida)	Florida's compliance with civil rights laws.
Mar. 16, 1970	Vice President Spiro T. Agnew	Vietnam policy.
Mar. 17, 1970	William P. Rogers, Secretary of State	Vietnam policy; Laos.
Mar. 18, 1970	George Romney, Secretary of Housing and Urban Development.	Administration is working for better housing.
Mar. 19, 1970	Gov. Raymond P. Shafer (Republican, Pennsylvania), Gov. Linwood Holton (Republican, Virginia.)	Republican Party's appeal to all segments of American population.
Mar. 20, 1970	U.S. Representative Rogers C. B. Morton (Republican, Maryland), U.S. Senator Hugh Scott (Republican, Pennsylvania).	Praising GOP leadership and appeal of the party.
Mar. 24, 1970	George Shultz, Secretary of Labor	Administration's actions in postal strike.
Mar. 25, 1970	U.S. Senator Edward Brooke (Republican, Massachusetts).	Proadministration foreign policy.
Mar. 26, 1970	Herbert G. Klein, Director of Communications	Administration's view of postal strike.
Mar. 30, 1970	John A. Volpe, Secretary of Transportation	Administration's view on air controllers slowdown.
Apr. 6, 1970	U.S. Senator Robert P. Griffin (Republican, Michigan)	Pro-Carswell.
Apr. 8, 1970	U.S. Representative Ancher Nelsen (Republican, Minnesota).	Supporting anticrime bill.
Apr. 10, 1970	U.S. Senator Howard H. Baker, Jr. (Republican, Tennessee).	Pro-Carswell.
Apr. 15, 1970	U.S. Senator Carl T. Curtis (Republican, Nebraska)	Favoring administration's space policy.
Apr. 16, 1970	U.S. Representative Gerald R. Ford (Republican, Michigan).	Dignity of the Supreme Court; anti-Douglas.
Apr. 17, 1970	U.S. Senator Barry Goldwater (Republican, Arizona), U.S. Senator William B. Saxbe (Republican, Ohio).	Supporting administration's space program.
Apr. 22, 1970	U.S. Representative Paul N. McCloskey, Jr. (Republican, California).	Administration's antipollution measures.
Apr. 23, 1970	Thomas F. Williams, Director of Public Affairs, Consumer Protection and Environmental Health Services, HEW; Walter Hickel, Secretary of Interior; Dr. Russell E. Train, Under Secretary of Interior.	Administration's work in area of ecology.
Apr. 24, 1970	Charles C. Johnson, Administrator, Consumer Protection and Environmental Health Service, HEW.	Administration's work in area of ecology.
Apr. 30, 1970	U.S. Senator Robert J. Dole, Republican, Kansas	Optimistic on steps President will take in Far East.
May 1, 1970	U.S. Senator John G. Tower, Republican, Texas	Cambodia.
May 5, 1970	Gov. James A. Rhodes, Republican, Ohio; U.S. Representatives Robert Taft, Jr., Republican, Ohio. U.S. Senator Mark Hatfield, Republican, Oregon	Ohio primary; various pro-Administration remarks. Cambodia.
May 6, 1970	U.S. Senator Robert P. Griffin, Republican, Michigan	Do.
May 12, 1970	Joseph E. Blatchford, Director Peace Corps	Students' occupying Peace Corps offices.
May 19, 1970	U.S. Senator John L. McClellan, Democat, Arkansas	Cambodia.
May 22, 1970	Melvin R. Laird, Secretary of Defense	Do.
May 28, 1970	Charles E. Walker, Under Secretary of the Treasury	Economy is improving.
June 1, 1970	U.S. Senator Margaret Chase Smith, Republican, Maine.	Against emotionalism in Government.
June 3, 1970	Clark Mollenhoff, Special Assistant to the President	Discussing his role as investigator for the President, alerting him on possible troubles or scandals.
June 11, 1970	Herbert C. Klein, Director of Communications	Cambodia.

goal, this variety of information programs will achieve it better than a formula for matching appearances.

Whatever the issue—Vietnam, racial strife, student militants, administration policy and its opposition—any detailed analysis of the network schedules will show that over a reasonable period of time the audience is exposed to the pros and cons for its own judgment.

For example, on a single weekday program—NBC's "Today"—45 pro-administration Federal officials and 35 opposition spokesmen appeared between January, 1970, and mid-June. A similar balance is found if you select a specific issue and trace its presentation in the network schedule.

Senator GRIFFIN. Mr. Goodman, if I may interrupt for a second, will you provide the committee with a list of those pro-administration Federal officials and the 35 opposition spokesmen who appeared on the "Today" show during that period?

OPPOSITION

Date	By—	Subject
Jan. 6, 1970	U.S. Senator Mike Mansfield (Democrat, Montana)	Vietnam.
Jan. 16, 1970	U.S. Senator Frank Moss (Democrat, Utah)	Air pollution; cigarette advertising.
Jan. 23, 1970	U.S. Senator Edmund G. Muskie (Democrat, Maine)	Vietnam.
Jan. 27, 1970	U.S. Representative Carl Albert (Democrat, Oklahoma), U.S. Senator Alan Cranston (Democrat, California).	Opposing President's veto of HEW bill.
Jan. 28, 1970	Hubert H. Humphrey, former Vice President; Mayor Peter Flaherty (Democrat, Pittsburgh, Pa.).	Opposing veto of HEW bill.
Feb. 18, 1970	U.S. Senator Abraham A. Ribicoff (Democrat, Connecticut).	School busing; integration.
Feb. 23, 1970	U.S. Senator Daniel K. Inouye (Democrat, Hawaii), Hubert H. Humphrey.	Against ABM and inflation measures.
Feb. 24, 1970	U.S. Senator Eugene J. McCarthy (Democrat, Minnesota).	Indochina war.
Feb. 25, 1970	U.S. Senator Edmund S. Muskie (Democrat, Maine)	Vietnam.
Feb. 26, 1970	U.S. Senator George McGovern (Democrat, South Dakota).	Vietnam, Laos, anti-Carswell.
Feb. 27, 1970	U.S. Representative James G. O'Hara (Democrat, Michigan), U.S. Representative Louis Stokes (Democrat, Ohio), U.S. Representative Carl Albert (Democrat, Oklahoma).	Against Vice President and the Southern Strategy.
Mar. 11, 1970	U.S. Representative Ken Hechler (Democrat, West Virginia).	Government's policies regarding coal mining.
Mar. 16, 1970	Mayor John V. Lindsay (Republican, New York City)	Federal Government not doing enough to cure urban problems.
Mar. 24, 1970	U.S. Representative Thaddeus J. Dulski (Democrat, New York).	Administration ineffective in postal strike.
Mar. 31, 1970	Mayor Charles Evers (Democrat, Fayette, Miss.).	Administration not doing enough for civil rights.
Apr. 3, 1970	Gov. John J. McKeithen (Democrat, Louisiana).	Opposing desegregation measures of administration.
Apr. 8, 1970	U.S. Representative Brock Adams (Democrat, Washington).	Opposing anticrime measure.
Apr. 10, 1970	U.S. Senator William B. Spong (Democrat, Virginia)	Anti-Carswell.
Apr. 15, 1970	U.S. Senator Howard W. Cannon (Democrat, Nevada)	Opposing administration's space programs.
Apr. 23, 1970	U.S. Representative Morris K. Udall (Democrat, Arizona), U.S. Senator Edmund S. Muskie (Democrat, Maine)	Opposing ecology measures of administration.
Apr. 24, 1970	U.S. Senator Gaylord Nelson (Democrat, Wisconsin)	Opposing administration on ecology.
Apr. 28, 1970	U.S. Senator George McGovern (Democrat, South Dakota).	Cambodia.
May 1, 1970	U.S. Senator Frank Church (Democrat, Idaho)	Do.
May 5, 1970	Gov. Albert P. Brewer (Democrat, Alabama), George Wallace (Democrat).	Alabama primary; race issue.
May 18, 1970	Clark Clifford, former Secretary of Defense	Vietnam; Cambodia.
May 19, 1970	U.S. Senator John Sherman Cooper (Republican, Kentucky).	Cambodia.
May 27, 1970	U.S. Senator J. W. Fulbright (Democrat, Arkansas)	Vietnam; Cambodia.
May 29, 1970	U.S. Senator Edward M. Kennedy (Democrat, Massachusetts.)	United States cannot police the world.

CONGRESSIONAL USE OF PUBLICITY

By Francis E. Rourke

Publicity has long had a variety of uses for Congress as for all legislative bodies. Of no small importance is the fact that such publicity provides an avenue whereby the legislature can vie with the executive in a quest for the attention of the community, in much the same way as it competes for the other means and ends of power that are at stake in conflict between the two branches of government. As long ago as 1908, Woodrow Wilson traced the president's supremacy over Congress to his ability to focus public attention upon himself,[1] and the executive advantage in this regard has been more than reinforced by developments since that time in the technology of mass communications. The presidential ascendancy characteristic of twentieth-century American politics is frequently traced to the priviliged access of the president to radio, television, and the news columns of the press.[2]

From this point of view the recent upsurge in congressional investigations primarily reflects an attempt on the part of the legislature to restore a balance of power in the area of publicity. No aspect of congressional activity other than investigations is as capable of attracting the attention of the public and of the communications facilities that both direct and reflect public interest. Investigations are a form of entertainment, even if they stir in the minds of some observers recollections of the Roman amphitheater or of the public trials and executions of revolutionary regimes.[3] But since investigations have such dramatic value—even reminiscent in their effect of Aristotle's venerable description of tragedy in his *Poetics*: "through pity and fear effecting a proper purgation of these emotions"—they can compete with the other forms of entertainment with which politics and political events are in competition for the voter's attention.[4] Otherwise, Congress might be entirely upstaged before the national audience by the presidential office and the activities of its incumbent. In short, the preoccupation of Congress with its investigative role may be said to spring from the very realistic legislative perception that a president cutting a cake has more news value for the media of communication than almost anything a congressman does in his non-investigative capacities.

As a method of redressing the balance of power with the executive with respect to command of public attention, the publicity connected with investigations may be said to serve the committees concerned.[6] This may be a more important factor in congressional choice among committee seats today than the traditional interest of the legislator in placing himself upon committees related in their jurisdiction to the particular economic and social interests of his constituency. . . .

For congressional blocs, whether organized on party or factional lines, the publicity evoking characteristic of investigations is of considerable practical utility, providing, as it does, the opportunity of inflicting public embarrassment upon executive agencies, or, if the legislative inclination so directs, private institutions or individuals. The manipulation of such publicity has become a strategic factor in party as well as factional warfare in our political system. From the point of view of some investigators, the most advantageous aspect of this publicity is the fact that their own investment before the public eye is merely one of legitimate legislative curiosity, while the group under scrutiny is necessarily put upon the defensive, a posture from which full recovery before the bar of public opinion is often very difficult to attain.

The power of publicity has found its most graphic illustration in contemporary legislative politics through the career of Senator Joseph McCarthy. The web of McCarthy's influence was woven almost entirely out of the fabric of publicity. It rested in part on the fact that there was a wide and deep public support for a vigorous anti-communist policy, however carried out, and McCarthy was able to identify himself as one of communism's most stalwart foes. And in part also, it stemmed from the intimidation of McCarthy's fellow politicians, as well as leaders in other walks of life, who were fearful lest a collision with McCarthy bring them the reputation of being sympathetic toward communism. But if publicity was the source of McCarthy's strength, it also proved ultimately to be his undoing. For in the Army-McCarthy hearings, where he and his staff were exposed in a baleful light, he suddenly found himself with a firm grip on the wrong end of the publicity stick, and it proved a disaster from which he never recovered.

Publicity has traditionally been used with great effectiveness by Congress to throw light upon the misdeeds of executive officials. More recently, it has acquired increasing prominence in connection with legislative investigations aimed at ferreting out wrongdoing in various areas of private life. It is this present-day preoccupation of many legislative committees with illegal or unethical activity within society that has transformed some legislative hearings into legislative courts and led to mounting pressure for reform of investigative procedures. Such pressure is quite similar to that generated more than a decade ago in favor of reforming the administrative process, when it appeared that executive agencies were overreaching their proper authority.[7]

While acting as auxiliary and *ad hoc* instruments of law enforcement, legislative committees have no power to impose punitive legal sanctions, except indirectly for a refusal to answer questions. Nevertheless, their direct power to punish is considerable. The core of this power is the ability of a committee to inflict the penalty of adverse publicity upon those called before it. This sanction has been used with telling effect in such widely diverse areas as the investigation of subversive activity, gambling, and the rigging of television quiz programs.

In calling witnesses to public hearings for the purpose, for example, of exposing what is considered to be either illegal or immoral activity, a legislative committee has the visible and usually justified expectation that such exposure will at the very least bring unfavorable public attention to the individuals concerned. Aside from the psychic deprivation or loss of public esteem that this exposure may represent for the person involved, such other extra-legal sanctions may follow in the wake of an appearance at a public hearing as loss of employment. Publicity may thus operate as a sanction in and of itself, or it may initiate the application of other informal penalties. The total impact of the sanction applied may bear some resemblance to the ostracism sometimes imposed by primitive societies. . . .

Legislative use of the publicity sanction as a method of control is not confined to its employment in the investigative process. Some statutes passed by the legislature also depend for their enforcement upon the effectiveness of publicity in preventing undesirable conduct. This is true of lobbying legislation, for example. The premise upon which the Federal Regulation of Lobbying Act of 1946 rests is that the mere publication of information about the activities of lobbyists will itself, given the disrepute in which such activities are presumed to be held by the public, help to keep lobbying within bounds. The same expectation is visible in the Internal Security Act of 1950, which requires Communist front groups to so identify themselves in their published material. There would appear to be little doubt that identification as a Communist organization would dissipate whatever persuasive effectiveness a political group might otherwise have upon the American public. It is, however, also clear that other legislation dependent for its effectiveness upon the publicity sanction may be toothless or bite very deeply, depending in good part upon the intensity of public disapproval of the activity against which the legislation is directed. It is still an open question as to whether recent efforts to regulate the internal affairs of trade unions through disclosure statutes will prove effective, given the fact that labor organizations like the Teamsters Union have, through long years of adversity, become accustomed to operating in an atmosphere of unfavorable public attention.

NOTES

[1] *Constitutional Government in the United States* (New York, 1908), pp. 67-69.
[2] See in this regard Sidney Hyman, *The American President* (New York, 1954), pp. 101-104. One of the principal avenues of presidential influence in the field of publicity is the press conference. For a recent treatment of this subject see Elmer E. Cornwell, Jr.,

"The Presidential Press Conference: A Study in Institutionalization," *Midwes of Political Science*, Vol. IV (November 1960), pp. 370-89. (See Cornwell, raphy—Ed.)

[3] Recent critical discussions of congressional investigations include Alan Barth, *C ment by Investigation* (New York, 1955); and Telford Taylor, *Grand Inquest Story of Congressional Investigations* (New York, 1955).

[4] See Morris Rosenberg, "The Meaning of Politics in Mass Society," *Public Opinion Quarterly*, Vol. 15 (Spring, 1951), pp. 14-15.

[5] Martin N. McGeary, *The Developments of Congressional Investigative Power* (New York, 1940), gives considerable attention to this function of the investigative process.

[6] It was reported in 1951 that no less than one hundred representatives were seeking seats on the House Un-American Activities Committee. See Irving Dilliard, "Congressional Investigations: the Role of the Press," *University of Chicago Law Review*, Vol. 18 (Spring, 1951), pp. 585-90, at p. 590.

[7] An interesting illustration of the correlation between a group's opinion and its interest is provided by the fact that the liberal-conservative alignment on the question of re-forming the law enforcement procedures of Congress is exactly the opposite from what it was in the struggle over reform of the administrative process. In the case of administration, Senator McCarran, for example, whose position may reasonably be described as conservative, was a sponsor of reform; in the case of Congress he was a target of reformers.

CONGRESS, PUBLICITY AND PUBLIC POLICY

By Nelson W. Polsby

. . . As institutions, the House and the Senate differ markedly in their essential character. The House is a highly specialized instrument for processing legislation. Its great strength lies in its firmly structured division of labor. This division of labor provides the House with a toehold in the policy-making process by virtue of its capacity to farm out and hence, in some collective sense, to master technical details. House members are frequently better prepared than senators in conferences,[1] and usually have the better grasp of the peculiarities of the executive agencies they supervise. This is an artifact of the strong division of labor that the House maintains: Members are generally assigned to one or two committees only; and floor debate is generally limited to participation by committee members. There is an expectation that members will concentrate their energies, rather than range widely over the full spectrum of public policy. Patterns of news coverage encourage specialization; general pronouncements by House members are normally not widely reported. Senators, because they are fewer, more socially prominent, and serve longer terms (hence are around long enough for newsman to cultivate), and

Reprinted by permission from *Public Policy*, Volume 18, Number 1 (1969) by permission of the editor and author.

allegedly serve "larger" districts, can draw attention to themselves by well-timed press releases almost regardless of their content.

The coordination of an organism like the House is difficult because it cannot entail excessive centralization of power. Decentralization is necessary for the House to maintain its capacity to cope with the outside world (that is, through its complex and specialized division of labor). And this in turn produces the House's major career incentive, namely the opportunity accorded a tenth to a fifth of its members to possess the substance of power in the form of a committee or subcommittee chairmanship or membership on a key committee. At present seniority acts as a bulwark of this incentive system, by guaranteeing a form of job security at least within the division of labor of the organization.[2]

Thus, as I once observed in another connection:[3]

> To that large fraction of members for whom the House is a career and a vocation, the longevity of members above them in the many hierarchies of the House—not the entirely predictable congressional election returns in their home districts—is the key to the political future.

The essence of the Senate is that it is a great forum, an echo chamber, a publicity machine.[4] Thus "passing bills," which is central to the life of the House, is peripheral to the Senate. In the Senate the three central activities are (1) the cultivation of national constituencies (that is, beyond state lines) by political leaders; (2) the formulation of questions for debate and discussion on a national scale (especially in opposition to the President); and (3) the incubation of new policy proposals that may at some future time find their way into legislation.

This conception of the Senate is, in some respects, novel, since it focuses on an aspect of Senate life that is much deplored by aficionados of the "inner club" conception of the institution, who often defend the curious thesis that the persons anointed by the mysterious chemistry of Senate popularity are the very elite that keeps this nation from the mob scene in *The Day of the Locust*.

I think, however, that there is considerable use in a democratic republic for an organization that encourages—as the Senate currently does—the generation of publicity on issues of public importance. One must grant there have been abuses in the pursuit of publicity by senators; but Senate "great debates," investigations, and hearings have also performed considerable public service.

Where the House of Representatives is a large, impersonal, and highly specialized machine for processing bills and overseeing the executive branch, the Senate is, in a way, a theater where dramas—comedies and tragedies, soap operas and horse operas—are staged to enhance the careers of its members and to influence public policy by means of debate and public investigation.

In both the House and the Senate the first commandment to new-comers is "Specialize." But this means vastly different things in the two house.[5] "Specialize" to a representative means "tend to your knitting": Work hard on the committee to which you are assigned, pursue the interests of your state and region. In the Senate everyone has several committee assignments. Boundaries between committees are not strictly observed: Occasionally a senator who is not a committee member will sit in on a hearing if a subject interests him. On the floor, quite unlike the House, virtually any senator may speak for any length of time about anything. Thus the institution itself gives few cues and no compulsions to new senators wondering what they should specialize in. For the Senate, specialization seems to mean finding a subject matter and a nation-wide constituency interested in the subject that have not already been pre-empted by some more senior senator.

It is a cliché of academic political science that in legislative matters, it is the President who initiates policy, and Congress which responds, amplifying and modifying and rearranging elements which are essentially originated in the executive branch. Not much work has been done, how-ever, on following this river of bills-becoming-and-not-becoming-laws back to its sources. Where do innovations in policy come from *before* the President "initiates" them?

Old Washington hands know the answer. There is very little new under the sun. A great many newly enacted policies have "been around," "in the air" for quite a while. In the heat of a presidential campaign or when a newly inaugurated president wants a "new" program, desk drawers fly open all over Washington. Pet schemes are fished out, dusted off, and tried out on the new political leaders.

There is often a hiatus of years—sometimes decades—between the first proposal of a policy innovation and its appearance as a presidential "initiative"—much less as a law. Commentators have greatly underesti-mated the role of the Senate in gestating these ideas, by providing a forum for speeches, hearings, and the introduction of bills going nowhere for the moment. This process of gestation accomplishes a number of things. It maintains a sense of community among far-flung interest groups that favor the innovation, by giving them occasional opportunities to come in and testify. It provides an incentive for persons favoring the innovation to keep up to date information on its prospective benefits and technical feasibility. And it accustoms the uncommitted to a new idea.

Thus the Senate is in some respects at a crucial nerve-end of the polity. It articulates, formulates, shapes, and publicizes demands, and can serve as a hothouse for significant policy innovation.

Hence proposals to increase the structuredness of the Senate, to force germaneness in debate, to tighten committee assignment procedures, and to reduce the number of assignments per senator misunderstand the nature of the Senate and the contribution it can uniquely make to the political system. What is needed in the Senate is as little structure as possible; its organizational flexibility enables it to incubate policy innovations, to advocate, to respond, to launch its great debates, in short to pursue the continuous renovation of American public policy through the hidden hand of the self-promotion of its members. . . .

NOTES

[1] Although the question has not been studied systematically or in great detail, this conclusion seems to be fair on the basis of a number of case studies. See, for instance, Richard F. Fenno, Jr., *The Power of the Purse* (Boston: Little, Brown, 1966), pp. 616 ff.; Gilbert Y. Steiner, *The Congressional Conference Committee* (Urbana: University of Illinois Press, 1951); James M. Landis, "The Legislative History of the Securities Act of 1933," *George Washington Law Review*, XXVIII (1959-60), pp. 29-49; or the following recent comment by Senator Lee Metcalf (formerly a member of the House Ways and Means Committee): "No matter what the Finance Committee does or the Senate does, when we come back from conference with the House we have given in to Wilbur Mills. He runs both committees" (*Washington Post*, January 14, 1969).

[2] Nelson W. Polsby, Miriam Gallaher, and Barry Spencer Rundquist, "The Growth of the Seniority System in the U.S. House of Representatives," *American Political Science Review* (in press; to appear in September 1969), goes into the history of seniority more fully. See also Michael Abram and Joseph Cooper, "The Rise of Seniority in the House of Representatives," *Polity*, I (Fall 1968), pp. 52-85.

[3] Nelson W. Polsby, "Two Strategies of Influence: Choosing a Majority Leader, 1962," in R. L. Peabody and N. W. Polsby, eds., *New Perspectives on the House of Representatives* (Chicago: Rand McNally, 1963), p. 244.

[4] Different points of view on the nature of the Senate are expressed by William S. White, *The Citadel* (New York: Harper, 1956); Donald Matthews, *U.S. Senators and Their World* (Chapel Hill: University of North Carolina Press, 1960); Joseph S. Clark, *et al.*, *The Senate Establishment* (New York: Hill and Wang, 1963); and Ralph K. Huitt and Robert L. Peabody, *Congress: Two Decades of Analysis* (New York: Harper and Row, 1969), especially pp. 159-208.

[5] A more familiar view of Senate specialization may be found in Matthews, *op. cit.*, pp. 95-97.

Congressional Perspectives
on the News Media

THE DAILY INTERACTION between members of Congress and the Washington correspondents determines much of what the public knows about Congress. The attitudes of members of Congress toward the reporters are important elements in these relationships.

Charles Clapp finds that congressmen are acutely aware of their dependence on the press. In terms of reelection, they place great emphasis on the importance of the local news media.

Rep. William L. Hungate (D.-Mo.) reports on his poll of members of the House and Senate in an attempt to measure their attitudes toward news media coverage of Congress and national events. While one can sense problems in the selection of questions and other methodologies in the study, it is a rare attempt to survey the attitudes of members on the news media. Its findings are not too dissimilar from the range of attitudes reflected by individual congressmen who have written or spoken frankly about the news media.

Two members of Congress, Rep. Shirley Chisholm (D.-N.Y.) and Rep. Bob Eckhardt (D.-Tex.) express contrasting attitudes toward the news media. Rep. Chisholm reflects the attitudes of newer minority members of Congress, expressed in this case by her refusal to attend the annual Gridiron Club dinner "on the grounds that the white male membership of the club was symbolic of the racism and sexism that exists in the news media." Rep. Eckhardt defends the news media against criticisms of their alleged liberal bias which he found not to be the case after conducting his own survey of newspaper editorial opinion.

In contrast to pro or con attitudes of members, Rep. Richard Bolling (D.-Mo.) and the late Rep. Clem Miller (D.-Calif.) make thoughtful and perceptive observations on relations between Congress and the news media. They describe the interdependence between the correspondents and the members. Both discuss the subject of member-correspondent relations and the variety and levels of news media and their relative significance. These views of the news media serve as transition to the next chapter on congressional correspondents.

THE VALUE OF PUBLICITY

By Charles L. Clapp

Although in discussing campaign techniques, attention has been focused primarily on those prominent during the campaign period, it is clear that many on-going activities of a congressional office are undertaken with an eye on election day and the electorate. In many instances, the same activities that are effective throughout the term are merely accelerated during the campaign period. Examination of a congressman's calendar would show, for example, an increase in the number of trips taken to his district during the months prior to adjournment in an election year.

Perhaps the most important goal of many House members is to develop in the voter the image of an active, dedicated representative. It is toward this end that many of their activities are geared. Activity is the key word, and in many instances it is creating the illusion of activity that is important rather than the reality itself. One congressman who flies home to his district twice monthly always schedules office hours on each occasion in his home city and one or more of the many small towns. He represents a compact district which a few newspapers cover, and each time he is home he places a small ad in all these newspapers. The ad displays his picture and says, "On (date) at (time) I will be in (city or town) at the courthouse to see residents on any problem they may care to discuss." All that is involved may be a two-hour stop in a small town, but by running the ad in all newspapers in the district, voters become aware of the time he spends on district problems.

The Press. Congressmen are aware of the role of the press in lightening or increasing their own burdens. Though many blame the press for the poor public image of the typical member of Congress and complain that reporters distort the record and fail to emphasize the important things, few express their unhappiness publicly. Newsmen whom the congressman may despise and fear are given a cordial greeting when they stop by the office. Reporters probably have easier access to the congressman's time than any other group, largely because, despite their shortcomings, they possess the power to advance—or hinder—the congressman's cause. As one western Democrat said in evaluating his standing in his district:

> One thing working for me is the amount of publicity I am given in the local press. Ninety percent of the press give me good support. When I go home in an off-year I have my campaign manager try to arrange a schedule showing fifty to a hundred appearances. I get prominent coverage on that schedule, and people start talking about how very active you are when you get home. This is very helpful and would not be possible without the friendly attitude of the newspapers.

Comments a midwestern Republican: "The news media do a great deal in determining how a person gets along with his district. The way they present you to the voters can make your task either easy or more difficult. Of course, this is all supplemented by your own public relations activities." Complained one Democrat:

> Unless I put an ad in the paper they never mention my name. The _____ company owns all the dailies and all the radio stations and all but one of the TV stations. They like my colleague and print the stuff he sends out. If I send out a news release they say, "_____ [referring to another member, not the speaker] and the rest of the delegation have introduced so and so or done so and so."

And a Republican expresses the feeling of many members of his party when he says the Republicans do not have a monopoly on press support:

> The press certainly isn't in the pocket of the Republicans as some people seem to say. As a matter of fact they're more likely to support the Democrats. I've had a terrible time in my own district because I just can't get the coverage. The _____ is a Democratic organ, although I must say they have endorsed me a couple of times. Last time they didn't come out and endorse me, but they did say that if the reader happened to be a Republican then he should support me. It was a sort of left-handed compliment.

Two Democrats discussed their relationships with the press:

> The first time I ran, a political science student made a survey of the coverage, given by the largest paper in the district, to the two congressional candidates in the last five weeks of the campaign. In terms of column inches my recollection is that my opponent had 620 and I had 50. I lost the election by half a percent that year.

> We have two dominant dailies in the state both of which are important in my district. I have thirty weeklies, but the dailies are the ones that feed the up-to-date news. They were giving me no coverage so I talked to the editor. I showed him the releases I had

been sending him and the coverage I had been getting. I said, "I don't know how many releases my opponent has been sending you, but you have been giving him this coverage." Although they are political opponents of mine, the paper has a sense of fair play, and from then on I got equal coverage with my opponent. If you can get that kind of coverage you don't have to spend much money.

Although congressmen as a group are publicity minded, many of them are forced to extraordinary lengths and expense to supplement normal news release procedures to ensure their district is aware of their activity. And some metropolitan representatives regard newspaper endorsement of their re-election as more important than any amount of advertising they might place, on the assumption that many readers watch for, and adhere to, the paper's recommendations. While newspaper publicity is regarded as valuable, placing political advertising in a newspaper is not considered as an important element in many campaigns today. Rural newspapers obviously are a better source for congressional releases and stories since the small staff is likely to welcome "news from outside" more readily and since there is less competition for coverage. For essentially the same reasons, they may also be a more effective means of getting through to the voter. As one rural district congressman put it: "I have twenty or thirty weekly newspapers, and I really use them. Rural people take those weekly papers and pass them around among themselves. People will go from one house to the other and borrow them. Because the newspaper is so important in the life of those people, I try to get my newsletters and things of that sort published there." As has been suggested elsewhere, some congressmen place ads at campaign time to ensure adequate publicity throughout their term rather than because of their belief in its effectiveness.

Radio and Television. Though extensive use is made of radio and television by candidates for Congress, these media rank well below the personal appearance so far as congressmen are concerned. They are particularly useful in that frequent brief appearances can be made with a saturation effect. Candidates of the party occupying the White House have found it helpful to get statements of endorsement from cabinet members and other high government officials and party leaders for use on these media. Usually, these are preceded and followed by statements of the candidates themselves, hopefully providing an association that will further their campaign. Television is regarded as especially helpful but too expensive to be used as often as candidates would like. One skilled legislator believes television is not only effective as a campaign tool but also regards it as a constructive force in elections:

TV is the very best of techniques. It is by far the most effective medium and I think it is good for the country, too. Unless a person is a consummate actor, folks can tell whether he is sincere and deserving. I am fairly convinced that TV has had and will continue to have a very good effect on improving candidates and their quality.

But one of the leaders of the House finds television less useful. In comparing the effectiveness of television, radio, and newspaper advertising he says:

> Television is virtually useless in a congressional campaign unless you are an extraordinarily good performer, and there is little competition for television time which is not the case in a commercial television situation where there are three or more stations. We use radio spots almost to a saturation point. We don't find our newspaper advertising worth a damn. Six years ago we had a polling group do some checking on some of our ads and discovered they weren't getting any response. The survey was not thorough enough to be truly scientific, but it was thorough enough to convince us.

This statement evoked a defense of television from another congressman:

> I don't agree with you about television. I have found it to be pretty helpful particularly in areas where there is just one station and you have pretty much a captive audience. Of course, I have an area covered by _____ stations [a city not in his district], and it is too expensive to use except for an occasional spot announcement. In other parts of the district where there is less competition I have found it very effective. People do watch it, and when I go around campaigning they say, "Oh, yes, I saw you on TV." I don't think it wise to spend too much time on TV—just enough to get your name across to the voters.

MR. AGNEW, YOU ARE WRONG ABOUT THE PRESS

By Bob Eckhardt

I have been quite disturbed by the continuing attacks by the Vice President on the nation's press. He has implied that the news media are a sort of agent of the liberal conspiracy, has vociferously attacked the eastern papers as being unrepresentative of the true feelings of the people and has constantly condemned the concentration of power among the news media as if such concentrations were anti-Republican and pro liberal.

I wish to report to you today on the results of a survey I took this summer of American newspaper editorial opinion. I felt that the subject

A statement from the office of Rep. Bob Eckhardt (D-Tex.) used with permission.

of diversity of newspaper editorial opinion was far too important to be talked about in vague generalities and on the basis of gut feelings and hunches. The people deserve to know what the newspapers are saying and whether or not it is what Mr. Agnew says they are saying.

My office sent questionnaires to 154 newspapers around the nation. They were sent to all 125 papers with a circulation of over 100,000. In states where there are no papers with a circulation this size, questionnaires were sent to the largest papers in the state. Responses were received from 84 of the larger circulation newspapers and 14 of the smaller ones for a total response rate of 64%. I am quite confident that I got a truly representative sample of newspaper editorial opinion and I think this is confirmed by the geographic breakdown of responses.

The responses to the questions asking party affiliation of the owners and editors did not prove to be significant. A more accurate indication of the political party to which the newspaper traditionally leans is presidential endorsements. In November of 1969, Vice President Agnew said the following in an address in Montgomery, Alabama:

> I do not seek to intimidate the press, the networks or anyone else
> from speaking out. But the time for naive belief in their neutrality
> is gone.

If "neutrality" means even balance between party support, my survey substantiated Mr. Agnew's statement—on the whole the press is not neutral: it is on his side. (I do not find this too discouraging as the Roper survey indicates that since 1963 television has taken over the lead from newspapers as most people's major source of news, especially about national candidates.)

Endorsement patterns are overwhelmingly Republican. Republicans have received a majority of the endorsements since 1932 in every election except that of 1964. The Republican margin is usually two or three to one over the Democratic candidate. In terms of circulation, it is often higher.

In 1956, 76% of the papers responding supported the Republican candidate for President, 69% in 1960, 14% in 1964, and 68% in 1968. The regional breakdown is even more impressive. The "liberal" eastern press does not lag behind the rest of the country in its support of Republican presidential candidates and clearly led the rest of the nation in Republican support in 1964. So we can say that when the Nixon-Agnew administration came into office in 1968 it had overwhelming support from the nation's press. Considering the closeness of the popular vote, if editorial opinion has any influence at all, an even division of it would have resulted in a popular vote victory for Hubert Humphrey.

Six issues were listed on the questionnaire and the papers were asked to indicate their editorial opinion on each. They were:

ABM (initial passage of Phase I)
Carswell (Supreme Court nomination)
Cambodian Operation (initial reaction)
Cambodian Operation (after June 30)
Vice President Agnew's Statements on Dissenters
McGovern-Hatfield Amendment.

Overall, consistently Republican papers were conservative on issues whereas Democratic newspapers were liberal. The papers which supported Humphrey were liberal (77% against the Cambodian operations and 67% against the confirmation of Carswell and Agnew's statements). The papers supporting Nixon in 1968 were more mixed (63% for the Cambodian operations and only 26% in favor of the confirmation of Carswell and in support of Agnew's statements).

The data on the editorial positions is very significant. First, on a national basis:

(1) 57% of the papers responding favored the building of an ABM sytem. This certainly reflects diversity of opinion.
(2) There was strong opposition to the Carswell nomination. The majority of the nation's papers did not, as the Vice President wishes to believe, support the nomination.
(3) There was a virtually even break on the Cambodian operations, again reflecting a healthy diversity of opinion.
(4) Almost two-thirds of the press came out against the Vice President's statements on dissenters. It would be easy for Mr. Agnew to generalize, as he often does, and say that this reflects the views of the biased liberal news media. However . . . .
(5) Three-quarters of the papers responding were opposed to the McGovern-Hatfield Amendment establishing a deadline for the withdrawal of American forces from Vietnam.

The data is interesting when viewed on a regional basis:

(1) The ABM system was supported in all regions except the midwest. Even there, there was only a very slight difference.
(2) All regions except the South opposed the Carswell nomination. However, if the Florida papers are removed from the sample, Carswell was opposed by a majority of the Southern newspapers.
(3) The Northeastern and Midwestern papers opposed the initial Cambodian move, the South split and the Western papers were strongly in favor. After June 30 some support was lost in the South.
(4) There was uniform unfavorable reaction across the nation to the Vice President's statements on dissenters.
(5) However, there was even stronger uniform opposition around the nation to the McGovern-Hatfield Amendment.

What conclusions can be gleaned from all this? Firstly, greatest opposition to Administration policies comes from the Midwestern papers, not the Eastern ones. Perhaps equally surprising, the greatest support comes from the Western papers rather than the Southern. As a matter of fact, Southern newspaper responses were not at all different from responses from newspapers as a whole. The charge that Southern newspaper editorial opinion is buried under a deluge of radical liberal Eastern establishment media opinion just does not hold water.

So three points stand out: Carswell had little editorial support, even in the South; the Eastern press is not the radical liberal monolith that the Vice President thinks it is, and any opposition that there is in the press to administration policies is not part of a liberal conspiracy. The administration, when it loses a majority of the large newspapers on an issue, loses by and large its basic supporters. Two-thirds of the nation's papers endorsed Nixon-Agnew in 1968 but 69% opposed Carswell, 65% were upset by the Vice President's statements on dissenters and only half the press supported the Cambodian operations.

I am not an Easterner or part of the so-called "liberal Eastern establishment." I do feel that some of the Eastern papers are among the best in the nation and I object to them being maligned by a misinformed Vice President. On all the issues I surveyed, the Eastern papers, as a body, agreed editorially with the nation as a whole. Where is this radical liberal monolith of which Mr. Agnew speaks?

We have much to be thankful for though. The newspapers may be Republican oriented but they are not a slave to the party and its leaders' policies. They may not be neutral but they afford a platform for diversity of editorial position on questions of important national policy. Would the Vice President prefer a press that blindly followed the lead of whatever administration happened to be in power? The Vice President's view that the media should be made to represent the majority of Americans would change the traditional role of the press as a check on government and as a purveyor of both majority and minority points of view. A press which merely reinforced popularly held viewpoints would contribute little to the development of the intelligent body politic which the founding fathers saw as the matrix of democracy.

The Survey

In July of 1970 questionnaires were sent to 154 newspapers around the nation. They were sent to all 125 papers with a circulation of over 100,000 and to a representative sample of smaller papers.

Responses were received from 84 of the larger circulation newspapers and 14 of the smaller ones for a total response rate of 64%.

The geographic breakdown of responses is as follows:

Northeast Region   (Connecticut, Maine, Massachusetts, New Hampshire, New Jersey, New York, Pennsylvania, Rhode Island, Vermont)
17 replies of 35 questionnaires—49%

Midwest Region	(Illinois, Indiana, Iowa, Kansas, Michigan, Minnesota, Missouri, Nebraska, North Dakota, Ohio, South Dakota, Wisconsin) 29 replies of 41 questionnaires—71%
South Region	(Alabama, Arkansas, Delaware, District of Columbia, Florida, Georgia, Kentucky, Louisiana, Maryland, Mississippi, North Carolina, Oklahoma, South Carolina, Tennessee, Texas, Virginia, West Virginia) 31 replies of 49 questionnaires—63%
West Region	(Alaska, Arizona, California, Colorado, Hawaii, Idaho, Montana, Nevada, New Mexico, Oregon, Utah, Washington, Wyoming) 21 replies of 29 questionnaires—73%

Only 42 respondees indicated the party affiliation of the newspaper's owner: 9 Democratic, 11 Republican and 22 independent.

Sixty returned questionnaires listed the editor's party affiliation: 14 Democratic, 18 Republican and 28 Independent.

A more accurate indication of the political party to which the newspaper traditionally leans is editorial presidential endorsements. As the results below show, except for 1964, endorsements have been overwhelmingly Republican.

ENDORSEMENT PATTERNS IN PRESIDENTIAL ELECTIONS
(R—Republican, D—Democratic, NA—No Answer)

1956	1960	1964	1968	Number
R	R	R	R	12
R	R	–	R	14
R	R	D	R	28
R	R	D	D	7
D	D	D	D	14
R	D	D	R	4
R	D	D	D	4
D	D	D	R	1
NA	NA	NA	D	1
NA	NA	NA	R	1
NA	R	NA	NA	1
D	NA	D	D	1
NA	NA	D	R	1
NA	NA	D	NA	1
NA	R	R	R	1

In 1956, 76% of the papers responding supported the Republican candidate for President, 69% in 1960, 14% in 1964 and 68% in 1968.

This endorsement policy was further broken down by region.

PRESIDENTIAL ENDORSEMENT POLICY BY REGION
(D—Democratic, R—Republican)

		Northeast		Midwest		South		West	
		D	R	D	R	D	R	D	R
1956	#	2	13	3	24	9	19	2	14
	%	13.3%	86.7%	11%	89%	32%	68%	12.5%	87.5%
1960	#	4	12	4	23	10	17	5	12
	%	25%	75%	15%	85%	37%	63%	29.4%	70.6%
1964	#	9	3	18	4	21	4	11	2
	%	75%	25%	82%	18%	84%	16%	84.6%	15.4%
1968	#	6	11	8	21	9	18	4	15
	%	35.3%	64.7%	28%	72%	33%	67%	21.1%	78.9%

Six issues were listed and the papers were asked to indicate their editorial position on each. They were:

ABM (initial passage of Phase I)
CARSWELL (Supreme Court nomination)
CAMBODIAN OPERATION (initial reaction)
CAMBODIAN OPERATION (after June 30)
VICE PRESIDENT AGNEW'S STATEMENTS ON
    DISSENTERS
McGOVERN-HATFIELD AMENDMENT

A conservative editorial pattern was defined as being *for* the ABM, Carswell, the Cambodian operations, the Agnew statements and *against* the McGovern-Hatfield Amendment. A close correlation between straight Republican endorsements and the conservative editorial pattern exists. The same is true of a straight Democratic endorsement policy and the liberal editorial pattern. (The opposite of the conservative pattern)

Of the 12 newspapers answering the survey who exhibited straight Republican endorsement policy, 8 followed the conservative editorial patterns: 11 of the 14 straight Democratic papers followed the liberal pattern.

The data on the editorial positions follows:

	FOR		AGAINST	
	#	%	#	%
ABM (initial passage of Ph. I)	52	57%	40	43%
Carswell Nomination	26	31%	59	69%
Cambodia (initial reaction)	47	51%	45	49%
Cambodia (stand after June 30)	41	49%	43	51%
Agnew's Statements on Dissenters	26	35%	49	65%
McGovern-Hatfield Amendment	18	26%	50	74%

RESULTS BY REGION
(F—For, A—Against)

		Northeast		Midwest		South		West	
		F	A	F	A	F	A	F	A
ABM	#	10	8	13	14	15	13	14	5
	%	55.5%	44.5%	48%	52%	54%	46%	73.7%	26.3%
Carswell	#	4	11	5	22	15	13	3	13
	%	26.7%	73.3%	19%	81%	54%	46%	18.75%	81.25%
Cambodia (initial Reac)	#	7	10	11	16	15	14	14	5
	%	41.2%	58.8%	41%	59%	52%	48%	73.7%	26.3%
Cambodia (After Jn. 30)	#	7	8	9	16	13	14	11	5
	%	46.7%	53.3%	36%	64%	48%	52%	68.75%	31.25%
Agnew	#	3	9	7	13	9	17	7	10
	%	25%	75%	35%	65%	35%	65%	41.2%	58.8%
McGovern-Hatfield	#	5	7	4	15	9	14	2	12
	%	41.67%	58.33%	21%	79%	39%	61%	14.3%	85.7%

Looking at just two issues in depth, the Carswell nomination and Vice President Agnew's statements on dissension.

CARSWELL NOMINATION AND AGNEW'S STATEMENT ON DISSENTERS
(F—For, A—Against, B—Balanced editorials F & A)

POSITION		NUMBER	PER CENT
Carswell	Agnew		
F	F	18	18%
A	A	40	41
*F	A	5	5
A	—	6	6
A	F	4	4
—	—	2	2
A	B	9	9
—	F	5	5
—	A	4	4
F	B	4	4
—	B	1	1

* 5 papers *for* Carswell and *against* Agnew are all Southern—1 each from Arkansas, Georgia, Florida, Texas, and Tennessee

AGNEW, CARSWELL, AND REPUBLICANS IN 1968

POSITION		NUMBER	PER CENT
Carswell	Agnew		
F	F	17	26%
A	A	21	32
F	A	4	6
A	–	2	3
A	F	4	6
–	–	1	2
A	B	4	6
–	F	4	6
–	A	4	6
F	B	4	6
–	B	1	2

AGNEW, CARSWELL, AND DEMOCRATS IN 1968

POSITION		NUMBER	PER CENT
Carswell	Agnew		
F	F	1	4%
A	A	18	67
F	A	1	4
A	–	2	7
A	B	4	15
–	F	1	4

MEMBER ATTITUDES ON NEWS MEDIA ROLE

By William L. Hungate

Mr. HUNGATE. Mr. Speaker, I recently concluded a poll of Members of the House and Senate to discover congressional attitudes on the role played by the press, radio, and TV media in covering congressional activities and national affairs.

Five hundred and thirty-three questionnaires were sent out, there being two vacancies in the House. One hundred and fifty replies were received by the stated deadline, November 1. Signatures were not required but 24 Members did sign. Comments were invited and 22 Members availed themselves of this opportunity.

I thank my colleagues for their time and courtesy in making these responses, which I hope will prove helpful, both to the press and to the Congress, in our constant evaluation of our mutual responsibilities toward the people of the United States.

I insert the results of the poll in the RECORD at this point:

Reprinted from the *Congressional Record*, 90th Cong., 1st Sess. November 6, 1967, pp. 31379-31380, by permission of William Hungate.

[Please check 1]

	Excellent	Good	Fair	Poor	No opinion
1. In general, what kind of rating would you give radio on its coverage of national issues?	7	58	62	20	3
2. In general, what kind of rating would you give TV on its coverage of national issues?	12	47	58	32	0
3. In general, what kind of rating would you give newspapers on their coverage of national issues?	18	56	41	29	0

	Highly accurate	Reasonably accurate	Occasionally accurate	Seldom accurate	Rarely accurate
4. Do you think the television reports on congressional activities are generally	2	77	51	10	7
5. Do you think the newspaper reports on congressional activities are generally	4	79	48	9	6
6. Do you think radio reports on congressional activities are generally	3	92	44	1	5
7. Do you think that Huntley and Brinkley's TV reports on congressional activities are generally	8	67	33	21	8
8. Do you think Drew Pearson's newspaper reports on congressional activities are generally	1	17	51	27	52
9. Do you think Paul Harvey's radio reports on congressional activities are generally	5	33	43	24	19

	Yes	No	No opinion
10. Would you favor a code of ethics to be adopted for application to all radio, TV, and newspaper personnel accredited to House and Senate galleries?	91	43	11

11. If you could only receive 1 weekly magazine to keep yourself accurately informed on the activities of Congress, which of the following would you prefer to receive?

Time	13
Newsweek	33
Life	2
U.S. News & World Report	82
Congressional Quarterly	5
The National Observer	2
(Numerous others 1 each.)	

12. Please list the news columnist you read most regularly (regardless of your opinion of reliability or the area covered).

Evans and Novak	29
David Lawrence	20
Drew Pearson	17
James Reston	13
Art Buchwald	10
(Several others from William Buckley to Ann Landers also ran.)	

CONGRESSIONAL QUESTIONNAIRE

There were many comments included in the replies. Some samples follow:

Four Members thought it impossible to generalize on newspaper coverage since, as one said, "depends on the newspaper—varying from rotten to excellent."

One thought:

> Some control should be put on radio, TV, and newspaper editorializing. Take for example, I ride to work every morning and hear Radio WMAL have an editorial everyday—they couldn't have that good a research department to know everything.

Two thought Paul Harvey was reasonably accurate but hedged their comments, one saying "Accurate in substance more often than not, but hardly ever accurate in perspective."

Comments on Drew Pearson were perhaps the most enthusiastic and ranged from one Member who considered him highly accurate to comments such as, "Only accidentally accurate" and "A paid purveyor of hatchets."

Two found Huntley and Brinkley TV reports "slanted," and one stated "These are performers—not newsmen," while another commented, "Their 30-minute program often seems stretched for content," and found radio programing pathetic.

Other samples included:

> It is my opinion that most reporters covering Congress rely on prepared handouts rather than investigation—and that almost all tend to use the same one or two Members (Members varying for each reporter) for all their news bits and opinions. With a few exceptions, they are lazy, pompous, prejudiced, egotists. * * *
>
> The press is a business. At times its interests as a business are not entirely consistent with the responsibilities it bears as a free system with Constitutional privileges and sanctions. In other words, "freedom of the press" is not a one-way street.
>
> There are certain columnists, such as Drew Pearson, who consistently distort the news. While their columns may bring public attention to certain issues which could not otherwise be focused so dramatically, they have done much to hamper the tradition of "privileged communications" with members of their profession. Drew Pearson has never reported any item accurately in which I was involved, which makes me doubt his veracity in regard to other Members.

Another Member commented in depth on the congressional questionnaire:

> In general, I think all of the news media do a good job in covering the Congress within the limits of each medium. The newspapers over-all are the best because they can devote the space to the

subject on a daily basis. I say this with respect to the major papers—
The New York Times, The Washington Post and The Washington
Star.

Television and radio news coverage are less comprehensive and
many of the major newsmen in the electrical media acknowledge
this. On certain subjects, however, television news exceeds the newspapers. This happens with the so-called "in depth" pieces the three
networks will utilize frequently. Radio news is rarely more than the
headlines and should not be expected to be much more than that.

I would add that the intelligent reader (if he wishes to remain
that way) must read and listen to more than one source for the sake
of accuracy. This presents a time problem but there is no other
solution.

I oppose a "code of ethics" for Congressional reporters because
I do not think this is a practicable idea. In fact, I am not even sure
what is intended in such a code. The press plays a more significant
role in our society than most citizens realize. Rather than restrictions,
it needs to attract the best possible people to become its practitioners,
a problem gaining wider recognition than heretofore.

Two other comments of interest were: "News of activities in Congress
is too sketchy for average Americans to realize what is really happening,"
and "I try not to be confused by reading any—never do I read an editorial."

GUESS WHO'S NOT COMING TO THE
GRIDIRON CLUB DINNER?

By Shirley Chisholm

As you know, I recently turned down an invitation to attend the
Gridiron Club dinner * on the grounds that the white male membership
of the club was symbolic of the racism and sexism that exists in the news
industry. I was aware from the most casual observation that a problem
existed but when my office started to do an in-depth survey of the hiring
practices in the journalism field, we found that the problem was even
more serious than we had ever suspected.

We looked at newspapers, magazines and television and radio stations
in our study and found that despite all the pledges to the contrary we

---

* The Gridiron Club is an exclusive establishment group of 50 Washington journalists.
Its annual dinner, to which public officials are invited and satirized, is considered by
some to be a major social and political event—see Bibliography, especially A. Dunn,
Essery and C. Phillips.

A speech released by the office of Rep. Shirley Chisholm (D-N.Y.) February 20, 1972,
used with permission.

have heard over the past few years from the press, it still has not made concentrated efforts to hire and promote minorities.

Let's start with what we found in the newspaper field. We wrote to 18 newspapers and asked for the number of Blacks among their reporters and editors. We queried mainly those papers in cities with large minority populations. We sent those letters out by air mail over two weeks ago. We received four replies. We don't expect we'll get many more. But the replies we did get are damning enough.

The *Washington Star*, for example, told us that in a city that is 71 per cent Black with a staff of 185 reporters and editors it has but nine reporters and editors who are Black.

The *San Antonio Express* and the *San Antonio News* replied that out of a staff of 74 reporters, they have two Blacks and nine Mexican-Americans. This is in a city with an 8.6 per cent minority population.

We called other newspapers directly to get the information. The *New York Times*, in a city which is 21 per cent Black, has 557 reporters and editors but only 20 minority reporters and editors.

The *San Francisco Chronicle*, printed in a city that has a 28.5 per cent minority population, has only 12 minority group members out of an editorial staff of 223.

Beyond those newspapers who ignored our request for information on the minority composition of their staffs, there are two who refused outright to supply us the information. It is ultimate hypocrisy that the papers that preach the loudest about freedom of information, civil rights and civil liberties refuse to provide information to the public about their own policies.

The *New York Post* told us that it was their "firm policy that we do not reveal figures to anyone except a government agency doing an officially authorized study."

The *Los Angeles Times* told us: "As a matter of policy we do not provide the figures requested by Rep. Chisholm and, in fact, do not maintain some of the data requested."

We secured figures about the *Times* from other sources. The *Times*, printed in a city with a 22.8 per cent minority population, has 175 reporters and editors, including a grand total of four Blacks and one Mexican-American, reporting the news.

When a Black congresswoman like myself comes to Washington, she realizes how lily-white the press corps is in this town. When I look from the House floor to the press gallery, it is exceedingly rare to see a Black face. When I do, it is usually a reporter for a Black paper and not a Black reporter for a white-owned paper.

That's probably why no Black reporters went to China with Mr. Nixon.

That lack of Black reporters is apparent. When our Black Caucus held its dinner last year, the Washington papers did run stories on it—

stories telling which white leaders were there. I suspect that this was because the white reporters who covered the event didn't know who the Black leaders were.

This is not only insulting but a liability to the newspapers who, theoretically at least, are supposed to be providing information to their readers, in this case the Black readers who make up the majority of the District of Columbia's population.

There are other instances when it makes sense from a self-interest point of view for a newspaper or a television station to have Blacks and other minority members represented on their reportorial staffs. First, when covering stories on minorities they can approach the assignment with a degree of background and rapport that white reporters do not possess. Second, as minorities become more conscious of their own group identification they have become more suspicious of white reporters. There have increasingly been instances when whites, including white reporters, have been barred from Black news events.

Of course, one of the reasons there was any increase in Black reporters at all is that many of the papers had to hire someone back in 1967 to cover the riots. One New England paper, for example, hired a Black woman reporter to write on the disturbances there. Unfortunately for her, she actually wrote what was going on. When her stories were edited beyond recognition, she had words with her editors and they decided to part company.

As part of our study, we also checked with the 18 papers from cities with large minority populations to see if they had any Black Washington correspondents, since after all, Washington correspondents are the cream of the journalistic crop and are responsible for transmitting what happens in the Capitol and the White House back home. Of the 73 reporters employed by these bureaus, there were absolutely zero Blacks.

I suppose this situation would be a little more defensible if the newspaper industry were doing better than other industries.

Using Equal Employment Commission figures, we checked the newspaper industry against industry as a whole in seven cities that had minority populations of more than 20 per cent. In all seven cities—far from finding that newspapers were doing a better job of employing minorities—they were doing much worse than the industrial average.

Using EEOC statistics, we find that in the newspaper industry as a whole, only 4.2 per cent of all employees are Black. In the professional class, the class which includes reporters, only 1.5 per cent are Black.

In the periodical field, things are a little better, but not much. The minority percentage among all employees is 7.3 per cent and among professionals it is 2.5 per cent.

In the radio and television field, the Federal Communications Commission has begun to require that stations file annual reports on the racial and sexual composition of their work forces.

Apparently the FCC isn't too concerned about minorities though, because it still hasn't compiled reports submitted last May. This year's figures may come in before the FCC gets around to programming its computer to compile last year's figures.

The National Association of Educational Broadcasters should be commended for being concerned enough to go through reports filed with the FCC and compile, by hand, the minority employment figures for public television stations.

The picture, however, is not very bright. As a matter of fact, it's pretty shocking. The percentage of minority persons employed by public television stations dropped from 12 per cent in 1970 to eight per cent in 1971.

The reason for this is the decline in public contributions to support public television. This has forced stations to cut back their staffs. As usual, minorities are the last hired and first fired. In this case, I will admit, minorities were fired first for a good reason—because in public television, Blacks and other minorities are concentrated in the job levels of professionals or technicians rather than the usual levels of service workers or laborers. It is the nature of public television that when staff cutbacks are made, they come first in the production department at the professional and technician levels.

What is the problem? Let's ask the press.

Mr. Leonard Arnold, personnel and industrial relations manager for the *New York Post*, told the Equal Employment Opportunity Commission at its 1968 hearings on white collar employment discrimination:

"Inexperienced reporters are seldom hired because the practice in the newspaper industry in large metropolitan areas such as New York is to hire experienced personnel or promote from within the organization."

By the way, the *Post*, which had refused to give us its reporter and employment figures, told the EEOC at that time that it had four Black reporters on a staff of approximately 53 or 54 reporters. To Mr. Arnold's knowledge, the *Post* had never had any Blacks in editor or manager positions.

John Mortimer, director of personnel and industrial relations for the *New York Times*, amplified Arnold's statement:

"Our chief failure has been our inability to take in new employees, whether minority or non-minority, who don't initially meet our requirements and develop them to the point where they do meet our requirements."

We wrote to a number of papers that have made efforts to recruit Blacks for reportorial positions. Evarts A. Graham, managing editor of the *St. Louis Post-Dispatch*, told of his paper's problems in recruiting Blacks:

"The generally inadequate education that most inner-city Blacks received has proved to be our most difficult problem in Black employment . . . We can teach standard journalism techniques but we cannot give a general education. I think you will discover that the Black enrollment in journalism schools has increased quite sharply in recent years."

In spite of all this talk, we overlook one thing: for years, Black newspapers and magazines have managed to find qualified Black reporters and editors.

There are several possible solutions that might be suggested. One suggested at the EEOC hearings to Arnold of the *Post* was that the three major papers in New York band together to provide training for potential Black journalists. Chicago newspapers, for example, have long operated a City News Bureau as a training ground for young journalists. There is no reason why this sort of operation might not be tried in other cities to develop the skills of Blacks who are interested in journalism but lack the skills that would allow them to go straight into reporting for a paper.

I think we should expect the nation's journalism schools to take the major part in increasing Black employment on papers. The number of Blacks employed as reporters, will in part be dependent on the number of Blacks graduated by our journalism schools. And the way to get Blacks into journalism schools is to recruit them, a function that can be shared jointly by schools and local papers. In Tulsa, for example, a media committee has sponsored weekly classes on the media in predominantly Black high schools.

We have written to 25 of the nation's largest and most prestigious journalism schools to ask them what they are doing to recruit and train more Black journalism students.

We cannot wait, however, for journalism schools to fill the need. Roughly one half of the reporters and editors now working have degrees in other desciplines. We must take steps now to recruit qualified Blacks with other degrees or skills or knowledge who have the intelligence, if not the academic credentials, to write a fair, objective news story. We can train and then use these individuals now instead of waiting for the four years it takes to go through a journalism school.

With attempts such as these, we can eliminate the excuse of papers that there just aren't any qualified Blacks around to be reporters.

AN OLDTIMER'S VIEW OF THE PRESS

By Richard Bolling

"That compound of folly, weakness, prejudice, wrong-feeling and right-feeling and newspaper paragraphs."
—Sir Robert Peel on Public Opinion

The public officeholder and the press continuously negotiate with each other over the spoils of free publicity and free news.

Outwardly, their relations are correct, sometimes friendly, and occasionally cordial.

The House Member wants favorable mention, including the correct spelling of his first name and his last name. The reporter for newspaper, magazine, television, or radio "wants the story." The House Member, orally or by mimeographed statement placed in the press gallery, gives the reporter a story that the Member wants his constituents to know. The reporter insists there is more to the story than the House Member is telling. This is very probably true. The reporter seeks additional information. The Member withholds it or offers a harmless generalization. Neither is entirely satisfied with the result.

The House Member is at a disadvantage with the press, which has a bias in favor of the 100-Member Senate, because mechanically it is easier to cover. The 435-Member House is too large for neat coverage. Power in the House is diffused, and its struggles are more difficult to identify, isolate, and analyze than in the Senate. Tactics and strategy are more closely concealed. The stricter rules of discussion, regulating the substance and time of debate, blunt the moments of high drama on the House floor. From the Senate press gallery, reporters can look down on a hundred men and women and see the personification of forces and philosophies. From the House press gallery, they see only a sea of heads. Therefore reporters have concentrated on the Senate and the White House for the bulk of the news.

Although House Members have a passably good relationship with correspondents from the newspapers in their own districts, most Members mingle with them warily. . . .

Wire-service editors impress upon their staffs that somewhere in the world a client newspaper is "going to bed"—that is, going to press. Every day hundreds of thousands of words are shoveled into the wire-service teletypes to satisfy harassed editors. This accounts for the fact that almost any mimeographed statement placed in the gallery is seized upon for news copy. City-reared Members, whose only view of a cow has been on a can of condensed milk, can get their names quoted in the press as experts in agriculture. A House Member whose travels consist of a triangular course between West Wetdrip, Washington, and the Army-Navy game in Philadelphia can make the news with outrageous remarks about our foreign-aid program simply by getting a press handout to the gallery early in the morning. A Member who can't keep his family accounts in balance can be quoted on the President's economic message to the Congress provided he looks at an advance copy and sends a statement to the gallery first thing in the morning. Thus, much of the wire-service copy is unselected and inconsequential.

The stories are gathered quickly and written quickly. The emphasis on speed brings with it a tendency to accept all statements of all House Members as being of equal merit—the press calls this "impartiality" or "objectivity." The insistence upon frozen formats such as this helped Joseph McCarthy's bully-boy career in the Senate. The concept of objectivity, superficially plausible, rules out the informed interpretation, the "in-depth" piece that explains why such a vote is meaningful and how Representative X's voting record on a given issue may be keyed to certain pressure groups.

The Capitol Hill bureaus of the press associations are staffed by able, knowledgeable men and women, but the compulsion to make a deadline blunts their effectiveness. It is not uncommon for a wire-service reporter to cover two or three committee hearings in a morning. He does this by going to the first hearing just before it opens, picking up available mimeographed copies of witnesses' prepared testimony, then going to the second and third hearings, where he also collects prepared testimony. He may stay a few minutes in each of the hearings, but he depends on being backstopped or "filled in" by the more fortunate reporters from daily newspapers who have just one hearing to cover. It is impossible to obtain an adequate story in this fashion. It implies that the once-over-lightly story will do for the "average reader." But instead there are blocs of readers, and some of them want considerable technical detail in news stories about their field of interest. An overly generalized story on higher education means that a college president in Oregon must make a call to Washington or await the next newsletter of his professional association in order to find out necessary details of a bill.

Compounding the wire-service reporter's problem is the wide variety of opinions held by the subscribers to the press associations. The reporter in covering a hearing on civil-rights legislation will be writing for the editors in Birmingham, Alabama; Oxford, Missisippi; and New York City and Chicago.

This results in what Ralph McGill calls "wood pulp pablum." The two major wire services, Associated Press and United Press International, are the sole source of news of the House for most newspapers and for almost all radio and television stations. Although there were 890 newspaper, magazine, and radio and television correspondents accredited in 1964 to the press galleries in House and Senate, there is too little continuous perceptive and accurate reporting. What scant commentary on the House there is is largely found in the syndicated columns and editorials.

One of the puzzling characteristics of newsmen is their tendency to report legislative business in terms suitable to a police story. Possibly this stems from the practice of training reporters on the police beat. The orthodox line of progression on the daily newspaper, which for some unexplained reason is supposed to produce first-rate reporters, is from police reporting to obituary reporting to general assignment to special assignments or "beats," such as city hall and the state house. After hanging around police headquarters long enough, the reporter often carries with him a policeman's view of events in which every man is so crooked he must screw his socks on in the morning. It makes for a simple cops-and-robbers picture of the world. It accounts for the concept of "the scoop"—for example, the Member's wife who is on his payroll—and the righteous hunting down of petty misdemeanors. It is not surprising that a newspaperman known for his aggressive reporting can say that when he sees a door shut on Capitol Hill "he wants to break it down." This is the attitude of the voyeur, not the reporter.

Newspapers thrive on wrack and ruin and catastrophe. Sweeping social changes in the world are converted into a scorecard of crises. If X number of bills are not passed by the House by a certain month, then it automatically follows that the House is "tied up" or "lagging" or "doing nothing." If a complex bill is held in a committee for a prolonged, legitimate discussion, then the bill becomes "controversial," "under fire," and "threatened with defeat."

In his formative stage, the reporter is pushed to master technique and develop an eye for minutiae. The middle initial of a man's name is regarded as of equal importance with the main point of a story. Once, in the house organ of the American press, *Editor & Publisher,* an editor was quoted as saying he would fire a reporter who used the word "however" instead of "but." There have been silly experiments with sentence lengths—one Chicago paper once adopted a "14-W" formula—no opening sentence or "lead" could contain more than 14 words. At an eastern journalism school a former newspaperman turned teacher would each year proudly tell the story of the occasion when, before the telephone was common, his city editor sent him back to the scene of a collapsed church steeple, an hour's journey, because he had not found "how high was the steeple." It may have been such pointless anecdotes as this that prompted A. J. Liebling in *The Wayward Pressman* to exclaim with impatience that this particular journalism school "had all the intellectual content of a school for A & P clerks."

Such is the outlook and experience that many reporters bring to Washington. It accounts for the condition of the American press—long on facts, sometimes trivial ones, but short on a sense of facts. Americans may have available the most numerous sources of information, as press people claim, but whether Americans are the most informed is debatable.

Much of the effort of the Washington press corps is expended in the area of "nonnews." Or what Daniel J. Boorstin at the University of Chicago calls the "pseudo-event," usually an interview scheduled simply to get the subject of the interview into the news columns. Probably more than one-half of any daily newspaper consists of pseudo-news. The proportion of actual events that occur without prompting by the press is decreasing. The Washington, D.C., press corps can be the most aggressive fight promoters in the world. There is many a report of a "feud" or "clash" or "row" within the House that exists only in the newspaper. One West Coast correspondent, covering the presidential signing of a major bill, reported that two Members of a state delegation jostled for position behind the President at the start of the White House ceremony. This story, with overtones of feuding, made the headlines back home. In fact, the two Members were escorted to their position behind the chair by a White House staff member before any other Members invited to the ceremony were admitted to the President's office.

Correspondents in Washington for out-of-town newspapers tend to compound the provincial character of the House by introducing into news stories the "local angle," emphasizing the views, opinions, and votes of the Member from the district in which the newspaper is located. When a local accent is given to a major foreign-aid story, the national issue inherent in the story becomes obscured and distorted. Often, Washington correspondents are closely attuned to the editorial position of their newspapers back home, and this gives a further slant to political stories.

In the American way, when reporters became correspondents or "journalists," they may acquire "clients." Spoilsmanship reaches its highest development in the cases of such Washington journalists. Their clients are an improvement over the usual panel of newsroom favorites that reporters can reach for that desperate on-deadline comment, the enlivening quote, or the controversial opinion to help brighten a light Monday-morning newspaper. These clients are House and Senate Members who are on the make with the press, radio, or TV men. These Congressmen are frequently seen on the Sunday-afternoon and early-evening panel shows; they are the source of the crutch story—the overnight wire-service story written for the first editions of the next day's afternoon newspapers. If the House passes a bill to bring peace on earth, the reporters doing the crutch story can turn to his client in the Senate for the quotations, often anonymous, that will permit the story to start out, "The peace-on-earth bill, passed overwhelmingly by the House, faces rough sledding in the Senate, key legislators said today. . . ." These clients are usually entrenched powers in the House and presidential aspirants in the Senate. In this state of symbiosis with a newsman, the Member of Congress can get his own ideas before the public. If the Member comes under attack, the correspondent can be relied upon to defend him. For example, Charles Halleck, John McClellan, and Barry Goldwater each has his Boswell.

A variant of this type of reporter is the correspondent who collects executive departments. A story out of the White House as to possible disarmament moves is certain to be followed by dire, anonymous warnings from well-protected scientific sources in the Defense Department. If these scientific sources get wind of what is up at the White House, their favorite science reporter will be called to shoot the disarmament moves out of the water even before they are launched. In the Senate in August 1962, George McGovern of South Dakota rose to suggest that the Soviet Union and the United States had acquired such an awesome nuclear arsenal that each had the potential to kill off the other's populations many times over—the so-called "overkill" concept. To those knowledgeable in the Byzantine ways of the Washington press corps, it was a reasonable certainty which reporter on which newspaper would quickly appear with a rebuttal to McGovern from unidentified sources.

Unlike Members of the Senate, relatively few House Members are beneficiaries of the "client" system. In any event, clientism is a disservice to the Congress and the American people. It understates the crucial role of issues and grossly exaggerates the power of individuals to shape situations and circumstances. It discourages a vigorous approach to news coverage. Not long ago, a newcomer to the Washington bureau of a major daily newspaper commented despondently that his fellow bureau members had protested his suggestion that the newspaper prepare a story on legislative conflicts of interest among Members of Congress. The reporter said his fellows pointed out that it had taken years to build up confidences and contacts with important Members and that such an exposé story would "rock the boat."

A capable newspaper man, Peter Lisagor of the *Chicago Daily News* explains the hazard of "psychological undertow." This, he explains, is the consequence of a reporter's frequent association with a particular important government official—a Cabinet office or a President. "You tend to soften the edges of criticism. . . . You tend to obscure, minimize things that the public generally ought to be hearing about, ought to know," Lisagor said. Newspapermen, too, like to be greeted affably and by first name by important persons.

Alan Barth, editorial writer for the *Washington Post*, phrased his thoughts on the matter in his acceptance of the Oliver Wendell Holmes Bill of Rights Award in 1964:

> "I do not mean to make light of the threats which reckless journalism may pose to rights of privacy, to the right to a fair trial and to other individual rights. These are serious problems. I am more concerned, however, with a different danger—with the danger that the press in the United States has become excessively responsible— has become, in fact, to an alarming degree, a spokesman and partner of the Government, rather than a censor." . . .

Another kind of correspondent regards the House and Senate as hallowed legislative museums rather than as viable organs of government to which major problems are brought for resolution. The emphasis upon form rather than context favors the entrenched powers and gives the American people a false sense of security about their national assembly. . . .

One indication that House Members feel they are not being adequately "covered" by the Washington press is the widespread use of periodic newsletters that Members send to constituents and the increasing utilization of home-district television and radio for two, five, and fifteen minutes by Members.

Over-all, the press coverage of the Congress, particularly the House, is inadequate. The "big name" Members are not necessarily the most competent or the most powerful or the most influential. They may be big names because they have big mimeograph machines, or a staff member with newspaper experience who knows that the way to get the boss a precious half-column of news, instead of a couple of paragraphs, is to time releases and speeches for publication in Monday-morning newspapers, when news is scarce.

Some of the most perceptive reporting is being published in the trade and specialty press, such as the *Wall Street Journal*, or magazines such as *Commentary, The New Yorker*, and *Science*. Our cluttered newspapers, with their lack of focus, make one appreciate the *London Sunday Observer*, the American Survey section of the *Economist*, or the American reports of the Manchester *Guardian* with their organized, lucid, and knowledgeable coverage of American domestic affairs.

The American press is not yet the adequate machinery of knowledge of which Walter Lippmann has spoken. Adequate coverage of politics would take account of that complex three-cornered interaction of the event itself, the reporting of the event, and the human reaction to it.

A reporter who knows the House well once said, "The only reform the House needs is full disclosure." A brilliant scholar has remarked that basic research, not reform, is the answer to what is wrong with the House. There is truth in both observations. Until the press systematically begins to reveal the weaknesses of the House as an institution, it cannot stimulate enough public interest to support a popular movement for reform.

The American press, a privileged institution with constitutional protections, has the opportunity to make known to voters the facts about how the House functions, where the true centers of power lie, the significance of seniority and the committee system, and the long dominance of the South and of rural Representatives in the House. The seasoned reporter knows that it is forces, not individuals, that ultimately underlie political struggles. Until the press gives its readers accurate information and analysis and a true perspective on the character of the House, it shares a responsibility for the present condition.

A NEWCOMER'S VIEW OF THE PRESS

By Clem Miller

Dear Friend:

It might be profitable to venture some observations on the relationship between this newcomer to Congress and the press.

First, there is the relationship with the home district newspapers. It is distinct and different from the Washington press. By and large, it is locally oriented, and properly so.

The key to this relationship is that it is a one-way street. The exchange almost always starts at this end, the Washington end, and flows out *to* the local newspaper. It is an arms-length affair. It is dominated by the mimeographed press release, which, in my case, has to be mailed to every newspaper in the First District. Occasionally we will wire the germ of a news item to a specific newspaper; even more rarely, we will telephone the item. We face a constant problem of the dailies and the weeklies. The timing of a release is vital to the newspaper. It does not get run in the weekly if it does not arrive on the spot at the right time. With different press days, with the unpredictable timing of developments in Washington, and with our limited resources, this process of communication is difficult and often frustrating for all concerned.

The role of the newspaper is usually passive, and occasionally hostile. Their news staffs are overworked and understaffed, have very limited budgets, and receive a never-ending flood of materials from all sides. The congressman gets his due along with a thousand other competing interests. Anyway, why should the editor worry when he has a senator and a congressman competing to deliver the news to him on a silver platter. That's the fact. The senator wants his name in the paper, so he is in there with a wire early. The congressman wants his name in there, so he is on the phone. This is the system. Newspapers like it. They call it "competition," and in America we always like to see the other fellow engaged in competition. Whether this is good for the newspapers or their readers is another matter.

Newspapers at home usually see no need to check with their congressmen on facts or on his position. The number of times that I have been contacted by *any* newspaper in my district in two years can be counted on the fingers of one hand.

Second, there is the relationship with the wire services, UPI and AP. At the opening of Congress in 1959 there was a brief flurry of contact from the wire service "regional men" handling California. Since then, there has been less contact. The reasons are the same. Overwork, under-staffing, and the flood of news. The UPI regional man for California, for example, is expected to cover all of the representatives and senators from ten or so western states. He is also responsible for reporting developments of possible interest to his service's clients—newspapers, and radio and TV stations—from several hundred committees and subcommittees on Capitol Hill as well as Floor activity in both houses. Harry Humphries of AP has always been most agreeable to talk to me if I call him. He will come around to the office and talk about it. But newsworthy occasions never seem to arise. The twist or angle which would make it news does not seem to be present. The effect of this is that constituents do not generally know what their congressman is doing, nor do they have a chance to find out. What is "news"? What is newsworthy in America today? Are the views of a congressman on current legislation, his voting record, etc., "news" to his constituency? Apparently not. I feel frustrated to the extent that I make little effort to promote this sort of thing, and con-versely, little effort is made to elicit it from me by newsmen.

A third category is one which might be described as the national press corps, the newsmen responsible for telling America what goes on in Washington and Congress. There is a large gallery immediately over the Speaker's chair reserved for the press. It is generally devoid of occupants. Except for crowded state occasions, there may be only one, two, or three newsmen bird-dogging the proceedings below. By and large, the reporting is quite perfunctory with little of the shading which gives political life its validity. While I believe this is unfortunate, it is understandable. The press has no time for shading today. This is the "age of the headline" and the "news capsule." Headlines come from the White House or from Senator Johnson's office, rarely from congressional debate. Congressman Chester Bowles made a foreign policy address last year. Not a line of the speech was reported by the press. Ditto for a speech by Senator Engle on our China policy. Another important speech on domestic economy was buried at the bottom of some other pronouncement. I suppose lapses like this can be defended because the timing was wrong or the speaker didn't get enough copies of the speech to the galleries, or because the general level of debate in the House is so low that the gold nugget was overlooked, etc., etc.

Sometimes, however, even by its own standard of judgment about news, the press fails. Such a major failure, to my way of thinking, was exemplified by the lack of coverage of the attempt by the Chairman of the Rules Committee to chastise a congressman for a critical radio broad-cast. For the first time in a decade the subsurface feud between northern Democrats and the Rules Committee majority broke out into the open. It may well prove to herald an historic turning point in the development of the House of Representatives. Yet, there was not a line, *not a line,* of this "effort to censure" in the newspapers the following day. A complete blackout. Was this due to inattentiveness on the part of the press? I do not know. What I do know is that it was a deplorable failure to report what I consider significant news—news that would inform and would promote understanding. So concerned is the press with the surface events of the day that the meaning of life in Washington is many times all but obscured or actually distorted beyond resemblance. The best case in point is the novel *Advise and Consent* which is full of surface but tells little about congressional politics.

It also means that some news gets lost. An interesting example comes to mind. Everyone was interested in what the congressional Democratic landslide of 1958 would produce. No radical changes materialized and the press lost interest. When the Democratic Study Group was formed in the House in September, 1959, the event went unreported. Prominent members of the press told me all through 1960 that the DSG was a flash in the pan. It would not survive, so it was not worth attention. However, lately a series of visitors not connected with newspapers have been coming to my office to talk about the DSG. The talk is discursive, ruminative, and stimulating. In various smaller periodicals, articles are now appearing about it. As yet, not one of the major news media or their interpretative writers has had a line published about this development. This is some indication of the news gap.

How the press gallery functions, I do not have the faintest idea. This is perhaps an admission of deficiency on my part. It is worth reporting only as illustrative of the chasm which exists between one junior congressman and the press.

If the press did not report Congress, Congress could hardly function. If the sound of congressional voices carried no farther than the bare walls of the Chambers, Congress could disband. We know this; it is brought home to us every day. Reporters appear very aware of their powers. From where I sit, it is a power they are not backward about using.

This suggests a basic rivalry between the press corps and congressmen. I must confess that I feel it. To the wise old birds in the Press Gallery, we politicians are trying to put something over on somebody. Exposure of this public show by politicians is a major portion of the routine of the newspaperman's job, and I agree it must be an important part. There is a tendency to fatuousness and fat-headedness which must be restrained. To the congressman, however, publicity is his lifeblood. It is his career, his fate, and it brings an emotion to his relationship with the press which the newsman does not comprehend, but which he can manipulate—very frequently with too much enjoyment to be bearable.

A good case in point was a recent newspaper series on nepotism which won its author a Pulitzer Prize. To my knowledge there was no news

sleuthing carried on with more vigor than this investigation into the
family members on congressional pay rolls. It was carried on in the finest
traditions of the journalistic profession. It was a joyous rousting-about of
the rascally politician. Actually, it shed little light, it contributed little.
It was harmful, I believe, to the public's understanding of Congress. This
should not be construed as the favoring of nepotism, but there was no
effort to tell the other side—the great financial difficulties which many
congressmen operate under in doing their jobs. It killed for this session
the addition of a staff man to each office, badly needed indeed under
congressional loads presently carried by most of us.

Then, there was the famous *Life* exposé of expense accounts. What
enthusiasm this engendered! There was another side to this story also
that was never told. The main point I am seeking to make is that much
of the press seems to regard its Washington role as it does police reporting.
The broader sweep of the meaningful "why" and the "wherefore" of
government is lost in the welter of what is on the police captain's blotter.

At a newspapermen's dinner one night I was the only politician
present. The talk was all about the trade—and to this outsider it was
fascinating indeed. After dinner the talk got on to campaigns, and I made
a few tentative assertions with suitable disclaimers of infallibility. Immediately I became the subject of a biting cross-examination by one of those
present. There was no intention to be rude or discourteous, but I became
uncomfortable and distracted. There was some unwitting contempt—this
gentleman from the press was on the highest level and knew all. There
was some real enjoyment on his part about what a monkey I was. He
leaned back, arms akimbo, gallus-snapping. He was supremely happy,
putting a congressman in his place. It was all quite unconscious and
unintentional, and he would have been mortified if I had told him of
the impression he made. I was quite angry, even so. This was a social
event, not an inquisition.

Finally, there is the relationship with a host of national correspondents who are busy explaining in their signed columns and interpretative
articles what the newspapers seem unable to do in the news columns. I
see these men closeted with the committee chairmen in the Speaker's
Lobby. I am introduced to them occasionally. I have had dinner with
them and found them delightful.

I have talked to them in the Speaker's Lobby, but it is difficult for
me to talk to newspapermen. I don't seem to have the hang of it. I don't
like to talk in clichés and the headline phrase does not come easily. Since
the press operates under terrifying time pressures, many newsmen think
in clichés. They want congressmen to talk in clichés. They become uneasy
if you tend toward too much "background" talk, or if your thoughts are
tentative. This, of course, is due to the modern demand for slogans.
Everything is compressed. People have no time to attend, to listen. We

have become a nation of headline readers. It is not at all surprising that the working press has come to require the same of politicians in its day-to-day reporting. The result is distortion, the inevitable distortion that comes from oversimplification and compression.

This is not to absolve myself. The job of a congressman, in major degree, is communicating—making our political world understandable. By dealing too much in the "grey" area of political life, and not presenting sharp, didactic alternatives, I do not make the job easier. I am constantly striving to do this, but my concept of the real political world does not make for an easy fit.

There are reporters who seek background. It is hard to get the knack of talking "background," "off-the-record," "on-the-record," unless you have a firm idea of the ground rules. Reporters become frustrated by the congressman who does not know the ground rules, who switches back and forth from "off-the-record" to "on-the-record," who interlards his talk with trivia or philosophy. The reporter's standard reaction to this sort of thing is to turn off his traveling pencil.

What all this means in terms of Congress is that the congressman who tailors his speech and remarks to the strictures of modern reporting is going to get in the news; and he who doesn't is going to have difficult sledding. It means that many capable legislators operate fairly silently, while others who might be of inferior competence are heard from quite frequently.

Very sincerely,
Clem Miller

6

The Congressional
Correspondents
and Their World

THIS CHAPTER TAKES a closer look at the variety of domestic correspondents and their work world—as they describe it. It includes two reports on a survey of the correspondents conducted for this book.

The first report, "The Variety of Correspondents," attempts to define and identify the types of news media representatives who "cover" Congress in many ways.

The second report, "The Correspondents Describe Their Work," presents backgrounds, job descriptions and attitudes of the correspondents and their relations with congressional sources. Information for this report was derived from interviews with 31 major congressional correspondents and from questionnaires completed and returned by 96 congressional correspondents, the majority of whom said they devoted most of their professional time on Capitol Hill.

To define and identify congressional correspondents, and to then examine their backgrounds, attitudes and relations with sources, a survey was conducted between Summer 1972 and Summer 1973—from the ITT hearings to the Watergate hearings.

The first step consisted of in-depth interviews with 31 of the more visible or obvious full-time congressional correspondents. The structured interview format was adapted from one developed and used in a previous study by Roger H. Davidson and his colleagues at The Public Affairs Center of Dartmouth College.[1]

The questions asked correspondents involved the percentage of working time devoted to Capitol Hill matters, correspondents' views of their functions as news reporters in relation to the business of Congress, chief sources of ideas for stories, their rating as news sources over congressional staff people over members of Congress, and any other matters the correspondents wanted to discuss.

The purpose of the interviews was to obtain an overall view of congressional coverage and to collect information for the design of a questionnaire to be sent to a broader sample of congressional correspondents.

Since some persons listed in the *Congressional Directory* as members of one or more of the Capitol news media galleries devote no time reporting on congressional matters,[2] an initial effort was made to sift non-congressional domestic journalists and all foreign journalists out of the *Directory* listings of media correspondents. The result was that 1,671 members of the press galleries listed in the 1972 *Congressional Directory* (92nd Congress, Second Session) were not included in the initial sample. These included all persons identified with foreign news organizations. Others included all but known congressional correspondents working for large major Washington-area news media, large bureaus and wire services. These domestic organizations have large numbers of reporters and editors residing in the Washington metropolitan area who are members of the Capitol press galleries but who seldom devote any professional time to congressional matters. These news organizations also generally have clearly identified congressional correspondents.

This initial sample included 722 domestic correspondents listed in the *Directory*, not counting the 31 correspondents interviewed. Of that number, 422 were listed under "Press Galleries—Members of the Press Entitled to Admission," 147 under "Radio and Television Correspondents' Galleries—Members Entitled to Admission," and 153 under "Periodical Press Galleries—Members Entitled to Admission."

Next, a short questionnaire was sent to the initial sample of 722. It asked what per cent of the correspondent's professional time was devoted to covering Congress; the per cent of this professional time spent in the House Gallery, the Senate Gallery, at the correspondents' news organization office, or elsewhere in the Senate or House office buildings, and the per cent of time spent in local-regional or national or other type of reporting.

Of the 227 questionnaires completed and returned (31% of the initial sample), 146 came from those accredited by the Press Galleries, 43 from the Radio and Television Correspondents' Galleries and 38 from Periodical Press Galleries.

From the results of the first questionnaire, an attempt was made to develop a more specific list of news media organization varieties, since the three major galleries—Press, Radio-TV and Periodical—were found to be too broad. (See varieties in Table 1, page 222.)

With the aid of the newly developed list of news media organization varieties, a telephone survey was conducted. Major news media organizations listed in the *Congressional Directory*, and not represented by the correspondents interviewed or by correspondents included in the returns of the short questionnaire, were called and asked to give the name of from one to three of their major congressional correspondents.

A five-page questionnaire was designed from information received in the interviews, in the first questionnaire and from previous surveys of Washington and British Parliament correspondents,[3] from a survey of influences on reporters' opinions,[4] and from a study of reporter-official relationships.[5]

The questionnaire was sent to all correspondents interviewed (31), correspondents responding to the short questionnaire (227), and to major congressional correspondents identified (49), including 14 Associated Press and 14 United Press International congressional correspondents—a total of 307.

The questionnaire was sent to the 307 correspondents who were associated with news media circulated or broadcast directly in 45 states. The states not directly represented—Arkansas, Delaware, Montana, New Mexico and Wyoming—probably were indirectly represented by national news media or by media in neighboring states. In addition, all of the states were represented by the circulation of *Congressional Quarterly*, which was included in the survey (Table 2).

The specialized newspapers and periodicals surveyed included a wide variety of subject matter.

Of the 307 questionnaires sent, 96 (31%) were completed and returned. The 96 responses were tabulated according to news media organization varieties the correspondents identified themselves with (five correspondents identified two media organizations each).

The survey was designed and directed by Robert O. Blanchard and conducted by him with the assistance of graduate journalism students at The American University: Carol Horner, Kay Hickox, Rick Beaudette, Wendy White, Thomas Murnane and Barbara Schechter. Carol Horner tabulated and coded the responses from the final questionnaire, conducted the telephone survey and tabulated the returns. Kay Hickox conducted most of the structured interviews with assistance from Wendy White, Tomas Murnane and Barbara Schechter. Rick Beaudette tabulated and coded the responses from the first questionnaire.

The survey was assisted in great measure by The American University Academic Computer Service.

Helpful advice and encouragement came from faculty colleagues Edward Bliss, Jr., Lewis W. Wolfson, and Jack E. Orwant.

The study team expresses special gratitude to the congressional correspondents who participated in the survey, especially those who cooperated in the interviews and who completed and returned questionnaires.

NOTES

[1] Michael O'Leary, (ed.), *Congressional Reorganizational Problems and Prospects*, The Public Affairs Center of Dartmouth College, 1964; Roger H. Davidson, David Kovench, and Michael K. O'Leary, *Congress in Crisis: Politics and Congressional Reform*, Belmont, Calif.: Wadsworth Publishing Company, Inc., pp. 42-47.

[2] Neil V. McNeil, "The Washington Correspondents: Why Do Some 'Drop Out'?", *Journalism Quarterly*, Vol. 43, No. 2 (1966), pp. 257-263; Bascom N. Timmons, "This is How it Used to Be," in Cabell Phillips (ed.), *Dateline: Washington*, N.Y.: Doubleday, 1949, pp. 44-46.

[3] Leo Rosten, *The Washington Correspondents*, N.Y.: Harcourt: Brace and Co., 1937;

William L. Rivers, "The Washington Correspondents and Government Information,"
Ph.D. dissertation, American University, 1960; and Jeremy Tunstall, *The Westminster
Lobby*, London: Routledge and Kegan Paul, 1970.
4 Ruth C. Flegal, and Steven H. Chaffee, "Influences of Editors, Readers, and Personal
Opinions on Reporters," *Journalism Quarterly*, Vol. 48, No. 4 (1971), pp. 645-651.
5 Delmer C. Dunn, *Public Officials and the Press*, Reading, Mass.: Addison-Wesley
Publishing Co., 1969.

THE VARIETY OF CORRESPONDENTS

By Robert O. Blanchard

Who are the congressional correspondents?

The White House, Defense Department, State Department, among
others, have press accreditation consisting largely of correspondents who
spend most, if not all, of their working time on matters in their jurisdictions. But this is not the case for the congressional news media galleries.
Accreditation on Capitol Hill is the basic accreditation and journalistic
social register in Washington. It is not limited to those devoting most of
their time to congressional matters.

"I would like to know," wrote one Capitol Hill reporter, "if over 2 per
cent of those holding congressional press cards ever really cover Congress!
It is my judgment they do not."

It depends on what is meant by the term "covering Congress."

Here are four comments representing four varieties of persons holding
Capitol Hill press cards:

> I've had no personal responsibility for covering the Congress
> since about 1942 and, as a *Washington bureau manager*, keep my
> gallery registration (and entry credentials) only for emergencies, of
> which there have been none involving me in recent years.—*Bureau
> manager for mid-Atlantic metropolitan daily newspapers.*
>
> As *news editor of the bureau*, I use registration for protective
> purposes. (A) great bulk of my time is spent operating . . . bureau.
> —*News editor for a major broadcast group.*
>
> We cover a large amount of Capitol Hill news—especially
> legislation relating to religion (e.g., abortion, family planning) or
> social issues (e.g., farm workers unemployment compensation, the
> war, etc.). But we seldom use our gallery passes for live coverage,
> relying instead on written testimony before committees, press releases,
> etc.—*Congressional correspondent for a major religious news service.*
>
> All or most [of my] time [is] spent on individual House mem-
> bers or Senators—covering a committee hearing for exploring an issue,

rather than covering Congress *in toto.—Congressional correspondent for a major East Coast metropolitan daily newspaper.*

Access to the news media galleries in Congress is not without limits.[1] Wrote an *editor of a consumer newsletter*:

> Because of a peculiar rule of the galleries, we are not given status there. Credentials are given only to those publications which take advertising. The excuse is that publications which are put out by lobbying groups cannot become gallery members under such restrictions. . . . We, along with other members of the Independent Newsletter Association, have been fighting this unfair rule for some time, with negative results.

In the meantime, this editor is registered as a correspondent for a commercial magazine, rather than an editor of an "independent publication which has no financing other than subscription fees and no connection with any lobbying organization."

In contrast, here is what one correspondent said who is accredited by the Standing Committee of Correspondents on Capitol Hill:

> For the past two and a half years I have been a *radio editor* at [one of the major networks] and have done virtually no reporting. None on Capitol Hill. Sorry I can't be of more help to you. I should be interested in the results of your survey.

These members of the congressional news media galleries are responding to a questionnaire which asked them how much of their professional time they devoted to covering Congress.

The temptation is great to first eliminate from this study all but the hard core, elite congressional correspondents—those working for the prestigious and influential general news services, daily newspaper and broadcast network bureaus. These, after all, are the correspondents who select the issues and the officials on which to report, thus creating in the general public's mind its general picture of Congress.

Yet there are varieties of correspondents who have considerable control over information flowing from Congress to special ideological, geographic and subject-matter audiences. And the power of these special audiences—when organized into interest groups, represented by powerful lobbyists and associations in Washington—can be great indeed. The influence of these groups in Congress often is greatly affected by information they receive from many varieties of Washington correspondents.

All of the correspondents—from the elite fulltime dwellers of the House and Senate galleries to the dabblers—have important roles in the function referred to as "covering Congress." A sketch of this spectrum of congressional correspondent varieties provides a context in which to examine the backgrounds and attitudes of correspondents of the more general print and broadcasting media, the topic of the next article.

Varieties of Time Covering Congress

Time can be one factor defining and identifying congressional correspondents. Four varieties are included in this study to refer to correspondents who devote certain percentages of time to covering Congress. These are:

1. Some Timers—less than 19%.
2. Short Timers—20 to 39%.
3. Half Timers—40 to 59%.
4. Most Timers—60 to 100%.

These terms are applied to 10 categories of activity:

1. Correspondents' total professional time devoted to covering the United States Congress;

Correspondents' congressional coverage time:

2. devoted to the House of Representatives;
3. devoted to the United States Senate;
4. in the House Gallery (includes House chamber or gallery offices);
5. in the Senate Gallery (includes Senate Chamber or gallery offices);
6. in their (media) organizations' offices (if their office is not in the gallery);
7. elsewhere in the Capitol or House or Senate office buildings;
8. in committee hearings (regardless of location);
9. "localizing" reporting (reporting local or regional "angles" to congressional affairs);
10. reporting national news.

These time factors determine, to a great extent, the type of information the correspondents receive and, thus, the type of stories and broadcasts they produce. Yet, these factors are dependent upon another of major importance to the correspondents—the media organization(s) they work for.

Variety of Media Organizations *

It is the correspondents' media organizations which seem to determine how much time they spend on Capitol Hill, where their time is spent on the Hill, what they do with that time, and, thus, what information they collect.

One veteran congressional correspondent expresses the differences in media organizations this way:

> They are utterly different. The greatest man in this area was Everett Dirksen, who understood the differences. When he talked with

* See Table 2 for the list of media organizations surveyed.

the wireman, he'd give him a headline phrase, a capsule, basically superficial; catchy approach to what was happening.

When he talked with the *New York Times* or other influential daily journal, he'd slip over into another area which had the profundities of it all and what it all meant.

When he'd talk to the news magazines, they'd not only get the profundities; [Dirksen] would avoid the catchy phrases. He had a reporter's eye. When he described a conversation with the President, he'd note that the President belches. He'd give the colorful little descriptive vignette that would let you see the scene yourself.

Television and radio are a different proposition. Radio, in particular, has a lot of reporters scrounging around the Hill with a little box they stick in the front of the faces of congressmen and senators. They are essentially dealing with talking news. Somebody said it. If the building fell down, the wire services would tend not to say the building fell down, they would say, "The *police said* the building fell down." The *New York Times* and the like are much more direct. Television's interest is variety. It's got part of the show biz with the interest in the catchy phrase. But [they] also [have] men like Roger Mudd who get an interpretative in-depth approach. They have the worst job of us all. They must tell their story in a couple seconds and that inhibits them.

General News Services. Perhaps the most important of the media organizations are the general news or wire services—the Associated Press, United Press International and their radio services.

"Although each year the Washington press corps grows larger as more individual newspapers respond to the increasing scope and complexity of government news," Jules Witcover observed, "the burden of reporting to the bulk of American readership continues to be borne by the two major wire services, the Associated Press and United Press International." [2]

Some correspondents, however, consider wire service coverage of Congress superficial:

> The wire services are superficial. Congress is like a huge machine of hand-outs, of generated news, and the wire services report this "news."
> The wire services over-simplify and miss quite a lot.

Other correspondents make similar evaluations in more positive terms:

> The wire services, which are the most widely read of all the news media, concentrate pretty much on straight factual reporting.

A wire service correspondent describes the services this way:

> The UPI and AP usually follow the same theory. I mean they are objective. Some of the others . . . have more leeway. They get more

opinion in. And I think some of them subconsciously slant their news articles to jive with the editorial policy of the newspaper.

Another veteran wire service reporter says:

> I think the wire services report more in a straight factual sort of way. But that's changed within the last ten years. More of them do interpretative kind of reporting about events in Congress, sometimes stubbing their toe. But generally they're doing a good job.

All of these evaluations point to one important fact—the general wire services serve large, general audiences and have between them as clients or members almost every daily newspaper in the nation, in addition to most radio and television newsrooms. When such a large and diverse audience must be served, it is not surprising that the news stories of congressional correspondents for the wire services are considered superficial, balanced, bland, objective, fair or otherwise general.

The important point, of course, is that both AP and UPI maintain bureaus in both the House and Senate galleries, staffed by 12 to 15 correspondents who devote most of their time to congressional matters. And these work-horse correspondents, through their bureaus, provide the daily log of congressional coverage.

These general wire services are not to be confused with daily newspaper news services, such as the *Washington Post-Los Angeles Times* News Service and the *New York Times* News Service. These services are growing and their more in-depth reporting is being used by more daily newspaper clients each year. They wholesale news. But these services are not burdened with the requirement of providing the daily minimum diet of congressional news to the nation. They draw mostly on the correspondents of the Washington bureaus of the newspapers with whom they are identified, which are national daily newspapers.

Daily Newspapers. The news media organizations in this variety include three major subvarieties—Washington bureaus for major metropolitan or national daily newspapers, Washington bureaus or services for newspaper groups or chains, and large and small Washington stringer bureaus which serve from one to many unrelated newspapers.

The metropolitan or national daily newspapers include the *national prestige press*, the daily newspapers which most officialdom reads in Washington and which most Washington correspondents use in their work. Not to be overlooked is the *regional prestige press* which public affairs opinion leaders and politicians in the nation's major regions consult in their work, or which, at least, have large circulations in major cities and are supporting Washington bureaus.

The metropolitan or national variety includes the Washington bureaus of such newspapers as the *Baltimore Sun, Boston Globe, Chicago Daily News, Sun-Times* and *Tribune, Christian Science Monitor, Des*

Moines Register and *Tribune, Los Angeles Times, New York Daily News, New York Times, St. Louis Post-Dispatch,* the *Wall Street Journal.*

Newspaper groups or chains include the growing multi-newspaper organizations—such as the Copley News Service, Gannett News Service, Hearst Newspapers & Hearst Headline Service, Knight Newspapers, Mc-Clatchy Newspapers of California, Newhouse News Service, Ridder Publications, Scripps Howard Newspaper Alliance, Thomson Newspapers, Inc.

From one to many unrelated newspapers include the larger bureaus, such as Donrey Washington News Bureau, Griffin-Larrabee News Bureau, Landmark Communications, Ohio-Washington News Bureau, Tufty News Bureau and numerous one, two, three, four-man or husband-wife stringer bureaus.

Ben H. Bagdikian has characterized correspondents from stringer bureaus as the "diggers and toilers." These correspondents serve a number of unrelated newspapers on a part-time basis. They report not the "deep currents of history, intricate social forces, portentous economic trends, and Byzantine world politics," Bagdikian said. Instead, they tell of "dredging obscure creeks in Florida, of Federal contracts for nuts and bolts in Connecticut, of slums cleared in Birmingham at central-government expense, and the prospects for higher tariffs on Hong Kong shirts." [3]

Two major correspondents for large metropolitan newspapers compared their roles with those of the diggers and toilers this way:

> Many newspapers 'localize' Capitol Hill news—but that [news] is usually poor, since only one correspondent must do it alone. The *N.Y. Times, Washington Post, Wall Street Journal,* Chicago papers and *Boston Globe* do in-depth, detailed reporting . . . Specialized publications usually advocate some interest.
>
> Smaller papers are more interested in parochial news. We [large daily bureau correspondents] don't really do much of that. If they, hometown members of Congress, do something newsworthy, yes. But we don't go out of our way to cover them. I probably use about 15% of their handouts, then I try to do some analytical pieces on their performance in Congress.

The daily newspaper varieties have two advantages over the broadcast varieties and the general news services—time and space.

As one veteran correspondent of a major Midwest newspaper said:

> Newspaper correspondents can be more selective and they can do more interpretative pieces than TV or the wire services. The *Wall Street Journal* and the *New York Times* are analyzing congressional actions and doing a very good job.

A fulltime congressional correspondent for a major network was even more specific about the advantages of metropolitan and national newspapers:

The A.M.'s (the morning newspapers) strike the best compromise. The best of them, like the [Washington] Post, [N.Y.] Times have reporters assigned to cover Congress. These reporters have a little extra time. They don't have to rush to the telephone with a breaking story. They can take time to gather all the facts, to put them into perspective and throw in a little interpretation. I would say the Washington Post is doing the best job of covering Congress. Along with the full time people covering the Hill, they also have those assigned to the State Department and the Pentagon, etc. Part of the reason for such a good job is that the reporters have time to sit and think before they write.

The first questionnaire of the survey revealed that the newspaper varieties have about the same percentage of congressional Most Timers. In the questionnaire tabulations the *daily newspaper* variety includes the large national and group dailies and the *other press* category includes the unrelated newspaper (stringer) bureaus—the diggers and toilers. The *daily newspaper* variety have 36% congressional Most Timers and the *other press* have 38% (Table 3).

Yet, there is a significant difference in the types of news they write about. In the *daily newspaper* group, 38% say they spend at least 20% of their time "localizing" their reporting—that is, reporting local or regional angles to the news. And 27% say they spend most of their time (60%-100%) localizing. In contrast, 61% of the *other press* variety say they spend at least 20% of their time localizing. Of these, 39% say they localize most of their time (60%-100%) (Table 11).

While about equal percentages of the two subvarieties—*daily newspaper* and *other press*—say they spend some time reporting national news, only 22% of the *other press* say they spend most of their time (60%-100%) in contrast to 37% of the *daily newspaper* group (Table 12).

Most newspaper correspondents seem to divide their time equally between the House and Senate. However, there is a significant Senate bias in the percentage of Most Timers. Between 16 and 19% of the newspaper correspondents are House Most Timers, while between 28 and 30% are Senate Most Timers (Tables 4 and 5).

Although only a few newspaper correspondents spend either Half or Most Time in the House and Senate galleries, those who do spend it in the Senate side (Tables 6 and 7). There is only one% Half Timers and no Most Timers newspaper correspondents in the House while there are about 10% Most Timers in the Senate gallery (Tables 6 and 7).

The daily newspaper correspondents seem to have more time to cover Congress than the other press correspondents. According to the time-spent questionnaire, 52% *daily newspaper* correspondents indicate they spend no congressional coverage time in their organizations' offices. Yet, only 15% are office Half or Most Timers. Of the *other press*, which includes the diggers and toilers, only 29% can afford the luxury of not having to spend congressional coverage time in their organizations' offices and 46% are Half or Most Timers in their offices (Table 8).

The *daily newspaper* correspondents also seem to have more time to attend congressional hearings—32% are Half or Most Timers in that category. The *other press* correspondents have only 18% in that category (Table 10).

A consistent number—about 70%—of all the newspaper correspondents spend some time in the House and Senate galleries (Tables 6 and 7).

This seems to indicate that, while few newspaper correspondents cover Congress from the press galleries, the gallery offices are used as important "check points" for telephone messages, press releases, distribution of reports and other information, and membership matters such as voting.

Special Interest Newspapers. In addition to the wire service and daily newspaper organizations, there are special interest newspapers with correspondents who spend some time on Capitol Hill. These include such publications a *American Banker, Baptist Press, Fairchild Publications, Oil Daily* and *Traffic World*. Correspondents from this variety, who represent five % of the responses to the final questionnaire, have much in common with most of the periodical correspondents.

Periodicals. While most of the newspaper correspondents work for general circulation publications, most of the periodical correspondents work for special interest publications such as *Advertising Age, Federal-State Reports, Electrical Wholesaling, Telephony, U.S. Medicine,* and *Western Stamp Collector.*

These are the ultra-specialists of the media organizations. They are dabblers on Capitol Hill—the Some and Short Timers who are seeking specialized information for specialized audiences. Periodicals have the lowest percentages of congressional Most Timers (8%) and the highest percentage of Some Timers (45%). This contrasts with the all-media percentages of 34 and 29%, respectively (Table 3).

Periodical correspondents indicate that only 21% are Most Timers in reporting national news and only 13% more are Some, Short or Half Timers. Since so few indicate they report local news, the assumption can be made that neither local nor national news fits the category of specialized information written for specialized audiences. This should account for the large percentage of No Timers among periodical correspondents for the local (92%) and national news (66%) question (Tables 11 and 12).

This assumption is reenforced by the lead periodicals have over all other media organization varieties in the time spent in congressional hearings—58% Half and Most Timers, compared to the all-media total of 28%. It is at committee hearings, of course, that the greatest amount of detail and specialized information, the foodstuff of the specialized periodicals, is generated (Table 10).

The correspondent of one specialized periodical expressed it this way:

> Virtually all our coverage of congressional events affecting technology policy and programs is through appropriate committees, their staffs and membership.

In the periodical category, there are two specialized publications important to this study—*Congressional Quarterly* and the *National Journal*. Results of the final questionnaire indicate that 45% of the correspondents rely somewhat or quite a bit on one or both of these publications for story ideas and 56% rely somewhat or quite a bit on one or both for information in their work. Only 15% of the correspondents in the survey said they never used either publication for information (Tables 27 and 28).

After the specialists have been considered among the periodical correspondents, the few, but very important, news weekly periodical correspondents should not be overlooked. These correspondents probably are the small percentage of Most Timer and Half Timer periodical correspondents who cover Congress (8% and 26%, respectively) (Table 3), who devote time in the House gallery (5%) (Table 6), in the Senate gallery (8%) (Table 7), and elsewhere in the Capitol or Senate or House office buildings (5% and 34%, respectively) (Table 9), and are the few periodical correspondents who report national news (21% and 5%) (Table 12).

It is to the news weekly periodicals that this correspondent for a major Washington daily newspaper was referring in this typical comment:

> The periodicals have a different function. Their main purpose is to take a week's events and put them into perspective—the meaning of the week's events. [They] should do this better than the daily newspaper, which grabs one undigested day and reports. Sometimes the papers try this with their Sunday editions. It may be significant that the [N.Y.] *Times* has stopped this, now just runs a couple of pages in the feature section.

Broadcasters. In broadcasting, there are three categories—*networks*, *broadcast groups* and *other broadcast*. The *networks*, of course, include the three major networks, the American Broadcasting Company, the Columbia Broadcasting System and the National Broadcasting Company, in addition to others such as the Mutual Broadcasting System and National Public Radio.

The second variety includes such *broadcast groups* as the Bonneville International Corporation, Cox Broadcasting Corporation, Metromedia and Radio News Bureau.

The *other broadcast* variety includes individual broadcasting stations represented by correspondents in Washington, such as the Jack Williams Washington News Service, Susquehanna Broadcasting Company, WBNS-TV, (Columbus, Ohio), and some of the Washington-area broadcast stations—the diggers and the toilers of the broadcast media correspondents.

The *broadcast groups* variety has the largest proportion of congressional Most Timers of any other category—71%, compared to the all-media average of 34%. The second largest percentage of congressional Most Timers is *other broadcast*—40%. The *broadcast networks* have 36% Most Timers (Table 3).

The relatively high percentages of Most Timers among the broadcasters reflect, to some degree, the relative lack of special information interests among broadcasters compared to the print media. There are few, if any, oil, financial, aviation, farm or other broadcast outlets compared to the print media newsletter. The large number of special interest newspapers and periodicals tends to decrease the percentages of print media Most Timers.

The *broadcast groups* variety has the highest proportions of Most Timers in reporting the local or regional angles in the news—59% (Table 11). The *network* variety correspondents, as might be expected, have the highest proportion of Most Timers in reporting the national news from Congress—82% (Table 12).

There are some strong House-Senate biases among the broadcast correspondents which distinguish them among themselves and from the print media. The *broadcast groups* correspondents, for instance, constitute the largest percentage (41%) of House of Representatives Most Timers, in contrast to the *broadcast network* correspondents (9%) and *other broadcast* correspondents (27%) (Table 4).

On the Senate side, the coin is reversed. The *broadcast network* correspondents indicate their preference for the Senate with 64% Most Timers, 36% Half Timers and no Short or Some Timers. The *broadcast groups* correspondents have 24% Senate Most Timers and 41% Half Timers. The *other broadcast* correspondents hold a similar proportion (27% and 40%) (Table 5).

The broadcast correspondents spend more time in the galleries than the print correspondents. The *broadcast network* correspondents have 18% Most Timers and 18% Half Timers in both the House and Senate galleries. The *broadcast groups* correspondents reflect both their preference for the House side and the galleries with 24% Most Timers and 12% Half Timers in the House Gallery. The *other broadcast* correspondents average 20% combined Half and Most Timers in both house galleries. These percentages contrast sharply with the all-media average of 4% Half Timers and 3% Most Timers in the House gallery and 7% Half Timers and 6% Most Timers in the Senate gallery (Tables 6 and 7).

These differences are determined, of course, by the nature of the media. The broadcast media require more extensive equipment and facilities. There are broadcast studios in the House and Senate galleries where the correspondents spend much of their time, while the print media—the "scribblers" as they are referred to by some broadcasters—are more mobile with only their pencil and pad and access to a telephone or typewriter as gear.

The role of the broadcast media in covering Congress elicits strong views from correspondents:

> Electronic media have to spotlight the issue of the day—they are oriented to the dramatic. Rarely is there more than one story a day on any of the networks that deals with Congress.—*Editor of a major periodical.*

> Television reporting is generally superficial, you have exceptions like Paul Duke and Roger Mudd, but none of them . . . do in-depth coverage.—*Congressional correspondent for a major West Coast metropolitan daily newspaper.*

> TV is always looking for a "hot shot" incident. They fell for Sam Ervin's gimmick to publicize his hearings on Army spying. Ervin held a family Bible in one hand, and a small cube on the other, and said the computerization of vast amounts of information is possible. The point of the hearings was missed.—*Congressional correspondent for a major Midwest metropolitan daily newspaper.*

> The structure of TV restricts it. But TV can sponsor debate between experts and politicians more interestingly than newspapers. TV and the press supplement one another.—*Congressional correspondent for a major mid-Atlantic metropolitan daily newspaper.*

> Take the tax reform bill of '69, for example. The radio-TV newsmen did not cover any substance of the bill. They seemed to assume that their audience didn't care. The electronic media stay away from technical matters and swarm around the story of the week or the story of the day.—*Congressional correspondent for a major national daily newspaper.*

> TV is the most superficial medium. But what they give is all some people want.—*Congressional correspondent for a major Northeast metropolitan daily newspaper.*

> Print guys in congressional reporting get a break because they can go into detail, when we have to sum it up so briefly.—*Congressional correspondent for a major broadcast group.*

> Time is the big factor in all reporting; the broadcast medium, for the most part, doesn't have a lot of time, so we have to overlook the mundane stories of the week. Most national broadcasters, I think, pick the stories that would affect most people and discard the others. The regional reporters, obviously, would be looking for things that affect their audiences on a smaller scale.—*Congressional correspondent for a major broadcast group.*

> Television is more immediate, it can only hit the highlights . . . TV has the visual—they can show how the war is really being fought in Vietnam. The use of television in congressional hearings has had

the same effect . . . I'm sure, partly as a result of television being permitted in the Senate hearings and not in the House, that the country has a greater awareness of what's going on in the Senate and very little awareness of what's going on in the House. Partly as a result there is a great deal of anonymity in the House, what it does and the people in it.—*Congressional correspondent for a major Washington daily newspaper.*

Newspaper . . . parent organizations want to slant news to a particular point of view . . . Working here for 30 years I know it is a fact. The now defunct *New York Herald Tribune* and *New York Times* would cover the same story—the story would differ enormously because their viewpoints would be different.

Television—national TV—can't do that. As a consequence it does not provide the daily steady coverage of Capitol Hill. I think TV goes in fits and starts on Congress. Ten years ago we had much more coverage on Congress than we do now. Now the tendency is to have longer segments that are more exploratory. The little pieces that simply tell what happened aren't used as much any more.—*Congressional correspondent for a major national network.*

The radio and television correspondents are headline hunters. —*Correspondent for a major national daily newspaper.*

Television, by the constraints of time, does not go into Congress in any depth.—*Correspondent for a major East Coast daily newspaper.*

Broadcasters briefly summarize the top stories of the day. That's all.—*Congressional correspondent for a national daily newspaper.*

I have five stations that are all news and they will use anything that they can get, really.—*Congressional correspondent for a small broadcast group.*

Radio and TV coverage of Congressional affairs is viewed pretty much as to what makes a good show. The ultimate end of the broadcast medium is to entertain and only incidentally to instruct. I've been on "Meet the Press" many times. I think in [periodicals] it is just the other way around. So if on a given day there's been a very serious debate in the Senate on foreign policy, and at the same time some Senator is discovered to have been going in for hair transplants to cover his baldness, you'll notice a difference of approach. TV will run an interview with that Senator and focus the cameras on his bald head. We won't pursue this story, but it will be only a picture with a caption or in the newsmaker section. But our big story will be on that foreign policy debate. For that reason, television does not treat the news in depth, unless it is for their specials. If they did, publications like [the one I work for], the *New York Times*, the *Wall Street Journal* would soon go out of business.—*Congressional correspondent for a major weekly periodical.*

Combining the time and media varieties reenforces known differences among various correspondents within the media varieties—between the news weekly and the newsletter correspondents in the periodical variety, between the general daily newspaper and the specialized daily or weekly newspapers in the newspaper variety, and between the network and broadcast group varieties. These figures also tend to dramatize some fundamental differences between the print and broadcast media—the broadcasters generally do not seek specialized information and many print correspondents do because they represent special interest groups.

NOTES

[1] See Chapter 2, "Accommodation and Regulation of the Corps."
[2] Jules Witcover, "Washington: The Workhorse Wire Services," *Columbia Journalism Review*, Summer, 1969, p. 9.
[3] Ben H. Bagdikian, "Diggers and Toilers," *Columbia Journalism Review*, Summer, 1963, pp. 36-38.

THE CORRESPONDENTS DESCRIBE THEIR WORK

By Robert O. Blanchard

Are the congressional correspondents part of the "tiny and closed fraternity of privileged men, elected by no one, and enjoying a monopoly sanctioned and licensed by the government," who "to a man live and work in the geographical and intellectual confines of Washington, D.C." and who "bask in their own provincialism" as former Vice President Spiro Agnew has characterized the national news correspondents?

Do the congressional correspondents fit the characterization of the national correspondents described by former White House aide, Daniel P. Moynihan, who said that:

—Journalism is becoming more and more dominated by a liberal Eastern Ivy League elite, strongly "influenced by attitudes generally hostile to American society";
—The Washington press corps relies heavily on information leaks which are often "antagonistic to presidential interests";
—The news profession lacks a tradition of self-criticism and self-correction.

Although these critics are vague about whom they mean by "the press," "journalism," "the press corps" and other terms, they usually are referring to the national correspondents and their coverage of the executive branch. This study, which is limited to the congressional correspondents, cannot respond entirely to these criticisms. But congressional correspondents have been subject to some of them.*

* See attacks on congressional correspondents reprinted in *Seminar* magazine, Number 22, December, 1971.

Congressional correspondents have been singled out for special characterization. Russell Baker, for instance, wrote in *An American in Washington* (Knopf, 1961):

> The Capitol reporter eschews the raucous spirit of the White House and affects the hooded expression of the man privy to many important deals. Like the politicians he covers, he tends to garrulity, coarse jokes and bourbon and learns to hate reform.*

These and other political and literary profiles of correspondents are impressionistic stereotypes at best. There are truths in them, but the accuracy of the pictures drawn is dubious. The results of this study, for instance, do not support the notion that the congressional correspondents hate reform. And, judging from their cooperative responses to two questionnaires and from long interviews with 31 fulltime congressional correspondents, they do not affect the "hooded expression of the man privy to many important deals."

Even if birthplace were reliable evidence that one is "Eastern" or "Western," there is too much diversity among the correspondents' home states to generalize (Table 13). Since a third of those with college degrees indicated they were undergraduate journalism majors, and since no Ivy League schools offer undergraduate journalism degrees, it might be assumed they are not part of the Ivy League elite (Table 16).

However, the congressional correspondent corps appears to be liberal. In response to a question asking for their political affiliations, 43% of correspondents identified themselves as "liberal" and another 14% as Democrat (Table 20).

This and other statistical materials on the backgrounds of the correspondents summarized below shed some light on the accuracy of various political and literary characterizations of the congressional press corps. Equally important are their own descriptions of work duties and habits, their professional attitudes and relations with sources, some of which also are summarized in this study.

However, it is not enough merely to consider the quantitative recording of birthplaces, incomes, political leanings, education, attitudes and similar information. There are cultural and social aspects to consider. There are, for example, correspondents who are more influential than others—influential in the importance and numbers of people in their audience *and* influential among fellow correspondents. And there are, for instance, various professional habits and customs among journalists generally and the Washington correspondents and congressional correspondents specifically which govern much of their behavior and decisions on what issues and officials to "cover."

Some of these factors are suggested in this study and are illustrated with quotations from correspondents interviewed. The material in this

* Quoted in *Columbia Journalism Review*, Spring, 1962, p. 10.

study, however, will neither silence nor vindicate either the critics or the correspondents. It can only add fuel to the debates and throw some additional light on the news media and their relations with Congress.

Backgrounds

The congressional correspondents' average age is 39 to 40 (Table 14). They are nearly all college graduates (Table 15), and most of them were either journalism or English majors in college (Table 16). About 27% hold Master's degrees, most of which are in journalism (Table 17).

Responding to a question asking how helpful their journalism schooling was in their early careers, 27% said "big help," 21% said "not much help," 4% said "no help" and 3% didn't know.

The relative youth of the correspondents is reflected in their years of experience in Washington (Table 18). Sixty-nine per cent, for instance, have had no more than 10 years experience in the nation's capital, nearly half less than 6 years (Table 18). An even higher percentage of correspondents have had less than 6 years covering Congress to the extent they do now—61%. Seventy-four per cent have been covering Congress no more than 10 years (Table 19).

In light of their relative youth and Washington and congressional experience, the correspondents are well-paid with a median annual income of about $20,000 (Table 21). However, many correspondents apparently work long hours for this income. While 67% of the correspondents work from 35-49 hours a week, 29% work "50 or more" hours a week.

Job Descriptions

Most of the correspondents surveyed (59%) are employed by daily newspapers, 17% with wire or news services, 6% broadcast groups, 5% special interest newspapers or periodicals, 4% national networks, 3% general interest periodicals and 1% news weeklies (Table 22).

Most of the correspondents (59%) write specialized news—43% routine news. Many correspondents do both, of course, in addition to writing a column (31%) and writing magazine articles (10%). Of the correspondents surveyed, 27% are bureau chiefs (many of whom also write and edit news) and 3% are newscasters (Table 23).

Reliance on Other Media

"Every morning," one congressional correspondent interviewed in this study said, "a group of guys comes together and decides what *the* story of the day is. The *New York Times, Washington Post, Washington Star-News, Baltimore Sun, Los Angeles Times* and *Boston Globe* lead the pack. [The others follow because] reporters are afraid of being embarrassed in front of their bosses."

Previous studies of Washington correspondents, particularly those of

Roston, Rivers and Cohen,* have found various degrees of "follow-the-leader" behavior among the correspondents. At minimum, correspondents are like other people: they read a newspaper or two a day and are exposed to other media of communication. In most cases they or their editors look for an "agenda"—a story or stories to follow each day.

In this study correspondents were asked which of the various media they relied on most often in their work. The responses indicate that the *Washington Post* is relied on by 62% of the correspondents, *Newsweek* by 27%, the *New York Times* by 23%, *Congressional Quarterly* by 20%, CBS Evening News by 17% and *Time* magazine by 12% (Tables 24, 25, and 26).

How much influence do these relied-upon media have on the congressional correspondents?

Their influence seems diminished when compared to other sources used by the correspondents. In response to questions asking what sources they rely upon for ideas, correspondents rated "newspapers and magazines other than your own" and "radio-television news broadcasts other than your own" lower than colleagues, editors, the *Congressional Record*, staffs of members of Congress, members of Congress and government-printed materials (Table 27).

Some correspondents suggest the power of the news media they expose themselves to by indicating their reliance on "the news of the day" which, to a large degree, is determined by the newspaper on their front steps in the morning—the *Washington Post* and, in some cases, the *New York Times*. These newspapers are also read by their editors, peers and news sources.

Q. In reporting Congress, what are your chief sources of ideas for stories (superiors, other reporters, news sources, etc.)?

Broadcast group correspondent—Well, I read four major newspapers every morning. I read all the national magazines. I read both wires . . .

Broadcast group correspondent—I'm the congressional correspondent, so I act as assignment editor and reporter. I make the decision based on what's happening on a given day.

Broadcast group correspondent—Well, really, it's the stories of the day, what breaks that day you work on.

Broadcast group correspondent—I don't have much opportunity to be creative up here. It's what is happening that day, what's happening that hour. I read four papers daily. I don't read weekly news magazines . . . reading *Time* or *Newsweek* is like having a bull session with other reporters. You really don't learn anything new . . .

* See Bibliography.

A metropolitan daily correspondent—My chief sources are readings. The *Washington Post*, in the editorial pages as well as in the news pages, is a good source. Also, I read the weekly news magazines to see what is gaining interest.

A metropolitan daily newspaper correspondent—The major source is the flow of news itself—what the big events of the day happen to be.

A network correspondent—Generally speaking, there is no such thing as an idea for a story. There is a story or there isn't one. Something happened or it didn't. Something was planned or it wasn't. . . . It is just something that happened and you are reporting something that goes on.

A Washington radio station congressional correspondent—First of all, there's what is happening on the floor. There are in the course of a day only three or four committee hearings that are of really significant news value. It's usually rather obvious what the stories are going to be on one day . . .

A metropolitan daily newspaper correspondent—The flow of news is really the chief source. I do not spend a lot of time with editors talking about stories. The stories evolve out of events that raise questions within my own mind.

A metropolitan newspaper correspondent—Essentially, it is the legislation before Congress . . .

Where do the relied upon media get *their* ideas? Correspondents from the major wire services, *Washington Post, New York Times, Time, Newsweek, Wall Street Journal*, ABC, CBS and others answered the "source of ideas" question this way:

Most congressional news presents itself. You have a daily grind of hearings, legislation and drafting of bills. Beyond that I get some (very few) suggestions from my bosses. And a few ideas come from editors who usually want regional stories . . . Most of our ideas we generate ourselves . . .

A good deal of stories are automatic. You don't have to depend on ideas. Bills come out of committee. Hearings are held. Bills are going to the Rules [Committee] where there may be a tug of war whether they go to the floor or are held back. Bill gets on the floor, then you have the Republican-Democratic, Dixiecrat, etc., efforts to hold it back. Some ideas come from editors. Quite often if you have been at a job too long you get a little blase; maybe every once in a while it is a good idea to have someone on the outside, an editor, nudge you a little. A lot of story ideas are a process of getting to know people, getting to know the House as an institution, and gradually you find ideas come to you by divine revelation. People call you, members of Congress, their staffs. Staffs of congressmen have as their job to build up their guy.

There are two stories, two type of stories—spot news and feature. My beat covers six committees, and every morning I check the list of hearings in the *Washington Post*, then confer with my editor about which to cover, which are necessary. We do regard ourselves as a journal of record in certain areas, such as reform. Feature ideas I get from all kinds of magazines, newspapers. Also, I get ideas at cocktail parties and from congressional staff members.

We have an assignment desk that churns up ideas, riding the news tickers in the New York office. The executive producer in the New York office is a very powerful fellow. His slightest whim will be converted into action in the form of assigning a correspondent and a camera crew. But on a beat like the Hill where I am on the scene and the producer is not, it is pretty much up to me to follow the breaking news and develop a story that is usually already in the news. I start the day by backgrounding myself on the big stories of the day. That involves reading the [*Washington*] *Post*, the [*New York*] *Times*, the *Wall Street Journal* and the ticker [UPI and AP wires] and if it's a hot [news] day, watching one of the morning news shows. I think of ways that I can explore whatever the big story is. At that point, it's a combination of my own ideas, and dovetailing them with what the producers are thinking about, and perhaps selling a story idea I have to the producer. We reporters, on my beat, talk with each other, but the Hill is considerably less incestuous in the passing around of stories than the other beats, such as the White House and the State Department, because there is so much more fertile ground up here. You don't have to write the same story that the other fellow does.

The first source is the reporter himself. I suppose equally important would be the congressional staff. The Senators are not immediately and instantly available to you. I usually go to the congressional staff, the chief counsel of the committee, or of the Senate Democratic policy lawyers, or a Senator's administrative assistant who will tell you things that are ideas. You will call over and just check on this and that and just begin to talk. Of course, the [network] management has ideas. I don't really work for [the network] itself, but for the [news show] and I respond to that. There's an awful lot of gang reporting on Capitol Hill.

Most ideas are my own. On [my publication], we don't cover a story the way the daily journals do; we have to have somewhat of a larger perspective. We look for some events, some things that happen, positions being taken by different people; we try to relate them, then draw theses out of them and then move on the story in these terms. There are a certain number of good stories just presented to you. It's very important to keep talking to everybody up there. There are a good number of senators and congressmen who will say, "I think you would be interested in this" and will tell you something that is happening. It may have nothing to do with the story . . .

I go to the congressional leaders, aides to the congressional leaders, or to the key senators or House members who are involved. Some of the best informed human beings are the aides . . . I read the *Congressional Record* every day. I don't turn to fellow newsmen for stories.

Basically, it's what is happening today or what's important. The debate on the war is there; or one person may have surfaced in the House. We may not report on him daily, but suddenly you realize there is a story there, for good or evil, an in-depth story that needs to be done. Of course, press releases help, not that you sit down and rewrite a press release; but you find out what is going on. Calls from congressmen's press assistants might give you a tip that you want to pursue, not that you follow the line that the representative has in mind. Listening to other reporters also helps you. It's a combination of many things, but you have to rely primarily on your intuition of what is important.

It's sort of a combination. Very little from my superiors. I have pretty free reign. The ideas come more from self-evident developments of the day, or the various ideas that are cast up as you listen to debate or go around talking with people.

Mainly news sources. After you've been around as many years as some of us have, you get all kinds of ideas without anybody telling you. You do the same things you did years ago, but times have changed since then. This is not a handout operation. Mainly you got to go out and get the information yourself. We go to members [of Congress] or staff people. There's all kinds of tips around. One of the best stories we had last week, we got through a tip from a guy who works in the basement of the Rayburn Building. We get a lot out of the *Congressional Record*, where they put everything.

Reliance on Other Sources

Most correspondents, especially the reporters for single large media organizations who can devote most of their time on the Hill, rely on a variety of sources for their information. Clearly, however, the staff members of Congress lead the list of sources.

Staff members of Senators are relied on "quite a bit" by 64% of the correspondents; House staff members by 60%. Nearly a third more correspondents rely on the staffs "somewhat" (Table 28).

Congressional correspondents for relied-upon news media enjoy relatively greater access to members of Congress. However, they too rely on staff members and other sources for information.

Q. When you prepare a story about an event in Congress, what types of sources do you normally turn to first for information (for example, newspaper files, press assistants, fellow newsmen, friends, etc.)?

On the House side there are 435 members who each represent a district of about one-half million people and yet they have no access to statewide or national press and most are eager to talk to the paper. House has a roll call—so you get 335 showing up on even on a bad day—so they're likely to be here. Also the Speaker's Lobby is open to the press—so it would be ridiculous to go any place else. Fellow newsmen are useful for finding out what happened in a place that you can't be. But I do not think any reporter should rely on any reporter for the facts they put in a story.

Most of my stories of such a current nature come from the official record of the event itself, or not even that, but from my observations of the proceedings themselves. One of the primary sources that I do use when I'm writing about issues is *Congressional Quarterly*. In other words, if I pick up a bill that comes over from the House, or after a trip from the city, I will use *Congressional Quarterly* as a source. I don't use newspaper clippings to any great detail, although I do do a lot of clipping for the stories I do and for informational purposes. I'm writing on deadline for a good part of the time and don't have time to use clips. I use press secretaries routinely, but if you ask me how important that is to my work, I would say not too important. Fellow newsmen tend to be an important source for information for stories in the Senate, the reason being that on any given day there are 20 or 30 events happening. Of those, two or three are significant enough to demand my attention. On really busy days there are 50 random events of which 10 or 20 require my attention. The way that I find out about these frequently is from other newsmen. I ask another guy, "What was the thrust of the hearing? Was it significant?" My office is in the gallery. I just ask reporters there routinely what happened when they come back from an assignment.

I don't know any press assistants. I like to deal with the participants themselves, the senators, the congressmen, the committeemen, the leadership. There are some staff people whom I do rely on, but very few. I don't like to deal with press secretaries because they basically are in the wrong line of work. They are in the publicity business for their own people. I want the information from the guy himself, in his own words and his own way. You don't want a curtain between you and the actor. However, there are occasions when an aide might be the key man to inform you what happened. An example some years ago, in 1966, there was a meeting of the Republican Leadership Conference at the Capitol—on August 23rd or 24th.

Richard Nixon was then a private citizen who had been out in Vietnam and Saigon. He'd said, among other things, that President Johnson should increase the military forces to 750,000 men. At that time, Senator Morton from Kentucky (who had been a supporter of the war) had shifted his own position on the war. A poll of his state indicated that Kentuckians—who are normally very militant on the war—had changed on the war. He had begun to assess the situation politically in terms of the 1968 election. He was absolutely sure that the Republican party should shift positions on the war and become the peace party. He had even figured out a way to do this. Chuck Percy had proposed an all-Asian peace conference. Morton wanted the Republican Party to adopt this as a way to resolve the war in Vietnam. Nixon's public statements flew in the face of this. When Nixon arrived in Washington, the conference was to start with lunch. He arranged to see Nixon privately in his office at 11:00 a.m. He told Nixon the facts of life—that this was not a Republican War, this was Lyndon Johnson's war and please cut out, right now, giving advice to Johnson on how to run the war. Later that afternoon, the Republican Leadership Conference came out for a peace plan. Nixon was very much for it; he'd seen the light. Now it was very difficult to find what Morton and Nixon said to each other. They met alone in a room—with one small exception; there was a staff member who had a very sharp mind and good photographic memory. He was very, very useful at that point. That's where I got the information for the story.

Our own newspaper files. And I keep my own files, my black sheets [carbon copies of stories]. If there is a bill on the floor, I try to carefully read a report that accompanies the bill. If it's on the House side, I frequently will go down to the Speaker's Lobby and talk with some of the people involved with the bill. If it's in the Senate, I will call them into the President's Room. Good files are very important. Suppose it's something that has to do with HEW—you have to keep your contacts there, so you know who to call up there.

Whatever written documents you have. In a way, these are more profound than people realize. What a guy wants to get on a written record determines how he ultimately behaves. Then I go to people whose business it is to know about the subject. This may be senators, aides, staff, White House lobbyists, business organizations— just anyone who has some interest in the subject.

If the House is debating a bill, I'm sitting in the gallery listening to the debate and getting the vote, I can write a story without relying on much of anything, except the history of the bill. I make quite considerable use of our library. [My bureau] has a very good library that goes back to the time the paper was founded, the files of the *New York Times*, and a very large selection of source books of all kinds— I may want to look in *Who's Who* to see what somebody has written.

Since the story must deal with the House, I would get hold of the House members who know the most, would talk with staff people (there is a pretty high professional level of the staff). The Democratic Study Group, a group of Democratic liberals, provides research. It has also become very deeply involved in reform procedures. There I would see the staff director of the Group. There's one guy around here who's the Speaker's sort-of general brain whose job is to try to keep on the big picture, what progress is being made, what amendments can be roadblocks. Another person is Frank Eleazer with UPI. He can usually gauge pretty well what the House is going to do in a given situation. Really one of the big jobs here is to try to figure out how it is likely to go on any one issue.

Newspaper files are my first source of information. Secondary are members of committee staffs, especially those that have proven reliable in the past. I *never* talk to fellow reporters about stories in progress.

I cover a beat, so my own past reporting is usually my primary source. Next comes the people involved in the event.

For covering the House, generally turn to the members. When it's lots of complicated pieces of legislation you turn to the committee staffs. For instance, the Ways and Means committee: the tax laws are so complex that if you didn't have experts who stay year after year through changes of chairman and changes of administration, you'd be hard pressed because those are the guys who really know what's in the law, what's in the bill. However, members, particularly in the House, are the principal source of information on a story. Files, to some extent. We don't have a morgue like they do down at the *Washington Post*. We have certain basic files to refer to. But we suffer from a lack of files. The various reference works that are available to members of Congress, like the *Digest of Bills*, the *Daily Record*, the *Congressional Record*, the documents they have around here. The committee has to file a report and an analysis on every bill that comes out. On most issues of any consequence there are special interest groups that can give you a point of view, help you find out things. For instance, Common Cause is interested in some issues. They have certain viewpoints, you may not accept their viewpoint, but they may be able to point out things that you might not have noticed otherwise. The Democratic Study Group does analyses of all the bills, really the best quick reference that's available. They generally give us some clues as to who's for it and against, and some clues of places you can look.

It depends on who has the information. If it is the type of thing a senator may have, you go directly to him. Sometimes his assistants will be as well informed or better on any particular subject than the senator himself. Sometimes it will be the Parliamentarian of the Senate himself if you want to know, for example, where a particular amendment can be brought up under a given set of circumstances. The key factor up here, there are 100 senators and then there are all kinds of other officials, and then there are staff members and committee members; you have to know where to go to find out what you want.

It would depend on the story. If it involved a couple of senators, you know pretty well ahead of time how accessible that senator is going to be. You know if he trusts you. Generally, I would go to the senator. In many instances, you know the senator won't tell you the truth or won't be very informative, you talk to his administrative assistant or you talk to some of the senators in his delegation, particularly when one is a Democrat and the other is a Republican. When you try to cover Congress nationally, it's very difficult to keep up with the internal politics. Since we don't get all the hometown papers up here, it takes some time to prepare yourself, to know what the political background is.

You go to source. I use the *Congressional Record*—I read it pretty closely every morning—I read the appendix.

Sources are critical on the Hill, especially when the big story peaks. It's at this point that good and honest sources are the most critical to me. I have a dozen people on the Hill that I can trust in the crunch. They can trust me and they won't try to use me at critical moments. This includes a few members of the Senate and key staffers who may talk more candidly than their bosses would. Key staffers—some are press assistants, administrative assistants and some just like to play the head counting game. Newspaper files and fellow newsmen are more for backgrounding.

I've made a practice of cultivating congressional aides because they're much more abreast of what's going on than the senators themselves. The one problem with the aides is that they are very reluctant to speak for attribution. You have to find out which aides are knowledgeable—it takes time.

Audience Perception

Interplaying with the ideas and information from sources are the correspondents' own judgments as to what leads to follow and what information to prepare for distribution.

It already has been suggested that the correspondents place great value on the "importance of the subject" in determining what issues and officials to cover. Yet, while 73% are influenced "quite a bit" by the "importance of the subject," 63% are equally attracted to "new and unusual aspects of the subject" 44% by "local angles of the subject" and 41% by audiences' "interests" (Table 29).

How the correspondents view their audiences is influenced to a large degree by the news organizations they represent, as reflected in representative responses to the question:

Q. When you prepare your copy, what type of audience do you normally have in mind?

A *wire service correspondent*—The general public. We've got so many papers and radio stations, we can't write it for one particular group. There are Republican papers, Democratic papers, independent papers. We write it straight down the line, or otherwise we get into trouble.

A *network correspondent*—A general public is no brighter than I am. It is important out there to bear in mind that the listener or viewer is not particularly bright and you must tell the story as simply and as clearly as possible. I always think in terms of short, clear phrases that can be readily grasped by whoever is listening.

A *metropolitan daily correspondent*—We have a large academic community in [my city] and they're certainly more interested than the average reader in Washington news. At the same time, you have a readership which has so many factors competing for the time . . . the climate. There's a great responsibility to inform them. The only way you can is to attract their attention; that means good writing and imaginative use of the material you have in such a way as not to bend it or distort it.

A *metropolitan daily correspondent*—My audience is primarily that of a well-educated, intelligent group of people. And, if I write a really good story, it can get into the *Washington Star*. On those stories I keep in mind policy-makers as part of my audience.

A *national daily correspondent*—Our readers are college-educated middle-class people and we keep that in mind.

A *metropolitan daily correspondent*—I have a city audience and a state audience, not a national audience. Much of my time is spent localizing news, relating it to my audience.

A *metropolitan daily correspondent*—My audience includes people of moderate intelligence who are interested in government and concerned about public affairs.

A *network correspondent*—We write for an audience we assume knows nothing about Congress and 99 times out of 100 doesn't know anything about the legislation at hand. There's no reason why they should. They're worried about taxes and the neighbor's dog. They haven't got time to fiddle around with the involvements of Congress.

A *network correspondent*—I really don't think of it that way—when I sit down to write it, I don't think about which peer group I'm writing for, I just sit down and write it.

A wire service correspondent—I wish I could answer that. We're supposed to be writing for the average American. But we have to go through our editors and newspaper editors. If we don't get through them, then the general public never sees it. So you have to try to accommodate all three of those things . . .

A Washington daily newspaper correspondent—My wife. She is smart, but doesn't know the details. If I'm covering an obtuse subject, I try to write for that kind of audience. Sometimes I write an obtuse story because it's only going to be read by the policy-makers. But by and large I try to write so that any one person can read the story . . .

News weekly magazine correspondent—I go on the assumption that I am writing for an intelligent and perceptive audience, for policy-makers and so on . . . Every Monday morning, just as soon as the copies of [my publication] are available to us, we send by messenger to all the top policy-makers in Washington compliments of [my publication]. Every member of Congress gets a complimentary copy, We're certainly not going to feed them pablum. It is a certain gratification to us that certain important articles are read into the *Congressional Record*. This occurs with virtually every issue of the magazine.

News weekly magazine correspondent—We are writing essentially for our editors in New York who are getting information from other sources than us and from all over the world. I must confess, though, that a good bit of writing at [my publication] has been for myself. It's been the kind of material that I find fascinating and that the editors find fascinating, but it rarely shows up in print for the simple reason that there's not enough space.

Professional Roles

Guidelines established by an occupational study of the professional values of American journalists suggest that the Washington correspondents are likely to have "participant" rather than "neutral" orientations toward their jobs.*

Their high amount of education, relative youth, their community and organizational setting and current job responsibilities, suggest they are journalists who believe that their role is to take an active and, to some extent, creative part in the development of the newsworthy.

However, previous studies of public affairs reporters by Cohen and Dunn,** among others, suggest that correspondents are often torn between the two concepts, the "participant" and "neutral."

* J. W. C. Johnstone, Edward J. Slawski, and William W. Bowman, "The Professional Values of American Newsmen," *Public Opinion Quarterly*, Volume XXXVI, No. 4 (Winter 1972-73).
** See Bibliography.

The responses from the congressional correspondents suggest that they have definite "participant" leanings, but that, on the whole, they have set equally identifiable limits to the extent of their participation.

For instance, 81% of the correspondents agree that their role is "to be an interpreter for the public by putting in understandable terms what Congress is doing and why it is doing it." This is clearly a participant concept; yet, this contrasts somewhat with the neutral prescription "to be an impartial, objective transmission link between Congress and the public," with which 53% of the correspondents agree. Although 64% agree with the neutralist role "to be a neutral observer who is detached from the events and activities he/she reports," this does not necessarily conflict with some participant values.

However, two other participant prescriptions which received 64% correspondent agreement do not prescribe neutral observers, detached from events—"to be a representative of the public as a watchdog against corruption and malfeasance" and "to determine the veracity of statements made by congressmen."

Most correspondents clearly reject extremist participant prescriptions, such as

—"to give advice and counsel to congressmen and their staffs when asked to do so"
—"to report actions or statements of congressmen which correspondents know are designed for news media consumption"
—"to advocate policy by presenting ideas and suggestions during direct encounters with congressmen and their staffs"
—"to advocate policy directly in stories by presenting proposals, analyzing the merits of pending measures or making a persuasive case for correspondent's view about the proper disposition of matter" (Table 30).

Congressional correspondents from relied-upon media seem to reflect the interpreter-with-limits view:

Q. What do you believe are the most important functions of the newsman in relation to the business of Congress?

Primarily of communicating the major developments in Congress to your reader. Particularly on our paper with so much emphasis on interpretation, we have to go further than wire service explanations—we have to go into what is involved and what are the various motivations, the current debate on Case-Church amendment. Why is Senator [Robert] Byrd of West Virginia pushing this modification that would essentially nullify the Case-Church amendment?

Judging a story as to its value and then distilling it down so that I can tell the viewer what the story means in 30 to 40 seconds. Part of being able to do this meaningfully and honestly requires maintaining contacts in Congress. This means an awful lot of leg work. It takes as much time for the TV reporter to put together a 20 to 30 minute story as it does for the newspaper reporter who turns out an 800-word story. The TV reporter (me), because of the limitations of his medium, must concentrate on the big story of the day, the story that makes the front page of the *New York Times* or the *Washington Post*.

It is most important to try to interpret the effects of the legislative process while reporting them. My job is to do for the public what it cannot do for itself. I am a kind of public representative in the sense that I am expected to be a detached observer who reports without any obvious weight to any specific values what happens up here. I don't see myself as the eyes and ears of the public on Congress. I see myself as someone whose job it is to interpret honestly and to report without exclusions the significant events.

Other than reportorial work, the most difficult thing is to maintain some distance from the members so you don't report a situation as if you were a member of Congress. And your reporting takes on a certain congressional tone after you've been up here awhile. That exists in all assignments; United Nations correspondents begin to talk like diplomats, correspondents assigned to Bonn begin to look German, correspondents assigned to France begin to look like wine tasters. You become identified with your beat, and it's very seductive to be up here quite a while and then play the game and get close to certain power individuals in Congress and do an awful lot of mucking around with them. The basic responsibility is to report what is going on with some meaning about why it is going on.

I've always thought it was to understand what was going on, not simply to skim the headlines but to know what is really behind the considerations each member gives to each issue, what his own problems are at home, what his own feelings are, how much of a conscience he has, how much he has to wrestle in making up his mind. And when he does vote against his own convictions, why is it justified. Also understanding the parliamentary situation. I think the regular correspondents up here have a deep understanding of it, but the occasional correspondents often do not. Their lack of familiarity causes them to often come up with stories that are morally and philosophically wrong if they're not factually incorrect. We're all guilty of the tendency to oversimplify here . . . An example of this: at the beginning of this administration, there was a lot of criticism by the White House of congressional inactivity. I checked and found that in repeated instances the President had sent up messages recommending that certain things be done. It has become traditional courtesy as well as a matter of practical necessity that Congress then waits for the executive branch to give it details of the legislation it has in mind. I found in repeated cases the President had recommended legislation in broad terms but then had waited months sometimes to send up specific drafts of legislation or even specific outlines. The result is that even if Congress had been inclined to give the President what he wanted, it wouldn't have had anything to begin with. And if it had started on its own and drafted legislation, as it has done in a number of cases, invariably the White House would have rared up and said, "This is not what we want." That's the sort of thing I mean about knowing exactly what goes on around here. Congress could have been criticized for not having acted on the President's recommendation, or the White House could have been criticized for not having sent up detailed requests of what it wanted. I don't see myself especially as an interpreter; all I want to know is everything that I can find out.

Our most immediate obvious function is to report the legislative activity, and it takes most of our time. I personally also feel we have also a greater responsibility—my own theory is we reporters are representing the public just as much as the congressmen are in a little different way. We have to find out if there are conflicts of interest, ethical violations. The Congress is very assiduous in keeping its eye on the executive branch, but there's nobody looking at the Congress except the press.

The main function is to inform the public. Another function is to get beneath the surface and explain whatever is happening. A third function is to explain how the institution of Congress functions.

If the system of government is going to work, there must be an informed electorate. The newsman must tell the man in Iowa what his congressman is doing on a day-to-day basis.

To try to find out what's going on and why it's going on and tell the people what he's able to find out in hopes they will benefit in knowing what Congress is doing. After all, it is a very important part of government which touches the lives of everyone. Congressmen are elected by people and I suppose they will elect better or worse ones if they know what they're doing. The short answer: to provide the public information they want to have or ought to have about this elected part of Congress.

The standard news reporting. Conveying the general consensus here, the movement. Accurately and fairly simplifying those complex procedures into meaningful reports.

To report the news. The word interpretation has bad connotations—but to put some meat on the stories, to give the reader the background and the foreground if possible, and to explain it as lucidly as possible.

The obvious one—explaining the action and motivation, pressures and frustrations of Congress to the reader.

The most important thing we do generally is to tell people what's going on. Legislation and appropriations and so on. It's not the most interesting, which to me is the institutional life of Congress and how the place actually functions. To me it's more important how something was passed, the forces that were competing to get a piece of legislation through.

I'm interpreting to the American people what Congress is doing. Also through covering Congress I think I'm getting as close to the American people as one can since Congress is the most perfect—though flawed—mirror of America. I see my job in two ways; I get a feel for what's happening in Congress. Secondly, through the medium of [my publication] I tell the country what is happening in Congress on a day-to-day or week-to-week basis.

We're up here to do a job and to try to communicate to the world what's going on. It's no lofty calling. It's a job, it's not a profession. We have a unique talent to try and make clear, to teach, to inform.

It's not one simple thing. Informing the public is a large function, involving 60-70% of a reporter's time. Muckraking has its function—investigating things that would not normally be publicized.

Q. How would you describe your own job as to your purpose in reporting news and the type of stories you are concerned with? Are you primarily a recorder, an interpreter, or a prescriber?

I don't see any difference between the reporter and the interpreter. Give everybody the *Congressional Record* and they will have to choose what they see as important and then tell what it means. You try to give the people an inwardness of things as fairly and accurately as you can. I try to think what the public wants to know or, at least, the likelihood of what they want to know.

It's an interpreter (I'm not an advocate at all), a role you gain with your experience. I'm certainly not a subscriber to the subjective new journalism. It's very hazardous. These youngsters assume that their interpretations are correct, and they may not be. You learn that only by experience. Interpretive journalism is only a matter of experience, spending considerable time up here where you get to know the motivations—which ones are sincere, which ones are to be trusted. If it were merely a recorder, my paper might as well buy the wire services; they perform that function very adequately. It's certainly not being an advocate of any particular cause, regardless of what my feelings might be.

Interpreter is the best word. We are reporting as accurately as possible, and then because of the very tight time frame we are working within, we have to interpret what has happened and then tell the story subjectively. You can't tell a story within 30 seconds with the full view from both sides. There are, of course, many stories we are just reporting. Those are usually the 35-second radio spots used to report a major action on the floor or some action taken by a committee. Even then we still try to slip in a sentence or two to tell what the action really means.

I report the news. Every now and then we write an interpretive piece; that is, when we get something we think needs interpreting. There is a lot of Congress that I only give cursory coverage to because I only have a five-man staff here. They are pretty well specialized. Some of them will cover finances, some of them will cover the military. I cover sort of the leadership up here, the floor action. I kind of keep up with the political situation. Who's doing what and why.

On television it's quite different from newspapers because on TV you don't have as much time to go into the screws and nuts and bolts of legislation. Generally speaking, for TV to go after a congressional story, it must be a pretty major one, a big vote, a confrontation between Congress and the White House, some particularly dramatic hearing. In television we look for movement and action on the screen. As a consequence congressional coverage doesn't measure up to the criterion of action unless it is a pretty dramatic hearing. We have to rely on dug-out chatter when we can't get into hearings. The product of covering a debate is considerably more bland than the debate itself; it means you're really not and can't give a true account of what happens on the floor. The other difficult thing for television: because it is restricted on the House side, television gravitates to the Senate side. As a consequence, television is in a large part responsible for elevating certain senators into positions that they don't deserve. They're easily identifiable, more well known and fewer of them, and they also like television.

I happen to be one of those who thinks that Congress is an absolutely essential element in our government. Over-sensationalizing criticisms are very often quite damaging, so I try to know as much as I can about the motives, what lies behind the decisions, so that if I do criticize, which I frequently do, it's sound to the point that even the members who may be the object of it can't complain because they've learned over a period of years that I know what I'm talking about. Combined with that is the fact that a great many of them have become friends, not in a social sense, but in a personal way; but they all know that will not prevent me from being rough with them, and I know that won't stop them from being rough with me if I get off on the wrong foot. I try to be extremely accurate, and to know the involutions of what goes on here. Ninety percent of what I know I do not use because it's not of interest.

I consider myself a reporter and most of what I do comes under reporting. We do a certain amount of interpreting, but we try to draw a pretty definite line between the interpretive writing and the report-ing, unlike what some newspapers do. We serve such a variety of clients on all sides of every issue that our reporter has got to do just that. We have some room for interpretive writing in various features and columns. For instance, we have this daily column on this Wash-ington Window in which we give a little leeway to do interpretive writing. The *Washington Post* on Sunday in their front news section ran an interpretive piece I did for the Washington Window without any slug on it. It was about the possible death of the revenue sharing bill. It was something I wouldn't have written as a straight news story because it expressed something I felt about what was going on about that [bill] rather than the facts. It was written as an edi-torial-type story, an analysis. And that is the way it moved on our wire. But mostly I'm a reporter. It's just a big job of reporting around here that you don't have time to analyze pieces even if you had all the leeway in the world.

Principally my job is that of recorder, a person who watches and asks questions, and listens, and tries to set down as accurately and fairly and completely as possible what it is that is going on. Now, inevitably, that requires some interpretation. The more the reporter knows about a story, the better able he is to put a particular event into perspective. For instance, the House passed a new minimum wage bill. If you read that it passed, you missed the whole point because the Democrats, with the very strong backing of Carl Albert, have been pushing for some things that were not approved. So it was really a defeat for Albert and victory for Nixon. When you get into opinion, I think that is fine as long as it is labeled.

I think Mary McGrory is one of the most perceptive reporters and brilliant writers in Washington. But obviously most of what Mary writes is opinion. She's got facts, but she looks at them from a par-ticular point of view. There's a place for that but it's not in the news column unless it's clearly labeled.

I view myself as a part chronicler and part interpreter—to ex-plain the facts to the reader. Interpretation means trying to explain the facts to the reader.

I use the Senate as a base to cover national affairs. I've only been here since January, 1971. I've been in Washington covering national affairs since 1965. But I am not really a congressional reporter in the sense that my paper perceives me as being the guy who covers the Senate from 9 to 5 or whenever it is in session. My job is to use this as a base to try and understand what's happening in Washington. I'm expected to range from here to the White House, to the Depart-ments, to the Democratic and Republican Committees, etc. In fact I spent most of my time of the past 14 months here; I wanted to get the foundation before I range out. My paper does not expect me every day to file news out of the Senate and I do not do that. What I do is try to find events of significance that need to be reported and to focus on them to add what I can to them beyond the actual events. A lot of my reporting—I come up here, if I come up here, about 10 a.m., unless for some reason I have an early appointment. From that time it is a busy day. Until about 1 p.m. I am likely to be tied up covering the news on a very objective basis. I will be writing factual news reports, in news story style. I'll be dictating them. In the afternoon I start thinking about what I'm going to do for the next day's paper. That story will be more interpretive or more exclusionary in terms of events. I will try to focus on what I consider the most important event. I will try to go beyond that day, and it will not say that "the Senate yesterday passed this bill." It will talk about what's in the bill, what led to its passage, what its prospects for passage are in the other body, or who the lobbyists were who were involved in it. My time is divided between supplying breaking news to [my publication] which I do in the morning, and writing overnights or more interpretive pieces which I do in the afternoon. Now those are completely different kinds of stories.

My main purpose in reporting news is to do a good job for [my publication]. I cover the House—each day I pick what I think are the big stories of that day, or one that we haven't dealt with adequately. Or it's something I don't know about that I'm going to have to know about, so I cover it not to write a story but just to listen. At this level, we need to do a little more interpreting. The reader today is in a hurry. He has the tube—he isn't home 'til seven, so he isn't going to spend a lot of time reading. Our job is to write clearly, distinctly, concisely and with depth, so that when Secretary of State William Rogers comes out of a closed Foreign Affairs Committee, you know the right questions to ask and stick them in the first five paragraphs.

There is a conflict between what must be covered now—and investigative pieces that take time. How much time can be used for investigative reporting is always set by the editor.

I look upon myself as a recorder and an interpreter. I do not think there is room in the newsmagazine business for the prescriber. The prescriber belongs in the journals of opinion that are frankly labeled as such like the *New Republic* or the *Nation*. These fulfill a needed purpose which is one of advocacy. [My publication] isn't in the business of advocating. I think in all the years I've been with [my publication] we have editorialized twice—at the height of the black disorders we took a strong stand saying more of our resources must be diverted to the black segment of America. The other was on the Vietnam War and that we should get out. In our profession, there are two kinds of reporters—the involved reporter or the objective reporter. Newsmen are fallible human beings and some of them find it difficult to separate their own emotions and their emotional reactions from the story they are covering. I belong to the objective school. I believe very strongly I must set my emotions and emotional

predilections to one side for a story, because I have a story not to fulfill my own emotional satisfaction but to interpret the Congressional
story to the two million six hundred thousand subscribers and pur-
chasers of [my publication] and to the estimated 13 million who read
it in all or in part. This means that when I am interviewing or talking
to a dove like Senator Church of Idaho, I know that Senator Church
believes I will set forth his position as fairly as humanly possible. The
same way when I talk with McGee of Wyoming, who's a hawk on
Vietnam. I'm convinced he feels that same way. Both happen to be
very good friends of mine. I can assure you that neither one knows
whether I am a dove or a hawk. I reserve those opinions for my home.

Relations With Sources

When correspondents talk to congressional staff members, members
of Congress and other sources, they generally seek interpretations of
events. For instance, 64% often ask sources "about a behind-the-scene
maneuver on some important issue." More than half ask a source to
"embellish your remarks made at meetings, conferences, on the floor, etc"
(Table 31). About as many correspondents often ask for on-the-record
reactions also.

In seeking their information, correspondents rely heavily upon their
professional credibility. Seventy-one per cent make it a point often to
demonstrate to a source that he can trust the correspondent by honoring
background and other confidential information, including quoting accurately (Table 32).

Although not as widespread, developing "personal, congenial relationships during informal social activities and visits to the sources'
offices" is practiced at least somewhat by 64% of the correspondents.

"Playing source against source to 'smoke' out the whole story" is
resorted to often by nearly a third of the correspondents and somewhat
by another third.

Quite a few correspondents resort to "appearing to be sympathetic
to a source" to get more information than he would get as a neutral or
hostile reporter. Although not relied upon often by many correspondents,
more than a third use it somewhat and another fourth use it very slightly.

A majority of the correspondents, however, do not give their sources
extra "ink" or "play" in a story just to puff them up as sources. It is used
at least slightly, however, by more than a third of the correspondents.

In general, the correspondents seem to enjoy a cooperative relationship with members of Congress. This is reflected in interview responses
of correspondents of relied-upon news media.

*Q. Generally speaking, do you feel that newsmen have a cooperative
or competitive relationship with Senators and Representatives?*

I don't think cooperative and competitive are accurate labels. A lot depends on the story. If you seek more exposition of what's in the bill, not an awful lot of competition is involved. If you determine motives, then it does become a competitive relationship. An awful lot depends on how much you know and what kind of questions you answer. There was a case during the ITT hearings. Peter Flanigan was denounced up here. The next day Mr. Flanigan orchestrated a rebuttal. He used as his conductor Norris Cotton of New Hampshire. Mr. Cotton, using documents supplied to him from Mr. Flanigan's office, came out on the floor to defend Mr. Flanigan. Up in the gallery were two young aides of Mr. Flanigan following Mr. Cotton's speech line by line. You could watch Norris Cotton speaking and the aides turning over the pages. I went down to Senator Cotton, who did not know I had seen the two aides up there. I asked him a series of questions, and his answers instantly confirmed that indeed Flanigan's office had handed this great Senator, who was an independent person in his own right, this canned speech which the Senator dutifully trotted out on the Senate floor and read like a Charlie McCarthy. If I had gone to Cotton not knowing those young fellows had been up there, the questions I would have asked would not have been to the point. That was competitive; he didn't know what I knew and he was dumb enough to answer truthfully.

Depends an awful lot on the individual reporter. A lot of them have a very low opinion of almost all members of Congress, others are a little more realistic. My own feeling is that they are pretty representative of the people who elected them. I don't feel competitive, antagonistic; some I don't like; on the same token some of the people who elected them I don't like. I suppose there have been some instances of conflict in objectives when they've tried to conceal something. But I think most of them are too smart for that. If they've been around long, they know that a good reporter is going to find out anyhow.

I don't know—both. My job is to find out regardless whether it will influence policy or not. It becomes a personal professional challenge to me to dig stuff out.

Normal for newsmen and public figures to be at odds. You can still be friends and still be at odds. Our purposes are not identical. Ours is to explain to the public the good and the bad. Of course the politicians are interested in only having the good. There is a cooperative story to many of them, but there's also some approach with them —you know they are for their self interest. We are not necessarily for that; our business is to explain as clearly as we can and as objectively.

Generally a cooperative relationship, but that doesn't mean we're getting into bed with them. We're cooperative in the sense that we each have an interest in getting out certain kinds of information. Any reporter worth his salt keeps his distance from the individual in personal terms. It's not so infrequent. Very often they don't want the information out if it is not politically opportune, embarrassing. It's just a matter of poking around, going around them, finding somebody else that will help.

Inevitably [correspondents and members of Congress] come into conflict. Also inevitably they come together at other points because of the congressman's goal. Ken Heckler led a crusade against the outrages of coal mines in West Virginia. He got that message out through the press. Another one was a campaign launched by Max McCarthy from Buffalo. He was horrified to learn this country is stockpiling chemical and germ warfare agents—he hammered and hammered until that was changed and lots of programs for this were stopped—including one in Wheaton, which was closed down. But all too often all they want to do is blow their own horns or keep something secret.

Newsmen and legislators generally have a cooperative attitude with each other concerning records, public affairs, the congressional business. The exceptions are when you get situations where legislators are in a minority position and in a position where they are holding legislative deliberations in less than the public light, in closed session or in a somehow remote session from the public light. Then there tends to be conflict. I think these are somewhat exceptional situations. There are some committees and some issues that tend to generate conflict between newsmen and legislators. One is the issue of D.C. and its government. The whole question of home rule is one where there tends to be tension between the congressmen involved and the newsmen who cover. That is sometimes true in the case of nominations. There can be tension about the process being used to investigate the nominee. It is sometimes true on specific appropriations. Sometimes you have a committee in favor of something like the SST—the Commerce Committee, an appropriations subcommittee.

Generally speaking—competitive, but I don't feel my operation is competitive. But then I'm a different kind of reporter. I don't believe in looking for scandal; I don't believe that politicians are venal or crooked. Of course there are some. I've got quite a lot of respect for quite a lot of the legislators up there. And in my relationship with them, that respect plays quite a big part.

The essential role of the reporter to the public official is a hostile one. If he steps out of line, you're going to nail him. He knows it and you know it. For example, Charlie Halleck was always very nervous with the press because he figured he was going to get himself in trouble. He used to follow the practice that you won't get in trouble for something you didn't say. There are still men in Congress like that, and in the leadership. But when you've been there awhile, you get a working professional relationship with a whole lot of guys. Normally the congressman or senator wants to explain himself, and there is no difficulty. There are times—not very often, when things get very sticky. I don't see the objectives are all that different. I know that congressmen tend to look at us as public relations agents for them, and some of them tend to get upset when it doesn't work out that way, but it shouldn't work out that way.

Most congressmen are more cooperative than not. Then I would add, it will depend at least to some extent on whether he knows the reporter to be an honest, accurate, fair reporter. There are many little bureaus of newsmen who cover two or three papers in the same state. They will spend almost all their time covering local angles of legislation and their congressmen. Usually they are on friendly terms and writing noncontroversial things, and their congressmen will go out of their way to be cooperative with them. Then those here to cover Congress as a national legislature—for them it's more difficult to get to know all members, and you probably would find you're kept at arm's distance. I think the Washington papers have the advantage or disadvantage. Whatever you write, the congressmen see, and they can form an opinion of your fairness and accuracy and if you come through okay, they talk with you. I have no trouble talking at least with most of the deep Southern congressmen who must disagree totally with every editorial in [my paper]; some of them are just very difficult for anybody to talk to—personality problems—but they can distinguish between me as a fair newsman and the editorial news side.

I think they are more cooperative. The only competitive relationship is when they are trying to hide something we want.

There is what I regard as a growing problem on coverage of the Hill in two directions. One: I see too many activist reporters consorting and on occasion conspiring with favored members of Congress to sell stories, to blow up stories. Two: There is a sizeable group in Congress among the conservatives who are growingly embittered at the press. Agnewism is obviously a factor in this. The press in Congress has an increasing credibility problem among some conservatives. This can create abuses on both sides. There are fewer closed doors in Congress than any place in Washington, but more doors are being closed. Reporters have to maintain a full crusade for access to the news, and I'm just saying the loss of credibility of some reporters hurts that crusade.

There's a built-in antagonism. I don't know if I would say competitive. We have a built-in wariness. Some senators are close friends, but I still try to maintain an aloofness with all of them. You never want to be in a position where friendship would interfere with your responsibility to tell the story objectively.

It depends on what you are doing. This gets right back down to a problem that starts at the lowest point in the newspaper business, covering the police beat. You have to be able to get along with the cops, and you have to be in a position to blow the whistle on the cops. Every newspaperman has gone through this, and you have to resolve it at every level. The question is how close do you get to your sources. If you get so close to them that you can't write anything ugly about them, then you might as well not know them. It's a problem for which there is not an easy, handy, all-purpose answer. A conscientious newsman can get to the middle ground. Obviously you've got to be on reasonably good terms with the Speaker of the House; on the other hand, you have to write a piece that says some of the people in the House don't think the Speaker is doing so well. This doesn't make him happy, but you have got to do that. And you have to write a piece every now and then about chairmen who got automobiles they ought not to have had. Mostly they don't take that bad. You rarely run across a member who feels you're supposed to be writing publicity about him.

Generally, it's cooperative. Probably, it should be more conflicting.

As I said before, they use us and we use them. Reporters are not hesitant to give a zinger to a senator or congressman who helped them get information the day before.

It's generally cooperative. Sometimes too cooperative.

Cooperative, for reasons I have already discussed. (Congressmen want their name in print; newsmen must constantly be in touch with congressmen.)

Q. How would you evaluate congressmen and senators themselves as news sources? Are they sensitive to the problems of news gathering or not?

This varies with the individual. Some have a keen sense of news. Some do not. Some are able to capsulize and focus their ideas, views and information when interviewed. For instance, Senator Alan Cranston of California happens to be a former newspaperman. He has a very good sense of news. It's always a pleasure to talk with him concerning some news event or piece of legislation with which he is involved. John Stennis of Mississippi, who is one of the great senators, is nevertheless not a good source—just doesn't think like newsmen. It took years before his aides could convince him that he had a responsibility to come up to the Senate Press Gallery to be interviewed by newsmen. There is something more: To find out what is going to happen in the House, I find out I go to a small number of the representatives because few of them are able to represent the course of events. If I want to know the Southern position, I'll go to Joe Waggoner from Louisiana. He's one of the shrewdest legislators in Congress. He knows what's going on and he's able to unite the Southerners. Or I'll go to the House Majority Leader Hale Boggs. If I want to know what liberal Democrats are going to do, I'll call sources on the Democratic Study Group which represents about 130 House members. But to go to the average Joe Blow in the House to find out what is going to happen on busing, and so forth, would be a waste of time.

Vary among themselves, but overall very good sources. They understand what you're after and are usually very cooperative.

Most of them are sensitive to our problems—that is, most of the ones you deal with. There is a large number of senators and congressmen with whom nobody in the press ever deals. They are the nonfunctioning members who do nothing and say nothing, and are not involved in the legislative process when it's time to vote. But the ones you deal with, especially the leadership, are sensitive. For example, Senator Stennis will put it to you this way: he feels he has a responsibility as a public servant to respond to your questions. He feels it in a constitutional way of thinking, others think of it in terms of personal publicity.

Some of them are—some are not. Most of them are. I find them very good news sources. I think I have better contacts in the House. That's where I spend most of my time. Of course they have their own causes to espouse, and you have to learn how to evaluate whether what they're saying is in self-interest or whether it's really important. Most of them have been in politics long enough to know the problems of the media; they know who they can use, who they can't and who they have to level with.

Yes, but that doesn't mean they are usually going to tell you anything that hurts them. There are no categories of them as news sources. Evaluate each source as you get to know him, how accurate he is, how good his judgment is, then make allowances for each guy and the way he operates. Also, it's important to determine whether he's in a position to know.

I think so, probably more than most other people in Washington. The congressman is much easier to deal with than the bureaucrats downtown. He has no boss, except for the people who sent him here. He's interested in getting out stories that indicate he is effective, with some kind of interest. Even as high up as the cabinet, the executive branch level, all have a boss, except the President. In the Congress there are two parties. It is always to someone's interest to get some information out. Congressmen are about as easy to deal with as any kind of species on the Hill.

Most of them are not sensitive to our problems, but they are sensitive to the desirability of getting along with the press. Most of them realize we are doing a public service around here, only in a little different sense than they are. The House members are cooperative and available. Of course, if you're looking for something they don't want you to have, as we sometimes are, then they get less available. They're in the gym playing paddleball or something.

Oh yes . . . They understand our problems. They'll tell you stuff you can't use their name on, but they'll give you good leads so you know where to go get the stuff. And of course, you get a Democrat who will tip you off about something going on with the Republicans. Neither side has a monopoly.

They vary. In all the years I covered Dirksen, he lied to me once the whole time. It involved a story in which he was personally and politically involved. It was an appointment that he was pressing. He denied having put a hold on the information. We knew he had. But he was always informative. Certain ones are very frank and open. Tom Eagleton is immediately accessible and always quite frank. Some you just know not to go to. Either they don't know you or would rather not tell you.

It varies. Some are excellent. Some are hopeless. Take Mansfield, he's his own press aide really. He's candid, reliable. If he doesn't know something he will tell you. They're generally cooperative. I find it interesting that a senator like Mansfield is more accessible to the press than some of the freshman ones who have inflated self-evaluations. I think my senators are okay now. They're pushing ideas, they want to get their names in the paper. Oftentimes it's not particularly newsworthy—and some of them never learn to recognize where the development is when it hits them in the face.

Some senators are no good at all as sources. This generally includes the crusty old establishment senators and some of those with secure seats who have no need to use the press. They just don't enjoy relations with the press. There are 30–35 senators who are pretty good sources. When their own interests are involved in getting a bill through, most of them are not going to level with you completely, but you can get helpful information even though they are trying to use you a little. There are a few who will be remarkably candid if they know and trust you, even though their candor may be contrary to their own interest.

I have to maintain sources across the full ideological gambit. That means I have to have people who trust me among the flaming liberals, the moderates and the conservatives and even among the reactionaries. You destroy your capacity to function as a reporter among all of these groups if you wear the badge of any one group on your lapel. I think this is the most important thing I can say to you and the mistake the advocacy reporter makes. There are moments when the advocacy reporter can't find out what the moderate or conservative faction is going to do because they have destroyed themselves by alienating all the conservatives or whatever because of their reputation of always slanting their stories toward the liberal wing.

Senators are absolutely useless as news sources because they consider themselves very important and don't actually know what is going on—unless it is about themselves. Also the senators are on about 18 committees and cannot possible keep up. On the House side, each member is on one major committee, and much more intimately involved in the preparation of legislation. None of them is sensitive to problems of news gathering. Their obligation is not to help you but to help themselves. It's just because they've never been newsmen. They'll cooperate and be very friendly up to a point, if they think what you are after is just information that will go into the paper and make them look like a creative member of Congress. But if you start asking them about their campaign spending or their connection with some bank, they don't think you have any right to know that at all. And we do. That's one of the continuing conflicts around—exactly what does the public have the right to know. I believe these are public people and the public has a right to know every goddamned thing you can find out about them. And you ought to put it in the paper if you can, without malice. I don't subscribe to the Drew Pearson form of journalism, but I do subscribe to the idea that these are public people and we have a right to know what they are doing.

Most of them are—especially if they learn to trust you. Now that doesn't mean they have to like you, nor does it mean that you have to favor them. If they think you are going to be as honest as you know how in handling a story, then I think they are extremely cooperative and helpful. After the first Civil Rights Bill in 1964, I personally was in favor of it, but rarely does anybody know how I feel, but in this instance they had a way of knowing. When the thing was over I got letters from the leading Southerners and just as many from the people in the other side saying I handled it with thoroughness and total fairness. Both sides were extremely cooperative in helping me keep track of it. Some reporters have a few senators whom they use, and they are generally favorably inclined and they get most of their news from them. I've never done that, at least in many years. There's nothing wrong with that system. You probably get just as much information, just as good information. But I just don't do it that way.

I think they are, much more so than any other area in town. I think congressmen and senators are an excellent news source. Generally there is no particular kind of legislator that I consider a better source. However, it has struck me that in the Senate there's a generalization that senators who tend to fall in the category of liberal or moderate and are from large states tend to be more responsive to press questions. Therefore, the South specifically and legislators who fall in the category as conservative, are generally not responsive sources. There are individuals whom I would not go to because I would feel ahead of time that I'm not going to get anything. That includes liberals and conservatives, small state senators and large state senators. It has occurred to me that, as a general rule, large state senators tend to be more aware of the press and more cooperative than small state conservatives.

It varies greatly. As a group, senators are more publicity minded —they have larger constituencies and need publicity through the mass media. In the House, older members distrust and avoid the press. Senators and representatives are more responsive to their local press.

They vary. All of them want publicity.

All of them are very sensitive about the way they look in print. But some are good sources and some are not.

In general, any one of the two term congressmen is very cooperative, anxious to get his name in print. Usually there is a tremendous accessibility on the Hill.

Q. In comparison with congressmen, how would you rate congressional staff people as sources?

I use the staff constantly and they by and large are much better news sources because they know what's more important going on. You deal with the committee staff when it's an issue before the committee—for example, like foreign relations, I have five or six I consult constantly, and they're very helpful in alerting me when some development is coming up. I take them to lunch frequently. On the personal staff, that's where an aide has a particular area of responsibility. Sometimes press secretaries are helpful, sometimes they are trying to promote, but by and large they're okay, and it's just that they are irritating at times when they are doing their flack work.

Staffs are extremely helpful. Some senators operate with small staffs, and some won't give you any information at all. It is virtually impossible to get any information at all about anything out of Margaret Chase Smith. No reporter knows where she lives. She's not listed anywhere. I suppose the only way to find out is to follow her home one night. When you call Mrs. Smith's office, there is this absolute wall of cinderblock that hits you square in the face. The Kennedy staff has always been very good—both Robert's and Edward's. They attract bright young people. There's a great difference in congressional staff, and I've never figured out what that was. You can make certain assumptions about potential presidential senators like Kennedy and Muskie—although the Muskie staff is not very good. The quality of the staffs run from 0–95. There are some press secretaries who can't give you answers about anything without saying, 'I'll call you back.' And there are others who can give you a quick answer and know what their boss is thinking. There are a lot of them, and I must say they are in the majority, who'll say I'll have to call you back, I don't know what the boss thinks about that; or they are just not aware of what the situation is back in Colorado or wherever. Generally speaking, most television calls to the senatorial office are to ask if the senator will be available for an interview, and not to sit down and go off the record with him. The television is an on-the-record operation; without the interview, the correspondent has to do a stand up piece, and in television that's not very exciting.

Very frequently when a senator's whole life revolves around a committee, you'll find the best staff men who operate in the senator's orbit are on the committee and not in his office. Take the Finance Committee—very informed. When you want to talk about Ribicoff's welfare plan, you go to the committee.

Depends a lot on individual staff members. In most offices, the top staff people know as much as the senator in certain areas. Usually things are kicked around with the staff for a while before it comes up to the senator. Some of the press people are very good. Others are scared to death of their bosses and will do anything they can to keep anything unfavorable from getting out. Some of them know their bosses don't want national publicity, and that's the only thing I can give them. The press man will serve more as a screen than anything else. Generally speaking, it just depends on just how well I know the press man, the committeeman or the senator. The committee people are usually very good, honest and open.

The personal staffs will know how the senator feels and will talk more freely while an employee on a committee cannot talk as freely.

The committee staffs are mostly pretty competent and pretty helpful. There are some exceptions. For instance, on the Appropriations Committee, the staffers are highly competent people who know what's in the bill, know what the agencies are doing; the committees couldn't operate without them, and we would be hard pressed without them, too. Personal staff—not too many House members that have press aides. The best guy when you can't get the congressman is the administrative assistant. There are some who have good press aides and they can be very helpful. I guess in most offices there is somebody assigned to press. I guess their job is to do handouts. They're not a principal source of information generally.

Personal staffs have a large interest in building up their congressman. I don't spend a great deal of time talking with staff. In the Senate you do, but in the House you have more access to the members. Particularly helpful is the Speaker's Lobby where members usually come through on their way to the chamber. Also we have men who go onto the floor and call out the members when we want to talk with them. The committee staff, professional staff—not just secretaries—are generally of high caliber, generally willing to be helpful. Sometimes members don't always remember the details that the staff has. The press aides; that's a rather spotty area in the House. There are some very good ones; the thing that they do that makes them stand out from the others is that they wander through the press gallery very frequently, making themselves available for background or fill-in. [Rep. Paul G.] Rogers from Florida has been getting an awful lot of press recently in a health subcommittee—he has moved a lot of bills. But one reason for so much press attention is that his press man is in the gallery frequently bringing out statements, and so forth. Some of the committee people have press people like that. Some other people may be cranking out statements that get delivered to the press gallery. They're there and you may see them and you may not see them.

Press aides usually don't know too much. They usually are not inside things. They just put out. The committee staff who work on legislation are more knowledgeable.

You must work both sides of the street up here. Certainly any effective Hill reporter must have to have a lot of sources among congressional staffs. And there are some very good staff people up here. I find congressional staffs of the superior members of Congress rate very favorably with the best public officials in town. Some press aides are just flacks, others are the most valuable member of the senator's staff. There are hidden press aides. The key man in advising a senator on what amounts to press relations may be a member of a committee staff. One example is John Goldsmith, who is on the staff of the Senate Armed Services Committee. A crack Hill reporter for many years, he really functions as the chief press aide for Senator Stennis.

Press aides are very helpful. Some secretaries and administrative assistants seem more difficult to get along with than their bosses. You've almost got to see the boss to get an appointment with some of these people. The press aides know that if they give us a bad steer, we won't trust them next time. Committee staffs are very helpful. You have to make contacts, but after you've been around here a little while, you know who will tell you and who won't tell you. Some of this stuff is very technical—you may be having a shipping bill one day and a farm bill the next. You just can't get it all; you need someone to explain it.

I don't use staff aides. At the same time, there are staff aides who are nothing less than brilliant. Carl Marcy of the Foreign Relations Committee is an incredibly well-informed man. He's a great scholar in his field, written in the field, lectured in the field. It's all on an individual basis. It all depends on what you are looking for. The committee staffs are excellent for providing background information on the areas you are dealing with. But when you get into the political areas, areas of conflict and controversy, they are worthless. They are very nervous of even being involved in this area. But political areas are the meat of some staffers.

Well, on the nitty gritty, the staff aides are frequently more valuable than the legislators. Dick Royce, chief of staff of the Public Works Committee, I would call on him to find out what was going to happen on a highway bill rather than the Committee Chairman, Jennings Randolph of West Virginia. Press secretaries are curiously not too well informed. If they have put out a hand-out, they will interview the senator or his legislative aide to get the information and then write a news handout. If I want to know about the latest information on the continuing investigations and get into the qualifications of Richard Kleindienst, I will go not to Kennedy's press secretary, but to the staff director of one of Kennedy's subcommittees who has been studying the information and been preparing the information. The personal staff are more helpful when you want to find out matters back in the state—for political information about political situations in Indiana and how it affects Bayh, I'll call his press secretary. But if I want to find out about his Equal Rights legislation, I'll go to the staff committee—but he will have second or third hand information about the political situation back in Indiana.

As news supplements, staff people in the Senate are invaluable. On the House side, they are useful regarding specific pieces of legislation where specific details are not known by the congressman. Jake Lewis, who works for Patman, is a good example. Personal staffs are totally useless—on the House side anyway. Press aides, well, we don't have them on the House side anyway. If a House member has a press aide, it's somebody who deals with the folks back home, it's not somebody with whom we deal.

Senate staff tends to be cooperative with the press with the exception of the snotty receptionist. Committee staffs tend to be less cooperative although still pretty cooperative. It varies from committee to committee, and it varies on the basis of the members of the committee and their attitudes toward newsmen. Press aides are very, very important to senators. The change of the press aide can sometimes completely affect the senator's own attitude toward newsmen and the release of the information. A press aide who understands the needs of the press will frequently argue with a senator ahead of time, explaining to him why it's important for him to disclose something or not to the press when they ask him to.

Staff members know as much or more than congressmen about a particular subject. Committee staffs are better than personal staffs; they want to remain more independent of congressmen.

In general, the staff people are useful; they know the subject matter and get to the point instead of wasting time. They are like newsmen in that they think rationally and deal with the facts. They are competent and willing to help newsmen.

Senate staffs seem more open and more helpful than House staffs.

Congressmen are more concerned about publicity, since there are so many more of them, and they will subtly harass you, and so do their staffs. They'll all try to use you. Personal and committee staffs are about the same.

Equally good. And sometimes better. It depends on the individual. I don't use press aides that much because most of the time they're not well informed. Normally I just use them for the routine kind of thing.

Many of them are very good. Some of them are no good at all. On the welfare reform bill I'm covering right now—John Stein on Senator Long's committee is very cooperative. He records what the senator says and then brings it over to the gallery for us. There are some very bright ones on the Hill now. I've often thought that a senator can be made or broken by the kind of staff he has. . . .

Relations With Sources: Sanctions

Even in a general atmosphere of cooperation, there are sanctions, however. For instance, congressional correspondents are sometimes supplied with false or unreliable information from sources. Almost as many are sometimes requested to correct alleged errors in their reports. More than a third have experienced having complaints made directly to their employer or editor. And, of course, refusal to grant an interview or access to his staff or office is not uncommon for a member of Congress who is angry at a correspondent (Table 33).

Correspondents from relied-upon news media described their experience with sanctions in their responses to the interview question:

Q. What kinds of sanctions are imposed on congressional correspondents? By whom? For what reasons?

An individual member or individual chief counsel may take a dislike to a man and just not give him any information. Sometimes members may say "I don't ever want to see that son-of-a-bitch again," but that doesn't happen very often. Some of the strongest sanctions are against radio and TV because they won't let cameras be set up, they won't let tape recorders be used in certain areas. Usually they have a pretty good reason. TV cameras do tie up traffic, can be fire hazards. We louse things up. There are very few places around the Capitol where we can shoot without special permission. Many places we can't shoot under any circumstances. This sanction, I don't think, is inspired by much more than the desire not to clutter things up. Or there are certain committee chairmen who object to television and radio simply because they are old dodderheads who never really have understood these new media anyhow. There are several still in the Senate who won't let them into their committee hearings, and a number in the House. Russell Long of the Finance Committee is one of them. Stennis used to be that way, but now he's relaxing a little bit. I think this is from a lack of awareness, and there may be some deep seated feeling if a committee member or a witness commits a commotion that is a little humiliating to the committee, if it is on film or on tape, it is more damaging than the written word.

In general each committee determines what part of its meetings are to be open or closed. In general the House committees mark up (vote on) the bills in closed sessions. We have a running battle about that. One notable exception to this rule is the Education and Labor Committee—one of the most partisan committees in the House, always arguing, fighting, yelling at each other. Certainly a free flow of everything, and it doesn't seem to be that they are inhibited by having the newsmen watch them cast their ballots. So many others are closed; Armed Services Committee—they claim national security— has been holding weeks and weeks of closed hearings on the military procurement bill. Maybe the press would have been able to catch some of the big mistakes like the $2 billion dollar overrun, but you never know. The House Appropriations Committee held all closed meetings, gave outrageous reasons like they didn't want lobbyists in there breathing down their necks. Now the House Appropriations holds open meetings as a result of the 1970 reform legislation. But the open hearings are generally those where the Secretary of the Department comes up and makes a very general statement. But when the details get interesting, they close the meetings. There are all kinds of meetings that go on around here that are little regional groups, the Democratic Study Group, the Southern Democrats have a Southern Caucus, the Black members have formed a caucus, and there are private unofficial groups. The House in my time has never had a secret meeting, although the Senate has.

There are no sanctions that I can think of. We do our own policing on Capitol Hill. There are the three galleries—press, radio, periodical. I'm a member of the executive committee of the periodical gallery. We have over 300 accredited members and our circulation [weekly] runs into the tens of millions. Now if these reporters, we, the elected members of the periodical gallery, censure them . . . Suppose we find a member of our gallery is involved in lobbying; we will withdraw his credentials because we extended them in the first place. Now these are the only sanctions I can think of.

No—we had a case some time ago of a fellow who broke into a congressman's office to get a news story he knew was in there. Actually I think he had had a few drinks. He didn't really break into it; he told the guard he was a staff member, who then let him in. The Correspondents' Committee didn't censure him or anything.* Actually what his paper did was to give him a raise. I guess we condemn, not

---

* According to the correspondent involved, he *was* censured—Ed.

censure. We get a lot of criticism from the members who complain about little things.

Television has sanctions imposed on it by Congress about where you can take your equipment. But, really, you can take your equipment anywhere if you can get a senator to say, "It's okay by me." That is, except in the chamber. I did a program five or six years ago with Dirksen, and he just made some phone calls and got us permission. So the rules can be fixed. But generally speaking, we're restricted to this small gallery we're in. You can set outside the senator's office with the senator's permission. We have certain places outside the building where we can go do stand-ups. To go outside the Senate Appropriations Committee requires you to call the sergeant-at-arms and then go through some rigamarole reminding you they have power over you. But on other sanctions, we operate just as general reporters do about on and off the record and background.

Hard to think of any specific sanctions. I would like to emphasize again the importance of the continuing crusade to keep all doors open to the press. There is far too much secrecy in this town. There are many documents that should be routinely open to the press that are refused to them. We are talking here mainly about major committees of Congress. Some of these work on a limited basis with the press.

I don't know what you mean. I have my own relations with the individual. If something is not given to me then I find another way. If somebody were to give me a stolen document, I would not question whether to use it or not, but whether it should be printed. As a matter of fact, when a person asked me about printing the Kissinger papers, I talked them into doing it.

Congress still has a number of closed sessions. I was shocked when I came to Washington to find out the number of closed meetings that do exist. The reform bill helped some, but most mark-up sessions, which is when the bill is actually changed or put into shape by the committee, most of those still are closed. One exception is the House Education and Labor Committee, which has completely open meetings. I'm not sure how much we would cover if all the meetings were open. The Appropriations Committee, which in the past has always had closed meetings, opened up last year and it was probably the most boring day I have spent, barring none. I suppose it is the idea that it should be open so that it is there if you want to cover it. I'm for opening everything. It's a slower process. There is grandstanding by some members. But at least it's convenience openly arrived at. Not really any personal sanctions. There may be if you irritate a certain source; he may refuse to talk to you and give his tips to other papers. But I think it all averages out. I have the theory that the Congress needs the press more than the press needs the Congress. We're conduits to their constituents.

One of the really nice things about Congress is the extraordinary openness. Almost everyone is available to the reporter at all times. You can arrange to see them. This is incredibly different from working with the administration. But it is almost impossible to see Nixon privately; it is done, but very seldom. The President holds very few news conferences. The Supreme Court is just as untouchable. The reporters have access to the Speaker's Lobby, where they can flag down 435 members at their leisure.

We operate under the jurisdiction of a Standing Committee of Correspondents which lays down certain loose rules. We cannot be press agents for anybody. We can't take money from some government agency by working on their side. We have to be of repute in our profession; that's supposed to assure that we operate under reasonably ethical conditions.

The obvious things—closed hearings which are particularly pronounced on our side. I can't think of any more sanctions except of time—not enough time to follow everything—but that's not a sanction. Newswise this place is as wide open as any place in town and more so.

Formal sanctions are few and reasonable. They have to do with the orderly process of covering Congress. You have to be an accredited correspondent. For the most part the accreditation process is reasonable, although not completely. . . . But that is something that is as much a problem of the press as it is the Congress because it is a self-policing function. It has denied access to important publications like the Village Voice, the so-called "underground paper" that is really not "underground" at all, and it has denied access to people like I. F. Stone. He's not accredited, but he's seldom kept out of important events though he would be kept out of a State of the Nation Address and things like that. There are sanctions by committee chairmen who will limit the number of press who may cover a specific hearing. Talmadge will not move from the room he normally uses for the Agriculture Committee because two or three as many reporters as usual would want to cover it. The most arbitrary and harmful sanctions are the Democratic and Republican leadership attitudes that they have the right to meet in party caucus in secret as if the Democratic and Republican parties were some kind of secret organizations that had nothing to do with the public business. The same sort of arbitrariness applies to sessions of some committees, especially the closed sessions. That's a problem much more on the House side than it is in the Senate. Congress leaves it up to the reporter's own committee to judge unethical or unprofessional behavior. There are very few cases where reporters have been barred. There are no specific guidelines laid down for ethical conduct. In fact, if the reporter were to be caught in the act of stealing a document from a Senate office, and he was prosecuted, he probably would lose accreditation.

The House rules say that a committee chairman, if he gets the vote of the majority of his committee, can close a committee meeting. We've objected to those rules, but there's little we can do except object. The House Appropriations Committee is opening up without fanfare—and eventually as each subcommittee chairman discovers that he can hold open meetings without trouble or revealing national secrets, I suspect they will all open up. We're not allowed on the floor of the House. I don't blame them. There are something like 2,000 reporters. It was stupid to close the Democratic Caucus; again, they seldom discuss anything that would hurt them. As a result of that, we have to go to our closer contacts in the Democratic Party to find out what happens. The result is a sort of jigsaw thing that may or may not have happened. If the story is distorted, it is the fault of the Democrats themselves. I don't think there should be any closed meetings. But a lot of other things go on around here that don't fall under formal sanctions—you know good and well that these guys meet in small groups and plot over cocktails the major decisions of the day. On the Rules Committee, I'm sure the most important decisions are made over coffee hour before they even come out into the Committee room. But that was true in Fairfax County.

There are no sanctions that I know of.

House members, especially, are less cooperative after an unfavorable article is written about them.

Congressmen and senators won't speak to a reporter for a while after he writes an unfavorable article.

I've never had any trouble with editors, and congressmen do not punish you for publishing unfavorable coverage. But there is a more nebulous thing—Capitol Hill is a world in itself, a community. And newsmen become a part of it, and as a result it becomes impossible for some reporters to be thorough, perceptive and questioning, or to cover Congress with detachment.

Is Congress Adequately Covered?

The following comments from major congressional correspondents came in response to an interview question:

Q. In general, do you think that Congress is well covered by the news media? If not, why not? Where do problems originate—the members of Congress, the legislative process, the reporters themselves, or the nature of policies of the media?

No, the Congress is inadequately covered. Take the wire services. If they were going to cover the Congress adequately, the AP and the UPI would have to bolster their congressional staffs by at least 70 per cent. Congress is covered, I guess, about as well as Congress in turn keeps track of the executive spending; it does this by appropriation hearings, by spot checking certain areas, and just by hit and miss. In turn, Congress is covered in a kind of spot checking way. We just kind of keep our eyes on the highlights.

There just aren't enough people here to staff all the hearings that go on and to adequately keep track of what's happening. The best work done in covering Congress is done generally by the trade press, because they zero in on a very narrow segment of one of their interests. They may be interested in just legislation pertaining to wool, or petroleum, and they do a very good job because they are restricting themselves to a particular area.

Yes and no. I think the newsmen are there to cover it. But the people back home don't always understand the importance of the issue, unless it's a very difficult issue for a congressional correspondent to sell his story to his station back home, a story about something like the higher education bill. In this case the coverage centered almost entirely on the busing, and not what the bill would do for higher education. This is probably a job of the news media, to educate the public to the importance of this thing. The public unfortunately is not too interested in the day-to-day workings of Congress.

In a general sense, yes. It is well covered in the sense that there are adequate reporters covering the events of Congress on a given day. It's not well covered in terms of the amount of information published by news organizations to explain Congress. In other words, the fault is not with the reporting or the news organization staffing of congressional beats; the fault is with the use of the material they get. And I think it tends to be under covered. This is especially true of the networks, although again, I think it's an individual thing. I think CBS tends to be a little better than NBC because Roger Mudd has more prestige at CBS than Paul Duke does at NBC. I think ABC . . . I don't know, I really can't say. Their correspondent up here is very good, but I don't see much of their news coverage. My general impression is that networks under-cover. I think that newspapers under-cover certain significant events too. I'm not talking about the Washington papers so much as the newspapers outside the city.

The problem may be in the nature of Congress as it is today, not with the congressman up there, but the congressman's view of his power. It may be that Congress is today more irrelevant to the government process than it should be because its power goes unexercised.

Probably I do. There's only so much space in the newspaper. However, the papers outside Washington are abyssmal. In Washington, we do the best job we can, and the paper does the best job it can within the limits of its time and space.

Yes. I don't think there are too many problems. I do have members who frequently don't want to talk about something because of restrictions from a committee or personal problems.

Not particularly. It gets more toward the orientation of the press, I think they are more oriented towards the White House and the executive branch for news. Congress comes out second best in the treatments and space.

No. A lot of it is the fault of the legislative process. They had this reorganization act. There's a lot of regulation to make public the financial activities of the members. But sometimes it's six months before it's published so it is no good when we get it. For instance— what's the member's outside interest they make hard to get hold of? That's all filed over here in the ethics committee—but it's not public. Just recently they raised the price of xeroxing copies of campaign reports filed by members—political contributors and lobbyists—used to charge a dime to get a copy. They raised it to a dollar.

It's exceptionally well covered by a small portion of the media. It's very well covered by the *Post*, the *Star*, the *New York Times*, the *Los Angeles Times*, the *Chicago Daily News* and the *Chicago Sun Time*, the *St. Louis Post Dispatch*. There is a sharp drop off after this exclusive group (also include the Minneapolis Cowles papers). Depends on the quality of the reporter and the amount of money the news organization spends on covering the Hill. (Currently all three of the networks do a good job. *Time* and *Newsweek* also do a good job. Another good coverage is the *Wall Street Journal*.)

I suppose so. I would say fairly well. There's an awful lot of hometown coverage of delegations that lacks a certain critical edge to it. It's a two-way street. . . In order for the reporter to maintain his credibility, he's got to produce the copy to keep the information coming, so he's got to play along with the delegation and with the bureau. So the senators guarantee some outlet back home. What you have is less the adversary relationship than it is the cooperative relationship, particularly those organizations which depend on their bread and butter for the friendship of the delegation. You can anger a delegation just so much, and then you find, as a reporter, they cut you off. Then you're cut off from the delegation that you're paid to cover, then you don't stay very long. So you find reporters going to the South Carolina night at the Hilton Hotel—maintaining their relationships with the Senator. When a group of Tennesseeans come to testify, you've got to cover them for the hometown paper at the expense of a story that might be more important.

Yes. The public gets as much as it will digest. There's an awful lot of rejection by the public of congressional news. We don't see it here so much, though. In the Midwest, far West, people aren't nearly so interested in what Congress does except the final verdicts on important issues. But they don't give a damn about the by-play.

The Senate is better covered than the House. I see a lot of people around here, but I don't know what they write. Most reporters gravitate towards the senator, it's better known. There aren't so many senators, the procedures may be a little less mystifying. The House is really a dark continent. I cover the House. The AP and UPI have about a five-man general bureau, the *Star*, the *Times*, the *Baltimore Sun*, but not many others, who do full time.

No. There's a decided failure of the congressional reporters themselves to know what they are writing about. There's a tendency among the reporters to take a pretty superficial view of Congress. They don't understand the rules, the history of American politics. In all journalism, it is a tendency to be superficial, popular. At one time there was a basic fault in the understanding of the editors of how important the congressional news really is. I suspect that 30-40 years ago the congressional reporter had more in print. But since the time of Roosevelt, the President has sort of preempted Washington affairs.

Yes. Congress is more open to the media than any branch of government. The glare of publicity is stronger on Congress than on any other branch of government. In the executive branch, the information is quite controlled. In Congress you have 535 primary news sources, then multiply this by those on the staffs, and you have an extraordinary number of news sources. As long as we have publications like the *New York Times*, the *Wall Street Journal*, the *Post*, *Time*, the *Los Angeles Times*, *Newsweek*, the *St. Louis Post Dispatch* I don't think there is any weakness in coverage. Really, these publications do a very good job of covering Congress. And as a result of the growth of the concept of the news magazines, the newspapers have begun competing with news magazines, have moved away from the "who, what, when, where and why," and try to give some depth to the coverage of their stories. I think the Americans are the best informed people on the planet.

I do think it could be done better. But considering the difficulties, overall, we're not doing a bad job. The area in which I think we could do a better job is the area of blowing the whistle on little irregularities; not illegalities so much as just slightly unethical things. It's very difficult. We're pressed for time. There's not a great market for it. In the wire service there's such a competition for wire service space. In Washington we could use all the space for Congress, but there has to be allowance made for the whole government here, the whole world, the other states, and other governments and the war in Vietnam. Even if you could get so much on the wire, the paper can print just so much copy. And they can't print near as much as we send them. I don't think there's too much borderline getting-by here. I do think not quite enough attention is paid to the extent to which members take care of themselves. This seems to me to be an issue of considerable interest to the taxpayers. We write about it. I think a little more attention might be paid to that area.

Better than most of the departments, by far better than the White House. Compared with other areas of government, yes. In the absolute, no. There are not nearly enough people to do the job. Thus, everybody has to do a lot of things; end up taking the cream of it and not getting into very much of what is going on here. But we just don't have time to do more. At the White House, the media are really a transmission screen; it's the only agency that operates by handout. There are no accesses to policy-makers, no opportunities to feel what is going on, or no feelings about what is going on that's very important.

Sometimes I think it's over-covered. We fall into the same trap that many members of Congress themselves fall into—thinking that the world starts and ends here in Washington. We don't get out into the country and really sound out what's happening out there, how certain bills or action taken up here fit into the local pattern. I think it is basically well-covered, but it could be improved by periodically dips out into the country. Some of the reporters are doing that, which is good.

I think the Congress is covered quite well under the limitations that exist—primarily air time. They're covered quite well by the networks on major issues. The broadcast groups do fairly well. But the trouble is that when you put all the radio and television stations together, there are only a few, just a small percentage that have any type of local representation here. So, simply then, I guess, the answer is no.

No, Congress isn't covered well. Across the nation, broadcasters are not generally committed to allocating enough money to cover it well. It's just that simple. Unless there's a massive commitment brought about by competition or by leadership to get this news coverage and representation not only of the Congress but elsewhere.

No. It's more a matter of manpower. The wire services do a very superficial job. To do an adequate job is very time consuming. I can only write one story a day, but maybe many things deserve attention. The House is neglected far too much. Also, having enough space in the paper is always a problem.

Congress should be covered more thoroughly, but the media have limits of manpower and space (or time) for news display. The electronic media coverage is very poor, and they should do a better job.

No. They could do a better job. (1) There is plenty of material available to most newspapers, radio and television that would enable them to do a better job. *Congressional Record, Congressional Quarterly*, and wire service reports. Inadequate use is made of this material. (2) Most media and news organizations only cover the final passage of a bill, not its developments. These problems are partly due to space limitations. And perhaps there is a lack of public interest, I don't know. Sometimes I think that the media can create interest if they want to, though.

No. News reporters duplicate information when they should be covering more events and people. The news isn't translated for the people who need it—it isn't fully explained.

No. There are things that often go unreported. For instance, the clash of competing interests and horse trading over a bill is not covered adequately on most pieces of legislation. It's hard for a citizen to tell what is happening and why.

No. There are limits of time, money and staff. And correspondents must constantly justify their existence by by-lines. There should be more investigative reporting.

You have about three or four news organizations that do a good job; about 100 do not. The coverage, in general, should be more competent, more probing, more thorough and more accurate than it is.

No. Everybody should be covered better, more thoroughly. Legislation is not made visible at all times, either to the congressmen or to the reporter. There should be a kind of a flow chart concerning legislation, including the date of hearings, the sponsor of the legislation, the staff people involved with it, and so on. Then we could better see what is going on, and would know what to cover.

Any reporting job could be done better, but it's not easy. I guess more stones could be looked under, as Jack Anderson does.

Yes, in the volume of coverage it is good. Newsmen try to put a perspective on the news. And there is not a secrecy problem in Congress as there is in the White House. There is a bipartisan relationship in Congress that the White House lacks, and indirectly and directly, that aids news reporters.

No. The Washington press corps could do a better job. Too often they just record speeches and statements by government officials, by senators, and by representatives. There is much of an attempt to cover Washington through press conferences, and too many reporters rewrite press releases.

Some reporters are just too lazy, especially those who are middle-aged or older. They get tired of legwork, and get too cozy with senators and representatives, and let themselves be used.

The coverage varies. Overall it's pretty good, though.

TABLE 1
NUMBER OF CORRESPONDENTS, BY MEDIA ORGANIZATION CATEGORY, INCLUDED IN SURVEY

SURVEY STEPS	GENERAL NEWS SERVICES	DAILY NEWSPAPERS	OTHER PRESS	BROADCAST NETWORKS	BROADCAST GROUPS	OTHER BROADCAST	PERIODICALS	TOTAL
Correspondents Interviewed	2	20	0	3	2	1	3	31
First Questionnaire	0	67	79	11	17	15	38	227
Telephone Survey	28	11	0	0	3	2	5	49
Final Questionnaire and Total	30	98	79	14	22	18	46	307
Responses to Final Questionnaire	16	57	12	4	6	0	6	96 (101)*

* Five correspondents checked two news media organization varieties

TABLE 2

NEWS MEDIA ORGANIZATIONS SURVEYED

GENERAL NEWS SERVICES

Associated Press

AP Radio

United Press International

UPI Radio

DAILY NEWSPAPERS

Arizona Republic

Ashtabula (Ohio) Star-Beacon

Atlanta Constitution

Atlanta Journal

Baltimore Sun

Boston Globe

Buffalo Evening News

Chattanooga (Tenn.) News Free-Press

Chicago Daily News

Chicago Sun-Times

Chicago Tribune

Chicago Tribune-New York Daily News
  Syndicate

Christian Science Monitor

Cleveland Plain Dealer

Copley News Service
  (16 newspapers in 2 states)

Daily Oklahoman

Daily Morning News

Denver Post

Des Moines Register and Tribune

Detroit News

Donrey Washington News Bureau
  (23 newspapers, 3 radio-TV stations,
  1 radio station in 8 states)

Enid (Okla.) Daily News and Eagle

Gannett News Service
  (52 Daily newspapers in 16 states and
  Guam)

Griffin-Larrabee News Bureau
  (28 newspapers in 10 states)

Gore Newspapers

Hearst Newspapers & Hearst Headline
  Service
  (10 newspapers in 6 states)

Houston Post

Kansas City Star and Times

Knight Newspapers
  (6 newspapers in 5 states)

Landmark Communications
  (6 newspapers in North Carolina and
  Virginia)

Lithuanian Daily News of Chicago

Los Angeles Times

Los Angeles Times Syndicate

Louisville Courier-Journal

Lowell (Mass.) Sun

McClatchy Newspapers of California
  (3 newspapers in California)

Madison (Wisc.) Capital Times

Milwaukee Journal

Minneapolis Star and Tribune

Newhouse News Service
  (19 newspapers in 7 states)

New Orleans States Item

Newsday

New York Daily News

New York Journal of Commerce

New York Times

Ohio/Washington News Service
  (7 dailies, 10 weeklies in 3 states)

Omaha World-Herald

Oregon Statesman

Orlando (Fla.) Sentinel and Star

Philadelphia Bulletin

Philadelphia Inquirer

Pittsburgh Press

Press Associates, Inc.
  (state and national labor newspapers
  —approximately 100 weekly clients,
  75 monthly)

Pueblo (Colo.) Chieftain and Star-Journal

Richmond Times-Dispatch

Ridder Publications
  (11 newspapers in 7 states)

St. Louis Post-Dispatch

St. Petersburg Times

Salt Lake City Deseret News

Salt Lake Tribune

Scripps-Howard Newspaper Alliance
  (17 newspapers in 10 states)

San Antonio Light

Seattle Times

Shreveport (La.) Journal

Tampa (Fla.) Tribune

Thomson Newspapers, Inc.
  (43 newspapers in 25 states)

Topeka (Kan.) Daily Capital

Tufty News Service
  (12 newspapers in 2 states)

DAILY NEWSPAPERS (Continued)

Tulsa (Okla.) World
Wall Street Journal
Washington Post

Washington Star-News
Watertown (N.Y.) Daily Times

SPECIALIZED NEWSPAPERS

American Banker
Fairchild Publications
(9 publications including Electronic
News, Home Furnishings Daily,
Women's Wear Daily)
National Catholic News Service
(News, feature, & photo service. 300
clients, mostly weekly Catholic news-
papers in U.S. and Canada, and a
wire service that goes to all 50 states.
Also, some overseas Catholic publica-
tions).
North American Newspaper Alliance
(Feature Syndicate for 150 news-
papers—merged with United Feature
Syndicate in Jan., 1973).

Oil Daily
Kenneth M. Schiebel Washington Bureau
News
(News Service which provides a
column, "Washington Farm Beat"
for over 50 newspapers and agricul-
tural trade publications such as:
Farmer-Stockman, The Packer,
Southeast Farm Weekly).
Science Service
(Publishes Science News, weekly news
magazine of science and offers a book
order service)
United Feature Syndicate

PERIODICALS

Advertising Age
Agricultural Services
(Monthly or semi-monthly columns
to about 35 commercial agricultural
publications such as: Poultry Tribune,
Poultry Meat, Progressive Farmer).
American Daily Review
Aviation Week
Baptist Press
Biomedical News
Bond Buyer Publishing Company
(Publishers of the Daily Bond Buyer,
a 4-column tabloid-size newspaper;
Money Manager, a weekly newspaper,
and Munifacts, a wire service of sec-
ondary municipal bond offerings.)
Broadcasting Magazine
The Bureau of National Affairs
(26 publications including Construc-
tion Law Report, Criminal Law
Reporter, Federal Contracts Report,
Occupational Safety and Health
Reporter, United States Law Week,
etc.)
Cable News
Chilton Publications
(18 trade publications including
Automative Industries, Electronic

Engineer, Gas Magazine, Iron Age,
The Spectator, etc.)
Compass Publications
(Publishers of materials for oceano-
graphic industry, government and
academia: a monthly magazine
Undersea Technology, a biweekly
newsletter and an annual handbook).
Congressional Quarterly
(CQ Service: 331 CQ clients in 50
states—287 newspapers and 44 broad-
casters).
Editor and Publisher
Electronics
(McGraw-Hill News Bureau)
Executive Business Media, Inc.
(Publishers of Catering Executive,
Club and Food Service News, College
Store Executive, Exchange &
Commissary News)
Farm News Service
(Columns for farm and "agri-
business" periodicals such as: Farm
Chemicals, Broiler Industry)
Federal-State Reports
Food Processing and Marketing
Forbes Magazine
Hospital Practice

Human Events
Industry Week
Investment Dealer's Digest
McGraw-Hill News Bureau
(33 publications including American
Machinist, Business Week, Coal Age,
Electrical Wholesaling, House &
Home, Modern Plastics, Textile
World, etc.)
Medical World News
Miller Publishing Company
(10 publications including Dairy
Herd Management, Feed Additive
Compendium, Hog Farm Manage-
ment, etc.)
Modern Railroads
National Journal
National Observer
Nautilus Press
Newsweek
Reader's Digest
Religious News Service
(450 Catholic, Protestant, Jewish &

Eastern Orthodox monthly, weekly,
or bi-weekly magazines & newspapers,
100 daily newspapers, 15 minute
weekly round-ups for about 200
radio-TV stations).
Research Institute of America, Inc.
(A business advising service which
publishes newsletters—weekly,
bi-monthly, monthly—on such
subjects as tax analysis, labor-
management, and regulatory
agencies.)
Telecommunications Reports
Telephony
Television Digest
Time
Traffic World
U.S. Medicine
Western Stamp Collector
Ziff-Davis Aviation Division
(Aerospace Daily, Aviation Daily,
Business Aviation)

NATIONAL BROADCAST NETWORKS

ABC News
CBS News
Mutual Broadcasting System

NBC News
National Public Radio

BROADCAST GROUPS AND OTHER "INDEPENDENTS"

Bonneville International Corporation
(6 radio and/or TV stations in
6 states)
Cox Broadcasting Corporation
(6 radio and/or TV stations in
6 states)
Group W (Westinghouse Broadcasting
Company)
(9 radio and/or TV stations in
7 states)
Granik-Cody Productions
(Washington-Worldwide Broadcast
News Service)
Metromedia Radio News Bureau
(11 radio stations in 6 states and
D.C.)
RKO General Broadcasting
(17 radio and/or TV stations in
7 states and D.C.)
Sterling Productions/News Services
Division
(Now called Washington Radio &

Television News, Inc.—12 TV
stations in 11 states).
Storer Broadcasting Company
(10 radio and/or TV stations in
8 states)
Susquehanna Broadcasting Company
(10 radio stations, one radio-TV
station in 6 states)
Time-Life Broadcast, Inc.
(used to operate 5 radio and/or TV
stations in 4 states; as of June 1, 1972
McGraw-Hill Broadcasting Co.
purchased 4 of the stations)
Triangle Stations, Inc.
(6 stations in 4 states)
WGN Continental Broadcasting
Company
(3 radio and/or TV stations in
3 states)
Jack Williams Washington News Service
(Independent TV correspondent for
12 TV stations in 9 states)

BROADCAST STATIONS

KERO-TV, Bakersfield California
   (Part of McGraw-Hill Broadcasting
   Company)
WAVA AM-FM (Arlington, Va.)
WBNS, WBNS-TV (Columbus, Ohio)
WJAR-TV (Providence, R.I.)

WMAL AM-FM-TV (Washington,
   D.C.)
WTOP News AM-FM (Washington,
   D.C.)
WTTG-TV News (Washington, D.C.)

TABLE 3

CORRESPONDENTS' TOTAL PROFESSIONAL TIME DEVOTED
TO COVERING THE UNITED STATES CONGRESS

		TIME CATEGORY			
	No Timers	Some Timers 1-19%	Short Timers 20-39%	Half Timers 40-59%	Most Timers 60-100%
MEDIA CATEGORY					
		Percentage of Correspondents (N = 227)			
All Media	3	29	14	18	34
Daily Newspapers	8	34	9	13	36
Other Press	3	24	11	24	38
Broadcast Networks	0	18	27	18	36
Broadcast Groups	0	12	18	0	71
Other Broadcast	0	40	13	7	40
Periodicals	0	45	18	26	8

TABLE 4

CORRESPONDENTS' CONGRESSIONAL COVERAGE TIME
DEVOTED TO THE HOUSE OF REPRESENTATIVES

		TIME CATEGORY			
	No Timers	Some Timers 1-19%	Short Timers 20-39%	Half Timers 40-59%	Most Timers 60-100%
MEDIA CATEGORY					
		Percentage of Correspondents (N = 227)			
All Media	14	4	19	45	19
Daily Newspapers	19	6	16	42	16
Other Press	10	1	18	52	19
Broadcast Networks	9	0	46	36	9
Broadcast Groups	0	6	18	35	41
Other Broadcast	13	0	20	40	27
Periodicals	16	8	16	50	11

TABLE 5

CORRESPONDENTS' CONGRESSIONAL COVERAGE TIME DEVOTED TO THE UNITED STATES SENATE

MEDIA CATEGORY	No Timers	Some Timers 1-19%	Short Timers 20-39%	Half Timers 40-59%	Most Timers 60-100%
		Percentage of Correspondents (N = 227)			
All Media	11	4	13	44	28
Daily Newspapers	13	6	9	43	28
Other Press	11	1	11	46	30
Broadcast Networks	0	0	0	36	64
Broadcast Groups	0	6	29	41	24
Other Broadcast	7	0	27	40	27
Periodicals	13	8	13	53	13

TABLE 6

CORRESPONDENTS' CONGRESSIONAL COVERAGE TIME SPENT IN HOUSE GALLERY (CHAMBER OR GALLERY OFFICES)

MEDIA CATEGORY	No Timers	Some Timers 1-19%	Short Timers 20-39%	Half Timers 40-59%	Most Timers 60-100%
		Percentage of Correspondents (N = 227)			
All Media	37	42	14	4	3
Daily Newspapers	31	52	16	0	0
Other Press	32	51	17	1	0
Broadcast Networks	36	27	0	18	18
Broadcast Groups	18	18	29	12	24
Other Broadcast	33	20	27	13	7
Periodicals	66	29	0	5	0

TABLE 7

CORRESPONDENTS' CONGRESSIONAL COVERAGE TIME SPENT IN SENATE GALLERY (CHAMBER OR GALLERY OFFICES)

MEDIA CATEGORY	No Timers	Some Timers 1-19%	Short Timers 20-39%	Half Timers 40-59%	Most Timers 60-100%
		Percentage of Correspondents (N = 227)			
All Media	33	40	15	7	6
Daily Newspapers	31	42	18	5	5
Other Press	27	46	19	6	3
Broadcast Networks	18	18	27	18	18
Broadcast Groups	24	41	18	6	12
Other Broadcast	20	40	20	7	13
Periodicals	61	32	0	8	0

TABLE 8

CORRESPONDENTS' CONGRESSIONAL COVERAGE TIME
IN THEIR ORGANIZATIONS' OFFICES (IF NOT IN GALLERY)

		TIME CATEGORY			
MEDIA CATEGORY	No Timers	Some Timers 1-19%	Short Timers 20-39%	Half Timers 40-59%	Most Timers 60-100%
		Percentage of Correspondents (N = 227)			
All Media	48	9	14	14	14
Daily Newspapers	52	10	22	9	6
Other Press	29	8	18	23	23
Broadcast Networks	46	27	0	0	27
Broadcast Groups	59	29	6	6	0
Other Broadcast	67	7	7	7	13
Periodicals	63	0	8	18	11

TABLE 9

CORRESPONDENTS' CONGRESSIONAL COVERAGE TIME
ELSEWHERE IN CAPITOL OR SENATE OR
HOUSE OFFICE BUILDINGS

		TIME CATEGORY			
MEDIA CATEGORY	No Timers	Some Timers 1-19%	Short Timers 20-39%	Half Timers 40-59%	Most Timers 60-100%
		Percentage of Correspondents (N = 227)			
All Media	39	21	20	15	6
Daily Newspapers	36	15	25	18	6
Other Press	34	32	22	6	6
Broadcast Networks	55	18	18	9	0
Broadcast Groups	41	35	12	6	6
Other Broadcast	53	7	27	7	7
Periodicals	42	8	11	34	5

TABLE 10

CORRESPONDENTS' CONGRESSIONAL COVERAGE TIME
IN COMMITTEE HEARINGS

TIME CATEGORY

MEDIA CATEGORY	No Timers	Some Timers 1-19%	Short Timers 20-39%	Half Timers 40-59%	Most Timers 60-100%
		Percentage of Correspondents (N = 227)			
All Media	33	21	18	17	11
Daily Newspapers	28	13	25	16	16
Other Press	32	33	18	9	9
Broadcast Networks	55	27	9	9	0
Broadcast Groups	47	24	12	6	12
Other Broadcast	60	7	13	13	7
Periodicals	21	8	13	42	16

TABLE 11

CORRESPONDENTS' CONGRESSIONAL COVERAGE TIME
'LOCALIZING' REPORTING (REPORTING LOCAL
OR REGIONAL ANGLES)

TIME CATEGORY

MEDIA CATEGORY	No Timers	Some Timers 1-19%	Short Timers 20-39%	Half Timers 40-59%	Most Timers 60-100%
		Percentage of Correspondents (N = 227)			
All Media	52	6	7	7	28
Daily Newspapers	55	8	6	5	27
Other Press	34	4	11	11	39
Broadcast Networks	91	0	0	9	0
Broadcast Groups	6	24	6	6	59
Other Broadcast	40	0	0	13	47
Periodicals	92	3	5	0	0

TABLE 12

CORRESPONDENTS' CONGRESSIONAL COVERAGE TIME REPORTING NATIONAL NEWS

TIME CATEGORY

MEDIA CATEGORY	No Timers	Some Timers 1-19%	Short Timers 20-39%	Half Timers 40-59%	Most Timers 60-100%
		Percentage of Correspondents (N = 227)			
All Media	31	16	14	9	30
Daily Newspapers	22	13	15	12	37
Other Press	24	24	20	10	22
Broadcast Networks	9	0	0	9	82
Broadcast Groups	24	29	12	0	35
Other Broadcast	20	20	20	13	27
Periodicals	66	3	5	5	21

TABLE 13

CORRESPONDENTS' BIRTHPLACES BY STATE

BIRTHPLACE	PERCENTAGE OF CORRESPONDENTS (N = 96)
U.S.A. (no state specified)	27
New York	12
Illinois	7
Massachusetts, Mississippi, New Jersey, North Carolina, Ohio	4 each
Pennsylvania, Texas	3 each
Colorado, Michigan, Nebraska, Oregon, Virginia, Wisconsin, District of Columbia	2 each
California, Connecticut, Delaware, Florida, Idaho, Kansas, Maine, North Dakota, Oklahoma, Tennessee, West Virginia	1 each

TABLE 14

CORRESPONDENTS' AGES

AGE CATEGORY	PERCENTAGE OF CORRESPONDENTS (N = 96)
20-29	17
30-39	37
40-49	32
50-59	7
60-69	5
over 69	2

TABLE 15

CORRESPONDENTS' LEVELS OF EDUCATION

HIGHEST LEVEL OF EDUCATION	PERCENTAGE OF CORRESPONDENTS (N = 96)
High School Graduates	2
Some College	10
College Graduates	44
Graduate Study	21
Graduate Degrees	23

TABLE 16

CORRESPONDENTS' UNDERGRADUATE MAJORS

SUBJECT	PERCENTAGE OF CORRESPONDENTS (N = 96)
Journalism	33
English/Literature	21
Government/Political Science	13
History	8
Economics	7
Liberal Arts	2
American Studies, Business, Foreign Language, Psychology, Radio-TV, Speech	1 each

TABLE 17

CORRESPONDENTS' GRADUATE SCHOOL MAJORS

SUBJECT	PERCENTAGE OF CORRESPONDENTS (N = 96)
Journalism	24
Government/Political Science	5
Foreign Language	3
History	2
Economics	2
English/Literature	1

TABLE 18

CORRESPONDENTS' YEARS COVERING WASHINGTON

YEARS	PERCENTAGE OF CORRESPONDENTS (N = 96)
1-5	48
6-10	21
11-20	16
21-40	12

TABLE 19

CORRESPONDENTS' YEARS COVERING CONGRESS TO THE EXTENT THEY DO NOW

YEARS	PERCENTAGE OF CORRESPONDENTS (N = 96)
1-5	61
6-10	13
11-20	15
21-40	6

TABLE 20

CORRESPONDENTS' POLITICAL IDENTIFICATION

	PERCENTAGE OF CORRESPONDENTS (N = 96)
Liberal	43
Independent	35
Democrat	14
Republican	4
Conservative	2
None of These	1
Don't Know	1

TABLE 21

CORRESPONDENTS' YEARLY SALARIES

SALARY CATEGORY	PERCENTAGE OF CORRESPONDENTS (N = 96)
Under $10,000	6
$10,000-$13,999	13
$14,000-$16,999	19
$17,000-$19,999	13
$20,000-$24,999	30
$25,000-$29,999	9
$30,000 and above	9

TABLE 22

TYPES OF ORGANIZATIONS EMPLOYING CORRESPONDENTS

MEDIA ORGANIZATION	PERCENTAGE OF CORRESPONDENTS (N = 96)
Daily Newspaper	59
Wire or News Service	17
Radio-TV Group	6
Special Interest Newspaper or Periodical	5
National Network	4
General Interest Periodical	3
News Weekly	1

TABLE 23

CORRESPONDENTS' DESCRIPTION OF THEIR PRESENT DUTIES

DUTIES	PERCENTAGE OF CORRESPONDENTS * (N = 96)
Write Routine News	43
Write Specialized News	59
Write a Column	31
Bureau Chief	27
Write Magazine Articles	10
Edit News	6
Newscaster	3
Other	5

* Total reflects duplication of duties

TABLE 24

NEWSPAPERS RELIED ON BY CORRESPONDENTS

NEWSPAPER	PERCENTAGE OF CORRESPONDENTS (N = 96)
The Washington Post	62
New York Times	23
Washington Star-News	4
Wall Street Journal	3

TABLE 25

PERIODICALS RELIED ON BY CORRESPONDENTS

PERIODICAL	PERCENTAGE OF CORRESPONDENTS (N = 96)
Newsweek	27
Congressional Quarterly	20
Time	12
U.S. News and World Report	4
National Journal	2
Business Week	2
Other	9

TABLE 26
RADIO-TV PROGRAMS AND STATIONS RELIED ON BY CORRESPONDENTS

BROADCAST PROGRAM OR STATION	PERCENTAGE OF CORRESPONDENTS ($N = 96$)
CBS Evening News	17
WTOP-Radio	4
ABC Evening News, Meet the Press, NBC Evening News, WGAY Radio, WTOP-TV, CBS Morning News	2 each
Other	7

TABLE 27
IDEA SOURCES RELIED UPON BY CORRESPONDENTS

SOURCES	DEGREES OF RELIANCE Not At All	Very Slightly	Somewhat	Quite A Bit
	Percentage of Correspondents (N = 96)			
Reporter-Colleagues in correspondents' organizations	8	21	45	18
Producers in correspondents' organizations	26	5	16	3
Editors in correspondents' organizations	12	28	33	15
Other sources within correspondents' organizations	25	10	7	1
Newspapers and magazines other than correspondents' own	1	25	50	12
Radio-TV news broadcasts, other than correspondents' own	29	32	10	2
Congressional Quarterly, National Journal	16	23	35	10
Congressional Record	8	23	41	19
Reporter-colleagues from other organizations	19	42	28	2
Staff of Senators or Representatives	4	16	38	38
Staff of Senate or House Committees	8	16	35	31
Senators	8	28	33	23
Representatives	7	25	34	23
Lobbyists and other interest groups	20	32	26	10
Government-printed material available in galleries or in office (press releases, hearing transcripts, reports, executive branch publications, etc.)	3	24	47	18

TABLE 28
INFORMATION SOURCES RELIED UPON BY CORRESPONDENTS

DEGREES OF RELIANCE

SOURCES	Not At All	Very Slightly	Somewhat	Quite A Bit
	Percentage of Correspondents (N = 96)			
Reporter-colleagues	15	38	31	6
Senators	3	10	44	39
Representatives	2	7	48	38
Staffs of Senators	1	4	28	64
Staffs of Representatives	1	5	29	60
Committee Staffs	5	33	57	4
Other Congressional staffs	7	4	10	10
Correspondents' organizations' files, library	12	15	35	26
Correspondents' personal working files	–	8	35	50
Lobbyists and other interest groups	7	34	39	12
Executive branch agencies, departments	2	13	50	26
Congressional Record	2	22	42	27
Congressional Quarterly, National Journal	15	18	30	26
Government-printed material	6	26	37	21

TABLE 29
PERCEIVED INFLUENCES ON CORRESPONDENTS' REPORTING

DEGREES OF INFLUENCE

INFLUENCES	Not At All	Very Slightly	Somewhat	Quite A Bit
	Percentage of Correspondents (N = 96)			
The importance of the subject	2	2	19	73
"Local angles" of the subject	17	15	16	44
New and unusual aspects of the subject	1	5	24	63
Readers'/viewers'/listeners' opinions	50	24	10	4
Readers'/viewers'/listeners' interests	10	10	29	41
Correspondents' editors' opinions	46	23	15	5
Correspondents' editors' interests	23	24	24	18
Correspondents' personal opinions	21	39	20	8
Correspondents' personal interests	12	27	34	16
Correspondents' news organizations' or clients' policies	55	24	5	6
Correspondents' reporter-colleagues	40	30	14	3

TABLE 30

CORRESPONDENTS' OPINIONS TOWARD ROLE PRESCRIPTIONS

OPINIONS

PRESCRIPTIONS	Agree	Tend to Agree	Unde-cided	Tend to Dis-agree	Dis-agree
	Percentage of Correspondents (N = 96)				
To be a neutral observer who is detached from the events and activities he/she reports	64	17	5	5	5
To serve as an impartial, objective transmission link between Congress and the public	53	21	3	13	7
To be an interpreter for the public by putting in understandable terms what Congress is doing and why it is doing it	81	13	–	–	1
To be a representative of the public as a guardian against special interests	48	25	3	7	9
To be a representative of the public as a watchdog against corruption and malfeasance	64	20	2	4	5
To remind politicians, through reporting, that they should be serving the public interest	48	27	3	5	9
To expose secrecy and seek to publicize secret proceedings	53	26	6	5	4
To determine the veracity of statements made by Congressmen	64	21	1	5	2
To stir things up by asking questions	35	29	5	8	14
To stimulate action on worthy legislation	18	18	9	20	25
To give weight and attention to news reports in order to influence the priority Congress attaches to a given policy	10	9	18	20	33
To advocate policy directly in stories by presenting proposals, analyzing the merits of pending measures or making a persuasive case for correspondent's view about the proper disposition of a matter	10	5	6	21	50
To provide information in stories which Congressmen find useful in making decisions	22	25	19	10	20
To advocate policy by presenting ideas and suggestions during direct encounters with Congressmen and their staffs	4	2	5	27	54
To report actions or statements of Congressmen which correspondent knows are designed for news media consumption	6	12	10	22	35
To give advice and counsel to Congressmen and their staffs when asked to do so	6	12	7	28	40

TABLE 31
CORRESPONDENTS' RELATIONS WITH SOURCES: INFORMATION SOUGHT

INFORMATION CATEGORIES	DEGREES OF USE			
	Not At All	Very Slightly	Somewhat	Quite A Bit
	Percentage of Correspondents (N = 96)			
Asking a source to embellish upon remarks made at meetings, conferences, on the floor, etc.	3	8	28	55
Asking a source about a behind-the-scene maneuver on some important issue	3	2	27	64
Asking for private, off-the-record interpretations of the meanings of events, statements	4	17	32	41
Asking for on-the-record reactions to statements or actions made by other officials	1	5	28	60
Other	–	–	–	4

TABLE 32
CORRESPONDENTS' RELATIONS WITH SOURCES: METHODS OF EXTRACTING INFORMATION

METHODS	DEGREES OF USE			
	Not At All	Very Slightly	Somewhat	Quite A Bit
	Percentage of Correspondents (N = 96)			
Appearing to be sympathetic to a source to get more information than correspondent thinks he would get as a neutral or hostile reporter	18	25	38	14
Playing source against source to "smoke out" the whole story	10	21	35	28
Developing personal, congenial relationships during informal social activities and visits to sources' offices	8	23	29	35
Demonstrating to source that he can trust correspondent (by honoring background and other confidential information, quoting accurately, etc.)	2	2	20	71
Giving sources extra "ink" or "play" in reports to cultivate them (reporting a little more favorably than correspondent would normally, finding more news in a statement or action than normally, etc.)	54	28	7	3

TABLE 33

FORMS OF SANCTION ENCOUNTERED BY CORRESPONDENTS FROM SOURCES

SANCTIONS	FREQUENCY OF USE			
	Often	A Few Times	Once	Never
	Percentage of Correspondents (N = 96)			
Insistence that correction appear in print or on the air	3	40	7	45
Request by source for apology from correspondent publicly	8	3	84	1
Complaint, or threat of complaint, to employer or other authority	3	34	12	47
Elimination from mailing list or distribution list	1	4	9	78
Prohibition from attending hearings or conferences	1	8	6	80
Refusal to grant interview or access to staff or office	3	37	6	49
Supplied with false or unreliable information from source	8	44	4	38
Other	1	3	–	–

7

Solons and Scribes

THE INTERACTION BETWEEN members of Congress and the varieties of congressional correspondents probably has received more attention than any other area of Congress-media relations.

A new general picture of relations between members and correspondents is presented by Delmer Dunn. He is followed by Douglass Cater and Donald R. Matthews, whose books have been standard reading for students of Congress-media relations.

Less known is Richard L. Riedel's description of correspondent-senator relationships as he viewed them during his many years as an employee of the U.S. Senate. Many of those years he was responsible for "press liaison" between senators in the Senate chamber and reporters in the President's Room nearby. Although a personal, sometimes gossipy, name-dropping report, it is otherwise an unobtrusive description of this point in the reporter-senator web of relationships.

Correspondents Stewart Alsop and A. Robert Smith provide two case studies of correspondent-senator interaction beyond the President's Room. Alsop presents an insightful comparison between Lyndon Johnson as a news source in the Senate and a news source in the White House. Smith's account of Senator Wayne Morse's relations with reporters gives a view of the sanctions and rewards with which at least one senator attempted to control or influence the news judgment of reporters.

Member-correspondent partnership in congressional activity is described by the late Bert Andrews, a participant in Richard Nixon's rise to prominence in the 1950's, and by Noel Epstein, a correspondent reporting on the activity of a colleague.

Laurence Stern and Edwin Knoll describe news media reporting of alleged corruption or unethical behavior on Capitol Hill.

Is Congress covered well by the news media? This was the final question asked the correspondents in Chapter 6. It is discussed further in this chapter in articles by Michael Green, a correspondent for a West Coast newspaper group, and by Lewis W. Wolfson, a former Washington correspondent and bureau chief who is now an associate professor of communication at The American University. Green argues that the House of Representatives is not covered adequately, particularly with in-depth, personalized reporting. Wolfson describes how the members of Congress whose districts are virtually in the shadow of the Capitol receive little coverage from community newspapers or from two of the major newspapers in the area—the *Washington Post* and the *Washington Star-News*. The case study was written from material gathered under Wolfson's direction by a team of graduate students in the Public Affairs Graduate Journalism Program at the American University. The students interviewed the five suburban members of the House and their press aides, their opponents in the 1972 election, and editors and reporters for the *Post*, *Star-News* and 22 suburban newspapers. Congressional coverage in both metropolitan dailies and 29 suburban newspapers was examined for the first three months of 1973. *Post* and *Star-News* coverage was followed for an additional four months.

Ben H. Bagdikian's article, which appears in Chapter 8 where congressional publicity is considered, also is appropriate in this Chapter. He summarizes the belief that correspondents do not cover Congress adequately. Furthermore, he says, they participate as "partners in propaganda," reinforcing careerism in Congress, and thus its unresponsiveness to the voters and the weakness of congressional checks on the executive branch. He describes a Nader-sponsored project, the Capitol Hill News Service, established to counter the publicity monopoly enjoyed by many members of Congress in their home districts.

———

SYMBIOSIS: CONGRESS AND THE PRESS

By Delmer Dunn

It is difficult to read a newspaper or watch a national television news program these days without hearing charges of "credibility gap" or "news management" with countercharges of "slanted news" or "nonobjectivity." The intensity and persistence of such discussions suggest that both political reporters and public officials regard the relationship between the press and government as fundamental to the democratic process. Analysis of press work in congressional offices shows it to be a central element of office structure and responsibility.

Reprinted from *To Be a Congressman: The Promise and the Power*, edited by Sven Groennings and J. P. Hawley, by permission of Acropolis Books Ltd. Copyright © 1973.

COMMUNICATING THROUGH THE PRESS

To be an effective senator or representative, one generally needs to develop both skills and routines in working with the press. For several purposes it is important for legislators to make news. Of primary importance is showing constituents that their man is doing a "good job" in Washington. The most notable examples of press communications designed to fulfill this function are the many routine announcements of bills introduced and grants made by the Federal government to the benefit of the home district. Regular newsletters offering commentary on national problems also serve this function.

While not all representatives and senators are "publicity hounds," most reap satisfaction from personal publicity. This publicity, of course, can have more substantial payoffs than personal satisfaction. Senators and representatives believe that the better known they are, the greater are their chances for re-election. Publicity which emphasizes their names is a primary means of building this identity with their constituency. Senators and representatives who seek to become national political figures recognize that the press offers opportunities to communicate their policy views throughout the country. Building a reputation for policy leadership cannot be done solely through direct personal contact. The media become crucial to the success of persons seeking higher office.

Congressmen also desire to make news in order to create an image of themselves as active and concerned leaders. A government commission recently recommended such "symbolic output" in calling upon the President of the United States to better indicate his responsiveness to students by showing greater willingness to listen to them. An official's concern may be expressed entirely apart from government actions actually providing goods and services or initiating the regulation of behavior. By disseminating symbolic outputs, the media enable a legislator to respond to the full range of society's needs and wants. Through news photos and television coverage of a walking tour of a ghetto, the senator or representative can demonstrate his interest in the problems of the poor. By visiting malnourished families or scenes of disasters he can demonstrate, the press permitting, that he is actively seeking out the problems of society and attempting to alleviate them.[1]

Officials also need the assistance of the press as they seek to introduce ideas and develop support for them. The Senate has increasingly become a place where new ideas for public policy are "incubated." [2] Before there is any hope of approval for such a policy, an interested senator can introduce the idea in the form of a bill and seek public support for it. While doing so he can communicate to others throughout the country that an official is interested in their ideas and perhaps provide them some incentive or encouragement to sustain their original interest. In addition, he can introduce the policy idea to others and suggest ways of using it to solve problems. Or perhaps he may attempt to dramatize the extent of a problem. By talking about the problem and presenting possible solutions, over the years a senator can make such matters acceptable in public discourse. Ideas that may at first seem radical become familiar and less imposing, and problems that once went unnoticed gain amplification. A few years ago "busing" and "pollution" were not part of the national political vocabulary. Today they are, as an increasing number of people perceive these subjects as grave public problems. Likewise, "medicare," though popular with many citizens 25 years ago, was viewed by some as suspect, if not heretical. But it became more familiar and less suspect throughout the fifties and early sixties until finally, in 1964, it was enacted into public policy. The role of the media is crucial both in transmitting and cultivating ideas during their incubation and in the growth of their acceptance.

Learning from the Press

One reason senators and representatives desire to make news is that publicity has an impact on the policy process. They learn from the media and assume that other officials do also. The media, for example, constitute a source of ideas. When the *New York Times* executes a study of what it perceives to be a national problem, the resulting work can provide a seedbed for policy ideas. A report on the state of medical education could generate numerous policy ideas. Likewise, a dramatic television documentary, ripe with ideas for new policy initiatives concerning a public problem, might produce extensive publicity. In addition, columnists frequently offer ideas and suggestions which an official finds congenial. These suggestions, of course, have further implications. Others read the same stories or watch the same television programs, including reporters and editors, who define what is and is not news. Their future news judgments may be affected by the suggestions, as the columns and programs at least tend to heighten their interest. As a consequence, an official taking action with regard to subjects examined in the media is in a good position to have his actions accepted as news. Indeed, an official may "plant" ideas for such documentaries and feature stories in an effort to dramatize the need to act on a program in which he has long been interested.

What senators and representatives learn from the media helps them in evaluating their own activities. Success is frequently determined, in their own judgment, by the extent and character of publicity. Failure to gain publicity may result in a legislator's decision to drop an idea. However, if his proposal is well received, he is likely to increase his attention to it if he thinks it has the potential of yielding even more news.

Officials also learn from the press how to order their priorities. Events, problems, and policy proposals which receive emphasis in the media *a priori* become important. By calling attention to an item, the media elevate its importance. They cause senators and representatives to devote more interest to the matter, because legislators from experience will be certain that the policy makers with whom they will be talking will also discuss such emphasized events and activities. Moreover, constituency mail often concentrates upon the top items in media presentation. Another reason for enhanced legislator interest is that events and activities emphasized by the press may provide a clue as to which interest groups will be activated and perhaps be calling upon officials to present positions or demands.

These uses of the press are evaluative in that they help officials decide what is important and where to place emphasis. Senators and representatives also learn from the press in two additional ways that increase its importance in the policy-making process.

The press frequently transmits substantive information that senators and representatives find useful in their work. Congressmen read newspapers to discover what is occurring on the Hill itself. The myriad of committee meetings makes it impossible to keep abreast of everything. Much business in the Senate and House is conducted with few members actually present on the floor. And while the late Senator Richard Russell is reputed to have read the *Congressional Record* from cover to cover each day to keep up with floor activity, few legislators find time to do so. Summaries of lengthy presidential messages, complex bills, and commission reports which appear in daily newspapers provide a shortcut in the lives of busy men to keep abreast of many activities.

The major legislation introduced each day and the most significant proposals of outside groups generally receive press attention. Again, the condensed versions in the newspapers provide helpful time-savers in the lawmakers' personal information-gathering activities. Finally, lawmakers utilize newspapers to keep up with events back home. Involvement in Washington frequently produces a feeling of isolation from the home district which can be particularly worrisome for elected representatives. Although one may keep in touch through periodic visits and telephone calls, these means do not yield the comprehensive constituency contact that newspapers from the state or district can provide.

Lawmakers, as do their counterparts in other governmental systems, also utilize the media to gauge constituency reaction.[3] Editorial reaction, particularly in papers back home but also in those which circulate daily in Washington, provide clues as to what their constituents are thinking. Senators and representatives watch letters-to-the-editor and reports of group activity as well as editorial commentary to measure opinion and reactions to policy proposals or political events.

ELEMENTS OF THE MEDIA

The job routines of representatives and senators provide numerous opportunities to those who desire to make news. Accredited to cover the Capitol are 2,182 political reporters representing 811 newspapers, magazines, news bureaus, wire services, radio and television stations.[4] Thus there are about five reporters for each senator or representative. The structure of the lawmaker's job coupled with pluralism within the news industry dictates certain variations of making news.

The media are differentiated into the "national" media and the "local" or "regional" media. The national media consist of the radio and television networks, the wire services and the major East Coast newspapers which circulate in Washington on the day of publication, often called the "prestige press." These newspapers include the *New York Times*, the *Washington Post*, the *Washington Star-News*, the *Christian Science Monitor*, and the *Baltimore Sun*. There are several advantages in making the prestige press. Many senators, in particular, are cultivating a national constituency in order to create the possibility of generating future support for high office. If they hope to become presidential or vice presidential candidates, they must make themselves and their activities known beyond the borders of their state. The national media are, of course, crucial in fulfilling this goal. Moreover, they are important because it is through them that officials do much of their "talking" and "listening" to one another, thereby extending considerably the scope of their communication. For this reason, an official developing a policy proposal must utilize the national media to communicate the substance of his ideas to other policy elites. Even those who are not engaged in advancing policy ideas or presidential ambitions find it advantageous to receive national media publicity. In many states such exposure increases the lawmaker's prestige among his constituents. It also provides him satisfaction in knowing that his colleagues are reading about his latest activity or pronouncement as they drink their morning coffee. All of them read the national press for its domestic and foreign coverage, even if they disagree with the editorial viewpoint.

At times, of course, legislators and those who write about them are suspicious of each other's motivations, hold contrary views or develop animosities. One is reminded of the legendary exchange in which a lawmaker concluded an interview with an antagonistic reporter by asking sarcastically, "Well, is everything you are writing today the truth?" The reporter replied, "Yes, everything not enclosed in quotation marks!"

Legislators seek to develop particularly close working relations with the "regional" or "local" media serving the home state or district. Many metropolitan newspapers and stations have correspondents in Washington. Smaller newspapers often buy the services of a news bureau or participate in a pool of correspondents maintained by a newspaper chain. Regular contact between a Federal lawmaker and the local media is mutually beneficial. The senator or congressman sends a steady stream of grant announcements and other press releases of local interest to the media, enhancing his image of constituency service. The local radio and television stations and newspapers solicit his reaction to major events, for he, as their audience's voice in Washington, is a prime source of news. At times legislators are cornered in the Capitol corridors to provide spontaneous interpretation of news just then unfolding. In 1972, for example, legislators were contacted almost immediately for their comments on the attempted assassination of Governor George Wallace and President Nixon's decision to mine the harbors of North Vietnam.

Understanding congressional press relations requires differentiation not only between national and local media but also between their use by senators and representatives. While senatorial advantages are strongest with regard to the national media, they at times extend to the local or regional media as well. Senators are more interesting news targets than congressmen for several reasons. Many openly aspire to higher political office, and journalists pay close attention to potential presidential candidates because these politicians command broad public interest. In addition, the Senate generally considers questions of broad public policy more openly than the House of Representatives, whose procedures frequently structure debate rather rigidly and, some think, predispose it toward superficiality. Recently, for example, some senators have attempted to alter military and foreign policy, and the drama of their efforts has attracted extensive reporting. The Senate's greater prestige further increases media interest in its deliberations, while rules for media coverage are more flexible in the Senate than in the House. Its open committee meetings may be covered by television cameras any time. By contrast, not until 1971 were television cameras allowed to cover House committee meetings, except during brief periods when the Republicans controlled the House in 1953-1955. Even now they cannot do so without committee approval.

Although representatives, by comparison to senators, rarely make the national media, there is some reversal with regard to the local or regional media. Representatives usually have deeper roots within their constituencies than do senators. Most local media are very interested in stories with a local angle, and a representative may be in a better position to satisfy that news definition than his counterparts in the Senate. If the representative happens to live in a district with a newspaper or station large enough to have a correspondent in the capital, so much the better. He may receive attention in such media because he is a readily available source to a reporter, indeed one of the few sources about news of interest to the state or locality. But if the regional medium is also a metropolitan one, the representative is again at a disadvantage compared with other officials, including senators. Such media frequently have a state-wide audience and accordingly a greater interest in a senator and his viewpoints. They also frequently devote attention to urban politics, to mayors, councilmen, and other politicians whose business appears to have more immediate and direct impact than that transacted in the Congress. Thus a metropolitan area's several congressmen face rigorous competition from a state's two senators in securing extensive attention to their individual opinions and activities.

METHODS OF GAINING COVERAGE

Senators and representatives desiring press coverage can acquire it in a variety of ways. The most ubiquitous is the press release which the typical office on both sides of the Hill distributes several times each week. Some indicate bills which the member sponsors or co-sponsors. The subjects for most of these releases are attendance at important conferences, results of constituency polls, committee activities, letters to the President, major government grants, key votes, and general policy positions. If the member disagrees with the policy of the administration, he may utilize this means to inform his constituency or the national media of that fact. News stories indicating how various senators or representatives responded to a presidential speech, policy message, or activity, very often quote from a legislator's press release.

One variant of the press release is the weekly news column or radio or television program. In these, senators and representatives frequently develop themes—the volunteer army vs. the draft, the performance of President Nixon vs. the proposals of leading Democrats, tax reform, inflation, and the environment—discussing their view of a problem or situation and their efforts to ameliorate it with positive and progressive action.

The typical Senate and House office has automated mailing lists of newspapers in the state or district. Such lists are usually divided between daily and weekly publications, and sometimes the daily is further segmented into metropolitan and non-metropolitan papers. Most news releases go routinely to these papers through use of such a list. From time to time offices also send special news releases to papers in areas where some local interest item is emphasized. For radio stations, many offices use a "beeper." It consists of a tape recording, usually of the senator's or representative's voice. Radio stations are then called and fed the transcript, which they re-record for later transmission. Stations often present such releases as "interviews" with the member. Weekly radio or television programs are sent by tape or film directly to the stations. They are frequently professionally produced within the Senate or House itself, as both Houses maintain recording and filming studios offering services at minimal cost. Press releases designed for the national media take a different route. They are distributed to the House or Senate press galleries, to the National Press Club where many reporters have their offices, and to reporters who are known to be interested in the subject matter of the release and are considered "friendly" by the member.

Personal interviews are a second way that Washington lawmakers come into contact with the media.[5] It is the rare representative or senator who refuses to talk with a reporter. Probably no one, except perhaps large campaign contributors, enjoys better access to elected Washington officials. Such encounters range from a 60-second interview for a radio or television program to a lengthy session covering a variety of subjects. Most interviews, however, are specific. A reporter usually wants to know about a particular event occurring on the Hill or an activity in which a member is engaged. Of course he very often asks about other matters in the course of the interview and invariably provides the member with time for "free association" if he wishes.

Floor speeches [6] can also be made to generate press attention. Some observers assert that most activity on the legislative floor is "play toward the press," designed primarily for its newsmaking qualities. This is something of an exaggeration, but undoubtedly does explain much that transpires there. The lawmaker desiring to amplify remarks made on the floor can issue a press release which summarizes them, distributing it either to the papers back home or to the press represented in Washington.

Lawmakers frequently stage events to achieve publicity. The congressional investigation is one of the time-honored techniques for doing this.[7] An investigation, because it implies controversy, wrongdoing and conflict, contains many of the prime elements of news definitions. Committee hearings can have the same effect. Themes may be set, witnesses selected, and topics planned to wring the maximum news coverage out of them. When a senator or representative assumes the chairmanship of a committee or subcommittee, he gains a powerful publicity instrument. He can arrange investigations or hearings, or stage tours to demonstrate a national need for a program, thereby winning media exposure. The Senate "Hunger Committee," under the chairmanship of Senator George McGovern (D., S.D.), provides a recent dramatic example of a committee which was formed in part to educate; that is, to call attention to a problem which Senator McGovern believed needed national attention.

Finally, senators and representatives can call press conferences or briefings. Congressional party leaders do this to support or criticize the positions of the President. A group of senators or representatives sponsoring a resolution may call a conference to explain their purposes and to obtain publicity for their idea. A senator recognized as an authority in a policy area may call the press together to explain his reaction to a presidential proposal. If members can properly gauge their timing and catch an issue riding the crest of a high interest wave, they may be able to use a press conference to great advantage. These events do not occur every day. But when a railroad declares bankruptcy, a soldier is court-martialed, or a bitter military defeat is suffered, the time may be ripe for cashing in on the interest associated with this activity by introducing a bill or resolution, criticizing a President's policy, or offering an evaluation which will provide news to the media and publicity to the member.

ORGANIZING TO MAKE NEWS

The typical congressman or senator has a press secretary to marshal the lawmaker's press initiatives, to calculate the ways to increase his publicity, to answer routine reportorial inquiries, and to write the weekly newsletter for newspapers as well as the script for radio and television shows. The press secretary should have broad personal contact with reporters, know what their news needs are, be able to recognize a good story, and be aware of the possibilities of generating news for the benefit of his boss. Perhaps the most elusive of these qualities is being able to recognize a good story. An event in the office of Senator Lowell Weicker (R., Conn.) illustrates how a press secretary can sense a good news item that others might judge to be routine. A member of the Senator's staff related the story:

> A woman shipped her dog by air and found that it was dead upon arrival. She then wrote Senator Weicker to complain about airline handling of animal cargo. One of the Senator's secretaries, a lover of dogs, was about to mail a routine reply when she mentioned the situation to the press secretary, Hank Price, who spotted the possibility that the "dog letter" had news value. To get information on other such cases, he phoned the Federal Aviation Agency, the Department of Agriculture, and the Civil Aeronautics Board. The last had recorded at least a dozen similar cases, while the Humane Society, which he also contacted, indicated that there had been more than one hundred cases. Upon presenting this information to the Senator, the press secretary next found himself drafting a bill for the purpose of authorizing the Secretary of Transportation to draft rules and regulations governing transport of animals by air, which Mr. Weicker introduced on the floor of the U.S. Senate. The story became front page news in Connecticut. It had human interest; "everybody" has a dog. Appreciative mail flowed heavily into the Senator's office. One constituent, whose letter is well remembered, wrote that he had never voted for a Republican in his life, but he loved animals and would vote for Lowell Weicker in future elections.

Senate and House offices are organized differently to handle press releases. Senate offices usually have a full-time press secretary and at least one assistant who may be titled as the assistant press secretary or the secretary to the press secretary. The "full-time" press secretary may occasionally have other duties—perhaps to write speeches or to staff a small area of legislative activities. But his primary responsibility is to handle press relations. He usually has direct access to the senator, arranges appointments with reporters for him, and discusses ideas for new publicity.

Although many House offices do have a full-time press secretary, most do not. House members' staffs are generally about half the size of senators' staffs. Frequently an administrative assistant or a legislative assistant combines his duties with routine tasks associated with press relations.

As is true for most House activities, the member frequently performs his own staff work, whereas a senator normally must rely much more on his staff. Thus a representative may serve as his own press secretary. He usually knows all reporters for district newspapers from past contact in campaigning. Representatives take telephone calls much more frequently than do senators, some even answering their own telephone when in the office. Thus they often obviate the need for someone to set up appointments. Indeed, reporters may just drop in and be instantly admitted if the representative is in his office. Some congressmen have even been known to write their own press releases or weekly newsletters, something that few senators take the time to do.

Conclusion

Most Washington lawmakers regard press relations as very important. . . . Effective press [relations] determine the success of many of the legislator's other activities. The press serves almost constantly as a mechanism linking him with his larger political environment. Through it he obtains ideas, suggestions, opinions and reactions. He also uses the press to communicate to others his views and goals. If legislators cannot communicate effectively with their constituents, their re-election prospects may be threatened; losing touch is the path to defeat. For this reason, it is not surprising that reporters readily gain access to lawmakers. Regardless of occasional hostility and suspicion between them, the working relationship of newsman and legislator is fundamental to the democratic process; to be a congressman is to work with the press.

NOTES

[1] See Murray Edelman, *The Symbolic Uses of Politics* (Champaign-Urbana, Ill.: The University of Illinois Press, 1964), for a discussion of the symbolic output of government.

[2] For an extensive discussion of the Senate's role in policy incubation, see Nelson W. Polsby, "Policy Analysis and Congress," *Public Policy*, XVIII (Fall, 1969), p. 67.*

[3] For an extremely valuable discussion of how foreign policy officials and others use the press, see Bernard C. Cohen, *The Press and Foreign Policy* (Princeton, N.J.: Princeton University Press, 1963), especially pp. 196-241. See also, for a discussion of utilizing the media to gauge constituency reaction, Douglass Cater, *The Fourth Branch of Government* (Boston: Houghton Mifflin, 1959), pp. 12-13,* and James Reston, *The Artillery of the Press* (New York: Harper and Row, 1967), p. 63.

[4] *Congressional Directory 1970*, pp. 788-818, 832-841, 844-853.

[5] For a more detailed discussion of how public officials use personal contact to make the press see Delmer D. Dunn, *Public Officials and the Press* (Reading, Mass.: Addison-Wesley Publishing Company, 1969), pp. 138-141.

[6] For other discussion of how officials use speeches to issue information, see Donald R. Matthews, *U.S. Senators and Their World* (Chapel Hill: University of North Carolina Press, 1960), pp. 203-204,* and Cohen, p. 179.

[7] For discussion of how the investigation can be used to generate publicity, see Cater, pp. 56-65,* and David B. Truman, *The Governmental Process* (New York: Alfred E. Knopf, 1952), pp. 379-386.

* Selections reprinted in this book.

THE STUFF OF WHICH GOOD REPORTING IS MADE

By Douglass Cater

In the United States Congress, the reporter is no longer barred, except from certain committee meetings. His access to individual legislators is frequent and intimate. Near each chamber there are private rooms to which the members are willingly summoned in a never ending file for communion with the press. During a lively session the President's Room just off the Senate lobby is continuously crowded with little clusters of solons and scribes, two by two, exchanging earnest confidences. Special doormen stand ready at the request of correspondents to call still others away from the debate. At times this little anteroom contains more Senators than the Senate Chamber. The creation of the public image of the debate is more engrossing to most of them than the actual debate itself.

A few steps inside the Senators' lobby, a battery of tickers brings back the news minutes after it is dispatched. Nowhere else in Washington does one more keenly sense the cyclical movement of policy and publicity. Across the Capitol, a similar drama is being enacted in the House of Representatives. There, even the members' lobby is open to the prowling correspondent.

Even the fledgling correspondent in Washington finds an ease of access to congressional leaders which makes Congress for him a happy hunting ground of journalistic enterprise. The senior reporters assigned to the Hill share an intimacy with these leaders which lesser members of Congress seldom gain. At least once daily the wire-service representatives are invited in for sessions with the Speaker of the House and the Senate Majority Leader. On countless unnamed occasions the reporter may attend the informal convocations at which the earthier matters of politics are explored. Not infrequently he is a direct participant in the act of legislative policy making, a privilege he would hardly be accorded in the Executive departments.

There is good reason for his prerogatives. The play of the news helps to regulate the orderly flow of legislative business, or, alternatively, to thrust an unaccounted item out of the darkness of committee neglect into the limelight of full congressional attention. It stirs mutinies among the rank-and-file Congressmen or squelches them. The pressures of publicity can reinforce the unspecified Constitutional authority of the potentates on the Hill when they seek to pit their power against the Executive. Access to the news writers provides the Congressman a chance to contribute his interpretation to the first draft of history, which he hopes will in turn help shape the course history takes.

At times the raw competition to service the press takes on bizarre proportions. The following account appeared in a "Footnote to the News" column of the Washington *Post and Times-Herald:*

> A freshman Senator outslicked his veteran colleagues to pick off the easiest publicity plum available last week. He was Clifford P. Case (R-N. J.), whose reaction comment to the President's decision [to veto the Natural Gas Bill] was the first to hit the Senate press gallery. His prize was a prominent play in the afternoon newspapers.
>
> Behind his speed was the quick thinking and faster legs of Sam Zagoria, Case's administrative assistant and former Washington Post and Times-Herald reporter.
>
> Zagoria had run off several copies of the Senator's "isn't-it-grand" statement early Wednesday morning. He then parked himself by the Associated Press teletype in the Senate lobby. When the flash came through, he hightailed it back to the press gallery, one floor above, where eager reporters were waiting to write reaction accounts. Zagoria beat a runner for Sen. William A. Purtell (R-Conn.) by one minute flat.

On an average day the long table in the Senate Press Gallery is littered with the mimeographed news releases from the Senators. This predigested copy summarizes their views on every conceivable issue, domestic and foreign. The American legislator, uniquely among the parliamentarians of the world, is sensitively alert to the business of systematic press relations.

For the reporter, it is more than easy access which makes Congress a primary news source. The business of Congress is the stuff of which good news reporting is made. Congress is a continuing scene of drama and conflict and intrigue. Its battles can be described in terms of colorful personalities rather than amorphous issues that may confound the copy desk and confuse the reader. Washington is a highly fragmented capital city in which it is not always simple for the reporter to follow the thread of his story. But it is possible for him to glimpse the image of the total story in the congressional mirror, indeed, to see its outlines in a bold relief that may not be so apparent on direct view.

Perhaps inevitably there should be this "congressional bias" to the news. There is, in addition, a degree of protectionism that comes into play. Powerful pressures dissuade the reporter from being as zealous an exposer of Congress itself as he is of the Executive departments. His stock in trade in terms of news "exclusives" depends upon the preservation of a chummy relationship with members of Congress. A great amount of news is dispensed to him as a favor and must be regarded as such. There is not quite the same camaraderie about news gathering in the more austere precincts of the Executive.

On the other hand, the retaliation for unfavorable publicity can be much swifter and more vengeful from Congress. It is by no means unusual for a member, enraged by something appearing in print, to take to the floor in a violent attack against the offending reporter. Such is the club-like atmosphere of the two houses, that no member is likely to come to the reporter's defense. Abuse of the most vicious sort has been heaped on the head of the offending journalist while the Senators and the galleries listened in uneasy silence.

On April 10, 1950, Senator Harry Cain rose on the Senate floor to answer an assertion by *Time* Magazine that he was among the Senate's "expendables." For the better part of the afternoon he centered an attack on *Time's* congressional correspondent. "If ever I sat with a human being who was smug, arrogant, self-centered, vain and frustrated . . . This ulcer-burdened young American who could neither vote nor fight . . . The agent *Time* Magazine has today was a 4-F in peace . . . has undoubtedly encouraged other men to die, but he has never stood on the sidelines and watched them die.

"During our conversation," Cain concluded, "I lost the rich anger and indignation which has possessed me for several weeks. I lost even what had been my desire to laugh in the face of this pygmy. I did not even want to bat him around physically because that would have been like punching a bag of mush."

Not one Senator remonstrated against this disgusting tirade.

As one who has had the experience of being thus attacked by a senior Senator, this reporter can testify to the unpleasantness of the experience. Only after several efforts was it possible to find one of his colleagues willing to insert a factual reply in the *Congressional Record*. Privately, many were ready to vouchsafe their sympathies.

The reporter knows there is slim likelihood of any followup on his initiative should he publish evidence of corruption or wrongdoing on the Hill. For one who turns up malfeasance in the Executive Branch, there is always a congressional committee standing by eager to pick up and pursue the matter. In fact, the publication of the exposé and the com-mencement of the committee probe have sometimes been carefully coordi-nated in advance. Reporter and committee counsel work hand in glove to reap its full benefits. But Congressmen are seldom as prone to examine one another. Nor is the Executive Branch always alert to bear down on congressional abuses. It has no publicity mechanisms comparable to the congressional committee probe for airing such abuses.

I do not mean to imply there is a preponderance of virtue in the Executive Branch or of vice in the Legislative, but merely to point out that the publicity processes do not provide so strict a surveillance of the latter. There are countless instances when Congressmen demand special privilege that would provoke great furor if made by an administration official. The legislator moves in an area of protectionism that extends even to his unwise public utterances. Members of the press often apply a deliberate censorship. One neophyte reporter who unwittingly quoted in print a rash remark revealing bigotry on the part of a leading Congressman told me he was afterward chastised by several of his press colleagues for this indiscretion.

Women correspondents covering Capitol Hill circulate among themselves the names of those members of Congress with whom it is unsafe to be alone. One or two solons have been known to be real sex reprobates. But no word of their misdemeanors ever reaches the reading public. Senators have been seen to stagger drunkenly onto the Senate floor and deliver unintelligible harangues without creating a ripple in the press. Considering the great glare of publicity that beats down on Congress, the unillumined corners are the more curious.

This protectionism even covers some of the collective activities in Congress. Year in and year out minor frauds on public understanding are committed without being duly noted by the press. Each year, for example, the House Appropriations Committee or one of its subcommittees virtuously makes deep cuts in appropriations bills for funds already contractually obligated. Each year, this action is duly rewarded by newspaper accounts that the Committee has "slashed" the budget by such and such an amount. And later each year the Committee quietly restores the cut in its "supplemental" appropriations. Yet, one reporter told me, though tempted he wouldn't dare lead his story with the fact that "the congressmen have made this cut with the full expectation, as in former years, of restoring it later in the Session when the public isn't looking."

'COVERING' THE SENATE

By Donald R. Matthews

In a typical postwar year, more than a thousand newsmen were accredited members of the Senate press galleries. This group was not a homogeneous one. Some reporters represented small out-of-town papers, while others were employed by the Washington newspapers or belonged to one of the large Washington bureaus maintained by the *New York Times, St. Louis Post Dispatch, Chicago Tribune,* and other metropolitan dailies. Some were reporters for the three wire services—the Associated Press, United Press, and International News Service *—while still others wrote for news magazines. A few were columnists and radio-TV news

Reprinted from *U.S. Senators and Their World* by Donald R. Matthews by permission of the University of North Carolina Press. Copyright © 1960 by University of North Carolina Press.

* Since this was written, UP and INS have merged into United Press International (UPI).

commentators. These different kinds of reporters were interested in different types of news, and this fact influences both the frequency and the nature of their dealings with senators.

The Two Levels of Reporting

Most Washington reporters work for small out-of-town newspapers and seldom cover national news. Rather they specialize largely in stories with a local slant—the appointment of postmasters, the letting of federal contracts to local concerns, and the like—leaving the coverage of "top" news to the wire services to which their papers subscribe.

Such a division of labor makes a great deal of sense. The wire services maintain sizeable staffs in the House and Senate galleries, in the White House, and in the executive departments. The Washington bureaus of most out-of-town papers are very small (often a single reporter), and they must try to cover the entire town. The wire services, by working in shifts, can cover news events continuously. Their stories are transmitted over their leased wires more quickly than other reporters can write in their stories.

But wire-service reporting has its limitations. Despite the fact that they maintain regional services specializing in news of interest to specific regions of the country, wire services cannot possibly provide locally slanted news for all of their subscribers. Moreover, wire-service news stories are written close after the event for transmission to scores of widely scattered subscribers with different needs and political persuasions. They tend to be severely factual, lacking in background and interpretation, and scrupulously objective. In order to overcome these limitations, a few metropolitan newspapers with large Washington bureaus, the Washington dailies, and the news magazines cover top news for themselves.

Thus Senate news is covered on two different levels. The vast bulk of the reporters for out-of-town papers (plus the regional reporters for the wire services) spend only part of their time on the Hill and are concerned with locally slanted news stories. A small number of the wire-service reporters and men from the Washington newspapers, large metropolitan dailies, and news magazines spend all their time on Capitol Hill covering top news.

The Reporter's Limited News Sources

No matter which level of news he seeks, the reporter's important news sources in the Senate are likely to be few in number.

This is most obvious in the case of reporters writing locally slanted stories. Within the Senate, only the two senators from their paper's state are likely to know of or care about the news they report. These two offices, however, are extremely fertile sources of the news such reporters need. The two senators, if they are of the president's party, play a major role in the making of federal appointments to local citizens. Usually they and their staffs have actively advocated the granting of contracts, franchises, and other forms of federal largess to their constituents. Most executive agencies, after making decisions on such matters, automatically notify the senators before making the news public. Also, senators who have served for any length of time have built up informal information machines among political dependents scattered all over town. They are likely, again especially after they have some seniority, to serve on Senate committees of particular importance to the folks back home. Rather than making a daily canvass of the scores of departments, agencies, bureaus, commissions, and committees making decisions of local interest, reporters can, by maintaining close liaison with their senators and representatives, obtain the same information more quickly and easily. But this short cut has its price. As one such reporter said, "The stress on the local angle makes us very dependent upon the senators and representatives from —— and their staffs."

The relatively few full-time Capitol Hill reporters writing top news have many more potential news sources. Indeed, this is one of the attractions of Congressional reporting. "In the White House," one prominent reporter explained, "you sit around until someone gives you a hand-out and then you write a story on the basis of it. That's not *reporting*, that's *stenography*." In the executive departments, especially in the State and Defense Departments, "they can really punish a critical or unfriendly reporter who needs more than routine hand-outs to meet his obligations to his paper. Up here we can be a lot more independent." In actual practice, however, most top news reporters on Capitol Hill develop a limited number of news sources and lean on them heavily.

In part, this is the result of the time pressure under which most Washington correspondents work. "You just can't go around and talk with all of them, so you tend to fall back on the ones that you know are most helpful to you." For the wire-service reporters, especially, this is important. Yet this is not the only reason that the reporters of national news each have close regular contact with few members of the Senate. "If I had all the time in the world," one reporter for a weekly news magazine said, "there are some senators I wouldn't bother to see."

Correspondents also desire off-the-record background information and interpretation. "If what you want is background information not for quotation, it takes a fairly lengthy and close relationship before they will be completely open with you," and "a senator naturally talks more freely off-the-record when he knows you and has learned to rely upon your discretion." Even when such a confidential relationship is well established, the reporter must know his informant well enough to read between the lines. "I don't mean 'getting to know' in the sense of knowing where to reach them but really and intimately knowing them as persons. You've got to be able to distinguish between what they mean and what they say. For example, I talked to Senator ——— the other day about his stand favoring an additional cut in foreign aid. Now he didn't say so in so many words but I carried away the impression that 99 per cent of this was for [home state] consumption so I played the whole thing down."

Still another factor encouraging the reporter's reliance upon a relatively few news sources in the Senate is the chamber's internal patterns of influence. "I don't talk about this for obvious diplomatic reasons," one reporter for a nationally known paper said, "but there's not too much use in talking to more than five or six senators. After you've talked to them, you know what is going on." Another top news reporter elaborated on the point. "Take ——— or ———, for example, they have big hearts but no real influence. Much of the time they don't have a good idea about what is going on, or what will happen in the future. I could ask ——— how many votes a bill will get on final passage and he probably would tell me. But it wouldn't be as good an estimate as that of a more influential senator. ——— is just not a member of 'the club.' "

Finally, as still another reporter said, "Some senators have a good news sense—they are good reporters. If we call them off the floor they can summarize developments briefly in newsworthy form."

For all these reasons, then, it is no exaggeration to say, "Every newspaperman on Capitol Hill must have a sponsor. We all have three or four congressmen and senators with whom we are intimate and from whom we get most of our news."

Influence on the Reporter's Sources

What factors determine the specific "sponsors" or "sources" a reporter has on the Senate side of the Hill?

First of all, the newspaper or organization for which he works shapes the reporter's access to senators. "Senators like to see their names in the Washington papers—it's funny, even after a lifetime in politics they like knowing that their colleagues are reading about them over their breakfast coffee. They also like publicity in their hometown papers and in the New York Times and Herald Tribune. Reporters from these papers plus the wire services have the best access." Other factors also enter in. "Congressional reporting is a big and lucrative field and reporters work hard at developing contacts and news sources on the Hill." All reporters agree that "if they like you it helps a great deal." "I used to take quite a kidding about my terrific 'in' with ———," a reporter for a nationally important paper said. "I don't know quite why I had it—I disagreed strongly with most of his policies. Of course being with the [newspaper] helped a great deal. This is a stuffy way to put it, but we had respect for each other. And we liked each other." Ideology also affects a reporter's contacts and sources. Reporters who are liberals, or who represent liberal papers, tend to work with liberal senators and vice versa. "During the McCarthy exposures a whole new group of reporters arose who worked closely with him and his staff." This is especially the case with columnists, commentators, and interpretive reporters, for "by the time they have been around here long enough to write a column, their political views are pretty well known and they have easy access to the senators who agree with them."

This does not mean that reporters talk only to senators whose political position is similar to their own or that of their employer. Relations between political opponents here, as in the Senate itself, are generally cordial. It does mean, however, that reporters are seldom able to establish a confidential relationship with a senator over too wide an ideological chasm. If they want completely frank and uninhibited opinions or information from a senator to whom, for this or some other reason, they are not close, reporters are likely to get it from some other member of the press corps who enjoys greater access to the senator concerned. "A good bit of the time, reporters cover the Senate by talking to each other."

The way in which the Washington reporters go about covering Senate news causes wide variations in the frequency with which individual senators are in contact with reporters and differences in the types of reporters they normally see. All senators are in close and frequent communication with the bureaus of their home-state newspapers, but, since most of this news is routine, the actual contacts are usually handled by their staffs. The frequency of a senator's contact with national news reporters depends largely upon his influence within the chamber. The floor leaders, committee chairman, and elder statesmen are often in daily communion with these men, while the ordinary senators see them much less often. Senators with a sense of national news are also in demand. The particular top news reporters a senator sees depends, of course, on all sorts of factors, but, as a general rule, senators see top reporters who work for papers in which they wish to receive publicity, whose political position is similar to their own, or who are personal friends.

THE POLITICAL ROLE OF THE REPORTER

According to the "Fourth Estate myth," reporters are neutral observers entirely divorced from the situation on which they report. No matter how laudible this myth may be, one need not spend much time on Capitol Hill to observe that it departs drastically from Congressional realities. In fact, reporters play an important role in the operation of the Senate and profoundly shape the behavior of its members.

The Reporter's Definition of News and Senatorial Behavior

In order to survive, most senators must make "news" by the reporters' definition of the term. To advance to even greater political heights (i.e., the White House) a senator must become a national celebrity. Thus much senatorial behavior is shaped by the senator's perceptions of the reporters' notion of news.

Some senators try harder to anticipate press reaction to their behavior than do others. . . . [A] few senators take the view that "no one knows how you vote but everyone remembers what you say" and avoid publicity as much as possible. Others define the role of the senator largely in terms of public "education" or propaganda and expend a larger amount of their time and energy on seeking publicity than doing anything else. Most senators fall somewhere between.

Even so, most of what is said on the floor of the Senate is aimed at "making news" via the press galleries. Congressional investigations, too, are more often calculated to affect tomorrow's headlines than the statute books. The types of bills a senator introduces, the committee assignments he cherishes, how he votes on roll calls, and what he defines as an "issue" are influenced by anticipated press reactions.

Over the years, most senators develop a "sense of news"; that is, they are able accurately to anticipate what events will be considered "news" by which reporters. This is more complicated than it sounds, for different types of reporters seek different types of news. The Washington reporters for a senator's home-state papers may give a big "play" to a story which the regular wire services will ignore. To send the same kinds of stories to reporters operating on the two different levels of reporting can result in loss of confidence by both kinds of reporters in the senator's news sense and the downgrading of the importance attached to all future releases. "Why, ——— has no news sense at all," one reporter complained. "If the President of the United States dropped dead before his eyes it would not occur to him that this was news." If a senator wishes to receive favorable publicity, he had better not earn this kind of reputation. Most of them do not. Most of them learn what is "news" and how to make it. In other words, they behave in accordance with the reporters' expectations.

Reporters as Informal Advisors

Reporters do not always wait for the senators to learn by themselves how the press wishes them to behave. The preparation of a senator's routine news releases is, especially for relatively new members, often a joint endeavor of the senator's staff and the home-state bureaus. If the relationship between senator and reporter matures into one of close collaboration and respect, the reporter is very likely to become an informal advisor to his Senate news source. For example, Richard Nixon, while a member of the House Un-American Activities Committee, first seriously investigated Whittaker Chambers' "pumpkin papers" on the advice and insistence of Bert Andrews of the *New York Herald Tribune.** An alert newspaper reporter first suggested the televising of Senator Kefauver's crime investigation.

* See selection by Bert Andrews in Chapter 7.—Ed.

"Pressuring" Senatorial Action

This kind of relationship shades imperceptibly into the reporters' forcing action they desire from apathetic or reluctant senators through their influence over the news.

One good example of this was Senator Fulbright's . . . investigation of the stock market. Upon becoming chairman of the Banking and Currency Committee, Fulbright was asked by a reporter what the committee would be doing during the next session of Congress. The senator from Arkansas said he did not know for certain, plans were still indefinite. The reporter persisted: would the committee be looking into the housing situation, the policy of the Federal Reserve Board, the recent rise in stock market prices. The senator replied, yes, probably they would. The next day the reporter broke the sensational news that the committee would investigate the stock-market boom. In this manner the investigation got under way.

Another example of "pressuring" is the explosive investigation of Secretary of the Air Force Harold Talbott by the Permanent Investigating Subcommittee. Charles Bartlett, the Washington correspondent for the *Chattanooga Times*, received a tip from a businessman acquaintance that Talbott was conducting private business from his office in the Pentagon. Bartlett took the tip to the staff director of the committee, a personal friend, and they agreed to look into the matter. Five months later, both Bartlett and the committee staff believed that they had obtained sufficient information to merit a public investigation. The night before the committee was told of the results of the staff investigation, Bartlett, fearful either that the story might leak out or that the committee would not take action on the matter, published his story. The committee had no choice but to proceed.

Almost endless examples of this sort of thing could be repeated here. A reporter for the *Washington Post* helped trigger the . . . investigation of the natural-gas lobby; the Teapot Dome scandals were initially uncovered by a newspaper. So, too, were the "five-percenter" inquiries during the Truman administration.

The truth of the matter would seem to be that while newspapermen make news, they cannot—with the exception of a few columnists— admit it. "When we find some newsworthy item, we take it and 'bounce it off' some news source. For example, if we discover a scandal in an executive agency we generally take it to a senator or congressman and try to get an investigation, or at least his comments. Then it becomes news."

The Press, External and Internal Communication

A major source of the senators' information on the outside world is the public press. They do not, unlike the members of the executive, possess a far-flung information and intelligence network of their own. While the normal senator has great (and sometimes misguided) faith in personal observation and experience, it is clearly impossible for him personally to gather more than a tiny fraction of all the facts and ideas he needs. Most senators are avid newspaper readers, for their busy schedules and personal inclinations do not seem to permit the extensive reading of books. Most of them read the Washington papers, the *New York Times* or *Herald Tribune* (sometimes both), plus several leading home-state papers every day. (Their staffs usually either clip or mark news items of interest to them in other papers in the home state.) The Senate cloak-rooms contain the wire-service tickers and they are regularly consulted by all the senators. The *Congressional Record* contains, each day, a large number of news articles and interpretative columns inserted by the members for the possible edification of their colleagues. The basic themes of many a Senate speech have clearly been stimulated by, or borrowed from, the latest efforts of Krock, Reston, Lippmann, and their local equivalents.

This is obvious. Yet it is not so well known that the senators often find out what is going on in the Senate by reading the papers. Senators are incredibly busy people. Most of them have specialized legislative interests. Most important legislative events take place in the myriad committee and subcommittee meetings occurring all over the Hill. Senators have neither the time nor energy to keep tab on this hundred-ring circus. The newspapers help immeasurably in the senators' never-ending struggle to keep track of what is going on in the Senate. It is ironic but still true that the members of so small a legislative body should find it necessary to communicate with each other via public print, but often they do.

It is a great deal easier to say that reporters play an important political role in the Senate than to document precisely what that role is. The reporters' influence is so all pervasive that it is hard to isolate it from other factors. Even so, we have suggested a number of ways in which the reporters shape the behavior of senators. Their definition of "news" influences how the senators act and what the "issues" are, they sometimes serve as informal advisors to the senators with whom they work closely, they can and do "pressure" senators into taking action merely by the way they "play" a story, and they serve as an essential link between senators and the outside world and as a means of communication within the chamber. These factors must have been in the mind of one Senate staff member who, when queried concerning the role of reporters in the Senate, answered, "Hell, they run the place." But the blatant subservience of most senators to reporters is not solely a manifestation of the latter's power. It is also, as we shall see, one way in which senators try to control reporters.

THE TACTICS OF THE PUBLICITY HOUND

Reporters influence the behavior of senators, but senators possess considerable leverage over the reporters as well. For one thing, the senators vary in the amount of publicity they need in order to survive. A senior senator, thoroughly entrenched in his constituency, without presidential ambitions or a thirst for fame, can say, "When you've got the votes, you don't have to talk," and largely ignore the press corps. This immediately increases his attractiveness to the reporters, although most senators who adopt this stance are in such powerful legislative positions that they would be hotly sought after news sources in any event. The more usual situation is one of extreme senatorial sensitivity to publicity. "You ought to see a senator read the papers the day after he has made important news," one reporter said. "The *implications* he can read into every word!" The appearance of still photographers or TV cameramen regularly touches off vigorous senatorial jostling and elbowing contests. "They all want to be in the middle of the picture, standing next to the big man. I'll bet that sometimes they go home at night with real bruises."

Even the senators who, through personal choice or political necessity, are publicity hounds can influence what the reporters write about them and how often. Nor need they, in an effort to maximize the favorable publicity they receive, invariably knuckle under to the reporters' demand that they make news, by the reporters' definition. They can also manipulate the men who report the news.

The tactics of the publicity hound are few and highly standardized. They seldom fool anyone, but, within limits, they still work.

Overcooperation

Senators, their staffs, and (indirectly) the American taxpayer provide all kinds of services and special privileges to the press corps. The Senate press galleries—larger, more cheerful, more comfortable than perhaps any other in town, "a good place to run into friends and catch up on the latest gossip"—are the most tangible of these services and help explain why the Senate and senators are such favored sources of news.

But the senators' staffs also provide home-state bureaus, wire-service men, and the press galleries with press releases as a matter of routine, written in the proper form and appropriately timed to suit the reporter's convenience. "I try to be fair in writing up these stories," one senator's press assistant said, "but you can be sure that the boss's name is right up there in the story." Interested reporters are notified in advance by the senator's staff whenever he is scheduled to make a floor speech or a presentation to a committee. The texts of his speeches and statements are dispatched to the proper people at the proper time. The Washington press corps is so dependent upon this prefabricated material (which most of them gladly make their own) that extemporaneous speeches, the give and take of debate, and the flow of committee questioning of witnesses are seldom adequately covered in newspaper accounts of Senate proceedings. Another consequence of this practice is that the senators gain more control over the content of news dispatches than they otherwise would have.

Most senators are easily accessible to reporters—at least those they wish to please—at almost any time. "They are the only ones who can go into his office without any preliminary rigmarole," one legislative assistant said of his boss. "Why, if he were having dinner with the Queen of England and [name of reporter] wanted to see him, he could and right away. When they call, everything else in the office stops." One enterprising young newspaperman confesses that he obtains most of his interviews with senators by telephoning them at home in the evening, obtaining their unlisted numbers from Washington's Social List. He reports that his annual $15.00 investment in "the green book" is money well spent and that "they are always delighted to talk."

A senator can provide many other services to a reporter as well. "Why, [senator's first name] is practically another member of our bureau," one reporter explained. "If I am unable to get some information from an executive agency that I need for a story, I call ——— about it. Within thirty minutes I get a phone call from some big wheel in the agency with the information. ——— will do that even if the story will not include his name; it pays off in a better press." Thus the basic gambit of the senator-publicity hound is overcooperation. It results not only in good will but in a sense of indebtedness on the part of the reporter as well, and at least some control is exerted over the reporter's stories. After all he, or more likely a member of his staff, wrote some of the stories in the first place.

Off-the-Record Interviews, Leaks, and Exclusives

Off-the-record interviews, leaks, and exclusive stories are variants on this same technique with one important difference; they are not "across-the-board" policies applied to many reporters but special favors granted to a select few.

Reporters, as we have already seen, are dependent upon access to confidential and unauthorized information. Once they have found senator-sources of such information, they understandably wish to "keep their sources open" for the future. Moreover, the reporter is likely to feel beholden to his source. "Suppose," one radio-TV news analyst explained, "that ——— came up to me at a party and said, '———, you're doing a wonderful job. Now there are a couple of things I think you ought to know' and then proceeded to give me some valuable inside information. I darn well wouldn't lambast him on the program that night." Indeed, the warm glow of the experience might even result in his saying something nice.

Sometimes a reporter's flattery of a senator is coldly calculated "My critics have sometimes accused me of getting news by buttering-up certain officials, referring to them as 'able' Senator So-and-so, or the 'astute'

Secretary of So-and-so. That was once true. I think I can even fix the date when I swore off." In many interpretative and behind-the-scene news stories originating on Capitol Hill (including those written by the man who allegedly has sworn off), the reporter's confidential sources are as clearly identifiable as the "good guys" in a grade-B Western movie. Whether or not this is the reporter's conscious policy, is, from the senator's point of view, irrelevant. He has obtained a better news break than he otherwise would have received.

According to one senator's press secretary, "There's such a thing as being too cooperative with the press. If what you want is publicity, I'm convinced that often the best way to get it is to withhold stuff from the press, treat it as a 'secret document," and then leak it out a little at a time. The word will get around and then they all will be calling here to find out the inside information." In this day of the mimeographed hand-out, press agents, and press conferences, the Washington reporters are hungry for "exclusive" stories. "If a senator calls me in and gives me the story as an exclusive, rather than calling a press conference, I'll give it a bigger 'play' and so will the paper—there's no doubt about that." After all, it makes both the paper and the reporter look good.

In this manner competition within the press corps works in the senator's favor. They can, by the judicious use of off-the-record interviews, leaks, and exclusives, build up the reputations of friendly reporters and papers and even win themselves a few new journalistic friends. This gambit, it should be added, works not only within each of the media but between them as well. One Democratic senator, confronted by an unusually hostile press in his home state, suddenly began breaking news stories over his weekly radio program before releasing them to the newspapers. Just as suddenly, his newspaper coverage improved.

The Friendship Ploy

Many a reporter has found that his best stories are obtained at Washington parties. At social occasions the senators' usual loquacity is "intensified by the lulling warmth of the liquor, the geniality of the group, the camaraderie of the occasion, and the absence of those inhibitions against confidential speech which are found in the formal press conference, the presence of a stenographer, or the vigilant portrait of George Washington on the wall." As one old-time reporter has put it, "The most important news usually comes out after the second highball." As a result, some reporters do a good deal of entertaining, and in turn are entertained by members of the Senate.

It is difficult to determine who gains the most from such commercial friendships. The reporters pick up tips and inside stories, but the senators gain protection. As one powerful columnist has written: "The more you go out to dinner, the more friends you make and the more you diminish the number of people you can write about without qualms of conscience or rebukes from your wife." A member of a small Washington bureau put the same point a little differently. "I've found it not a good idea to be too friendly with senators from my paper's state," he said. "It complicates matters too much; if you have to clobber them they are liable to get mad . . . it's best to keep your relationships [with home state senators] on a strictly professional basis." "Take Drew Pearson," still another reporter said, "I'm sure that many members of the Senate thoroughly despise the man, yet they do business with him. And, at social occasions, I've seen them flock around him. It's a form of self-protection, I suppose."

Just as in their relationships with lobbyists, constituents, and Senate colleagues, the senators find, in their dealings with reporters, that at least the semblance of friendship pays off.

Noncooperation and Attack

The basic tactic of the publicity hound is to provide services and special favors to reporters which then may be withdrawn in the event the newsmen do not live up to their end of the bargain—i.e., render favorable coverage. The bargain, it should hastily be added, is invariably implicit and perhaps not even recognized as such by either side, but that makes it no less a bargain.

When a reporter does not live up to his end of the deal, his relations with the senator involved cool; the senator understandably loses some respect for the reporter's judgment and may take his inside dope, leaks, and exclusives elsewhere. The seriousness of this situation, from the reporter's standpoint, depends largely on which level of news he writes. The local-story reporter, with many fewer *potential* sources and less prestige on the Hill, can be hurt a great deal more than the top news reporter with a wider group of potential news sources. Neither kind of reporter, however, is likely to bring on such a situation needlessly or without considerable prior thought.

Very rarely one hears of a senator boycotting a reporter. Senator Morse of Oregon was recently so infuriated by an AP story that he banned all AP reporters from his office and press conferences for about a year.* More often, but still also rarely, a senator will publicly attack a member of the press corps. A few years back, for instance, Senator McKellar of Tennessee became so angry with Drew Pearson (who had written that he possessed an uncontrollable temper!) that he took the Senate floor and said of the capital's number one peeper into political keyholes:

> He is an ignorant liar, a pusillanimous liar, a peewee liar. . . .
> That statement is a wilful, deliberate, malicious, dishonest, intensely
> cowardly, low, degrading, filthy lie.

* See Selection by A. Robert Smith in Chapter 7—Ed.

When a man is a natural-born liar, a liar during his manhood, a liar by profession, a liar for a living, a liar in the daytime, a congenital liar, a liar in the nighttime, it's remarkable how he can lie. . . .

This human skunk cannot change his smell. He will always be just a low-life skunk. Mr. President, if I have been guilty of exhibition of temper, I hope the senators will forgive me.

The same reporter was once physically assaulted by Senator McCarthy.

Several recent Congressional investigations have been ill-concealed efforts to punish hostile news media. Senator Bricker of Ohio, for example, recently cast himself in the unlikely role of trust-buster in an investigation of the broadcasting industry. The radio and TV news commentators had, almost to a man, panned the proposed Bricker Amendment a short while before. And Senator Eastland spearheaded a Senate exposé of "Communists" on the *New York Times* staff after the paper had repeatedly and vigorously disagreed with his policies.

The trouble with these sanctions is that they do not work. A senator who boycotts a reporter, paper, or news service usually does himself more harm than good—the AP survived the Morse boycott with considerably greater ease than did the senator—nor are public tongue-lashings of reporters likely to result in a better press in the future. To punish the publicity media via publicity is a difficult trick, even when utilizing that awesome instrument for doing so, the Senate investigation. To the reporters, efforts to use such extreme sanctions against them merely indicate that the senators "just don't understand our business and are not likely to be good sources, anyway."

CONFLICT, COOPERATION, AND THE NEWS

The potential sources of conflict in the relations of senators and reporters are almost infinite. The reporters want news, and the senators desire favorable publicity for themselves and their programs; the two are by no means identical concepts. The newspapers and magazines for which most reporters work are identified with policy preferences which, be they "liberal," "conservative," or between, are always repugnant to some members of the chamber. The columnists and interpretative reporters, of course, face this problem in an extreme form. It is often unclear whether a reporter's discussion with a senator is "on" or "off" the record, and the reporter's use of information is a potential source of considerable strain. Given the conditions of the journalist's work, some inaccuracies are inevitable in Congressional reporting, and senators can be extraordinarily sensitive about small errors. There are, too, some things that senators would prefer not to expose to the bright glare of publicity. It is certainly to the senators' advantage to maintain large areas of semisecrecy about which reporters can learn only through leaks which place the reporters in their debt. The reporters, on the other hand, have a vested interest in free access to information, softened, to be sure, by their understandable desire for "beats" and "exclusives" which the present type of semisecrecy makes possible.

The Infrequency of Senator-Reporter Conflict

It is not surprising, therefore, that animosities, hurt feelings, and ill will often characterize the relations between senators and reporters. In the process of covering Washington political news, many reporters develop a thorough-going distaste for politicians, including senators. "When I first started reporting I was told to treat 98 per cent of all public officials with contempt. I propose no change to this rule—except to up the percentage to 99." They complain that "to some politicians, lying just comes naturally" and develop a profound distaste for "the monumental pomposity of most senators."

The senators and their staffs, on the other hand, complain fairly often of violated confidences; or inaccurate, distorted or misleading reporting; that "while reporters talk about freedom of information, all they really want is a public-relations man to write their stories for them"; and the reporters, by playing up "side shows" and personal conflict, paint a distorted picture of the Senate and senators.

Yet the surprising thing to the outside observer is that these animosities seldom break the surface. Given the potential sources of conflict, the relations between senators and reporters are remarkably free of friction.

One reason for this is that, through close and regular contact and despite the cynical talk, many reporters and senators begin to identify with each other and to understand each other's problems. For example, one publicity-oriented senator has bitterly complained for years of the lack of coverage he receives in his home-town newspapers. The reporters for the papers, it seems, have been able to "get off the hook" by showing him copies of all the stories about him that they have filed but which have not been printed, thereby re-directing the senator's wrath toward their employers. Many senators excuse the reporters in their preoccupation with scoops and sensations on the grounds that this is what the reporters' editors and readers want.

At the same time, the reporters of top news who spend full time on the Hill tend to become socialized into the Senate folkways and to develop a sympathetic understanding of the senators' plight. "Up here," one of these reporters said, "we tend to become identified with the Senate. It's a little like being a war correspondent; you really become a part of the outfit you are covering."

More than sentiment softens reporter-senator conflicts. Rational calculation does as well. Few groups are more dependent upon each other than senators and Washington reporters. They need each other so badly that the use by either side of sanctions stronger than noncooperation is not rational policy. The inevitable hostilities and frustrations of such a dependent relationship usually remain unexpressed or disappear rapidly: "If I write an unfavorable story about a senator, our relations may be a little cool for a few weeks, but it won't last long."

Senator-Reporter Cooperation and the News

Both senators and reporters have it in their power to build each other up. A senator, by giving a reporter preferential treatment, can enhance newsman's prestige among the press corps, his standing with his employers and readers, and his earning power. A reporter, by giving the senator a good break, can contribute substantially to the success of the senator's career. This kind of "back scratching" is far more profitable to both sides than conflict.

In local-story reporting, "it pretty much happens across the board." The mutual build-up is less common in national news reporting, but even in this kind of reporting "back scratching" is not unknown and the pay-offs in fame, power, and Pulitzer prizes are great. We have already mentioned the close collaboration of Richard Nixon and Bert Andrews (of the *New York Herald Tribune*) on the Hiss-Chambers case. At least partly as a result of their joint endeavors, Nixon became a national figure almost overnight and quickly won election to the Senate and the vice presidency, and Andrews won a Pulitzer prize. Arthur Vandenberg and James Reston (of the *New York Times*) are another example of a senator-reporter team which, through intimate collaboration, rapidly "built each other up" in their respective worlds. William S. White, then of the *Times*, had impressive "ins" with Robert A. Taft and the Southern patriarchs in the Senate. As a result of this arrangement, both Taft and the Southern leaders gained sympathetic national publicity, and White, a well-earned Pulitzer prize. And so it goes.

Senator-reporter "back scratching" has a decided influence on Capitol Hill news. The national news reporters' best sources receive a better press than their actions merit. The chamber as a whole escapes the searching criticism that some members of the press corps would like to give it, if they dared.

At the same time, one must be careful not to push this conclusion too far. There is a limit beyond which a reporter cannot go. He cannot suppress a really newsworthy story. "There are few secrets in the press corps. We all love to come up with exclusive stories but we don't succeed very often. If I held back on something fairly newsworthy, some other paper would most certainly pick it up." But the reporters are their own judges of newsworthiness, and their standards may easily vary from one situation to the next. In a marginal case, this judgment of newsworthiness may well be influenced by the reporter's desire not to "go out of my way to embarrass a reliable source." For instance, reporters admit to *not* writing stories concerning senators who took mid-session Florida vacations, had brushes with traffic policemen, were drunk and disorderly at Washington parties, and failed to return to their constituencies during summer recess. These are certainly not world-shaking events, but they might conceivably be viewed as "news."

Generally speaking, however, it is *how* a story is written, and not whether it is written, that is influenced by reporter-senator "back scratching." Let the reader beware.

Reporters, the Folkways, and Intra-Senate Conflict

While relations between senators and reporters are amazingly smooth, this very fact tends to stimulate conflict within the Senate.

The senator's locally oriented publicity is far less conducive to intra-Senate conflicts than are his efforts at making national news. Other members of the Senate are generally ignorant of the kind and amount of publicity a senator receives back home. They all know it is essential, and besides it does not affect them in any way. There is, however, one important exception to this rule: the other senator from the same state. Each senator watches the publicity of his colleague very closely indeed, and many a feud has been touched off by the fact that one senator seemed to be getting better publicity than the other. Sometimes full-scale "publicity battles" will break out between the two senators. In one case, a senator made a practice of arriving at work each morning armed with a personal count of the number of times his colleague's name appeared in the paper that morning compared with the number of times that his own name had been printed. These comparisons were invariably invidious, despite the best efforts of a succession of administrative assistants, until his colleague was defeated for re-election.

Even when such a battle does not break out, the kind and amount of publicity one senator seeks is generally affected by what his colleague is doing. One Midwestern senator, for example, had served with quiet efficiency in the Senate for some years when an ambitious, young, publicity-oriented man won the other seat. "At first," an assistant to the older man has said recently, "we thought we could go on as before and that the contrast between ——'s and ——'s styles would be to our benefit. But we pretty quickly changed our minds. One thing [the younger man] has done is to educate a lot of people about what is going on here. Now we get out as many, indeed a few more, press releases for home consumption than he does! The people in the Iowa offices do a lot less than we do and their state is about the same size and type as ours. But they don't have —— to contend with." The relations between two senators from the same state are almost always strained, and their competition for publicity in the same arena seems to be one reason for this coolness.

Competition for national publicity, however, is even more disruptive to intra-Senate harmony. One way to make national news is to play a significant part in the making of important legislation. This is not a role that can be played by all senators simultaneously and, given the present structure and folkways of the Senate, is most often and easily played by those senators with the least need for publicity. The ordinary senator can usually make national news only through such frowned upon practices as "grandstanding"—making sensational speeches engaging in "personalities," excessive partisanship, and other forms of behavior calculated to get his name in the headlines without legislative accomplishment—or through such "side shows" as Senate investigations of war profiteers, grafters, criminals, and Communists. If enough senators do not voluntarily engage in such activities, the reporters, especially those from the wire services, try to stimulate conflict. "They often call up my boss," one legislative assistant explained, "and say 'Senator so-and-so just made this statement. Do you want to attack it?' If he makes a tough enough statement they print it. Their attitude is 'Want to fight? I'll hold your coat.'" The reporters' desire for controversy-laden national news and the relatively uninfluential senator's desire to make it are highly subversive to the Senate folkways.

A VIEW FROM THE PRESIDENT'S ROOM

By Richard L. Riedel

When Senators come out to meet the press in the President's Room, they may be making the most important move of that day. If the Senator is a good news source, willing to talk about his committee activities and share his insights, he may be rewarded with a front-page story that will accomplish more than a dozen speeches to win public support. It is to a legislator's advantage to treat news correspondents well. With notable exceptions, most Senators go out of their way to help the press.

A private interview in the President's Room does not put Senators on the spot as television panels are known to do. It is apt to be a relaxed, respectful encounter between two knowledgeable friends who open up and share information because they trust each other. The Senator can give valuable off-the-record leads because he knows that he will never be quoted without his permission. Or he can caution the correspondent in the manner of North Carolina's Sam Ervin who sometimes says with a cherubic smile, "Just say you got it from a source nearest the truth!"

Longtime friendships between Senators and newsmen are mutually beneficial, but are the friendly exchanges in the President's Room suspect because they might stifle the independence and objectivity of the press? Would we be better informed if all newsmen were bloodhounds, sniffing out trouble and treeing Senators right and left? On the contrary, the public gains from the mutual trust between Senator and correspondent. The informed Senator can supply background information that will define the issues and personalities. Who supports and who opposes a bill and why? In what way is a bill likely to be amended? Which pressure group is most active in trying to influence Senatorial thinking? The public has a far more thorough analysis from a free flow of information among friends than it would have from the guarded comments of Senators who are suspicious lest a newsman violate his confidence.

There can be the other extreme. While all established correspondents have their main sources of information, William K. Hutchinson had two or three veritable pipelines on both the Democratic and Republican sides. Chief of the Senate staff of Hearst's International News Service for twenty years, Hutch would come to the President's Room with fire in his eyes and in a snarling undertone, ask for his Senator to meet him at the south door to the Chamber. Upon hearing who wanted him, the Senator would never refuse but go immediately to the rendezvous like a trained seal.

If a correspondent bites the hand that feeds him news, he may have severed that news source forever. It is human for a newsman to cast a better light on his Senatorial friends, but it does not follow that he must always agree with them or cover up for them. Most Senators have a healthy tolerance for dissent. Like Senator Richard Russell of Georgia, they ask only that their own position be stated fairly and not distorted. Russell's committee work and leadership of the Southern Senators gave him few spare moments for an interview, but he would always come, sometimes explaining to me, "I don't have time, but that man has been so honest in his reporting, I just must go to see him." Another time he would go out reluctantly to a different newsman, saying, "That fellow! No matter what I say, he'll twist it around to mean something else. Oh well, here we go!"

Objectivity in a newsman leads to genuine respect from Senators. The two Democratic Senators from Connecticut welcomed veteran Bob Byrnes of the Republican *Hartford Courant*. More important than politics is the fact that Bob has always been scrupulously fair.

Very few Senators go as far as Wayne Morse of Oregon in defining a fair article as a favorable one. Senator Morse became so incensed by a story written by Milt Kelly of AP that it was years before he would see anyone from the Associated Press. However, Morse would open up graciously to the correspondent of a certain conservative paper even though the newsman began by saying, "Senator, you know my paper will never compliment you, but I have to know the background of the education bill you are sponsoring." Out of respect for the newsman's honesty and his own devotion to education bills, Senator Morse gladly supplied his information.

Those of us who knew Senators through daily contact came to regard them as human beings more than as public figures. It is not unusual for a newsman to take a liking to a Senator whose beliefs are at odds with his paper's policy. Warren Francis, who with his wife Lorania covered Washington for the *Los Angeles Times* for over twenty years, found himself an admirer of the tireless Sheridan Downey of California, though the *Times* criticized the Senator severely for his welfare ideas. Not until the paper and Downey united to fight for California's share in the water rights of the Colorado River did the Senator realize what a valuable friend he had in Francis. Senators would do well to consider newsmen as individuals, not solely as spokesmen of their papers.

Tensions frequently reach heroic proportions at the Capitol, one of the world's most sensitive news beats. Senators under the strain of work and worry have momentarily blown their tops when I approached them for newsmen, responding in this key, "I don't ever want to see that stupid fellow again! He couldn't write a story straight if he wanted to!" In these darker moments I would go back to the newsman with a soothing story that the Senator was tied up or that he could not answer at that time, with never a hint at the verbal attack. In this way many of the feelings directed at the press have been ventilated in my presence and have evaporated harmlessly into the air.

Many Senators have realized and appreciated my protection. It could even have international implications if the newsman were the correspondent of a foreign paper. An influential Senator exploded one day when I asked him to see the representative of a paper in a Balkan country, "Tell him I don't give a damn about him or his government and I don't want to talk to him, period." I simply told the newsman that the Senator was busy, which was true enough. Later the Senator approached me anxiously to ask, "You didn't tell that foreign correspondent what I really said, did you?" With great relief he thanked me for smoothing over a situation which could have been embarrassing to him and to the United States.

Senator Barry Goldwater's reaction to the press was not limited to an occasional eruption. He was the one Senator who nursed an increasingly bitter attitude toward most of the newsmen. When any correspondent wanted to see him, Goldwater waved me away with an oath and said, "You know I don't want to see those damn newsmen! Can't you see I'm busy?" Some days he issued a general order that he would not come out for anyone. When correspondents had a question for him, I found it necessary to perform a flanking maneuver, knowing that even speaking to him would bring forth his wrath. Coming up behind him abruptly, I had to fire the question at him point-blank without any amenities. Often in sheer surprise he gave an answer in spite of himself.

For some time I gave him the cover-up treatment I always reserved for Senators with momentary frustrations, but the months of hostility grew into years of antagonism. As Senator Goldwater continued to spurn my every effort to smooth his press relations, the situation became more disillusioning and untenable every day. Finally he made it impossible for me to give bland excuses for him, leaving me no alternative but to tell the press exactly what the Senator had said. As his attacks reached their mark, noticeably his press invitations began to drop off.

Senator Goldwater left no illusions, but he does present a study in what might have been had he not been so belligerent. He cut a trim and dashing figure with his bronze, Arizona-desert tan, his dark-rimmed glasses, and his crisp, executive manner. It should have been a press agent's dream to cast him in the image of the Great Zorro, not astride a black steed but zooming away from Capitol Plaza in his Thunderbird or swooping down a canyon in his jet plane. There is about him a distant air of the fabulous man of wealth, accustomed to instant command and response. As a skilled photographer and a general in the Air Force Reserve, Goldwater possesses many possibilities for building up a legend of glamour. That he chose instead to build a wall between himself and the public's eyes and ears, the press, is beyond explanation.

Another conservative Republican took the opposite view. Though fatally ill, Eugene Millikin of Colorado would come out whenever a newsman asked for him. The portly Senator might be settled on a comfortable cloakroom sofa when I approached, but Millikin would smile wanly, stretch out both hands and say, "If you can help me out of here, I can make it!" I would hoist his heavy frame to a standing position and uncomplainingly he would go to the waiting correspondent. Senator Millikin's powerful brain and key position on the Finance Committee made him a valuable source of information while his graciousness endeared him to the entire press corps. He considered it an obligation to come, despite his infirmities, to enlighten the press and thereby the country.

While no Senator has been as antagonistic toward the press as Barry Goldwater, few have been as selfless as Eugene Millikin. The majority are caught in the revolving door of Senatorial urgencies. Somehow they must find time for their committee work, study, hearings, and meetings, and to appear on the Floor to answer quorum calls, to debate, and to vote. In hundreds of letters and scores of telephone calls and visits each day, Senators "run the maze of bureaucracy for their constituents," as Abraham Ribicoff of Connecticut puts it. There are also flying trips around the country on speaking dates. Altogether the Senatorial pace is almost inhuman.

Understandably a Senator cannot do everything. By a process of natural selection he responds more quickly to those correspondents who will give him the best return on his time: his home-state papers, the wire services who represent legions of newspapers, a national radio or television network, and the syndicated columnist whose words are widely read. The names of Ralph McGill or Marquis Childs, Eric Sevareid, Bob Novak or Rowland Evans impress even the most prominent Senators. "I'll be right out!" is their instant response.

When Allen Drury first came to the Capitol in 1943 with the United Press, Senators came out readily enough to see the lanky young reporter. By the time he had moved from *Pathfinder Magazine* to the *Washington Star* and on to the *New York Times* and *Reader's Digest*, Al had become a legend around the Senate as the author of the Pulitzer Prize winning novel *Advise and Consent*. He continued to come with the same modest smile, listening to and mentally recording every word of an interview in order to translate it into the trenchant language of his articles and books.

When Joseph Alsop appeared at the Senate, he might well have left the tents of the Arabs the day before on one of the self-assignments that have taken him all over the globe. "What's on the menu, Rit-chard?" Joe would ask as he jauntily seated himself on the bench outside the President's Room, whipped out his advance copy of *Time* or the latest book to read until I found his Senator. No one devours the printed word of others more avidly than the working press.

When his Senator hurried out to greet him, Alsop's reading material disappeared under his arm. He strode across the English tiles, thrust forward his hand and boomed out, "Sen-ah-tah!" As he literally propelled the legislator into the President's Room, Joe Alsop's exuberance was as intriguing as his sophistication was sobering. Perhaps the world's only effervescent cynic, he was more than a match for an intellectual like Senator William Fulbright.

Awe is not the only reaction columnists arouse among Senators. A reserved caution is the general mood when confronting Drew Pearson or his presently more active assistant Jack Anderson, who have dedicated themselves to finding the splinter in the official eye. Occasionally Jack Anderson would be seated on a sofa discussing the downfall of one Senator while on the opposite side of the room, columnist and Pulitzer Prize winning author William S. White would be seeking to build up another. Bill White has devoted himself so consistently to the Senate scene since hitting the Normandy beaches and covering the European theatre in World War II that he seems a part of the Senate itself.

Freewheeling columnists gravitate to independent Senators. The mere sight of Robert S. Allen barrelling from the west elevator would send me on a search for Senators Gruening, Morse, and Cooper who are solitary thinkers on many issues. Drew Pearson's one-time partner Bob Allen has

given Capitol corridors a fast-paced beating for forty years with time out
to serve as aide to General George Patton during the war. Patton was
probably the only man who could match Bob Allen in determination and
colorful vocabulary. Bob's loss of his right arm during the Battle of the
Bulge has not deterred him in the least. With his jutting jaw and low
boiling point, Bob Allen continues to be a symbol of the most vigorous
and unrestrained nature of the working press.

Women correspondents, particularly a columnist like Doris Fleeson
or Mary McGrory, inspire a certain courtliness in the majority of Senators
that enables the correspondent to get away with more pointed questions.
With a mind as sharp as her tongue, Doris Fleeson produced one of the
most memorable moments to occur in the anteroom outside the President's
Room. A young Senator John F. Kennedy of Massachusetts stood for
many long minutes listening to a pithy lecture from Doris in which she
vehemently reproached him for following the Establishment. Kennedy
took it all with patient good nature and no visible strain. He went on
seemingly to follow Doris' advice as he began to strike out more on his
own. Proving his regard for her, President Kennedy once closed his press
conference with the quip, "Now I must go read what Doris Fleeson has
to say!"

The first woman to blaze a trail in the Press Gallery was a Mrs. Briggs
who, the records show, represented the *Philadelphia Press* in 1870 during
the 44th Congress. It took an aggressive amazon like Isabel Worrell Ball
of the *Lawrence* [Kansas] *Journal* and the *Arkansas City Traveller* to
invade the all-male domain for any length of time, from 1900–03. She
was greeted with the enthusiasm of a case of smallpox, according to
veteran newsmen who noted that the cussing and hairy chests on a hot
day disappeared when she arrived.

From the time of Myra Richards and May Craig, two New England
ladies, the place of the newswoman in Washington has been secure. The
1920's brought Ruth Finney and Bess Furman to the Gallery while Ruby
Black joined in 1933 when Eleanor Roosevelt admitted only women
correspondents to her press conferences. Each of these early members was
married to a newspaperman. Today there are over 250 women members
of the combined press galleries.

Perhaps the most glamorous correspondent ever to come to the Senate
was a young reporter from the *Washington Times-Herald* Jacqueline
Bouvier. The President's Room played its part in furthering one of the
world's best known romances when an early meeting between Senator
Jack Kennedy and Miss Bouvier took place amid the heroic frescoes.

Recently returned from the Sorbonne after two years at Vassar, she
was very shy and ill at ease in the legislative setting. With a gracious smile
Miss Bouvier introduced herself in the breathless whisper that would
become world famous. It was all I could do to catch the words "Jackie

Boo-vhay." I had such difficulty deciphering her French pronunciation that I would inform the Senators almost under *my* breath that they were wanted by the *Times-Herald*'s Jackie "Boovvvvay," skimming lightly over her name.

The future Mrs. Kennedy would wait for her Senators, as all correspondents do, sitting on the bench outside the President's Room. Reserved as she was, she must have been aware of the effect she had upon my young assistants. They were totally overcome by her glamour, tittering in her presence to the point where I finally suggested that they walk away into the Lobby to spare her embarrassment. John Kennedy was only one of several Senators Miss Bouvier interviewed during her intermittent visits to the Capitol.

Senators can be naive about the press, but the opposite is rarely true. The freshman lawmaker, whose new nameplate is barely fastened to his desk, can be tempted to rattle off answers without first learning the questions. If he does, he gets a reputation for glibness or a narrow party outlook that may take him years to live down.

Then there is the grandstander who prefers to make an occasional nationwide splash as man of the day. A wise old-timer like Walter F. George understood the long-term value of complete coverage on the grass-roots level. He would always come for wire service and local correspondents whose stories reached every paper in Georgia.

It takes more than wanting headlines to get them. Even the best-prepared press releases do not help if they lack substance or timeliness. I have watched Senators read mediocre speeches that called for a revolutionary solution like a "meeting of the minds," after which they would glance up longingly at the Press Gallery to see if some newsman were dashing out to write it up. They would hurry out to the news tickers in the Lobby, searching vainly for word of their speech.

To be newsworthy, Senators must work hard on legislation, know their facts, and keep themselves available to the press. They must answer questions with directness instead of campaign oratory, and when they have no answer, admit it. Experienced correspondents are worldly-wise and well-informed individuals who expect a lot of a Senator. Empty clichés do not fool them.

On the other side of the interview, inexperienced newsmen can be exasperating unless they have studied enough to ask intelligent questions. Many Senators would echo Russell Long's ruffled comment about an uninformed reporter, "Why should I write his story for him? He needs to do his own homework!"

Directness is a key virtue for newsmen as well as Senators. I feel sorry for the new reporter whose shy introduction goes on ad infinitum, "How do you do, Senator? I don't want to take your time. I know you are a busy man, but could you answer a question for me? It won't take long."

The correspondent has already taken the Senator's time merely by calling him off the Foor and now he has drowned the Senator's interest in a flood of unnecessary apologies. The best approach is a smile, one word of greeting, and an immediate question to the point. "How are you, Senator! What action do you expect your committee to take on the Housing Bill this week?"

Unfortunately, hard work alone does not guarantee good publicity. Senators can work for months on constructive legislation, and newsmen may cover them well, but their efforts often result in a small story on an inside page. The hint of a scandal is shouted from page one, but many valuable Senators and their finest accomplishments rarely make the headlines.

Several Senators have had the rapport that clicks with newsmen as well as the nourishing information on which the press thrives. In first place would come William E. Borah . . . . Homer T. Bone of Washington rated high in press popularity, along with Joseph O'Mahoney, Homer Ferguson, H. Alexander Smith, and Leverett Saltonstall.

Today [1969] it is the inner calm of Eugene McCarthy of Minnesota that attracts the press. He is welcomed to the Press Table in the Senate Restaurant where he comes to share opinions over a morning cup of coffee. As Senator McCarthy makes off-the-record comments, he is doing his own news gathering. The questions asked him by the correspondents are an excellent gauge of the important undercurrents of the day.

McCarthy is more than a likeable friend and a droll scholar. He is a phenomenon of relaxation in a world of hypertension, the quiet conscience expressed with a take-it-or-leave-it shrug of the shoulders. Hidden within his underplayed tone is a surprising depth of analysis that envelops the listener instead of attacking him as more vociferous speakers do. Perhaps Senator McCarthy's disarming calmness, so contrary to the hectic pace of Washington, can be traced back to the year he spent as a Benedictine novice. Whether he is with the press, campaigning for the presidency, or simply visiting as a friend, Gene McCarthy takes everything in stride better than any Senator I have ever known.

Senator Alexander Wiley, one-time Chairman of the Foreign Relations Committee, did not wait to be asked. He would come out unannounced to josh the newsmen with a friendly, "What do you fellows know?" Pale and paunchy with his pockets full of packets of cheese, Senator Wiley was a walking Chamber of Commerce for the State of Wisconsin. Once he interrupted Bob Barr of Fairchild Publications to thrust a piece of cheese candy into the Press Gallery telephone booth where Bob was calling in his story. The Capitol parties given by the Senator and Mrs. Wiley were a delight to any lover of cheese.

While not the deepest thinker, Senator Wiley was one of the friendliest men ever to serve in the Senate. He often went out of his way to provide the comedy relief during a weary day. Stopping by the President's Room, he would say, "Let's get some pep out here, young fellows!" Then he would go into a remarkable tap dance with all his pounds pounding on the tile floor while we clapped in time to keep his rhythm. Like a perennial Santa Claus, Senator Wiley emitted a continual ha-ha-ha. He kept people from taking themselves too seriously, ribbing Senators and newsmen.

Senators who have been newsmen themselves have the special advantage of seeing both points of view. They anticipate the questions before they are asked and answer first things first in the factual language of the press. At least one-tenth of the Senators I have known have had some experience in the news world. Half of these were publishers in their pre-Senatorial days, such as Medill McCormack of the *Chicago Tribune* and William Benton of the *Encyclopaedia Britannica*. Others were reporters like Arthur Capper of Kansas who came to the Press Gallery in the 1890's. He went home to build a political career upon the broad base of his agricultural news empire which reached millions of readers throughout farming communities in the Midwest.

Blair Moody was the only one to step down immediately from the Gallery onto the Senate Foor when he was appointed in 1951 to fill the Michigan seat vacated by the death of Senator Arthur Vandenberg, another newspaperman. Well-known as Washington correspondent of the *Detroit News* for eighteen years, Blair caused a sensation among his press colleagues who proudly applauded him when he took the oath of office. Thereafter newsmen took delight in leaning over the gallery railing and occasionally dropping spitballs whenever Blair occupied the Chair as presiding officer. Handsome and youthful, Blair Moody was the first Senator I have called by his first name. He remained unchanged, the same hyper-tense individual searching for facts with hard-driving impatience. Though Blair continued his television appearances and fully utilized his press experience, he did not win the election following his appointment and suffered a fatal heart attack during his second try for the Senate in 1954.

The one member of the Press Gallery to make a second career of politics was Louis Ludlow, amiable Washington correspondent, author, and Member of Congress from Indiana. He had covered Washington for almost thirty years when he was elected to the House in 1929. A Democrat from a strong Republican district, Louie Ludlow was an untiring worker who served his people like a devoted minister. They responded by returning him to Congress for twenty years, where he never lost his sense of brotherhood for the press.

Mike Monroney first wrote of the political world for the *Oklahoma News* before coming to the House and later to the Senate. Intent and nervous, like so many newsmen, Monroney was always on the move and one of the most capable legislators. He translated his energies into constructive legislation such as the improvement of aviation and the measure for which he is best known, the LaFollette-Monroney Act of 1946 providing for the reorganization of Congress. Three years before Mike Monroney came to the House, his fellow reporter from Oklahoma City Jack Bell came to Washington to cover the Capitol. As chief of the Senate staff of the Associated Press, Jack is the one who looks and acts like the arrived Senator, while Senator Monroney has retained the unaffected manner of the press corps.

Henry Cabot Lodge, Jr. stands out as the Senator whose previous ten years of newspaper work may well have been responsible for the breadth of his outlook as a legislator. The sheltered but unspoiled grandson of Henry Cabot Lodge became a reporter after being graduated from Harvard. When I first met him, he was with the Washington bureau of the *New York Herald Tribune*. His experiences with the press gave Lodge a taste of life that made him plainspoken and understanding of the needs of the average citizen. When he came to the Senate in 1937, no one was more concerned with the problems of unemployment and old-age insurance than the handsome young man from Massachusetts.

The press greeted Cabot Lodge as one of their own, a factual man of action who could shoot back answers as quickly as they were asked. I was amazed at the quality of his press interviews that approached Borah's in sharp perception. The twinkle in his eyes and tilt of the head had all the charm of his grandfather without the reserve and scholarly preciseness. However, I could sometimes sense a struggle between the plainer side of his personality and his aristocratic heritage. In times of extreme pressure a touch of the frosty aristocrat would crop up in Lodge when he would say to me, "I haven't time to go out there to see anyone. I'm here to make *history!*"

Once during a dull day in the late 1930's, Senator Lodge replaced Vice President Garner in the Chair. The young Senator leaned back a little too far until his chair upended noisily, hitting the flag behind him. The next moment Lodge found himself literally wrapped up in the American flag. When Ed Haakinson of AP came dashing down to find out what happened, Senator Lodge reluctantly agreed to see him. Knowing that the mishap would not add to the dignity of either the Cabots or the Lodges, he had to be convinced that the story was newsworthy. Finally Lodge agreed to its publication saying, "All right, but be sure to say it must have been a Democratic chair!" That was one of the few times Senator Lodge forgot his newspaperman's sense of values.

Cabot Lodge is one of those men who has followed conscience rather than expediency. When he made the difficult choice of going into active combat during World War II rather than remaining as one of the Senate's military experts, he met his sense of duty, winning admiration and service medals, but losing his seniority when he returned to the Senate in 1947.

While his grandfather played a major role in shaping the earlier postwar world as a partisan figure of deep conviction, the younger Lodge joined Arthur Vandenberg in pushing the bipartisan Marshall Plan through the Senate. In seeking to moderate his party's policies, he lost the support of conservative Republicans by opposing Robert Taft for the leadership. Lodge helped convince General Eisenhower to accept the presidential candidacy. In the end he lost his Senate seat to John Kennedy by working harder for Eisenhower than for his own reelection. As vice presidential candidate with Richard Nixon in 1960, Cabot Lodge lost another close race with Kennedy.

Going on to serve as ambassador to the United Nations and to Viet Nam, he has made the most of each difficult assignment with the spirit of a good soldier tackling his job without regard to glory. By considering himself the servant of the nation rather than first promoting Henry Cabot Lodge, he has made his career the very essence of statesmanship.

Being a Capitol correspondent can have its element of danger as Charles Stevenson, then of the United Press, proved in the spring of 1933. In that budget-minded era he wrote an article for *Liberty Magazine* detailing what the government furnished to various officials. The Senate Disbursing Officer Charles F. Pace was enraged by the article, for while it did not mention him by name, his car and chauffeur were included as unnecessary expenditures.

Early one morning Pace charged into the Press Gallery in an excited state. A nervous man at best, he began waving a gun around and demanding to see Stevenson. Fortunately Charlie had not yet arrived. Joe Wills and others in the Gallery calmed Mr. Pace down until he pocketed the gun and went on his solemn way.

The incident was the sensation of the day. Charlie Stevenson heard about it while covering a hearing on the House side when he was warned to watch out for Pace. The other Stevenson in the Gallery, known as "Stevie," was chief of the Senate staff of the Associated Press. To make the distinction clear, Stevie posted the following notice on the Gallery bulletin board, "My name is Francis Xavier Stevenson. Henceforth will my friends please call me Mr. Smultz?" When the Rules Committee investigated, it was found that Pace's revolver was an old Army .45 automatic that was too rusty to shoot in any case.

A decade later after years of otherwise peaceful service, Mr. Pace asked his chauffer to drive him down to Haines Point. There he stepped out of his official limousine and disappeared into the muddy waters of the Potomac in a successful suicide. A very healthy Charles Stevenson now heads the Washington bureau of *Reader's Digest*.

The atmosphere at the President's Room might bristle occasionally but only once did press relations come close to physical combat. One day in the 1930's I brought Senator Kenneth McKellar of Tennessee out to see Bob Horton of Scripps-Howard without realizing that the Senator was angered by an article Horton had written. He no sooner caught sight of the newsman than he began to tell him off as only the volatile McKellar could. In a chain reaction the Senator grew more and more excited, shaking his clenched fists in Bob's face. Suddenly he stepped back and started to swing at Horton with his right fist. I had been watching the entire show, and when I saw that McKellar was actually going to hit Bob, I stepped between them and said, "Please!" That was all that was necessary. They both walked away, McKellar to cool off in the Chamber and Bob Horton to tell his colleagues in the Press Gallery about his close call. The interview was ended permanently for they never spoke again. Later Senator McKellar thanked me for saving him from an embarrassing situation.

A decade earlier Senator McKellar was being interviewed by a newsman on the far side of the President's Room while another Senator and correspondent occupied a sofa nearby. I was in the anteroom outside when suddenly there was a tremendous crash mixed with the sound of breaking glass. Simultaneously a great cloud of dust came rolling out the door. Knowing that McKellar was in there, I wondered what he had done this time! So much dust filled the room that it was impossible to see inside. Immediately two very shaken Senators and the newsmen emerged, stepping through the debris of broken glass and plaster. Luckily they were uninjured. No one knew what had happened until the dust settled and we could inspect the damage.

Like the tale of Chicken Little who spread the word that the sky was falling, the story went out that the huge chandelier had fallen. Actually only the center panel of thick plaster immediately over the chandelier had broken loose, but its shattering descent had stripped off most of the lovely etched globes and the crystal pendants. The whole imbroglio had struck the Lincoln table below with a hollow boom.

Constantino Brumidi had covered every inch of the President's Room with his elaborate frescoes, so that nothing could fall without damaging his work, but only three cherubs met disaster. Though another artist endeavored to replace them later, the new cherubs do not have Brumidi's vivid three-dimensional quality. With carefully regulated humidity and plaster preservatives, none of the painter's work has toppled since.

With all of its overwhelming ornateness, the President's Room does capture and hold a sense of history. And well it might, for history has been made within its four walls. Each President since Abraham Lincoln has used the room briefly. Until Franklin Roosevelt's first administration it was thought essential that a President sign bills before Congress actually adjourned. I have watched Presidents Wilson, Harding, Coolidge, and Hoover sit at the large table with its green felt padding to sign the last-minute legislation passed by an outgoing Congress. A dramatic restoration of the custom came on August 6, 1965, when Lyndon Johnson chose to come to the President's Room to sign the Voting Rights Act upon an ancient desk. It was said to be the one Lincoln had used when he signed a bill on the same date in 1861 to free slaves who had been drafted into serving the Confederate Army.

Thousands of news stories have originated from interviews in the President's Room. Fortunately the news is not often as sensational as it was the summer day in 1947 when I brought a very pale Senator John Bricker of Ohio out to tell the press about his brush with death only moments before. The Senator had been walking to the subway car in the Senate Office Building when a disgruntled constituent fired two shots at him that luckily missed their target, taking some chips out of the wall. The sound of the gun going off in the tunnel was deafening but Senator Bricker had the presence of mind to run forward and jump on the subway car. The operator gave the electric vehicle full power and they sped away toward the Capitol and safety. Within minutes the police nabbed the man with the gun and took him away for observation, correspondents had *the* Capitol story of the day and photographers caught a shaken Senator Bricker telling me about it in the President's Room.

Since the advent of the flashbulb around 1930, more Senators have been photographed in the President's Room than in any other part of the Capitol. In the old days, pictures were almost always made outdoors in daylight, but occasionally an early photographer, such as Herbert French or Buck May, would be granted special permission to use powder-flash equipment in the Reception Room. The photographer crouched under the black cloth thrown over the camera. His feet protruded while he held the flashpan above his head in a Statue of Liberty manner. Counting to himself, "Ready-open-boom!" he uncovered the lens as a cap detonated the powder. Like a miniature atomic mushroom, a cloud of smoke would puff to the ceiling and descend to envelope everyone in a dense haze. Groping their way out, Senators were usually able to get back to the Chamber before the smoke had drifted out an open window. When they discovered the white dusty "fallout" all over their clothes, Senators vowed never to allow a powder flash in the Capitol again—until the next time.

Flashbulbs and then strobe lights made later photographers more popular with the Senate and they were allowed to use the President's Room like other newsmen. For a while they were permitted to photograph the Senate in session from the Gallery and, by special permission, to take pictures on the Floor after the session had ended. But because some pictures were taken showing an almost empty Chamber and were published with captions which implied that Senators were not on the job, the privilege was withdrawn. Only one picture has been taken in recent years:

the National Geographic Society photographed the full Chamber on September 24, 1963, at the time of the atomic test ban treaty vote.

The exacting life of a news photographer has produced the most lively members of the press corps. Beyond the technical mastery of their equipment and an intuitive sense of what is newsworthy, they are professional artists with a gift for composition. Every photographer is continually on the lookout for that rare shot that will win a prize in the annual contest of the White House News Photographers Association, the organization of those who cover the national scene from Washington. So valuable are good photographs to politicians that both parties now have acquired permanent staffs. Longtime White House photographers Arthur Scott and Clyde Wilkinson focus on the GOP for the Republican Senatorial Campaign Committee, while brothers Al and Frank Muto photograph their Democratic counterparts. Veteran White House photographer Bill Forsythe has been the only superintendent of the Senate Photographers Gallery. There he keeps his World War II helmet ready for whatever comes. The rugged career of news photographer has never been and never will be for the faint of heart.

Radio was an infant in crystal sets and headphones during my page days. Electronic technology grew with such speed, however, that on March 4, 1925, Calvin Coolidge's inauguration was broadcast nationwide.

The pioneer radio men serving the Senate in the late 1920's were a hearty trio: Bob Trout of WJSV [WTOP] of the Columbia Broadcasting Company, Hurlif Provensen of WMAL which joined the American Broadcasting Company, and Graham McNamee of WRC of the National Broadcasting Company. They had to drag their heavy equipment with them for not until 1939 was the Senate Radio Gallery established.

As the only staff member assigned to the press at the Senate Floor, I became the first person to help these pioneers make contact with Senators for their live broadcasts. In those early days not many legislators grasped the political possibilities of radio. Very few had ever broadcast before doing so at the Senate, and most were leery of speaking before microphones, not knowing how they would sound on the air. I would try to persuade them with a "Really, Senator, the microphone won't bite!" Even then some refused point-blank and others would tremble as they came out to confront the mikes for the first time.

Newsreel photographers came soon after the radio correspondents, giving the moviegoers of the nation their first sight of Senators in motion. Early newsreel men would escort their Senators outside to make daylight pictures. When sunlight failed, they would burn flares to supplement the lighting. The first newsreels, like the first feature movies, were shown with titles, but eventually sound was added which made the Senatorial image complete. Paramount newsmen used sound for the first time during President Roosevelt's second inauguration in 1937 when ten-ton trucks were needed to haul the equipment around. In the rain Bob Denton's camera shorted out and knocked him twenty feet. When the finished production was put together, each camera had recorded the inaugural address in a different sound level. One moment Roosevelt's voice would be a tenor while the next shot would send him down to a bass or up to a high squeak. Today with the technical difficulties long since solved, television has replaced newsreels.

Television came to Washington first as a demonstration in the 1930's. Senators and staff people were driven down the Mall to a location in front of the Department of Agriculture where we were interviewed by Bryson Rash, then a young announcer for NBC. Later at the National Press Club not far away, we could watch others broadcasting with Bryson on the Mall. To recognize the image of a Senator almost a mile away seemed an amazing achievement to me that day.

Thirty years later on November 22, 1963, the combined television networks asked me to broadcast from the studio in the Senate Radio-TV Gallery. Before the largest audience in history, I sadly told of the Senate's reaction to the tragedy of President Kennedy's assassination, relating how I had broken the news to Senator Teddy Kennedy who was presiding in the Chair that afternoon. A hundred million people could share the sorrow simultaneously.

In less than two generations we have progressed from the novelty of hearing a Senator's voice on early radio amid a shower of static to the familiarity of seeing legislators in our homes by way of television. Whether broadcast through the immediacy of TV and news photos or the written words that pour out over the wires of the Press Gallery, most of the nation's news of the Senate begins in a quiet meeting between correspondent and Senator in the President's Room.

SENATOR LYNDON JOHNSON:
A CORRESPONDENT'S VIEW

By Stewart Alsop

I was first exposed to the curious obtuseness of Lyndon Johnson where the press is concerned on a trip to the LBJ Ranch in 1958, for an article on the then Majority Leader for the *Saturday Evening Post*. My wife and I had flown to San Antonio, where Senator and Mrs. Johnson met us at the airport, greeted us cordially, took us to a political dinner where the Senator made a speech, and then drove us to the ranch. Johnson was at the wheel, driving at a furious pace, and I was in front with him, while my wife was in the back seat with Mrs. Johnson.

Throughout the long drive, Lyndon Johnson relentlessly stressed the same theme. The *Saturday Evening Post* was a conservative, Republican magazine. He knew, of course, that therefore I couldn't write a fair, objective article about him. He knew I would have to belittle him, and downgrade him, and stick a knife between his ribs. He knew, but he wouldn't hold it against me—a man has a job to do, and he has to do it. And so on . . . and on.

Finally I could stand it no longer.

"What you have been saying," I burst out, "is just as insulting as though you'd called my wife back there a whore."

There was a stunned silence. The car slowed to a crawl. After a few minutes, a long arm reached out, and began kneading my shoulder. Thereafter, the Majority Leader, a prickly subject for an article, then as now, went out of his way to help, and gave me a rare and rather fascinating on-the-record interview—all, I suspect, as a result of my outburst. But what is significant is that Lyndon Johnson was quite genuinely surprised that I should have resented what he said.

Perhaps it is not altogether surprising that he should have been surprised. Reporters on certain Texas papers are not noted for their journalistic independence—it is widely believed in the press corps that when Johnson was Majority Leader, reporters from Texas papers friendly to him actually submitted their copy to him before filing it.

Moreover, throughout his reign as Majority Leader, Lyndon Johnson generally enjoyed a good press, even in the national news weeklies and the big metropolitan dailies in the North. The symbiotic relationship of press and politicians is closer on the Hill than elsewhere in the government, and generally less antagonistic. The Senate especially is a small world of its own, and reporters as well as Senators learn the value of Sam Rayburn's old rule: "To get along, go along."

Reporters covering the Senate soon learned, moreover, to go to almost any lengths to avoid being subjected to what was then known as "Lyndon's Treatment A." I first experienced Treatment A in 1957. Here is my contemporary account of the experience, related when it was still painfully vivid in my mind:

> This reporter experienced Treatment A during the post-Sputnik era, when Johnson's defense hearings were dominating the headlines. The reporter wrote an article, to the effect that Democrats as well as Republicans were vulnerable on the defense issue, which contained the following two fatal sentences: "As for Johnson, his voting record on defense has been good. But he is obviously open to the charge

that he only summoned his Preparedness Subcommittee to make a serious inquiry into preparedness after the issue had been dramatized by the Sputniks."

On the day the article appeared, the reporter was summoned to the Majority Leader's small, ornate, oddly impressive office in the Capitol. Treatment A started quietly. The Majority Leader was, it seemed, in a relaxed, friendly, and reminiscent mood. Nostalgically he recalled how he had come to Washington in 1937, a mere freshman Congressman, and how Franklin D. Roosevelt had prevailed on the chairman of the Naval Affairs Committee to put "young Lyndon Johnson" on his powerful committee. That was, it seemed, the beginning of Johnson's interest in the national defense, which had continued ever since.

By gradual stages, the relaxed, friendly, and reminiscent mood gave way to something rather like a human hurricane. Johnson was up, striding about his office, talking without pause, occasionally leaning over, his nose almost touching the mesmerized reporter's, to shake the reporter's shoulder or grab his knee. Secretaries were rung for. Memoranda appeared and then more memoranda, as well as letters, newspaper articles and unidentifiable scraps of paper, which were proffered in quick succession and then snatched away. Appeals were made, to the Almighty, to the shades of the departed great, to the reporter's finer instincts and better nature, while the reporter, unable to get a word in edgewise, sat collapsed upon a leather sofa, eyes glazed, mouth half open. Treatment A ended a full two hours later, when the Majority Leader, a friendly arm around the shoulder of the dazed journalist, ushered him into the outer office. It was not until some days later that the reporter was able to recall that, excellent as Johnson's record on national defense undeniably is, the two sentences he had written had been demonstrably true.

In his Senate days, most of the reporters who covered Johnson were personal friends or at least friendly acquaintances. Most of them liked him, and even those who didn't were heavily dependent on the Majority Leader for news—or on the men around him, like Bobby Baker and George Reedy. Several days a week, after the Senate adjourned, eight or ten reporters would crowd into Johnson's small, impressive, Brumidi-decorated office on the gallery floor; or later, into the vast, unimpressive, Texas-decorated office suite off the Senate floor, known as "the Taj Mahal," which Johnson co-opted for himself in 1959. Drink would flow generously, courtesy of the Majority Leader (who drank Scotch and soda, and complained constantly that his soda wasn't fresh enough), amidst much talk, almost all of it Johnson's. Even in those days Lyndon Johnson would never tip his hand, and he was not much use as a news source. Even so, the gatherings were pleasant and often amusing, and a certain family feeling grew up between the Majority Leader and the Senate reporters.

A similar feeling has never grown up between the President and the White House reporters—quite the contrary. The lack of this feeling at first surprised, and then angered, President Johnson. For a while, after he inherited the Presidency, Johnson tried hard to establish the old ambiance on a much wider scale. (More even than most men, the President is a prisoner of his past, and tries ardently to re-create it.) He would invite the regular reporters into his office, or onto the Truman balcony, for drinks or coffee, and he would invite publishers, columnists, and the like for lunch in the private dining room, often preceded by a swim in the White House pool and followed by talks which might last all afternoon.

But the relationship between the press and a President is inherently different from that between the press and a Senator, however important the Senator, and this effort by the President to re-establish the relationship with the press of his Senate days was inevitably a failure.

The failure irritated the President all the more because the press is actually installed inside what Lyndon Johnson sometimes refers to as "my place"—the White House. (Theodore Roosevelt, who came closer than any other President to managing the news successfully, was the first to set aside a room in the White House for the press.) Because the reporters were actually inside the White House, the President, according to one who knows the workings of his mind well, thought of them as *his* men, in much the same category as his staff. Thus when a White House reporter wrote something he disliked, he felt as though he had been nourishing a viper in his bosom.   .

This was true above all when a reporter wrote something like Philip Potter's aid-to-India story—an accurate account of something the President intended to do. President Johnson has never understood how this sort of story gets reported and written; he has never understood the paleontological method of reporting, by which a few details and a few telephone calls make it possible for a shrewd reporter to reconstruct a whole situation.

When a newspaperman wrote an accurate story of a certain complicated decision affecting future action in the foreign policy field, McGeorge Bundy, then still the chief White House foreign policy staff man, read it, and asked the reporter a favor. "Would you mind giving me a memorandum on how you came to write that story?" he asked. "I'd like to show it to the President. I know you got the story legitimately, but this President never believes a reporter can get a story like that unless a secret paper is filched or a Cabinet member suborned." (The newspaperman said he would think it over, but finally decided that he could not write a convincing memorandum and protect his sources at the same time.)

Quite often, of course, the President himself is the chief source of a major story. For example, in 1966 the President at a news conference said: "We must continue to raise the cost of aggression at its source."

Philip Geyelin, then with the *Wall Street Journal*, drew the obvious conclusion: that major U.S. air strikes against North Vietnamese targets were imminent. He did some careful checking around, confirmed his conclusion, and wrote a piece to that effect which was sent out over the Dow Jones ticker. The President, reading the article, instantly concluded that there had been a security-compromising leak, and ordered the FBI to investigate. There had, indeed, been a leak—and the leaker was Lyndon B. Johnson.

Latterly, the President has abandoned all attempts to re-create with the press the family atmosphere of the Senate days. He has three surviving personal friends among the journalists—William S. White, Max Freedman, and Marianne Means (who, on an early visit to the LBJ Ranch, made the immortal remark: "Oh, Mr. President, you're *fun!*"). These three are invited to Camp David, and attend social and/or state functions at the White House rather regularly.

He also sees a select group of newspaper and television reporters quite often on a business basis. These include: Hugh Sidey, able White House correspondent of Time-Life; Edward P. Morgan; Merriman Smith of UPI (the President was genuinely moved, and did what he could to help, when Smith's son was killed in Vietnam); Charles Roberts of *Newsweek*; occasionally Max Frankel of the *New York Times*; quite often Ray Scherer, White House correspondent of NBC; Garnett Horner of the Washington *Star*; Dan Rather of CBS; Frank Reynolds of ABC; Frank Cormier of AP; and a few others. He also regularly grants audiences to important visiting firemen—for example, C. L. Sulzberger, foreign correspondent for the *New York Times*, almost always sees the President when he comes to Washington.

But these contacts are strictly business; except for his three surviving personal friends, the family atmosphere is all gone. The President has come to regard the press as a cross he has to bear. In this respect he is no different from his predecessors, except that he resents his cross-bearing more than any of them. He expressed his true feelings about the press when, in 1967, he strode into the White House press lobby with the King of Thailand, who was on a state visit to Washington.

"This is the press room," he told the King. "This is where they try you and convict you and execute you all at the same time."

As for the feelings of the press about the President, a few reporters deeply admire him, and a few dislike him to the point of hatred. The feelings of most are a mixture of admiration and dislike. The reporters who cover him talk about the President endlessly, and the quality of their ambivalence is suggested by a series of remarks which I jotted down in my notebook during one of the President's off-year election forays in 1966:

"I never know if he's looking at me—you can't tell by his eyes."

"Ever notice his blink rate? He hardly ever blinks."

"He's a man who always does the right thing, always in the wrong way."

"Think there's any chance he might step down in sixty-eight? He might just do it, you know, just to prove us all wrong."

"He could go out of office the most unpopular President in history— and one of the best."

"You know, there's something pathetic about the old bastard—he wants so much to be loved, and he never will be."

Looking at the President making a speech to a crowd in a street in Des Moines: "By God, maybe we're all wrong. These people just love that corn."

SENATOR WAYNE MORSE:
A CORRESPONDENT'S VIEW

By A. Robert Smith

On the afternoon that the Senate finally fastened upon him the ignominy of his assignment to the District of Columbia Committee, Morse strode briskly from the chamber. In a Capitol corridor he was intercepted by an Associated Press reporter, G. Milton Kelly, who asked the senator's reaction to his setback. Morse used bitterly disparaging terms to describe the other senators and what they had that day done to him, says Kelly. So in writing about the episode, the veteran AP reporter chose the colorful expression "smoking mad" to describe Morse's reaction.

When Morse saw Kelly's story, he took the Senate floor to brand it a "lie." He had not been smoking mad, he protested. He had been "amused." This is one of the most useful words in the English language for Wayne Morse. He uses it to characterize his reaction to political events which, in lesser men, would evoke anger, fear, bitterness, dismay, or disappointment.

"Of course I did not agree with the result. I said 'the fight has just started.' I said it good-naturedly, as far as the principle that I defended on the floor of the Senate was concerned. There was no anger about it. I fight hard, but I fight professionally," boomed out Morse. Growing more amused as he warmed to his topic, he described the Associated Press as a "slanted-news reporting service" with a "bunch of clever writers skilled in the use of snide, reputation-assassinating adjectives."

When the Senate that afternoon adjourned for the day, Kelly entered the chamber and approached Morse before the senator had departed. "I understand I have had the honor of being called a liar by you," remarked the veteran newsman. Morse, he related later, refused to discuss it and ordered him to leave "or I'll have you removed." When the Senate convened next day, Morse was on his feet demanding an apology from the Associated Press for the "insulting and brazen manner" of its reporter. Finally Morse made clear what was gnawing at him. Kelly's dispatch, he felt, had "smeared" him because the expression "smoking mad" created the impression "that I was a poor sport." Morse told the Senate that if Kelly "had any brains at all, he would have known he would have left that impression when he wrote that I left the floor 'fighting mad' [sic] . . ." In a word, Kelly should have protected him. He should not have informed Oregon voters that their senator was in a state of unamused fury. What would they think of his sportsmanship?

"I happen to be one member of the Senate," he thundered bravely, "who is not afraid of the press. If there is anyone in the press who thinks he is some little third-degree artist, let him get it through his skull now that I do not propose to be insulted on the floor of the Senate by any man in the press gallery. . . . I wish to say to the AP that until I receive an apology for the conduct of their correspondent on the floor of the Senate yesterday afternoon, I never want a member of the AP ever to darken the door of my office, because as of now they are *persona non grata*, as far as the junior Senator from Oregon is concerned; and I would not give them a conference on any subject, because I do not trust their intellectual honesty, I do not trust their journalistic ethics. I think the Associated Press will understand that language."

What one must understand about this language is that Wayne Morse, perhaps more than the average thin-skinned politician, scans the press with a very subjective eye. Newspapers and their editorial writers and columnists rise and fall in his esteem in direct ratio with how they treat his latest exploits. During his first days in Washington on the War Labor Board, Morse received magnificent publicity as a colorful new figure in the often dull area of labor relations. He won editorial tributes for his tough-mindedness in standing up to John L. Lewis. How it affected Wayne Morse may be seen in a letter he wrote on one such occasion in June 1943 to Professor Andrew Weaver at Wisconsin:

> I am enclosing a copy of my decision in the coal case. I consider my special concurring opinion the most significant decision I have ever written. It apparently was good enough for Eugene Meyer, publisher of the Washington *Post* to invite me over to his office yesterday afternoon for lunch which was attended not only by his managing editor but also by his head editorial writer. I won't tell you much about what he said because even I have a streak of modesty in me. Suffice to say that he said he considered my special concurring opinion one of the most outstanding acts on the basis of principle which has come out of Washington in many a day. . . .

When Morse found a particularly glowing article about himself, he passed it along to a friend at the University of Oregon, such as he did in 1943 with a St. Louis *Post-Dispatch* article which he suggested might be circulated by the university publicity office. "Let the suggestion come from you and not from me, if you get the point," Morse wrote his friend. "It is just one of those little things which might help keep the 'personal fences' in repair back there." When he noted an uncomplimentary press reference, in these early days of his career he held his tongue, publicly.

Not until 1951, when the Chicago *Tribune* read Morse out of the G.O.P. after he defended Truman's dismissal of General MacArthur, did the senator openly scold a newspaper. Colonel McCormick then owned the Washington *Times-Herald* as well as the *Tribune*, and through these mighty organs he advised the G.O.P.: "The time has come for the Republican caucus to assemble and formally vote to bestow Morse to the Administration party, where he belongs. He is not a Republican. He retains the fiction of Republican allegiance only because he can do the Republicans more damage posing as one of them than by openly avowing that he has been an Administration supporter right along." Characteristically Morse was the one to call the Senate's attention to the colonel's advice. He called this criticism "a great personal compliment" because these newspapers are "the mouthpieces of reaction, the instruments for a type of American fascism [and] are good examples of what would happen to the Republican party if the editor of these papers ever became the true spokesman of the Republican party."

The *Tribune* responded by dispatching a reporter to Oregon to look into Morse's background. From a few anti-Morse Republicans, the newspaper developed a story which portrayed Morse as a pinko ex-professor who was a member of the Institute of Pacific Relations (then under investigation by the McCarran Committee) and a pal of Harry Bridges. From its Washington-bureau chief, Walter Trohan, the Chicago *Tribune* then published a story revealing that Dean Morse's election to the I.P.R. had been "announced by Joseph Barnes, editor of the New York *Star* and former foreign editor of the New York *Herald Tribune*." The story observed that Barnes had four times been identified "as a former Red" by witnesses before the McCarran Committee but that Barnes had denied Communist connections. Observing that Morse had been demanding an investigation of the China Lobby is the No. 1 item on the Communist party program for action on China policy, according to photostats of American party documents made available to the Chicago *Tribune*. The article sought also to link Morse through the I.P.R. to other targets of the day, including Professor Owen Lattimore, Ambassador Philip C. Jessup, Alger Hiss, Earl Browder, and Harry Dexter White.

While this assault from the far-right wing of the press was happily received by those who had grown to despise Morse in Oregon, it was another newspaper that came to Morse's defense. Editor Tugman in the Eugene *Register-Guard* dismissed the *Tribune's* innuendo about the suspect I.P.R. as follows:

> Arnold Bennett Hall, the president of the University of Oregon, was promoting the Institute of Pacific Relations and, indeed, had a dream of getting the darn thing to headquarters in Eugene. It was the fashionable thing to be Pacific-minded. Professors made summer tours to the Orient. A team of Oregon debaters traveled up and down the Pacific basin arguing with Australians, Filipinos, Chinese and Japanese. Mrs. Murray Warner was providing the treasures for the Museum of Oriental Art on the University campus. Merchants of Eugene were providing the cash for the building. Chambers of Commerce were whooping about the Pacific trade. Everybody was Pacific-minded.

Tugman allowed that Morse had done "many injudicious things in the course of his career," but joining the I.P.R. was not one of them. "This paper has supported Wayne Morse, and probably will continue to do so, for the simple reason that we believe his virtues outweigh all his faults."

The following spring, however, Tugman took Morse sternly to task for supporting President Truman's seizure of the nation's steel mills. The issue became an inflammatory one in the Senate, complete with cries for Truman's impeachment. As the only Republican senator who supported Truman, Morse felt the heat more than most. He lashed out at the press for "ignoring the seriousness of the situation" and not playing up the danger of allowing the great steel furnaces to grow cold while the boys in Korea remained in action. Specifically Morse was incensed because the papers all but ignored testimony of Defense Secretary Robert Lovett in a hearing at which Lovett answered a Morse question by saying the Pentagon was "very gravely concerned about any stoppage" in steel production. This wasn't *news*, however, for Lovett had earlier made a speech on the subject to the American Society of Newspaper Editors which was fully reported in the press. Yet Morse criticized the New York *Times*, New York *Herald Tribune*, New York *World-Telegram*, Washington *Post* and Washington *Star* for devoting only five column inches of news space to Lovett's testimony, but later devoting 979 column inches to the court decision ruling the seizure unconstitutional.

Editor Tugman wrote that Morse's "effort to blame his troubles on the press is the silliest thing he has ever done, and that's a large statement. In kindness, we diagnose this outburst as 'a tantrum' such as we've seen him throw before. Morse has great abilities, but he would be a more valuable Senator if he would think more and talk less." Morse fired back a long letter accusing Tugman of imbibing in an "emotional drunk." The newspaper published it on the front page.

When Morse bolted the party that fall, he incurred the wrath of additional newspaper editors who had earlier supported him in his Republican heyday. Shortly before the election he told a Chicago *Sun-Times* reporter that the two greatest dangers to America are "Red Communism and yellow journalism." He cited the New York *Times* and the St. Louis *Post-Dispatch* for fair journalism and the Chicago *Tribune* as "a good example of yellow journalism." Replied Colonel McCormick, "Senator Morse is a well-known liar."

From that time on, complaints about the press became a curious obsession. After the election, when Morse made his first trip into Oregon since bolting the party, crowds turned out in large numbers to hear him explain his party turnabout. When he arrived at the University of Oregon, 1000 persons were there to hear him. In this homecoming setting, where Morse and Tugman had been allied in many past causes, the senator now sought to discredit the editor before his fellow townsmen. Morse was bleeding from an editorial in which Tugman had questioned his sincerity. He could not let this pass unchallenged.

Tugman's editorial noted a dispatch I had sent to the *Register-Guard* relating that preconvention conversation in which Morse had told Alice Johnson of the Seattle *Times* and me of his thoughts about issuing a call for a new party if Taft were nominated. I had reported this remark as a kind of footnote to history, after Morse bolted the party, to show that his departure was not an impulsive act. Tugman also noted a story in the *Oregon Journal* from Roulhac Hamilton which quoted Morse right after the convention as saying that Eisenhower isn't "big enough" or "hasn't the mind" for the presidency. Tugman's point was that Morse could hardly have been sincere in later ecstatically writing from London to General Eisenhower and promising to stump the country for him.

Before challenging the editorial, Morse called in Hamilton and told him that I had denied the portion of the editorial which referred to my dispatch. Hamilton says he realized Morse was up to his old schoolboy snow-job tricks, for a secretary in the senator's outer office was trying without luck to find me. Hamilton advised Morse that the editorial looked accurate to him, as far as his contribution was concerned. When I was subsequently invited in, the senator heard the same answer. We had indeed written the stories from which Tugman quoted. Morse told me he had no recollection of telling us what we reported. I told Morse my only doubt about my story was caused by some uncertainty as to whether he regarded those remarks, made in a quiet chat just outside the Senate chamber, to be off-the-record. But the senator took the position that he had never made such remarks, on or off the record. He said this was what he intended to tell anyone in Oregon if the issue came up. I said I understood his position, and we parted amicably.

When the senator gamecock got warmed up before the huge university crowd, which included Tugman, he didn't wait for someone to raise the issue. In his effort to discredit the editor's opinion, Morse claimed that Hamilton and I had "authorized" him to say, "It's not true." Morse sought to convey that we had repudiated our stories and Tugman's editorial references to us. In fact, we had not authorized Morse to say anything, nor had we repudiated our stories. Tugman published Morse's speech on page one, flanked by contrary statements from us newsmen. We were then barred from Morse's office. Editorially Tugman observed that it appeared that Morse had "adopted the precedent of the great Theodore Roosevelt of repudiating newspaper quotes whenever they turn out embarrassing."

This was not Morse's first adoption of the Teddy Roosevelt precedent. In 1950, still a Republican, he composed a statement taking other liberal Republicans to task. He gave a copy to Charles (Doc) Watkins, an Associated Press reporter, and later telephoned Watkins twice to make changes before the story was written. The statement was newsworthy; Watkins' story hit the front page of the Washington *Star* that afternoon.

Another AP reporter, Ernie Warren, learned that Morse subsequently had written letters to several offended senators blaming the reporter for the story. Watkins covered the offices of all Pacific Northwest members of Congress for the AP, but after this incident this pleasant, thoroughly non-combative reporter stayed clear of Morse. Subsequently they met by chance in a Capitol Hill corridor. Morse stopped and candidly apologized to Watkins. The reporter recalls the senator explained, "I had to have a fall guy, and you were it."

On his 1952 tour of Oregon after bolting the party, an *Oregon Journal* reporter, Don Sterling, Jr., sought to pin Morse down about his mounting complaints about the press. The senator said:

> Don't misunderstand me. I'm not a paranoiac—I don't have a persecution complex. But I predict in the next few years you will see the greatest campaign of lies and smears in history to get rid of the liberals in the Senate.

His bill of particulars against the press was brief. In 1947 he recalled the AP had quoted him as telling the Senate he would oppose the Taft-Hartley bill even though he thought most of his constituents favored it. He blamed the AP for not carrying his subsequent remarks explaining that he meant he was better informed on the subject than many constituents who unwisely favored that labor act. He reiterated his complaint about press coverage of the steel-seizure issue. And he cited the recent rhubarb with Tugman, Hamilton, and me.

Years later, the city editor of the *Oregonian*, J. Richard Nokes, tried to elicit from Morse a bill of particulars for his massive indictment of the press. The senator brushed the whole matter aside.

A constructive case could be made respecting the shortcomings of the

American press at large, starting with its devotion to blood, sex, and society shenanigans, all of which are abysmally popular with readers. But Morse's criticism has been fiercely subjective and unspecific. In the spring of 1953 he declared, "I doubt whether in the last four months 10 per cent of the stories that have appeared in the press about the junior Senator from Oregon have had a 20 per cent relationship to the facts." He was "sad" to have to criticize the press, but "someone in public life . . . ought to stand up against a misinformed press."

His tiff with AP reporter Kelly blossomed into a full-scale attack by the senator upon the Associated Press, the world's largest news-gathering agency and a non-profit co-operative owned by the member newspapers which it serves. "I know how vicious and dangerous is the AP as a propaganda organization for poisoning the minds of the American people against any official whom they are out to smear," he said in the Senate. He suggested that a motto for the AP, using its initials, would be "Always Polluted."

There is no doubt that a wide majority of newspapers editorially prefer Republican-party candidates and policies—a fact of great usefulness to Wayne Morse in his early election campaigns. But the success of the Democratic party since the New Deal, broken only by the G.O.P.'s recruitment of a popular war hero as President in the fifties, indicates at least that the popular will is not readily determined by editorial writers. Complaints about press coverage of political campaigns, whether from Adlai Stevenson or Richard Nixon, come inevitably from the loser.

One point raised by Morse deserves attention, however, for it concerns whether or not the press affords him fair treatment in the news columns. To fortify his assault on the AP newspapers, Morse read the Senate an editorial from the York Gazette and Daily, a liberal tabloid published in the Pennsylvania-Dutch country. Editor C. M. Gitt, a Henry Wallace supporter in 1948, was sympathetic to Morse's complaint that the "reactionary" publishers were giving him little attention. The AP is dominated by the larger publishers, wrote Gitt, and "those persons whom the big boys in the association are interested in get the publicity and the coverage and those persons, such as Senator Morse, whom only a few of the members of the Associated Press are interested in, get practically none or very slim coverage."

There is some justification for saying that an individual newspaper may give the silent treatment to a politician who incurs its disfavor. Such a newspaper is Hearst's Seattle Post-Intelligencer, which periodically has acted as though Washington State Senators Warren G. Magnuson and Henry M. Jackson, both Democrats, had vanished into outer space. No matter what the senators did during their periods of banishment from the news columns, the readers of the P-I would find no mention of their senators in that newspaper. It is said that once when the sports editor cautiously injected Senator Magnuson's name into his column, it was dutifully deleted by higher authority. The reason for such discrimination apparently was not ideological, however. Both senators had sinned against this morning newspaper by making important announcements about new defense contracts for the Seattle area at a time during the day when this big news could be published *first* in the afternoon *Times.* Had the *P-I* been given the break, Magnuson and Jackson would doubtless have been noble names in the *P-I* editorial offices thereafter. Even a former *P-I* reporter, Russ Holt, who was Jackson's press secretary, could not get his leader's name back in the paper for six months.

No one who has plowed through Morse's vast accumulation of press clippings, pasted neatly into a monumental stack of scrapbooks, would believe for an instant that he has been banished from any news columns. In 1953, at the peak of his campaign against the press, Morse received front-page attention everywhere he went on a tour of his home state. The *Register-Guard* faithfully reported "his crowd was sympathetic to Morse's blistering attack on the Eisenhower Administration." The *Oregon Statesman,* along with a front-page picture of the senator and Mrs. Morse, carried several stories on his local visit to Salem, one of them reporting he had "a friendly audience" which "punctuated Morse's speech with several rounds of applause and kept the Senator answering questions for 45 minutes afterward." A reader complained to the *Register-Guard* about a picture of the senator on the front page of the Sunday edition which showed him with some youngsters at a tree-planting ceremony. "How can you call that stuff news, especially when you know that he'll turn right around and accuse the press of misrepresenting him whenever it suits his fancy?" the irate reader asked. Editor Tugman replied:

> In covering Senator Morse, or any other public character, the news department never has any instructions except to be there and to report as accurately and completely as possible whatever is done or said. If Senator Morse, or any other public character, chooses to cry "unfair" (as he often does) that is merely one of our occupational hazards. Morse is a controversial figure (like McCarthy) and he has many of the same talents for making headlines. He has made many false and insupportable accusations against the Oregon press but that has not affected their reporting of his visit.
>
> In any showdown, the press can stand on its record, perhaps even better than the Senator. We have great faith in the ability of the people to appraise their public men in the long run. At the moment we are not quarreling editorially with anything the junior Senator says or does. This is his time to "howl"; it is our job to tell about it. It's the American way and we know no better way in public matters.

Morse's complaint has not been that the press has ignored him. "I say to the people of my state that they have not read an accurate story in the Oregon newspapers, outside of the Medford *Mail Tribune* for some five months on any controversy in which the junior Senator from Oregon has participated," he said in mid-1953. The liberal *Mail Tribune* was unique in perhaps only one respect at that time: its editor, Robert W. Ruhl, had editorially sided with Morse, even in his assault upon the AP. Ruhl's newspaper was served by the rival news agency, United Press, which faithfully reported Morse's purple adjectives about the AP.

Another Oregon newspaper, the Pendleton *East Oregonian*, equally as liberal as the *Mail Tribune*, commented that Morse "has a stuck needle. Everyone who disagrees with Morse, according to the Senator, is a liar." Noting Morse's blanket charge of unfair treatment, the *East Oregonian*'s editor, J. W. Forrester, Jr., wrote, "Such a statement seems too ridiculous to warrant more than scant attention. But we can't forget that Senator Joe McCarthy has made it pay off politically and Morse is a far more able orator." The *East Oregonian*, which has always supported liberal candidates for office, notably the Neubergers, has been on Morse's black list of "reactionary newspapers" ever since—a complaint he voices with regularity upon visits to Pendleton. Morse, in a word, applies but one litmus test in determining whether a newspaper is reactionary or liberal: has it been true-blue to Wayne Morse, or has some acid editorializing made the senator see red?

To apply his test, Morse is an avid reader of what Oregon newspapers publish about him. The senator does not read all the newspapers in his state. Indeed, in late years he has canceled his subscriptions to all the Oregon papers he once received at his office. He subscribes, instead, to a news-clipping service, as do many politicians. A private enterprise based in Portland gets Morse's business. Its staff of readers comb the daily prints for any mention of the name of Wayne Morse, take scissors in hand, and soon send off a bundle of fresh clips to the senator. After he has passed judgment on what sort of press he is getting, the clippings are pasted into scrapbooks.

When Morse banned a number of reporters from his office, he did not cut himself out of the news. His speeches in the Senate were faithfully covered by newsmen sitting above in the press gallery. And his office kept the press releases flowing—even to the banned newsmen. Once Roulhac Hamilton, one of the banned correspondents, found himself stuck at the last moment without a dignitary to interview on his radio program to Oregon. Although it seemed pointless, he asked Morse's office whether the senator might like to go on. A model of accommodation, Morse hiked all the way to the far end of the Capitol to the House Radio Gallery for the recording session. "He did a beautiful job," recalls Hamilton.

When the program was finished, Hamilton sought amplification of a point he thought would make a good newspaper story. Drawing back, Morse asked, "Are you asking me as a radio broadcaster or as a correspondent for the *Journal*?" Hamilton had in mind writing a newspaper story on the point at issue. He says Morse replied, "I'm sorry, but I don't give interviews to the correspondent for the *Journal!*" Off he went through the studio door.

If this seems like a weird distinction, it reflects Morse's subjective approach to the news media. Radio is very kind to him. Every week he makes a tape recording and sends copies of it to a string of radio stations in Oregon. He picks his own topic and has fifteen minutes in which to have his say, every word to be sent out on the air waves to his faithful listeners. No editorial observations by the station are injected. No one's counter views are sought. The newspapers, for all the space and head-lines they give him, are ever ready to give Morse his comeuppance editorially.

The most prominent exception to criticism in the newspaper world, as far as Morse is concerned, is Drew Pearson. Speaking of the columnist, Morse told the Senate in January 1961, "I think he is the most able and the most effective journalistic muckraker we have had in the United States in our time, if not in our whole history." He said he meant the term in a highly complimentary sense as one who seeks to expose corruption by public men and corporations. Pearson's bouquets to Morse have been equally sweet over the years.

The Morse-Pearson relationship is well served by their unique usefulness to one another. Morse is adept at supplying Pearson with inside scoop material. Pearson reciprocates by portraying the senator in heroic terms.

Morse learned this trick of the trade in his first years in Washington on the War Labor Board. An item from a Pearson column in 1943 records this purported exchange from a White House conference on the coal strike of that spring:

> ICKES: You can't mine coal with bayonets. The fundamental issue is to settle the strike. I would have settled it if the War Labor Board had let me alone.
> MORSE: Mr. President, either your Secretary of the Interior is ignorant or he is maliciously misrepresenting the facts. The fundamental issue is whether one man, John L. Lewis, shall be allowed to defy the sovereignty of the U. S. Government.

An amusing illustration of the Morse-to-Pearson pipeline is seen in a column about that auto trip Morse took with President Truman to Ball's Bluff. A Massachusetts citizen clipped the Pearson column and sent it to the President along with a photograph he had taken of Colonel Baker's grave at San Francisco. Truman examined the photograph with interest, but when he read Pearson's column he bristled. Reporting that at one point Truman nearly swerved off the road, the columnist gave this account of Morse's adventure with the President:

Their first conversation was about the fact that the President was driving himself, the Senator discreetly inquiring when the President had last driven. Truman admitted he hadn't driven for a couple of years, but said he still remembered how. As the trip continued, it was evident that whatever the President lacked in skill as a chauffeur, he made up in zestful driving. With the Secret Service men sitting nervously in the rear, the President enjoyed every minute of it.

In his reply to Captain John J. Sheehan, Truman thanked him for the photograph but added, "The clipping you enclosed by Pearson was wrong in every particular—he never tells the truth about anything intentionally. If he does, it is by accident, and he usually lies later to offset it. There was no conversation on the subject on the way down and I am still able to drive a car as well as ever. I don't think you will find that Wayne was in any way uneasy on the trip. We had a fine visit with General Marshall and discussed the idea of the state of Oregon erecting a memorial to Baker. That was the whole program and there was nothing else to it."

Once Morse took up the cry of "yellow journalism" against the "reactionary press," he found it impossible wholly to desist. A candidate for a master's degree at the University of Oregon, Robert B. Whipple, even wrote a thesis on the subject: "The Change and Development of Editorial Attitudes of Selected Oregon Daily Newspapers toward Senator Wayne Morse." Like Morse, Whipple stressed the shift of editorial opinion from pro-Morse to anti-Morse when he bolted the Republican party. The reverse of the coin is also true: Morse was never troubled by the press while it supported him, but once the criticism began, he quickly discerned "the great fallibility of the newspaper editors," as he put it in a letter to Whipple.

In 1955 Morse quietly dropped his indictment of the wicked Associated Press, without receiving the apology he had so loudly demanded in 1953. What he received was much more valuable and gratifying—a long, friendly article about his favorite subject, Wayne Morse, written by the AP's Pulitzer prize-winning reporter Don Whitehead. The story, complete with photo of the Morse family at tea, was given prominence in the Sunday Oregonian, filling four full columns opposite the editorial page. The newspaper headlined the article: "Morse Gains New D. C. Stature; Vote to Decide Senate Lineup."

The AP was not out to butter up Morse by concocting a favorable story. The story related that Morse was suddenly the key man in the Senate after the 1954 election, when the Independent senator's vote could have given either party control of the Senate. The AP was doing its customary impartial, creditable job by offering its member newspapers a lengthy profile of the senator who was suddenly big news—even though he was the same senator who had slandered the AP in bygone days of desperation. Whitehead reported that "the politicians have been forced to give a new and higher prestige rating to the rebel Senator from Oregon." No more did Wayne Morse describe the AP as vicious and dangerous, poisoning the minds of the American people.

Later correspondent Hamilton and I, after three years of banishment, were also restored to good favor. Editor Sprague of the *Oregon Statesman* in January 1955 suggested to Morse in a letter that he resume normal press relations with me on a strictly professional basis. The senator replied that this was a fine sentiment, but "I do not believe that I should be asked to hold personal interviews with a correspondent who I honestly believe is so unreliable that in order to protect myself I should have present at a conference a stenotypist to take down verbatim every word spoken between us." Subsequently Hamilton and I jointly wrote Morse to propose periodic press conferences with a stenographer present for the mutual protection of all participants. We were instantly summoned to his office, and there greeted like prodigal sons.

After a spate of jolly banter about our children and his grandchildren, the senator grew serious: "Now, as to this proposal. I see no reason in the world why grown men can't sit down in the same room together without having some stenographer present to take it all down." Without any spoken reservations, the senator ended his cold war against the working press, that day in the autumn of 1955. "But there is just one thing about this," added Morse, his brow deeply furrowed with the gravity of his next point. "There will be some who will say, 'Ah, there's Morse, making his peace with the press because he is coming up for re-election next year.'" Pondering the thought that anyone could be so cynical, we waited expectantly for the senator to conclude. Leaning across his desk and virtually embracing us with a look of humble sincerity, Wayne Morse averred, "But as long as you men don't think that is the case, then it doesn't matter to me what they say."

Mr. Hamilton, with consummate skill acquired in long years of journalistic jousting with con men in and out of public life, replied with the barest trace of mischief in his eyes. "Why, no, Senator, we wouldn't think anything like that." On this merciful note, peace was restored.

Wayne Morse's war on the press coincided with his gravest time of trouble, during his frustrating period as an independent, as a senator without a party, without visible means of political support, possibly a senator without a future. Everything had gone wrong, in one sense, as Morse viewed his troubled position as the most junior member of the Senate Committee on the District of Columbia.

Fictional though the Independent party was, it served the momentary political needs of this man without a party. Having deserted or been kicked out by the Republicans, he could not rush headlong into that party he had so frequently condemned for its alleged devotion to government by men and not by law.

Adlai Stevenson said in the 1952 campaign that the Democrats had a light in the window for Morse; and Hubert Humphrey said he would swap three Southern Democrats for Morse any day. But for Senator Morse, whose early success at the polls had been dependent upon strong utterances of contempt for the Democratic party and some of its liberal proposals, a complete transition would take at least a little time and a plausible explanation.

———

CORRESPONDENTS AS PARTICIPANTS: CASE I

By Bert Andrews

Wednesday, August 12—Nixon called and asked me to drop over to see him.

He sparred around for a bit when I reached his office. He said he wasn't sure how much he could safely tell me. I told him I had never yet been accused of breaking a confidence, and that he could talk as freely as he wanted to on an off-the-record basis. I added that I would, of course, want to be free to use the information if it became possible to use it without injuring the investigation. He agreed to that.

Nixon told me he had stopped the idea of using a lie detector in the Bentley business because of the more important issues being raised by the Chambers testimony. He asked me to read the testimony on a confidential basis. Nixon said he wanted an outside judgment on whether Chambers really knew Hiss as he claimed. I did read the testimony and it seemed almost certain that Chambers must have known Hiss well. Later Nixon had William Rogers (later to become U.S. Attorney General in the Eisenhower Administration), an investigator for the Senate Internal Security Committee read over the material, as well as both John Foster Dulles and brother Allen. All came to the same conclusion: Chambers must have known Hiss.

There is a big difference between being certain of something and proving it.

"Our investigators haven't had much time to work," Nixon told me. "We have established two facts. Hiss did live in the Twenty-eighth Street apartment at P Street that Chambers described. He did have a dog. That's about as far as we have gotten. It is still largely a case of Chambers' word against Hiss's word. I don't know which one to believe. I'd like to get your judgment. Will you drive up to Chambers' farm with me?"

I said I would. We set the date for the following Sunday, August 15. Meanwhile, the committee dropped the Hiss-Chambers case like a hot potato and went into other matters.

We talked about nothing but the case on the two-hour drive to Westminster. Nixon said that he had told Chambers he was bringing "a newspaperman" up to see him, but had not told him who the newspaperman was.

"He may not want to talk in front of you," Nixon said.

He was right. I was introduced after Chambers had ushered us into the living room of his farmhouse. His wife and children were not present. When Chambers heard my name, he puffed on his pipe and looked at me for a full thirty or forty seconds.

"Oh, I remember," he said. "Aren't you the man who wrote *Washington Witch Hunt?*" I said I was. He shook his head slightly. "I thought you were unfriendly to the Committee," he said. I asked him why he thought that. He said it was because of the book.

I was annoyed. I told him I had gone into the case of ten State Department employees who had been discharged, only because I thought it was a case of railroading. None of the ten had ever been told what they were accused of, or who their accusers were. And that they had been given no right of appeal.

"Don't you see," I continued, "that if you are telling the truth, you are in danger of having similar procedures used against you?"

He took his pipe out of his mouth and asked me what I meant.

"Ask Congressman Nixon here," I said. "He'll tell you that the Committee is very close to dropping this whole case because it is loaded with dynamite and because they don't have enough evidence. If they drop it, what happens then? It's still a case of your word against Hiss's. And Hiss's record is so much better than yours the chances are you will still be indicted for perjury just because his story will be believed over yours. After all, nobody has really believed your story for the last nine years, have they?"

Chambers nodded.

"To me," I went on, "this is a great news story, either way it goes. I'm not partisan for either you or Hiss. If you are lying, Hiss ought to be exonerated. If Hiss is lying, I don't think you should be railroaded any more than I thought the people in the State Department should have been."

Chambers still hadn't made up his mind. Nixon said: "I know Bert as a reporter—an honest one. I am personally anxious to get his opinion of what he thinks of you and your story. I'd advise you to trust him. But I warn you that he'll want to ask you some blunt questions."

Chamber was silent for another thirty or forty seconds. He was, I was to discover, a man given to such long periods of contemplation that people first meeting him sometimes wondered whether he had gone into a trance.

"Well," he said, "let him go ahead and ask them."

"What about the rumors that you are a chronic drunk?" I asked.

"That's easy to answer and to prove," he said. "I don't like hard liquor and never drink it. I may have five or six bottles of wine—a year. Any of my associates can tell you that I do not drink."

"How about the story that you have been in a mental institution or an insane asylum?"

"I have never been in any kind of a sanitarium—period," Chambers said, emphasizing the word *period*. . . .

Chambers was a man who would answer all questions but volunteer nothing. Looking back, I wonder why in the world Nixon and I never asked him if he had any documentary evidence. I truly believe he would have produced it. But we never thought to ask that one. . . .

Chambers answered many other questions before Nixon and I left to drive back to Washington. On the trip, and in my apartment for several hours, we talked over what we had heard.

I told Nixon the House Committee had disgusted many observers because it had smeared witnesses on insufficient grounds or without giving them chance to get their stories on the record.

Time and again, I pointed out, there had been insufficient preparation by the investigators. The result often was that if a witness offered a bland "No" in answer to a question, the Committee had no idea of what to ask him next.

I told him Representative John Rankin of Mississippi had hurt the Committee by assailing Jews and Negroes.

I told him that, regardless of investigators' reports, I thought the handling of the case involving Dr. Edward U. Condon had been shameful, in that he was smeared as "the weakest link in our atomic security" without ever having been called to the stand.

Nixon said: "I agree with everything you say. But where do we go from here?"

We agreed that there had to be a confrontation between Hiss and Chambers and it ought to be held in secret. If there had been a mistake in identity, an unqualified apology could be made to Hiss.

"How about the Ford car that Chambers mentioned in the executive session?" I asked Nixon.

He said the Committee had not been able to trace it.

"How hard have you worked?" I asked. "I'll bet that somewhere in the District of Columbia some records about that car survive. Why don't you put the whole staff of investigators to work on it? Maybe one investigator just politely inquired at one place and accepted a plea of no information. But there must be a dozen places to check. Did some one own it before? What is Hiss's story of what became of it? Did Hiss trade it in when he got a new car? Most people do. Or did he sell it? At any rate, who got it? And why can't you trace the subsequent owner?"

Nixon was amused at the speed at which I was talking.

"Go ahead and laugh," I said. "But I'll bet it can be done. And what about the houses? Chambers said he and his wife lived in the Twenty-eighth Street apartment for from three to six weeks after the Hisses moved to P Street. Can't you check the dates? Did Hiss have a lease? Did he have sublet privileges? Were the gas and lights still on in the Twenty-eighth Street apartment when Chambers said he was there?"

Nixon laughed. "You've made up your mind, haven't you?" he asked.

"I've made up my mind on one thing," I said. "I'm positive Chambers and Hiss did know each other. No one could invent all the little items that Chambers has told. I don't believe, either, anyone could learn them merely by studying a man's life. It just doesn't make sense."

We left it this way: A confrontation scene would be arranged. The investigators would be ordered to explore every rathole to find out what had happened to the 1929 Ford. But first the Committee would talk to Hiss privately—just as Nixon and I had talked to Chambers privately— and see what more it could learn. . . .

[In the ensuing months, Hiss filed a libel suit against Chambers and Chambers released State Department papers which supported his claims that he and Hiss had met years before.—Ed.]

The lawyers for both sides examined the papers. They were thunder-struck. They called in Judge W. Calvin Chesnut. He was flabbergasted. A telephone call was put in to Washington for Alexander Campbell, head of the Criminal Division of the Department of Justice.

Campbell rushed to Baltimore. He examined the papers, agreed they were important, took them back to Washington, and impounded them. Secrecy was imposed on all concerned. But there was a leak. It resulted in this paragraph in the *Washington Post* of December 1 in a column by Jerry Kluttz:

"Since Alger Hiss sued Whittaker Chambers for libel, attorneys for both men have been taking detailed expositions from witnesses, including the two principals. Some very startling information on who's a liar is reported to have been uncovered."

Mr. Kluttz was only slightly wrong. Chambers had been questioned. Hiss had not. It was still a good beat.

On the same day a United Press dispatch went out of Washington —a result of a deliberate leak from the Department of Justice. It was a complete contradiction of the Kluttz item. It said that the perjury part of the Hiss-Chambers case was about to die for lack of evidence, and it added: "Unless something new turns up soon, officials said, there would be little use in going to a grand jury with the information obtained so far."

The two stories were so far apart that I had Jack Steele, my chief assistant in the *Herald Tribune* bureau, query Mr. Campbell. Mr. Campbell had seen both items. All he would say was: "I just can't comment on these stories. I can't answer any questions about the Hiss-Chambers case. Number One—this is too hot. Number Two—I just can't say anything about it."

Mr. Campbell's remark that "this is too hot" for comment was enough to indicate that something big was in the offing. I got on the telephone. I talked to Judge Chesnut in Baltimore. He would say only that no depositions had been filed in the court itself, and that he could make no other comment. I talked to Mr. Hiss. He was sorry, but he felt he had to refer all questions to his attorney. I talked to Chambers. He said: "On advice of counsel, I am unable to answer your questions."

I talked to Mr. Marbury in Baltimore. He said: "I couldn't possibly answer your question as to whether new evidence was uncovered." I tried another tack, asking him if the depositions were in Judge Chesnut's possession.

"The answer to that is no," Mr. Marbury said. This alone convinced me that the depositions were in existence somewhere, even though Judge Chesnut didn't have them.

I talked to Richard Cleveland, Chambers' attorney, in Baltimore. He said, "I can't disclose any information revealed as a result of this pretrial examination."

Finally, I talked to Nixon on Wednesday, December 1. He and Mrs. Nixon were preparing to entrain for New York at 8 o'clock the next morning to start their first vacation in three years, a sea trip to Panama.

"I think Chambers produced something important at the Baltimore hearing," I told him. "I have a hunch that he may have another ace in the hole. Why don't you try to find out?"

Nixon, with the rueful air of a man who has a thousand things to do before leaving on a trip, said he would. I left him. He and Bob Stripling drove to Chambers' farm.

Nixon said afterward:

"We didn't even have to open the subject. Chambers told us he knew why we were there. He said he could not talk in detail because he had been warned he might be held in contempt of court if he did. I tried one question. I asked him: 'Did you drop a bombshell at the Baltimore hearing?'

"Chambers thought a long time before he answered. Then he said: 'Yes, I did.' He implied he had still more information. I asked him for it. He shook his head and said he didn't want to get in contempt of court."

Nixon and Stripling drove back to Washington late Wednesday night. Nixon telephoned me at my home about 10 P.M. He said he wanted to see me. I took a taxi and traveled the three miles across town to his office. He told me of the trip to Westminster and the lack of results.

"You were too nice to Chambers," I told him. "Did you just ask for anything he had? Or did you slap a subpoena on him?"

Nixon said he hadn't really thought of a subpoena. I told him: "Look, before you leave town get hold of Bob Stripling. Tell him to serve a blanket subpoena on Chambers to produce *anything* and *everything* he still has in his possession. He couldn't possibly be held in contempt for giving you documents if he has any that haven't been subpoenaed by the court."

"I'll think it over," Nixon said. We parted about 12:30 A.M., December 2. I promised to notify him by wireless to the ship of any developments. He told Stripling and his staff to keep me informed.

Very early Thursday morning Nixon telephoned Stripling to meet him in his office by 7 or 7:15, so Nixon could still make the 8 o'clock train. Stripling got caught in a traffic jam and missed Nixon at the office. However, Nixon left Stripling a note, which read:

"It is highly important that you serve subpoenas on Chambers immediately for everything he has. I mean *everything*."

Nixon phoned his office from the station just before train time. He reached Stripling and reemphasized the importance of the assignment.

Stripling knew Chambers was to be in Washington that day to testify in a loyalty case hearing. He telephoned to Westminister and asked Chambers to come to see him after the hearing. At noon Chambers arrived at Stripling's office and Stripling handed him the subpoena. It called on Chambers to deliver "all papers, documents and other matters you may have" concerning a long list of individuals, headed by Hiss. Chambers accepted the subpoena. He arranged to meet Committee investigators Wheeler and Appell at 5:30 P.M. The three drove to Baltimore, where Chambers had parked his car. Chambers switched to his car and led the way to the farm.

It was about 10 P.M. The night was dark. Chambers did not enter the house at first. He walked to a pumpkin patch, stooped over, and looked around. Then he returned to the two investigators and said he couldn't find what he was seeking. He went to the house and turned on some yard lights. They gave slight illumination to the pumpkin patch. Chambers picked up one pumpkin, examined it, and dropped it.

Then he picked another one.

It was like a pumpkin prepared for Hallowe'en. The top had been severed in a circle. The pumpkin had been hollowed out and dried, as had been the top. The top had been replaced. Chambers lifted off the top.

As the investigators gathered around him, he reached inside and brought out three small aluminum cylinders. Each was wrapped in adhesive tape. Two more rolls were brought out. They were wrapped in oiled paper. One of them had been slightly crushed. Chambers said he didn't think the film inside the crushed one was any good, adding, "I think it has been lightstruck." He put the pumpkin back in its place.

"Is that all?" Wheeler asked, mindful that the subpoena called for anything and everything Chambers had pertinent to the investigation.

"That is all," Chambers answered.

Wheeler and Appell got into their car and started back to Washington. On the way they stopped at a cafe to mark the cylinders for identification. They delivered the films to Bob Stripling on the morning of December 3. The three took one roll of microfilm into a washroom. They locked the door, stood in the darkness, and unrolled a section of the film. The first words they saw were:

"DEPARTMENT OF STATE
STRICTLY CONFIDENTIAL"

Stripling told William Arnold, Nixon's secretary, what had been found. Arnold telephoned me. I went to Nixon's office and talked to Stripling and Arnold. Stripling sent a cable to Nixon on board the ship. Several hours passed without an answer. Stripling telephoned Mundt in South Dakota. Stripling and I took turns talking to him.

The investigators had a rush job done of enlarging and printing the films that were already developed. Mundt took our word for it that the documents shown in the film were "sensational." Mundt dictated this statement from his home:

"Documents secured by subpoena from Whittaker Chambers indicate that a final conclusion is imminent in the long-discussed Hiss-Chambers espionage case with which the House Committee has been concerned.

"There is now in the possession of the Committee, under twenty-four hour guard, microfilmed copies of documents of tremendous importance which were removed from the offices of the State Department and turned over to Chambers for the purpose of transmittal to Russian Communist agents. These documents are of such startling and significant importance and reveal such a vast nework of Communist espionage within the State Department that they far exceed anything yet brought before the Committee in its ten year history.

"These microfilms have been the object of a ten-year search by agents of the United States government and provide definite proof of one of the most extensive espionage rings in the history of the United States.

"On the basis of the evidence, it appears that conclusive proof has been established that secret documents of direct significance to our national security were fed out of the State Department by a member of the Communist underground to Whittaker Chambers, who at that time was operating as one of the Washington contacts for the Communist underground operating in America.

"As chairman of the subcommittee handling this matter, I shall proceed to Washington as soon as possible. I am getting in touch with other members of the subcommittee to ascertain the earliest possible date for a public hearing. The evidence is so shocking that I do not feel justified in delaying action a day longer than required."

Stripling and I talked things over. He had had no answer to his wireless message to Nixon. I sent one, and I pulled some strings with the transmitter company to see that it was expedited.

My message read:

INFORMATION HERE IS THAT HISS-CHAMBERS CASE HAS PRODUCED NEW BOMBSHELL. CHAMBERS HAS BEEN QUESTIONED IN LIBEL SUIT BROUGHT BY HISS. INDICATIONS ARE THAT CHAMBERS HAS PRODUCED NEW EVIDENCE. ALL CONCERNED ARE SILENT. HOWEVER, JUSTICE DEPARTMENT PRACTICALLY CONFIRMS INDICATIONS, SAYING CASE TOO HOT FOR COMMENT. INFERENCE IS NEW INFORMATION IN JUSTICE DEPARTMENT HANDS. MAY LEAD TO REOPENING OF NEW YORK GRAND JURY'S INQUIRY AND MORE INTENSIVE PERJURY INQUIRY HERE. IN VIEW YOUR COMMITTEE'S ROLE, CAN YOU TELL ME WHETHER COMMITTEE WILL REOPEN ITS INVESTIGATION. ALSO WHO WILL BE CALLED AND WHEN. ANY OTHER DETAILS APPRECIATED. PLEASE RUSH ANSWER COLLECT.

From the steamship "Panama" came Nixon's answer:

HAVE ADVISED STRIPLING TO INVESTIGATE AND ADVISE ME REGARDING NEW HEARINGS. WILL REOPEN HEARINGS IF NECESSARY TO PREVENT JUSTICE DEPARTMENT COVER-UP. WILL ADVISE DATE, WITNESSES, ETC., UPON HEARING FROM STRIPLING.

After learning more about the papers I was able to flash Nixon again:

DOCUMENTS INCREDIBLY HOT. LINK TO HISS SEEMS CERTAIN. LINK TO OTHERS INEVITABLE. RESULTS SHOULD RESTORE FAITH IN NEED FOR COMMITTEE IF NOT SOME MEMBERS. NEW YORK JURY MEETS WEDNESDAY. COULD YOU ARRIVE TUESDAY AND GET A DAY'S JUMP ON GRAND JURY. IF NOT, HOLD HEARING EARLY WEDNESDAY. MY LIBERAL FRIENDS DON'T LOVE ME NO MORE. NOR YOU. BUT FACTS ARE FACTS AND THESE ARE DYNAMITE. HISS'S WRITING IDENTIFIED ON THREE DOCUMENTS. NOT PROOF HE GAVE THEM TO CHAMBERS BUT HIGHLY SIGNIFICANT. STRIPLING SAYS CAN PROVE WHO GAVE THEM TO CHAMBERS. LOVE TO PAT. (SIGNED) VACATION-SPOILER ANDREWS.

Nixon sent another message saying he wanted arrangements made for him to leave the ship. The House Committee, through Secretary of Defense James Forrestal, had a Coast Guard plane sent to take Nixon off the ship at sea. Mrs. Nixon had to continue on their long-planned trip alone.

[The following letter was reprinted in the appendix of A *Tragedy of History*—Ed.]

May 15, 1952

Mr. Bert Andrews
New York Herald Tribune
National Press Building
Washington, D. C.

DEAR BERT:

In reading Whittaker Chambers' book, *Witness*, I was reminded again of the decisive part you played in the investigation. As you will recall, Chambers mentions the time that you and I drove up to his farm to see him on Aug. 15, 1948. What he did not know at that time was that the whole course of the investigation was determined by that visit.

I had become convinced from the manner in which Chambers spoke of Hiss that he was speaking of a man he knew rather than relating facts about a man whose life he had studied.

I recognized, however, that it was possible that my judgment could be wrong and consequently decided to obtain the opinion of someone I considered to be a completely impartial appraiser of the facts. I felt it was particularly essential to do this because to allow a fraud to be perpetrated upon the Committee would not only be a great wrong to Hiss and the others named by Chambers but it would be a death blow to effective and necessary investigation of the Communist conspiracy in the United States. It was at this point that I asked you to go up to Westminster with me.

I had two motives in asking you to do this. My first reason was that I knew that you had the reputation for being an impartial and objective observer, that you didn't "write with your heart" and that you always called them as you saw them. A second reason was that I knew you had been critical of some of the Committee's methods in the past. This meant that if you became convinced that Chambers was telling the truth no one could level a charge of bias against you and your opinion would, consequently, have great weight with those members of the working press who were covering the hearings, almost all of whom were completely convinced that Chambers was lying and that Hiss was telling the truth.

I remember that you suggested several lines of inquiry which aided immeasurably in getting the facts which eventually broke the case.

There were other times when our paths crossed during the investigations.

All the incidents caused me to state in a letter to the *New York Herald Tribune* on March 12, 1951, after the final word on the conviction of Hiss:

"Now that the Supreme Court has finally written the decision in the case of Alger Hiss, I should like to take this opportunity to give due credit to a man on the *New York Herald Tribune* who was as responsible as any other one individual for bringing out the facts which led eventually to the trial and conviction.

"There will be understandable efforts made now that the final decision has been handed down, to determine what individual or individuals were responsible for Mr. Hiss's exposure and conviction. As in all such cases there were a number of people who deserved credit for the parts they played. But I know from firsthand experience that Bert Andrews' name should be among the first when the credits are given out for those who participated."

Sincerely,

/s/ Dick

RICHARD NIXON

CORRESPONDENTS AS PARTICIPANTS: CASE II

By Noel Epstein

One afternoon last spring, Sanford (Whitey) Watzman, a reporter for the Cleveland Plain Dealer, was sitting in the House press gallery feeling rather pleased. "Nobody noticed," he said, "but they passed my bill today."

It wasn't an idle boast. For more than a year, Whitey Watzman, reporter, had been doubling as Whitey Watzman, Congressional strategist; he had played a significant behind-the-scenes role in winning House adoption of a measure authorizing the Pentagon to check contractors' books for possible overcharges on about $5 billion a year of defense work not put up for competitive bidding.

Indeed, it was Whitey Watzman who conceived of the legislation. It was Whitey Watzman who privately urged members of Congress to introduce it. It was Whitey Watzman who provided prompting to help keep it moving. It was, in many respects, Whitey Watzman's bill. And, standing a good chance of final passage by the Senate before adjournment this fall, it could become Whitey Watzman's Law.

The fact is that the influential Washington press corps' powers extend considerably beyond reporting and interpreting the news unfolding

Reprinted by permission from *The Wall Street Journal*, Volume 79, Number 51 (September 11, 1968) by permission of the publisher. Copyright © 1968 by *The Wall Street Journal*.

in the capital. Unknown to their readers, newsmen here, and particularly investigative reporters, sometimes are the prime promoters or offstage prompters in the Congressional hearings, legislative battles and other events they are chronicling, theoretically with detachment. This practice of "not only getting it from the horse's mouth but being inside his mouth" is "almost a way of life for many columnists and some reporters here," says Laurence Stern, an assistant managing editor of the Washington Post.

Assuring Publicity

Busy members of Congress generally welcome such newsmen's assistance, and for good reason. It often supplies them with fresh, ready-made issues to seize upon and, perhaps more important, it almost guarantees that their efforts will receive prominent attention in the reporter's publication—which is often a newspaper published in the officeholder's home territory.

For reporters, the double role can gain wider recognition for news stories they initiate or feel strongly about, while also promoting causes they believe to be in the public interest. (Congressional press gallery rules forbid any lobbying by the 1,050 member correspondents from the daily press and the 400 radio and television and 500 periodical representatives, but this bar is aimed mainly at preventing legislative pressure work by reporters for special interests and for profit.)

Charles Nicodemus of the Chicago Daily News is among those who have climbed "inside the horse's mouth," helping to draft speech material and then reporting the ideas as those of the officeholder he aided. He played just such a duet with Republican Rep. Paul Findley of home-state Illinois during the 1967 dispute over the Government-authorized sale of M-16 rifles to Singapore while the weapons were in short supply for Vietnam troops—a story Mr. Nicodemus uncovered.

A Congressman Sounds Off

"When I first got word of what was cooking, I wanted someone to raise hell in public about it," he says. "So I got in touch with Findley, who I had worked with before. . . . I fed him stuff and he sounded off about it, and he asked the State Department or Defense about other things." Mr. Nicodemus won a distinguished service award from Sigma Delta Chi, the professional journalism society, for these and related stories.

Currently back in Chicago as the News' political editor, Mr. Nicodemus remarks that he is "the first to say there are real problems involved" in playing such dual roles. But he adds: "You come to feel that when you're dealing with a crucial subject like this, where guys' lives are involved, someone ought to be doing something about it. And if a reporter is the only one around with the time or inclination, he'd better well do it."

Some other Washington reporters, like Pulitzer Prize-winner Clark Mollenhoff of the Des Moines Register and the Minneapolis Tribune, expend much effort trying to promote Congressional investigations. Mr. Mollenhoff says he has been attempting to interest "countless Senators and Congressmen" in a broad inquiry into what he considers the questionable way North American Aviation Inc. received major contracts for the Apollo moon-landing program. In May and June of 1967, Mr. Mollenhoff wrote several articles on the subject, tied to the Senate hearings on the Apollo fire that killed three astronauts, but the issue has been dormant since.

"I wish I could stir five times as much interest," he says. "But the committees are touchy about getting into it. They work closely with the agencies they supervise, and too often they aren't the policemen they're supposed to be."

A Potential Danger

A somewhat comparable conflict of interest, however, is one of the dangers critics see in reporters' close collaboration with officeholders they cover. The Washington Post's Mr. Stern, for one, says "the integrity of their stories and their ability to look at an official impartially become compromised." (Dual-role practitioners, however, maintain that they would criticize in print any of the Republicans or Democrats they deal with, if criticism were due.)

Doubters also complain that voters may get a distorted impression when a cooperating officeholder receives heavy press attention—since his outpourings really are partly the reporter's ideas. They suggest that the reporter might take a leave of absence or work full-time for the legislator if he feels that strongly about an issue.

But others, like Los Angeles Times correspondent Robert Jackson, tend to applaud the newsman who also dons the participant's hat, so long as the goal is in the public interest. "Frequently, nobody is looking out for the public, whereas you have all sorts of lobbyists working for moneyed groups," he says.

In between these conflicting views are those of Edward Barrett, until recently dean of Columbia University's Graduate School of Journalism. He finds reporters' double role "very disturbing" but "wouldn't put down a blanket prohibition against it." He does feel, though, that the reporter "has an obligation to disclose his involvement to his editors and probably to his readers." Mr. Barrett concedes that "finding a way to do this presents difficulties," but suggests "one possibility might be a notation at the end of the story telling of the reporter's participation."

While this probably would discourage many officeholders from cooperating and almost surely would lessen the impact of many such stories, it certainly would provide readers with intriguing and possibly mountainous footnotes if the full details were included. Consider, for example, the long and arduous adventures of Whitey Watzman:

In April 1967, Mr. Watzman wrote for the Cleveland Plain Dealer a 10-part series based on little-noticed reports by the General Accounting Office, Congress' watchdog agency, which assailed Pentagon waste. The GAO, in spot checks over 10 years, had uncovered $130 million in overcharges by defense companies on certain types of negotiated, noncompetitive contracts that now total about $5 billion a year.

The GAO verdict and the thrust of the Watzman series: The Pentagon wasn't enforcing the Truth-in-Negotiations Act, which requires the negotiating companies to furnish accurate, complete and up-to-date cost estimates. The GAO urged the department to adopt one regulation requiring companies to furnish supporting evidence for cost figures and, touchier still, another regulation letting department auditors peek at company records after jobs were done to see if original estimates and final costs jibed.

An Important Phone Call

But despite heavy play on page one, the Plain Dealer series received no notice outside Cleveland. "That was when we decided to begin a lengthy campaign to get more attention for this," Mr. Watzman says.

Among the first steps was a phone call by Mr. Watzman, whose paper has the largest circulation in Ohio (nearly 400,000 daily and about 540,000 Sundays) to the office of Ohio's Sen. Stephen Young, of Cleveland. "Whitey spoke to me," says Herbert Jolovitz, Sen. Young's administrative assistant. "He said he thought it would help if a speech were made. I took it up with the Senator, and he liked the idea."

On April 20, Sen. Young delivered a Senate speech criticizing the Pentagon, praising Whitey Watzman, calling for a Congressional investigation and inserting the Watzman series in the Congressional Record. The next morning's Plain Dealer carried a story headlined "Young Asks Defense Dept. Buying Probe."

"Anybody can get stuff in the Congressional Record," Mr. Watzman says. "But at least it was giving some added circulation to the story."

At about that time, he recalls, "I had heard that Sen. Proxmire's subcommittee was going to hold hearings in this general area, so I called up. He spoke to Ray Ward, a staff man on Wisconsin Democrat Proxmire's economy in government subcommittee, and suggested that the truth-in-negotiations issue be included in hearings scheduled for the following month. He got no commitment.

An additional tactic seemed to be needed, and the Plain Dealer's Washington bureau chief, John Leacacos, conferred with the paper's publisher and editor, Thomas Vail. At Mr. Leacacos' suggestion, it was decided that copies would be made of the Watzman series, and on April 26 they were sent, along with a covering letter by Publisher Vail, to all

26 members of Ohio's Congressional delegation, plus some other influential Washingtonians. Mr. Vail's letter said the Plain Dealer couldn't understand Congress' unawareness of the charges aired in the Watzman stories and asked for any reaction the Ohioans might have.

"We have the same right as any other concerned citizens, and we did what they would do—wrote to our Congressmen," Mr. Watzman says. "What we did beyond that was in furtherance of our objective to cast light on and correct a bad situation. The test in my mind is whether you do this on behalf of a special interest group or on behalf of the public."

Among those receiving the Vail letter was Ray Ward, who showed it and the Watzman series to Sen. Proxmire. The Wisconsin Democrat immediately decided to include the truth-in-negotiations issue in his subcommittee hearings, and he brushed up on the subject in a talk with Mr. Watzman.

Prospects looked brighter. Whitey Watzman arrived at the mid-May hearings anticipating that the wire services and publications with national circulations would at last latch on to his story. But he was in for a letdown. Sen. Proxmire's truth-in-negotiations quizzing came late in each of the hearing sessions, and by that time other reporters of consequence had left the hearing room. So except for Plain Dealer stories on the GAO and Sen. Proxmire attacking Pentagon officials, plus an editorial praising the Senator, there still was hardly a peep about the dispute.

It seemed obvious to Mr. Watzman that other strategies were necessary, and he decided to speak to Republican Reps. William Minshall of Cleveland and Jackson Betts of Findlay, Ohio. To them he made a new suggestion: A resolution by Ohio's GOP Congressmen.

Seeking More Drama

The resolution was introduced to the group by Rep. Betts, explained by Rep. Minshall, adopted by all 19 Ohio GOP Congressmen and reported in the May 23 Plain Dealer: "19 Ohioans Call McNamara Lax." Citing the Watzman series again, the resolution urged the GOP leadership to press for action to halt Pentagon waste of contract funds.

Though the Plain Dealer noted that this was the first time that the 19 legislators, making up the House's biggest GOP delegation, had "spoken publicly as a group on a major controversy," it was an exclusive story again for the Plain Dealer, the last thing the paper wanted. Clearly, something still more dramatic was needed. It was then that Whitey Watzman conceived of his legislation.

So Whitey wrote letters to Rep. Minshall and Sen. Proxmire, proposing his bill. They liked it. They asked the GAO to draft a measure specifically granting the Pentagon the record-checking authority, and on June 6 identical bills were introduced in the House and Senate.

"It was my bill in the sense that I suggested it, but it was very much the Minshall-Proxmire bill in the more important sense that they were the capable lawmakers who quickly comprehended the need and did the hard fighting," Mr. Watzman remarks.

New Developments

Eleven days later, the Pentagon took its first step, in response to the quizzing at the May Proxmire hearings: It proposed, and later adopted, regulations requiring negotiating companies to submit supporting data for their cost figures. But the touchier record-peeking question raised by the Minshall-Proxmire bill remained unresolved. On this, there was divided opinion at the Pentagon; auditors there were eager to look into defense company books, but procurement officials were opposed, saying they feared contractors would feel second-guessed if their records were open to scrutiny after a noncompetitive fixed-price contract had been negotiated.

Though the House Armed Services Committee had referred the Minshall-Proxmire bill to the Pentagon for comment, none arrived, and so no hearings were scheduled on the bill. New developments were needed, and they soon came:

—Sen. Young, on advice of Mr. Watzman, asked the GAO for additional reports on Pentagon waste; he got them and delivered another Senate speech.

—On their own, Sen. Proxmire announced the resumption of his subcommittee hearings, the GAO submitted favorable comment on the Minshall-Proxmire bill and Democratic Rep. L. Mendel Rivers, chairman of the House Armed Services Committee, ordered a subcommittee investigation of the Truth-in-Negotiations Act.

—Republican Congressman Charles Whalen of Dayton, Ohio, got hold of more GAO reports at Mr. Watzman's urging; when he saw them, he decided to make a House speech. Rep. Frank Bow of Canton, Ohio, after a talk with Whitey Watzman, criticized the Pentagon in his newsletter to constituents. Whitey phoned Rep. Minshall ("I knew what he would say, of course") and ran a story headlined "Minshall Charges Stalling on Truth Bill." He called the Pentagon for reaction to this charge and received no comment; he wrote that, too.

—Dayton's Rep. Whalen, a member of the Armed Services Committee, introduced another bill identical to the Minshall-Proxmire measure. And Democratic Rep. Porter Hardy Jr. of Virginia, presiding over the panel's investigating subcommittee, attacked the Defense Department for still not submitting comment on the measures.

Finally, on Nov. 2, Assistant Defense Secretary Thomas Morris delivered to Rep. Minshall and Sen. Proxmire copies of a new Pentagon regulation requiring a clause in all affected contracts allowing department auditors to open company books; at the same time, the Pentagon dropped any opposition to the Minshall-Proxmire bill. Whitey Watzman's strategy had worked.

"I didn't care that much about the bill any more," says Mr. Watzman. But Rep. Minshall and Sen. Proxmire still cared, maintaining that a Pentagon regulation could be withdrawn at any time. With the legislators still pushing for it to become law, the measure cleared the House Armed Services panel last April 26 and was adopted in the full House on May 6.

THE NEWS MEDIA AND THE BOBBY BAKER CASE

By Laurence Stern and Erwin Knoll

Muckraking, still an honorable form of journalistic enterprise at the city hall and state capital levels, has long gone out of fashion among the elite corps of reporters assigned to the Congress of the United States. The national legislature makes so much news that most of the reporters assigned to it cover only the surface flow of events—such formal happenings as committee hearings, floor debates, parliamentary maneuvers, and the genial press conferences staged regularly by the leadership. A state of symbiosis has grown up between press and lawmakers, enabling both to go about their business in an atmosphere of mutual tolerance. The viability of this relationship is rooted in an unwritten code that the press, and especially the journalistic "regulars" who cover the daily operations of Congress, will behold only the official face of the legislative branch and avert their eyes from the tattletale gray patches of private impropriety.

When the Bobby Baker scandal broke into print last fall it came, therefore, as something of a journalistic anomaly. Stories of personal wrongdoing emanating from Congress about its own members are a rarity in Washington bureau dispatches. When such scandal flares, it usually centers on a hapless member of the Executive Branch.

At the outset the Baker Affair had a divisive effect on the Capitol Hill reportorial community. "It has the smell of dead fish," grumbled one veteran Senate correspondent about the early allegations. The regular Senate hands, to whom Baker had long been an invaluable news source, responded to the early flow of revelations with skepticism and even a touch of annoyance at those colleagues who persisted along the Baker trail.

This is a point that deserves emphasis. The initiative and enterprise that went into development of the story did not come from the Senate Press Gallery, but rather from a group of journalistic outsiders and irregulars. For example, the story was brought to the surface by Jack Landau, an alert Federal District Court reporter for *The Washington Post*, who recognized immediately the explosive implications of a civil suit to which he had been tipped.

Once the Baker Affair surfaced, Senator Joseph S. Clark could not resist twitting the newsmen who regularly covered the World's Greatest Deliberative Body. "Where have you guys been all these years?" Clark needled. Clark's question still haunts some of the newsmen and editors who pride themselves on their grasp of political realities in the Senate. Where, indeed, had they been while Baker—between trips to the Senate floor—was amassing and directing a paper empire that he valued at more than $2,000,000?

There had been clues, to be sure. Some newsmen had been guests at the gala opening of Baker's sumptuous motel, the Carousel, in the seaside resort town of Ocean City, Maryland. Newspapers in the Capital celebrated the event as a major social event of the 1962 summer season—and it was. That a $19,600-a-year Senate employee with no known private resources could plunge suddenly into a million-dollar business venture apparently was accepted unquestioningly by all. The Carousel opening was dutifully recorded on Washington society pages.

A little earlier the same year, John J. Lindsay, of *The Washington Post* (now with *Newsweek*), had disclosed Baker's affiliation with a Silver Spring, Maryland agent, Don B. Reynolds, who had written $200,000 in insurance on the life of Lyndon B. Johnson (and who was later to become Baker's principal public accuser). Painstaking research among Maryland corporate records had confirmed the story for Lindsay, but Baker had denied taking any active part in the firm's affairs. Reynolds subsequently testified that he had paid Baker some $15,000 for helping to bring in business from his many Capitol Hill acquaintances. After a one-shot story, there were no follow-throughs.

By the time of the Carousel opening, a diligent examination of public records could have provided a catalogue of Baker financial affiliations that included: a motel partnership with a fellow Senate employee, Small Business Committee clerk Gertrude C. Novak; a $54,000 Small Business Administration loan for repair of hurricane damage at the motel; a thriving Washington law practice; and an active insurance business. Further investigation into the law firm might have revealed to such additional affiliations as the Serv-U Corporation, a fast-growing West Coast vending machine firm; the celebrated Quorum Club on Capitol Hill, and a travel agency, Go Travel, Inc.—all listed in District of Columbia records as enterprises incorporated by Baker's law firm.

If Baker's name emerged in the news during this period, it was only in occasional profiles of a bright young man on the way up the Washington social and political ladders. In these appreciative pieces tribute was invariably paid to Baker's acumen as a Senate head-counter, to his personability, and to his devotion to duty. One exception was an article by *Chicago Daily News* correspondent Jim McCartney, who related Baker's boast that he controlled ten Senators.

Nonetheless, the genesis of the Baker case, insofar as the press is concerned, must be dated September 12, 1963. That was the day when *The Washington Post* published on page 3-C, deep in the local section, a story by District Court reporter Landau that was headlined: "Senate Official is Named in Influence Suit." Baker's name was not mentioned until the third paragraph, but Landau's article gave the details on the civil suit filed against the Senate official and two associates by a vending machine operator, Ralph L. Hill. Hill claimed, in effect, that he had bought Baker's influence to get a lucrative vending concession in a defense plant and that Baker's influence was subsequently used to break the contract.

There had been considerable initial soul-searching by the *Post*'s editors on whether news of the suit should be reported, since it was a complaint in a private dispute. Finally, the executive editor, J. R. Wiggins, and the city editor, Ben W. Gilbert, decided to clear Landau's story without so much as a call to the newspaper's counsel.

Following publication of the initial story, additional manpower was assigned to the Baker story by the *Post*. The result was a page-one story published on September 22, 1963, that identified for the first time Baker's heavy financial interest in the Serv-U vending concern, which did most of its business in defense plants. At this point the *Post*'s only direct competition on the story was a little-known trade publication, *Vend* magazine, organ of the vending machine industry. Both published the story of Baker's affiliations with Serv-U on the same day. It was one of those rare instances when a highly specialized trade journal became a newsstand sellout in Washington.

After September 22, reportorial curiosity was further whetted by a sudden freshet of leads from disenchanted former associates of Baker, from casual acquaintances who could speak of specific episodes, and from anonymous telephone tipsters. Those who professed to know hinted darkly to newsmen of call-girl operations on Capitol Hill, of abortion rings, and of clandestine business deals in which prominent Congressional figures were alleged to have participated. One of Baker's former associates passed out the telephone number of a prostitute who boasted to several newsmen of a list of patrons almost large enough to constitute a quorum of either House. Her confessions were tape-recorded by a Washington private detective who subsequently granted paid audiences to newsmen who wanted to hear the recordings. (Stories based on the tapes were eventually published in the Hearst newspapers, the New York *Daily News*, and the *New York Post*. Only the *News* named the woman—and printed her picture.)

Some of the initial reports that came to the press from the gossip mines of Capitol Hill later proved to be substantially accurate; others turned out to be distortions or utter fabrications. Nevertheless, to the small corps of newsmen who were pursuing the story and trying to sift fact from fantasy, the Bobby Baker Affair was assuming a new importance. This stemmed in part, to be sure, from Baker's close relationship with Lyndon B. Johnson. But there was also the additional suspicion that a far bigger story lay beneath the surface of the Baker case. One news magazine correspondent made this memorable observation at the time: "What we have here is the story of the invisible government of the Senate—of how things are really done in Washington." The way things were really done in the world of Bobby Baker, reported Julian Morrison in the *Washington Daily News*, included the use of Senate limousines on private business and the juggling of Senate pageboy salaries.

Only a handful of newsmen was engaged in the lonely, investigative stage of the inquiry preceding Baker's resignation on October 7. Without the early stories, it is doubtful that Baker would have resigned or that the Senate would have directed the Rules Committee on October 9 to embark on a full-scale investigation.

While the Rules Committee made leisurely preparations for an investigation—an activity that was foreign to its normal housekeeping role—disclosure was heaped upon disclosure by a growing phalanx of reporters devoting all or most of their time to the story. In a massive display of gang journalism, *Life* magazine deployed platoons of reporters and photographers throughout Washington to bivouac in major hotels, roam the city, and extract whatever intelligence could be beguiled or bought on Baker's operations.

It was at this point that press coverage of the Baker case entered its Lavender Period. On October 21, the Advance News Service—Washington Bureau for the Newhouse newspapers—disclosed that Baker owned the lavender-carpeted townhouse near the Capitol that was occupied by his comely secretary and another Senate Girl Friday. This story titillated the imagination of some editors who had been unmoved by the disclosures of possible financial conflict of interest and political skulduggery. Five days later Clark Mollenhoff, Washington correspondent of the Cowles publications, filed an even more sensational report that a mysterious "German beauty" had been whisked out of the United States because of her intimacies with high-level Washington personages.

This development made the Baker case an international cause célèbre from Times Square to Red Square. Photographs of the alluring West German brunette side by side with Baker's Capitol Hill secretary were blazoned across front pages. "Senators, Model Held Parties At Baker House," blared the *New York Post* on the same day that the New York *Daily News* proclaimed: "German Pip Charmed On-The-Town VIPs." In London the sedate and intellectual *New Statesman and Nation* crisply headlined an article on the Baker case: "America's Profumo Scandal." Australian newspaper readers were cautioned: "U. S. on brink of sex scandal."

Ultimately the press reached the limits of its investigatory powers. In the Baker case, Senator John J. Williams of Delaware was able to complement the work of newsmen by relating their findings, both published and unprinted, to the leadership. He called in witnesses whose testimony had been of interest only to the press and he invited newsmen to bring in material that they were unable to develop themselves.

Although Williams had no investigative staff of his own, nor even the power of subpoena to carry out his private inquiries, he had built up a reputation in the Senate for spotlighting official wrongdoing in both Republican and Democratic administrations. He was the catalyst by which the Baker case was transformed from a newspaper investigation into an official inquest by a Senate committee.

On December 17, 1963, when the Rules Committee convened its first public hearing in the Senate Caucus Room, the theater for the Senate's most publicized investigations, the Baker case was formally inaugurated on Capitol Hill as a News Event. There were television cameras and May Craig sitting in customary prominence at the press corps' head table. There was a full turnout of wire service correspondents and Washington bureau regulars. The Baker Affair was no longer "dead fish." It was an investigation that could be chronicled in the calendar of Congressional events posted by the Senate Press Gallery.

Ironically, when the klieg lights were turned on, the spotlight of press initiative was turned off. Newsmen became increasingly dependent on official disclosures, and coverage of the Baker case gradually slipped back into the traditional pattern of reporting testimony. There were a few exceptions—notably revelations of some of Baker's Caribbean financial interests and his intercession for Nevada gamblers. These were reported respectively in *The New York Times* and the *Washington Evening Star*—both of which came to the story late but caught up quickly.

The concentration of reportorial energy and attention on the pursuit of Baker's myriad financial dealings produced important ancillary dividends. They included these revelations: Representative John W. Byrnes, a Wisconsin Republican, had interceded with the Treasury Department in behalf of the Mortgage Guaranty Insurance Corporation of Milwaukee (MAGIC), which later favored him with the opportunity to buy valuable stock at below-market prices (*Washington Evening Star*); Senator Olin D. Johnson of South Carolina had interceded with Dominican authorities for a gambler-constituent whose investments were endangered after the downfall of Trujillo (*New York Times*); Senator John J. Sparkman, second-ranking Democrat on the Banking and Currency Committee, had bought stock in a newly-chartered Washington national bank with a one-third down payment (*Los Angeles Times*); a cargo airline had provided free transportation for Capitol Hill staffers and lobbyists to a Las Vegas fund-raising dinner in honor of Senator Howard W. Cannon, Democrat of Nevada (Scripps-Howard).

Lyndon B. Johnson's accession to the Presidency imposed heavy inhibitions on newsmen who had been exploring the nature of the relationship that existed between Johnson and Baker. The press reflected the national desire to maintain unity in the wake of catastrophe. On the morning of November 22, insurance man Don Reynolds gave Rules Committee investigators the first evidence injecting Johnson's name into the Baker inquiry. Although the details of Reynolds's session with the committee staff were known to several reporters, the story did not appear in print until January.

Of all the private sources of information, Reynolds knew the most about Baker's business dealings and had the most documentation to back up his assertions. As a witness, he provided some of the most damaging testimony—although only in the form of published transcripts, since the Rules Committee never called him in open session. He became the center of the Johnson Administration's first news management controversy.

"Persons within and close to the Johnson Administration have attempted to use secret Government documents to impugn the testimony of a witness in the Robert G. Baker case," Cabell Phillips reported on page one of *The New York Times* on February 8. In the background of the controversy were Reynolds's allegations that he had been pressured into buying advertising time on the Johnson family's Austin, Texas, television station, and that he had paid for an expensive gift stereo set for the Johnsons. After Reynolds had given his testimony at two executive sessions of the Rules Committee, publishers and other key newspaper executives began receiving telephone calls from high figures in the Johnson Administration who pictured the insurance agent as an unreliable witness and cautioned against publication of his charges.

Phillips reported, and others confirmed, that "in several instances, individual newsmen and news executives have been read excerpts from what purported to be reports by either Air Force intelligence or the Federal Bureau of Investigation. These reports purported to contain derogatory information on Mr. Reynolds' background and his reputation for veracity."

The effect of these calls was varied. The *Washington Evening Star* revised a story about the stereo gift after a White House call, only to acknowledge later that its reporter had been right in the first place. The Hearst Headline Service, first to publish the story, made its decision to go ahead after a frantic round of telephone calls between Washington and New York. *The Washington Post* decided to await the expected release by the Rules Committee of Reynolds's testimony about the stereo set and advertising kickbacks to the Johnson station.

In any event, the Reynolds charges were widely publicized in all media when uncensored transcripts were released by the Committee—although they had to compete for news play with the concurrent release of President Johnson's budget message.

At this point, columnist Drew Pearson and his associate, Jack Anderson, began to publish a series of sharp attacks on Reynolds, quoting extensively from what they described as official records. In one instance, Pearson appended to his column the text of an Air Force memorandum on Reynolds's war record that bore a January, 1964, Pentagon stamp. In a "confidential note to editors," according to one published account, Pearson wrote: "For your information and because of possible concern over libel in columns on Don B. Reynolds, I am giving for your private information a copy of an Air Force report on Reynolds's background. Information contained in columns is from various sources, though the following is a fairly good summary."

The White House denied that it had any part in compiling or releasing the dossier on Reynolds. The Justice Department also denied any complicity in the leak. The Defense Department refused to make any comment on the episode, even in response to Senatorial inquiries.

The source of the leaks remains a mystery to this day. And the problem of how to handle unattributable, derogatory information from official files—a problem posed in its most acute form during the McCarthy era a decade ago—remains unresolved. In dealing with the Pearson revelations, *The Washington Post* twinned the first critical column with an answering statement by Reynolds. Other Pearson subscribers carried only the column. In a few instances the Pearson column was killed.

A chronic problem underscored by the Bobby Baker Affair is the strong pressure on Congressional beat men to confine their reportage to the visible legislative surfaces. Admittedly, covering the Senate is a complex and exacting assignment—one that is competently performed by most of the mature professionals in the Press Gallery. It is argued that Senate reporters are too burdened with daily coverage responsibilities to ferret out corruption in the Legislative Branch. However, the disclosures of the Baker case drive home the harsh truth that self-interested actions concealed behind the parliamentary facade are an intrinsic part of the story.

One Senate aide paid tribute to the role of the news media in the Baker case with the observation that "without the newspapers this would have been over long ago." He alluded to the fact that press disclosure provided the frame of reference for the Rules Committee investigation. Unarguably, the press did itself credit in the Baker Affair, displaying the investigative initiative it can bring to bear once its interest has been whetted.

Still, the question propounded by Senator Clark—"Where have you guys been all these years?"—remains a perplexing one. Had it not been for a seamy business squabble that spilled over into the courts, how long would it have been before the press recognized that the private financial interests of the Senate's Number One news source were also news?

NOBODY COVERS THE HOUSE

By Michael Green

Behind the closed, guarded doors leading to the House chamber one Wednesday morning several months ago, a dramatic and unexpected confrontation took place. Occurring at what was to have been just another routine monthly meeting of the House Democratic caucus, a customarily tepid conclave which normally fails to summon the interest of the Congressmen themselves, the confrontation totally bypassed the press. Even had the doors not been closed, reporters most likely would have shown scant interest. Conversely, had they been interested, the closed doors would have been no bar to their extracting ample accounts of developments inside.

But that morning, events unfolded in a public vacuum. Not only were they dramatic, they were politically significant—a first early signal of the determined, open rebellion by a few House reformers that was to break out two months later in defiance of the institution's customs and leaders. The issues raised were important to the country. The frustration and anger voiced against the House establishment revealed a sudden new boldness, not quite like the kind of militancy in evidence before, pushing back the boundaries of political civility in the chamber which in the past had always marked the acceptable outer limits to demands for change by young reformers.

Even without such hints of significance, the confrontation was in itself newsworthy. Out of the sea of anonymity which engulfs most Congressmen most of the time, and nearly all junior Congressmen nearly all of the time, an obscure, previously conservative and well-behaved, two-term Congressman from California named Jerome R. Waldie stepped forward and was recognized. For the next few amazing moments, he gave 78-year-old Speaker John W. McCormack a dressing down to his face, in front of his assembled colleagues, that was without contemporary precedent and shocked all in attendance.

The charge was "a dismal lack of leadership." The tone, though sternly polite and dignified, was unmistakably personal. The immediate criticism centered on the Speaker's attitude toward Administration policy on Vietnam, but went beyond it to question the performance of all in

Reprinted from *The Washington Monthly*, Volume 2, Number 4 (June 1970) by permission of the publisher.

the House leadership and the antiquated procedures that had made the House seem as obsolete in the last third of the 20th century as any institution in society.

Predictably, the reaction by McCormack and by those faithful party regulars who habitually attend him was one of outrage. The reaction of the public was non-existent. For good reason: not a line appeared in the nation's press the following morning. Nor on the television screen that evening. Nor anywhere the day after, nor the day after that, save for one afternoon daily clear across the country, which buried the story on an inside page at the bottom in one of the back sections.

Nearly a week passed before Congressional reporters finally stumbled across the story by accident. Even at that late date, the confrontation, was considered significant enough to rate as news, and Washington papers carried several accounts. But the story might just as easily have never appeared.

Ordinarily, the failure of the press to discover and report this solitary incident when it occurred might be dismissed as an understandable omission, given the multitude of events that compete for a reporter's attention and energy and all the judgments which must be made at various levels as to the value of an event as news.

But an examination of the position now occupied by the House in the political life of the country, in relation to public awareness of it and concern over it, and specifically to the need for reform, suggests a chronic failure by the press that goes far deeper than any single oversight. It extends to the coverage of all kinds of activities in the House, whether related to reform or otherwise, with serious implications for the future of the democratic process itself.

At a recent press conference, Representative Allard K. Lowenstein (D-N.Y.) warned that if the House were to become any more ignored than it was already, it would become as obsolete as the House of Lords and the country would simply evolve into government by Presidential decree.

If the public is without alarm, perhaps it is because Lowenstein's words went virtually unreported, as had Waldie's confrontation with the Speaker. And even had his warning been heard, could it be said the press had so prepared the public that it might have understood the meaning of his words?

The disturbing truth is that the increasing irrelevance of the House in American life is attributable at least in some proportion to the degree to which its activities and people remain a mystery to the public, and that the hope for urgently needed reforms is doomed in large part by this same public ignorance. The current state of general House coverage by the press is a key ingredient in the despair Congressional reformers feel over their chances for success in the uphill battle they face. At least some of them, though not impolitic enough to say so publicly, now see the issue of reform in the House as being inseparably intertwined with the need for change in the coverage the press gives to Congress. Without changes in press coverage, they hold out little hope for the kind of public pressure which alone might drag the institution into the modern world.

The larger casualty of the present state of affairs is the political process itself. At a time when the system is beset on all sides by accusations of unresponsiveness, often made in violence, the elected representatives supposedly closest to the people are among the least known officials in Washington, and the institution that in theory most directly links the people to government is furthest removed from their eyes and comprehension. Is it any wonder, in words Waldie used to challenge the Speaker, that "no one really looks to the House or its leadership as an authority or as a hope in this trying period for our country"?

Examples of the great Congressional coverage gap extend to a disturbing array of issues and events. The conclusions to be drawn can only be disheartening.

The press has failed to keep the public abreast of even the basic developments related to the reform effort.

For the past year, a subcommittee of the House Rules Committee considered legislation to modernize some of the antiquated House procedures. Its work went virtually unreported. Without the stimulus of public pressure, the subcommittee soon abandoned all substantive proposals for reform. It decided not to deal with the questions raised by the seniority system, lobbying practices, conflict-of-interest, secret committee meetings, unrecorded votes, and similar basic issues. It is doubtful many in the country even knew the subcommittee existed or that legislation was being drafted. Certainly, few constituents knew how their own Congressmen stood on these issues in testifying before the subcommittee. By the time legislation was actually drafted, the determination of reformers to add meaningful amendments on the floor existed without the benefit of public comprehension and support. Coverage by the press was too minimal to have any effect.*

The press has failed to show the real forces at work and to chronicle the shifting alliances for and against change.

The champions of House reform in prior years have looked curiously pale of late. When Waldie followed up his initial confrontation with the Speaker with a challenge at a subsequent caucus, in the form of a "no confidence" resolution against the House leadership, the old reformers shunned him. Similarly, when the once-militant Democratic Study Group offered a mild resolution calling only for a study of the seniority system

* This apparently was written before the passage of the Legislative Reorganization Act of 1970.—Ed.

even that move was thought too bold by many of the older champions. Rep. Morris K. Udall (D.-Ariz.), who challenged McCormack for the speakership only a year ago, suggested privately it was not the right time to make waves. He hopes to bid for the speakership again next year. The aging, autocratic committee chairmen found unexpected allies in their moves to prevent the reorganization bill from ever reaching the floor, even with its watered-down and largely meaningless proposals. Such old-time labor liberals as Representatives James G. O'Hara (D.-Mich.) and Frank Thompson (D.-N.J.) shifted uncomfortably at the thought of the rules subcommittee bill emerging. Their exaggerated fear was a possible move on the floor to split the House Labor and Education Committee and pack the new labor panel with anti-union conservatives, a move few thought was really in the works or would have a serious possibility of success, anyway. Conservatives, in turn, feared liberal amendments from the floor aimed at introducing meaningful House reform.

The strange posturing and maneuvering by the reformers of old was disturbing, but, thanks to the press, their reputations as champions of change have remained untarnished. Their fearful whispering not to "make waves" stayed a private affair. Their evolution within the system they once confronted openly and subsequent replacement by a newer group of young militants standing in the shoes they once wore, went unreported by the press.

The press has failed to pursue its own as well as the public interest.

One of the few real hopes of bringing about eventual reform in the House has centered in efforts to open it up to public scrutiny. Perhaps the single most important proposal considered by the rules subcommittee was to permit live TV coverage of the House and its committees.* It was fitting and ironic that the proposal was rejected by the subcommittee in a private session behind closed doors. But the proposal's enemies were not numbered from just among the ranks of the House power structure, which prefers not to have the public view what goes on. The opponents included the writing press.

Samuel J. Archibald, Director of the Washington Freedom of Information Center . . . tried in vain to mobilize editors and publishers to support the proposal. He found "no interest at all" among working newsmen in the House Press Gallery, most of whom strongly opposed it. He found "very minimal interest" on the part of various editorial and publishing associations—"very minimal." The death of the proposal, and the deeper issues involved in its rejection, were virtually ignored by all media, including television news itself.

The press has failed to show the average Congressman as he really is.

The anonymity of those Congressmen opposed to reform, who remain unknown both to the country at large and to their own constituents, is a special aspect of the perennial failure to achieve reform. If a few colorful, entrenched committee chairmen like L. Mendel Rivers (D.-S.C.) head of the Armed Services Committee, have received wide publicity, the bulk of anonymous Congressmen who support the antiquated system have not, even in their own districts. They include a wide variety of types, each opposing change for his own reasons. Many do not think of themselves as anti-reform. Rather, they see no need for it, some professing genuine astonishment at the reformers' complaints.

A Democratic colleague of Waldie's from California serves as an example. Rep. John J. McFall, 52, with 14 years in Congress, is one of those honest, amiable, pleasant-faced members whose name and status are always lost on observers in the Congressional gallery, if not to most of his colleagues as well. A "zone whip" for the Democratic leadership, assigned to keep tabs on members in a limited geographical area on important votes, he also heads the party's research activities in the House, though in seniority he still ranks well down the list on the Appropriations Committee. Well-liked by colleagues of all persuasions, he is a part of the comfortable existing order. It was McFall who helped put together McCormack's rebuttal to Waldie's charges.

Sitting back in his office swivel chair recently, head down on his chest, thumbs rotating around each other on his lap, feet spread apart and socks drooping around his ankles, McFall expressed honest puzzlement over the reformers' complaints. "I really don't understand what they're talking about," he said. "I really don't understand. I really don't."

That, say the reformers, is no small part of the problem. But it is not one likely to ever be considered in McFall's home district. For the seven terms he has served in Congress, his actions affecting the lives of all in the country, no newspaper in his district or outside of it has reported, either regularly or occasionally, his actual day-in and day-out performance in the midst of Congressional life as it really is. His attitudes, maneuverings, relationships, and thoughts remain unknown to the public. John McFall's socks have never drooped in his hometown paper. In fact, when he very nearly lost his last reelection campaign, it was not because he had displeased his constituents but because, a post-election survey showed, so many of them didn't remember quite who he was. So it is, to a greater or lesser extent, with most members of Congress; they are known to editors and readers back home only by their press handouts and occasional visits. Who they really are and what they really do over a period of 14 years is not "news."

The press imposes its own self-censorship.

At a recent press conference crowded with reporters, Speaker McCormack, third in line for succession to the Presidency, blew his top. Turning on a reporter who had written a matter-of-fact, even sympathetic account of McCormack's years in Congress and current troubles, the Speaker denounced the newsman as "a goddamned sonofabitch." The reporters seemed stunned. None was sufficiently stunned, however, to write anything about the outburst. No one seemed sure exactly why, except perhaps that McCormack is an old man, given to frequent outbursts these days over both real and imagined slights, and it did not seem the tasteful thing to do.

All the foregoing provides only glimpses of the deeper and more basic problem, which is that the average Congressman lives and works today far from the beaten path of press coverage; and the abuses of the system he either fights or engages in, and the failure of the system in dozens of its intricate parts, are far removed from the attention of the public and any possible response from it. Because the press never shows the system and its participants to the public, pleas for reform can only fall on confused ears, producing hesitation and uncertainty in place of loud demands for action. In a recent interview, Allard Lowenstein asked incredulously: "Do you know that we were not allowed to have a roll call vote on whether to deploy the ABM? And that on the Vietnam resolution the President wanted passed because it was vital to his plan for peace, there were no hearings, and discussion was limited to four hours—which averages out to 30 seconds a member—and there was no way to introduce amendments? And we've voted on amendments to bills that appropriate billions of dollars without having the amendments *explained*, let alone discussed?

"If only the country understood what goes on! But the whole procedure is designed to make that impossible."

It is clear the country does not know what goes on and that the system does make it impossible. It is also true that for all practical purposes, the press is a part of that system.

The relative absence of Congressional coverage today has many causes. In part, it reflects the low esteem to which the House itself has fallen in relation to the Senate and to the other branches of government, with a corresponding reduction in its news priority. The secrecy of the House, which bars reporters from committee sessions where billions of dollars are allocated, plays a major role, as does the sheer bulk of the institution.

Yet, it can be argued that the House is now the last, best hope of democracy as a participatory process, and therefore the most important institution of all—important as both a cause and potential remedy of the feeling of political impotence which afflicts the American body politic.

But the Congressional press corps is poorly equipped to serve as a bridge for bringing the House into the arena of modern life. The fault is both physical and attitudinal, resting more with press management than with the reporters assigned to Washington, most of whom function at a high level of competence within the restricted news spheres.

In physical terms, most medium-sized dailies in the country either maintain ludicrously understaffed bureaus or, most often, no bureau at all to cover local Congressmen on the Hill. They rely on wire copy. Here the deficiency in coverage is most obvious. For by the nature of a wire service reporter's preoccupation with the major news event of the moment, there is neither the opportunity nor the inclination to be concerned with the average Congressman. All the dailies back home receive is mimeographed press releases from the Congressman's own Washington office.

The result is a yawning gap in coverage more serious than is generally known. The fact, for example, that not a single major newspaper in the San Francisco-Oakland area, with its millions of people, maintains a Washington bureau is regarded as something of a scandal among Hill reporters themselves. Even when a paper maintains a bureau, however, the appearance is likely to be deceiving.

One California newspaper chain maintains a two-man bureau. But the two reporters are assigned to cover a total of nine Congressmen, two Senators, the Departments of Interior, Agriculture, HEW, and HUD, and occasionally the White House. Quite obviously, there is no time to do the job that needs doing. Another newspaper chain, based in Michigan, has one man to cover eight Senators and countless Congressmen for newspapers in four states spreading as far west as Oregon. The story is the same.

Even where a major newspaper or news service maintains a large bureau, the average voter may find it no easier to discover what his Congressman is doing and what he is really like. *The Los Angeles Times* has nearly two dozen reporters in town. But an esoteric publishing philosophy which stresses the more occult and ivory-tower dimensions of major stories leaves local Congressmen and their maneuverings as dimly reported as ever and the House as mysterious.

The attitude of publishers and news editors back home is primarily responsible for the failure of coverage in Washington. They have a highly ritualistic view of governmental coverage which holds unquestioned sway year after year and in its own way is as unresponsive to the times and as impervious to change as other hardened institutions of society, including the House itself.

What is generally omitted from coverage of Congress, almost alone of the categories of people and events with which a newspaper regularly deals, is journalism that might portray Congressional life so as to engage public interest. The human face of Congressmen and their aides, in all the day-to-day expressions of their small human foibles and unreported triumphs, mirror the forces at work in the population as a whole. They color the story and, in so doing, reveal it. But the public is not allowed to know this story. Readers are told only in dry, clipped accounts the numerical fate of legislation. They are shown the final score, seldom the action itself. The smells and faces and humanity of the players is lost to them and with it the opportunity for interest. The daily weather report is more interesting to the public and seemingly has more demonstrable relationship to their lives.

Journalistic tradition holds certain kinds of writing appropriate only to certain categories of coverage. Thus, there is business writing and sports writing, governmental coverage and garden columns, and the one is not to be confused with the other. Red Smith belongs on the sports pages. No one wonders what magic interest might be aroused in the public if he suddenly began covering Congress and appeared on the front pages. By the same token, if the present style of government reporting were extended to the coverage of sports events, the American people would lose interest in sports overnight. If Broadway Joe Namath's socks are seen to droop, millions of Americans via the press will hang on the unravelling threads. But for their news about government, the American people must suffer the dullest, driest, and most dehumanized accounts being published in the English language. Perhaps, as will be argued, the average Congressman is just not all that interesting or glamorous. But certainly there must be potential in someone like Dapper Dan Flood (D.-Pa.), the Shakespearean actor-turned-Congressman, with his twirled villain's mustache, dark glasses, Gaylord Ravenal voice, and white buck shoes, who controls billions of dollars in appropriations every year. Unfortunately, there appear to be no Damon Runyons now assigned to the Congressional press corps who might be equal to him. It is doubtful anyway that a distant editor trained to the present type of coverage could be persuaded by his reporters that Dan Flood actually exists.

The tradition of journalistic drabness in governmental coverage is not very old. It was not so long ago that William Allen White could report from the thick of political action or H. L. Mencken could freely dismiss a Congressman as a "boob" in his coverage. When Mark Twain was covering Congress for a time in the last century, one account began, "Dear Reader: Suppose that you were a Congressman. And suppose that you were a thief. But I repeat myself." Well, they don't write like that anymore.

It is high time that we started writing about the House as it is. What happens in Congress is a deadly if silent war within our political boundaries; we need more Ernie Pyles to cover it by living, eating, and getting shot at alongside the political troops while writing about combat conditions. Perhaps the confusion and puzzlement the average citizen now feels might be replaced by comprehension and involvement. At least government would have a face. The electorate would need not seek after strange devils to explain the mysterious coming of political winds. The process, by being human, would become rational, and even to lost souls in forgotten cities all things might seem possible within the system as it was meant to be.

If the possibility or even certainty exists of abuse by politically motivated reporters in providing this kind of intimate coverage, one also needs to ask the price of public apathy and Congressional unresponsiveness. It may still be easier to balance subjective coverage between reporters of different political hues than to rebuild Detroit.

In the current state of governmental coverage, the public has long since given up trying to understand elected behavior. Voters in a district, of course, may always hold their own Congressman accountable. But perhaps he has publicly supported the legislation they favor, as a majority of his colleagues may have, and yet it has died in the murkiness of some closed committee room—if he was in that room, his constituents need never know how he voted. It should be of little wonder that the system breeds despair and that the average citizen feels politically impotent.

It would not be accurate to say the press has failed utterly to communicate the need for change. The public has a general awareness by now, due to constant repetition over the years, that a seniority system that places aging, Southern autocrats in charge of powerful committees somehow works to the disadvantage of the country as a whole. It grasps, as well, the issue involved in the continued rule or non-rule of McCormack, third in line at age 78 for succession to the Presidency. The symbol here is powerfully visual. Particularly when McCormack sits behind the President at televised State of the Union messages, the gaunt visage of a man who has simply become too old for the job he holds conveys an unmistakable conclusion.

But the crisis of the House requires more than vague public uneasiness in order to be resolved. It requires intimate public knowledge, day by day, of the deeper evils of the system as it functions on a primary level and of the manner in which those evils are worked. This, in turn, requires a scope and depth and humanity of coverage on a continuing basis that so far shows no signs of appearing.

It requires, in the end, an urgent understanding by citizens that they alone have the power to force the institution to become responsive, not only in terms of the great social problems facing the country, but, first, in reshaping its own procedures to meet those problems. Somehow, it has not occurred to constituents who make their voices heard in Congress on a myriad of issues from crime to taxes that they have the power to influence the House toward its own reform. Somehow, it has escaped their notice that the way the House conducts its affairs is as much their business as any other issue and has great long-range impact on their lives. This is the real failure of the press.

What is required for public understanding is that coverage honor the truism set forth by Honoré de Balzac when he observed: "Men are so made that they can resist sound argument, and yet yield to a glance."

It should be the daily job of the press to record not only the bills that are moved and the votes that are cast but the glances that are exchanged and the human motivations that are behind them. Only then will the art of governmental reporting imitate life as it is with all its potential for change.

THE PRESS AND WASHINGTON'S OWN SUBURBAN FIVE

By Lewis W. Wolfson

While Richard Nixon is feverishly scratching marginal notes on White House news summaries, and the lowliest Arlington County building inspector may have to fight off cheeky reporters, the hands of Washington's five suburban members of the House of Representatives scarcely need tremble when they pick up their local newspapers.

The local press pretty much pays them no mind. And when the papers do write about Gil Gude, Larry Hogan, Marjorie Holt, Stan Parris or Joel Broyhill, the congressmen can mostly treat the *Washington Post*, the *Star-News*, *Alexandria Gazette* or *Oxon Hill Times* as comfy political security blankets. At worst, they are slightly prickly. More usually, the congressmen can see ahead only cloudless days of press publicity for branch bank ribbon-cuttings and their fearless co-sponsorship of somebody else's bills.

While the dailies offer deep thoughts about White House and congressional powerbrokers, 2.3 million suburban constituents get scarcely any news of substance about their own congressman. Ironically, Harry Rosenfeld, *Post* assistant managing editor for metropolitan news, himself refers to the *Post* as the "dominant" and maybe the "only" channel for Washingtonians to read about their congressman. But *Post* editors took two years to think it over before finally assigning a reporter fulltime to the Maryland and Virginia congressional delegations early last year. Soon

Reprinted by permission from the *Washingtonian* magazine, Volume 9, Number 5 (February, 1974). Material for this study was gathered by a team of graduate students in the Public Affairs Journalism Program at the American University. Editors: Laird Anderson, Richard Beer, Carol Crist and Robert Peirce. Interviews and content survey: Marjorie Bonnett, Peter Davidson, Diane Gregg, Carol Horner, Gil Klein, Jimmie Murphy, Cathryn Ritzenberg, Christopher Thorn, David Thompson and Robert Wiegand.

afterwards, the reporter was shifted to Watergate stories and the experiment was shelved. Rosenfeld insists that they'll come back to it again sometime.

Meantime it's slim pickings for the readers. For example, during the first 90 days of the 93rd Congress, the *Post* carried only 11 stories in which any one of the five suburban congressmen was mentioned more than in passing. Even then, nine of the 11 were simple "spot" news stories, apparently prompted by statements, press releases or other congressional handouts. In the entire year, the *Post* carried a total of only 10 articles that focused at any length on activities of the suburban five —or fewer than one a month. Whole weeks went by without their names even appearing in the paper. The *Star-News* coverage for the same period was, if anything, worse.

Out in the suburbs, flourishing community newspapers carry more stories about the congressmen, but manage to say less. Many of them regularly pass off the member's press release boasts as genuine news stories, reprinting them verbatim. 1972 Maryland congressional candidate Werner Fornos calls the suburban papers "the lackeys of the congressmen."

Washington is by no means unique in the way that news of Congress falls between the cracks. Local congressmen usually settle somewhere between school superintendents and sheriffs in most newspapers' pecking order of political coverage—well behind governors, state legislators, councilmen and the like. Editors tend to feel that what a congressman says and does in far-off Washington simply does not have much meaning to the homefolk.

But it is hard to fathom why, with Capitol Hill only a phone call or busride away, even the *Post* and *Star-News* largely ignored the hometown congressmen. Readers can find little in the press about the suburban five's performance on issues of transportation, energy, health, political reform, war powers—to say nothing of the news in the thousands of constituent pleas that pour into Capitol Hill offices. Broyhill and Hogan both estimate that they get as many hometown queries as any House member, and both in fact operate as much like mini-mayors as they do as national legislators. "They even get him at the stoplights," says a Broyhill staffer.

During campaigns, reporters swarm all over the countryside. But in an off-year—like 1973—coverage virtually disappears. Do the suburban five —Republicans all—go down the line with Richard Nixon on Watergate, the economy, the White House vs. Congress? Alas, about all we've gotten in the press in the past year is Broyhill vs. D.C. and Hogan on abortion.

The congressmen think they are victims of what Parris calls "a circumstance of geography." Because there are 435 House members in town, they are not treated as singular political figures as they might be in New York or Miami and, surely, in many smaller communities.

Larry Hogan says that when he speaks out of town, "the press is there hanging on my every word . . . They ask you about . . . all the national issues. And what you say is on the front page the next day. Around here, my own papers couldn't care less." Joel Broyhill thinks that television especially is "loaded with stuff" about the local congressmen in other cities.

Now, he's "not complaining," mind you, says Broyhill, although he is saddened by the press's failure to acknowledge that woolhat Broyhill of yesteryear is now statesman Broyhill. Why, these days he even makes the *Wall Street Journal* for his statements as third-ranking Republican on the *very* vital House Ways and Means Committee. But not the *Post*.

He can make a statement on some tax or other matter to Ways and Means, Broyhill says, and then slip out of that "very important meeting to go upstairs to a District of Columbia committee meeting. I'll stay up there for about 15 or 20 minutes and make some statement about a storm sewer or street repair . . . and I may be on television (about that) that night. And there will be a major story on it in the newspapers the next day. . . .

"But what I say of a national nature is not important to these Washington newspapers . . . And if I can't make Walter Cronkite on my Ways and Means statement, I won't make Max Robinson on it. I'll make him on my storm sewer statement. . . ."

The suburban congressmen are not far wrong in believing that they get the small type after the *Post* and *Star-News* have given the headlines to the House and Senate District committees, Walter Fauntroy, or some carousing out-of-town congressman who has run his car into a lamppost. For years, both papers have had two "local" Capitol Hill reporters, but both have written mostly about D.C. affairs. Broyhill has hardly been treated as representative of 465,000 northern Virginians.

"The flamboyant quotes from Broyhill that Mayor Washington is a good ribbon-cutter have gotten more play than what Broyhill is really doing about the suburbs," says William Curry, formerly *Post* assistant Virginia editor, who now handles District affairs. The same holds true for Gude and Hogan. "If you went and measured the number of times Larry Hogan's name appeared in the paper, you'd see that once he got off the House District Committee, it went way down," says Irna Moore, until recently *Post* editor for Maryland news.

On the other hand, it's hard to tell if the congressmen really understand what would happen if thousands more constituents suddenly started reading about them regularly.

Could the suburban five cope with a lot of Congress-conscious Woodwards and Bernsteins sniffing around their offices about bills for special interests or disclosure of personal finances, or veteran political reporters firing off analysis of how their performance rates against House colleagues?

Freshman Marjorie Holt bravely maintains that you should, indeed, "know what your congressman is doing because it does affect you." She says the press should help constituents to know how a member votes, why he voted that way, what he's doing in committee and what, if any, "leadership or influence" he may wield in the House.

But we interviewed the new congresswoman just about the time she was hopping mad at the daily *Annapolis Evening Capital*. Going beyond the handouts, as any good newspaper should, the *Evening Capital* had carried stories that she felt had garbled her stands on the war, and on impacted area school aid.

"The trouble with some papers," Ms. Holt told us, is that "they report (something) in a way that doesn't sound at all the way that I wanted it to be." Other papers, such as the *Baltimore News-American*, give her "good cooperation," she felt. "They will let me say whatever I want to there . . ." The *Anne Arundel Times* and the *Villager* do all right, too: "They take my press releases and release them the way I want them released, and to me this expresses what I'm trying to convey to my constituents."

It is an old story to Jack Kneece who had been the Star-News' Capitol Hill reporter for two years until leaving the paper recently. "They'll usually say . . . 'You distorted this,' or 'I didn't want you to emphasize that.'" When called on it, Kneece says, the congressman will say, "'Well, of course, I made the remark, but I didn't have any idea you were going to do that with it.'"

The Public Relations Machines

Congressmen like the kind of "news" that is "channeled directly to their district without an independent, or hostile press (as middleman). Many of them know very well that they can get reelected . . . without any help from the major media," says Robert Blanchard. . . .

"News" is what's greased by handouts, instant radio statements and heavy mailings of newsletters under their free postal frank. Press releases regularly pop up in print untouched by suburban editors' hands. The legislators are snapped forthrightly snipping a ribbon at the newest local branch bank, or at work at their desk, sleeves rolled up (one such Stan Parris promotional picture appeared in three different papers in his district within a week). At virtually no cost to them, they can crank out 30-to-45 second news items all day long from their offices to area radio stations that are hungry for news voices.

Well-paid Hill press aides and a well-oiled public relations machinery proclaim their vigor in the high councils of government. A constituent reading press-release inspired suburban newspaper headlines early in this Congress had to believe that first-termer Stan Parris, for example, was a Hill dragon-slayer: "Stan Parris Blasts District Judge," "Parris Asks Investigation of Rent Hikes," and "Parris is Waiting for Paris" (on peace talks). Meanwhile, his Virginia colleague was busy legislating to the accompaniment of press releases: "Broyhill Pushes Tax Benefit for Retirees," and "Broyhill Bill Aims to Aid Widows Get Death Payments."

For Marylanders, Larry Hogan was tossing out more red meat on busing and abortion through "The Hogan Report," his weekly "column" for the suburban papers.

Freshman Marjorie Holt was learning how to cover herself with the homefolk—"Holt: School Funds to County Not Cut," and "Army Officials Tell Rep. Holt: No Job Losses at Meade"—and most photogenic Gil Gude was being snapped as he checked on C and O Canal restoration, and gamely administered mouth-to-mouth aid to the Heart Association's shapely mannikin, Resusci-Annie.

"Their appetite is insatiable," says former Montgomery County *Sentinel* editor Roger Farquhar. "They quiver when you call them up and they think they'll get their name in the paper."

But they don't wait for the phone to ring. Broyhill, for example, sends news releases to 30 daily and weekly newspapers, four television stations and 12 radio outlets. Hogan's mailing list includes 140 news outlets and individual journalists, according to press secretary Marian Barb.

Most of the congressmen and their press aides like radio best. "We try to hit the morning and evening traffic hours . . . You've got a captive audience sitting in their cars," says Broyhill aide Tom Adams. Newspapers and television have a way of writing their own version of the story, he says. But with radio tapes, "you can tailor the subject to your member's view."

Broyhill uses the Republican Congressional Campaign Committee's service for delivering taped instant analyses to 12 area radio stations at once. A Parris aide claims that his man is "the seventh most active congressman in the country" in the use of the service. Gude has even offered free pamphlets on cooking and child-rearing to gauge the listener-ship for his free 'public service' radio statements. Feedback was slim.

What does draw feedback is the congressional newsletter. Hogan's 1972 foe, Edward Conroy, thinks that newsletters, not the news media, are "far and away" the biggest factor in people's noticing a congressman. Broyhill's Adams calls them "the most effective way" to put across the congressman's views.

Broyhill last year upped his newsletter mailings from one every two months to 10 a year. In February, for example, 164,000 registered and potential voters in northern Virginia received a newsy one-page note from the congressman about federal spending, declining mail service and rent increases. In his close, Broyhill wrote, "I urge you to give me the benefit of your views so that I might better represent you in the Congress."

His office was deluged with replies. Hundreds of people wrote in, some penning comments onto the newsletter itself. Some even corrected the diction. But, while an estimated four out of five applauded Broyhill, the office wasn't about to repeat what Adams wryly referred to as that "tragic mistake." In subsequent newsletters Broyhill retreated to, "Let me again thank those of you who have given me the benefit of your views on previous newsletters."

Three of the five local congressmen also have their own newspaper columns. Freshman Parris, who quickly swung into things on the Hill with a $20,500 a year "Media Director," answers a selection of six letters a week in his column. It's informative but, not incidentally, also leaves constituents with a warm feeling that Stan Parris is their friend, and a bulldog on their behalf.

Did a constituent fail to get a sought-after street repair or social security check? The congressman tells readers how he personally straightened out their frustrating collision with a government office. He knows what it is to fight City Hall: "(This) is typical of the bureaucratic delays . . . suffered by all of us," he writes to C.R. of Alexandria, assuring him that a check for $202.94 is "in the mail" from Massachusetts to cover the damage caused when one of that state's National Guard vehicles collided with his car.

Papers are asked to run the Parris column as "a public service," and a blurb advises readers that they should write to the congressman c/o the *Manassas Journal-Messenger* or *Springfield Independent* (which carry the column), in effect turning the newspapers into a district office for Parris. Press aide Richard Leggitt says that they have had "tremendous results" from the column.

Since June, Congresswoman Holt has fed a bi-weekly column to 15 weekly newspapers. According to an aide, 10 of them usually carry the entire release. Larry Hogan not only dispatches his weekly Hogan Reports to his press mailing list, but he also owned his own house organ for a while, with a sizeable interest in a Prince Georges County weekly.

Hogan and partners shed the Clinton *Star-Leader* in 1973 after owning it for less than a year. But while their interest lasted, the paper carried considerably more coverage on owner Hogan than other weeklies had on suburban congressmen—even though Clinton is in Ms. Holt's district.

Five people who can count themselves as leading experts on the effects of all this congressional ballyhoo are the Democratic candidates who were strewn about the countryside after the Nixon sweep of Maryland and Virginia in 1972.

"Larry Hogan's nose for the press is excellent," says Edward Conroy, 11 years a state legislator, who challenged Hogan in Maryland's fifth district. "There is no question about the man's public relations ability. He is excellent in his ability to knock out press releases. You could get in the Congressional Record every day about something if you chose to do so and, in time, his name is going to become a household word . . . It's extremely frustrating for a candidate who runs against a professional public relations expert to compete in this atmosphere, very difficult. Every candidate who has ever run against Hogan has said the same thing."

Conroy thinks that Hogan has parlayed a comfortable formula out of news releases and newsletters, a flair for "issues that inflame the public" (abortion, amnesty, busing), and the absence of serious examination by the press. People have the impression (a mistaken one) that Hogan has initiated much major legislation, says Conroy. The Hogan image of being constantly in motion makes people feel that "he moves large numbers of congressmen in any direction (he wants to) on Capitol Hill."

Fairfax County commonwealth's attorney Robert F. Horan Jr., who was beaten by Stan Parris in a fairly close race in 1972, ungrudgingly admires how his old opponent has painted himself as "a very active, forceful, energetic member of Congress" in the press. But, "you really have to search extra hard to find out how he is voting or whether he is showing up at committee hearings," says Horan. "That's the guts of a congressman's performance, not what he is putting out in his press releases. It would take independent investigation to determine that, and you will not get that from the media."

Horan thinks the political PR machinery created in the last 10 years has taken the fight out of reporters. "The first thing a guy does when he gets a job (in government) these days is to hire a flack," he says. There are still a few reporters, he feels, "who never accept anything at face value. You can tell them until tears run out of your eyes what happened, and (they) . . . are checking around to see what the other side of the story is . . . (But) the new style reporter will tend to buy it from the press release and embellish it. He'll write a very nice piece. But it's not necessarily reporting."

Post and *Star-News* editors feel that they at least cover the congressional elections fully. But the challengers think it's the time when the congressional PR machines can most easily steamroller the voter.

By that time, they say, the money is flowing, the campaign literature is flowing, and veteran campaigners like Broyhill and Hogan are pouring it on about all the great things they've done in Congress. Horan feels that even if the media were very good at it, "the last eight weeks of a political campaign is a little late to be finding out what (a congressman's) stewardship has been for the past two years."

The man who has twice tried to beat Broyhill by "taking his voting record to the people," Fairfax County attorney Harold O. Miller, points out that a Post reporter often is thrown into covering a congressional race without having met the congressman or his challenger, much less having plumbed the subtleties and ambiguities of Hill affairs.

"When Congressman Broyhill says he voted for the Water Pollution Control Act, (the reporter) doesn't know that Broyhill had first voted to cripple it. When that lost, he then voted for the final bill. So, a challenger like myself will say that Joel Broyhill voted to cripple the Water Control Act in 1970 and Broyhill will say, 'What a pack of lies. I voted for that bill.' . . . Or, he'll tell people that he voted (for) the agency that's building Metro . . . But he doesn't tell you that he voted year after year not to give (it) funds. No one ever seems to be able to address this in news coverage in a knowledgeable way."

The Post, Star-News and the Suburbs

While the Washington papers were out covering Watergate and Home Rule, their hometown—including three of the 10 wealthiest suburban counties in the country—was growing out from under them. The powerful *Post*—like the federal bureaucracy it so often needles for its creakiness—was maddeningly slow to respond to this new power in the suburbs.

The paper didn't exactly have to go out on a limb. A lot of U.S. dailies who look to the Watergate-sleuthing *Post* as the guiding light of journalism already have been covering the local congressmen for years through their Washington bureaus. But the *Post* has been trailing the pack in this and, astonishingly, with Congress right in its own backyard.

Post editors long have known what should be done: stories on the congressmen's work for constituents, their place in committee and party councils, their views on issues and reasons for voting—a story on "Joel Broyhill as a congressman, not as a demagogue," says Irna Moore. "What kind of man he is, how he operates in the House, what his power is in the Republican caucus, how important he is on the Ways and Means Committee. Everything that has nothing to do with his role on the District committee. I don't think we've ever really written about it."

But while some 2.3 million congressional—and *Post*—constituents waited, the editors talked "for at least two years, if not longer" about assigning a reporter to cover the Maryland and Virginia delegations, according to metropolitan editor Rosenfeld.

"Every one of my editors has talked about . . . how 'we gotta do this.' . . . We've all agreed on it for a long time. But we probably have the pressures of the institution . . . and it takes us longer than it should to find the right person to make sure that this is going to work." A slightly different version, from Ms. Moore, is that reporter Herb Denton had done a good job in covering local Maryland politics "and there was no opening to send him to Annapolis, so that (job) was created for him." In fact, it was done not by establishing a new Hill slot, but by lopping off one of the two D.C. affairs reporters.

Denton, a 30-year-old black reporter from Arkansas who has been with the *Post* for five years, came off a beat as one of three reporters in Prince George's County. As he learned his way around the Hill early last year, he came up with a story on the congressmen's fight with Nixon over school aid cuts, and a notable piece on lobbyists' efforts to influence the Washington congressmen's votes on using the highway trust fund for mass transit.

But Denton also was still backstopping D.C. affairs reporter Martha Hamilton, and he was pulled off the beat from time to time to do other stories. By mid-summer he was covering Watergate fulltime, and then was given an editing post for Maryland. Everything else was moved to the backburner.

So, 11 months after it was launched, little has been done with the *Post*'s new suburban congressional beat. Readers have yet to see the stories on the editors' own agenda, to say nothing of the enterprise work that makes a strong beat—continuing fresh story ideas, tips acquired, investigations pursued, thoughtful portraits of congressmen filled in.

Stories sometimes disappear into a no-man's land in the *Post* bureaucracy between the metropolitan and national desks. Other metropolitan reporters may catch a Maryland or Virginia assignment on the Hill, but never any of the *Post*'s 25 national correspondents. Suppose Mac Mathias proposes overhauling the congressional committee system, recalls Ms. Moore. "Well, what kind of story is that—is it a national story, or a local, Maryland story? No, it's not a Maryland story. And we'd bounce it back and forth, and it'd fall in the cracks every time."

Even simple things—like making sure that suburbanites can check out at a glance how their national legislators vote on important issues—have fallen between the cracks. Editor Curry recalls how he erupted a couple of years ago when a front page story noted how certain congressmen had voted on a bill. "They were all from Podunk. It was real Afghanistanism. Nowhere did it say how the local delegations voted. My temperature rose like mercury on a hot day."

He fired off a memo that charged the *Post* with spending more time collecting items for the crime clock, the daily log of police reports, than on the suburban congressmen's votes. After that, the *Post* started running a weekly roundup of votes culled from *Congressional Quarterly*. But in time the column disappeared, only to pop up occasionally in some odd corner of the paper. Rosenfeld himself was unsure of whether it was still being run in the paper.

It's not really a question of space or manpower, Curry says, but "lack of commitment to get it into the paper." "We have a lot of reporters. We usually have too many," says Ms. Moore. To her, it's a question of the *Post*'s getting over past indecision about "just what kind of local newspaper we are, and what we are to do about covering these local congressmen."

Crosstown, the *Star-News* may carry a good suburban congressional story now and then, but it generally lags behind even the *Post's* halting coverage. The paper still uses the system of having the two local Hill reporters concentrate on the House and Senate District Committees (and, like the *Post's* Denton, *Star-News* Senate reporter Martha Angle was shifted to Watergate coverage during the summer).

David Burgin, who became metropolitan editor last year and who has himself covered Congress, felt that the paper "probably" gives an outsized share of its Hill coverage to D.C. affairs. One of the suburban five usually has to make a big splash to rate a story. Burgin's predecessor Scot Smith said that the press, the *Star-News* included, simply does not do a good enough job of getting below the surface on the Hill.

The congressmen and their aides are at it all the time, stroking, hustling or needling reporters. "They all have axes to grind . . . ," says reporter Kneece who was interviewed before he left the *Star-News*. "For example, I had a couple of beers yesterday with Stan Parris's press aide, Dick Leggitt, and he had a story he wanted me to do . . . about how Parris could do nothing to prevent the reduction of impacted (school) aid funds to the suburbs.

"He was very frank . . . He said, We want you to do this story because Herb Harris is going to run against Stan, and Herb is going to make this a big issue. And, he said, If you can do a story saying that Parris is really helpless in this whole thing, we'd really appreciate it. Well, how would you answer somebody like that? If it's a legitimate story, okay. But you're not going to go out of your way to do something . . . You're not their lackeys . . ."

Once you write one puffy piece about a congressman, says Kneece, he'll "think of you as a mouthpiece," and keep coming back for more. When he first started covering former D.C. Committee Chairman John McMillan, the South Carolinian granted a rare interview to southerner Kneece, and some favorable stories resulted. But, "when I was forced to write other things—when he started pulling little tricks—McMillan got very angry and thought I was sort of a turncoat. You can't get yourself into that box."

The Suburban Press

Out in the suburbs, where community papers sprout with the crab grass, the picture is bleaker for the reader, if not necessarily for the congressmen's publicity efforts. "There are no strong local papers," Broyhill assistant Tom Adams told us. For the most part, he said, they just "rewrite our press releases."

A good 80 per cent (conservatively) of these papers' coverage is based on the congressmen's press releases, and the rest is mostly secondary references to them in other stories.

It apparently is common practice for releases to go straight from the Hill and into a local newspaper word for word. Unbeknownst to the reader, a congressman's legislative boasts or self-serving quotes may be lifted whole from the releases and shovelled into print with no further checking. In one two-month period we found 84 stories (in 29 papers) that were based on press releases, and nearly half (41) of them were verbatim reprints of the release.

Agnes Deviney, editor of the *Herndon Tribune*, told us that she likes "to print them (releases) straight. Then the responsibility is on the congressman." (She also said, "I feel that editors must help their congressmen.").

The editor of the *Oxon Hill Times*, George Trees, also was open about the practice, perhaps because he himself had once been a Hill press aide:

"A congressman can keep his name before a newspaper if it's nothing more than with good effective PR blurbs. We're not above (using) that sort of thing if it's a good story about local people . . ." Had he sought out any stories on Ms. Holt (it was early in her new representation of Oxon Hill)? "She has a PR (person) and if the PR can't . . . give me a local story, then I don't feel it's my problem to worry about it," he said.

Trees felt that a small community paper has to be "myopic." "To me a good burning local issue is when somebody's son makes Eagle Scout. I don't feel I'm supposed to compete with other papers . . . (or) report on the world." Congress is "pretty far away." "I generally take the attitude . . . that if they dropped an atomic bomb on Marlow Heights, I wouldn't cover it. It wouldn't be a local story," he said.

Nearly every one of the 22 suburban editors we interviewed said that it is not really their job to cover the congressmen. They run local newspapers with local concerns, they told us. They believe, with an almost childlike faith, that the two titans of newspapering in whose shadow they operate are covering the congressional story, and they cannot possibly compete. Some editors told us they follow the *Post* and *Star-News's* lead on such stories. Only two of the 22 recognized that the big dailies aren't doing the job.

It is easy to feel sympathy for the harried suburban editor. But just when we thought that, perhaps, they could not do much more, we would come across a refreshing piece of enterprise.

The weekly *Prince George's Sentinel* did not just settle for Hogan's handouts, but actually sent a reporter to an anti-busing rally at the Capitol, and he provided readers with an interesting story filled with quotes and good color. Virginia's *Globe* newspapers did a roundup of the views of Broyhill, Parris and the two Virginia senators on priorities for Congress. The *Globe* also was one of the few local papers that logged key congressional votes regularly.

Not that anyone can expect Washington's local editors to all be William Allen Whites, laboring over the cold type with gnarled fingers and homespun editorial integrity.

Some retain their ideals and scrape by financially from week to week ("We've literally done without food, clothes and dental work to put the paper out," says the *Herndon Tribune*'s Agnes Deviney). Others see the burgeoning suburbs as a chance to make money rather than as a battle-ground for better journalism. All vow that they are dedicated to serving the community, but some student interviewers wondered how you can look like a house organ for politicians' press releases and still claim to be a "community" newspaper.

One American University graduate student was even prompted to start his own bureau to provide small newspapers and radio stations in Virginia with local-interest news of Congress. Indeed, the local papers might well take a leaf from papers around the country, some even smaller than the 5,000 circulation *Oxon Hill Times*, which use such congressional news services. Short of this, an editor or reporter doesn't have to be a Hill buff to pick up the phone to give his readers more than a congress-man's boasts about himself.

Suburban Washington papers need to step up to their audience more. "The people out here are about as well informed as anybody," says the *Globe* Newspapers enterprising young editor Greg Forte, "but they really don't have too much information available to them . . . We have the responsibility of giving the congressmen close continuous coverage, and we haven't been doing it."

The Worst Covered Story

Congress may well be one of the worst covered stories in Washington. Some of the people we talked to, like Ms. Holt's 1972 opponent, Werner Fornos, called it *the* worst covered story. Congressman Gude said it's too bad there are so many competing levels of government here because "three-fourths of the local newspapers ought to be filled with what we're doing here." Gude's last Democratic opponent, Joseph Anastasi, thought that a comparative study of the local media would show that you find out "less about the House than about any other level of government."

For many people, a congressman is unique. He is their one link with the impenetrable federal bureaucracy—"the one federal official that people think of in local terms," says Harold O. Miller, who twice lost bids for Congress against Broyhill. People go to their congressman here for every-thing, "even for potholes in the street," says Miller.

But a congressman needs to hear from more than just complainers or cheerleaders, and Bethesda might as well be Pocatello and 2,200 miles away for all the press-generated dialogue Gil Gude or any of his four local colleagues has with the mass of their constituents. To many people their congressman probably isn't much more than a face on a billboard every two years, and even the name may escape them.

The one sure way to turn this around would be for the *Post* and *Star-News* to get over what one *Post* editor calls their "schizophrenia" about setting out to do what, deep in their hearts, their editors have known ought to be done on hometown congressional coverage:

Double Coverage. For years the Washington papers have been wasting a unique opportunity to report on both dimensions of their hometown congressman's performance: his Hill activities, and what's on the minds of people back in his home district.

The *Post*'s Rosenfeld himself talks about how "Congress is in our own backyard," but little has been done about it. Both Rosenfeld and the *Star-News*'s Burgin insist that their county reporters do cover the congressmen in their districts, but we found no evidence of it in the paper. The only substantial coverage of the congressmen on either end is during election campaigns, and that may well be the worst time to get a sensible reading on a political performance.

Rosenfeld says that about one-third of the *Post*'s 70 metropolitan reporters cover largely the suburbs. The *Star-News* has about 50 metropolitan reporters, divided roughly into a third each for D.C., Maryland and Virginia, according to Burgin. Surely, each paper has at least one reporter in the pack who could be assigned to the Maryland-Virginia congressional beat and kept on it, even when Watergate beckons.

Front Page/Metro Page. National newspapers or not, the *Post* and *Star-News* also ought to take a fresh look at their news priorities.

If Wilbur Mills's back problems merit page one of the *Post*, should Gil Gude's decision to consider running for governor of Maryland—page one news in most any other city—be given seven paragraphs on an inside page (or be pushed even further back as it was in the *Star-News*)? Should news of California or New York (where *Post* reporters are stationed) get more play than news of the hometown congressmen?

Gude or Hogan for governor seems to be a good time to look at Gude and Hogan as congressmen, and other takeouts on Congress of the sort the *Post* does so well on D.C. or national personalities and issues. Readers should be able to find out whether Washington's congressmen take the lead in doing serious work on public problems in Hill affairs—or whether they are publicity-seekers, caretakers for special interests or seat-warmers.

What They Think/How They Vote. Surely, the dailies could run the major congressional votes regularly, and explain these in context so people can judge whether their congressman's actions hurt or help them. Members should be quizzed about major votes and other important issues.

Rosenfeld worries that more coverage will mean more PR for the politicians. "We're not here as press agents. We're here to reveal to people how the legislature works . . . We're not recording every chicken scratch;

we're describing the chicken . . . ," he says. But if an editor or reporter learns how it "works," shouldn't he be able to sort out the substance from the press agentry? And we surely get a lot of chicken tracks in the *Post* on other politicians.

What's needed from the dailies is the kind of Pulitzer-prize winning commitment that sends the *Post* after a Watergate scandal, cutting loose reporters and editors and space to carry the story day after day. Marjorie Holt may not rate Watergate-sized headlines, but the way she and other suburban congressmen operate may have much to do with what kind of government people are going to get.

Most Washingtonians probably are just as soured on government's workability as the rest of the country. The idea that Congress somehow can be made more responsive to the people may seem to many to be a wild romantic notion about government best left back in high school civics.

But, these are the days of Common Cause's citizen lobbying and Nader reports on congressmen and, now, on the news coverage of them. Congress is even conducting its own study of media relations. More than anything, the Watergate hearings have dramatized congressmen's power to inform. The legislative branch is big news. But, as it confronts the President, who but a few gnomes of Capitol Hill really understands about its powers and impotence? Hearing more about what one's own congressman is up to might be a good place to start.

8

Congressional Publicity
in Action

CONGRESS HAS DEVELOPED techniques to create publicity, to communicate an individual member's message directly to his constituents, and to carry its proceedings from the chambers and committee rooms to locations around and outside Washington—with and without the cooperation of the news media.

These techniques have been developed partly as a congressional response to the power of the executive branch's command of modern channels of mass communication. The open congressional hearing has become a favorite forum to meet the needs of both the news media and Congress. Douglass Cater describes the formative periods of the modern congressional hearing designed for news media coverage. The hearing format as he illustrates in this classic analysis also serves the careers of individual members of Congress.

In addition to providing competition for executive publicity, the congressional hearing also helps satisfy the drive of broadcast journalists for news to compensate for their lack of access to congressional proceedings. William Small provides examples of this from his CBS Washington Bureau's coverage of the early congressional debates over the Vietnam War. He also describes the struggle between Congress and the President—primarily through manipulation of television—over the public's attention to their points of view on Vietnam.

A more recent and refined example of the publicity-generating congressional hearing is freedom of the press investigations by the Constitutional Rights Subcommittee of the Senate Judiciary Committee, chaired by Sen. Sam Ervin (D.-N.C.). The selection by Laurence Leamer would be just as appropriate for Part Three, where examples of Congress-media cooperation in the conduct of hearings and issues of press freedom are considered.

Sen. Ervin was subsequently selected to chair the Senate Select Committee on Presidential Campaign Activities (see Introduction to Part

Three). The effects of the Watergate hearings—and attendant publicity—on the careers of the members of the Ervin committee is considered in a "Style" section story by Jeannette Smyth of the *Washington Post*.*

The congressional hearing is only one of many channels of publicity devised by members of Congress. A selection from a book written for freshmen congressmen by Donald G. Tacheron and Rep. Morris K. Udall (D.-Ariz.) illustrates the variety of institutionalized channels of communication available to members of Congress who seek maximum control over the flow of information to congressional districts.

Selections from the Ralph Nader Congress Project and by Ben H. Bagdikian (see Introduction to Chapter 7) describe the incumbents' domination of the "media of electioneering" with the aid of reporters.

THE CONGRESSIONAL HEARING AS
PUBLICITY VEHICLE

by Douglass Cater

Amid the publicity drives of Congress the investigative committee exerts the most powerful thrust. It is geared to the production of headlines on a daily and even twice daily basis. It is able to create the news story which lingers week after week on the front pages to form an indelible impression on the public mind. No institution of the Executive Branch is capable of such sustained and well-manipulated publicity.

It is a bewildering discovery for the newcomer to Capitol Hill to come upon the publicity trapping of the congressional probe. Within the marble conference rooms of the dignified old congressional buildings, the technicians of the mass media have taken over. Row on row of reporters occupy the forward seats. Crouching directly before the beleaguered witness are the still photographers, ever ready to thrust their cameras into his face to record each symptom of anger, grief, or perhaps only confusion caused by the noise and fuss. In the Senate committees a backdrop of klieg lights and TV and movie cameras completes the stage setting for this bizarre function claimed to be part of the "legislative process." . . . .

One witness who was questioned for more than ten hours before a committee has put down his recollections of that event:

* See also: Robert Walters, "The Howard Baker Boom," *Columbia Journalism Review*, November/December, 1973.

Reprinted from *The Fourth Branch of Government* by Douglass Cater by permission of Houghton Mifflin Co. Copyright © 1959 by Douglass Cater.

The physical setup a witness faces is most disconcerting . . . There were, I think, seven microphones or recording devices in front of me, so placed that it was impossible to have my papers before me in any way that gave easy access to the documents . . . The bright lights necessary for television were shining in my eyes all the time they were on, throughout the day. It meant that when I lifted my eyes to look toward committee members, I was almost blinded. It was extremely difficult to read from documents . . .*

The startling thing is that the committee members accept this intrusion of the image makers without question. Only the rare committee chairman ever attempts to impose limits on what the press can do. Committee members don sun glasses to protect themselves against the klieglight glare and endure unprotestingly the heat and clamor. Even during the celebrated MacArthur hearings, affected by highest military security at a time of war in Korea, the compulsion to accommodate the press was overriding. Teams of stenotypists and mimeographers fed to the waiting reporters a fast-moving stream of verbal transcription of the witnesses' testimony read and cleared in haste by a military censor. It was as if the business of the nation would come to a halt unless the latest word was served up to the waiting public.

The most notable committee investigations are seldom in point of fact "investigations." They are planned deliberately to move from a preconceived idea to a predetermined conclusion. The skill and resourcefulness of the chairman and a sizable staff are pitted against any effort to alter its destined course. Whatever investigating is done takes place well in advance of the public hearing. The hearing is the final act in the drama. Its intent, by the staging of an arresting spectacle, is to attract public attention, to alarm or to allay, to enlighten, or, yes, sometimes to obscure.

In 1943, the counsel of a House committee investigating the Federal Communications Commission distributed a confidential memorandum to Committee members which inadvertently fell into the hands of outsiders. It had been prepared for the Committee by a reporter for International News Service, whose talents later carried him high in the employ of the Republican National Committee. Its seven points remain a classic disquisition on the publicity requirements for an "investigation":

1. Decide what you want the newspapers to hit hardest and then shape each hearing so that the main point becomes the vortex of the testimony. Once that vortex is reached, *adjourn.*
2. In handling press releases, first put a release date on them, reading something like this: "For release at 10:00 A.M. EST July 6," etc. If you do this, you can give releases out as much as 24 hours

* G. Bromley Oxnam, *I Protest* (New York, 1954).

in advance, thus enabling reporters to study them and write better stories.

3. Limit the number of people authorized to speak for the committee, to give out press releases or to provide the press with information to the *fewest number possible*. It plugs leaks and helps preserve the concentration of purpose.

4. Do not permit distractions to occur, such as extraneous fusses with would-be witnesses, which might provide news that would bury the testimony which you want featured.

5. Do not space hearings more than 24 or 48 hours apart when on a controversial subject. This gives the opposition too much opportunity to make all kind of counter-charges and replies by issuing statements to the newspapers.

6. Don't ever be afraid to recess a hearing even for five minutes, so that you keep the proceedings completely in control so far as creating news is concerned.

7. *And this is most important:* don't let the hearings or the evidence ever descend to the plane of a personal fight between the Committee Chairman and the head of the agency being investigated. The high plane of a duly-authorized Committee of the House of Representatives *examining* the operations of an Agency of the Executive Branch for constructive purposes should be maintained at all costs.

The memo furnishes blatant evidence of the extent to which publicity considerations can mold the committee investigation. The allusion in point 5 to "the opposition" simply means those who are being investigated. It is a rare investigation, and certainly a poorly publicized one, which has not passed judgment on the "opposition" long before the hearings.

Publicity is frequently the end product and not the sideline of the committee's work. In some of the more notable probes the final committee conclusions have been a matter of scant importance. After two particularly sensational ones of recent years—the MacArthur dismissal inquiry and the Army-McCarthy hearings—the chairmen sought to dispense with the formality of a report altogether, each making vague assertions that the public had "the facts" and could form its own judgments. The responsibility to come up with remedial legislation is often forgotten in the shuffle. The cleansing power of publicity is considered remedy enough.

No one can seriously dispute the usefulness of the congressional committee investigation. As Senator J. William Fulbright has declared, "It provides the legislative branch with eyes and ears and a thinking mechanism." Over the past four decades, as investigations grew into a major activity of Congress, it is possible to outline an impressive record of the looking, listening, and cogitating that Congress has accomplished through its committees.

But it also provides the Legislative Branch with a broadcasting mechanism. Here many of the dilemmas of the investigating committee arise. Much committee practice that would cause little concern if conducted only before the limited audience of Congress provokes tremendous concern when it is enacted on a floodlit national stage, observed by millions.

In his book *Grand Inquest,* Telford Taylor has pointed out that the modern committee investigation with all its publicity fanfare was developed with the active connivance of the Executive Branch of the government. "Observing the immense success, both psychological, and legislative, of the Pecora hearings," he wrote, "the leaders of the Roosevelt Administration rightly concluded that investigations were unsurpassed as a means of formulating and awakening public support for the governmental measures they had in mind."

It is ironic that these leaders did not foresee the inherent dangers in committee probes conducted for the most part by senior members of Congress holding scant loyalty to the Administration in power. Before very long, the congressional investigation had been effectively turned into a means for "formulating and awakening" public opposition to the Administration and its measures. Commencing in 1939 with the Dies Committee of the House of Representatives and continuing right up to the present, the committee probe has been a formidable weapon in the hands of powerful individuals and groups in Congress seeking to dissipate popular support for the Executive Branch. In an age of big government, it has proved a more effective weapon at times than the power of the purse string or the purely law-making powers of Congress.

It is not surprising that this should be so. The investigating committee, unhampered by the need for a clear definition of purpose, guided by the flimsiest rules of procedure and relevancy, its leadership not necessarily representative of prevailing opinion in Congress and not subject to review for its misdeeds, has nearly unlimited discretion. It can stage the kind of spectacle that will produce news and attract public attention.

With the steady build-up of the public image of the chairman and certain key members, cast in their half judge, half prosecutor role, there develops what Telford Taylor calls "the illusion of investigative omnipotence." The committee decides which witnesses and facts are considered relevant to public opinion and in what order of priority. Against this, an illusion of Executive incompetence can be created as day after day the accusations are called forth at a rate which no dreary recital of the answering facts can hope to match. In the battle for the headlines the rebuttal can hardly compete if it cannot be summarized in a few catchy words.

But the illusion extends still further. At one point or another many of these investigations founder on the rock of what is called "executive privilege." Since Congress has devised no way to test the constitutional limits of its right to probe the executive and the courts are notably reluctant to arbitrate, the conflict goes unresolved. But in the testing before the court of public opinion, it is always Congress that casts itself in the role of judge, conveniently forgetting its role as plaintiff. The Army-McCarthy hearings, for example, dealt, as one knowledgeable observer put it, with "the basic constitutional problems of the correct relationship between the two main branches of the American government." Yet, the hearings were conducted by the same investigative subcommittee which had been a party of the dispute. Only Chairman McCarthy temporarily stepped down.

These celebrated hearings remain a landmark of publicity gone riot. Day after day for two months the testimony was carried *in toto* to the waiting television public. A great department of the government was kept in a state of suspension while its leaders were made to perform in the congressionally staged drama.

Reporters who have sat through countless hours of these investigations can vouchsafe how difficult it is for a witness to overcome the enormous publicity advantage of the biased committee. Of course, memorable exceptions have occurred. In 1947 the flamboyant Howard Hughes, aided by a skilled public relations man, succeeded in igniting backfires of publicity that forced his inept inquisitor, Senator Owen Brewster, to retreat. More recently, there was a similar attempt by a witness to play directly to press and public when the House Special Subcommittee on Legislative Oversight began to probe the affairs of New England tycoon Bernard Goldfine and particularly his dealings with the Assistant to the President, Sherman Adams. Goldfine, accompanied by a retinue of lawyers and publicity agents, set up headquarters in a Washington hotel, staged press and television conferences day and night, timed releases to compete with committee-inspired headlines, and pursued a calculated public relations policy to make himself appear, as one aide put it, "a simple, innocent, underdog type being persecuted by a powerful congressional subcommittee." The efforts reached a climax at a hastily summoned midnight press conference in Goldfine's suite. In the course of it, one of Goldfine's agents fished a microphone out from under a doorway to an adjoining room. A committee investigator and a reporter secreted in the next room had been "bugging" their private conversations.

Philip Deane, of the London *Observer*, cabled his English readers a graphic account of his visit to the Goldfine publicity headquarters:

> We were shushed into silence while the television news was switched on. One of the well-known commentators was speaking of the latest developments in the Goldfine case. When mentioning Goldfine himself, the television star lost control and an Homeric laugh spread across his distinguished face . . .

"Great! Great!" said Mr. Jack Lotto, Public Relations Counsellor to the Goldfine interests. "That's what we want; we want people to laugh."

"Please," said a European journalist, earnestly puzzled, "did you say you wanted people to laugh at your employer?" . . .

"It's like this," explained a fellow journalist. "When McCarthy attacked Senator Millard Tydings, of Maryland, Tydings tried to defend himself with dignity and failed miserably. His Public Relations firm made a fascinating study of this and decided that the only way to fight an attack by Congressional investigation is to raise more noise than your opponent, make the whole thing into a farce."

"People don't think of you as a villain when they are laughing at you," said Mr. Williamson thoughtfully.

"Doesn't Goldfine mind being made a clown?" asked the European.

"You're thinking in terms of your own country. People here are different," said the American journalist. "Actually, there's a good deal of sympathy for Goldfine. He has done less than most business men do. He gives vicuña coats. Others give mistresses to married men. Have you seen salesmen entertaining buyers at Las Vegas?

"This is sad because Goldfine is cute and he is not such a bad example of the great American dream—poor immigrant boy makes good. Lotto here is applying the conclusions of the Tydings case, defending the Goldfine integrity by destroying the Goldfine dignity while incidentally, the whole United States Administration goes down gloriously in a cloud of fudge."

The net effect of this and similar publicity brouhahas has been to divert the public's attention from the underlying ills in government which need legislative attention. Amid the aimless airing of charges, the quest reduces itself to a confused chase after individual villains rather than a purposeful inquiry to get at the root causes and to devise lasting solutions.

The proliferation of publicity-inspired investigations has taken us in the direction of what might be called the mass media mandate. Decisions tend to be taken not in an orderly, procedural way but on the basis of what is instantly explainable through the mass media to the public. The trouble is that a great many of the complex issues of our time are not susceptible to this kind of explanation. To attempt to do so only serves to distract government from its more important tasks and to burden the public with choices it is not equipped to make. It opens the way for the demagogue who is prepared to oversimplify the grave issues of our time and to regard publicity as an end rather than a means in the drive for power.

CONGRESS, TELEVISION AND WAR PROTESTS

By William Small

War fever grew, early in 1965, when Viet Cong guerillas on February 6 attacked a U.S. military compound at Pleiku, killing eight Americans and wounding 126 others. In retaliation, 49 U.S. planes swept in from the sea, bombed and strafed Dong Hoi, North Vietnam. The bombing came just a few hours after Soviet Premier Alexei Kosygin had arrived in Hanoi, reportedly on a peace mission. Three days later, the Viet Cong attacked an American billet at Quinhon, killing twenty-three Americans.

Escalation was underway. Advisors became combat troops. A total of 23,000 rose to 181,000 by year's end. There were over 1,600 deaths from hostile action.

America began to realize that a major effort was underway. Some began to choose sides. The terms "hawk" and "dove" slowly emerged, given national prominence for the first time, perhaps, in an hour-long television debate on March 8, 1965: "Vietnam: the Hawks and the Doves."

CBS Newsman Charles Collingwood quickly traced the developments from the French defeat in Indo China to the current growing escalation, spurred by events of the previous month. He called it the point of "crossroads" and turned to his hawks and doves, the first hawk being Senator Gale McGee (Dem., Wyoming) who said bluntly "planned escalation of the war in Vietnam is a necessary forerunner to any meaningful negotiations." This obviously was the Administration posture. Senator George McGovern (Dem., South Dakota) firmly replied, "there are problems all around the world that do not lend themselves to a military solution, and particularly a military solution imposed by foreign troops." In essence, the two Democrats had set the tone for the hawk-dove debate of the next four years.

The audience for that broadcast, as for similar debates, was small. The impact, however, may have been most meaningful. Television was beginning to spell out the importance of the issues by virtue of the special programming. Television was beginning to characterize the legitimacy of dissent by according the "other side" such prominence. The tactile promptings of the daily reporting from Vietnam and Washington were being supplemented by special broadcasts indicating the special nature of the subject.

Reprinted from *To Kill A Messenger: Television News and the Real World* by William Small by permission of Hastings House, Publishers, Inc. © 1970 by William Small.

TV Debates on Vietnam

At CBS, Friendly planned for a series of debates to continue the "Vietnam Perspective" broadcasts. One was scheduled for Sunday, January 30. Called "Congress and the War," we arranged for participation by Senators Stennis, Mundt, Morse, Clark and Representatives Boggs and Ford. Sevareid was to moderate; I was to produce.

On Saturday night, it started to snow. Early Sunday morning, I awoke to discover a record snowfall. My automobile was completely covered with drifting snow. I called Friendly and told him that it looked impossible, we could never get the crew and the guests into our studio for the broadcast. We would have to turn the time back to the program we had pre-empted: "Sunday Sports Spectacular." Minutes later Friendly called back. The sports people had planned on a live broadcast, cancelling it when they were pre-empted for "Vietnam Perspective." We would have to somehow get the broadcast on the air.

I called a nearby garage and asked if a tow truck could make it to my home in Bethesda. "Mister," said the garage man, "Impossible. A thousand guys are calling. You'd have to say some magic words to get me to your place."

"How about fifty dollars?"

"That's magic. I'll be there."

He came and we plowed through drifts to Sevareid's home, two miles away. Sevareid came out through hip-high snow and downtown we went.

The television crew came straggling in, car pools working their way through drifts of snow until the genius that was their boss, Charles Chester, had enough men to get us on the air. One of them battled his way up to Capitol Hill where Senator Mundt lived and brought him in.

The tow truck driver, his job in jeopardy, stayed with us long enough to get Senator Morse from the northwest end of town. We never did get Representative Gerald Ford who walked half a mile through heavy snow to a point where our second tow truck picked him up but he lived in Virginia and the bridges were all blocked with stalled autos. Local police picked up Senator John Stennis and brought him in. The only taxi driver we could find (and we quickly hired him for the next few days) went to Georgetown and brought in Senator Joseph Clark. Somehow, Congressman Hale Boggs managed to not only drive in from Bethesda without difficulty, but even managed to stop at church on the way in.

Our Washington staff struggled in. Sylvia Westerman and other girls in ski outfits, men in boots and heavy coats. When it was time to take air, we were ready with the single exception of Gerry Ford who was still valiantly trying to make it across clogged bridges, calling in periodically with progress reports.

The weather was cold but the debate was hot. For ninety minutes under the strong hand of Eric Sevareid, they covered the issues, concentrating on whether or not to resume the bombing.

Fred Friendly, in his memoirs, described the broadcast thusly:

> Morse and Stennis were evenly matched, and for ninety minutes the two of them turned our Washington studio into the floor of the United States Senate. Toward the end of the program Stennis interrupted an attack on Morse and the doves to say: "This has been a real Congressional debate, (with) nationwide television coverage," and afterward Stanton called to say that it had been one of the best produced, most useful programs of its kind we had ever done.

There was an exciting response in Washington, in the press and in the mail. If it had made an impression on the White House that is not known. The next day, President Johnson ordered the bombing resumed. He also asked Ambassador Goldberg to take the Vietnam peace issue to the United Nations.

On Tuesday, CBS News presented a thirty-minute discussion with Senator J. William Fulbright, Chairman of the Senate Foreign Relations Committee and now the leading dove in high office. Fulbright was critical of the resumption of bombing, praised the action in the U.N. and asserted that "we were misled by this preoccupation with what has been called so often the international conspiracy of communism."

It was during this broadcast that Senator Fulbright confessed that he had erred in sponsoring the Tonkin resolution. Friendly later called it "a portrait of a tortured man." It certainly was a rare bit of television. . . .

Fulbright's "confession" of error in the Tonkin matter and his views generally made front page news the next day. On that day, I called Friendly to ask about hearings on foreign aid before Fulbright's committee. A few days earlier, Dean Rusk had testified and there had been an absorbing series of exchanges between the Secretary and dovish members of the Committee, including Chairman Fulbright. The witness that next day was David Bell, head of the Agency for International Development. The chief of AID is hardly the best known figure in the Administration but Friendly had been so disappointed in the comparatively brief treatment given Rusk, I felt he ought to know that the Foreign Relations doves had another Administration spokesman coming before them.

"Can it be covered live?" asked Friendly.

"Yes."

"I'll let you know."

He let us know—the answer was "yes." The other networks, as is customary, were told that there would be live cameras at the hearing. They asked that it be pooled. Early the next morning, CBS and NBC carried the hearing live. Probably no one was more surprised at this sudden notoriety than the witness himself, David Bell.

Bell could only speak to the AID program but the questioning, the extended remarks, and the exchanges between members of the committee turned it into a lively, unstaged Senatorial debate on Vietnam. CBS carried the morning session as did NBC. After a luncheon break, CBS returned to the hearing. NBC at first did not, then opted to join in continuous coverage. Friendly estimated that it cost CBS alone $175,000 in lost revenues.

Not everyone in the CBS family was pleased. Executives outside of the News Division were troubled by the costs and the precedent. Some affiliates complained bitterly because they, too, were losing considerable revenue (and had no voice in the decision).

It was announced that the next witness before Fulbright's committee would be General James Gavin, whose enclave theory was then popular among doves as a means to cut back on the military effort. CBS announced that it would carry Gavin. So did NBC.

In a sudden move that *Congressional Quarterly* described as "taking the spotlight from the Senate hearings," the President announced that he was flying to Hawaii to meet the leaders of South Vietnam. Gavin's day on the Hill was exciting television but only a prelude to an evening full of special reports on the Hawaii war conference. Around midnight, Johnson's plane had arrived in Los Angeles. Vice President Humphrey had flown there to meet him and was to continue on to tour Southeast Asia. . . .

Early in 1968, Fulbright was to hold more hearings on Tonkin and despite a carefully documented defense by Defense Secretary McNamara, there were serious questions about the entire incident which "legalized the war." Committee member Frank Lausche (Dem., Ohio) said of an unpublished committee staff report on the matter, "Every statement in this secret report tends to prove that we should not have done what we did . . ." Senator Albert Gore (Dem., Tenn.) said, "The Administration was hasty, acted precipitately, inadvisably, unwisely, out of proportion to the provocation." He said the "Congress and the nation were misled about the . . . operation."

The Vietnam commitment had risen to half a million American soldiers. The Vietnam opposition similarly escalated—at one rally alone, in New York on April 15, 1967 some 100,000 protesters took part in spelling out displeasure with the war. All three networks carried special documentaries on the war. They were frequently critical.

In October, over 55,000 persons took part in a March on the Pentagon. It ended with a nighttime "siege" of the Pentagon parking lot, hundreds of arrests, and one brief clash between demonstrators and troops at the Pentagon door.

Harris and Gallup polls showed diminishing support for the war.

On November 30, Senator Eugene McCarthy (Dem., Minnesota) announced that he would enter four Presidential primaries to demonstrate opposition to the Johnson policy in Vietnam. Though New Hampshire was not one that he named, it became the first and most significant of his primary races.

And then, in early 1968, came Tet. . . .

As the Tet attack was finally contained, Rusk was persuaded to appear in open session before Foreign Relations for the first time in two years. For two days, Rusk gave a superb defense of the Administration position—testimony carried live during the day on NBC and in prime-time condensations by ABC and CBS at night. The dexterity of Rusk's performance was matched by the eloquence of his detractors on the committee. All participants had come to the hearings well prepared, well briefed.

Jack Gould, in the *New York Times*, noted the observation of a committee member sympathetic to Rusk, Senator Karl Mundt (Rep., South Dakota), that somehow the Administration has not been successful in getting its point of view across to a country now seriously divided. Added Gould, "It might be argued that a spontaneous television program, embracing conflicting points of view, might be even more effective in reaching the general public. Television has the ability to personalize staggering problems, something the print media cannot hope to duplicate."

Rusk's testimony ended when Chairman Fulbright noted that though the hearings were on foreign aid, he "believed" the Secretary had reason to suspect that the Vietnamese war would come up. Rusk allowed himself an easy smile and responded that he, too, had an inkling that the topic would arise.

Washington buzzed with instant critiques of Rusk's performance. Most agreed he had done well. Even his critics called it a brilliant defense of the indefensible. At the White House, the "reviews" were ecstatic. From the President on down, all were overjoyed with Rusk. . . .

THE SAM ERVIN SHOW

By Laurence Leamer

Senator Sam Ervin, Jr., always gets good and wound up talking about the dangers that computers pose to personal liberty, and so, last May, he'd been glad enough to come down to Atlantic City to address the farewell luncheon of the Joint Computer Conference. He inclines to think of computer technicians as men employed at dark sorceries, arranging data on coded tapes and thus threatening ordinary citizens with a web of secret information. Mindful of the insidious technology available to the members of his audience, the Senator gave them one of his best speeches. He offered Biblical quotations and some of his best down-home North Carolina stories, but none of it took too well. The Senator is not a sophisticated raconteur, and anyway, everybody was in a hurry to leave.

No one really should have expected the computer experts to take to Ervin, for the North Carolina Senator is just too confounded old-fashioned. He is a lover of good food, of bourbon and ginger, and hard work; and now, in his seventy-fifth year, the food and liquor, if not the work, show in his face. He has jowls deep as a goiter, a nose that glows red on color television, age lines running down the sides of his nose and along his chin much as they do on a ventriloquist's dummy, heavy eyebrows that angle almost rakishly down toward his nose, and a thick mane of white hair that appears not the absence of color but its quintessence. In a word, his face is a perfect caricature of the old-time Southern Senator, and when cartoonists draw his face, often they will soften his features, not exaggerate them.

Driving back to Washington in a spring drizzle with three of his subcommittee aides, Senator Ervin wasn't worrying about the reception the computer experts had accorded him. He was rambling on with Rufus Edmisten, a North Carolinian and a pretty decent yarn-teller himself, reminiscing about some old boy they had known back in the mountains. Then, out of the blue, Ervin turned to Lawrence Baskir, chief counsel and staff director of the Constitutional Rights Subcommittee: "You know, Larry, I think we better have hearings on the First Amendment and freedom of the press. Why, I think we should come right out and say that television should be as free as newspapers. If it's not a question of freedom of the press, then it's a question of freedom of speech."

Thus the provenience of the hearings held last November by Ervin's Constitutional Rights Subcommittee, hearings that were later scheduled to resume in February. The Senator didn't need to explain anything to Baskir. The staff members are very much *his* people, and Ervin knew they would set up a free-press hearing that would do him proud and conform to *his* vision of what freedom of the press is all about.

Learning of Liberty

Sam Ervin's notion of liberty has evolved from his life in Morganton, North Carolina (population 10,000). Morganton sits on the western edge of the Piedmont Plateau. It's still the kind of place where a man can go up to his neighbor and speak his mind; a man can even start his own newspaper if he pleases, and if he wants to write that the moon is made of blue cheese, that's fine too, and anyone who agrees with him can buy the paper.

As a boy Sam Ervin was addicted to learning and toy soldiers, his face full of twitches, his arms full of books. His father taught him that the worst threat to liberty comes from government, and he helped to instill in the boy a sense of independence and individuality as fierce as his own, a sense that tangled with his son's shyness and reserve, and that he wore camouflaged, cloaked in the mores and language of the town.

When he returned to Morganton in 1922, Harvard law degree in hand, Ervin still had those simple country ways. He still had eyebrows that jittered up and down when he got nervous, and an occasional stutter, and in court he depended on his wits and his stories, and not on any sort of thundering oratory.

In those years when Sinclair Lewis was writing of Babbitt and Main Street, Ervin was a town booster, a patriot, a joiner, commander of the local National Guard unit, a member of the Masons, the Knights of Pythias, the Junior Order, the Sons of the American Revolution, the Society of the Cincinnati. His was a patriotism and a boosterism that so far transcended the puerile, self-serving ideals of the emerging industrial and commercial order that they scarcely should be spoken of in the same language. He could almost always be found with a book in his hand, learning of his country, his county, or his people. He traced his people back to their Scotch-Irish origins and their arrival in the colonies in 1732, and he traced back the genealogies of his uncles, aunts, even distant relatives—all taproots to his past. He was not searching out nobles, notables, the making of a family crest, but a deepening of his sense of the uniqueness and richness of the American experience.

Ervin's vision of a free press is both simple and profound; simple because his ideas do not venture far from the world of the Founding Fathers and the early printing presses, profound because no matter how the media might defame his beliefs, his region, his very being, his struggle to maintain a free press continues with unabated zeal.

His particular interest in the present hearings was also encouraged by Walter Cronkite, who, at about the same time the Senator spoke to the computer technicians, came to the Old Senate Office Building to expound the troubles of television news broadcasting. It was natural that Cronkite should come to Ervin, for the Senator and his staff already had conducted hearings on the threats to freedom implied by computers, government dossiers, and the Army's surveillance of civilians.

What Cronkite came to tell Ervin the Senator already believed: television should be as free as possible from governmental control. In his earlier hearings, as in almost every speech, the Senator had described the modern battle between freedom and slavery as one being fought in a thousand government offices—with newfangled legislation, bureaucratic initiatives, and computer printouts as the weapons of tyranny, and the Constitution as the last, best, and only defense of liberty.

In the Pentagon Papers case, for the first time in the history of the Republic, the government had sought, prior to publication, to restrain a newspaper from printing critical documents. Police were posing as newsmen, and the courts themselves had been subpoenaing the notes of professional journalists. Television had endured similar harassments.

A Jeffersonian liberal to the very marrow of his bones, Ervin *knew* that as long as government kept even one small finger on freedom of the press, the day might well come when government would reach out and crush that freedom in its fist. The Senator is given to hyperbole, and he believes the nation to be in the midst of a grave Constitutional crisis. To Ervin the Constitution is the most precious of American possessions, and he speaks of it with language and emotion that are rarely heard these days even on the Fourth of July.*

Cronkite's lament thus was heard by a man who believed that television had to be a free marketplace for ideas as well as products. Liberal meddlers had already ended tobacco advertising on television. Since tobacco itself wasn't illegal, Ervin believed the action to be unconstitutional, and many legal scholars agreed with him. Then there was the fairness doctrine that said if you aired one side of an issue, you had to give somebody a chance to air the other side. One U.S. Court of Appeals had gone so far as to rule that consumer groups had to be given air time to run ads countering commercials for high-powered autos and leaded gas. Now Women's Lib groups, ladies from Boston upset about children's television, New Leftists, kooks, pressure groups of all kinds were lining up to get on the air. Conservatives, for their part, were talking about laws to make sure television acted "responsibly." They were all good-minded people out to improve society, but Ervin knew they would end up destroying the very freedom they were tinkering with.

Lost Irony

When Bill Pursley, a dedicated young lawyer on the Constitutional Rights Subcommittee staff, began putting together a list of witnesses for the hearings, he took account of the Senator's opinions. The list of witnesses practically wrote itself. He couldn't have just one network president, although he felt one would be sufficient; he had to ask all three. It wouldn't be right to invite just Walter Cronkite, so he asked all the network anchormen. Then, let's see, there were the press associations, certain

---

* In this perspective, it is no irony that Sam Ervin, adamant defender of the First Amendment, is also the Senate's most brilliantly effective opponent of civil-rights legislation. He takes as his dictum Justice Brandeis's statement that "the greatest dangers to liberty lurk in the insidious encroachment by men of zeal, well-meaning, but without understanding." In his tenacious defense of State's Rights, Ervin is the best that Southern conservatism has to offer; his tragedy is the tragedy of his age and his class and the ideas they lived by. His hometown has passed him by now; his grandson attends an integrated school; and the people there, black and white alike, are proud that the racial situation has worked out as well as it has.

prominent Constitutional scholars, and by the time he'd gotten through there just wasn't that much time for anyone who might be critical of the networks.

With this remnant of time, Pursley had to be especially careful. Ervin was seeking to educate the Senate, and nothing could be worse than having some freaky radical jump up and down in front of the television cameras making the Senator out as the guardian of the underground press, the Daniel Ellsbergs, the Jerry Rubins of the world.

The hearings would be, then, as Lawrence Baskir, the chief counsel, said, "a version of freedom of the press cleaned up for the Establishment." They would proceed as ritual drama, in which, to a large extent, reality is predetermined. (There is nothing devious about this. Senator Ervin runs as fair and open a hearing as is found in Congress, but all hearings develop a kind of legal brief intended to convince Congress and the American people of whatever it is the committee wants to announce.)

Because the mass media accept the *reality* of Congressional hearings, in much the same way shopgirls once accepted the reality of professional wrestling, Ervin and his subcommittee entered into the customary collusion between press and government. The hearings that were to have raised the most profound questions of press freedom became a convenient pseudo-event that various commentators, journalists, and politicians could exploit for their own purposes.

The irony was lost on Ervin. He distrusts the modern theories of the press advanced by people such as Walter Lippmann and Nicholas Johnson, the outspoken commissioner of the Federal Communications Commission. Lippmann once observed that the television networks are so powerful that it is as if there were only three printing presses in the entire country, a situation the Founding Fathers hardly could have envisioned. The Johnson argument holds that the networks constitute an information oligarchy (60 per cent of the American people say they get most of their news from television) and that instead of a free marketplace of ideas the networks operate a closed shop, run by people to whom controversy is anathema because it interferes with the business of selling things. "You simply have to make a distinction between government controls designed to enhance freedom and to restrain it," Johnson has said in response to the Ervin argument against government intervention. "The antitrust laws are regulations that allow free enterprise to function. That's the kind of regulation we're talking about."

The law appears to support Johnson. In the 1934 Communications Act, Congress decided that the best way to apportion the public airwaves was to have the FCC make private licensees the temporary custodians of particular frequencies. The licensees would be free to make a profit, but in exchange the public interest had to be served.

It is the FCC's mandate duty, then, to see that this greatest of communications media does not become, or indeed remain, merely a conduit for selling soap and razor blades. "It is the right of the viewers and listeners, not the right of the broadcasters, which is paramount," wrote Justice Byron White in expressing the Supreme Court's opinion in the 1969 *Red Lion* decision, the most important and eloquent expression of this modern free-press theory. "It is the purpose of the First Amendment to preserve an uninhibited marketplace of ideas in which truth will ultimately prevail, rather than to countenance monopolization of that market, whether it be by the government itself or a private licensee. It is the right of the public to receive suitable access to social, political, esthetic, moral and other ideas and experiences which is crucial here. That right may not constitutionally be abridged either by Congress or by the FCC."

Fooling with Realities

Perhaps the most revealing encounter of the hearings took place on the third day. Several hundred spectators, half a dozen television cameras, and more than a score of reporters crowded the Senate caucus room. Senator Ervin hardly noticed. Innocent of the ways of the media, Ervin never realized that his staff had scheduled the committee witnesses to obtain maximum publicity. On the third day the witness would be Walter Cronkite.

In their approach to the television cameras, no two men could offer a more perverse contrast than Ervin and Cronkite. Ervin's deep, lumbering mind would have served him well over a century ago alongside a Webster or a Calhoun on a Senate floor where debate was charged with vitality and importance. He believes that the reality of a political event is conveyed by the vigor of the ideas and the truth of the arguments, not by the presence of the media. In this he is almost an anomaly, not only in the Senate but among Americans generally. Even so conservative a man as Robert Byrd of West Virginia will play to the television cameras, having several paragraphs of sharp, graphic prose stitched into his usually florid speeches, an addition that reads like a television commercial—which, in a sense, is what it is. Ervin will have none of that. With his long, rambling stories and broad forensic gestures, he is an unmitigated disaster on television.

He hurried into the caucus room just after 10:00 A.M., taking his place at the enormous felt-covered committee table that extended through half the length of the room. He was the only member of the subcommittee who bothered to appear on time. Sitting alone at the vast table, he began in a voice that seemed hesitant, an old man's voice. He welcomed Cronkite with his customary stateliness of phrase.

Cronkite read from a prepared statement, his text as lean and crisp as that of the *CBS Evening News*. A man thoroughly familiar with the medium of television, he did not raise his voice. He pumped his every sentence full of spontaneity and earnestness. He caressed the medium, playing with it; and the lights stayed on him, the cameras gorging themselves with good film.

"There are things we are not doing that we ought to do," Cronkite began. "There are challenges we have not fully met."

Cronkite had little choice but to read his testimony. The etiquette of Congressional hearings requires that witnesses provide neatly mimeographed statements to pass out to committee members, staff, and particularly the press. The Washington press corps feeds off press releases, news briefs, PR handouts, and prepared statements, and some reporters turn surly if a witness should dare speak extemporaneously.

Americans seem unable to give to another man's ideas and feelings anything that borders on complete attention, and practically everyone in the room was zooming in on Cronkite, then Ervin or a cameraman, a face somewhere, a moment or so scanning the room, back to Cronkite, fooling with the realities of the hearing much the way one fools with a home movie camera. Probably no one in the room was listening to the testimony with quite Ervin's intensity. Many Senators will sign letters, catch up on minor paper work, even daydream at hearings, but when Ervin is truly involved with a hearing he has an intensity of concentration that is awesome. They are no ritual to him. He learns from his witnesses; and in other hearings on other days, he has learned things that have led directly to legislation.

In the past few years, almost despite himself, Ervin has become something of a minor hero to the national press. The issues he speaks to are of such importance that he just can't be ignored. For the most part Ervin is pictured as an eighteenth-century libertarian, an absolutist on questions of civil liberties, and an avowed opponent of strong government. This is as much a caricature of Ervin as was the earlier view that he was simply a racist. Ervin's libertarianism is, in fact, both constrained and subtle; his struggle to preserve the meaning of the Constitution in a century rapidly approaching 1984 is both magnificent and rather limited.

It was perhaps inevitable that the media would stereotype Ervin anew since in recent years he has made his national reputation through his subcommittees, the committee system being in large measure a client of the media. In the past two decades, primarily by exploiting the media, Congressional committees have achieved unprecedented and often nonlegislative power. They have come to serve as a surrogate press, but they are rarely neutral or benign in their interest.

By merely reporting what committees do—not what they don't do— the national media caricature the whole governmental process. Ervin's hearings on the Army's surveillance of civilians, for instance, appeared to be a frontal attack on the forces of illiberalism and the developing tyranny by dossier. That it was Sam Ervin, a hawk, a proponent of big military spending, a Southern conservative, in a word a patriot, who was leading the attack gave the hearings an unimpeachable credibility. In articles and editorials the press heralded their newfound champion of civil liberties, but the press did not know or care to know that Senator Ervin had placed clear limits on just what his subcommittee was to delve into.

"They help us find our way"

"How could we be improved by outside monitors without destroying the independence which is essential for a free press?" Cronkite asked. "Vice President Agnew was right in asserting that a handful of us determine what will be on the evening news broadcast, or for that matter, which he didn't specify, in the *New York Times*, or the *Christian Science Monitor*, or the *Wall Street Journal*, or anywhere else. Indeed, it is a handful of us with this immense power, power that not one of us underestimates or takes lightly."

Cronkite is the great switchman shuttling the truth on and along his track at CBS as best he can, a noble, good, and modest man, as impartial and fair as can be, or so his testimony implied. He danced through the pages, in turn concerned, worried, earnest; and he called for an end to the fairness doctrine.

Ervin's questioning, a colloquy really, seemed to meander on all around the issues but, when transcribed and placed in the written record, it would serve to deepen Cronkite's and Ervin's view of press freedom. Ervin never even hinted that the scarcity of network news and information programs, which during the last fiscal year took up 2 per cent of total broadcast time, might have helped prevent a full and frank discussion of public issues. Nor did he ask questions that would have led one to realize that Cronkite had been less than candid. The CBS newscaster's performance had been masterly, but at times he had ridden that well-traveled border between deviousness and truth where public-relations men make their living. He said there was far more diversity in radio and television than in print; however, as Fred Friendly, once Cronkite's superior as president of CBS News and now the Ford Foundation's television consultant, suggested in testimony two weeks later, such assumptions were "suspect." Cronkite talked of "the wired cities of tomorrow" when with cable television we "will have an almost unlimited number of channels available," but he did not mention that the networks are fighting to cripple cable television.

While Ervin and Cronkite were having their discussion, Senators Roman L. Hruska of Nebraska; Hugh Scott of Pennsylvania, the Senate minority leader; and Ted Kennedy of Massachusetts came into the room and sat down at the committee table. At least one or two of the Senators may have been attracted to the hearings solely by the scent of the media. Scott, it turned out, had never attended a Constitutional Rights Subcommittee session before, and he would not appear again at these freepress hearings. Kennedy, who had spent something less than an hour at the previous day's session, would not return either. Hruska was making his first appearance also.*

After Hruska asked several questions, Ervin called on Senator Scott. Unfortunately, several of the television cameramen were changing film reels.

"Thank you, Mr. Chairman," Scott said. "I will try not to say anything important, Walter, until the cameras come back on."

"I was wondering how you fellows stand these lights," Cronkite said over the laughter of the audience.

"We can stand the lights in view of what they connote because they help us find our way," Scott said.

"Maybe we are like our old partner, a Reconstruction lawyer in North Carolina," said Senator Ervin. "A lawyer lost a point of law arguing before him and he said that the more lights you shed upon him the louder he got. Maybe that is our condition."

"I think that when I attend some of the executive sessions of the Judiciary Committee," the minority leader said, and asked several questions.

Senator Kennedy came next. "I want to extend a warm welcome to Mr. Cronkite as well," he said, "and apologize that I was unable to be here for your statements and for your comments." The Massachusetts Senator began by asking Cronkite whether the networks had been intimidated by the Vice President's attacks and by other harassments—the same question, as he pointed out, that he had asked Dr. Frank Stanton, the president of CBS, the day before. Next Kennedy asked a question that had been handed him by a subcommittee staff member. After receiving an answer he thanked Cronkite once again.

None of the Senators asked Cronkite the questions that would have prevented his testimony from becoming solely a platform for the networks' view of freedom. They did not seem to know that this should have been a debate of historic proportion, that there was a decision known as *Red Lion*, that this was the first opportunity Congress and the American public had had truly to grapple with these monumental issues.

The Senators could have had an opportunity to learn something of the other majority First Amendment theory, since the morning's second witness was Jerome Barron, professor of law at George Washington Uni-

---

* Senator Hruska did appear regularly from that day on and from his conservative perspective made as large a contribution to the hearings as anyone other than Ervin. Strom Thurmond (S.C.) was the only other Senator ever to attend. The other subcommittee members are: Birch Bayh (Ind.), Robert Byrd (W. Va.), Hiram Fong (Hawaii), John McClellan (Ark.), and John Tunney (Calif.).

versity. Professor Barron's theory of public access to the media has made him the best-known scholarly proponent of this contemporary free-press theory. The subcommittee staff had only called Barron the previous afternoon, and he had not had time to prepare a formal statement: "I was lucky that I was able to hear most of Mr. Cronkite's testimony this morning, and I think the best way for me to start is perhaps to give my reaction to it. I might borrow something from you, Senator Ervin, to frame that reaction. You said the First Amendment was drafted not only for the brave but for the timid, and I would like to put an addendum to that. The First Amendment was not drafted for the broadcast networks, and yet I think really that is a conclusion which we got from Mr. Cronkite's testimony."

Even before Barron began talking, Senators Scott, Hruska, and Kennedy left the room. While he was talking the television cameramen were gathering up their equipment, slamming film cameras into boxes. At least half the reporters had left or were leaving, and most of the audience was slowly shuffling out of the room.

"I have said before in print," Barron continued, "that I think that it is one of the great public relations trumphs of the twentieth century over the eighteenth that the broadcasters have managed to identify themselves so completely with the First Amendment. I think the problem comes because we are groping for a Constitutional theory which will somehow be adequate to the communication problem of the twentieth century. I think all of our difficulties stem from a rather myopic view of what freedom of speech means in broadcasting. I think the conventional view has been that freedom of speech in broadcasting is exhaustive when the freedom of speech of the communicator is protected. In other words, if Dr. Stanton, Mr. Cronkite, Mr. Reasoner, Mr. Brinkley had their say, then freedom of speech in America is safe; but they are three or four people out of 200 million. I don't think it is conspiratorial or anything like that; it is a combination of the marriage of technology and the pressure of the concentration of the economic system, which has given them this enormous power. I don't accuse them of seeking it, I realize in many ways they just find themselves at the throttle, but our problem is, what are we going to do about it. . . . And it is nothing short of amazing to me for a representative of broadcasting to contend that now they should be free from all regulations and yet they don't suggest everybody should be licensed anew as an original proposition. To that extent they are not willing to abdicate or abandon government aid."

Barron is a man full of all that confounded liberal *smartness*, a man who, as the Senator might put it, believes that all the wisdom in God's creation is found on the banks of the Potomac, and Ervin had no use for his ideas. Yet he questioned him with just the same civility and purpose that he had shown to Walter Cronkite. The Senator hadn't noticed the cameras before when they were grinding away, and he didn't notice them now when they were quiet, and he spent a good half hour drawing Barron out, giving the man a chance to develop his case as fully and as profoundly as he could. He didn't quit until one o'clock or so when he called a lunch break so he could go over to the Capitol barbershop for his daily shave.

A Commercial for the Networks

There had been something so admirable, so likable, about Senator Ervin and the manner in which he conducted the hearings. Even those mountain stories, he couldn't resist telling them but then he would hurry through, the words spilling down his chest so that much of the time it was impossible to understand, but everyone would laugh anyway. When he talked of the meaning of a free press—unaware of reporters or cameras or anything but his ideas, as if his very words might reaffirm belief in liberty—he was truly inspiring. He believed that the ideas of a Jerome Barron or a Nicholas Johnson had a brilliance to them that had not worn into wisdom, and that there was a danger to liberty in their solutions, but he did not see that they had come far closer than he to understanding why freedom of the press in America is so often such a sham.

He did not see that in this anonymous, urban society the mass media are the vocal chords of free speech. One hundred thousand demonstrators can march in Washington against the Vietnam war, but unless their protests make the evening news they have no reality. Ervin believed ultimately in the goodwill of free men, and he believed that in the long run broadcasters would be fair. He did not see that television is so powerful, and the diversity of ideas in America so wide, that no man or small group of men can be given total control. He just did not see this, and he did not see that in his free-press hearings Professor Barron and his ideas had been denied their freedom of speech.

That evening on the network news programs, the TV reporters merely introduced their films of Walter Cronkite and his reasoned appeal for freedom of the press, followed by what appeared to be probing questions from Senators who, in fact, had not even heard Cronkite's full testimony. Ervin's hearings had been turned into a commercial for the networks, and by the end of the first week he began receiving letters from people back home asking why he was supporting the liberal networks. He wrote back saying that he was only supporting freedom of the press; he did not understand how his very lineup of witnesses had made it easy for the networks to use him and his beliefs.

NBC covered the hearings for seven of the eight days and ran testimony from seven witnesses who in a broad sense could be considered pro-industry as against two who were not. Christie Basham, Washington producer of the NBC *Nightly News*, was trying to do what in the network's sense of the word was a fair and responsible job, but once she accepted the reality of the hearings she just could not. "We tried to cover different points," she says. "We had a long cut of Cronkite partially because he was animated. By watching Cronkite's testimony you wouldn't have gotten the story of the hearings but you would have learned something. You would have learned what Cronkite feels about television. That's more valuable than what an outsider feels. Of course, it's an interesting question whether we should be covering such hearings at all." In fact, if NBC, CBS, or ABC really had cared to define the free-press issue by doing their own reporting, they could have done so in less than half the total time they spent on the hearings. The same could be said for the print media since its coverage of the hearings was by no means superior to television's.

During the hearings the public learned almost nothing about this historic debate over the nature of the First Amendment; and Sam Ervin, a man for whom ideas and beliefs are almost tangible, helped to foist clichés and half-truths on the nation. For years the integrity of his beliefs and of his earnest struggle to protect the Constitution had prevented him from becoming one of the manipulators or the manipulated. But with his new fame and the urgency of his struggle, he, too, was now part of the media apparatus.

Once Ervin and his subcommittee grew dependent on "news," they were living in a world where there were few boundaries between reality and unreality, and truth has the consistency of cotton candy.

TV LIGHTS, INVITATIONS, KISSES AND PHONE CALLS

By Jeannette Smyth

Sen. Herman E. Talmadge (D.-Ga.) turned down an offer of a $10,000 honorarium and a free trip to Acapulco for a speech there.

The switchboard at Sen. Edward J. Gurney's (R.-Fla.) Northwest Washington apartment building lights up with calls from women wanting to know if the wavy-haired 59-year-old is "unattached and available." (He has been married for 33 years.)

A woman in Dallas wants to marry 77-year-old Sen. Sam J. Ervin Jr. (D.-N.C.), who—after 19 years in the Washington phone book—got an unlisted home phone number to avoid the press.

Sen. Daniel K. Inouye (D.-Hawaii), who lost his right arm in World

Reprinted from the *Washington Post*, Volume 96, Number 225 (July 18, 1973) by permission of the editor.

War II, says "there's no question" that the Senate Watergate committee hearings are the most difficult influence on his life that he has yet encountered.

The televised coverage of the marathon hearings in the Senate Caucus Room has changed the lives of all seven senators who form the committee. It has brought them fame and glory and high profiles. It has brought unwanted attention, too, attracting mobs they don't quite know how to handle, for example, or increased amounts of do-me-a-favor mail from people who'd never heard of any of the seven before the televised hearings began May 17.

One Ervin aide says they may have to hire a guard to run interference through crowds of journalists and tourists who dog "Uncle Sam's" tracks.

Recently, an aide in Sen. Howard H. Baker Jr.'s (R.-Tenn.) office wailed, "If I get one more letter from somebody who wants a job, they can have mine!" (In response, a mischievous colleague dashed off a gag letter, purportedly from the widowed mother of five starving children, and was delighted when the joke was taken seriously.)

The volume of mail for the Watergate senators has increased as much as five times since early this year. Tourists flock to committee members' offices, wanting souvenirs or autographed pictures.

Speaking invitations from all over the country are coming in. Requests for Ervin, Baker and Gurney have doubled, according to aides, with Ervin's up 100 per cent over last year and Baker's up from 30 or 40 requests a week to 100 requests a week since the televised hearings began. Gurney's appointments secretary says she could book him two major speeches every weekend, as compared to one mediocre groundbreaking every weekend pre-Watergate.

Unsolicited honorarium offers to Ervin and Baker have increased by an average of $1,000 per speech. Some offer Ervin an honorarium as high as $5,000. And for the first time, Sen. Joseph M. Montoya (D.-N.M.) has signed a contract with a speaker's bureau (Montoya has private real estate income, a spokesman says, and turns his speaking fees over to a New Mexico scholarship fund).

When 6-foot-6 Sen. Lowell P. Weicker Jr. (R.-Conn.) went to a Mets-Braves baseball game recently at New York City's Shea Stadium, he outbatted superstars Hank Aaron and Willie Mays "three to one" in numbers of autograph seekers, an aide said.

The television exposure could prove to be a boon in terms of campaign advertising for the four Watergate committee members whose terms expire next year—Sens. Ervin, Inouye, Talmadge and Gurney. And though most staffers insist their man isn't running for national office, at least four senators—Baker, Inouye, Talmadge and Gurney—are urged to do so by letter-writing fans.

People keep writing and phoning to say how happy they are to see that America has "honest"—and "charismatic," "sexy," "adorable"—politicians working for them.

Four Watergate committee members have become the John, Paul, George, and Ringo of Watergate. They are Baker, Inouye, Gurney and Talmadge.

Baker, 47, leads the hit parade with about 100 mash notes and is said to be embarrassed about it. The notes range from that of a lusty 69-year-old who wrote (anonymously) "I could vote for you for President all day, and all night, too!" to the cheeky babysitter from Bardstown, Ky., who penciled "You broke my heart Sen. Baker! I was all set on marrying you (so what if you're 30 years older??) when I found out you were already married."

Baker's wife, Joy, daughter of the late Sen. Everett Dirksen (R.-Ill.), is unconcerned. "I got used to it. My daddy had a lot of those," she said.

Sen. Gurney's fans apparently prefer the telephone. He's gotten "quite a few" marriage proposals, he says, asking if he's "unattached and available." Gurney, whose wife is an invalid, seems a little horrified by his new sex-object status. Asked how a gentleman answers questions about availability, his voice flared a little. "I just say I'm not!" he cried.

(Gurney fans should know that he does his own grocery shopping, suffers from war wounds sustained in the Battle of the Bulge with Patton's Third Army, and carries a chair cushion to ease his injured back.)

If Baker and Gurney are taken aback by female adulation, Talmadge and Inouye are taking it in. Talmadge, 59, who may have been feeling his age after the recent birth of a fourth grandchild, is amazed by the young women who rush up to him in the Capitol subway to give him a kiss. Two days after it first happened, Talmadge showed up for work in a sports jacket—for the first time in recent memory, according to an aide.

(Talmadge fans should know he keeps getting rather good cigars from TV fans.)

In a recent poll of Atlanta beauty shops, Sen. Inouye, 49, was voted "the sexiest man on the Watergate committee." (Georgia's Talmadge came in second on his own turf. Baker was third. "It's the Oriental mystery," one senator noted.) Asked if he'd heard about it, Inouye simply laughed a long, sexy baritone chuckle and said his wife, Maggie, voted the same way.

But Inouye is not entirely sanguine about the effect of the Watergate hearings on his life. For one thing, a bank of blinding lights for color television faces the senators' table and burns into senatorial retinas day after day. Inouye found he wound up with "horrible headaches" every day. He took to wearing sunglasses until a woman called to say they made him look like "a member of the Yokohama Mafia." He's had a new pair of slightly tinted glasses made, and can still be glimpsed shading his eyes during testimony.

Personal remarks, suggestions and criticisms are common. One woman wrote 42-year-old Sen. Weicker "I love your mod glasses, but please do something about that tie you wear all the time." Others write Sen. Talmadge that he has demolished their stereotype that Southerners are ignorant, or to tell Sen. Baker to get a haircut and contact lenses and to smile more. "When you do, Wow!" wrote a 15-year-old Washington state girl.

Washington hostesses apparently haven't jumped on the bandwagon yet. None of the Watergate senators admits to an increase in social invitations, perhaps because summer is off-season. The senators point out they're too busy to accept anyway, or like Sen. Weicker, like to go to bed early.

"I've been so darn busy," said Sen. Gurney. "I'm not much of a social bug. I don't like parties that much, and I have to save most of my socializing for Florida."

One senator says he's sent his family home, partly because of threatening telephone calls. "I wouldn't want my son to pick up the phone and hear some of that," he said.

He's not changing the phone number, but a bachelor life of hamburgers and eating out of cans does not amuse him. It's part of the fallout of Watergate.

————

KEEPING IN TOUCH WITH THE PEOPLE, GETTING ALONG WITH THE PRESS . . .

By Donald G. Tacheron and Morris K. Udall

A normally active congressional office not only reacts to constituency demands. In one way or another, quite apart from their overt campaigning, most House members encourage requests for information or assistance. Just answering the mail is not enough, an experienced Congressman indicated during the 1963 Seminar for Freshmen, adding:

> . . . we like, I think, to encourage mail from back home. For no matter how close you live, no matter how close you keep in touch with your district, no matter whether or not you have a district office or office hours in your district—there tends to be something of a vacuum between the people that you represent and you as their legislator, their Representative in Congress.

As is the case with service work, the value placed on "keeping in touch" is an amalgam of civic virtue and political necessity.

While Congress is in session, the average member spends about six days a month in his district. He also makes about eleven radio and television appearances a month and devotes about five hours a week to press work and writing chores. At least in part, activities such as these are self-serving. They are designed to reveal the Congressman's brilliance, effectiveness, and sense of dedication, thereby establishing or maintaining his political base. But they also have wider implications for the democratic process. In delivering speeches and engaging in other activities in the district, in writing newspaper stories, magazine articles, and books, in making radio and television broadcasts, the Congressman engages in civic education, reaching out to—and, he hopes, involving—citizens who otherwise might not take an active interest in policy issues and public affairs.

Another speaker at the 1963 Seminar stressed the importance of this aspect of the Congressman's job. Members of the House, declared Washington reporter David Broder, are in an ideal position "to convey some of the realities of this world to the people at home who are, unfortunately, dependent on newspapers and television for most of what they can grasp as to what is going on." Continuing, Broder said:

> I don't know what you should tell them about the shape of the world. That is something for you to decide for yourselves, but I do think you should be as frank in defining for your constituents the problems and the prospects of this nation, both at home and abroad, as you are in telling the bureaucrats downtown the facts of life about the problems and the wishes of your constituents in matters in which they are concerned.
>
> I think you have to take the serious responsibility of telling your people as honestly and as frankly and as fully as you can what kind of shape we are in as a nation and what kind of a world we are living in. This is a responsibility that you share with those of us in the press who, Lord knows, meet our own responsibilities imperfectly on keeping the people informed. And if there were one wish which I could express to you it would be that, as you enjoy the security that your membership in this distinguished body has given you, you will recall your obligation to be a teacher to your people.

Direct Personal Contact

Congressmen generally agree that there is no substitute for "direct personal contact . . . in the business of getting elected and in the business of informing your people." For the member whose district is near Washington, maintaining contact is usually not difficult. He may meet with constituents on weekends and some weekdays while Congress is in session. For example, one experienced member schedules office hours in his district throughout the year:

> . . . I feel that, in many ways, just answering mail is not enough. Certainly it is true in my area, and I make a point of holding more or less regular office hours in my district where I get the problems that are really insoluble. You know, you find them pouring out their souls to you. But it does give them an opportunity to talk to their Congressman, which I think is valuable. I do also write newsletters on a regular basis, primarily to newspapers, and then I have a supplementary mailing list to individuals. [It is] an effort to close the gap between here and home.

Closing the gap presents a greater problem for members who are not able to return to their districts frequently. Travel costs mount up, and the allowance does not go far. As a result, many members must rely primarily on correspondence to develop and maintain personal relationships with constituents, to serve and to inform them, and to get some idea of their attitudes on various issues. A west coast Congressman describes his dependence on the mail:

> If you are from states that are close to Washington—and I would classify the area from Chicago to New York probably as within that general area—a member can get home fairly frequently. That is if they want to get home on a weekend, they can. If they want to have office hours on Saturday mornings in their district, they can, sometimes Fridays. We on the west coast in most cases have found that it's impractical to try to get home on regular weekends. The airplane costs about $301 round trip for a single trip. For just a weekend that is hardly worthwhile. So most members from the west coast go home infrequently. As a result we are more dependent upon the means of communication through the mail than are members that are closer to their districts. I use the newsletter. I also endeavor to make sure that the mail is answered, and answered promptly and thoroughly. I usually issue a questionnaire each year, which is done by many members of the House. This does provide another means of communication with the people in your district. I think that the west coast members have to rely to a greater extent on means of communication of this type than is true with some of the districts close to Washington.

Stimulating Public Interest

Experienced members advise their junior colleagues that no single method of establishing contact and informing constituents will be effective in all congressional districts. The following comment is representative:

> I want to bring up this other point in talking about what works for one district: No two districts are exactly alike and no two Congressmen are exactly alike, so my advice would be, instead of taking a whole lot of advice, there is not a man up here in Washington that knows your district any better than you do. After all you got elected down there, and you know what it took to get elected and you know

the people that you are representing—and if you don't know them you had better get out and learn. You just do that thing that you think is the best way to inform your public, I mean your people. Certainly, get all the advice that you can, but let what you do be your decision.

"Classroom" on wheels. The same member goes on to describe what works for him—a mobile office equipped to serve individual constituents or groups such as high-school classes in government:

> I have found that during the years that I have been observing members of Congress, particularly in my district, that the one big complaint most always heard was that our other Congressman comes home and he sees Bill Smith and John Jones and then drives on out of town. . . .
>
> To counteract the same criticism being made of me (and I guess they will find some other one) I seized upon this idea of a mobile office whereby the people could know where I would be at certain times. In that office I could have all sorts of information, which I do have, and which we pass out, and we have the high-school government classes come by.
>
> Well, it has just worked tremendously to my advantage. It may not work for you; it may not work for another Congressman; but I don't know how else I could have gotten pictures of the mobile office with me standing in front of it on the front pages of the [papers]. I couldn't have bought the publicity. The four sides of this mobile office are white with red, big boxcar letters, with dignity, of course, but with some blue also. Regardless of the direction from which they are traveling into the main part of each of eighteen counties in my district . . . they know that [I am] in town because the name is there. They can't miss it. I have had as high as two hundred people in one day to sit across my office desk asking me questions, and, of course, I have a little adjoining office and two or three helpers there. . . .
>
> Now a lot of people tell me they couldn't possibly do all of that, but I will tell you there is not a man in my district that can tell me much about my district today because I was there last fall, even though we had a short adjournment. I was in every county in my district. I talked to any constituent who wanted to see me, and that is the beautiful part about it. How can anybody in my district say, "Well, you can't see the Congressman. He never comes around"?
>
> It is impossible for them to say it. Newspapers carried it, the TVs are happy to carry. They come there and interview you and all that sort of thing, and everybody knows that on Monday between certain hours, the Congressman from the First District will be at this town. They name the square, the corner of the courthouse square, or what street. Then on Tuesday you may be twenty miles away at this other town. If they are not home that day they can drive twenty miles if they really want to see you.

"*Grass roots Congress.*" Another member, Representative James A. Mackay, adapted the New England Town meeting technique in order to stimulate public interest in national and international problems. An article in the *Christian Science Monitor* described his experiment:

. . . Rep. James A. Mackay of Georgia's Fourth Congressional District, which includes part of Atlanta, says some of his colleagues in the House are interested in the effectiveness of his "Grass Roots Congress." If they deem it successful, they have told him, they will start similar "congresses" in their own districts.

After five months of study and preparation, beginning last June, 250 of Representative Mackay's constituents met Dec. 3–4 at nearby De Kalb College. They heard a report from him on legislation passed during the first session of the 89th Congress. Then chairmen of nine citizens' panels on subjects likely to come up during the next session of Congress gave Mr. Mackay their thinking and advice.

He didn't promise to base his future votes on their recommendations, but said they would influence his thinking.

Mr. Mackay, a freshman member of Congress from a newly created Georgia district, proposed the "Grass Roots Congress" to a selected group of his constituents last spring. There was need, he said, for closer communication between the people and the federal government. . . .

Some 400 people agreed to take part in the work of one or more of thirty-one panels set up to study specific problems as diverse as foreign relations and water resources. Representative Mackay sent them appropriate House bills, committee reports, and government studies on their respective subjects to digest. He assigned a member of his staff . . . to correlate the work of the panels.

Of the thirty-one panels, nine "followed through" to the extent of having reports ready for submission to the "Grass Roots Congress." . . .*

"*Dial-a-Congressman.*" In January 1966 another member, George Grider of Tennessee, began setting aside two hours each week for long-distance telephone chats with constituents he was unable to see during visits to his district. Under his "Dial-a-Congressman" plan, constituents with problems or opinions they wished to discuss personally were invited to come to the Memphis office Monday afternoons from 3 to 5 P.M. and place a call—free of charge—to the Congressman at his Washington office.

Representative Grider reported receiving about twenty calls each Monday afternoon. "For the most part," he told *Roll Call* newspaper, "the calls are a microcosm of the mails. You might say that all of them might have been handled by my staff just as effectively. The essential value of the calls lies in the fact that Congressmen are great attention-getters. The constituents, when they talk with me personally, know that through

* By Joseph H. Baird, *The Christian Science Monitor*, December 10, 1965.

me they have a voice in what happens, both in the district and outside. They feel that I can focus attention on their concerns—and democracy won't work unless people with problems [can] get attention."

Meeting the Press

Congressional newcomers frequently confess to a sense of frustration in their dealings with the press. In a newsletter to his constituents, the late Representative Clem Miller of California described the "chasm which exists between one junior Congressman and the press". . . .*

Some observers may disagree with Representative Miller's over-all appraisal of press performance. A Washington reporter was, in fact, given equal time to respond in one of the Congressman's subsequent newsletters. Representative Miller's comments, however, go to the heart of the matter for those involved in political communication from the nation's capital: The Fourth Estate comprises many houses, and the key that will open all the doors to one may not get the bearer through the front gate of another.

Guidelines for Give-and-Take with the Press

Despite the diversity of press capability and interest noted by Representative Miller, a number of general practices are considered mutually profitable to members and the press. Those most frequently mentioned by Washington newsmen and experienced Congressmen are:

Accessibility and initiative. Reporters tend to cultivate those Congressmen who produce news for them, if for no other reason than that their professional status depends in part on their ability to reach and tap a wide variety of news sources. Because in the newsroom timeliness is next to godliness, reporters customarily develop alternative sources, so that they can secure information quickly in the event one source is unavailable to them. These factors suggest that the member who is readily accessible is likely to be asked for views on various matters more frequently than one who is often unavailable to the press.

At the same time, there is no reason for the Congressman to wait anxiously for his telephone to ring when he feels that he has something to contribute. Reporters read each other's material and the interests of leading newsmen and commentators indicate to some extent which topics are likely to become current and choice among the press corps in general.* Newsmen, particularly those on regional or Washington bureau desks, look for ways in which to give developing stories a local angle. Moreover, some observers suggest that the press as a whole is becoming more interested in background and interpretation—and that suggestions for topics

---

* This excerpt is included in "A Newcomer's View of The Press" by Clem Miller, Chapter 5.—Ed.
* See "The Influence of the Elite," in William L. Rivers, *The Opinion Makers* (Boston: Beacon Press, 1965), pp. 41-56.

deserving this kind of treatment are welcome. A prominent newsman
makes this point:

> We need you desperately in the press. In terms of trying to ex-
> plain to us what are your views about these things . . . not the narrow
> view of what will get you elected, but the view of what you bring out
> of the heart of the country as to what is best for the country in the
> long run. . . .
>
> It is true that the press is oriented to the Senate. There is no
> doubt about it. But the press, I think, performs a function in this
> town which is a vital function. It can help you. You can greatly
> help us. There is a tendency, I think particularly in the Executive
> branch of the government, to think about the press as a problem,
> which it is—I would be the first to admit it. But it is also an op-
> portunity and its role, I suggest to you, is changing all the time. It
> used to be primarily concerned with the "scoop," with what is
> happening today, with trying to wheedle out of you what went on in
> executive session in some particular committee. You may be sure that
> it is still going to try to do that, but, at the same time, in the last
> generation it has changed quite a bit. The radio has taken away from
> the newspaper the primary role of being the first purveyor of the news.
> The television has taken away from the press the great picture story,
> the great descriptive story. And in a way this has been a good thing,
> because it has forced the press, particularly in Washington, into
> the educational function. It has forced it to do what it should have
> been doing all along, explaining endlessly the complications of
> legislation.
>
> I find a singular lack on the part of Congressmen and Senators of
> approaching newspapermen, or when they see things in the press that
> are wrong merely griping about it instead of calling up and saying,
> "Here is an aspect of a really important bill that I think, if you don't
> mind my saying so, merits your taking some time to study and ex-
> plain." I can't speak, of course, for all my colleagues, but we certainly
> on the [_____ newspaper] would welcome any suggestions at any
> time of any sort whatsoever of that kind, because we know that once
> you get into your committee meeting and spend hours and days on
> bills you will know a whole lot more about these problems than we do
> and we certainly would welcome your help. This has nothing what-
> soever to do with the fact of your regional representation or the fact
> that you are new men.

Expertise and judgment. Development of a specialty or of expert
knowledge in a particular area is likely to bring a member to the attention
of the press. An experienced member explains why:

> Make a reputation for yourself, and my thought here is that one
> way by which one advances is to develop a specialty. There is some area
> of interest, some area perhaps of experience, some area where you com-
> bine your past experience with your interest, where you can by certain
> application and diligence come to learn more on that subject than any-

body else. I have in mind the great reputation built in the House by [Representative _____] who has come to be accepted as so much of an authority on China that even the Chinese consult him. And if you have an interest or a specialty (and you get to be extremely good on it) it isn't necessary to speak very often on the floor because there are other outlets. . . .

It gives you an opportunity to be called upon in the television forums and radio debates, because, after all, the people who are looking for members of Congress to appear on their programs want them to have something to say and something to say that they know something about. It isn't enough merely that you have a generalized knowledge or that you were extremely active back home in the American Legion or in some other organization. And, therefore, you are much more likely to be called for on television, radio, and general forums, and thereby get better known, if you have developed these specialties of your own.

Similarly, the ability to recognize the important and ignore the trivial is regarded as an advantage, as a newsman suggests:

A great public commotion about an issue is no assurance it will become a matter of central importance to the electorate. In other words, just because there is a lot of froth and noise and clacking around in Washington about something doesn't mean a blessed thing. Oftentimes it doesn't, and one of the sensitivities, I think, of the great people in Congress is that they can tell the difference. They know how to discriminate between what's plain stuff and what's meaningful.

Candor and truthfulness. An experienced Congressman explains the value of free and frank exchanges with newsmen:

I was once in the district attorney's office for a good many years, and I worked with an assistant district attorney who would never tell the press anything. I have been a naval intelligence officer during the war when we decided to tell the press everything, and, believe me, the second system is better, because you will find that as you develop confidential relations with the press that they are for the most part to be trusted.

I believe a full, frank meeting with the press in which you tell them the background of what you are doing and make it very clear what you feel can be quoted as against what you think cannot be quoted—it will be respected. So I choose the open relationship with the press rather than the close-mouth position. It is something like Sophie Tucker, who said, "I've been rich and I've been poor, and, believe me, rich is best." So I would be a little rich in the information you give out as long as you have established a basis of confidence.

And you will find that everybody down here is talking to the newspapermen and talking more freely perhaps at cocktail parties than anywhere else (more freely than is advisable there, perhaps) but . . . there is nothing wrong in getting your ideas and getting out information which is favorable to your point of view. . . .

On some occasions, of course, comment may breach a confidence or injure a colleague. A newsman suggests that, in such cases, silence is golden:

> If you can't tell the truth, the thing to do is just don't say anything. To become branded as a liar (and, believe me, quite a few public figures deservedly and perhaps not too deservedly are so branded) finishes you as far as the—I mean the network, the word gets out in this town, something awful, and you just don't mean anything any more. Your word means nothing, and people still laugh at your jokes and welcome the little tidbits you might hand out, but there has to be a very cold Monday before you mean anything.

Invective and errors. Public officials seldom win public quarrels—especially long-distance quarrels—with editors and publishers. As an experienced Congressman puts it:

> Never . . . quarrel with either the press or the clergy, because the press will get you in the footnote no matter what you say. In the way in which they write your comment critical of the press, they will always get you. You write a letter to the editor and you criticize the paper; notice the headline or the footnote, the editorial note that goes on it which only doubly destroys you. And I do not believe it is, generally speaking, feasible to criticize the clergy because they can always appeal to a higher court than you can.

However, reporters are fallible. Ordinarily they do not mind being advised of their honest errors, as a newsman indicates:

> I don't think that reporters generally (certainly those I know) are ever angered by a political figure calling him up and saying, if he sincerely so believes, that something that the reporter wrote was not accurate. We make mistakes almost as much as politicians, but, believe me, for all our sins very few if any reporters are venal, while all reporters, certainly the hundreds that I have known, are sensitive and have points of view. I think that basically what reporters want is the facts as they can honestly interpret them.

Whether it is *always* desirable to call errors to the reporter's attention and to ask for corrections is another matter. Some members find that, unless the error is of great importance, the record can be corrected most gracefully in another forum, without direct reference to misstatement of the case elsewhere.

News Release Techniques

Congressmen have at their disposal resources and facilities designed for, or adaptable to, use in dealing with news media. In House practice, these are employed in a wide variety of techniques to make it easier for the newsman to get the facts and report them accurately.

Use of press assistants. Whereas some members prefer to handle their own press relations, working directly with district editors and publishers whom they know personally, a substantial number of Congressmen delegate this responsibility to a staff employee who has had newspaper or related media experience. The 1965 *Congressional Staff Directory* lists only thirty-six individuals with the title of press assistant, press secretary, or public relations aide, but this figure is misleading; in many offices, the administrative assistant is a former newsman, and a major portion of his time is devoted to work with reporters and editors in the district and elsewhere.

Statements and releases. Some congressional offices produce highly polished press releases for distribution on a regular schedule. Others do not attempt to write releases at all, preferring to make the raw materials —copies of speeches backed up by personal interviews, for example—available to those reporters who can be enticed in a casual telephone conversation to drop by. On occasion, of course, these techniques are combined. A release containing excerpts from a speech or statement may be accompanied by the full text; and newsmen, particularly those representing media with outlets in the district, may be notified by phone that the material is both available and significant.

In any event, newsmen and experienced members alike recommend that texts of speeches be made available to the press, in advance of their public presentation whenever possible. Thus, reporters are given an opportunity to familiarize themselves with their contents, and the possibility of misquotation or error is reduced. Accompanying press releases containing excerpts give the members an opportunity to emphasize those portions of their remarks which they think are most important, at the same time reducing the possibility that reporters will overlook significant statements in their haste to meet a deadline.

Reporters maintain that they do not want the story to be written for them, that the press release need only contain basic information about the occasion for the speech and pertinent quotations from it. However strong this preference may be, it is not unusual for well-written releases to turn up substantially verbatim in newspapers and broadcasts. Releases are most frequently published in weekly or smaller daily newspapers, which have limited editorial staffs; but even the larger dailies and the wire services occasionally use them as they have been written.

Generally, members who prepare releases for publication as written attempt to follow standard newspaper format: One to three pages, double-spaced, in clear and concise language, with editorial comments about the author's brilliance and effectiveness either implied or attributed to someone else.

Distribution of materials. Copies of speech texts and press releases are customarily made available in the House Press, Radio-Television, and

Periodical galleries, which provide facilities for correspondents employed by the major newspapers, wire services, news broadcasters, and magazines. These galleries are situated adjacent to the House Chamber in the Capitol. Between twenty-five and fifty copies of releases and texts are usually sent to the Press Gallery, with perhaps ten each to the Radio-Television and Periodical galleries.

Many congressional offices maintain an up-to-date list of all district newspapers and broadcasting stations, complete with press and news broadcast deadlines for each. On important news breaks—establishment of a federal facility in the district, or the award of an important government contract, for instance—the information is often telephoned or wired to the news outlets most likely to be interested. Less timely releases, and other materials, are customarily mailed well in advance of local outlets' deadlines, with a release date prominently displayed as part of the heading.

Photo services. The House Republican and Democratic campaign committees employ photographers who are on call to record meetings between members and their constituents, individually or in groups. Usually this service must be requested well in advance, for these photographers are seldom available on a moment's notice. Many members keep a camera handy in their offices and take their own pictures of constituents. These can be mailed, or if the camera develops the picture immediately, passed out at the time. Extra prints of photographs are useful for publicity or filing purposes.

Radio and television. Radio and television station licensees are required to devote time to public-service programming. Perhaps as a result of this requirement, local outlets have been found by Congressmen to be relatively receptive to tape, film, or telephone reports from the nation's capital. Among techniques developed to exploit this opportunity are:

- The one-minute television report. Usually such a report comments on major news events of general significance or on items of special interest in a particular district. Because of the time needed to make the film and ship it to local stations, reports of this kind usually have to be planned somewhat in advance.
- The radio-television "beeper" report. Used for commenting on news events as they occur or reporting on legislative activity of particular local concern, this report can be produced with little advance planning, for the physical arrangements involve only a call to local radio stations. In agreement with local stations, some members are prepared to make such reports whenever an event occurs that lends itself to this technique. The Capitol switchboard can also set up a conference call so that the report can be given to several stations at once, thereby minimizing telephone costs.
- Regular radio or television programs. These can be sent to local stations on a weekly, biweekly, or monthly basis. They usually are three- to five-minute presentations that require considerable advance

planning in order to present effective discussion of a topic at some length.

• The interview. This format is recommended by experienced members for five- to fifteen-minute programs. It is customary to invite other federal officials (a cabinet member, an Assistant Secretary, or a prominent Senator, for example), or state or local dignitaries visiting in Washington, to participate in these programs, which usually focus on topical issues of direct concern to the district.

An experienced Congressman suggests that it usually is better to keep radio and television tapes short:

> It is easier to fit the shorter tapes into a regular news program on a TV station than if you send out a longer length tape. This is also true with radio time. Five minutes or less tends to be more usable on news programs in the radio stations in your district. The recording facility has suggested if you do pick a longer period, such as fifteen minutes, that an interview type of program usually seems to go over better than just a straight discussion on your part alone. These are just suggestions. They have suggested that you try to make arrangements for your local stations, either TV or radio, to carry your programs on a specific set time each week. People will become accustomed to the time, know the time and can turn on their sets at that particular time if they are interested in hearing you each week. That way you usually get the best reception.
>
> If you send out one- or two-minute tapes, either radio or TV, you have a chance of having them put right into a news broadcast they might have on that day, and be picked up as current news, which of course gives you wide coverage.

Although production requirements delay television reports somewhat, a film may sometimes be produced on the day of an event and transmitted to local stations in time for evening news broadcasts. Delivery of a film-strip may be speeded by sending the negative, rather than having the film fully processed. Technical details of this method of meeting airline shipping schedules, as well as other aspects of television and radio reporting, are available in the House Television and Recording Studios.

Publication by Mail

Competition for the attention of the Washington press corps is intense—and distasteful to some. Moreover, items about "those fellows back in Washington" must compete with local news for space and time in newspapers and broadcasts in the district. To supplement information available to their constituents through commercial outlets, most members rely heavily on direct mail and the use of the frank to distribute, in quantity, various publications and government documents.

CONGRESSIONAL NEWSLETTERS

Because they have encountered difficulties in gaining access to the news media, many members have gone into the publishing business themselves, informing their constituents of their activities through a "Letter from Washington" or "Congressional Newsletter." The use of this technique has increased steadily in the past several years:

> I think when I first came down in 1950 it was the exceptional Congressman who wrote a newsletter. I would say today that it is pretty much the exceptional Congressman who doesn't write a newsletter. Somehow or other we have found, I guess by experience, that we don't really get through to our people through the media. And each one in our own way is coming around to the point that we have to develop other techniques to get through to them.

Not all members agree, however, that publication of a newsletter is a good idea or a technique to be adopted without consideration of the production problems involved. One experienced Congressman points out that, while a newsletter is easy to start, continuing publication may be a different matter:

> I am an old newspaperman from way back, but I never have written a newsletter because I know what a problem it is to keep something going after you have one time started it. Now with some members it has worked beautifully, and I intend to start a newsletter maybe this term, I'm not sure just yet. I have done my informing in other ways, and there are plenty [of] other ways whereby you can inform your constituents about what is going on here and that which you want them to know.

Variations in format and content. Newsletters come in many diffferent shapes and sizes. Some are handsomely printed and include a picture of the Congressman; others are everyday mimeographed sheets. Some contain in-depth treatment of a single topic; others are composed of several items, giving the Congressman an opportunity to set forth his position on various issues, to explain how certain events or legislation will affect the people of the district, and to comment on significant developments in related areas of government and foreign affairs. Some members give their newsletters a lighter, more personal touch, adding chatty comments about visitors to their office and the doings of their children and grandchildren. This approach is described by one experienced member:

> . . . I do believe that it helped me more in vote-getting than any single thing I did that I kept them advised. They don't ask for weighty information. They don't ask that you agree with them, I may say. What they do want is to know that you care enough about them to write home and that makes the big hit, that you are still aware of the

fact that they sent you here. . . . Try it out if you like the idea and you will be surprised how many people have read [the newsletter]. . . . Include in it some little homely news, at the bottom maybe a list of the visitors who came in. Keep a visitors' guest book. People are honored to be asked to sign it. Keep the guest book and then write in that newsletter that "Mr. and Mrs. So-and-So came in this week to see me. They were on their way through to Florida . . . and I was so happy to see them," and mention all these people. They love to see their names in print even if your newsletter has a small circulation.

Some newsletters are published on a weekly or biweekly basis, while others appear only once a month or at irregular intervals. Some go to only a few hundred people, but most are distributed far more widely. As a general rule, most newsletters are sent to all news media in the district; and some newspapers, especially weeklies, reserve a regular space for those which appear regularly. Most members also send their newsletters to party officials throughout the district.

Newsletters may be mailed under the franking privilege as long as they adhere to the franking regulations. Even so, however, a newsletter can become an expensive item, especially if it is published on a weekly or biweekly basis and distributed to a large mailing list. . . .

USE OF QUESTIONNAIRES

Although little agreement exists as to their merits, apparently the trend is toward more general use of questionnaires. Some Congressmen feel that questionnaires stimulate constituent mail unnecessarily and overburden the staff with requests for assistance of one kind or another. Others feel that they may possibly become committed, against their better judgment, to supporting a legislative proposal *only* because of the published results of a questionnaire. Those who use them, however, are willing to take on any extra work involved, arguing that questionnaires provide a valuable check on constituent attitudes and create good will by giving those who respond a sense of participation in the operation of the national government.

Distribution and design. Questionnaires can be sent either to everyone in the district, using simplified address forms, or to all registered voters. If a list of voters is not available, a fairly representative sample can be obtained by taking names at random from telephone books—for example, every fifth or every tenth name. Some newspapers, especially weeklies, will publish a blank questionnaire so that readers may clip it out and send it in. If this cannot be aranged, a member can announce in the press that he is conducting a poll and that he will send a questionnaire to any constituent who requests one.

To make the results more meaningful, besides questions relating to issues, respondents can be asked to indicate their political affiliation, the area in which they reside, and perhaps their occupation. Some members make a practice of sending a tabulation of the results to everyone who was sent a questionnaire, whether or not they answered it. This procedure is rather costly, and the more general practice is to send results only to those who request them and to all newspapers and radio and television stations. Some Congressmen also insert the results in the *Congressional Record* and then have reprints made for mailing purposes.

. . . AND, FRANKLY, GETTING REELECTED

By Mark J. Green, James M. Fallows and David R. Zwick

There is one more edge, perhaps the greatest advantage incumbents have: domination of all the media of electioneering—the mails, the newspapers, radio, and television. Aside from the postage allowance, the basis of incumbent domination of the mails is, of course, the franking privilege. One new representative was told by his father (a former representative), "Son, I have three pieces of advice for you if you want to stay in Congress. One, use the frank. Two, use the frank. Three, use the frank." Franked mail is marked with a bold, florid signature that supposedly says, "This mail is my official business," but that all too often means, "I want to be reelected." The volume of franked mail goes up as elections come closer, as one might expect.

Although the frank is supposed to be used only for "official business," and not to aid a member's reelection, Congress has defined official business very broadly. The widest of the many loopholes in the law permits any excerpt from the *Congressional Record* to be mailed as official business at taxpayer expense. When this rule is combined with the custom that permits any member of Congress to stick anything he wants into the *Record*, the opportunity for abuse becomes clear. Congressman Alvin O'Konski prepared for his 1972 reelection campaign by sending a flood of material into the *Record* in December, 1971 (long enough before the election that it would not become a campaign issue)—including the "Biography of Alvin E. O'Konski" and an impressive list of his successes in supping from the pork barrel. Even as this is written, Cong. O'Konski's life story—excerpted from the *Record*—is filling mailboxes in Wisconsin's tenth congressional district. Other members insert flattering words about local businesses, scout troops, garden clubs, debate teams, and church

From *Who Runs Congress? A Ralph Nader Congress Project* by Mark J. Green, James M. Fallows and David R. Zwick. Copyright © 1972 by Ralph Nader. Reprinted by permission of Grossman Publishers.

groups, and mail them to the flattered parties. One congressional aide, whose boss indulges in the technique frequently, flatly admitted that the *Record* is "a great political gimmick."

Usually the use and abuse of the frank is done with more circumspection as congressmen ply their voters with newsletters, questionnaires, reprints of speeches on issues of interest, and the like. While helping keep the public informed, these letters and questionnaires also assist the incumbent's reelection. First, they increase the representative's visibility. Gerald Ford, the House minority leader, sends newsletters to his Michigan constituents weekly; as a result his voters are far more likely to recognize his name than other voters are to recognize their members' names. Second, the content of the newsletters, if not frankly political, often leans that way. In 1966, William C. Love analyzed the materials sent to constituents by senators and congressmen. In the House, Love found that 38 percent of the representatives could be classified as "self-promoters," 22 percent as "persuaders," and 17 percent as combination promoter-persuaders; much smaller percentages were found to be "reticent" or "educators." The Senate was worse: 44 percent were promoters, 28 percent persuaders, and 19 percent a combination of the two. What is more significant is that freshman senators and representatives were much more likely to be self-promoters than the secure veterans, who tended toward the "reticent" end of the spectrum.

Challengers, forced to rely on stamps instead of signatures, cannot hope to compete. To send one mailing to each of the 150,000 households in a typical congressional district would, at 8 cents apiece, set a challenger back $12,000 just for postage—not counting the printing (which the member, but not the challenger, can obtain at cost) or envelopes (which the member, but not the challenger, can obtain free). Twelve thousand dollars is just about half what is usually spent by congressional candidates.

One 1965 study found that about a third of the members of the House said that newspapers in their districts printed their news releases verbatim, and that another third wrote their own columns for the local press. Domination of the press is another media advantage enjoyed and gleefully exploited by incumbent members of Congress. It is the one perhaps most dependent upon the glory and trappings of office, which shroud the congressman until he doffs his statesman's gown and reenters the political fray, at election time. Typical congressmen pour out well over a hundred press releases each year; atypical congressmen, those from not-so-safe seats, pour out many more.

This formidable press barrage naturally does more good for congressmen from rural areas than those from big cities. The small-town editor, anxious to fill his columns, and having no Washington bureau to prepare stories for him, relies on the newsmaker more than, say, reporters for the *New York Times*. In Congressman David Obey's rural Wisconsin district, all the daily newspapers and half the weeklies publish his newspaper column, which appears every week. Obey and his peers are able to obtain columns and columns of free publicity that are simply not available to anyone hoping to challenge them, and at the same time these columns act as the filter through which news reaches his constituents. Exclusion of one's opponents from the relevant media can be as effective as an incumbent's domination of it.

When Murray Watson challenged William Poage in their east Texas Democratic primary, local newspapers totally ignored Watson's candidacy. "Watson's name never appeared in the paper except in ads," said Roger Wilson, his aide. The papers refused to print Poage's votes on environmental and consumer issues. "We finally ended up running them as ads," said Wilson.

Domination of the broadcast media, radio and television, follows a similar pattern. More than half of all representatives have their own regular radio or television broadcasts, which are eagerly aired by stations who must demonstrate their willingness to air public-service programming if they wish to keep their FCC licenses. The shows are taped for peanuts in the Senate and House recording studios, which have a mock congressional office, with an elegant desk and a window giving a glorious view of the Capitol dome in the background. Incumbents are also sought out whenever they make news, or whenever the station wants them to comment on the news. In 1965, members of the House told researchers that they averaged four television appearances and eight radio appearances every month while Congress was in session. Members of the Senate, who are sought out by the networks for national coverage, have it even better.

Some congressmen go to further lengths to assure themselves adequate exposure on the broadcast media. In 1969, there were fourteen members who owned more than $5,000 in stock in radio and television stations, and eight more were the owners or principal investors in them. One investor is Congressman O'Konski, the man who larded the *Congressional Record* with his own biography. O'Konski owns radio WLIN in Merrill, Wisconsin. He even keeps his district office there, and thereby pays himself the government subsidy that is given for maintaining a district office. The possibilities for conflict of interest in all these cases—when the station's license comes up for renewal, for example—are as obvious as the advantages to incumbents.

Members of Congress have to give up their free television and radio programs when they announce that they are candidates for reelection (which is one reason they delay the announcement as long as possible), but that does not mean that they give up their power in radio and television. One of the big advantages they have over their opponents is financial. The House and Senate recording studios charge members of Congress only the cost of materials when they use the studios. Everett Dirksen used the studios to record his smash-hit single, "Gallant Men," and thus got a leg up on other recording stars. The Nader Congress Project has found that to make a year's worth of weekly reports an incumbent pays $2,500, but his challenger would have to pay production costs of about $60,000.

The result of all this attention in the mails and the press and on television and radio is a much higher degree of voter recognition for the incumbent than a challenger can hope to obtain except by extraordinarily high spending. Though only half the voters know the name of their congressman, far fewer have ever heard of his opponent.

What do they know about the incumbent, besides having heard of him? Voters asked this question will usually answer, "He's a good guy," or "He does a pretty good job." Only rarely do they know what he thinks or how he votes. One remarkable survey taken by the American Business Committee on National Priorities found that "in almost every instance, between 80 percent and 100 percent" of the voters were unaware of how their representatives had voted on key issues that had drawn national attention. The Business Committee polled ten congressional districts represented by important legislators; in all of them, a majority of voters expressed opposition to continued funding of the SST. But eight out of the ten representatives voted for the SST, and apparently could get away with it, since 85 percent of the voters didn't know how they had voted and the 15 percent that thought it knew was wrong as often as it was right.

Congressmen cannot afford to ignore their constituents entirely when it comes to voting on major issues. There is at least a small group of informed citizens who follow what their member does, and cast their votes accordingly. It's unwise to alienate what political scientists call "the informed swing voter." Speaker Sam Rayburn counseled congressmen, "When in doubt, vote your district." But clearly some districts don't much care. Only this can explain some of the surprising representation sent to Congress. South Dakota, for example, has regularly returned George McGovern, a very liberal Democrat, and Karl Mundt, a very conservative Republican, to the Senate, although each represents the same constituency. Senators from Oklahoma and North Dakota are similarly contrasting—one very liberal, the other very conservative.

What all this seems to mean is that voters are more likely to vote for the image of a man than for his legislative record, and are more likely to vote for the image of a man than for the party to which he is attached. In fact, one of the reasons put forward for the recent upsurge in the trend to return incumbents indefinitely is that as party labels have less and less impact, the candidate who is best known to the public—the incumbent—will be the candidate who wins.

CONGRESS AND THE MEDIA:
PARTNERS IN PROPAGANDA

By Ben H. Bagdikian

Shortly after he was elected United States Representative from the 10th District of Pennsylvania in 1962, Joseph M. McDade went to the top editors of one of his hometown papers, the Scranton *Tribune*, second largest in his district, and told them he'd like to put one of their reporters, Bob Reese, on his payroll. Reese would remain in Scranton and continue on the paper's news staff.

The editors agreed, and, for the last eleven years, Reese has drawn a salary from both the paper and the congressman. Mr. McDade is not an unimportant member of Congress. He is on the powerful House Appropriations Committee and ranking member on its subcommittee controlling money for the Department of Interior; he is also a member of the Select Committee on Small Business.

When Congressman McDade wants to dispatch some advantageous information back to his district, he often asks Reese to write a news release. Reese sends it to one of McDade's offices for approval and then distributes it to the district's twenty-four daily and weekly newspapers and the various radio and television stations. Reese, who ordinarily covers City Hall and the police in Scranton, says he does not cover McDade directly, but he told CJR that, when he hands his own release to his *Tribune* editor, it usually is handed back to him to write for the paper as a news story.

Recently the newly formed Capitol Hill News Service, a product of Ralph Nader's Congress Project, revealed the fact that Reese gets $5,000 a year from Congressman McDade. This story clearly has something to say about journalistic ethics. But it also symbolizes in its own blatant way something more subtle and pervasive in the present political mess in Washington.

The crisis in federal governance is sometimes blamed on the news media, and in a way this is partly true. The media, however, are to blame not merely for what they do, but for what they do not do. The problem is not only their approach to the Executive Branch and the White House in particular, but also the fact that by omission and commission most of the printed and broadcast news media of the United States have permitted themselves to become propaganda arms of Congress. This development, in turn, has contributed to the growing impotence and insensitivity of the Legislative Branch of the federal government, while the Judicial

Reprinted from the *Columbia Journalism Review*, January/February, 1974. ©

and the Executive have become overpowering. Unnoticed by most voters and contrary to popular notion, the House, presumably the most sensitive legislative instrument in the government, has become a sluggish body of semi-permanent membership, almost as creaky as the British House of Lords whose members inherit their membership.

This has special meaning in the 1970s, when the White House scandals have immobilized much of government and demoralized public confidence. For a year after Watergate there was only one body clearly responsible under the Constitution to resolve the crisis—Congress. But Congress, having become sclerotic, refused to act and either impeach the President or absolve him. This unresponsiveness arises from many factors, but a significant portion of the blame lies with American journalistic institutions.

Ironically, it is the Congress that is supposed to be most reflective of new public sentiments, especially the House, whose members have to go back for re-election every two years and thus theoretically let voters judge how well they have served the district. It used to work that way. *Congressional Quarterly* tells us that in the 1870s more than half the members of each session of the House were newly elected, but that by 1900 only a third were first termers and that by 1970 the figure had dropped to 12 per cent. Of 330 incumbents running for re-election in 1972 (the other 135 having retired, died or given up in primaries), only ten incumbents —3 per cent—were defeated.

Obviously, as these figures show, the renewal of the House on the basis of performance and changes in public desires is not working. One important reason is that the news media simply don't tell the folks back home what their member of Congress really does. Worse than that, most of the media are willing conduits for the highly selective information the member of Congress decides to feed the electorate. This propaganda is sent to newspapers and broadcasting stations, and the vast majority of them pass it off to the voters as professionally collected, written and edited "news."

An acquaintance of mine with an obsession for reading every local publication in the state of Wisconsin recently sent me a curious collection of newspaper clippings.

From the Blair, Wis., *Press:* "At least one producer has given up its efforts to triple the wholesale price of natural gas that eventually is piped to consumers in 132 Wisconsin communities, according to Rep. Les Aspin (D.-Wis.).

"The Cotton Petroleum Company has. . . ."

From the Argyle, Wis., *Agenda:* "At least one producer has given up its efforts to triple the wholesale price of natural gas that eventually is piped to consumers in 132 Wisconsin communities, according to Rep. Les Aspin (D.-Wis.).

"The Cotton Petroleum Company has. . . ."

From the Denmark, Wis., *Press*: "At least one gas producer has given up its efforts to triple the wholesale price of natural gas that eventually is piped to consumers in 132 Wisconsin communities, according to Rep. Les Aspin (D.-Wis.).

"The Cotton Petroleum Company has. . . ."

From the Cadott, Wis., *Sentinel*: "At least one gas producer has given up its efforts to triple the wholesale price of natural gas that eventually is piped to consumers in 132 Wisconsin communities, according to Rep. Les Aspin (D.-Wis.).

"The Cotton Petroleum Company has. . . ."

It seemed possible that Rep. Les Aspin might have some insight into this, so a visit to his office and a request for any press release he might have distributed on the subject was made. A familiar legal-size sheet of mimeograph paper was unearthed; it bore the heading: PRESS RELEASE FROM CONGRESSMAN LES ASPIN. And the news release began:

"At least one gas producer has given up its efforts to triple the wholesale price of natural gas that eventually is piped to consumers in 132 Wisconsin communities, according to Rep. Les Aspin (D.-Wis.).

"The Cotton Petroleum Company has. . . ."

The papers had run the release word for word as journalistic news. This is hardly a rare phenomenon. Hundreds of press releases, paid for by the taxpayers, are sent to the media by members of Congress, and hundreds are run verbatim or with insignificant changes, most often in medium-sized and small papers, with only rare calls to check facts and ask questions that probe beyond the pleasant propaganda.

It is no accident that most members of Congress have at least one former journalist working for them (Sen. Lowell Weicker of Connecticut has four). The ex-reporters turn out competent-sounding stories as press releases and know how to plant them with a minimum of questioning. Naturally, there is no press release—or news story, usually—if something embarrassing happens to a member of Congress, or if there is some sleight of hand in committee that would anger his constituents, or if he is carrying water for corporations that have nothing to do with the welfare of his constituents. Also there is no release if a member doesn't want to anger people with his feelings about a particular national issue. If there is no correspondent to ask his opinion, he can keep it to himself—or, more likely, distract attention with a release in the style of *Rebecca of Sunnybrook Farm* about a rivers and harbors appropriation for local marinas.

There are few Washington correspondents to ask individual members pertinent questions the voters back home need answered. The recent Ralph Nader Congress Project calculated that of the nation's 1,750 daily papers, 72 per cent have no Washington correspondent or contract with stringers. The same is true of 96 per cent of TV stations and 99 per cent of radio stations.

There are about 1,400 domestic Washington correspondents. The majority of them practice herd journalism, crowding into White House and State Department briefings or sexy hearings on the Hill. Everyday congressional workings are regarded as an impenetrable and unrewarding can of worms. About 400 of these 1,400 correspondents cover Congress specifically, but they also follow the herd, most of them working for national news organizations that concentrate on big issues and a few leaders. This is a natural and necessary concern, but it means that most members of Congress are left uncovered.

This gap pretty much leaves the field to the printed press release and an even more effective instrument of political promotion: television footage represented as news when in fact, it is government-subsidized propaganda.

It is instructive to tour (after maneuvering with high-level members to get permission) the $500,000 studios maintained by the House and Senate for members to make their own video, film and audio tapes and duplicate them for use on local stations.

The House facilities, for example, are in the basement of the monstrous Rayburn Building. They have two video studios, each equipped with color cameras. The first studio is for tape, and the second is for film (largely to service the growing number of cable TV systems). There are also four radio recording studios with master controls. The entire facility is outfitted with processing and duplicating equipment that is unmatched by any local or network studio in Washington—and all of it is available at bargain prices. A five-minute color video tape duplicated about twenty-five times for simultaneous presentation on local TV stations costs a senator or representative about $150, usually paid from his official expense allowances—one-tenth to one-twentieth of the amount that would be charged by a non-subsidized firm.

The result is sometimes a weekly or monthly radio or TV report from a member of Congress on local broadcasting stations—or, more often, footage spliced into the regular local news and presented to the viewer as professional coverage. Occasionally the member of Congress appears with an aide who sits with his back to the camera, thereby appearing to be an interviewing journalist; the aide lobs soft questions for the member to knock out of the park. These sessions are presented on stations all over the country as "news" shots, although the Federal Communications Commission says it is a violation of rules for a broadcaster to run any footage, video or radio, that has been paid for in any way by the donor without announcing that fact to the audience. The offense is punishable by a $1,000 fine per unannounced showing; nevertheless, the spots run every day without informing the viewer that he is watching contrived propaganda.

The practice is most common in medium-sized and small cities, but these smaller stations form the majority of the nation's 705 commercial

TV and 6,800 commercial radio stations. And because they are in communities with fewer media than the big cities, their impact per broadcast on a particular congressional district can be great.

Most of the "news" items sent out by the congresspersons (delivered for use in the local studio the next day) are not labeled by the station —but there may be a few clues. The House studio, for example, has two basic sets. One is an "interview" set where the representative converses with a visiting fireman or a prestigious government figure, a Cabinet officer, perhaps. The set itself may give a clue that the scene is a taxpayer-subsidized piece of propaganda. There are two gold chairs behind an oval coffee table that has a brown wooden globe on one end and a bowl of green ivy on the other. On the table may be two books, one blue (in fact, the 1966 *Congressional Directory*) and the other, for nice color contrast, red (in fact, *Foreign Relations of the U.S., 1911*).

There is a choice of backgrounds for the representative. He can choose a scholarly-looking "library" background with legal-like bound books. He can also appear in front of a blue curtain or a carefully contrived photograph of the Capitol as though seen through his office window. Unfortunately, this view of the Capitol is not seen from the office of any senator or representative, either in size or perspective, but it has appeared in thousands of TV shots, implying that the local politician occupies a high-status office overlooking the great dome.

Another background is a special screen on which a slide or movie (provided by the member, not the studio) can be projected, either for a stable background or for action footage that dramatizes the subject the member wishes to discuss.

The other basic set is the "office," with a big congressional desk, the standard black-leather high-backed chair behind it, a desk pen, perhaps the blue and red books, and the choice of backgrounds available on the other set.

There is one other scene, not exactly a full set. It is a paneled wall with two hooks on it from which may be hung the standard gold-painted nameplate of every standing committee of the House—Agriculture, Appropriations, Armed Services, so on; thus, the member may be photographed as though standing outside a committee room from which he has just emerged to share with his voters the inner secrets and wisdom. It may be hard for the viewer to detect this set in his "news" except for one added distinctive feature. The congressional studio has such modern and expensive equipment that its TV footage is clearly superior in quality to the average material shot by a local television crew.

Last year 352 of the 435 members of the House repaired to their studio, most of them every week. Members from the big cities tend not to use it because their metropolitan stations won't run the stuff and their audiences are tougher media critics. Also these senators and representatives are more likely to be covered by genuine journalists coming from larger local news organizations.

Do these studios ever make campaign shots for candidates? The stock answer from studio staffers—sixteen in the House studio alone—is that they have no control over content or use. The answer, however, is yes: the studios do make many campaign tapes and films for incumbents at the taxpayers' expense.

From the standpoint of the local radio and television station, source-produced "news" shots can be either material shot in the congressional studio or a commercial plug made by the candidate. It is common now for candidates to provide free footage for local stations. During the 1972 Democratic nomination wrestling, for example, Edmund Muskie was fighting for support from precinct leaders in Iowa. His staff obtained an effective videotaped endorsement from Sen. Harold Hughes of Iowa, an enormous boost. They edited the tape to 3 minutes and 45 seconds, hired two airplanes to fly duplicates of the tape to 10 Iowa TV stations and then had Muskie workers check on its usage. All the stations ran the tape and the average air time was 3 minutes and 15 seconds. But at least Muskie filmed the interview on his own and paid for it out of his campaign funds.

With congressional studios collecting only nominal costs and providing free staff services, it is not difficult to see why it is so hard to defeat an incumbent. The size of this advantage was not lost on one representative from a Western state who once told the New York City Bar Association's committee on ethics, "A challenger needs $25,000 just to get even with me."

With most TV stations, including those in the smaller markets, making better than 25 per cent on sales, the failure to reject political propaganda footage as "news" is not only a violation of FCC rules but journalistically sinful. These stations can well afford to roam the congressional beat themselves and provide original, unbiased coverage. The same is true of the average paper, which makes the same kind of profits. A one-person, full-time Washington bureau can cost $30,000 a year. Most big and medium-sized papers could make this expenditure, but most don't. For instance, until the San Francisco *Chronicle* recently opened a one-person bureau, no daily in the media-rich Bay Area had a full-time Washington correspondent. (The Hearst San Francisco *Examiner* is served by the eight-person Hearst bureau that covers for nine papers in six states with a total of 145 members of Congress. Most of its daily report is concerned with national rather than local angle news.)

It is not farfetched to say that this dearth of firsthand Washington correspondence contributes to the failure of Congress to renew itself as the social environment changes—the incumbents have too strong a tax-subsidized propaganda machine and the news media are too tolerant of it for the voters to get the sort of balanced input they need to make informed decisions.

(It is interesting to note election results in areas where there *is* original congressional coverage. In 1972, for example, of 60 new members elected to the House, including some filling vacancies, 57, or 95 per cent, came from the minority of House districts with a newspaper or broadcasting station that maintains some direct Washington correspondence.)

Lack of adequate coverage has probably contributed to the longevity of many congressional leaders, some of whom have performed admirably and some miserably, but all without discernible effect on home districts.

Sen. Mike Mansfield, Majority Leader of the Senate, has many newspapers and broadcasting stations with significant circulation among his constituents in the state of Montana. Of that total circulation, however, only 4 per cent receive coverage from newspapers and stations with Washington correspondence of their own. The figure for West Virginia, home of the Senate's second in command, Sen. Robert Byrd, is 12 per cent. Rep. Harley Staggers, also of West Virginia, famous for his subpoenas of CBS and criticism of the media and the powerful chairman of the House Committee on Interstate and Foreign Commerce, comes from a district where none of the local media has anyone of their own covering the congressman while he is in Washington.

Rep. George Mahon of Texas, who as chairman of the House Appropriations Committee controls more federal money than any other Congressperson, comes from a district that has only one paper with any Washington correspondence—a two-person stringer bureau that also covers most of the state's 26 House and Senate members for nine other papers outside Mahon's district. The Associated Press reporter assigned to that area told the Nader group she covers all members from Texas, Oklahoma, New Mexico and Arizona—altogether 44 members of Congress and their related committees. For all of his virtues, Mr. Mahon—re-elected 16 times —has not been closely covered for the benefit of the 477,000 people in his district.

There is concrete evidence for the view that close coverage in Washington can bring about more changes in Congress. In 1972 Sen. Jack Miller, a Republican, was considered certain for re-election from Republican Iowa, which clearly was for Nixon (and voted for him). But not long before the election, James Flansburg, a local reporter for the Des Moines *Register*, and Clark Mollenhoff, the paper's Washington correspondent, wrote about and kept following up an amendment pushed by Miller for the benefit of a Bermuda insurance company, an embarrassment that his previously unknown Democratic challenger, Dick Clark, has credited with his victory.

For many smaller papers, of course, a $30,000-a-year Washington bureau would be either impossible economically or an unreasonable imbalance of effort. Some smaller papers solve the problem by using stringer bureaus that either serve on an annual retainer-plus-fee-per-story basis or just receive a fee per story. While the big bureaus have glamour and national impact (the New York *Times* with its 43 people; the AP with 74), the majority are stringer-manned outfits few people outside of Washington have ever heard of. Organizations and individuals are listed in the back of the *Congressional Directory*, but it is uncertain how much and what kind of work they do. The *Directory* shows two Washington correspondents for the Bogalusa, La. *News* (circulation, 8,619). But these same two, if tracked through the rest of the *Directory*, also cover for six papers in four states with a total of 36 congressional members. The Gannett News Service has an eleven-person bureau, but it serves a chain which at this writing has 57 papers in states with a total of 188 senators and representatives.

With all their problems, Washington bureaus that serve large chains and stringers are beneficial if the local editor insists on news important to the home district and pays reasonably for it. These are big "ifs." Most bureaus have trouble with the home office not knowing or caring enough about their local delegations, agency actions, or the Washington scene in general. Eileen Shannon, writing in the October 1973 ASNE *Bulletin* on "Hometown Reporting from Washington," describes the aches and pains of the local reporter in Washington but also the obtuseness of editors with a strange view of Washington corresponding.

"It is hard to describe what I felt," she wrote, "when I was wakened one balmy summer night in 1971 and asked to please get a copy of the Pentagon Papers. Touched, yes, deeply touched." Shannon was not alone. At a time when the FBI and Henry Kissinger, let alone the Washington *Post* and Los Angeles *Times*, were having trouble unearthing the Pentagon Papers, a number of editors back home casually asked their stringers or bureau people to hustle up a set for that night.

For the newspaper and broadcasting station that cannot support a full-time bureau, or thinks it can't, there is now an alternative: the Capitol Hill News Service (CHNS). Growing out of the Nader Congress Project, and given a six-month seed grant of $40,000 from Nader's Public Citizen fund, CHNS was created to provide close congressional coverage in those states with the largest concentration of uncovered members of Congress at prices any news organization could easily afford.

When it began operating last September, CHNS offered its services for a free trial period, but its grant runs out in late March, and by that time CHNS has to be self-sustaining commercially or close to it. Salaries are a problem. It was clear CHNS could not pay current rates for Washington correspondents. While their median salary is not accurately known, one common figure a few years ago was $17,000.* The minimum for a reporter with four years of experience on the Washington daily papers

---

* It's more like $20,000. See Chapter 6—Ed.

is $20,000 a year. At that rate salaries alone would drive CHNS out of business in less than six months.

CHNS has a five-reporter staff. Leader of the group is Peter Gruenstein, 26, a lawyer by trade but drawn into journalism by free-lance writing for the *Christian Science Monitor*, San Francisco *Chronicle*, the *Nation* and *Progressive*. He put an advertisement in *Editor & Publisher* and *(More)* for correspondents who would work for no more than $8,000 a year. In Washington it is hard to hire a filing clerk for that. Two hundred people answered the ads. Gruenstein thinks 40 to 50 were hirable, including applicants working for the New York *Times*, the Washington *Post*, *Newsday* and *Newsweek*. He hired David Holmberg, 35, a respected Capitol Hill reporter for the Washington *Star* and before that for the now defunct Washington *Daily News*; Lauralyn Bellamy, 26, recently on the staff of *Broadcasting* magazine; Chris Matthews, 27, a free-lance reporter for the Philadelphia *Daily News*, Washington *Post* and Washington *Star*; and Clay Steinman, 23, former editor-in-chief of the Duke University daily paper and AP stringer and at the time a reporter for the Vancouver, Washington, *Columbian*.

Deploying this tiny army was done with Naderian precision. A "media profile" was compiled for each member of Congress, the key factor being the percentage of papers and stations with Washington coverage in each member's district or state. The figures varied from Rep. William Hudnut of Indianapolis, with 99 per cent of his district's circulation served by a correspondent, to Rep. J. Edward Roush, of Huntington, Indiana, with zero coverage for a 152,000 circulation. A distressing number of districts had their own Washington reportage for only 0, 1, 2, 3 or 4 per cent of their media circulation, distressing, that is, for the body politic but obviously fertile territory for a professional news service.

The CHNS decided to provide coverage for every congressional district in Indiana, Montana, Nebraska and West Virginia plus districts of twelve members from Pennsylvania and those of a few individual members, all subject to change. The five reporters cover 20 Republicans and 28 Democrats, or approximately ten Congresspersons each.

After a couple of months of free service to 279 newspapers and 750 broadcasting stations, CHNS asked for news organizations to sign contracts. Judging by its work in the early stages, the service looks respectable from any standpoint and obviously is an advantage over the past void. In addition to local material it sends out national stories. One of these was a listing of forty-three members of Congress who ran without opposition in the last elections but who nevertheless received $592,000 in contributions and kept most of the money, some of it from lobbying groups unconnected with their home districts. Another CHNS national story reported apparent illegal printing of campaign literature (including bumper stickers for Gerald Ford) by a government-subsidized printshop.

Other national stories were not earth-shakers but gathered useful information for the average voter. One story, for instance, pointed out that members of Congress (who receive salaries of $42,500 a year and large expense budgets) get subsidized haircuts for $2 (there is a "Select Committee on the House Beauty Shop"). The story also told about the sixteen-volume set of the U.S. Code that a member can send free to a favored lawyer in his district. It reported the fact that there is a full-time government employee who does nothing all day but run U.S. flags up and down a special flagpole on the roof of the Capitol so that members may send influential people in their districts a flag that "was flown over the Capitol" —the recipient, of course, assuming that it was the flag seen at the very top all day long.

On the state and district level CHNS revealed that Rep. Ken Hechler, who for the past fifteen years has brought West Virginia high school students to Washington to study their government in action, quietly raised the money for their expenses from corporations including aircraft and aerospace companies such as Hughes Aircraft and Fairchild-Hiller. Mr. Hechler is chairman of the House Subcommittee on Aeronautics and Space Technology and passes, among other things, on the NASA budget. Also, as earlier noted, CHNS printed the story about reporter Reese being on Representative McDade's payroll. Area files so far have had useful roundups on votes and opinions of local members of Congress on issues important to their districts, raising questions ordinarily never asked. There is no evidence that the service has any predilection for liberals or against conservatives. At times CHNS overreaches as it did on a story about a Montana congressman headed MELCHER LEAVES ROOM: LOSES VOTE. It was true that Melcher was out of the room when an important committee vote affecting his district was taken, but the story said the vote was 11-to-4, unlike the impression in the headline that Melcher's absence reversed the vote. At other times CHNS doesn't reach far enough. The McDade story was therapeutic—and many Pennsylvania papers and stations used it—but if CHNS had pushed a little further they would have discovered that the situation had been going on for eleven years and added the significant fact that it was done with the prior approval of the paper's editors.

But these are not important criticisms of a service that is providing needed information where none existed before—and for a staff that works long hours without fancy supporting services. The fees are ridiculously low. For newspapers of under 10,000 circulation, the charge is $15 a week, and the scale slides to a top of $50 a week for papers with more than 50,000 circulation. Radio stations pay $10 a week for less than 25,000 circulation, $15 a week for between 25,000 and 100,000 circulation, and $20 for more than 100,000. Television rates are $15 a week for under 100,000 circulation and $20 a week over that. The organizations are permitted to slug their copy "From Our Washington Bureau" or "From the Hometown Washington Bureau"—or to announce, "From our Washington correspondent, the following report . . ."

One month after CHNS sent out the first request to subscribers to start paying, the results were not overwhelming. Gruenstein says he needs $1,200 a week to break even. At the one-month mark he had contracts amounting to $178.50 a week. Verbal comment generally was positive—some of it wildly enthusiastic—but not many signed up, usually citing either budget arguments with the boss or the paper shortage.

The cost of the service for a newspaper is less per week than most pay for a medium-popular comic strip. And while most papers have, in this time of paper shortage, cut down on news rather than advertising, an occasional half-column or full-column story on their Congressperson could easily replace some of the dubious froth that continues to appear.

There may be good reasons why news organizations would not subscribe to a near-give-away professional news service. But the slow response is more likely due to the inertia of times past when low priority was placed on telling the local voters what their representatives in Washington were doing on their behalf.

One day not long ago, Lauralyn Bellamy of CHNS quietly entered an otherwise uncovered committee hearing whose members included a congressman in her area of coverage. When she entered, the congressman was in a mental state common at committee hearings not covered by the press (aside from total absence): the man's eyes were glazed over close to winkin', blinkin' and nod. A moment later he noticed Bellamy, sat upright, shuffled a few papers, listened to the witness intently and asked piercing questions. Gruenstein has a simple aphorism for the phenomenon:

"People being watched act differently from people not being watched."

The American body politic is hemorrhaging from Executive people unwatched. But the remedy, a responsive and daily accountable Congress, has also gone largely unwatched in any way significant for local voters. Most members still do not have to answer pertinent questions for the voters back home, and most continue to propagandize their constituents at the constituents' expense with the cooperation of the local news media. This process started a long time ago but the price of an immobilized government has now come due.

Part Three

CONFLICT AND
COOPERATION

GOVERNMENT-MEDIA RELATIONS IN the United States often have been dominated by one major question: what is liberty of the press? Many issues raised by this question have been resolved by the U.S. Supreme Court. But, as Alexander Hamilton prophesized, many free press issues, including many which reached the Court, have been resolved primarily by public opinion. And the extent of public tolerance or intolerance of press freedoms and restraints often has been influenced or reflected by Congress—through legislation, debate and investigation—in a continuous process of conflict and cooperation with the news media.

Throughout American history, Congress has been both the hero and villain of press freedoms. On one hand, for instance, the Federalist Congress enacted the Sedition Act, one of the greatest threats to freedom of the press in the history of the Republic. Yet, as Leonard Levy argues, the reaction to the Act, initiated in the congressional debates by the Jeffersonian Republicans, led to interpretations of the First Amendment far more libertarian than ever intended by the original supporters of the First Amendment.*

There have been significant confrontations and important cooperation between the Congress and the news media during the past 180 years. Parts One and Two present some examples of these. Many of them have been over issues of access and accommodation and the result of the daily interdependence and interaction of members and correspondents.

In addition to these, there have been some important institutional conflicts and instances of cooperation. The examples in Part Three involve relationships between news media organizations and Congress and its committees. They involve significant press freedom issues.

For instance, Congress has become the point of confrontation for the issue of whether First Amendment *press* freedoms do, indeed, apply to all of the *news media*—that is, broadcast journalism as well as print journalism. Some of its members and subcommittees have been investigating the content of network news documentaries as their influence on American public opinion has become more apparent. These investigations, which have brought other members of Congress to the defense of broadcast journalism, provide contemporary examples of Congress acting both as a threat to and defense of what the news media consider their rights guaranteed by the First Amendment.

During the 1950's there was a very close Moss Committee-media rela-

* See his introduction to *Freedom of The Press from Zenger to Jefferson*. (New York: The Bobbs-Merrill Company, Inc., 1966).

tionship in their freedom of information (FoI) crusade against executive secrecy. The cooperative FoI venture culminated in 1966 in the largely symbolic and only partially effective Federal Public Records Law (FoI Act). And more recent congressional hearings and investigations over the weaknesses of the Act have revived somewhat this now almost ritualistic cooperative relationship.

More recently, the news media have sought help from Congress for statutory protection against federal disclosure of confidential information and its sources (shield legislation). This cooperation was sought after the U.S. Supreme Court ruled 5-4 in *Branzburg* v. *Hayes* that the First Amendment does not provide a newsman with immunity from having to reveal confidential sources and information to a grand jury. Mr. Justice White, in his opinion for the majority, suggested that Congress could provide such protection. This decision raised doubts among representatives of the news media as to whether the U.S. Supreme Court could be relied upon, as it had been so often this century, to protect and expand press freedoms under the First Amendment. These doubts began to appear after the Court's dubious "support" of the news media in its majority decision against the government after its censorship of the Pentagon Papers.

Similar doubts about the reliability of the courts were raised more than 20 years ago when news media representatives sought ways of attacking growing post-war secrecy. Harold Cross found that the courts, including the U.S. Supreme Court, supported discretionary powers of the federal bureaucracy to withhold information from the public. He called on the news media to turn to Congress, not to the courts, for relief.* Not unlike Cross, Justice White clearly indicated that Congress was a potential source of relief for the news media for shield legislation.

Congress has powers to define the limits of protection against forced disclosure of confidential information and its sources. But what Congress can give, Congress can take away. While enacting the Freedom of Information Act, Congress professed a wish to open government information to the public and the news media. However, in attempting to define the limits of access, Congress also created statutory protection for some categories of government which had not before been closed to the public and news media. Now, partly as a result of this experience with the FoI Act, many representatives of the news media are reluctant to accept any statutory attempts to define and protect newsman's privilege.

The Senate Watergate investigation is a contemporary example of cooperation between Congress and the news media in exposing alleged wrong-doing in the executive branch. In their mutually reenforcing investigations, both Congress and the news media were attacked for

* Harold Cross, *The People's Right to Know*. (New York: Columbia University Press, 1953), p. 246.

conducting trials by publicity and jeopardizing the fair trials for those charged, thus raising the fair trial vs. free press issue.

In arguing their right to conduct public hearings, congressional leaders were strong in their defense of a free press. The media generally defended Congress. The extent to which the public was persuaded, both the news media and Congress enjoyed wide-ranging freedom to conduct and publicize the hearings and investigate, report and comment further on all aspects of the Watergate scandals and related issues of political corruption in the Nixon Administration.

Clearly, the news media have been more successful flexing their own powers and cooperating with Congress in its oversight and investigatory powers, than they have been in urging Congress to enact legislation which allegedly protects freedom of the press. Largely due to their own investigations and willingness of reporters to go to jail, and with cooperative congressional investigations and hearings, the news media enjoyed at least a temporary break in the public hostility and official harassment which characterized the five or six years previous to Watergate. This was accomplished without any new legislation or court decisions favorable to the news media.

9

Broadcast Journalism Rights:
First Amendment Conflict

THE CBS DOCUMENTARY "The Selling of the Pentagon" was the subject of considerable attention in the 92nd Congress. This episode in Congress-media relations is an example of both conflict and cooperation between Congress and the news media. It also represents a congressional attempt to use investigation and debate as means of influencing public opinion on unresolved First Amendment issues. In this case one of the major issues is the extent to which the First Amendment applies to broadcast journalism.

The significance of "The Selling of the Pentagon" confrontation in Congress was not lost to the editors of the *Educational Broadcasting Review* who reprinted selected statements from the hearings. Jerome Barron's introduction to these selections, written for the *Review*, is included in this chapter. It reflects his well-known view that the media should be more accessible and responsive to the public. It also reflects his preference for judicial, rather than political, resolution of the conflict between the government and the news media.

Until, and if, the courts resolve the conflict, the untidy "partisan involvements and antagonisms of Congressmen and broadcasters" are likely to determine the climate of public opinion—and, perhaps eventually, court opinion.

A leading figure in the political battle is Rep. Harley O. Staggers (D.-W.Va.).

"Broadcast journalism," he said, "precisely because it enjoys the benefits of a limitation of access by others, is not identical to print journalism."

His subcommittee's minority provided an eloquent response to Staggers' arguments as well as a challenge to the news media:

"Government is powerless either to render journalism responsible or to restore public confidence in it. Only the journalists have that power."

The committee report reached the House on July 13, 1971. It debated H.R. 534 which called for a contempt of Congress citation against the

Columbia Broadcasting System and its president, Dr. Frank Stanton. The resolution was defeated.

Selections from the debate are included in this chapter.

'THE SELLING OF THE PENTAGON':
PARTISAN INVOLVEMENTS AND ANTAGONISMS

By Jerome Barron

A CBS telecast almost precipitated a confrontation between government and the electronic media such as New York *Times* publication of the Pentagon Papers actually provoked for the print media. The two events were oddly similar. Both involved the Pentagon. The CBS television program, "The Selling of the Pentagon," attacked the public relations efforts of the Defense Department. The telecast of the program represented to conservative Congressmen and administration spokesmen an invidious attack on the nation's spirit as well as its will to be militarily strong. For proponents of the program it was a milestone in broadcast journalism, a courageous investigation of a tax-supported campaign to propagandize in favor of militarism and war.

A special investigative subcommittee of the House Committee on Interstate and Foreign Commerce, chaired by Congressmen Harley O. Staggers (D.-W.Va.), sought to subpoena all the tapes, films, outtakes and script material that had been prepared by CBS in the production of "The Selling of the Pentagon." The crucial issue was whether the outtakes, film shot for use in the program but not actually used, must be submitted to the Congress.

From the point of view of the House Committee, the capacity of television to propagandize a nation was something that was within the scope of both legislative control and legislative inquiry. It was a paradox that the Congressional inquiry into whether the networks had propagandized arose out of a CBS exposé of an alleged governmental effort to propagandize. In the view of CBS, the editing processes of television were obviously protected by the First Amendment. Surely the government would not be permitted to subpoena a newspaper editor's notes. How therefore could a governmental inquiry into film editing on television be justified?

On July 1, 1971, a majority of the House Committee on Interstate and Foreign Commerce voted to recommend that the House of Repre-

Reprinted from *Educational Broadcasting Review*, Special Issue (Winter 1971-72), by permission of the National Association of Educational Broadcasters.

sentatives cite CBS and Dr. Frank Stanton for contempt of Congress. But the full House decided to recommit the matter to Committee. The vote to recommit killed the citation for contempt. As a result, a case that might have resulted in a great judicial decision which would have identified the First Amendment responsibilities and obligations of government and broadcasting, respectively, was aborted.

Superficially, the aborted Staggers-Stanton controversy stands in sharp contrast to the Pentagon Papers case, the print media—government Armageddon. After all, publication of the *Pentagon Papers* case did in fact result in Supreme Court vindication of the press publication of the Pentagon Papers. But the theory for that vindication was hardly an endorsement of an absolutist conception of press power or freedom. The truth is that the frontiers of responsibility for government regulation of the media and media accountability to the larger society are really as ambiguous and unsettled with regard to the print media as they are in the broadcast media. . . .

The Report of the House Committee on Interstate and Foreign Commerce on the Stanton-Staggers controversy demonstrates that the Committee relied on familiar ground. The Committee argued that the Congressional right to investigate is only limited by the requirement that the investigation have a valid legislative purpose. Furthermore, the information or testimony sought must be relevant to legislative purpose. For its part, CBS asserted that the First Amendment guarantee of freedom of the press is a barrier to any government inquiry into the workings of the broadcast press. The Committee replied that the First Amendment does not protect calculated falsehood. It made no sense, according to the Committee, to assert the First Amendment as a defense to a subject the First Amendment does not protect.

The rub, of course, is that CBS contented that what it did was not calculated falsehood but honest film editing, the scrutiny of which would violate freedom of the press in its most fundamental sense. The House Committee replied that the broadcasters and the networks have long claimed to be the trustees for the public. A trustee, said the Committee, is by definition accountable to those he serves: The members of Congress are the elected representatives of those whom broadcasting serves.

A Committee of Congress was asking to be allowed to make the ultimate determination as to what material should come under its subpoena power, even when the material sought was in the possession of the broadcast press. Dr. Stanton, on the other hand, insisted that the ultimate judge of whether material sought by Congress should be divulged was, in the last analysis, a broadcaster decision. Why? *Times* man, Max Frankel, writing about the *Pentagon Papers* case, said the reason the final decision-maker must be the newspaper editor is because the First Amendment says so. Does the First Amendment say that? And if it does, does it say that for the broadcaster as well? . . . Because the crisis was averted and the House drew back from taking on the broadcast networks, judicial consideration of whether broadcast journalism has a First Amendment privilege to refuse to respond to the exercise of the Congressional subpoena power was not obtained. Should we regret that the collision did not occur? Would a collision have resulted in a clear decision? The constitutional status of the government's refusal to divulge papers in its possession and the press's power to publish them is muddier rather than clearer as a result of the *Pentagon Papers* case. In the *Pentagon Papers* case, there were nine separate opinions from the Court. There could hardly have been more. . . .

If a broadcast controversy raising the issues of the Stanton-Staggers controversy ever does reach the Supreme Court, the reaction of the Court is difficult to predict. . . .

Recent Supreme Court history . . . illustrates that broadcast journalism is unlikely to be accorded a greater latitude than the print media. Currently, a triad of cases, on the issue of newsman's privilege, the refusal of newspaper journalists to respond to a government subpoena, is before the Court. In these cases, newspapermen are contending that the First Amendment shields newsmen from having to reveal their sources. Whether the Supreme Court will hold that there is a First Amendment basis for newsman's privilege, and if there is such a privilege, whether it is absolute or qualified remains to be seen.*

An interesting phenomenon is that important sections of the newspaper press have not made the broad arguments for immunization from responsibility that broadcasters have made. In the *Pentagon Papers* case, counsel for the *New York Times*, Alexander Bickel, suggested that some prior restraints might be constitutional. The test advanced was whether the publication of a document would have a direct link to a grave event which was immediate and visible. In the *Caldwell* case, one of the newsman's privilege cases presently before the Supreme Court, the *New York Times* similarly declined to argue that an absolute First Amendment privilege protected newsman's sources. . . .

We are now in the midst of a struggle over the First Amendment theory to apply to broadcasting. There are at least three theories in conflict. There is the old theory, which from a larger perspective was always basically inadequate, that the inherent limitation of the spectrum was the justification for broadcast regulation. There is the classic view of laissez faire liberalism that government should have nothing to do with

---

* *Caldwell v. United States,* 434 F. 2d 1081 (9th Cir. 1970); cert. granted, *United States v. Caldwell,* 91 S. Ct. 1616 (1971). *In the Matter of Paul Pappas,* 266 N.E. 2d 297 (Mass. 1971); cert. granted, 91 S. Ct. 1619 (1971). *Branzburg v. Pound* 461 S.W. 2d 345 (Ky. 1970); cert. granted, *United States v. Caldwell,* 91 S. Ct. 1616 (1971). [The court's decisions on these cases are discussed in Chapter 10—Ed.]

the processes of communication. Finally, there is the new theory that the basic or paramount concern of an approach to the First Amendment should make the pivotal interest that of the reader, the listener, and the viewer.

Perhaps, it is still too early to guess which of these theories will dominate First Amendment interpretation. But one thing is clear: At least in broadcasting an absolutist approach to the rights of the broadcaster is dead. In the press it may still be possible to argue that protection for freedom of the press is exhausted in the property rights of the publisher. But in broadcasting the property involved does, after all, belong to the public. The public is under-represented in both access to television and in access to information about television's inner workings. Yet the dominant legal approach to free expression problems in broadcasting is now an access-oriented one.

Yet the movement for participation of the public in broadcasting is, as yet, little appreciated or understood. Typical of the usual response to controversies of the Staggers-Stanton type is that portrayed by Tom Wicker. Wicker's column in the *New York Times* entitled "CBS Stands Up" pictures CBS as a David facing a government Goliath. A more realistic appraisal would show a power struggle between two Goliaths, the broadcast networks and the government. In a column published the day before the House of Representatives voted on the contempt citation, Wicker speculated that Staggers had a good chance to secure success. Wicker wrote, "Legislators are reluctant to offend or oppose powerful leaders whose favors they may need later."

But Staggers lost, and the death struggle between two Goliaths did not transpire. Some of those who supported the contempt citation speculated that legislators feared others besides their leaders in Congress. They speculated that they feared the CBS affiliates around the country whose good will they wished to retain if their faces and views were to be given exposure on the local news in their home communities. . . .

In conclusion, what can be said by way of generalization which might be helpful in understanding these battles between powerful government and powerful media? Some observations of Mr. Justice Frankfurter provide, I think, a constructive conclusion.

In *Dennis v. United States* (341 U.S. 494-1951), Mr. Justice Frankfurter set himself to the task in a concurring opinion of identifying the values in conflict between a society's concern for both freedom of expression and national security. He warned against the unhelpfulness of "uncritical libertarian generalities." And yet, that has very largely been the journalistic and academic response to the great issues which the documents in these pages record.

To equate broadcast journalism with Tom Paine's printing press may be an appealing analogy at a broadcasters convention. As a basis for legal theory, it is an analogy which is particularly shallow. Justice Black, who made his name synonymous with an absolutist interpretation of the First Amendment, was not misled by such analogies. The *Red Lion* case, where the Supreme Court postulated an interpretation of broadcast journalism which was predicated on an access-oriented interpretation of the First Amendment, was an unanimous decision. Justice Black participated in that unanimity. He participated because the imposition of responsibilities on broadcasters did not, in his opinion, nor in the opinion of his colleagues, in any way transgress the spirit or letter of the First Amendment. The fairness doctrine, the personal attack rules and the politician editorializing rules were all designed to provide a structure for dialogue. What is also needed in the area of congressional oversight of broadcasting is a structure for accountability.

Any structure which lodges complete or ultimate power with either the broadcasters or the government is unsatisfactory. Others reading the pages that follow may vigorously disagree with this conclusion. Many will conclude that broadcasters should be trusted to have the last word on the production of television programs that reach millions because trusting the broadcaster in the last analysis has less risks than trusting anyone else. For me, the best arbiters of these questions are the judges who hopefully will be free from the partisan involvements and antagonisms of Congressmen and broadcasters.

THE FIRST AMENDMENT AND BROADCAST JOURNALISM: A DEBATE, 1971

Excerpts from the *Congressional Record*'s version of the debate over the Staggers' Subcommittee recommendation that the House of Representatives cite CBS and Dr. Frank Stanton for contempt of Congress

July 13, 1971

Mr. STAGGERS. Mr. Speaker, I would like to make my explanation of this very brief.

Mr. Speaker, to me the question is a very simple one. This subcommittee issued a subpena, a duly authorized subpena, and it was duly served. The question is whether it was complied with. However, as you have heard and read, it was not complied with. In view of the fact that it was not complied with, those who were cited in the subpena were in contempt of the Congress of the United States. That means all of this Congress, not just one person, one committee, but the whole Congress of the United States was defied when they said, "We will not deliver the materials that were requested."

So, that is the simple question today. I think that the vote ought to be right now as to whether they were in contempt. However, I do not think that would be fair to the House. I would like to present what brought it about.

There has been an awful lot of talk about the first amendment. I do not believe the first amendment is involved in this question in any way whatsoever.

This has been the principal issue of those on the other side, that this is an invasion of the first amendment.

Let me say to you that if it involved any man's thoughts, any man's notes or concepts, or anything that he had in his mind, I would say yes. But it does not. This involves only the actual shooting of scenes in public. Most of them, seen by more than the person; the cameraman and all the prop boys who were around. If anybody wanted to say that we were taking their notes, it would have to be the cameraman who took down the voices and the pictures, and not somebody who was asking the questions. But the cameraman, he is the man who actually did the work, acted in good faith. That is the reason I cannot see that the first amendment is involved.

So many say that we are trying to get the reporter's notes. There were no notes. They took a picture. They took the recordings. And they took 11 months to take this into some darkroom somewhere and to say, "All right, this man said something that we did not want him to say. So we are going to take an answer from another question over here, and make him say something he did not say." And he did not say it. We know this because we have the testimony, the sworn testimony, of the Assistant Secretary of Defense that he did not make them in this sequence; he did not say these things. We have the deposition of a colonel who said he did not make the statement that was attributed to him; that it was made by a foreign minister of another nation, Laos. And yet they present it and put it as his concept, as though he said it at a certain time.

Now, I think that America is done with this deception. We have had enough of it. And you women and gentlemen of this House of Representatives are the guardians of the public's interest. Every license that is given to any station says "for the public interest, convenience, and necessity." And it can be taken away from them at any time.

The airwaves have been held by law and by the courts to belong to all the people of this Nation. The Chief Justice whom we have now has been quoted extensively as saying that these are the people's airwaves, and that they ought to be interested in them, and when things are wrong that they ought to do something about them.

We represent the people of America. The gentleman from Michigan

(Mr. GERALD R. FORD), represents all of his people who cannot get to New York to complain. The gentleman from New York (Mr. OGDEN REID) does the same thing. He has an obligation to represent his people to the best of his ability, and to see that it is truth and not fabrication that is offered to the American people—and that goes for every other Representative in this House of Representatives. There are those who would like to say that we have all the information that we need. We do not have that information. We have the sworn testimony of one man. We do not have the outtakes of any portion of the program. There might be 20 or 30 or 40 different places where they misquoted or misplaced these things, we do not know.

The SPEAKER. The time of the gentleman from West Virginia has expired.

Mr. STAGGERS. Mr. Speaker, I yield myself 3 additional minutes.

Mr. Speaker, the situation is that we need these facts before we can legislate.

There are those who say we have enough, but we cannot legislate in a vacuum. No Member wants to legislate without knowing all the facts. I know the Members would not want to do so; no Member of this House would want to do so, and if he did do so he would be doing wrong if he did not have all the facts.

We want the facts. That is all we want. All we want them to do is supply us with the outtakes. They have refused to do so. When Dr. Stanton appeared before our committee and we asked him certain questions; he refused to answer those questions. If this House ever makes the decision that that is not in contempt of this Congress, then God save and help America.

This is a letter that was written to me that we talked of in the hearings:

> DEAR REPRESENTATIVE STAGGERS: Your subpena on data on the "Selling of the Pentagon" has stimulated CBS to do some selling on its own.

He includes a letter addressed to professors. This is a letter which was sent to us which we found was not supposed to be sent to us. It was sent out by CBS and addressed to a professor at a school in Texas. It states:

> Some of the demands contained in the subpoena served on CBS in connection with the "Selling of the Pentagon" I am sure you agree, are deeply disturbing.
> If you share our view that they are entirely improper, we would urge you to telegraph the Special Subcommittee on Investigations, House Interstate and Foreign Commerce Committee, deploring the subpoena and asking its withdrawal.

This is the letter that was sent out. We do not know how many were sent out.

I asked Dr. Stanton when he was before our committee and I said— a thousand—2 thousand—how many?"

He did not answer—and I do not know—he said he would supply them for the RECORD.

This went to journalism schools and to universities in America and to the broadcasting stations.

Let me tell you how many came to us from these different sources.

We got nine from press organizations deploring it, and using the same words used in this letter. Ten came from journalism schools.

Sixteen from individuals associated with the universities.

Twenty-three came from broadcasting stations and associations.

Sending out thousands of these across America—this in fact was it. Everyone of them who replied used the paragraphs that were sent out. I say they were wrong, completely, in sending this out.

When we first wrote the subpena served on Dr. Stanton, he wrote me a letter expressing the hope that it would be modified so as to call for only such materials as were actually broadcast and information directly related to that.

I want you to understand this: And all other material directly related thereto. He said that he wanted us to change it.

Our subcommittee had the rest of the information that we needed by that time, and we changed it to do that: The subpena called for only those outtakes related to the broadcast.

He came before our committee again and refused to do what he said in the letter that he would do.

Mr. CELLER [D.-N.Y.]. Mr. Speaker and Members of the House, I counter my fellow chairman, the affable gentleman from West Virgina, and that counter leaves an ashen taste in my mouth. But there are overriding considerations in my opposition, reluctant as I am to utter them.

The first amendment towers over these proceedings like a colossus and no esprit de corps and no tenderness of one Member for another should force us to topple over this monument to our liberties; that is, the first amendment.

Does the first amendment apply to broadcasting and broadcasting journalism?

The answer is, "Yes."

In the case of American Broadcasting Co. against United States, 110 Federal Supplement 374 (1953) the court said:

> * * * no rational distinction can be made between radio and television on the one hand and the press on the other in affording the Constitutional protection contemplated by the First Amendment. (Affirmed by the United States Supreme Court in 1954.)

See also Rosenbloom against Metromedia which was a decision of
the Supreme Court passed down only last month.

Does the administration say that the first amendment applies equally
to the press as well as to broadcasting? The answer is, "Yes." See the
address of Attorney General Mitchell before the American Bar Association on August 10, 1970.

President Nixon at a San Clemente press conference recently said
that he did not support the subpena. He said:

—as far as bringing any pressure on the networks, as a Government
is concerned, I do not support that.

Are the notes, unused memoranda, unused film and written interviews of a press reporter immune from governmental scrutiny? The answer
is, "Yes."

It was so held in the Caldwell case decided in the Court of Appeals
for the Ninth Circuit, 434 Fed. 2d, at page 1081 (1970). The case is
now pending in the Supreme Court. In that case the Court of Appeals
said that—

It is not unreasonable to expect journalists everywhere to temper
their reporting so as to reduce the probability that they will be required to submit to interrogation. The First Amendment guards
against governmental action that induces such self-censorship.

The court protected the source material—namely, interviews with
Black Panthers—from grand jury scrutiny.

Are the clips, outtakes, and other source materials of the broadcaster
also impervious to governmental subpena? The answer is, "Yes."

There may be no distinction between the right of a press reporter and
a broadcaster. Otherwise, the stream of news may be dried up. Those who
offer the TV reporter information might refuse cooperation if their names
were divulged. I cite the recent case of New York against Dillon, decided
June 23, 1971, New York Supreme Court, on a motion to quash a subpena for outtakes.

Do I share the grave and well-motivated concern of the Committee
on Interstate and Foreign Commerce with the real danger of deceptive
practices and abuse of the media in the exercise of their rights? Yes, but
these are hardly new concerns. James Madison addressed himself to these
evils of the press. He said:

Some degree of abuse is inseparable from the proper use of every
thing; and in no instance is this more true than in that of the press.

The press and TV often are guilty of misrepresentation and error.
Some of this is inevitable in free debate. But "the media, even if guilty
of misrepresentation, must be protected if freedom of expression are to

have the breathing space that they need to survive." See New York Times against Sullivan.

The importance of the issue before us warrants amplification of the questions I have raised and the applicable law:

Question: Does the First Amendment apply to broadcasting and broadcast journalism?

Answer: As reflected in the following cases, it is clear that the First Amendment applies to broadcasting and broadcast journalism just as it does to the written press.

1. "Broadcasting and television are entitled to the protection of the First Amendment of the Constitution, guaranteeing freedom of speech and of the press."

American Broadcasting Company v. *U.S.*, 110 F. Supp. 374 (1953), affirmed 347 U.S. 284 (1954), a case rejecting an FCC interpretation of a criminal statute concerning broadcast lotteries.

2. "Preliminarily, we note that the fact that the news medium here is a radio station rather than a newspaper does not make the First Amendment discussion, in particular with regard to freedom of the press, any less germane. Radio and television were, of course, unknown media when freedom of the press was written into the Bill of Rights, but no rational distinction can be made between radio and television on the one hand and the press on the other in affording the constitutional protection contemplated by the First Amendment."

Rosenbloom v. *Metromedia, Inc.*, 415 F. 2d 892 (1969), affirmed June 7 by the United States Supreme Court, 39 U.S. Law Week 4694, a case extending standard of actual malice in libel actions to cover issues of public importance as well as public officials and public figures.

3. "Each method [of expression; e.g. books, movies, etc.] tends to present its own peculiar problems. But the basic principles of freedom of speech and the press, like the First Amendment's command, do not vary."

Joseph Burstyn, Inc. v. *Wilson*, 343 U.S. 495 (1952), a case extending First Amendment protection to motion pictures and voiding a New York State law that required movies to be licensed by a censor.

4. "The First Amendment draws no distinctions between the various methods of communicating ideas."

Superior Films v. *Department of Education*, 346 U.S. 587 (1954); Douglas, J. concurring in a *per curiam* opinion.

Question: Are there serious dangers inherent in interfering with the media in the exercise of its functions?

Answer: Definitely. Interference with the media has a chilling effect on free speech which militates against the public interest.

1. [We must consider this case against] "the background of a profound national commitment to the principle that debate on public issues should be uninhibited, robust and wide-open and that it may well include vehement, caustic, and sometimes unpleasantly sharp attacks on government and public officials."

"Whether or not a newspaper can survive a succession of such judgments [awarding recovery for libel of public officials] the pall of fear and timidity imposed upon those who would give voice to public criticism is an atmosphere in which First Amendment freedoms cannot survive."

New York Times v. Sullivan, 376 U.S. 254 (1964), a case denying recovery for libel of a public official in the absence of actual malice, reckless disregard of the truth.

2. "The First Amendment exists to preserve an 'untrammeled' press as a vital source of public information."

Grosjean v. American Press Co., 297 U.S. 233.

3. "The very concept of a free press requires that the news media be accorded a measure of autonomy; that they should be free to pursue their own investigations to their own ends without fear of government interference."

"[I]t is not unreasonable to expect journalists everywhere to temper their reporting so as to reduce the possibility that they will be required to submit to interrogation. The First Amendment guards against governmental action that induces such self-censorship."

Caldwell v. U.S., 434 F. 2d 1081 (1970), a case quashing a subpoena by a Grand Jury summoning a N.Y. Times reporter to testify regarding his interviews with Black Panthers. (To be argued next term in the United States Supreme Court.)

4. First Amendment freedoms need "breathing space" to survive. NAACP v. Button, 371 U.S. 415 (1963).

Question: Even if legally supportable, should the House force this constitutional confrontation?
Answer: It should not.

1. [The First Amendment] "is much more than an order to Congress not to cross the boundary which marks the extreme limits of lawful suppression. It is also an exhortation and a guide for the action of Congress inside that boundary. It is a declaration of national policy in favor of public discussion of all public questions. Such a declaration should make Congress reluctant and careful in the enactment of all restrictions upon utterance, even though the courts will not refuse to enforce them as unconstitutional."

Zachariah Chafee, "Free Speech in the U.S.", 1941.

2. "Some degree of abuse is inseparable from the proper use of every thing; and in no instance is this more true than in that of the press."—James Madison. 4 Elliot's Debates on the Federal Constitution, p. 571.

3. "Authoritative interpretations of the First Amendment guarantees have consistently refused to recognize an exception for any test of truth—whether administered by judges, juries or administrative officials—and especially one that puts the burden of proving truth upon the speaker." New York Times v. Sullivan, above.

4. In opening the Special Subcommittee meeting of June 24, the Chairman of the House Interstate and Foreign Commerce Committee stated the Subcommittee already had in its possession sworn testimony

and other evidence indicating CBS engaged in questionable manipulative techniques in producing "The Selling of the Pentagon".

5. Additional materials that may be required are obtainable from sources other than the broadcast journalists themselves; e.g. from persons interviewed and electronic specialists.

Question: Are broadcasters' "outtakes" equivalent to the written notes of newspaper reporters?

Answer: Yes. They are part of the inherently judgmental process through which the broadcast journalist gathers and organizes his materials.

Question: Have these "outtakes" been afforded judicial protection?

Answer: Yes, on the basis of both state statutes expressly protecting them and on First Amendment grounds.

Section 79h of the New York Civil Rights Law (1970) "specifically protects a broadcast journalist from contempt citations for refusing or failing to disclose any news or the source of any such news coming into his possession in the course of gathering or obtaining news . . . for broadcast by a radio or television transmission station or network, by which he is professionally employed, or otherwise associated in a news gathering capacity".

In *New York* v. *Dillon*, on June 23, 1971, the New York Supreme Court quashed a subpena commanding CBS to provide the court with outtakes pertaining to a documentary on drug usage.

Section 1070 of the California Evidence Code similarly precludes use of compulsory court process to compel production of outtakes.

An order of the Superior Court in California, on 7/20/70, quashed on First Amendment as well as the statutory grounds a subpoena calling for "outs" of Westinghouse Broadcasting.

We must keep in mind that in this instance CBS has afforded the Vice President, the Secretary of Defense, and the Chairman of the Armed Services Committee an opportunity to criticize on the air the documentary in question.

That this is not a party matter is quite clear. The White House Communications Director has been quoted as saying the subpena "is wrong and an infringement on freedom of the press." The Republican United States Senate Policy Committee, in December of 1969, took the position that

> Whether news is fair or unfair, objective or biased, accurate or careless, is left to the consciences of the commentators, producers and network officials themselves. Government does not and cannot play any role in its presentation.

In his May 1 news conference in California, the President stated his agreement with the above policy statement and, when questioned specifically with respect to the CBS controversy, said:

As far as the subpoenaing of notes is concerned, of reporters, as far as bringing any pressure on the networks, as a government is concerned, I do not support that.

In summary, I am convinced that as a matter of law if the Congress votes this contempt citation and the matter is brought to the courts by the Department of Justice, the position of the House will not be sustained. Further, as a matter of policy, I believe we are embarking on a dangerous path and, what is more, we are doing it without any evidence of compelling need. There is no need to attempt to impose this legal question on the courts since all of the information necessary for the Committee's legislative purpose is either presently in its possession or available through other sources.

I urge the House to reject the pending resolution. . . .

Mr. EDWARDS [R.-Ala.]. Mr. Speaker, CBS apparently used extremely poor judgment in its production of "The Selling of the Pentagon." For that, we as individuals, can condemn them and we should. We can hope the American people will join in that condemnation. That is their right. We can insist that CBS give fairer treatment in its coverage of the important issues facing this Nation. Many of us have been doing that for some time. In fact, I am one of their most vocal critics.

But however strongly we feel about CBS or NBC or ABC or any of the newspapers or other media, we must not trespass as a legislative body, as a branch of the Federal Government, on their constitutional right to use their own editorial judgment.

If a newspaper reporter interviews me, there is no assurance that he will write every word I say. And while I may not like the way he handles his story, surely I would not suggest that the Congress has a right to inject its judgment in place of the reporter's or that Congress has a right to review his notes to see what he left out of his story. I suggest the same is true of the broadcast media.

It would be ever so easy to vote "yes" today. CBS has maligned the South, colored the news, handled the coverage of the war in a biased manner, played up the bad and played down the good—all of this and more. But I would not exchange all this, as bad as it may be, for the evil that would infect this Nation from a controlled press. Oh, there are times when I get so exasperated with them I would like to ban all TV, but that exasperation is nothing compared to what it would be if we had a press that had to answer for its editorial judgment, however bad, to a committee of the Congress.

I have great respect for the Committee on Interstate and Foreign Commerce and its chairman. The Washington Post suggested this morning that the very able chairman had his reputation on the line on this issue.

I doubt that. But more importantly, the Congress has got its reputation on the line, and we must not let emotion, or anger with the news media, or concern for the reputation of a Member cause us to make a grave constitutional blunder.

Mr. Speaker, the chairman and a majority of the committee are, in my humble judgment, dead wrong. Sure they are offended by the fact that Dr. Stanton ignored their subpena in part. But if I were in Dr. Stanton's position, I would ignore the committee, too, because the subpena goes too far and flies in the face of the constitutional protection of a free press. In any case, what the committee is asking the House to do is to make extremely bad law. In my opinion, the courts of this land will not hesitate to throw out the contempt citation as violation of the first amendment right of freedom of the press.

I would not run CBS as Dr. Stanton does, not by a long shot. But Mr. Speaker, that is not the issue here today. You know, Dr. Stanton's problem is that he is right this time, but he has cried wolf so long that nobody believes him, or wants to believe him.

When Vice President AGNEW and others have taken the press to task, Stanton has cried like a stuck pig. He and his counterparts in the media world have cited "Government censorship." He does not understand that we have as much right and duty to criticize the press as it has to criticize us. And so, he has cried wolf too often. And frankly, I would sort of like to stick it to him now. But my friends, we overstep our bounds, and exceed our prerogatives, and offend the Constitution, when we attempt by subpena to go behind a news story or television broadcast.

If a reporter does me wrong, I can refuse further interviews, or publicly condemn him and his paper or television station. If he does my country wrong, or one of its institutions, I have a right to set the record straight, to call his errors to the attention of the people. But I do not have the right to have the legislative branch call his editorial judgment into question. That is where I believe the Constitution draws the line on interference with freedom of the press.

And so, whether we like Stanton or not, whether he has cried wolf too often or not, whether we like CBS or not, whether we approve of "The Selling of the Pentagon" or not, the Congress of the United States has no right to hold Dr. Stanton and CBS in contempt. It can be no other way, else we will have taken the first big step down the road toward Government control of the press. If that day ever comes, then this Republic as we know it shall not long endure. . . .

Mr. O'HARA [D.-Mich.]. Mr. Speaker, CBS certainly can broadcast news and opinions as it sees fit, but I do not believe that it can deny the U.S. Congress its right to inquire into the techniques employed or to examine the television tape recordings used in the broadcast. That is all that has been asked for—not the reporter's private notes, but television tape recordings.

But in any event, Mr. Speaker, the resolution before us does not try to decide the constitutional question. All the resolution does is to refer a prima facie case of contempt to the U.S. attorney for appropriate action— and that is the only way that a judicial determination of the constitutional question can be obtained.

Mr. Speaker, the right of the Congress to obtain information for use in discharging its legislative duties ought not to be abandoned lightly on the basis of self-serving claims of an embarrassed TV executive without even seeking a judicial determination. I hope for that reason the resolution will be agreed to. . . .

Mr. BADILLO [D.-N.Y.] . . . Even if we were to grant the legitimacy of the subcommittee's effort to obtain the outtakes for "The Selling of the Pentagon," I would still oppose the issuance of a contempt citation because such action poses dangers to basic American freedoms. If we approve this motion we shall be establishing a precedent that may lead us into greater and greater control and supervision of news broadcasts and documentaries. Any degree of control or supervision makes a mockery of our constitutional guarantee of freedom of the press, and of the public's right to know.

Mr. Speaker, I believe we are caught up in a wave of anxiety over the content of the print and broadcast media. The motion we are debating today is the product of the assumption that the CBS network and, by extension, all news gathering agencies, are engaged in the intentional deception of the public. I think it is far more likely that a different assumption is the more correct one from which to begin any discussion— that the media are presenting an accurate and truthful picture of American society today. . . .

Mr. CONTE [R.-Mass.]. Mr. Speaker, I rise in opposition to the pending resolution to cite the Columbia Broadcasting System and its president for contempt.

I am sure that most, if not all, of the Members have done a great deal of soul-searching on this issue. We have all received a great volume of mail, legal briefs, and arguments concerning this matter. We have listened to our colleagues cogently advocate their positions.

I personally feel that the subpena in question is legally objectionable. I set forth my reasons in a letter to the esteemed chairman of the Interstate and Foreign Commerce Committee on May 6, 1971. Those reasons have been reiterated here in various forms by those who join me in this opposition, so I will not repeat them.

We can argue as to how the Supreme Court would rule on this question for days and weeks. But I believe we can and should decide this question ourselves—and we should decide it in favor of the network and its president.

This is our affair and it should be decided by us as elected representatives of the people, not necessarily in an assumed role as a Supreme Court justice.

I think we can all agree that the freedom of the press, including the broadcasting media, must be maintained. I believe we can also agree that approval of the contempt citation in this case would result in an encroachment on this freedom. Whether we label it a "fettering," a "chilling effect," or "censorship," we all must agree that an endorsement of the subpena, especially an endorsement through punitive sanction, will result in a restraint that otherwise would not exist.

We would also agree that Congress has legitimate investigative powers, including the power to subpena. But Congress should use these powers only when needed, and with discretion.

Even if we were all in agreement that the subpena in question would survive the test of a Supreme Court decision, we should not let the matter rest there. We should discipline ourselves. We should not be content to look at the decisions of the Supreme Court and work within the broadest possible limits of those decisions. Our concern with freedom of the press should be as great or greater than that of the judicial branch. We can and should do more to protect the freedom of the press because we are not bound, in affording such protection, by the legal niceties of constitutional law.

We have the obligation to decide, using our own judgment, whether the subpena and subsequent citation were appropriate in this case. In the recognized light of the fact that they will result in an undesirable restraint, we should find them appropriate only if we find them necessary. We should find them necessary only if we find that they would serve some legitimate purpose. . . .

Mr. PELLY [R.-Wash.]. Mr. Speaker, the evidence brought forward by the House Committee on Interstate and Foreign Commerce certainly indicates that the practices used by the Columbia Broadcasting System in the production of "The Selling of the Pentagon," were deceptive at best. Defrauding the American people through dishonest film editing practices is reprehensible.

But, it does not seem to me that delivering these "outtakes" will make any difference to the committee. This raw material does not seem to me to be necessary to determine if the network deliberately distorted the facts. CBS president Frank Stanton now admits that editing policies have been changed.

Yet, the charges by the committee are well taken. We can look back to other CBS endeavors, such as "Hunger in America" which was proved to be, in part, staged.

Much as I deplore what I consider to be a lapse of editorial responsibility by CBS, it does not seem to me that it is necessary to bring about charges of contempt. CBS has shown the American people its practices, and the committee has well publicized CBS' lack of credibility.

It brings to my mind, Mr. Speaker, the advice given some time back by Vice President Spiro Agnew, when he warned the TV industry that it should discipline itself. Maybe now they will take that advice without the Congress having to bring about that discipline itself.

In a way I would like the question of the first amendment to go to the Supreme Court. However, Mr. Speaker, I do not feel it is proper in this case to cite Mr. Stanton for contempt. I shall vote to recommit the bill to committee, or I will vote no, whichever is the case. . . .

Mr. GUDE [R.-Md.]. Mr. Speaker, I rise in opposition to the resolution of the House Interstate and Foreign Commerce Committee to cite CBS and its president, Dr. Frank Stanton, for contempt for failing to comply with a subpena issued by the Subcommittee on Investigations.

The issue at stake in this vote is not whether Congress approves of the CBS documentary "The Selling of the Pentagon," or even whether Congress condones the editing techniques employed by CBS in the production of this program. Instead, what we are being asked to decide is whether Congress should sit in judgment on a network's decisions in this area.

I feel strongly that this contempt citation, if approved by the House would have a chilling effect on the freedom of the press, and would substantially discourage the presentation of controversial, and unpopular points of view by the news media.

The Federal Communications Commission studied the issues surrounding this controversy and concluded that the CBS editing decisions were a matter of journalistic judgment into which governmental inquiry would not be proper. The FCC also concluded that CBS has provided significant opportunities for contrasting viewpoints to be heard, and, therefore, complied with the fairness doctrine.

Mr. Speaker, I have only the highest regard for the distinguished Chairman of the Committee on Interstate and Foreign Commerce, and I understand his concern over this matter. I feel a personal obligation to preserve the integrity and scope of the first amendment's guarantee of press freedom. This obligation transcends any present concern I might feel over the alleged indiscretions of the CBS officials, and I, therefore, urge that the resolution be defeated. . . .

Mr. BROWN [R.-Ohio]. Mr. Speaker, the protection of the press springs from the right of the individual citizen to speak his views even though he may be the only one to hold those views. His version of the truth is sacred to him and his right to hold those views should be sacred to the government of a free society—even though the majority may hold that truth is the opposite of those views.

The pursuit of truth is the historic search of mankind and, according to the Judeo-Christian culture, will make man free. But it follows that the search for truth is much easier in an environment of freedom because freedom permits the multiplicity of views where all shades of truth can be found.

It is this search for truth through multiplicity of voices which has been at base of several Federal laws throughout our Nation's history. Second class postal rates to encourage newspapers and legislation to require UHF tuning capacity to expand the range of use of the broadcast spectrum by television are but two examples. The concept of a free press finding the truth works best where there are many presses in the hands of many different people of divergent view.

We should face frankly what is the greatest danger in the freedom of the networks to broadcast their version of the news—and that is that the three major networks night after night command an audience of most of our population to the same view of truth as they see. But the question remains as to whether even that concentration of power over the dissemination of a version of truth should be subjected to a single power; namely the power of government. Three voices seeking truth may be a thousand times worse than three thousand; but one voice determining truth is infinitely worse than three.

In an effort to make this power of concentrated ownership available to more viewpoints—rather than limit its use or judge its discernment of truth—the "fairness doctrine" has been enunciated by the Federal Communications Commission and the "equal time" provision in political campaigns has been written into the basic communications law of our land. But to an extent both such requirements are artificial efforts to further proliferate those viewpoints and therefore, they are not as effective as if they were the result of the harsh reality of economic competition or technological capability.

The potential for further proliferation of voices exists in the technology of cable television and satellites which will further expand the choices of methods by which viewpoints are transmitted. In considering the concentration of audience of the present broadcast networks, the Congress would be much better advised to consider how it can hasten the day when there are more methods of transmission of views and more individual ownership of those methods. This is a much sounder and altogether more constitutional approach in line with our tradition of freedom and private enterprise than any steps to regulate the networks in the quality of truth they choose to disseminate.

The networks may, indeed, be at the height of their power today in influencing Americans and persuading them to the positions held by a small group of executives in a narrow geographical and philosophical fringe of our Nation. But the power of that challenge to our national diversity should not be responded to with an exercise of power by this House which would deny this or any other minority of its right to exercise its biased views simply because of what those views are.

I shall vote against the citation for contempt or to refer this issue back to the committee on Interstate and Foreign Commerce in the firm belief that my committee can serve truth and the freedom of speech better by attempting to proliferate the voices which seek truth in our land than by trying to identify truth by some official Government agency and then limit the voices that do exist to the espousal of that government inspected version of truth. . . .

Mr. WHALEN [R.-Ohio]. Mr. Speaker, the indispensibility of first amendment guarantees of free speech and a free press is unquestioned in our society. The Supreme Court has consistently declared that the first amendment is to be given broad and sweeping coverage. And the rationale most frequently cited by the Court for a broad interpretation of first amendment freedoms is that the investigation and criticism of governmental bodies is a requisite for a free and democratic society. The Court has stated:

> The free press has been a mighty catalyst in awakening public interest in governmental affairs, exposing corruption among public officers and employees, and generally informing the citizenry of public events and occurrences . . .

Although the first amendment literally reads "Congress shall make no law," the Court has broadened its interpretation of the amendment to mean that no agency of Government, or court, shall abridge the freedom of speech and the press. The Court has ruled that commercial gain is irrelevant in determining the scope of first amendment freedoms. In 1967, the Court ruled:

> Books, newspapers, and magazines are published and sold for profit does not prevent them from being a form of expression whose liberty is safeguarded by the first amendment.

Certainly, therefore, there is no justification for denying first amendment freedoms to television newscasters.

As the New York Times has editorially observed, if the press is to fulfill the role of independence guaranteed by the first amendment "the line of separation between it and the Government must be kept unmistakable. That line is jeopardized by the subpenas various news magazines, television networks, and newspapers" have received from Federal authorities for "notes, files, film, and other material."

Today, the House is being asked to take an unprecedented step across that "line of separation" by citing CBS for contempt for refusing to turn over unused outtakes from the television documentary, "The Selling of the Pentagon."

The program itself was courageous journalism, informing the public of questionable uses of the military's public information budget. As the Supreme Court has emphasized, that type of newscasting—scrutiny of public bodies—can only be welcomed in a free society.

Some have argued, however, that the program was flawed by distortions and inaccuracies. Certainly no one would contend that the press is—or could be—perfect. But as Life magazine pointed out—

> People who criticize the CBS documentary are having plenty of
> chance to be heard, which is one way to get distortions righted.

Another recourse is for those individuals who claim to have been quoted out of context to seek redress in the courts.

Regardless of the merits or defects of the program, what constructive purpose can be served by congressional interference in the news judgments of CBS?

Newsmen in the print and electronic media must daily make thousands of news judgments, including only a minute portion of all the material they receive in the "finished product." Newsmen will make mistakes, of course. But, as the Boston Globe has noted—

> Freedom of the press includes the freedom to make those mis-
> takes, and as long as the press is truly free and competitive, there is
> a built-up assurance that mistakes will be corrected.

The alternative to a free and independent news media, and the disadvantages that inevitably accompany it, is far more ominous than any newsman's error. Government control over news judgments in the preparation of the news would render first amendment freedoms impotent.

Those who seek to subpena unused materials claim that there is something less than abridgment of the first amendment involved in such an act. But history has indicated that each encroachment on the freedom of the press leads to further erosion of first amendment freedoms.

First, the "chilling effect" of the subpena issued by the Congress has probably manifested itself already. Broadcast journalism has never been vigorous in its scrutiny of Government. As CBS News President Richard Salant said, a common tendency for some in the broadcast industry is to say, "Let's skip this one, let's not make waves, let's stay out of trouble." That tendency has undoubtedly been reinforced by the Government's intervention into the creation of one of the few TV programs that has examined Government with a critical eye.

Second, the Government is attempting to exercise unwarranted authority in demanding unused materials from a news agency. It is the equivalent of asking a reporter to produce all the notes he took in gathering information for a particular story. If this action is sanctioned, journalists will be put on notice that their unused thoughts, notes, files, and film can be examined on demand by the Government. At least one consequence is clear: Free, independent journalism will be stifled by the Government.

Third, assuming that CBS did make errors in the disputed program, and that all CBS materials were seized by the Government, what legislation can emerge other than proposals for some type of Government interference in the journalist's preparation of the news? Would Government seek to control the content of news programs and documentaries before they are broadcast? Or would the Government threaten to intervene after a program has been broadcast, searching through files and notes with some intent to prosecute if the Government's "interests" are believed to be at stake? It appears obvious that any legislation intended to police the Nation's news agencies would at best amount to harassment; at worst, to censorship.

President Nixon recognized the necessity for the untrammeled flow of news when he spoke out against the Government bringing any pressure on the networks. The Chairman of the Federal Communications Commission, Dean Burch, has noted the similarity between a reporter's notes and broadcast outtakes, and has voiced his opposition to Government subpenas. FCC Commissioner Nicholas Johnson has argued that the Nation's news media have an "absolute right" to refuse the demands of Government prosecutors for reporters' notes and unused television film.

Perhaps former FCC Chairman Newton Minow put it best, however. In recommending that the media refuse to honor Government subpenas of news film, he said that the media's reply to such requests should be: "Judge me on what we broadcast; the rest is none of the Government's business."

Mr. HOLIFIELD [D.-Calif.]. Mr. Speaker, I rise in support of the position of the gentleman from West Virginia (Mr. STAGGERS).

My review of this matter convinces me that the action recommended to this House by the Committee on Interstate and Foreign Commerce best serves the purposes of the first amendment.

We are not dealing here with a case of prior restraint of the press. For it appears that the press may publish anything it desires, whether the material is stolen or honestly gathered; whether it is true or false; or whether it is libelous or slanderous. I cite the case of Rosenbloom against Metro-Media, Inc.

Neither are we dealing with the confidentiality of news sources about which the law appears to be well settled.

What is involved here is the right of the people to know—and to know the truth, with particular reference to a federally licensed TV channel monopoly.

As Mr. Justice Black pointed out in his recent opinion in the New York Times case, the first amendment belongs to the people. It is not the property of those who publish for profit nor is it the property of the Federal Government.

The enlightenment of people on the great issues of our time cannot be achieved by a media which warps and distorts facts, and which cannot be called to question in any forum.

It is the people's right under the first amendment to know when the "news" or other events, presented to them by a Government-licensed monopoly, are biased.

Mr. Speaker, I have had two unfortunate personal experiences involving what appears to be television network bias within the past 10 months.

The first involved a documentary for the CBS Morning Report prepared by Mr. Joseph Benti. Before giving Mr. Benti over an hour of interview time, I was assured that his program on "The Dangers of Radiation" would be balanced.

To my amazement, when the program was aired during the week of August 10 to 14, 1970, I found that only 2½ minutes of my filmed answers were used in the so-called 1-hour documentary. The balance of the hour was used for arguments against my position.

On the other hand, the producers of this film took great pains to comb the countryside for persons to interview on the other side of the issue. Most of this material was purely conjecture and all of it misrepresentative of the consensus of responsible scientific opinion. The entire program was generously laced with the biased editorial comment of the interviewer.

Ironically, CBS, in order to prove its own preconceived notions that the Atomic Energy Commission has misrepresented the facts, resorted to considerable "fact-twisting" of its own. . . .

The other instance, Mr. Speaker, also involved the position of nuclear power in the existing energy crisis. In this instance, I gave a 1 hour interview of my time to NBC for use on a program entitled "The Powers That Be," which was shown on May 18, 1971. Five and one-half minutes of my statement was used and approximately 50 minutes was used by the movie star commentator and other persons to present comment and arguments which were critical of my position. I do not consider 50 minutes' time on a 1 hour program to criticize a 5½-minute statement of a controversial matter a fair division of time.

On this program, a well-known comedian was the narrator; music with overtones of genocide was added; and all questions asked of me were omitted. Once again, the commentator inserted biased editorial matter, and the majority of the interviewees were scientists whose theories have been thoroughly discredited. The theme, again, was that our Federal Government is guilty of misleading the public. The so-called documentary film ended with a music background of the old religious song "Nearer My God to Thee."

Mr. Speaker, these two cases have been sufficient to convince me that I should not grant future pretaped interviews on any important national problem to the television media. I would have no objection to a formula of fair debate on a live program where time would be divided equally between proponents and opponents of a given issue.

Mr. Speaker, I contend that our failure to support the Committee on Interstate and Foreign Commerce today will have its own "chilling effects." This phrase is frequently used by Mr. Stanton of CBS in his defensive arguments.

Continued irresponsible use of the powerful broadcast monopoly to interpret great issues only in accordance with its own particular bias "chills" the right of the public to hear and see the truth.

Further, an unaccountable broadcast industry will have a "chilling" effect upon the willingness of public servants to speak out on important issues.

Perhaps the greatest "chilling" effect of all, Mr. Speaker, would be upon the ability of this House to make the laws under the mandate of article I of the constitution.

If this House, through its committees, is unable to compel evidence upon which to base its legislation, where will we look for guidance? How can we assure that the public interest is being served by a federally licensed monopoly?

In summary, Mr. Speaker, these are the reasons why I will vote in favor of the resolution which is before us:

The first amendment did not create a select group of persons who are immune from all accountability, as some would have us believe. The amendment simply established the right of the people of an unrestrained press.

The press is accountable to the people and to the people's representatives who must make the laws. The people have a right to know when they are reading, hearing, or seeing a biased account of events based upon the political or philosophical views of some editor, producer, or reporter.

It is also very interesting to note that a TV corporation protects its media position by requiring an interviewee to sign a legal form which protects the TV corporation from any type of legal liability which might arise from an interviewee's remarks. At the same time they sign no legal form protecting the interviewee from misrepresenting his remarks or subordinating his position by massive use of time in relation to the time allowed to the interviewee's arguments.

If the "chilling" effect of a contempt citation results in a greater degree of truth in broadcasting, the purposes of the first amendment will be served in the highest degree possible. . . .

Mr. DENT [D.-Pa.]. . . . Talking about experiences, during the fight in this House on reciprocal trade, I spent 2 days in a glass factory, doing everything, gathering the glass and cutting it and everything. I attended a meeting of the whole organization, and I spoke to them. I spent about 2 days before the cameras. Later at home I got all my friends and neighbors in. I spent a little money to see my starring performance, and I put together a buffet and refreshments.

I made a little mistake. I started to light a cigar, and before the match went out I was off the air. Before the documentary was over, if the people did not see any more of me than what I had seen of myself, I am sure they did not know who was being starred because they certainly used the rest of that time to tear my position apart.

The thing you must understand is always to listen to radio and view television with a sense of humor; just remember, they do not mean half the things they say. . . .

Mr. PICKLE [D.-Tex.]. Mr. Speaker, we need not be here today. It is a tragedy when two great institutions—the Government and the press—get deadlocked.

We need not be here and we would not be here had CBS lived up to its own past history of cooperation. In the past, the network has given up outtakes, as requested. This time, they refuse. This time they refuse to even answer the only question the committee asks. Did the network mismatch questions and answers in a filmed interview to make the subject appear to be saying something he did not.

Mr. Speaker, the public has a right to know whether CBS willfully transposed questions and answers. We are not concerned with the content of the program. We are not concerned with censorship. We are not concerned with Government standards of truth. We are not concerned with bias.

We are concerned with discovering whether there is adequate legislation designed to protect the public.

There is no newspaper which compares to the networks—there is no national newspaper in the United States.

There are three networks which are all powerful in reaching the length and breadth of America. These networks are using a public commodity—there are only so many airwaves available. These airwaves belong to the people. The courts have said this many times. These people have a right to protection from deceitful practices. Perhaps legislation is the only answer.

Mr. Speaker, the first amendment—the free speech amendment—

cuts both ways. I believe nothing should be done to curtail the first amendment protections for the press. Further, I believe nothing should be done by the press—particularly the networks—to curtail the rights of a man being interviewed to access to free speech. By jumbling questions and answers, the networks abridge an individual's right to free speech. Certainly, the public needs protection from this abuse.

This is an extremely tough decision before the Congress today. It will take courage. It will take courage because our decision today will have far-reaching, long-range effects on the rights of the public.

Therefore, Mr. Speaker, I think certain observations must be set forth in a logical fashion:

First. It is strange that no one—not the broadcast industry and not any Member of Congress—has defended this act of mismatching questions and answers. Apparently, everyone admits that what CBS has allegedly done was wrong.

Second. In effect, CBS admits what they did was wrong. On the very day before the subcommittee was to consider the contempt resolution, CBS issued a new set of operation guidelines governing interviews. In effect, CBS was saying "We're not guilty—and we promise not to do it again."

Many times CBS has come forth with new rules to police themselves, which is good. I believe I can remember the network issued similar rulings shortly after the rigged quiz show scandals in 1959.

Third. If CBS did commit a wrong-doing by mismatching questions and answers, what recourse, what protection does the public have from these practices? That precisely is what the committee is asking: Is new legislation needed?

Fourth. On previous occasions, our committee has supenaed outtakes when there was strong evidence that deceptive practices were committed. Today, some of the strongest proponents supporting CBS—proponents from my side of the aisle—are the same people who previously voted with the committee to acquire the outtakes on other cases.

Admittedly, personal opinion comes into play on each instance. In the past, I have voted against my own committee in refusing to demand outtakes when I thought it was a fishing expedition. What falls on the cutting room floor should remain there—unless there is strong, clear evidence that deception or fraud was practiced. And, it makes no difference whether the question involves a civil or a criminal charge. Deception is still deception.

Fifth. Congress is not attempting to pass judgment on all the facts of this particular program. Congress is not attempting to sit in censorship. Congress is not attempting to offer a critique on whether the documentary was positively biased or slanted.

Congress is asking but one question: Is there adequate protection for the public? I repeat again, these airways belong to the public. They are invaluable.

Sixth. CBS keeps dropping back to the first amendment. Yet, by its refusal to discuss whether the editing process mismatched questions and answers—the network is, in effect, taking the fifth amendment.

Mr. Speaker, the first amendment cuts both ways. A man being interviewed has the right to know that what he says in a filmed interview will not be jumbled by a technician wearing white gloves in the editing room.

Seventh. Many Members challenge the case before us on the basis that "the case is not strong enough." Perhaps they are right. But, must we wait for massive deception before we act? The basic principle is a question of right and wrong. The public has a right to know the truth. Our case may not be the strongest possible—I have so expressed this opinion in committee—but the principle of right and wrong is at stake, regardless of whether the deception was big or little. Clearly, we must proceed with courage.

Mr. Speaker, I urge the House to pass this resolution. It is obviously in the public interest. If need be, I think we should pursue this question all the way to the Supreme Court. I readily agree that the networks should be free to speak on any issue. I will insist that the public, too, shall have that right.

Mr. HOWARD [D.-N.J.]. Mr. Speaker, the Members of the House of Representatives are today being asked to either approve or reject the contempt of Congress charges against Columbia Broadcasting System President Frank Stanton and the network.

Mr. Speaker, we might not always agree with what newspapers, television, and the rest of the news media have to say, but we must zealously guard their right to say it as provided under the first amendment.

In my opinion, there is absolutely no difference whatsoever between attempting to force a newspaper reporter to reveal his written notes and attempting to force a television network to provide its unused film from a news documentary.

This is not a matter of deciding if television is doing an adequate job or not, because I feel that in many ways it has failed to give the American viewer good programing.

The question the Congress faces is one of freedom of the press and for that reason, I must respectfully oppose the distinguished chairman of the House Committee on Interstate and Foreign Commerce and the majority of its members who voted out the contempt citation.

We are not here today to decide if the disputed program, "The Selling of the Pentagon" was a good program or even if it was a fair program, but we are here today to decide if we are going to continue to respect freedom of the press as provided under the first amendment or not.

The first amendment makes it abundantly clear that neither the Congress nor anyone else has the right to decide for the people of the United States what they should or should not be told by a free press.

Once we begin to make inroads against a free press there will be further suggestions that other areas should be controlled and the result will be that we have violated the first amendment and at the same time, done a disservice to the people of the United States.

I do not always agree with the things I see in the newspapers or on television; I have had the personal experience—as I am sure almost everyone here in the House has—of seeing inaccurate statements printed in the press.

The members of the press are human beings and have faults much the same way as we do and this naturally results in mistakes. But on balance, the press has served this Nation very well and I am not about to be one of the persons who would begin putting restrictions on a free press.

What this House is being asked today is to vote again on the John Peter Zenger trial which occurred in New York City in 1775 and which resulted in Mr. Zenger being found not guilty of seditious libel.

The Bill of Rights was not added to the Constitution as mere afterthought but it was a result of the concern on the part of many of the delegates to the Constitutional Convention and of several of the State legislatures that the Federal Government was endowed with too much power and could exercise the same amount of control that the British had.

Today, we are faced with a new threat to freedom of the press. It is a subtle threat and if it is approved by the House, its value as a precedent-setting measure would lend enormous weight to the argument of those who would further limit freedom of the press.

Thank you.

Mr. MINSHALL [R.-Ohio]. Mr. Speaker, during the June 24 hearing by the Subcommittee on Investigations on CBS' controversial editing of "The Selling of the Pentagon," Dr. Stanton bewailed the lack of a broadcaster's equivalent to the printer's ellipses, which are used to indicate omission of words or phrases from a quote.

Let me read briefly from the printed copy of those hearings:

> Dr. STANTON. We have been searching for a long time in broadcast news, both for radio and for television, to find the equivalent, for example, of the three dots that the printer has. We have not found that particular device.
> Mr. MANELLI. Would that not simply be to let the jump cut take place without—maybe you can define these terms. If you do not put in the reverse, which was in the Henkin interview, when you cut the tape

it will be quite obvious to the person watching the screen, isn't that true?

Dr. STANTON. That is a very good question. We have experimented with jump cuts and I am not sure all the members of the committee are familiar with this.

Mr. MANELLI. Would you define it for the record?

Dr. STANTON. Sir?

Mr. MANELLI. Would you define what you mean by jump cuts?

Dr. STANTON. A jump cut is a cut in the film where you take out some material for editing purposes and you don't do any bridging at that particular point so that a man might have his head over here in one scene and you cut and his head suddenly goes over here.

Mr. MANELLI. Does that not take the place of the three dots?

Dr. STANTON. That could take the place of the three dots but I think we would be before you for a different reason.

Mr. MANELLI. Why?

Dr. STANTON. Ridicule of the person interviewed because at one moment he may have a pipe or cigarette in his mouth and the next minute it is gone. It creates all types of problems.

Mr. MANELLI. Don't the people being interviewed object, not for that, but because their appearance is that they are saying things which they didn't say and that appearance is enhanced by interjecting cutaways to the interviewer so that you cannot see that the splice has been made? That is really the more basic complaint, isn't it?

Dr. STANTON. That is a matter of editing judgment and that is what we are talking about here, it seems to me. As far back as I think a year ago we made up a special film to see how these things would work, various techniques, to try to find the three dots because that is something that we don't have.

As author of the truth in news broadcasting bill, H.R. 6935, I believe I have found Dr. Stanton's elusive ellipses for him. Much of the controversy which provoked today's debate centers around this lack. Certainly had CBS clearly identified the portions of its documentary that were edited out of context at the time of broadcast, there could have been few recriminations afterward. It may never be known if CBS was merely victim of television's rigid time requirements and condensed the interviews not wisely or too well, or if CBS editors cut-and-pasted interviews out of context with deliberate intent to defraud.

I strongly suggest that enactment of my legislation would help prevent such unhappy controversies from occurring in the future. Very simply, H.R. 6935 would supply Dr. Stanton's "three dots" by requiring the clear and explicit labeling of broadcast news and news documentaries that have been staged, edited or altered out of context. This would alert the viewing public just as plainly as does the label a food manufacturer must place on his product if artificial coloring or flavoring have been added.

On radio, my bill calls for a disclaimer by the announcer before and after such sequences, in much the same way we now hear the familiar announcement, "The preceding was recorded." For television, broadcasters would superimpose a disclaimer on the screen during transmission of the sequence, precisely the same way they now label some portions of moon shots as "simulated." It would work no greater hardship on broadcasters than that.

As I have stated on this floor before, it seems remarkable to me that the networks have not voluntarily adopted my proposal. As honest reporters, who are constantly proclaiming that "the people have a right to know," it is a solemn obligation they owe their audiences. The right to know includes the right to know whether the news being broadcast into American homes is the whole story, only a part of the story, or the broadcaster's version of the story.

Last spring, I sent a copy of my remarks on my truth in news broadcasting bill to Dr. Stanton, among many others in the news media. I received no acknowledgement from him, but in view of the attention H.R. 6935 has received in radio-television trade journals, I find it difficult to believe he is unaware of its existence. Yet in his June testimony before the Subcommittee on Investigations he states that he and his colleagues are at a loss in finding a substitute for the printed ellipses. Either they are not looking very hard, or there is a lack of sincerity in their search.

Whatever action is taken by the House today, I sincerely hope that truth in news broadcasting will soon be accorded hearings by the committee chaired by my good friend and very able colleague, the gentleman from West Virginia (Mr. STAGGERS). Enactment of H.R. 6935, which I include at this point in the RECORD, contains no threat of first amendment infringement and some very solid guarantees that the American public will be able to more accurately evaluate the validity of news programs broadcast into their homes.

The bill follows:

H. R. 6935

A bill to amend the Communications Act of 1934 to provide for more responsible news and public affairs programing

Be it enacted by the Senate and House of Representatives of the United States of America in Congress assembled, That part 1 of title III of the Communications Act of 1934 is amended by adding at the end thereof the following new section:

"NEWS AND PUBLIC AFFAIRS PROGRAMMING

"Sec. 331. (a) No licensee may broadcast any program which contains a filmed or video-taped sequence purporting to be factual reporting if the event shown has been staged, edited, or altered in any way, or if interviews have been arranged, edited, or altered so that questions and answers are no longer in their original context, unless

such sequence is explicitly labeled throughout its entire showing as having been staged, edited, rearranged, or altered, as the case may be.

"(b) No licensee may broadcast by radio any recorded, audio-taped or otherwise audio-transcribed sequence purporting to be factual reporting if the event has been staged, edited, or altered in any way, or if interviews have been rearranged, edited, or altered so that questions and answers are no longer in their original context, unless such sequence is explicitly described by any announcer both before and following the broadcast of the sequence as having been staged, edited, rearranged, or altered.

"(c) Any live sequence, whether for television or radio broadcast, that is staged or is a dramatization purporting to be factual reporting must be clearly identified as a staged or dramatized sequence in accordance with the methods described in paragraphs (a) and (b).

"(d) Complete transcripts of unedited interviews must be available for distribution on request and at a nominal fee immediately after broadcast of any interviews that have been edited, altered, or rearranged.

"(e) Whenever a broadcast station presents one side of a controversial issue of public importance, such station shall afford reasonable opportunity for the presentation of contrasting views."

Mr. RARICK [D.-La.]. Mr. Speaker, I rise to support the committee and will vote to hold CBS in contempt of Congress because I believe in the right of our people to know the truth.

I cannot see where in the action today any first amendment violation is involved inasmuch as the constitutional amendment reads:

Congress shall make no law . . . abridging the freedom of speech or of the press.

Congress, in this instance, is not making any laws but rather attempting to investigate the threats to free speech which have been brazenly manipulated by the CBS network people using licenses extended by a Federal agency.

If by the widest stretch of the imagination there has been a first amendment violation, it has been the censorship—even more than that, the willful distortion, by the CBS network operating through its affiliates, using the licenses granted by congressional authority being exploited to misinform our people.

There is a decided difference between freedom of speech and freedom of the press and the right to use the ether waves which are classified as being vested with a public interest and owned by all of the people and therefore supervised by Congress and the FCC.

In recent months we in Congress have beheld judicial approval of action taken by the FCC in denying licenses to TV stations and radio stations in the common interest of the American people. One such incident was the revocation of the TV license in Jackson, Miss., on grounds that it did not program its TV coverage to conform with the racial proportions of the community. None of the champions of free speech, including the right to distort TV signals here today, were ever heard to utter one word on the theory of denial of free speech to the owners of the Jackson, Miss. TV station.

And Americans have learned that the pettiness of banning the playing of Dixie and displaying the Confederate flag on TV has been as a result of guidelines from the FCC bureaucracy, without any first amendment violation cry.

Certainly, since the FCC was created by and operates under the laws of Congress and has demonstrated quasi-dictatorial powers over the speech matter and programing on TV and radio stations, it is absurd to think that Congress—charged with the responsibility of protecting the first amendment rights of the people to free speech and free press so they can be fully informed—cannot insist that CBS network, as the beneficiary of its affiliates' licenses to operate an opinionmaking monopoly, not willfully lie in what is told the people.

Many people today experience the feeling of the world as upside down. What is reported to them as being good, they find to be bad and what they are told is bad, they end up finding is good. As one constituent told me:

> I have to stand on my head to understand the new vocabulary and what is going on in America.

Those who the people are told are for war, are found to be for peace; while those who act and talk of peace are those who prolong the war and keep it from ending. Likewise, in the matter at hand, it is CBS, cloaking itself with the first amendment, who is the censor of free speech and free press and who would deny the American people the right to know.

Jesus said:

> And ye shall know the truth and the truth shall make you free.— John 8:32

If this body does not adopt the resolution before us today, truth will continue to be a stranger in our land and the freedom of our people will continue in jeopardy. . . .

Mr. GONZALEZ [D.-Tex.]. Mr. Speaker, we are here under the baleful eye of the CBS logo, talking about contempt of Congress. But the issue is really the right to know. The issue is whether someone except CBS is to be the arbiter of truth.

When a newspaper prints an error, its competition is generally glad

to correct the story. When a magazine prints an opinion there are dozens, even hundreds, to print other opinions. But when a television network errs or lies there is no competition around that seems willing to broadcast a correction; and networks do not like to state opinions, at least out in the open. Yet no individual in the country has enough access to television networks to call an error an error; and CBS assuredly is unwilling to confess it is wrong, or has been wrong, or even that it has an editorial point of view.

So who is to protect the truth?

Ideally it should be the competition from other networks. But we know that this has not assured fair reporting, because there is no competition between the networks, except for ratings and prestige.

Maybe some day in the far distant future we will have as many television outlets as we have magazines and newspapers, and there will be sufficient competition to assure that the networks report with accuracy and care. But today the fact is that we do not live in such a perfect world as that. We live in the world where the baleful eye of CBS reigns with a mighty hand.

The might of that hand was made clear to me when CBS broadcast its famous "Hunger in America" show, which featured many scenes in my district. I demonstrated, and repeated investigations subsequently demonstrated that the show contained outright errors—or lies—about San Antonio, and greatly distorted the actual situation in the city. Yet CBS has never felt that it had to so much as admit it could have been wrong, much less correct the record. The show is still being used all around the country, unchanged from its original form, though I know all too well its inaccuracies, and though others including Orville Freeman have said it was "bluntly and simply a travesty on objective reporting."

I said many months before "The Selling of the Pentagon" was ever broadcast:

> The facts and opinions carried over the network outlets have powerful ability to create public opinion or influence it. The combination of film and sound has always been a powerful one; it produces great drama, elicits strong emotions, sets loose fervid thoughts. Television networks have great power, and therefore, they bear great responsibility in their use of it. But the fact is that the networks are responsible only to themselves, not to the public. How, then, is misinformation to be corrected when it comes from the networks? How are false statements to be corrected? Wherein lies the redress when the networks fail in their responsibility?

We have before us a grave problem. It is more than a matter of a contempt citation. It is a problem of arriving at some means of giving the public some protection against the abuse of network power. If a contempt citation is a poor tool, it is the only one we have available, at least right now. And besides, I would ask, what does CBS have to hide? Certainly they would not want to hide the truth.

Mr. STAGGERS. Mr. Speaker, I yield myself the balance of the time.

Mr. Speaker, I would say that this issue has produced the greatest lobbying effort that has ever been made on the Congress of the United States. I would like to quote from the TV Digest:

> NAB marshalled its 50-man Future of Broadcasting Committee for personal contacts with all Members of the House.

Mr. Speaker, one Member has told me that he has been contacted 12 times in 1 week. Another Member who was out walking, and saw me, told me that he had been contacted 15 different times.

If this Congress is going to be intimidated by one of the giant corporations of America, and give up to them, then our Nation will never be able to exist as a free nation, a nation of free men. It will have to answer at all times to the big corporations, and it will have to do what they want us to do. They must not be permitted to intimidate this Congress on this issue.

All we are asking is to have the Supreme Court of the United States settle the question, not this Congress.

Mr. Speaker, the slogan up there says, "In God We Trust." Are we going to change it to "In the Networks We Trust?"

This Nation was built on the principles of honesty, integrity, goodness and love. We can draw a lesson from that, and no giant corporation has the right to tell us what we should do and what we should say. All we are saying is that the Supreme Court should settle the case under the law.

I say to every Member of the House that I want you, before you vote, to search your consciences and to strike out from your consciences everything except the essential truth about this matter, and then say, "I am going to vote the right way, and I am going to vote the way my people would want me to vote, and not the way a great corporation wants me to vote, with all its tremendous wealth and awesome power, and its millions if not billions of dollars." If you do not vote your consciences then your people will be telling you that you are wrong. And I can guarantee you that because, by every indication we have received, by 6 to 1 the people have said that the contempt citation is right. . . .

Freedom of Information
and Shield Legislation

NEWS MEDIA SPOKESMEN have argued that the right to know and access to government information are guaranteed by the First Amendment: How can a free press exist if it cannot gain free access to information?

Finding little sympathy in the courts for this interpretation of the First Amendment and facing an ultra-secret post-war executive branch, the news media organized themselves in the 1950's. They turned to Congress for help.

After many years of political activity and cooperation with Congress, the news media claimed success with the enactment in 1966 of the Federal Public Records Law, also known as the Freedom of Information Act. This law's purpose was to reduce executive secrecy by guaranteeing public (and, therefore, news media) access to information in the federal bureaucracy. But more than six years' experience suggests that the law is of little use to the news media and is little used by the news media.

Why did 10 years of Congress-media cooperation produce so little success? What does this experience portend for the outcome of contemporary news media efforts to seek legislative relief from an unfriendly executive branch and unsympathetic courts?

In the first selection, the nature and extent of cooperation between Congress and the news media is summarized in the context of the Freedom of Information Act. It refers to the establishment of the Moss Committee during which there was close Congress-media cooperation. It describes the decline of the subcommittee's watchdog activities in the 1960's and its revival in 1972 under the chairmanship of Rep. William Moorhead (D. Pa.). During the 92nd Congress the Moorhead Committee conducted hearings to investigate the weakness of the FoI Act and suggested amendments. It remains to be seen, however, whether this renewed legislative attempt will succeed in achieving the news media's long-sought goal of free and open access to federal government information.

In the meantime, a generation after the opening of the freedom of information confrontation between the executive branch and the news media, a similar confrontation has developed over the issue of shield legislation.

As in the 1950's, the news media turned to the courts in the 1970's. In this test of the newsman's right to protect the confidentiality of his sources, the U.S. Supreme Court did not resolve the issue in favor of the news media.

As in the 1950's, the news media then turned to Congress for relief. A selection by Fred P. Graham and Jack C. Landau summarizes news media efforts with the 93rd Congress for legislation which would "shield newsmen from being compelled to tell courts, grand juries or state or federal inquisitors information received in confidence or the identity of whoever told it to them."

Unlike the 1950's, however, a growing number of news media representatives began to doubt the wisdom of shield legislation. The experience the news media had with FoI legislation tends to confirm this position presented in a selection by Charles L. Bennett, an Oklahoma editor.

―――――

A NEW FOI WATCHDOG NEEDS WATCHING

By Robert O. Blanchard

Coinciding with the momentous events surrounding the publication of the Pentagon Papers has been the apparent revival of the long-dormant government information watchdog committee in Congress.

The new congressional freedom of information spokesman is Rep. William S. Moorhead (D.-Pa.). He replaced Rep. John E. Moss (D.-Calif.) in April [1972] as chairman of the Foreign Operations and Government Information Subcommittee of the House Government Operations Committee—for 15 years known as the Moss or FOI Committee.

The Moorhead Committee's recent hearings have halted the subcommittee's eight-year decline as a government information watchdog.

But it cannot be assumed yet that the revived subcommittee, even with a new chairman and new staff, will be any more effective in the long run. If past experience is any guide, the press—represented by media FOI spokesmen and committees—will determine how effective, or ineffective, its congressional agent will be.

Media FOI spokesmen were responsible for the establishment of the

Reprinted by permission from *The Quill*, Volume 59, Number 8. (August, 1972).

Moss Committee in 1955—then called the Special Subcommittee on Government Information—at the height of press-executive branch confrontation not unlike the present.*

Continued press support was responsible for the subcommittee's effectiveness in checking many executive branch information abuses during the Eisenhower Administration. But press tolerance of congressional stalling in the 1960s—and its susceptibility to congressional rhetoric in place of action—was equally responsible for the Moss Committee's decline as an effective watchdog of the Kennedy and, particularly, the Johnson Administration. By the time of the Nixon Administration, the subcommittee was all but defunct.

In the beginning, the Moss Committee courted and heeded the views of the chief press FOI spokesmen of the American Society of Newspaper Editors, Sigma Delta Chi, the Associated Press Managing Editors, the National Newspaper Association, and the American Newspaper Publishers Association.

Unfortunately, while they had Congress's ear these and other media FOI spokesmen did not ask for enough. They sought legislation to check excessive government secrecy. But they permitted the Moss Committee's "freedom of information" bill to protect a host of government secrecy categories—including the presidential privilege to order secret anything he considers to be "in the interest of national defense or foreign policy."

Even more serious was the media FOI groups' view of the Moss Committee's watchdog function only as a means to legislative ends. They did not pressure the subcommittee to maintain a continuous vigil on executive agency information practices.

Even while their support of the Moss Committee was exposing secrecy, embarrassing government officials responsible for it and causing release of information, the media FOI leaders were subject to criticism from some other journalists. They were, after all, involved in making news. They were participating in congressional hearings (called "panels" in an attempt to soften the fact), publicizing hearings, committee prints, reports, press statements, member speeches and proposed legislation.

The only way this activity could be justified was for the media FOI spokesmen to overtly defend the right of media professional organizations to engage in pressure politics as do other professional organizations. Unfortunately, FOI spokesmen—many of them editors—were (and still are) unwilling to articulate this point.

Thus, as some of the worst Eisenhower-Nixon Administration secrecy abated and the sophisticated press men of the Kennedy Administration dashed into Washington, the freedom of information issue was reserved

* See Robert O. Blanchard, "Present at the Creation: The Media and The Moss Committee," *Journalism Quarterly*, Summer, 1973.

for hinterland editors who did not understand the inner workings of government.

After all, it was repeatedly said and written about the FOI issue, the "talented" and "hard-working" correspondent could really "dig" and get the "inside" story. The price seemed cheap enough. The information was off-the-record, for-background-only, from an exclusive interview, not-for-attribution, or for trial balloons. The real scoop was the selective leak of classified information.

In this atmosphere, in the Era of Consensus, the media FOI spokes-men—particularly the ASNE—slowed down their political activities which once had created and sustained a political atmosphere for an alert congressional watchdog.

It should be a surprise to no one that in this atmosphere, congressional FOI spokesmen—themselves wooed by Presidents and their sophisticated congressional liaison tacticians—should relax their vigil. There remained little political capital in FOI.

The state of affairs was only made worse by the denial of both press and congressional FOI spokesmen that they were relaxing their vigil. To the charge, first published in the summer of 1966,* that the press FOI groups were in a state of decline, Moss said:

> There is no cause to lament the demise of the FOI organizations.
> From my observation post, it is obvious these groups were never more active or aggressive in the crusade for the people's right to know and for freedom of the press.

The Freedom of Information Committee of ASNE defended Moss from the same source of criticism:

> The complexion of the (FOI) battle has not changed . . . because a Democratic administration has come to power and Moss is majority whip (as critics charged).
> The new public records law itself is a milestone. And Moss assured us that there will be public hearings on it as soon as sufficient experience with it has accumulated.

This was in 1967. The ASNE FOI committee never did succeed in getting Moss to hold his promised hearings on the effectiveness of that "milestone"—the Federal Public Records Law—even though there has been a vast accumulation of criticism and evidence that it was not being enforced.*

There were many warnings about the weaknesses of the law and the need for compensating political and congressional surveillance. Kenneth

---

* R. Blanchard, "Watchdog in Decline," *Columbia Journalism Review*, Summer, 1966.
* R. Blanchard, "The Freedom of Information Act—Disappointment and Hope," *Columbia Journalism Review*, Fall, 1967.

Culp Davis, a leading authority on administrative law, said this about ASNE's "milestone":

> That the Congress of the United States, after more than ten years of hearings, questionnaires, studies, reports, drafts, and pulling and hauling, would wind up with such a shabby product seems discouraging. The drafting deficiencies cannot be explained away as the product of extreme complexity, intractable subject matter, or unruly struggles between irreconcilable political philosophies. The failures in this instance are in the nature of inattention and indifference.

In 1969, Ralph Nader and his raiders released a documented indictment of the law:

> The Act . . . explicitly provides for nine exemptions which offer a vast amount of discretion—so vast that to call these exemptions loopholes would be to indulge in the grossest kind of understatement.

The ASNE also assured Moss's critics in 1967 that the Moss Committee was "active on all major fronts: the White House, the Pentagon, Vietnam, the Dominican Republic, and major federal agencies, including NASA."

However, Moss acknowledged inaction. Responding to an Associated Press inquiry in 1966, he made this remarkable statement about the Johnson Administration's information record:

> On the basis of complaints we receive, this administration has a reputation for an almost *perfect score in not abusing the handling or withholding of information.* We get fewer complaints now. If anyone feels I'm playing politics, let him bring in a complaint. (Emphasis added.)

In its heyday, when it was playing havoc with the information policies of the Eisenhower Administration, the Moss Committee did not *wait* for complaints. The subcommittee staff aggressively sought examples of executive information abuses from members of the press. Although the Moss Committee staff consulted with reporters, editors and publishers in Washington and throughout the nation, they avoided responding *ad hoc* to individual complaints.

Throughout its "golden era," 1955-1963, the Moss Committee quietly gathered the evidence and then staged hearings or published reports, delivered speeches, wrote press releases—all documenting an over-all charge of administration-wide information abuses.

Not so in the 1960s, and this has made all the difference.

Today's media FOI spokesmen should consider three important principles or experiences as they develop their rapport with the Moorhead committee.

First, is the undeniable and too often underestimated watchdog powers of Congress.

Not even the Moss Committee's inaction in the 1960s can take away from the performance of the Special House Subcommittee on Government Information. From 1955-1960, Moss presided brilliantly over a model of congressional oversight. It was as effective in catching attention of the press and manipulating it as it was responsible and judicious with the agencies it was investigating.

But mere activity was not the only element of its effectiveness. Two scholars on government information, Dan Nimmo and Francis Rourke, found that the Moss Committee's effectiveness was often in what is called the "law of anticipated reaction." The credible threat of Moss Committee exposure swept the bureaucracy and was a deterrent to secrecy.

Another element of effectiveness was the subcommittee's continuity. Rourke discussed this factor as it related to the subcommittee:

> (The Moss Committee) served the very useful purpose of giving continuity to the task of legislative oversight of executive information practices—a function which the legislature otherwise performs only on an *ad hoc* basis as cases involving the withholding of information come to the attention of individual legislators or committees.

These factors, combined into a continuous threat of exposure to executive agencies, were not significant parts of the Foreign Operations and Government Information Subcommittee which succeeded the Special Subcommittee on Government Information in 1963. As Rourke observed:

> This subcommittee did not prove to be nearly so effective a force under Kennedy and Johnson as it had under Eisenhower. The zeal of Democratic congressmen for exposing the misdeeds of executive agencies diminished by a measurable amount when the White House was controlled by a Democratic rather than a Republican president.

Responding to this type of criticism in 1966, Moss cited a long list of *ad hoc* cases from his files which were brought to the attention of the subcommittee. But these cases were seldom published in a subcommittee report or print, or reviewed in hearings.

In place of the threat of exposure and the continuity of oversight, Moss described a curious consensus-style of surveillance of the Johnson Administration. This description might help explain how it was possible for the executive branch to practice widespread duplicity and secrecy in the 1960s, unchecked by the Moss Committee. Moss wrote:

> . . . . Following the Subcommittee's all-out information battles during its formative years there has been *far less need to engage in the tactics of formal hearings* or to apply other forms of public pressure to

focus attention on or to solve information withholding problems . . .
The difference in handling the problems in the 1960s as compared
to the era of the Eisenhower Administration is that the Subcommittee
has had the *close cooperation* of and responsiveness from the top level
officials of the Kennedy-Johnson Administration. Thus, it has been
possible in most instances to get the information problems solved
before they become a public issue. (Emphasis added.)

This leads to a second set of experiences the press should take into
account in its relations with the Moorhead Committee: media group
political collaboration with Congress.

The classic cooperation between the media FOI groups and the Moss
Committee ranged from day-to-day coordination of the timing of press
releases and subcommittee reports to participation in hearings. It began
in the 1950s as an effective "buddy system," but ended in the 1960s with
the Moss Committee staff as big brother.

The subcommittee was established, in great part, in response to the
FOI crusade spearheaded by the ASNE. The subcommittee's first three
years was largely a public rehash of research and rhetoric generated by
the ASNE. Somewhere along the line, the Moss Committee became infallible in the eyes of FOI groups. They began to depend more and more
on the subcommittee for the initiative and guidance on what to do.

They even permitted—if not requested—the subcommittee staff to
draft sections of their annual FOI reports. Of course, the initiative, guidance and rhetoric was carefully orchestrated by the subcommittee staff to
harmonize with Moss's new, cooperative relationship with the Democratic
Administration. In return, the FOI groups defended the Moss Committee
from criticism.

FOI groups' adoration of the Moss Committee also blinded them to
Moss's growing identification with and socialization in the House of
Representatives—which in this century has become a careerist institution.
With the help of the national prominence gained as chairman of the
subcommittee, Moss secured his district in California. He has been a
safe-seat congressman. He has long passed what H. Douglas Price has
called the "fourth term crisis." This usually leads congressmen to the
adoption of the mores, traditions and ways of behavior of a congressional
careerist looking toward the future and power-through-the-leadership.

These factors, in addition to Moss's position as deputy whip, certainly
took their toll on Moss's interests and energies as an FOI spokesman.
Thus, when he was forced this year to choose between the chairmanship
of the FOI Committee and the chairmanship of a Commerce subcommittee, he chose the latter. He did this only after reform-inspired legislation limited every congressman to one subcommittee chairmanship.

This leads us to the last great experience which the present media

FOI spokesmen should keep in mind when dealing with the Moorhead Committee.

The press-Moss Committee collaboration turned into cronyism almost without the media recognizing the change. It was accomplished by the subcommittee through the application of the arts and sciences of an old political shell game. The more infamous and familiar examples of this process are government regulatory agencies going to bed, as it were, with the industries they are supposed to regulate.

The techniques of this game are described in a classic analysis by Murray Edelman, "The Symbolic Uses of Politics." Political forms, he said, serve overtly as a powerful means of expression for mass publics while behind the scenes, they convey special benefits to particular groups, but not necessarily the publics.

Although probably never a mass public issue, the FOI crusade was a broad coalition of press, bar and scientific groups with common gripes over post-war and Cold War administrative and executive secrecy.

But a major goal of the movement was freedom of information legislation. The goal has been achieved—the Federal Public Records Law— but, other than its symbolic value, is not meeting expectations.

Francis Rourke has suggested that many reform movements, including the FOI crusade, become self-defeating this way:

> I am much impressed by the fact that some of the (media) groups involved in freedom of information . . . have struggled so hard for reform legislation, even though it is difficult to see how much legislation could be really effective.

Congressional committees and interest groups tend to "measure their achievements or provide themselves with a *raison d'etre* by getting legislation enacted," he said.

The legislative oversight function—the watchdog activity—important and as effective as it is "does not seem to confer sufficient legitimacy" for these groups.

They seem to need a legislative coonskin to nail in their annual FOI reports.

The new generation of media FOI spokesmen should demonstrate to Moorhead and his staff that it can count on them as alert and cooperative constituents while the subcommittee functions as a continuous check against executive secrecy and propaganda. They should appreciate the value of the watchdog function and their role in implementing it in the political process. They should measure the results, not the rhetoric, of the subcommittee. In short, they should keep a close watch on this watchdog.

THE FEDERAL SHIELD LAW WE NEED

By Fred P. Graham and Jack C. Landau

Last June 29 [1972] the U.S. Supreme Court ruled that the First Amendment does not grant newsmen a privilege to withhold from grand juries either confidential information obtained during legitimate news-gathering activities or the source of that information. In addition to this specific 5 to 4 holding in the *Caldwell-Pappas-Branzburg* cases, Justice Byron R. White implied even broader limitations against the press by repeatedly stating, in one form or another, that reporters have no more rights than "all other citizens":

> We see no reason to hold that these reporters, any more than other citizens, should be excused from furnishing information that may help the grand jury in arriving at its initial determinations. . . . Newsmen have no constitutional right of access to the scenes of crimes or disaster when the general public is excluded, and they may be prohibited from attending or publishing information about trials if such restrictions are necessary to assure a defendant a fair trial before an impartial tribunal.

What is important about these statements is that the issue of press access to public disasters or public trials was extraneous to the *Caldwell* case; and in fact the statements appear to be erroneous as a matter of public record.

1) A great many "other citizens" have privileges not to testify before grand juries. There are more than 300,000 attorneys who may, in all federal and state courts, invoke the attorney-privilege to protect confidential information from clients which might solve a case of heinous murder or treason; about 300,000 physicians who may withhold confidential information about crimes under certain conditions in federal and state courts; and several hundred thousand clergymen who have a recognized privilege, in one form or another, in federal and state courts to protect confidential information obtained from penitents. (The priest-penitent issue, however, is somewhat murky because there has never been a Supreme Court case in that area.)

2) So far as we know, newsmen may not be prohibited from attending public trials. In fact, the only Supreme Court cases on the subject state that newsmen must be admitted and that they may not be held in contempt of court for publishing public trial events.

3) It has never been decided that a representative of the public—in

Reprinted from the *Columbia Journalism Review*, March/April, 1973, ©.

the person of the news media—is not guaranteed some access to public disaster areas. It is true that public officials would have a strong argument against admitting 1 million persons to a disaster area in New York City. But the current concept is that the public "has a right to know" and that, while the number of visitors may be restricted, to guarantee a flow of information the public is entitled to be represented by a reasonable number of journalists.

The point here is that Justice White felt so strongly about the *Caldwell* case that he interpreted issues against the news media which were not even litigated and made statements of constitutional policy which, consciously or unconsciously, appear to misrepresent existing constitutional law to the detriment of the media. It is therefore imperative for journalists to realize that, while they must continue activity in the courts—meeting every censorship challenge head-on—they must seek a redress of their grievances at the legislative level—an invitation, no matter how gracelessly offered, by Justice White in *Caldwell*:

> Congress has freedom to determine whether a statutory newsman's privilege is necessary and desirable and to fashion standards and rules as narrow or as broad as deemed necessary to address the evil discerned and equally important to refashion those rules as experience . . . may dictate.

Congressmen responded by introducing twenty-eight * bills granting various types of newsmen's privileges in the last session and twenty-four bills within the first fortnight of the new session. Hearings were held on some of these bills . . . by a Subcommittee of the House Judiciary Committee chaired by Rep. Robert W. Kastenmeier of Wisconsin . . . and Sen. Sam Ervin of North Carolina, who chairs the Constitutional Rights Subcommittee of the Senate Judiciary Committee. . . .

The Kastenmeier hearings were perhaps more educating for the press than for Congress. The news media displayed a disturbing lack of unity (with various organizations supporting different bills); a disheartening public exhibition of intra-media rivalry between a book author representative who accused TV of producing "warmed-over" documentaries, and a broadcasters' representative who declared, "I see the authors didn't mention Clifford Irving" (both comments were edited out of the formally published committee hearings); and a failure to present convincing factual evidence of the necessity for new legislation.

In an effort to consolidate the media position, Davis Taylor, publisher of the Boston *Globe* and chairman of the American Newspaper Publishers Assn., invited major media-oriented organizations to participate in an Ad Hoc Drafting Committee to prepare a bill which could be used as

* This number had doubled by mid-1973.—Ed.

a model. The committee included representatives of the ANPA, the American Society of Newspaper Editors, the Newspaper Guild, the National Assn. of Broadcasters, the Sigma Delta Chi journalistic society, the American Civil Liberties Union, the Reporters Committee for Freedom of the Press, the New York *Times*, *Newsweek*, ABC, CBS, and NBC. The ANPA has endorsed the whole bill; many other groups support only various portions of the bill or have not yet taken a formal position. . . .

Problem One: Which members of the "press" should qualify for a federal "shield law" privilege which at least protects the source and content of "confidential" information? (Underground newsmen? Freelance news writers? Lecturers? Researchers? Book authors?)

Pending suggestions: The narrowest commonly used definition is contained in several state shield laws which grant only protection to "newspaper, radio, or television . . . personnel." All of the pending Congressional legislation is considerably more expansive, ranging from bills which protect "persons directly engaged in the gathering of news" to the broadest possible definition of "any person who gathers information for dissemination to the public." This would appear to include even dramatists and novelists.

Comment: This threshold question—of who should receive shield law protection—poses most disturbing moral, political, and legal problems which could easily fragment the media.

Those who argue for the broadest definition—describing researchers and would-be authors as members of the press—present a strong historical and constitutional case that the First Amendment was written against a background, not of multinational communications and great news empires, but of individual letter writers, Committees of Correspondence, and citizen pamphleteers. Justice White, in the *Caldwell* opinion, emphasized the historical validity of a broad definition for members of the press by noting that the "liberty of the press is the right of the lonely pamphleteer who uses carbon paper or a mimeograph machine." The Authors League, in its testimony, stressed that many major political scandals of recent years have been unearthed by individual authors working alone, rather than by investigative reporters for major newspapers, magazines, or TV networks. In effect then, a broad definition—including authors, researchers, and freelancers unconnected to any established news organizations—would, in many ways, make the newsman's privilege virtually coordinate with the freedom of the speech protection of the First Amendment and would mean, in practical terms, that any person interested in public affairs could probably claim shield law protection.

Those who argue for a narrower definition favor limiting the privilege to persons connected with recognized news organizations. They argue that the author-researcher definition is so broad as to create the privilege for virtually any person interested in public events. Such a broad definition might invite many fraudulent claims of privilege, perhaps even "sham" newspapers established by members of the Mafia (as Justice White hinted); would alienate Congress and the Courts; and would give opponents of a shield law their most powerful political argument against creating any privilege at all. Furthermore, they argue that while the legendary individual author from time to time does engage in muckraking on a grand scale in the most hallowed traditions of Lincoln Steffens, the great majority of investigative reporting is conducted by employees of established news organizations. It is they who are going to jail and it is they who need the coverage more than any other identifiable group.

Suggested solution: While politics and pragmatism would dictate limiting the privilege to news organization employees, morality and history would dictate that the greatest possible number of journalists be covered without attempts to include all purveyors of information and opinion. Therefore we suggest that the bill grant the privilege to "recognized members of the press" and permit the courts to decide who should and should not qualify. The bill should specifically state that the privilege covers the underground and minority press (the true heirs of the eighteenth century pamphleteers), the student press, and at least previously published "legitimate" freelance nonfiction writers. . . .

Problem Two: Which proceedings should be covered by a shield law (grand juries, criminal trials, civil trials, legislative investigations, executive agencies)?

Pending suggestions: These range from the narrow coverage . . . . which would grant the privilege only before federal grand juries and criminal trials, to the broadest coverage, which would protect a news reporter before any executive, legislative, or judicial body.

Comment: There is general agreement among the press as to which government proceedings should be covered—all of them. If a newsman is protected only from testifying at a criminal trial, his testimony can still be coerced by a legislative body or by an executive agency which has the contempt power, such as state crime investigating commissions. Furthermore, it seems unfair to deny to a criminal defendant confidential information which might help to acquit him but at the same time give the information to a state legislative committee which may have no better purpose than to further some ambitious Congressman's stepladder toward the governorship.

Suggested solution: News reporters should be privileged before all judicial, executive, and legislative proceedings. . . .

Problem Three: What types of information should be protected?

a) Confidential sources of published information (e.g. Earl Caldwell was asked to disclose the confidential source of material published in the New York *Times.* William Farr was asked the confidential source of a Manson trial confession published in the Los Angeles *Herald-Examiner*)?

b) Confidential sources of unpublished information (e.g. TV news reporter Paul Pappas was asked what occurred inside Black Panther head-quarters; CBS News was asked the identity of the person in New York who supplied a Black Panther contact in Algiers in connection with a *60 Minutes* story on Eldridge Cleaver)?

c) Unpublished nonconfidential information (e.g. Peter Bridge was asked further details of his nonconfidential interview with a Newark Hous-ing Commission member; CBS News was asked to supply outtakes of nonconfidential interviews in *The Selling of the Pentagon*; the St. Louis *Post-Dispatch* was asked for unpublished photos of a public antiwar demonstration)?

d) Published nonconfidential information (e.g. Radio station WBAI in New York City was asked for tapes of published interviews with un-named prisoners involved in the Tombs riot; WDEF-TV in Chattanooga was asked for the tapes of a published interview with an unnamed grand juror)?

Pending suggestions: The narrowest commonly accepted protection is contained in several state shield laws which protect only the "source" of "published" information, giving no protection, of course, to the confi-dential source of background information never published and no protec-tion to the unpublished confidential information itself. All the pending Congressional bills protect both the *source* and the *content* of "confiden-tial" information whether or not the information is published. Interest-ingly, all the Congressional bills also protect the source and content of "nonconfidential information," which could even protect TV outtakes or a reporter's notes of a Presidential speech ("nonconfidential informa-tion").

While the broadcasters generally support the printed media's desire to protect "confidential" sources and information, the real TV interest in the shield law debates will center on the nonconfidential information problem, from both a practical and philosophical point of view. The classic cases cited by the TV news executives concern the difficulties of television cameramen covering riots, dissident political demonstrations, and student disorders—"nonconfidential" events whose film records could be used by the FBI or local law enforcement to identify participants for criminal prosecution. TV executives and, to a lesser extent, news camera-men recite incidents of stonings by demonstrators, breaking of cameras, and destruction of equipment because demonstrators believed that jour-nalists were collecting evidence for the police. The TV news executives argue that their news operations are not an "investigative arm of the Government" and that their cameramen must be able to represent to hostile demonstrators and to the general public that the only film the FBI will see is the film that is actually shown on the tube. But this raises a logical dilemma: Is a film outtake of a public demonstration to be given the same protection from a subpoena as a "confidential" source in the Watergate bugging scandal?

Television also has a practical financial objection to permitting its film to be subpoenaed. It is expensive and time-consuming to run through reel after reel of film, an objection similar to that of newspapers whose morgues have been subpoenaed.

Suggested solutions: It is our suggestion that the shield law privilege might be bifurcated like the attorney-client privilege: There could be an "absolute" privilege to refuse to disclose the source or content of confidential information; there could be a "qualified" privilege to refuse to disclose nonconfidential information—such as outtakes of a public demonstration. The outtakes would be available only if the Government demonstrates an "overriding and compelling need."

This two-level absolute-qualified privilege would be similar to the privileges available to attorneys. Attorneys may refuse to disclose the content of confidential communications from their clients and in some cases even the identity of their clients. However, attorneys have only a limited privilege to refuse to turn over nonconfidential "work product" evidence —such as an interview with a witness to a crime who is now unavailable. There are three advantages to offering to a news reporter or cameraman the absolute-qualified privileges held by attorneys.

FIRST: The press is not asking Congress to create a novel or unique concept by establishing a specially privileged class of citizens. In fact, the press is merely saying that confidentiality is as important for the performance of newsgathering as it is for the performance of legal representation; and to deny the press a privilege which Congress has granted to an attorney would be saying that the right of the public via the press to learn about the Bobby Baker or Watergate scandals is to be accorded less protection than the right of a member of the public, via his lawyer, to be represented in a land transaction or a patent case.

SECOND: The attorney-client relationship is so well established that a whole new body of law would not have to be developed for the multitude of unanswered questions which naturally arise with establishment of a new and untested right. (How is the privilege asserted? Who has the burden of proving it is properly invoked? etc.) . . . .

Problem Four: Should there be any specific exceptions to the privilege to refuse to reveal confidential and nonconfidential information or sources? (Libel suits? Eyewitness to a murder? Information about a conspiracy to commit treason?) . . . .

Comment: Most of the bills would not have protected Earl Caldwell because the grand jury in the *Caldwell* case was allegedly investigating a threat by Eldridge Cleaver to assassinate the President. Once the Congress suggests that newsmen may protect confidential information except for national security or libel or felonies or to prevent injustices, the media will end up with a bill which is full of procedural loopholes, moral dichotomies, and legal inconsistencies.

Furthermore, judges have proved ingenious in discovering ambiguities in statutes in order to force reporters to testify in situations that would boggle the nonlegal mind. Paul Branzburg was ordered to name his source of a drug abuse story despite a state law protecting reporters' sources! The Kentucky courts ruled that he saw the sources making hashish and thus they became "criminals" and not news sources. A California law protects reporters' sources, but a Los Angeles judge waited until William Farr temporarily became an ex-newsman and then ordered him to talk; the California legislature promptly passed a new law protecting former newsmen. The moral is that shield laws should be as broad and tight as words will permit, or judges will find ways to evade the intent of the statutes.

Critics of the unqualified privilege often fall back on a stable of horribles ("what if a kidnaper had your child and a reporter knew where?") to argue for leeway to compel testimony in extreme situations. But some states have had unqualified laws for years and no such incident has ever occurred. Either a reporter believes that it is his duty to talk or he feels so strongly against disclosing the information that no judge or turnkey could break his silence.

Of all the qualified bills, ... [the one calling for] exception for the "national interest" would place a heavy burden on the Government or a private litigant—a burden that would appear to be satisfied in those rare situations similar to the Pentagon Papers litigation.

The conceptual difficulties of attempting to cover all confidential and nonconfidential information under the same broad legal standards have persuaded us that the privilege perhaps could be tailored to the major problems of confidential and nonconfidential information rather than attempting to make a series of subjective evaluations for certain types of crimes or proceedings. Libel presents an unusual situation; in other testamentary confidentiality situations such as the attorney-client privilege, if the client refuses to waive the privilege then he is subject to an automatic default judgment as the penalty for invoking the right.

Suggested solutions: Attorneys, clergymen, and psychiatrists cannot be forced to violate the confidences of their clients, penitents, and patients, even upon a showing of an investigation into espionage or murder. In fact, how many attorneys know that their own clients or other persons are guilty of heinous crimes but are protected by the attorney-client privilege? It seems grotesque to accuse a news person of being an unpatriotic citizen because he has a privilege to refuse to disclose confidential information of a serious crime, when attorneys (50 per cent of the Congress are lawyers), physicians, and clergymen are considered upstanding citizens if they invoke their privileges to refuse to divulge the same criminal information to a grand jury or a trial. Therefore it is suggested that any exemptions for confidential information be drawn as narrowly as possible and that there be a heavy burden of proof for forced disclosure of nonconfidential information.

Problem Five: Should the shield bill apply only to newsmen involved in federal legislative, executive, and judicial proceedings? Or should the bill cover newsmen involved in attempts by state government agencies to obtain confidential sources and information? . . . .

Comment: No single issue divided the ANPA Ad Hoc Drafting Committee more than the question of federal-state coverage. While lawyers all agree that Congress can cover federal proceedings, there is serious disagreement—both on constitutional and political grounds—as to whether the press should aggressively push for state protection in the federal bill.

If statistics were the only issue, then the media would all agree that Congress should cover state proceedings because the subpoena problem is much more serious now in the states and counties than in federal jurisdictions. Ever since Atty. Gen. John N. Mitchell promulgated his Justice Department Subpoena Guidelines in July, 1970, the Justice Department, which had issued a large number of subpoenas to the press in the prior eighteen months, has issued only thirteen subpoenas. The celebrated cases today are mostly state cases: William Farr, Peter Bridge, Harry Thornton, David Lightman, James Mitchell, Joseph Weiler, Joseph Pennington.

Furthermore, there are only eighteen state shield laws in effect and they offer varying degrees of coverage. A federal-state law would fill the void in the remaining thirty-two states, thus eliminating the necessity of new legislation in these states and of corrective legislation in most of the existing states whose laws offer less protection than the ANPA bill. . . . .

Suggested solution: The federal government is only one of fifty-one jurisdictions. In fact, when one remembers that the Farr-Bridge-Thornton cases were processed in the county courts, there are the federal government; fifty states; and some 3,000 county court jurisdictions. Under the Justice Department guidelines, there is a lessening danger from the federal government. Therefore, we consider it absolutely essential that, despite the political difficulties of this position, the shield law protect every news reporter in the nation—not just those who, by happenstance, are involved in federal proceedings.

Assuming that the media can agree on which bill they want, can the press persuade Congress to pass the legislation? Three years ago, the newspaper publishers succeeded in obtaining passage of the Newspaper Preservation Act with its exemption from the antitrust laws, over the public opposition of the then antitrust chief, Richard McLaren. Two years ago, the broadcasters, within forty-eight hours, were able to muster enough support to protect CBS president Frank Stanton from being held in contempt of Congress, over the objections of Rep. Harley Staggers, who was attempting to obtain nonconfidential outtakes of *The Selling of the Pentagon.* The conclusion is quite simple: What the media owners want from Congress, the media owners get from Congress. The only question that remains is whether the First Amendment is of as much concern to the media owners as was exemption from the antitrust laws.

THE POTENTIAL DANGERS OF SHIELD LEGISLATION

By Charles L. Bennett

When we talk about the idea of shield laws around our shop, we don't exactly do it as disinterested parties indulging in an academic exercise divorced from any real threat in this area.

We recently published a story to the general effect that the CIA had a definite and purposeful role in the planning of the My Lai massacre in Viet Nam. This story was based on more than two years of research, resulting in what we viewed as convincing circumstantial evidence of the CIA involvement, and upon information given to us by five persons involved in the whole affair and whose identity we are pledged to protect.

This is perhaps the most sensitive, but only one of, the stories we are or have been involved in where there is or was a threat of legal action aimed at forcing us to disclose our sources and peripheral information. So we are not on the sidelines, but in the front line.

I wanted to say that first to underline the fact that we, like most if not all of you, are entirely convinced that, to be a newspaper, we, like you, have to handle stories in which a part of our obligation is to use confidential sources and information that must be protected from disclosure.

There is no question that the Watergate exposures required the use of confidential sources. But to say that the Watergate exposures illustrate the need for a shield law—as has been contended—seems to me to be contrary to reality, since the Watergate disclosures were accomplished without benefit of a shield law.

So, we are not convinced that shield legislation at the federal level is needed or desirable. In fact, we are persuaded that enactment of such legislation could, and most likely would, be—instead of an aid to carrying out our free press obligations to our public—a serious detriment and, perhaps, a fatal blow.

From remarks by Charles L. Bennett, managing editor, *The Daily Oklahoman*, at an American Society of Newspaper Editors' panel discussion, Washington, D.C., May 4, 1973.

Our objections to a federal shield law come in three general sizes:

First: Despite all the adverse actions and decisions in recent months, we are not convinced new legislation is needed to protect our, and thereby the public's, vital interest in our ability to use and protect confidential sources and to keep our work products—unpublished notes, etc.—confidential.

Second: We believe there are effective steps that can and should be taken by newspapers, individually and collectively, that would do more to help us protect, when needed, the confidentiality of our sources and information than would the passage of any federal shield law.

Third: We believe passage of shield legislation at the federal level could, and very likely would, open the door to federal legislative power over the press that would be far more damaging to both our and the public's interests than are the conditions under which we now operate.

I'd like to mention only a couple of points on each of these three areas of objection.

On the first: The adverse ruling on the Caldwell case by the Supreme Court is, we believe, not necessarily the last word by that body on this subject. It shall be remembered, among other things, that Caldwell refused to even appear before the grand jury. What the outcome of his case might have been if he had appeared and clarified his position we will, unfortunately, never know. Some lower court rulings already have gone our way, rather than in that direction. Given more cases which reach the Supreme Court and involving different sets of circumstances we believe future rulings may well be more favorable to our view.

For nearly 200 years we have fought along the battleline that the rights of the free press belong to ALL the people—not to newsmen or editors or publishers or owners of news media—and that we act only as agents of the public's right to know, with exactly the same rights accorded by constitution and law to all citizens. By and large, over that period, that view has worked effectively and has been supported by the public. Now, in the face of short-term harassment, we talk of abandoning the tested and proved status in favor of some untried special status that gives privileges separate and apart from those of the ordinary citizen. That looks to us, in the longer view, very much like bailing out of a flying airplane—without a chute—for fear the motors might, at some indefinite moment, fail.

On the second point: That there are other, and more effective, steps we can and should be taking that would be more surely useful than passage of a federal shield law, there are two I would like to mention:

One is that, in several jurisdictions, there has been a trend toward interposing jury trial between the person (newsman or otherwise) held in contempt and the judge who so holds him. Encouragement of this procedure in ALL cases involving the confidentiality of newsmen's sources and material would put our problem into a legal arena where we can fight effectively, not only legally, but in the court of public opinion.

The other is related: As many have said, we have done a terribly poor job of explaining and justifying our case to the public—our readers —who are the beneficiaries of and who, eventually, will be decision makers on this whole issue. If we would work half as hard at enlisting the public in our, and their own, cause as we do in fighting those who attack us directly we might still lose some battles, but would be far more assured of winning the war.

On the third: The dangers of enacting federal shield legislation:

Any qualification of the rights of the press—as to whom the privilege may apply, under what circumstances or whatever—automatically opens the way to changes, amplifications, extensions of those qualifications. To what eventual end this could lead, only your imagination—under perhaps even LESS benevolent relations between press and government at some future time—only your imagination can tell you where this kind of government regulation of the press might end: licensing of newsmen, licensing of newspapers, specific limitations and rules as to what can and cannot be printed—all these things, and more, are distinct and real possibilities once you not only concede that Congress does, contrary to the First Amendment itself, have the right to "pass laws abridging freedom of the press." We currently are not only conceding Congress has a right so to legislate, we are begging it to do so.

Finally, three quotes:

James Kilpatrick: "We will err, I believe, if we embark on a cure that could be worse than the disease . . ."

Vermont Royster: "Once it is conceded Congress can legislate about the press, no man can know where it might end . . ."

John S. Knight: "Proponents of shield legislation would be well advised to ask themselves whether the remedy they propose will ultimately sustain or destroy press freedom."

Fair Trial vs. Free Press

PERHAPS SOME OF THE most dramatic and obvious examples in recent times of Congress-media cooperation have involved the Senate hearings on the Watergate scandals.

The hearings of the Senate Select Committee on Presidential Campaign Activities and their coverage by the news media became the center of a major public and professional debate over whether the publicity of non-judicial inquiry creates "witchhunts" prejudicial to subsequent judicial inquiries or whether they are necessary to restore public faith in the government.

A central figure in this debate, as well as in the hearings, was Sen. Sam J. Ervin, Jr. (D.-N.C.). The full account of how and why he was selected by his Senate colleagues (more likely, by the Senate Democratic leadership) to head this committee has yet to be made, but there were at least two contributing factors. First, Sen. Ervin had the appearance, at least, of fairness. He was 76, with no apparent political aspirations other than, perhaps, reelection to his Senate seat. He was a gentleman. He was a former judge. Furthermore, he had been a relatively obscure Senator nationally until his almost incidental rise to prominence as chairman of a Constitutional Rights Subcommittee of the Senate Judiciary Committee which conducted hearings on the Army's surveillance of civilians and later, freedom of the press. These hearings gave him a national image as a defender both of the Constitution and individual rights.

But there were other Senators who met these criteria. The second, and probably the major, contributing factor leading to Ervin's selection was his status as a "minor hero to the national press" as Laurence Leamer expressed it:

> Ervin's hearings on the Army's surveillance of civilians, for instance, appeared to be a frontal attack on the forces of illiberalism and the developing tyranny by dossier. That it was Sam Ervin, a hawk,

a proponent of big military spending, a Southern conservative, in a word a patriot, who was leading the attack gave the hearings an un-impeachable credibility. In articles and editorials the press heralded their new-found champion of civil liberties . . .*

After Ervin's hearings on freedom of the press, Leamer said, Ervin had acquired a "new fame" which, with the "urgency of his struggle [to protect the Constitution] he, too, was now part of the media apparatus."

The first major challenge to Ervin's investigations came from Archibald Cox, the then-special Watergate prosecutor appointed by the then-Attorney General Elliot Richardson. He sought to delay the Senate investigation or, at least, stop national news media coverage of the hearings. George Lardner, Jr. of the *Washington Post* summarizes the challenge, followed by excerpts from the ruling of John J. Sirica, chief judge of the U.S. District Court in the District of Columbia, denying Cox's request for a delay of the Senate investigations.

The major issue, from Cox's point of view, was that the nationally publicized hearings, which were compelling witnesses to testify under grants of immunity from prosecution, would prevent fair trials from ever being held for persons charged with wrongdoing in the Watergate scandals. This argument was supported by others represented here in a speech by then-Vice President Spiro Agnew and an editorial from *The Times* of London. The arguments for continuing the hearings are represented in an editorial from the *Washington Post* which responds both to Agnew and *The Times*.

Jules Witcover analyzes the "trial by publicity" issue, comparing and contrasting the Watergate hearings to previous widely-publicized congressional hearings. He concludes that the Select Committee's treatment of witnesses has been fairly mild in comparison to some previous investigations.

Bob Woodward and Carl Bernstein, the *Washington Post* investigative reporters who were credited with uncovering the Watergate scandals, report on the White House attitude toward the hearings, Ervin and the Select Committee.

In reading about the Watergate hearings, it is helpful to recall the ever-present conflict between the President and Congress and the role of the news media in this conflict.** Although bitter and sometimes personal, the White House attitude reported by Woodward and Bernstein was part of the larger struggle for power between these two branches of government. After many years of preeminent executive power and news media attention, Watergate may have sparked a new period of congressional dominance in national decision making—with the assistance of the news

* See "The Sam Ervin Show," Chapter 8.
** See Chapter 4.

media. Periods of congressional dominance during post-war years in American history have been common. But the role of the news media in this process seems to grow in importance each time.

———

THE BATTLE OF WATERGATE TV

By George Lardner, Jr.

The debate . . . is between special Watergate prosecutor Archibald Cox, who would love to see Watergate back in the classified ads, and the Senate select Watergate committee headed by Sen. Sam J. Ervin Jr. (D.-N.C.), who considers a more prominent pursuit of the truth of paramount importance.

So far, Ervin appears to be winning the instant argument over nationally televised hearings for the expected revelations of former White House counsel John W. Dean III and former Nixon campaign deputy Jeb Stuart Magruder.

But the issue goes deeper than that. When crimes are traced to the White House, can both fair trials and a free press have their day?

Sworn in May 25, Cox waited less than a week before raising the point, first privately asking chief Senate Watergate counsel Samuel Dash and Ervin to postpone their hearings, and then, when they declined, pressing the committee with an outspoken public letter.

In a passage that defense lawyers seem sure to toss back at him one day, Cox even asserted the fear that pretrial publicity about the scandal could "prevent fair trials from *ever* being held" (emphasis in letter).

Somewhat more guardedly, one of his top deputies, Phillip B. Heymann, contended in federal court here four days later that television coverage of Dean's and Magruder's testimony would seriously—"not hopelessly, but seriously"—threaten the prospect of fair trials "at an early date."

"We're between the devil and the deep blue sea," Heymann told reporters after the hearing in acknowledging that the arguments would doubtless come back to haunt the prosecution. "Sure, what we're arguing now will be used by defense lawyers later."

Evidently, however, Cox feels strongly that televising Dean's and Magruder's testimony—if compelled from them under grants of immunity from prosecution—into millions of homes across the nation could cripple his hopes of any convictions. Without restrictions on news cover-

Reprinted by permission from the *Washington Post*, Volume 96, Number 188 (June 11, 1973).

age, Cox warned U.S. District Court Judge John J. Sirica in a 13-page brief, the result might be "complete amnesty to these witnesses and all those who acted in concert with them."

A Biased Nation?

The concept of a country's entire populace disqualified from jury duty because of notions conveyed by the televised testimony of two men is somewhat startling, but Cox was plainly asserting it.

"While it is impossible to judge at this time the precise impact of this publicity on the conduct of the forthcoming cases, there is, at the least, a significant possibility that the committee's recommendation will imperil the government's ability to empanel an unbiased jury for the trial of any offenses charged," Cox declared.

It is a stance that has produced sharp, and conflicting reactions in the legal community, including some arched eyebrows over former Solicitor General Cox's potential savvy as a criminal prosecutor.

Even with Watergate, "you can have both fair trials and a free press," says University of Pennsylvania law professor Louis B. Schwartz, who recently served as staff director on a national commission to reform the federal criminal code. "It's like the Kennedy assassination. It's a case of enormous provocation. And in cases like that, there is an unavoidable compromise. A certain amount of screaming is permissible when the thing screamed about is big enough. The press has done only what it should do."

At the same time, Schwartz feels, there are plenty of antidotes, "a whole series of legal remedies" that can ensure fair trial. Among them are continuances of the trials "until the furor has died down," careful examination of prospective jurors for prejudice, and firm and explicit instructions from the judge to the jury to "start fresh" with what they hear in the courtroom.

"I would never say it's acceptable or desirable for people to come into a jury box with an opinion," Schwartz said. "But there is no rule that every juror must enter the box without an opinion."

Unlike murders and other bloody crimes involving just one defendant who may be the target of a community's ire, he added, Watergate is a complex case certain to include a variety of defendants whose individual involvement is far from settled in the public's mind.

Legitimate Worry

"Cox had something legitimate to worry about," Schwartz said of all the Watergate publicity. "If I were prosecuting the case, I'd feel it my responsibility to voice my concern to Sen. Ervin.

"But he took a stronger line—and got cuffed for it, quite properly.

Archie is not the most sensitive guy to political lines and boundaries. Maybe it's the solicitor general in him. The solicitor general has always exercised a godlike judgment role. He's the keeper of the royal conscience. That's not exactly what's called for here."

Washington attorney Nathan Lewin is another who sees no need for the press to pull back on Watergate.

"If Daniel Ellsberg, Jack Ruby and Sirhan Sirhan could get a fair trial," he says, "these guys certainly can. I don't know if people have more of an opinion about John Dean than Jack Ruby. And I submit that the average guy does not have an opinion about whether John Mitchell is guilty of the offense of bugging and tapping or obstruction of justice."

Lewin also disagrees with Cox's claims, in his letter to the Watergate committee, that continued disclosures at the hearings and in the press would encourage the concoction of "fabricated explanations" and increase the difficulty of getting truthful information from potential witnesses.

"Almost everything he said in that letter does not apply to Watergate," Lewin declared. "The best breaks have come after stories appeared in the press. And only a reckless, incompetent lawyer would tell his client that he can stop worrying once he appears on TV. When the times comes, Cox is going to be pulling out all the arguments on the other side."

Reardon Supports Cox

The special prosecutor however, is not without supporters for the side he's on now. Among them is Associate Justice Paul C. Reardon of the Massachusetts Supreme Court, best known as the architect of the so-called Reardon Report, a 1968 fair-trial, free-press study that was the basis for the first major overhaul of the American Bar Association's code of ethics in 60 years. The report recommended sharp restrictions on out-of-court statements about pending criminal cases, standards that Reardon says are beginning to be enforced in many states.

As Reardon sees the Watergate case, "the press has done an excellent investigative job," but "certainly we're very fast approaching the point where it's becoming impossible" to have fair trials.

"It's in the notorious case that the system comes under its greatest strain," Reardon said. "And this is unparalleled in our history. Cox has said it may prove impossible to prosecute those who are guilty. But there's another side. There are possible indictees who may be innocent. At the present juncture, their rights are being eroded—in a way that's not in the best tradition of the Constitution."

Reardon, whose initial intervention led to a 1969 Massachusetts Supreme Court order forbidding a public inquest into the Chappaquiddick accident involving Sen. Edward M. Kennedy (D.-Mass.), said he feels the Watergate publicity has reached a point where it poses dangers not only to the Sixth Amendment's fair-trial guarantees but also to the

First Amendment's guarantee of a free press. He said he sees a risk of restrictive court decisions growing out of continued publicity and suggested that the press is being short-sighted in pursuing it.

"They [the press] don't know who their friends are," Reardon said. "I think people ought to start pulling back." He said he was confident that "the truth will come out in the adversary process" of the courtroom, without any further prodding from the press or Congress.

Still other lawyers suggest that perhaps the time has come to compromise openly the traditional notion of an impartial jury.

"The fact is that the only jury you'll get in Watergate now that is fair in the traditional sense is an awfully uninformed jury," says one prominent Washington attorney. "It's impossible to find anybody who isn't an idiot who hasn't heard about the sensational aspects. What we're probably going to have to recognize is that in the television age, we probably have a new ballgame and that we've got to settle for less. Perhaps just jurors who have 'no fixed opinions.'"

Judge Sirica has promised a ruling Tuesday on the Senate committee's application for immunity orders for Dean and Magruder, which Cox contends should contain restrictions against radio and television coverage of their congressional testimony.

At Friday's court hearing, however, committee counsel Dash maintained that all the pertinent court precedents were really on his side.

Court Precedent

One that could prove prophetic for any Watergate trials was a 1952 decision by the First U.S. Circuit Court of Appeals in Boston involving Denis W. Delaney. A Democratic appointee, Delaney had, in order, been ousted by President Truman, indicted by a federal grand jury, investigated by a House subcommittee at heavily publicized hearings, and convicted on Jan. 22, 1952, three months after the hearings, for taking bribes and falsifying tax returns.

In reversing Delaney's conviction, the Court of Appeals said it had no quarrel with the House subcommittee which was fully entitled "to decide whether considerations of public interest demanded at that time a full-dress public investigation," even though Delaney was already under indictment. But the court added that "so far as the modern mass media of communication could accomplish it," Delaney's character had been "pretty thoroughly blackened and discredited as the day approached for his judicial trial."

The trial judge, in declining to put off Democrat Delaney's trial any longer than he did, had observed that most of 1952 was an election year anyway, with no one month before November offering better prospects than another month. But the appeals court held that Delaney's trial should have been postponed until "the hostile atmosphere engendered by all the pretrial publicity" had substantially evaporated even if that meant a delay "until after the election."

The appeals court emphasized at the same time that it was dealing with a former public official already under indictment. In cases involving damaging publicity for unindicted officials, the court said:

"Such a situation may present an important difference from the instant case. In such a situation, the investigative function of Congress has its greatest utility . . . Also, if as a result of such legislative hearings, an indictment is eventually procured against the public official, then in the normal case there would be much greater lapse of time between the publicity accompanying the public hearing and the trial . . ."

Tailoring that to the Watergate case, Dash contended that since indictments are still said to be three months off, with trials "six months to a year away," the effects of pretrial publicity now would be minimized.

If it hasn't been, defense lawyers, again relying on Denis Delaney, could ask for more time.

A one-time student of Cox's at Harvard law school, Dash took great relish at Friday's hearing in offering one other precedent for Judge Sirica's consideration: a 1962 Supreme Court decision upholding the conviction of Carpenters Union president Maurice A. Hutcheson for refusing to answer questions put to him by the Senate Labor-Management Rackets Committee.

The Supreme Court sustained Hutcheson's contempt-of-Congress conviction by a 4-to-2 vote. Justice John M. Harlan wrote for the majority:

". . . Surely a congressional committee, which is engaged in a legitimate legislative investigation need not grind to a halt whenever responses to its inquiries might potentially be harmful to a witness in some distinct proceeding . . . or when crime or wrongdoing is disclosed."

It was, Dash observed, a victory for the government and for the official who argued the case before the Supreme Court: Solicitor General Archibald Cox.

———

FAIR TRIAL AND THE WATERGATE HEARINGS

By John J. Sirica

While the Special Prosecutor [Cox] acknowledges that the Court cannot withhold entry of the immunity orders here at issue, he nevertheless asks the Court to make such orders conditional. The specific

Excerpts from an opinion by John J. Sirica, Chief Judge, U.S. District Court, District of Columbia, "In Re: Application of United States Senate Select Committee on Presidential Campaign Activities (Misc. No. 70-73)," June 12, 1973.

conditions recommended are listed from the Special Prosecutor's memo-randum.

1. Requiring, as in the case of criminal trials, the exclusion of the broadcast media (radio and television), when an immunized witness is required to furnish self-incriminating testimony, at least in the absence of an express waiver by the witness and his counsel of any objection to such potentially prejudicial coverage.
2. Limiting the grant of an order directing the witness to testify before the Committee to testimony given in executive session.
3. Conditioning the grant of the Committee's application on the assurance that it will receive the testimony only in executive session and will not publicly release the transcript of the testimony or any summary of it pending completion of the Committee's investigation.
4. Supplementing one or more of the above by directing the witnesses not to discuss or comment upon their testimony with members of the press or with any persons other than their counsel, members of the Committee and its staff, and prosecuting officers of the Department of Justice.
5. Supplementing one or more of the above by conditioning the grant of immunity on an understanding that the Committee and its staff will not make public statements about the witnesses' testimony pending completion of the Committee's investigation.

In oral argument, counsel for the Special Prosecutor apparently abandoned most of the above recommendations and urged upon the Court a single restriction: that the immunity orders direct the witnesses to testify only outside the presence of television cameras and radio microphones, thus permitting them to assert a Fifth Amendment privilege based on the type of news coverage given their testimony.

Insofar as the Special Prosecutor's proposals ask the Court to judge the wisdom of granting immunity to these witnesses or the appropriate-ness of coverage by the broadcast media, the foregoing discussion suffices to show that the Court lacks completely any power of intervention. Inso-far as the proposals ask the Court to exercise inherent powers in the interest of preserving the rights of potential defendants, additional con-siderations forbid judicial interference with the Select Committee's investi-gation and procedures.

The Special Prosecutor has cited a variety of cases which highlight the sort of judicial protections which he seeks. Prominent among these are: *Sheppard* v. *Maxwell*, 284 U.S. 333 (1966), *Miranda* v. *Arizona*, 387 U.S. 436 (1966), *Estes* v. *Texas*, 381 U.S. 532 (1965), *Rideau* v. *Louisiana*, 373 U.S. 723 (1963), and *Delany* v. *United States*, 199 F.2d 107 (1st Cir. 1952). As precedents for judicial intervention in legislative matters he cites such cases as: *Powell* v. *McCormack*, 395 U.S. 486 (1969), *Dom*-

browski v. *Eastland,* 387 U.S. 82 (1967), and *Kilbourn* v. *Thompson,* 103 U.S. 168 (1881).

These decisions, however, are not precedents for what the Special Prosecutor proposes. The one distinguishing feature found in each of the cases regarding fair trials and defendants' rights is the fact that indictments were extant and defendants identifiable. The Court here cannot confront any such "case or controversy." Counsel for the Special Prosecutor at the hearing represented to the Court that indictments in the matter being investigated by the Select Committee are sure to be forthcoming, although a time cannot be estimated, and that Mr. Magruder and Mr. Dean would very probably be named as defendants in such indictments. To broadcast nationally the possibly self-incriminating testimony of Messrs. Magruder and Dean, compelled pursuant to the orders herein, would, asserts the Special Prosecutor, endanger (1) the ability of any persons named by the witnesses in their testimony to obtain a fair trial, (2) the validity of future indictments, and (3) the ability of the Government subsequently to prosecute the witnesses. The fact remains, however, that there are no indictments, no defendants, and no trials. However much the Court may sympathize with the Special Prosecutor's wish to avoid serious potential dangers to his mission, it cannot act on suppositions, and the Special Prosecutor himself has been unable to show where any court has so acted. The matter is simply not ripe for judicial action.

Where a court has indictments or trial proceedings pending before it, it can draw on a well-stocked arsenal of measures designed to preserve the integrity of proceedings and the rights of individuals. It may act to change venue, grant a continuance as in *Delany, supra,* restrict extrajudicial statements as in *United States* v. *Tijerina,* 412 F.2d 661 (10th Cir. 1969), *cert. denied* 396 U.S. 990 (1969), control the courtroom as per *Sheppard* v. *Maxwell, supra,* etc. But even supposing that a court might be able to act in a premature situation such as the instant one, it is clear that the court could not go beyond administering its own affairs and attempt to regulate proceedings before a coordinate branch of government. The case authorities cited by the Special Prosecutor cannot sustain intervention in this situation under the immunity statutes. On the contrary, decisional law mandates a "hands-off" policy on the Court's part. A sampling of cases will suffice.

Delaney v. *United States,* 19 F.2d 107 (1st Cir. 1952), is a leading case involving pretrial publicity provoked by a congressional hearing. After Delaney was indicted on matters relating to the administration of the Internal Revenue laws, he was subjected to adverse publicity by hearings dealing with tax matters conducted by the so-called King subcommittee. The Circuit Court reversed Delaney's conviction because of the District Court's failure to grant a continuance, but noted that this indictment could still stand and that, with an appropriate continuance, Delaney could have received a fair trial. The Court stated further:

> We mean to imply no criticism of the King committee. We have no doubt that the Committee acted lawfully, within the constitutional powers of Congress duly delegated to it. *It was for the Committee to decide whether considerations of public interest demanded at that time a full dress public investigation* [of Delaney.] 199 F.2d at 114. (emphasis supplied)

The Court emphasized that the *Delaney* case involved an individual already under indictment. In a statement that portends the present situation, the Court said:

> We limit our discussion to the case before us, and do not stop to consider what would be the effect of a public legislative hearing, causing damaging publicity relating to a public official not then under indictment. Such a situation may present important differences from the instant case. In such a situation the investigative function of Congress has its greatest utility: Congress is informing itself so that it may take appropriate legislative action; it is informing the Executive so that existing laws may be enforced; and it is informing the public so that democratic processes may be brought to bear to correct any disclosed executive laxity. Also, if as a result of such legislative hearing an indictment is eventually procured against the public official, then in the normal case there would be a much greater lapse of time between the publicity accompanying the public hearing and the trial of the subsequently indicted official than would be the case if the legislative hearing were held while the accused is awaiting trial on a pending indictment. 199 F.2d at 115.

In his concurring opinion in *Hutcheson* v. *United States*, 369 U.S. 599 (1962) Justice Harlan observed:

> . . . [S]urely a congressional committee which is engaged in a legitimate legislative investigation need not grind to a halt whenever responses to its inquiries might potentially be harmful to a witness in some distinct proceeding . . . or when crime or wrong doing is disclosed. *McGrain* v. *Daugherty*, 273 U.S. 135, 179–180. 369 U.S. at 618.
>
> . . .
>
> Nor can it be argued that the mere pendency of the state indictment *ipso facto* constitutionally closed this avenue of interrogation to the [Congressional] Committee. 369 U.S. at 63.

The recent Supreme Court decision in *Doe* v. *Macmillan*, _____ U.S. _____ 41 U.S.L.W. 4752 (1973) holds that public distribution by a congressional committee of libelous or actionable material may impose liability on persons outside the legislative branch, for example, those who do the publishing. Thus, as a practical matter, a committee might in some cases want to be satisfied with internal distribution of information so as not to subject others to liability. Nowhere in the decision, however, does the Court even hint that the judiciary has power to direct a congressional committee so to act.

It is apparent as well that a committee's legislative purpose may legitimately include the publication of information. As the Supreme Court stated in *Watkins* v. *United States*, 354 U.S. 178, 200 (1957):

> [There is a] power of the Congress to inquire into and publicize corruption, maladministration or inefficiency in agencies of the Government. That was the only kind of activity described by Woodrow Wilson in *Congressional Government* when he wrote: "The informing function of Congress should be preferred even to its legislative function." (citation omitted). From the earliest times in its history, the Congress has assiduously performed an "informing function" of this nature.

See also *Hearst* v. *Black*, 87 F.2d 68 (D.C. Cir. 1936).

In conclusion, the Court finds that the Select Committee requests have met the two procedural requirements established by § 6005. The Court is, therefore, compelled to grant unconditionally the immunity orders sought. Inasmuch as the Court is without discretion in this matter, it is not invited to comment on the wisdom or unwisdom of granting immunity in this case or to express its opinion on the desirability or undesirability of implementing the Special Prosecutor's proposals. To comment would be not only gratuitous but graceless. The Court's decision and action, therefore, cannot be interpreted as anything more than the Court acting as it is required by the law to act.

DUE PROCESS OF LAW

The Times of London

The President of the United States is in the unenviable position of being tried by his fellow countrymen in three different forums, each of which has its own particular deficiencies and two of which have the power

An editorial from *The Times* of London, June 5, 1973 which appeared in the *Washington Post*, reprinted by permission of *The Times*.

to offer freedom from prosecution to those whose evidence may accuse him. That is not to say the President is innocent, or that he would be innocent if any precisely formulated charges had been brought against him. It is perfectly possible for a wholly guilty man to be tried in a wholly unjust way. Indeed, many of the men who have been lynched in the course of history were lynched for crimes they had actually committed. That does not alter the fact that what Mr. Nixon is now receiving is a Washington variant of lynch law, and that while he may or may not be innocent, he may never be proved guilty by a process so clearly lacking in justice.

The three forms of trial, which are taking place simultaneously, are the Ervin committee in the Senate (and this leaves out other related inquiries by five other Senate or congressional committees), the grand jury, and the media, including The New York Times and The Washington Post.

The Ervin committee is investigating precisely because the Senate thought the due process of law was working too slowly. The senators are trying to ask fair and relevant questions; there is no allegation that this is a Senate committee on the lines of the McCarthy committee, though it has approximately the same powers and rules. Yet Senate committees are not courts: they do not have an adversary procedure; they do not have cross examination by counsel for the accused; they can take and certainly do take hearsay evidence. The Ervin committee has already been warned by Archibald Cox, the special prosecutor, of "risk of damage to investigations and any resulting prosecution." The enormous publicity given to hearsay evidence in televised hearings is so prejudicial that it alone would seem to preclude the possibility of fair trial for any accused, even including the President himself if there were impeachment proceedings.

The second tribunal is the grand jury. No student of British law will forget that we abandoned the grand jury procedure because of its notorious weaknesses as an instrument of justice. Grand jury proceedings provide the prosecutor with opportunities to introduce prejudicial evidence, which would not be admissible in a trial. The Watergate grand jury proceedings have been held in camera but have been widely leaked. The public has therefore a partial and unreliable account of these proceedings; that must be more damaging to the administration of justice than if there were a full account or no account at all. The publication of alleged reports of proceedings held in camera would be contempt of court under British law.

The third tribunal is the press, with television. But for the work of The Washington Post the real elements of the Watergate scandal would not have been uncovered. However, now we have a simultaneous process of trial by newspaper allegation, beside the Senate hearings and the grand jury. The American press, and particularly The Washington Post, deserve their full credit for forcing the Watergate affair into the open. They are however now publishing vast quantities of prejudicial matter, that would be contempt under British law, which again must tend to prejudice the fair trial of any accused, or, if it came to that, of the President.

The latest and most damaging example of this is the evidence given by John W. Dean III. According to The New York Times and The Washington Post, Mr. Dean told Senate investigators that he conferred with President Nixon thirty-five to forty times between January 1 and April 30 of this year. The subject of these conversations was alleged to be the concealment of the fact that White House men were behind the break-in of June 17 last year, the Watergate burglary. Mr. Dean also alleged that the President agreed to buy the silence of the accused. These allegations have been denied specifically by the White House, though it is agreed that the President saw Mr. Dean, who was indeed the White House counsel at the time.

This is evidence of the greatest possible importance. It is not too much to say that if Mr. Dean's evidence is true, Mr. Nixon is not fit to remain the President of the United States. Mr. Dean's evidence, if believed, would convict the President on two counts, firstly of conspiracy to prevent the course of justice and secondly of deliberate, continued and systematic lying to cover up his own part in that conspiracy. In practice, if Mr. Dean's evidence comes to be accepted, it could well lead to the successful impeachment of the President of the United States, and it is the first evidence in the whole case which takes the central matter straight home to the President, not by hearsay but by direct account.

This evidence of Mr. Dean's has come out first in two great newspapers, the most important national newspapers of the United States. Perhaps one should consider what the quality of Mr. Dean's statement is as evidence. In the first place it was given to Senate investigators whose committee has the power to give or withhold immunity from prosecution to witnesses before the Senate committee. Mr. Dean has stated that he will not be the fall guy, and one way in which he could avoid being the fall guy would be to obtain immunity for himself in return for his evidence against other people. There is a long legal tradition that the evidence of those who wish to turn Queen's evidence should be treated with suspicion.

Mr. Dean's evidence was a preparatory statement; it was not given on oath; it was not given in open hearings; it was not given in open court; it must have been subject to questioning by the staff of the Senate committee, but not to public examination. It was most certainly not open to cross-examination by counsel for the President. On these grounds alone it is hard to think how evidence could be less satisfactory. Yet on this evidence could well be based public conclusions which could destroy a President of the United States.

The case is in fact worse than this. Any cross-examination would have put to Mr. Dean the apparent contradictions between this statement, now so unfortunately leaked to the press, and the earlier statement made by Mr. Dean's "friends" in an interview published by Newsweek on May 6. Mr. Dean's friends reported that Mr. Dean did think that Mr. Nixon knew of the cover up, but gave only the slender evidence of an interview in September 1972, in which the President stated: "Good job. Bob told me what a great job you've been doing." Mr. Dean took this to refer to the cover-up. By May 6 we are therefore already dealing with a Mr. Dean who is a hostile witness to President Nixon. He makes no mention then of the 35 meetings, but provides much more remote evidence for his belief that the President knew what was happening.

That is not a crucial inconsistency; Mr. Dean could well have been dribbling out the truth, a little last month, a little this month. In the same interview, however, Mr. Dean's friends quoted another story of Mr. Dean seeing the President. Mr. Dean admitted that he had never conducted the supposed inquiry into White House involvement, and told the President so on March 21, 1973. "The President came out of his chair" in apparent shock. So by Mr. Dean's first account we have the President shocked by a fact which, if Mr. Dean's second account were true, the President could scarcely have failed to know. That little physical detail of President Nixon bouncing out of his chair when he hears that Mr. Dean has been organizing a cover-up tells strongly in the President's favor, particularly as it comes from a hostile witness, and particularly as it refers to a date as recent as March 21 of this year.

That is not to say that this contradiction cannot conceivably be explained. What it does do is illustrate the danger of prejudice inherent in press reports of unsworn, untested, uncorroborated evidence. This is leakage of evidence likely to prejudice the Senate committee, which when it is presented to the Senate committee will further prejudice any trial that may depend upon it. It is prejudice very close to the fountain of information on which justice at some later stage is supposed to be done. The Dean leak is lethal, if believed, and yet of minimal evidential value; it alone could make a fair public trial impossible.

The tragedy is that the whole case is concerned with justice. What the President is accused of that really matters is to have interfered with the course of justice. That would be as grave an offense as a President could commit. Yet are not the Senate committee who are taking and publishing hearsay evidence to the whole country also interfering with the course of justice? "It is much more important for the American people to know the truth . . . than sending one or two people to jail," said Sen. Ervin, the chairman of the committee. That is not only interfering with the course of justice, but justifying the decision to do so.

And what about the press? Of course the American law of contempt is very different from ours, but the principles of fair trial are the same. How can one justify the decision to publish the Dean leak? Here is a real piece of hanging evidence, the missing element—if it is believed—in a chain of proof. Here is a piece of wholly suspect evidence—unsworn, unverified, not cross-examined, contradicting previous evidence, subject to none of the safeguards of due process, given by a man who may be bargaining for his freedom. How can the newspapers defend themselves from the very charge that they are bringing against the President, the charge of making a fair trial impossible, if they now publish evidence so damning and so doubtful with all the weight of authority that their publication gives?

TV'S INCANDESCENT AND DAMAGING PRESENCE IN THE HEARING ROOM

By Spiro Agnew

The Scripture tells us, "To every thing there is a season." The season of summer, in television, usually brings little but reruns and unknowns in place of regular stars. But this summer it's different. Somewhere on your TV dial, morning, noon, and night for the next several weeks or even months, you will be able to find a gripping drama—the Senate investigation of that web of crimes and controversies that has come to be known as Watergate.

Let me say at the outset that as entertainment these hearings have undeniable audience appeal. And I do not doubt that they are sincerely motivated as to legislative fact-finding and public education. But the point which many people have now begun to question is whether this is the right time for the Senate hearings to be going forward.

One of the Senate's most respected elder statesmen, Sam Ervin of North Carolina, the eminent constitutionalist and civil libertarian who heads the Watergate Committee, was asked not long ago if the hearings might not jeopardize the judicial proceedings—a point that Special Prosecutor Cox himself has now publicly raised.

The Senator answered, and I quote, "It is much more important for the American people to find out the truth about the Watergate case than to send one or two people to jail."

This statement brings us to the heart of the current concern over

A speech by then-Vice President Spiro Agnew before The National Association of Attorneys General, St. Louis, Mo., June 11, 1973.

whether prosecutors and juries or Senators and network TV crews should be in the lead on this Watergate investigation. Let's probe a little further into the implications of the thinking of my esteemed friend, Chairman Ervin.

Getting the truth out into the open, he says, is more important than just jailing people. I could not agree more. Jailing the convicted criminal is only one part of what justice is all about. Justice in its deepest meaning involves the assurance that we live in a society where the individual is truly free; the confidence that we are ruled by a government of laws, not of men; and the demonstrated proof that innocence and guilt alike are rewarded or punished as they deserve.

There can be no justice without public trust, and there can be no trust without a systematic and thorough airing of the whole truth about affairs that concern us all.

I cannot agree, however, with the suggestion that determining the truth and convicting the guilty are two entirely separate processes, one for the Congress to pursue and the other for the courts. The truth itself is what a court relies upon in deciding whether to convict or acquit a defendant. And because human freedom, fortune, reputation, and in some cases life itself hang in the balance with the making of that decision, our judicial system has developed the most careful procedures that exist anywhere in our whole society for testing and verifying, checking and double-checking, the truth about what men did or did not do and why.

Justice Felix Frankfurter once wrote, ". . . the history of liberty has largely been the history of the observance of procedural safeguards."

How very pertinent his observation is to us as the Watergate story unfolds. What is critically lacking, as the Senate Select Committee does its best to ferret out the truth, is a rigorous set of procedural safeguards.

Lacking such safeguards, the Committee, I am sad to say, can hardly hope to find the truth and can hardly fail to muddy the waters of justice beyond redemption.

Some people have argued that rules of evidence and guarantees of due process don't matter so much in the Ervin hearings because nobody is really on trial up there. The mission of the hearings, this argument runs, is purely one of information gathering. But Chairman Ervin himself has suggested otherwise. "My colleagues and I are determined," he said on the day the hearings began, "to uncover all the relevant facts . . . and to spare no one, whatever his station in life may be."

To me, ladies and gentlemen, that phrase "spare no one" sounds very much like an adversary process, a trial situation. There is no escaping the fact that the hearings have a Perry Masonish impact. The indefatigable camera will paint both heroes and villains in lurid and indelible colors before the public's very eyes in the course of these proceedings. This is essentially what is known in politics as a "beauty contest" and the attractiveness and presence of the participants may be more important than the content of the testimony. Particularly disturbing are the compliments to some witnesses and the stony silence accorded others at the close of their testimony.

There is no question whatever that some men despite their innocence will be ruined by all this, even though I am sure that the Senate intended nothing of the kind when it commissioned this investigation.

That is why it ought to concern all of us that in at least seven basic ways, the orderly procedures by which facts are elicited and verified in a court of law are lacking each morning when Senator Ervin's gavel comes down and the Senate's trial of the Nixon Administration before the court of public opinion resumes. These departures from the rules of fair play—rules fundamental in Anglo-American jurisprudence—occur not by the malice of any individual or the design of any faction, but simply by the nature of a legislative hearing as compared to a courtroom proceeding. But they are no less troubling to fair-minded observers for that reason.

Let's examine these seven missing safeguards:

1. *In the Senate hearing, there is no absolute right of cross examination afforded the persons accused or named by a witness.*

Thus there is no opportunity to test the accuracy and veracity of a hostile witness. The right of cross examination is a basic right in a judicial trial. This right is particularly important when a witness himself stands accused or already convicted and hence has a motive to implicate others to mitigate his own offense or to exonerate himself. To get at the truth, it is vitally important that each individual not only have an opportunity to present his own version of the facts, but that he also submit to vigorous cross examination by those opposite him in the adversary proceedings.

2. *In the Senate hearing, the right of persons accused or named in testimony before the Committee to be represented by counsel is severely abridged.*

The defendants' right to representation by counsel in a criminal trial is guaranteed by the Constitution itself. At the Senate hearings, in contrast, witnesses may have counsel at their side for advice only; their lawyers can take no active part in the colloquy among Committee, staff and witnesses.

3. *In the Senate hearing, there is no firm guarantee of an opportunity for persons accused or named by a witness to rebut that testimony by calling other witnesses or introducing other evidence; there is not even a formal assurance that the accused person himself will have a chance to testify.*

The right to rebut testimony is fundamental to a fair trial, and yet is being observed in only the most casual way in the Watergate hearings. James McCord, for instance, made a number of charges against his former attorney, Gerald Alch. Mr. Alch had not been scheduled as a witness, and it is unclear whether the Committee ever would have called him had he not happened to be immediately available and demanded a chance to speak. Thus we might never have heard Mr. Alch contradict Mr. McCord —and the public might never have known that James McCord has possibly perjured himself before the Committee.

4. *In the Senate hearings, there is no guarantee of an opportunity for persons accused or named by a witness to introduce evidence which tends to impeach the accuser's credibility by establishing bias or interest on the part of the person making the accusation.*

Such an opportunity is available in every judicial trial and should also be guaranteed in the Watergate hearings, especially when we are dealing with people whose jail sentences may depend in large measure on what they tell the Committee.

5. *In the Senate hearing, unlike a trial, the witness is permitted to introduce hearsay evidence.*

Even though the Chairman has in good faith repeatedly emphasized that hearsay testimony is not receivable as truth, it is difficult for tens of millions of viewers to disregard what they have just heard.

As Justice Jackson said in an opinion on the 1949 case of *Krulewitch* v. *U.S.*, "The naive assumption that prejudicial effects can be overcome by instructions to the jury . . . all practicing lawyers know to be unmitigated fiction . . ."

In the Watergate hearings, the witness is not only permitted to give hearsay but positively encouraged to do so. When a witness testifies to what some third party told him, he frequently is then asked to elaborate on details of the hearsay statement and pressed to say whether his informant mentioned still other persons. The effect of such lines of questioning is to strengthen the public's erroneous impression that the rumor and hearsay can be considered as reliable evidence.

6. *In the Watergate hearings, the witness is permitted to testify as to his inferences, his impressions, even his speculations.*

In a judicial trial, such so-called opinion testimony is totally inadmissible as evidence. Guilt or innocence, truth or falsehood, are determined in a court by facts, not guesswork.

In contrast, who can forget the May 23rd dialogue between Senator Montoya and witness John Caulfield on the alleged offer of Executive clemency to James McCord:

> Q. "Now, you mentioned that Mr. Dean had instructed you to say that it comes from way up at the top."
> A. "Yes, sir."
> Q. "What did you conceive that to be at the time?"
> A. "Well, sir, in my mind I believed that he was talking about the President."

Later in the same appearance, Mr. Caulfield said that he had never had any conversations with the President with regard to Executive clemency and that Mr. Dean had never specifically said the alleged offer came from the President.

Thus we were left only with Mr. Caulfield's personal opinion—an opinion that would never have been permitted in a court of law because its truth can't be tested.

The stark differences between the Watergate hearings and our basic concepts of justice came screaming out that night when the Washington Star's banner headline announced: "Felt Nixon Knew, Caulfield Says."

The next day, The New York Times carried a similar banner on an inside page: "Caulfield Asserts He Believes President Authorized Clemency Offer to McCord."

By any standard, this kind of thing can only be termed a gross perversion of justice.

7. *The last among the missing procedural safeguards is the prohibition against cameras.*

The reason that cameras are banned from most judicial trials is that they introduce an emotional and dramatic factor which gets in the way of a deliberate, dispassionate pursuit of truth. The court can too easily become a theater.

In a judicial trial, the public are only spectators. In the Watergate hearings, however, the American people have been cast as the ultimate jury by Senator Ervin and his colleagues; and television for better or worse thus becomes an indispensable vehicle for interjecting the people into the process of judgment. Moreover, the audible sighs, snickers or groans of the people in the hearing room are dramatically relayed to the millions of TV viewers, thus potentially affecting the way they receive the information.

Television's incandescent presence in the hearing room has additional damaging effects. It tends to complicate the search for truth by making both witnesses and Committee players on a spotlighted national stage, and it tends to impede the search for justice by creating a swelling flood of prejudicial publicity that could make it virtually impossible to select an impartial jury when and if new indictments are returned in the Watergate case.

Thus even if the Senate hearings succeed in reliably establishing the guilt of some individuals in the Watergate case, they will probably do so at the expense of ultimate conviction of those persons in court. And this is bound to leave the American people with an ugly resentment at the spectacle of wrongdoers going scotfree.

For those who have done no wrong—and experience would lead us to assume that they far outnumber any who have—the prospect of justice is bleaker still. Irreparable harm may well be done to the good name of the innocent by accusations leveled in televised hearings and never conclusively refuted in a court of law, the only institution in our system whose exoneration of an accused person is definitive and final.

In listing these seven deficiencies in the procedures of the Senate Watergate hearings, I do not mean to imply that the Ervin committee is proceeding in a haphazard or disorderly fashion. Far from it. They have a carefully drawn and published set of rules to guide their investigation. Even where those rules may seem to approximate judicial fairness, however, a closer reading reveals that they are not ironclad guarantees of due process after all for their application is left to the committee's discretion.

It is easy to understand the urgency which many attach to seeing the Ervin hearings go forward, since the judicial process was at first stalemated by the silence of many key figures, and then later shadowed by the lingering concern that the Administration was essentially investigating itself, without an independent figure leading the prosecution.

But now those conditions no longer prevail. One major witness after another is coming forward to tell what he knows, and a Special Prosecutor of impeccable integrity has taken command.

There is no denying that a judicial trial sometimes falls well short of airing all the circumstances and ramifications surrounding a crime or controversy, particularly when guilty pleas are entered as they were in the first Watergate trial last January. The courts can't do it all. What a court can do, however, with far greater precision and fairness than any legislative committee, is to establish the central facts of individual culpability—the task that now stands first on the Nation's Watergate agenda.

Instead, one is now left with the feeling that hearings which began on the premise that it is more important to bring out the truth than to jail people may wind up blocking the imprisonment of some who are guilty, smearing the reputation of many who are innocent, and leaving the truth itself very much in doubt.

Many have therefore suggested that it would be helpful if this unavoidably loose process—so harmful to so many and potentially so injurious to our country in ways even reaching far beyond our shores—could at least be deferred until the Special Prosecutor has a chance to develop his case, as Mr. Cox himself has urged.

In all likelihood, however, the hearings will proceed despite the reservations I have voiced. The Senate has every right to exercise its constitutional prerogatives, and appears intent on doing so. On that presumption, there are several points I hope the Nation will bear in mind over the weeks to come.

First, let's all understand that a great deal of what we see and hear in these hearings would be indignantly ruled out of any court of law in the United States.

Second, let's be conscious as we watch and listen that probably a considerable number of very fine people, entirely innocent of any wrong-doing whatever, could come out of this un-judicial proceeding tragically besmirched, terribly humiliated, and irretrievably injured—and therefore let us strive to suspend our judgments until all the facts are in; and let us remember the ancient injunction that every man among us is deemed innocent until proven guilty beyond reasonable doubt.

Third, I would hope that my good friends and old sparring mates in the Nation's press will consider that circumstances have changed dramatic-ally in the last several months. From a situation where the news media—to their great credit—were one of the principal forces pushing for full disclosure, we have now moved into a situation where excessive haste to print the spectacular may actually frustrate the processes of truth and justice.

The journalism profession never tires of telling us that it is a public service institution, not merely a profit-making enterprise. The weeks and months ahead will put that contention to an acid test by challenging reporters and editors to think twice about those sensational leaked-source stories that might boost circulation but which could also malign the innocent and help to acquit the guilty.

Finally, let everyone understand that as I have here extolled the virtues of our court system, I no less subscribe to the immense value of the Congressional investigative process—a process which I regard as one of the essential pillars of sound government in our system. What I have said here is not directed in any way to the weakening of that essential feature of the legislative process. Nor is it meant to impugn in the slightest the sincerity or objectivity of any member of the investigating committee, for each of whom I have only the highest respect.

I have simply endeavored to express my earnest personal belief that in this particular circumstance, as the court proceedings struggle toward justice and as the Senate hearings reach in their way toward truth, it does appear that the latter can hardly fail to injure the former—and I feel that every American citizen should understand that.

Justice Benjamin Cardozo, one of the greatest American jurists of this century, left us a wise reminder when he wrote, "Justice is not to be taken by storm. She is to be wooed by slow advances."

The storm of public indignation aroused by this sordid Watergate affair is an understandable reaction, and a healthy one. But the raw and undisciplined forces of such a storm cannot by themselves achieve justice, as Cardozo warned. Those forces must be harnessed by the instincts of fair play that are so basic to our society, and they must be channeled through the established institutions best equipped for the difficult dual task of protecting the rights of the individual and enforcing the law of the land.

This will not be the shortest or easiest way for America to untangle the tragedy of Watergate and repair the damage done—but beyond a doubt it is the safest and wisest way. I ask all of you, as dedicated servants of the rule of law, to join with me in working for this goal.

————

DUE PROCESS AND THE PRESIDENT

The *Washington Post*

"Getting the truth out into the open [Senator Ervin] says, is more important than just jailing people. I could not agree more. Jailing the convicted criminal is only one part of what justice is all about. Justice in its deepest meaning involves: the assurance that we live in a society where the individual is truly free; the confidence that we are ruled by a government of laws, not of men; and the demonstrated proof that innocence and guilt alike are rewarded or punished as they deserve.

"There can be no justice without public trust, and there can be no trust without a systematic and thorough airing of the whole truth about affairs that concern us all."

—Vice President Agnew, June 11, 1973

Had the Vice President stopped right there, with these six sentences excerpted (only moderately out of context) from his speech on Monday, we would have been pleased to see them written in stone. But Mr. Agnew, of course, proceeded to brush aside these and other sensible things he had to say in his address to the Attorneys General in St. Louis, and to join those who would close down the Watergate hearings, silence the news media, and leave it to the courts to determine the "whole truth" about the monumental scandal and corruption that have come to be called "Watergate." "There is no escaping the fact that the hearings have a Perry Masonish impact," Mr. Agnew went on to say. "The indefatigable camera will paint both heroes and villains in lurid and indelible colors before the public's very eyes . . ." Reciting those elements of a judicial proceeding which he finds lacking in the Senate hearings, he argued that what a court can do, "with far greater precision and fairness than any legislative committee, is to establish the central facts of individual culpability—the task that now stands first on the nation's Watergate agenda."

An editorial reprinted by permission from the *Washington Post*, Volume 96, Number 190 (June 13, 1973).

The Vice President is far from alone in the view that the Ervin committee proceedings and the on-going investigative reporting of the multiple facets of Watergate threaten to prejudice the prosecution of those who may be guilty of crimes, while unfairly damaging the innocent. The White House has cried out against a plot to "prosecute a case against the President in the press . . . an unprecedented assault on judicial and administrative due process . . . an [effort] to destroy the President." Secretary of the Interior Morton has opposed the Ervin committee "because there's too big a tendency to try people in a forum that is not designed for that." Sen. William Proxmire, a Democrat with no record of softness for Mr. Nixon, has argued that the President is "being tried, sentenced and executed by rumor and allegation."

Now that is pretty strong stuff and we would not dismiss it out of hand; the smearing of the guiltless is always a danger when scandal almost literally envelops a government; pre-trial publicity is often something of a hindrance to the effective prosecution of criminals. But before concluding that both things are now happening to an intolerable degree it might be wise to consider how much of this hand-wringing over due process of law is pertinent, and how much of it proceeds from an excessive effort to shield the President from the due processes of a political system which also explicitly provides for a free press, for free expression and for the vigorous discharge by Congress of its constitutional responsibilities.

And it might also be wise to consider the quite extraordinary implication of this argument when it is applied on behalf of the President. For what this argument does, in effect, is to relieve the President of the United States of the responsibilities and the risks inherent in his great office. It reduces him to the ranks of an ordinary criminal suspect, for whose protection against a repressive monarch the right of due process was expressly written into the Constitution. That he has such a right as a citizen is not the point. That he should be so endangered by the charges raised against him that he should feel obliged to rely on this right represents, in our view, a retreat on his part and on the part of his defenders which is more genuinely damaging in its way than anything that has been said against him by those who, for one reason or another, wish him ill.

And yet that is the plain implication of an eloquent defense of the President in an editorial from the Times of London, which appears elsewhere on this page today.* We are reprinting it, not because we agree with it but because it represents a presumably disinterested view from afar, and because it forcefully expresses the thinking of Mr. Nixon's supporters in this country—so much so that White House propagandists are circulating it approvingly.

* It is reprinted in this chapter, preceding Agnew's speech.—Ed.

"What the President is now receiving is a Washington variant of lynch law," the Times declares, and it rests its case very largely on the publication of this newspaper and in The New York Times of a report that Mr. John Dean had told government prosecutors and Senate investigators that he had discussed aspects of "the Watergate coverup with President Nixon or in the President's presence on at least 35 occasions this year." The Times of London calls this "hanging evidence" of complicity in the obstruction of justice, which, if believed, could "destroy a President." But on the basis of its own reading of Mr. Dean's reliability the Times editorial goes on to argue that it is also "wholly suspect" evidence and the editorial asks: "How can the newspapers defend themselves from the very charge that they are levelling against the President, the charge of making a fair trial impossible, if they now publish evidence so damning and so doubtful with all the weight of authority that their publication gives?"

Well, there are several things to be said in response to that. One is that the American public will now apparently have a chance to see for itself how damning or doubtful Mr. Dean's testimony is, when he gives it publicly before Senator Ervin's committee; his sworn testimony will be subject to challenge by Senators and staff members and subsequent witnesses; perjury would not exactly fit the purpose of a man who is said to be desperately trying to avoid going to jail. As for the weight of newspaper reports, it is as nothing compared with the weight of an American President, capable of commanding all three television networks simultaneously in his own defense. The Times contends that British newspapers would not be allowed to publish material as prejudicial as that now appearing in the American press. But the fact is that what is now being published is no different in essence from the early investigative reporting of Watergate to which the Times graciously and glowingly gives "full credit."

Moreover, as Britain's Guardian has pointed out, while such a press campaign might be more difficult to mount in Britain, it would also be "less necessary." In this regard, we would put this question to the Times: For how long would a British Government remain in office, if it had lied systematically to the press, and by extension to Congress and the public, for 10 months; if it had grossly misled the public on a critical issue—the nature and extent of its own investigation of alleged corruption in its midst; if two of its principal figures and assorted lesser lights had been forced to resign; if two of its former Cabinet members had been indicted for crimes; if "illegal as well as unethical" conduct had been conceded to have occurred in the campaign that brought it to office; if it had plainly engaged in a massive effort to obstruct justice; if it had approved a broad campaign of admittedly illegal security measures in clear violation of individual rights?

Would the Times of London in such circumstances be talking earnestly about due process for the Prime Minister?

This is the heart of what is wrong about the Times' argument; we are not Britain; we have a different set of checks and balances, which grant a President a fixed, firm term of office while holding him answerable, every day, to the judgment of the people he serves. It is only in this sense that the President is "on trial" before the Ervin committee or in the press. And it is for this reason that the Watergate crisis, which is in a very real sense a crisis of confidence in government, cannot await the determination, on narrow legal grounds, of criminal guilt or innocence. As the Vice President himself acknowledged, "a judicial trial sometimes falls well short of airing all the circumstances and ramifications surrounding a crime of controversy."

It is an authentic tragedy that we should have arrived at a point where it is not easy for the Congress or the press to exercise their rights and responsibilities without the risk of prejudicial, pre-trial publicity potentially injurious to the President. But it was not the press nor Congress which brought us to this sorry state. And we will not rise from it by suspending the due processes of the American political system for the sake of affording due process of law to the President. We are dealing here, not with specific isolated crimes, but with a whole style and manner and method of governing. We are dealing, in the end, with the President's capacity to govern, which derives, in turn, from public trust. And the Vice President is right: *There can be no trust without a systematic and thorough airing of the whole truth about affairs that concern us all.*

––––––

TRIAL BY PUBLICITY?

By Jules Witcover

"It's a great trial they're conducting up here, isn't it?" an exasperated John N. Mitchell blurted out last Wednesday at the close of the day's interrogation by the Senate Watergate committee.

The remark came as Sen. Lowell P. Weicker (R.-Conn.) concluded a tough cross-examination in which the former Attorney General admitted he had failed in his responsibilities as a lawyer and "officer of the court" by not reporting illegal White House acts.

Earlier the same day, the committee vice chairman, Sen. Howard

Reprinted by permission from the *Washington Post*, Volume 96, Number 223 (July 16, 1973).

H. Baker Jr. (R.-Tenn.), had pointedly denied, however, that the Watergate hearings constituted a trial of Mitchell or any other man.

"The responsibility of this committee," he said, "is not to fix blame. . . . We have no defendants. We are not trying to establish the guilt or innocence of anyone. We are trying to prevent this in the future by legislative relief."

Sen. Sam J. Ervin Jr. (D.-N.C.), the chairman, in opening the hearings on May 17, noted that "it is clear that we have the full responsibility to recommend any remedial legislation necessary." And the resolution creating the Select Committee on Presidential Campaign Activities said it should determine "the necessity or desirability of the enactment of new congressional legislation to safeguard the electoral process by which the President of the United States is chosen."

Yet the contention that the Watergate hearings are, in fact, a trial of all those alleged to have been involved in the break-in or subsequent cover-up, up to and including President Nixon—a trial before the court of national public opinion—cannot be dismissed out of hand.

Although the committee has no direct punitive power—it can neither indict nor convict any individual—the public airings of its hearings, particularly on nationwide television, puts the reputation of each witness on the line. And perjury in testimony, of course, can bring judicial action.

In his May 17 statement, Ervin also observed that while the purpose of the hearings "is not prosecutorial or judicial, but rather investigative and informative," the committee was "determined to uncover all the relevant facts surrounding these matters, and to spare no one, whatever his station in life may be."

So far, Ervin appears to be as good as his word, and Mitchell is not the only one who's complaining. On Friday, Sen. Carl T. Curtis (R.-Neb.) charged that the committee, with a $500,000 budget, was not "serving any lawful purpose," but rather its purpose "is to attack the President" and the hearings should be ended.

The accusation, from a long-time conservative, is reminiscent of charges that filled the air during the McCarthy investigatory hearings of 20 years ago, charges mostly sounded by liberals, that the only purpose was exposure, with no legislative intent.

McCarthy was berated repeatedly for using Senate hearings to expose, intimidate and destroy the careers of those who crossed swords with him or incurred his dislike. Men like Owen Lattimore, a State Department adviser, an Army dentist Maj. Irving Peress, and Army Gen. Ralph Zwicker were among his best-publicized victims.

McCarthy charged Lattimore first with being "a bad security risk" and wound up calling him "the top Russian espionage agent," all without proof. When Peress exercised his constitutional protection against self-incrimination and refused to testify, McCarthy called him—and others who did the same—"a Fifth Amendment Communist." And when Zwicker refused to cooperate, McCarthy, in humiliating televised hearings in the same Senate Caucus Room now housing the Watergate hearings, said Zwicker was "not fit to wear" his uniform.

These and other McCarthy excesses put congressional investigations generally under fire, with constant demands from civil libertarians that legislative intent be demonstrated, as proof that such investigations and hearings were not merely reputation-destroying witch hunts.

In the militant anti-communist climate that existed in the country in the 1950s, being accused of leftist leanings, or even viewpoints, often was enough to end an individual's government, and even outside professional, career. Certain Hollywood writers and actors were blacklisted so long they were driven into other fields.

Though this climate has waned appreciably in the intervening years, public exposure on television still can be devastating, and that is the gist of the Mitchell and Curtis complaints.

There are, of course, significant differences between the Watergate hearings and those earlier investigations. Real, not imagined, crimes have been committed, and there is a demonstrable need for tougher federal legislation governing presidential campaigns.

Once the hearings get past the first phase, investigation of the Watergate break-in and subsequent cover-up, they are to focus, in Ervin's words, on "allegations of campaign espionage and subversion and allegations of extensive violations of campaign financing laws."

Also, parallel judicial procedures are going forward through special Watergate prosecutor Archibald Cox. Mitchell, for one, already is assured of a real trial, having been indicted in New York on charges of perjury and obstruction of justice in connection with a Securities and Exchange Commission investigation of Robert L. Vesco, an international financier and Republican contributor.

And the manner of interrogation, to date at least, has been mostly courteous and responsible—a far cry from the reckless brutality of McCarthy and other earlier congressional investigator interrogators. Nor has there been much showboating by the senators or committee counsel before the tempting television cameras.

Perhaps one of the more aggressive, embarrassing bits of cross examination occurred Thursday when Assistant Majority Counsel Terry Lenzner, referring to White House logs, reduced Richard A. Moore, a White House special counsel, to stammering confusion.

Moore, a white-haired, red-faced man who looks considerably older than his 59 years, could not remember details about specific White House meetings that the 33-year-old Lenzner pressed him on. Lenzner, a former Justice Department civil rights investigator and a defense attorney for Father Philip Berrigan in his conspiracy trial, at one point charged Moore with telling the committee staff one thing in private and another in public. To this, the hapless Moore replied: "I'll let my answer stand—whatever it was."

Moore's name surfaced in the Watergate matter only recently. Former White House counsel John W. Dean III testified that Moore had attended meetings with Dean and President Nixon that led to Dean's telling Mr. Nixon all he knew about Watergate last March 21. Moore has not himself been implicated in any way in the break-in or cover-up, but in a sense it could be said his competence was put "on trial" before the TV cameras by Lenzner's interrogation.

In a letter printed in The Washington Post Saturday, a reader criticized Lenzner for "unintended but callous prolongation of agony" to Moore, and observed sympathetically to Moore that "what you have forgotten is probably more than this bright young man knows as yet."

Lenzner said Saturday he had received no other criticism. He read a telegram from a viewer in Columbus, Ohio, that said: "Thank you for your kind questioning toward an obviously incompetent old man. Please keep showing citizens the decay which must be cleaned out."

Two other flashes of aggressive questioning also stand out in recent days. The first was Weicker's biting reminders to Mitchell of his professional and ethical responsibilities as Attorney General and lawyer, which precipitated Mitchell's lament about being on "trial." The second was a sharp challenge to Mitchell's credibility by Chief Counsel Samuel Dash near the close of his testimony.

Noting two cases where Mitchell's committee testimony had differed "diametrically" from what he had said in a civil suit deposition on Watergate, Dash bluntly said:

"What I have to say to you on that, Mr. Mitchell, is that since you may have given false testimony under oath on prior occasions, is there really any reason for this committee to believe your testimony (on other matters)?"

But the Watergate hearings have yet to produce very much of the kind of hammering cross-examination for which men like McCarthy, Sen. John L. McClellan (D.-Ark.) and Robert F. Kennedy as chief counsel of the labor rackets committee became famous.

As congressional "trials" go, this one so far has been conducted mostly with the gloves on. Undeniably, exposure is an immediate product. But in light of the clamor already building on Capitol Hill and in the country for election reform, legislation almost certainly will result down the road.

———

NIXON AND HIS AIDES BELIEVE
HEARING IS A WITCHHUNT

By Bob Woodward and Carl Bernstein

President Nixon and his top aides believe that the Senate Watergate hearings are unfair and constitute a "political witchhunt," according to White House sources.

Despite apparent bipartisan and public support for the hearings and the manner in which they are being conducted, the sources said that the President in the last weeks has expressed bitterness and deep hostility toward the two-month-old proceedings.

"The President," one source said, "sees the hearings as an attempt to get Richard Nixon and do it just damn unfairly." According to four separate sources, the hostility toward the hearings is also pervasive in the White House staff, especially among former assistants to H. R. Haldeman and John D. Ehrlichman, the deposed former top presidential aides.

One White House source said he saw the struggle with the Senate Watergate committee as not just politics but a battle for survival. "The Ervin Committee is out to destroy the President," he said.

The bitterness, according to the sources, extends to the point where some White House aides openly mock the members of the Senate committee. In a reference to Sen. Sam J. Ervin Jr. (D.-N.C.), the committee chairman, one White House aide put on a Southern accent and told a reporter:

"I just little ole country bumpkin Sam and this nasty politics offends my pea-picking heart." The aide, who holds a middle-level position in the White House, then dropped the Southern accent and said that "Senator Ervin is out to slice the President and it offends me to see him come on so sweet when he isn't."

Another high White House aide said that Sen. Howard Baker (R.-Tenn.), the committee vice chairman, "has effectively deserted the President and the resentment runs high over here."

Five White House aides agreed to discuss the individual members of the Watergate committee, and all said they found Sen. Lowell Weicker (R.-Conn.), an outspoken critic of the White House, the most offensive. In several outbursts of moral indignation, Weicker has denounced the political espionage, dirty tricks, cover up and deception which come under the heading of Watergate.

Reprinted by permission from the *Washington Post*, Volume 96, Number 228, (July 21, 1973).

One White House source said that the President himself has de-nounced Weicker with an unflattering obscenity.

Two of the sources also criticized Sen. Edward J. Gurney (R.-Fla.), who is the strongest defender of the President. "Gurney is doing the only decent job of questioning," one source said, "but he is not pushing enough."

All the sources asked to remain unidentified. Several of them said that Leonard Garment and J. Fred Buzhardt, the White House attorneys representing the President on the Watergate, generally represent a so-called soft-line of cooperating with the Senate Watergate committee.

One of the advocates of a hard-line in the White House said: "This is not a legal struggle as Garment and Buzhardt see it—instead it is a political struggle and we must counterattack politically and in the media."

The sources generally agreed that there is a cloud of gloom around the White House that must be eliminated. Avenues of possible counter-attack, the sources said, could be to:

· Charge that the Senate committee is blowing the Watergate out of proportion and diverting too much governmental attention to it, keeping the President from solving more important problems such as those of the economy.

· Blame the Watergate committee for "McCarthyism"—hearing un-supported charges and creating an atmosphere in which the latest polls show that 35 per cent of the people believe the President had knowledge of the Watergate bugging prior to the June 17, 1972, break-in, though there has never been such an allegation by any witness.

· Charge the news media with bias and sensationalizing of all Water-gate allegations, including the televising of former presidential counsel John W. Dean's allegations against the President by all three television networks while the Senate committee witnesses who defend the President are broadcast on only one network.

· Release a detailed defense on the expenditure of $1.3 million for the President's homes in San Clemente, Calif., and Key Biscayne, Fla., show-ing that the money was spent for legitimate security measures. (There is a feeling in the White House that the issue was badly handled by the General Services Administration, which released the figures.)

Though some White House aides do not feel a counterattack should be mounted, the sources said nearly all aides feel that there is no reason the President should appear chastened by the Watergate.

"As the bitterness runs high," one source said, "there is little recep-tivity to the lessons of Watergate that we might learn."

BIBLIOGRAPHY

This is a selected list which contains information pertinent to some aspects of Congress and the news media not referred to or included elsewhere in this book. See the footnotes of the selections for additional references.

BOOKS

Allen, Robert S. and Drew Pearson. *Washington Merry-Go-Round*. New York: Horace Liveright, 1931.

Ambler, Charles Henry. *Thomas Ritchie: A Study In Virginia Politics*. Richmond: Bell Book & Stationery Co., 1913.

Ames, William. *A History of the National Intelligencer*. Chapel Hill: The University of North Carolina Press, 1972.

Bailey, Stephen K. *Congress Makes a Law*. New York: Vintage, 1950.

Bibby, John F. and Davidson, Roger. *On Capitol Hill: Studies in the Legislative Process*. New York: Holt, Rinehart & Winston, 1967.

Brown, Glenn. *History of the U.S. Capitol*. Washington, 1902.

Brownlow, Louis. *A Passion for Politics: The Autobiography of Louis Brownlow*. Chicago: University of Chicago Press, 1955.

Bryan, W. B. *A History of the National Capitol*. New York: Macmillan Co., 1914–1916.

Carlson, Oliver. *The Man Who Made News: James Gordon Bennett*. New York: Duell, Sloan and Pearce, 1942.

Cater, Douglass. *Power in Washington*. New York: Vintage Books, 1964.

Chafee, Zechariah, Jr. *Government and Mass Communication*. Chicago: University of Chicago Press, 1947.

Clark, Champ. *My Quarter Century of American Politics*. New York: Harper and Bros., 1920.

Clark, Delbert. *Washington Dateline*. New York: Frederick A. Stokes Co., 1941.

Cohen Bernard C. *The Press and Foreign Policy*. Princeton: University of Princeton Press, 1963.

Cornwell, Elmer E. *Presidential Leadership of Public Opinion*. Bloomington: University of Indiana Press, 1965.

Davis, Elmer. *History of the New York Times*. New York: The New York Times, 1921.

Dunn, Arthur Wallace. *Gridiron Nights*. New York: Frederick A. Stokes Co., 1915.

Essery, J. Frederick. *Covering Washington: Government Reflected to the Public in the Press, 1822–1926*. Boston and New York: Houghton Mifflin Co., 1927.

Filler, Louis. *Crusaders for American Liberalism*. New York: Harcourt, Brace and Co., 1939.

Gobright, Lawrence A. *Recollections of Men and Things at Washington During a Third of a Century*. Philadelphia: Claxton, Remsen and Haffelfinger, 1869.

Goldwater, Barry. *The Conscience of a Majority*. Englewood Cliffs, New Jersey: Prentice Hall, 1970.

Jones, Alexander. *Historical Sketch of the Electric Telegraph*. New York, 1852.

Kendrick, A. *Prime Time, the Life of Edward R. Murrow*. Boston: Little, Brown and Company, 1969.

Kraft, Joseph. *Profiles in Power: A Washington Insight*. New York: New American Library, 1966.

Lippmann, Walter. *Public Opinion*. New York: Harcourt, Brace & Co., 1922.

McNeil, Neil. *Forge of Democracy*. New York: David McKay, 1963.

Marbut, Frederick. *News From the Capital*. Carbondale: Southern Illinois University Press, 1971.

Mazo, Earl. *Richard Nixon: A Political and Personal Portrait*. New York: Harper and Bros., 1959.

Merrill, John C. *The Imperative of Freedom: A Philosophy of Journalistic Autonomy*. New York: Hastings House, Publishers, 1974.

Minow, Newton N., John Barlow Martin, and Lee A. Mitchell. *Presidential Television*. A Twentieth Century Fund Report. New York: Basic Books, 1973.

Nimmo, Dan D. *Newsgathering in Washington*. New York: Atherton Press, 1964.

Pearson, Drew and Jack Anderson. *The Case Against Congress*. New York: Simon and Schuster, 1968.

Phillips, Cabell. *Dateline: Washington*. New York: Doubleday, 1949.

Phillips, David G. *The Treason of the Senate*. New York: Monthly Review Press, by arrangement with Academic Reprints, Stanford University, 1953.

Poore, Benjamin P. *Perley's Reminiscences of Sixty Years in the National Metropolis*. Philadelphia: Hubbard Brothers, 1886.

Reston, James. *The Artillery of the Press*. New York: Harper & Row, 1966.

Rosten, Leo C. *The Washington Correspondents*. New York: Harcourt, Brace and Co., 1937.

Rovere, Richard H. *Senator Joe McCarthy*. New York: Harcourt, Brace and Co., 1959.

Sargeant, Nathan. *Public Men and Events*. Philadelphia: J.B. Lippincott & Co., 1875.

Seymour-ure, Colin. *The Press, Politics and the Public*. London: Methuen & Co. Ltd., 1968.

Shils, Edward A. *The Torment of Secrecy*. Glencoe, Illinois: The Free Press, 1956.

Smith, William Ernest. *The Francis Preston Blair Family in Politics*. New York: Macmillan, 1933.

Stealey, O.O. *Twenty Years in the Press Gallery from the 48th to the 58th Congress.* New York: 1906.

Talese, Gay. *The Kingdom and the Power.* New York: Bantam Books, 1970.

Tunstall, Jeremy. *The Westminster Lobby.* London: Routledge and Kegan Paul, 1970.

Townsend, George Alfred. *Washington, Outside and Inside.* Hartford, Conn.: James Belts & Co., 1874.

Wechsler, James A. *Reflections of an Angry Middle Aged Editor.* New York: Random House, 1960.

Weisberger, Bernard A. *The American Newspaperman.* Chicago: University of Chicago Press, 1961.

ARTICLES AND PERIODICALS

"ASNE (American Society of Newspaper Editors) Report on the Wechsler Case," and "Additional Comment on the Wechsler Case," *Neiman Reports*, VIII, no. 4 (October, 1953).

Bagdikian, Ben. "A Golden Age of Oracles," *Columbia Journalism Review*, Winter, 1966.

———. "Diggers and Toilers," *Columbia Journalism Review*, Summer, 1963.

———. "How Editors Pick Columnists," *Columbia Journalism Review*, Spring, 1966.

———. "Journalist Meets Propagandist," *Columbia Journalism Review*, Fall, 1963.

———. "News as a Byproduct," *Columbia Journalism Review*, Spring, 1967.

———. "Oracles and Their Audiences," *Columbia Journalism Review*, Winter, 1966/67.

"Committee Secrecy: Minor Impact of Reform Act," *Congressional Quarterly*, XXX, No. 7 (February 12, 1972).

"*Congressional Record*: A Daily Publishing Triumph on Congress' Doorstep," *Congressional Quarterly*, XXVII, No. 48 (November 28, 1969).

Dilliard, Irving. "Congressional Investigations: The Role of the Press," *University of Chicago Law Review*, XVIII (1950–51).

Doig, Ivan. "Keafauver vs. Crime: Television Boosts a Senator," *Journalism Quarterly*, XXXIX No. 3 (Autumn, 1962).

Dunn, Delmer. "Differences Among Public Officials in Their Reliance on the Press for Information," *Social Science Quarterly*, XLIX, No. 4 (March, 1969).

———. "Transmitting Information to the Press: Differences Among Officials," *Public Administration Review*, XXVIII, No. 5 (September/October, 1968).

"Freedom of Information Attitudes of the 91st Congress," Freedom of Information Center Report No. 214 (January, 1969).

Goldman, Ralph M. "Congress on the Air," *Public Opinion Quarterly*. XIV, No. 4 (Winter, 1950–51).

Grotta, Gerald L. "Philip Freneau's Crusade for Open Sessions of the U.S. Senate," *Journalism Quarterly*, XLVIII, No. 4 (Winter, 1971).

Javits, J. K. "The Case for Televising Congress," *The New York Times Magazine*, January, 13, 1952.

Kampleman, Max. "When Press Bites Man," *Columbia Journalism Review*, Spring, 1968.

King, Larry L. "The Road to Power in Congress," *Harper's* (June, 1971).

Koop, Theodore R. "Equality of Access for Radio in Covering Washington News," *Journalism Quarterly*, XXXIV, No. 3 (Summer, 1957).

Littlewood, Thoms B., "The Gallery Card War: Skirmishes over VOA," *Columbia Journalism Review*, January/February, 1974.

Loevinger, Lee. "The Journalistic Responsibility of Broadcasting," *Television Quarterly*, VIII, No. 1 (Winter, 1969).

McNeil, Neil V. "The Washington Correspondents: Why Do Some 'Drop Out'?" *Journalism Quarterly*, XLIII, No. 2 (Summer, 1966).

Marbut, Frederick B. "Early Washington Correspondents: Some Neglected Pioneers," *Journalism Quarterly*, XXV, No. 4 (December, 1948).

Moynihan, Daniel P. "The Presidency and the Press," *Commentary*, LI, No. 3 (March, 1971).

Mullen, James J. "How Candidates for the Senate Use Newspaper Advertising," *Journalism Quarterly*, XL, No. 4 (Autumn, 1963).

Partian, Eugene G. "The Use of Broadcast Media in Congressional, Legislative and Quasi-judicial Proceedings," *Journal of Broadcasting*, IV, No. 2 (Spring, 1960).

Richardson, Francis A. "Recollections of a Washington Newspaper Correspondent," *Records of the Columbia Historical Society*, II (1903).

Rivers, William L. "The Correspondents After 25 Years," *Columbia Journalism Review*, Spring, 1962.

Schneier, Edward. "The Intelligence of Congress: Information and Public Policy Patterns," *Annals*, No. 388 (March, 1970).

Shanor, Donald R. "Can a Congressman Sue a Columnist?", *Columbia Journalism Review*, Spring, 1967.

Sherrill, Robert. "The Invisible Senator," *Nation*, VIII (May 10, 1971).

Siebert, Frederick. "The Right to Report by Television." *Journalism Quarterly*, XXXIV, No. 3 (Summer, 1957).

Stevens, John D. "Congressional History of the 1798 Sedition Law," *Journalism Quarterly*, XLIII, No. 2 (Summer, 1966).

Taylor, Telford. "The Issue is Not TV, But Fair Play," *The New York Times Magazine*, April 15, 1951.

Wiggins, J.R. "Background on Investigations of the Press," *Neiman Reports*, VII, No. 4 (October, 1953).

Witcover, Jules. "Washington Letter: Finding a Press Seat at the Conventions," *Columbia Journalism Review*, Spring, 1968.

———. "Washington: The News Explosion," *Columbia Journalism Review*, Spring, 1969.

Yoakum, Robert. "The Dodd Case: Those Who Blinked," *Columbia Journalism Review*, Spring, 1967.

———. "Further Notes on Dodd," *Columbia Journalism Review*, Summer, 1967.

———. "Dodd Case: Loose Ends," *Columbia Journalism Review*, Summer, 1968.

Index

ABM, 141, 144, 145, 327; congressional hearings on, 71, 74, 88
Abzug, Bella, 50
Adams, George W., 42
Adams, Sherman, 350
Adams, Tom, 335, 336, 340
Advance News Service, 318
Advertising Age, 175, 224 (table)
Advise and Consent (Drury), 162, 273
Advocacy reporters, 206
Agency for International Development (AID), 354, 355
Agnew, Spiro T., 117, 118, 180, 363, 419, 422, 459, 472-79 ("TV's Incandescent and Damaging Presence in the Hearing Room"); Eckhardt on, 139-46
Albert, Carl, 198
Alch, Gerald, 475
Allen, Robert S., 273, 274
Alsop, Joseph, 273
Alsop, Stewart, 239, 283-88 ("Senator Lyndon Johnson: A Correspondent's View")
American Banker, 175, 224 (table)
American Bar Association, 462
American Broadcasting Company (ABC), 70, 78, 85, 176, 184, 217, 225 (table), 234 (table), 282, 356, 367, 418, 449
American Broadcasting Company v. United States, 413, 415
American Business Committee on National Priorities, 387
American Civil Liberties Union, 449
American in Washington, An (Baker), 181
American Newspaper Publishers Association (ANPA), 441, 448, 449, 454
American Society of Newspaper Editors (ASNE), 291, 441, 442, 443, 445, 449
American University, 167, 240, 331

Ames, William E., 8
Anastasi, Joseph, 32
Anderson, Jack, 221, 273, 321
Andrews, Bert, 239, 258 and n., 267, 300-309 ("Correspondents as Participants")
Angle, Martha, 340
Annals of Congress, 7, 8; see also Congressional debates
Annapolis Evening Capital, 334
Appell, Donald T., 305, 306
Appropriations Committee, House, 60, 61, 213, 214, 216, 253, 326, 388, 394
Appropriations Committee, Senate, 62, 214
Archibald, Samuel J., 325
Aristotle, 128
Arkansas City Traveler, 274
Armed Services Committee, House, 62, 71, 88, 213, 314, 315, 326
Armed Services Committee, Senate, 62, 210
Army-McCarthy hearings, 129, 348, 350
Arnold, Leonard, 152, 153
Arnold, William, 306
ASNE *Bulletin*, 395
Aspin, Les, 390
Associated Press (AP), 44, 54, 155, 160, 161, 167, 171, 172, 185, 216, 219, 223 (table), 253, 264, 265, 270, 278, 288, 289, 293, 294, 296, 298, 299, 394, 395, 443
Associated Press Managing Editors, 441
Authors League, 44

Badillo, Herman, 420
Bagdikian, Ben H., 173, 240, 388-98 ("Congress and the Media: Partners in Propaganda")
Baird, Joseph H., 374 n.

Baker, Bobby, 315-22, 452
Baker, Howard H., Jr., 368, 369, 370, 482-83, 486
Baker, John W., 160
Baker, Russell, 181
Baker Affair, 315-22, 452
Ball, Isabel Worrell, 274
Baltimore American, 31, 42
Baltimore Republican, 30, 34
Baltimore Sun, 172, 182, 219, 244
Balzac, Honoré de, 331
Banking and Currency Committee, Senate, 259, 319
Baptist Press, 175, 224 (table)
Barb, Marian, 335
Barnes, Joseph, 290
Barone, Michael, 94, 95 *n.*
Barr, Bob, 276
Barrett, Edward, 311
Barron, Jerome, 364, 365, 366, 405, 406-10 ("'The Selling of the Pentagon': Partisan Involvements and Antagonisms")
Barth, Alan, 158
Bartlett, Charles, 259
Basham, Christie, 366
Baskir, Lawrence, 357, 360
Baukage, H. R., 66
Bayard, Richard Henry, 37
Bayh, Birch, 211, 364 *n.*
Beaudette, Rick, 167
Beeper, 246, 380
Bell, David, 354, 355
Bell, Jack, 278
Bellamy, Lauralyn, 396, 398
Bennett, Charles L., 440, 455-57 ("The Potential Dangers of Shield Legislation")
Bennett, James Gordon, 8, 28, 29, 34, 35, 36, 38
Benti, Joseph, 427
Benton, William, 277
Bernstein, Carl, 459, 486-87 ("Nixon and His Aides Believe Hearing Is a Witchhunt")
Berrigan, Philip, 484
Betts, Jackson, 313
Bickel, Alexander, 408
Bill of Rights, 432
Black, Hugo, 410, 427
Black, Ruby, 274
Black Panthers, 414, 416, 451
Blaine, James G., 42, 43
Blanchard, Robert O., 167, 168-80 ("The Variety of Correspondents"), 180-221 ("The Correspondents Describe Their Work"), 334, 440-46 ("A New FoI Watchdog Needs Watching")
Bliss, Edward, Jr., 167

Bobby Baker case, 315-22, 452
Boggs, Hale, 204, 353
Bolling, Richard, 73, 74, 77, 78, 79, 82, 83, 88, 89, 135, 153-59 ("An Old-timer's View of the Press")
Bone, Homer T., 276
Bonneville International Corporation, 176, 225 (table)
Boorstin, Daniel J., 156
Borah, William E., 276, 278
Boston Globe, 172, 173, 182, 425, 448
Bouvier, Jacqueline, 274
Bow, Frank, 314
Bowles, Chester, 161
Bowman, William W., 192 *n.*
Boynton, H. V., 42, 43
Brandeis, Louis D., 109, 359 *n.*
Branzburg, Paul, 453
Branzburg v. Hayes, 402
Branzburg v. Pound, 408 *n.*
Brewster, Owen, 350
Bricker, John W., 265, 281
Bridge, Peter, 451, 454
Bridges, Harry, 290
Brinkley, David, 76, 148, 365
Broadcast groups, 225-26 (table); and congressional coverage time, 226 (tables), 227 (tables), 228 (tables), 229 (tables), 230 (table); *see also* Broadcast networks; Radio; Television
Broadcast journalism, access and accommodation for, 58, 66-89 *passim*
Broadcast networks, 225 (table), 429; and congressional coverage time, 226 (tables), 227 (tables), 228 (tables), 229 (tables), 230 (table); public access to, theory of, 409; *see also* Broadcast groups; Radio; Television
Broadcasting magazine, 396
Broder, David, 371
Brooks, Erastus, 30, 32, 36
Brooks, Jack, xi
Brooks, James, 32
Brooks, Wayland, 46
Browder, Earl, 290
Brown, Clarence J., 422
Broyhill, Joel, 331, 332, 333, 335, 336, 337, 338, 341, 342
Brumidi, Constantino, 280
Bundy, McGeorge, 286
Burch, Dean, 426
Bureau of National Affairs, 224 (table)
Burgin, David, 340, 343
Burke, Aedanus, 8, 9, 11
Business Week, 225 (table), 233 (table)
Buzhardt, J. Fred, 487
Byrd, Robert C., 193, 361, 364 *n.*, 394
Byrnes, Bob, 270
Byrnes, John W., 319

Cable television, 363, 391

Cain, Harry, 252

Caldwell, Earl, 450, 452, 456

Caldwell v. United States, 408 and *n.*, 414, 416, 447, 448, 449, 452, 456

Cambodia, 104, 107, 111, 112, 125, 141, 142, 144, 145

Campbell, Alexander, 303, 304

Cannon, Howard W., 320

Capitol Hill News Service (CHNS), 240, 388, 395, 396, 397, 398

Capper, Arthur, 277

Cardozo, Benjamin, 478

Carpenter, Thomas, 8, 15, 17-18

Carswell, G. Harrold, 141, 142, 144, 145, 146

Case, Clifford P., 193, 251

Cater, Douglass, 55, 239, 250-53 ("The Stuff of Which Good Reporting Is Made"), 345, 346-51 ("The Congressional Hearing as Publicity Vehicle")

Caulfield, John, 475, 476

Celler, Emanuel, 413

Center, The (Alsop), 283

Chafee, Zechariah, 416

Chambers, Whittaker, 258, 267, 300-08 *passim*

Charleston Courier, 31, 32, 33

Chattanooga Times, 259

Chesnut, W. Calvin, 303, 304

Chester, Charles, 353

Chicago Daily News, 158, 172, 218, 310, 317

Chicago Sun-Times, 172, 218, 292

Chicago Tribune, 42, 116, 172, 253, 277, 290, 291, 292

Childs, Marquis, 273

Chiles, Lawton, 63

China Lobby, 290

Chisholm, Shirley, 135, 149-53 ("Guess Who's Not Coming to the Gridiron Club Dinner?")

Christian Science Monitor, 172, 244, 363, 374 and *n.*, 396

Church, Frank, 104, 193, 200

CIA, 455

Cincinnati Commercial-Gazette, 42

Civil rights, filibuster over (1964), covered by TV, 67-70

Civil Rights Bill (1964), 207

Clapp, Charles L., 135, 136-39 ("The Value of Publicity")

Clark, Dick, 394

Clark, Joseph S., 316, 321, 353

Clay, Henry, 36, 37

Cleaver, Eldridge, 451, 452

Cleveland, Richard, 304

Cleveland Plain Dealer, 309, 312, 313

Cohen, Bernard C., x, 183, 192

Cold War, 446

Collingwood, Charles, 352

Columbia Broadcasting System (CBS), 55, 66-72 *passim*, 78, 85, 105, 120, 176, 183, 184, 217, 225 (table), 234 (table), 282, 345, 352-56 *passim*, 363, 367, 394, 405, 406, 407, 409, 410, 449, 451; and congressional debate on First Amendment (1971), 410-38 *passim*

Columbia Journalism Review, 108, 181 *n.*, 315, 346 *n.*, 442 *n.*, 447

Columbia University, Graduate School of Journalism at, 311

Commentary magazine, 159

Commerce Committee, Senate, 62, 106

Committees of Correspondence, 449

Common Cause, 94, 189, 344

Communications Act (1934), 360

Communism, 129

Computers, Ervin's views on, 356, 358

Condon, Edward U., 302

Congress, 7, 8, 93-103 *passim*, 105, 106, 109, 117, 120, 169, 193-97 *passim*, 201, 202, 214, 215, 250; coverage of, by news media, question of adequacy of, 216-21; direct mail used by, 381; and "fourth-term crisis," 445; and Freedom of Information (FOI) Act, *see* Freedom of Information (FOI) Act; "Grass-Roots," 374; and "keeping in touch," 370-84 *passim*; and media, as partners in propaganda (Bagdikian), 388-98; and organizing to make news, 248-49; perspectives of, on news media, 135-64 *passim*; and press, 136-38, 240-49, 375-80; Press Galleries of, 40-47 *passim*, 52, 53, 66, 154, 162, 166, 213, 227 (table), 246, 251, 254, 261, 277, 379, 380; and protectionism by correspondents, 252, 253; and publicity, 128-34, 345-98 *passim*; and radio, 138, 139, 380, 381, 386; and television, 138, 139, 380, 381, 386, 391, 392, 393; *see also* Congressional correspondents; Congressional Hearings; Congressional debates; House of Representatives; Senate

Congressional correspondents, 165-67, 239; ages of, 230 (table); audience perception by, 190-92; backgrounds of, 182; birthplaces of, by state, 230 (table); and coverage of Congress, question of adequacy of, 216-21; coverage time of, 226-30 (tables); educational levels of, 231 (table); "follow-the-leader" behavior of, 183; graduate school majors of, 231 (table); idea sources relied upon by, 234 (table); influences on reporting by, 235 (table); information sources relied upon by, 235 (table); and

Congressional correspondents (*Continued*) job descriptions, 182, 233 (table); newspapers relied upon by, 182, 183, 184, 185, 233 (table); numbers of, by media organization category, 222 (table); organizations employing, types of, 233 (table); as participants, 300-15; periodicals relied upon by, 183, 184, 233 (table); political identification of, 232 (table); professional roles of, 192-200, 236 (table); and protectionism for Congress, 252, 253; radio programs relied upon by, 184, 234 (tables); and relations with sources, 200-16, 237 (table); reliance of, on other media, 182-86, 233-34 (tables); reliance of, on other sources, 186-90, 234-35 (tables); roles of, professional, 192-200, 236 (table); salaries of, yearly, 232 (table); sanctions imposed on, 212-16, 238 (table); and sources, relations with, 200-16, 237 (table); television programs relied upon by, 183, 184, 234 (tables); and time, coverage, 226-30 (tables); types of organizations employing, 233 (table); undergraduate majors of, 231 (table); variety of, 168-80; and years covering Congress, 232 (table); and years covering Washington, 231 (table); *see also* News media; Newspapers; Press; Reporters of Senate News

Congressional debates: on access for official press (1800), 15-28; on First Amendment and broadcast journalism (1971), 410-38; on reporter's place in House (1789-90), 8-15

Congressional Directory, 44, 45, 53, 166, 392, 395

Congressional Globe, 8, 30, 31

Congressional Hearings: by Constitutional Rights Subcommittee of Senate Judiciary Committee, 357, 359-67 *passim*, 458; on "Equal Time for Congress" (Communications Subcommittee of Senate Commerce Committee, 1970), 103-27; on "Modern Access for Broadcast" (Special Subcommittee on Legislative Reorganization, 1969), 70-89 *passim*; as publicity vehicle (Cater), 346-51; on Watergate, *see* Watergate hearings

Congressional Quarterly, 58, 60 and *n.*, 167, 176, 183, 187, 220, 224 (table), 233 (table), 234 (table), 235 (table), 339, 355, 389

Congressional Record, 5, 29, 54, 55, 88, 93, 95, 100, 105, 146, 183, 186, 189, 190, 192, 196, 220, 234 (table), 235 (table), 243, 252, 260, 312, 337, 384, 386

Congressional Register, 8, 9

Congressman, The: His Work as He Sees It (Clapp), 136

Conroy, Edward, 335, 336, 337

Constitution, 93, 94, 100, 101, 105, 116, 120, 123, 358, 359, 362, 367, 389, 419, 432, 458, 459, 462, 474

Constitutional Convention, 7, 432

Constitutional Rights Subcommittee of Senate Judiciary Committee, hearings by, 357, 359-67 *passim*, 458

Conte, Silvio O., 420

Coolidge, Calvin, 66, 280, 282

Cooper, John S., 104, 273

Copley News Service, 173

Cormier, Frank, 287

Correspondents, congressional, *see* Congressional correspondents

Cotton, Norris, 201

Cox, Archibald, 459-64 *passim*, 469, 472, 477, 484

Cox Broadcasting Corporation, 176, 225 (table)

Craig, May, 274, 319

Cranston, Alan, 204

Cronkite, Walter, 76, 86, 333, 358, 359, 361-67 *passim*

Cross, Harold, 402 and *n.*

Crutch story, 157

Curry, William, 333, 339

Curtis, Carl T., 483, 484

Curtis, Thomas, 99, 100-03 ("The Executive Dominates the News")

Daily Record, available to Congress, 189

"Dangers of Radiation, The" (CBS documentary), 427

Daniels, Dan, 72

Darling, Joseph, 54

Dash, Samuel, 460, 463, 464, 485

Davidson, Roger H., 165

Davis, Kenneth Culp, 442-43

Dean, John W., 460, 463, 466, 470, 471, 475, 476, 481, 485, 487

Deane, Philip, 350

Debates, congressional, *see* Congressional debates

Defense Department, 113, 122, 158, 168, 255, 314, 321, 406

Delaney, Denis W., 463, 464, 466, 467

Democratic National Committee, 56, 105

Democratic party, 41, 215, 216, 282, 294, 299, 300; platform of (1972), 63

Democratic Study Group (DSG), 162, 189, 205, 213, 324

Dempsey, John J. ("Jack"), 66

Dennis v. *United States*, 409

Dent, John H., 429
Denton, Bob, 283
Denton, Herb, 338, 339
Des Moines Register, 172-73, 311, 394
Des Moines Tribune, 173
Detroit News, 277
Deviney, Agnes, 341, 342
Devol, Kenneth S., ix n.
"Dial-a-Congressman" plan, 374-75
Dies Committee, House, 349
Digest of Bills, 189
Dirksen, Everett, 69, 170, 171, 206, 214, 369, 386
Dodd, Thomas J., 71, 75
Dominican Republic, 107, 111, 112, 443
Donrey Washington News Bureau, 173
Downey, Sheridan, 271
Drury, Allen, 273
Due process of law, and Watergate, 468-72, 473, 479-82
Duke, Paul, 178, 217
Dulles, Allen, 300
Dulles, John Foster, 300
Dunn, Arthur Wallace, 149 n.
Dunn, Delmer, 95 and n., 96, 192, 239, 240-49 ("Symbiosis: Congress and the Press")

Eagleton, Thomas F., 206
Early, Stephen T., 45
Eastland, James O., 265
Eastman Kodak Laboratories, 71
Eckhardt, Bob, 135, 139-46 ("Mr. Agnew, You Are Wrong about the Press")
Economist, 159
Edelman, Murray, 446
Editor and Publisher, 49, 156, 224 (table), 396
Edmisten, Rufus, 357
Education and Labor Committee, House, 213, 214, 325
Educational Broadcasting Review, 405, 406
Edwards, Jack, 418
Ehrlichman, John D., 486
Eisenhower, Dwight D., 279, 292, 441, 443, 444, 445
Eleazer, Frank, 189
Electrical Wholesaling, 175
Ellsberg, Daniel, 462
Engle, Clair, 161
Epstein, Noel, 239, 309-14 ("Correspondents as Participants")
Equal Employment Opportunity Commission, 151, 152, 153
Ervin, Sam J., Jr., 178, 269, 345, 367, 368, 448, 458, 459, 460, 461, 469, 471, 472, 473, 474, 476, 479, 483, 484, 486; Leamer on, 356-67

Essery, J. Frederick, 149 n.
Eugene Register-Guard, 291, 292, 295
Evans, Rowland, 273
Evening Star, 42
Executive, Chief, see President

"Face the Nation," 117
Fairchild Publications, 175, 224 (table), 276
Fairness doctrine, 120, 121, 359, 363, 410, 422, 423
Fallows, James M., 384-87 (". . . And, Frankly, Getting Re-elected")
Family Assistance Plan, 108
Farquhar, Roger, 335
Farr, William, 450, 453, 454
Fascell, Dante B., 63
Fauntroy, Walter, 333
Federal Bureau of Investigation (FBI), 287, 320, 395, 451
Federal Communications Commission (FCC), 106, 117, 121, 122, 151, 152, 347, 360, 361, 386, 391, 393, 422, 423, 426, 435, 436
Federal Public Records Law, see Freedom of Information (FOI) Act
Federal Regulation of Lobbying Act (1946), 130
Federal-State Reports, 175, 224 (table)
Fenno, John, 7, 14
Ferguson, Homer, 276
Fifth Amendment, 465
Filippov, Ivan A., 48
Finance Committee, Senate, 62, 108, 209, 272
Findley, Paul, 310
Finney, Ruth, 274
First Amendment, 357, 359 n., 361, 364, 365, 367, 401, 402, 405-10 passim, 439, 447, 449, 455, 457, 463; and broadcast journalism, debate on (1971), 410-38
Flanigan, Peter, 201
Flansburg, James, 394
Fleeson, Doris, 274
Fleming, Edwin, 43
Flood, Dan, 329
Fong, Hiram, 364 n.
Forcade, Thomas King, 49, 50
Ford, Gerald R., 353, 385, 396, 412
Ford Foundation, 363
Foreign Affairs Committee, House, 55, 62, 76
Foreign Relations Committee, Senate, 71, 75, 77, 88, 104, 118, 120, 210, 276, 354, 356
Fornos, Werner, 332, 342
Forrestal, James, 307
Forsythe, Bill, 282
Forte, Greg, 342

Fourth Branch of Government, The (Cater), 250, 346
Francis, Lorania, 271
Francis, Warren, 271
Franked mail, 384, 385
Frankel, Max, 287, 407
Frankfurter, Felix, 409, 473
Franklin, Benjamin, 122
Frederickson, Paul, 46
Freedman, Max, 287
Freedom of Information (FOI) Act, 402, 439, 440, 441, 443, 446
Freedom of the Press from Zenger to Jefferson (Levy), 401 *n.*
Freedom or Secrecy (Wiggins), 59 *n.*
Freeman, Orville, 437
French, Herbert, 281
Freneau, Philip, 7
Friendly, Fred, 68, 120, 353, 354, 355, 363
Fulbright, J. William, 76, 77, 82, 99, 103, 107, 108, 109, 113-25 *passim*, 259, 273, 348, 354, 355, 356
Furman, Bess, 274

Gales, Joseph, 8
Gallup poll, 355
Gannett News Service, 173, 395
Garment, Leonard, 487
Garner, John Nance, 59, 60, 278
Gavin, James, 355
Gazette of the United States, 7
General Accounting Office (GAO), 312, 313, 314
George, Walter F., 275
Georgia Journal, 31
Gerstel, Steven, 49
Geyelin, Philip, 286
Gilbert, Ben W., 317
Gillette, Guy, 66
Gitt, C. M., 294
Goldberg, Arthur J., 354
Goldfine, Bernard, 350, 351
Goldsmith, John, 210
Goldwater, Barry, 110, 157, 271, 272
Gonzalez, Henry B., 436
Goodman, Julian, 126, 127
Gore, Albert, 355
Gould, Jack, 356
Government Operations Committee, House, 62, 63, 440
Graham, Evarts A., 152
Graham, Fred P., 50, 440, 447-55 ("The Federal Shield Law We Need")
Grand Inquest (Taylor), 349
Granger, Francis, 36
Green, Mark J., 384-87 (". . . And, Frankly, Getting Re-elected")

Green, Michael, 239, 240, 322-31 ("Nobody Covers the House")
Grey, David L., ix *n.*
Grider, George, 374
Gridiron Club, 135, 149 and *n.*
Griffin, Robert P., 113, 115, 117, 127
Griffin-Larrabee News Bureau, 173
Groennings, Sven, 240
Grosjean v. *American Press Co.*, 416
Gruening, Ernest, 273
Gruenstein, Peter, 396, 398
Gude, Gil, 331, 333, 335, 342, 343, 422
Gun control, 110, 113
Gurney, Edward J., 367, 368, 369, 487

Haakinson, Ed, 278
Haldeman, H. R., 486
Haley, William, 108
Hall, Arnold Bennett, 291
Halleck, Charles, 157, 202
Halls of the Mighty (Riedel), 269
Hamilton, Alexander, 105, 401
Hamilton, Martha, 339
Hamilton, Roulhac, 292, 293, 296, 299
Handy, F. A. G., 43
Hanna, Sam, 49
Harding, Warren G., 280
Hardy, Porter, Jr., 314
Harlan, John M., 464, 467
Harper's Magazine, 356
Harris, Herb, 340
Harris poll, 107, 108, 355
Harrison, William Henry, 34
Hartford Courant, 270
Harvey, Paul, 148
Harwood, Richard, 50
Hatfield, Mark O., 141, 144, 145
Hawley, J. P., 240
Hearings, congressional, *see* Congressional Hearings
Hearst Newspapers, 173, 270, 320, 393
Hechler, Ken, 202, 397
Hewlett, Frank, 49
Heymann, Phillip B., 460
Hickox, Kay, 167
Hill, Ralph L., 317
Hiss, Alger, 267, 290, 300-09 *passim*
Hogan, Larry, 331, 332, 333, 335, 336, 337, 341, 343
Holifield, Chet, 426
Holmberg, David, 396
Holt, Marjorie, 331, 334, 335, 336, 341, 342, 344
Holt, Russ, 295
Hoover, Herbert, 280
Horan, Robert F., Jr., 337
Horn, John, 68
Horner, Carol, 167, 331

Horner, Garnett, 287
Horton, Bob, 280
House of Representatives, 93, 94, 95, 100, 106, 131, 132, 133, 154, 174, 177, 189, 207, 208, 209, 213, 240, 245, 250, 322-31; Appropriations Committee of, 60, 61, 213, 214, 216, 253, 326, 388, 394; Armed Services Committee of, 62, 71, 88, 213, 314, 315, 326; and correspondents' coverage time, 226 (table), 227 (table); decentralization necessary for, 132; Dies Committee of, 349; Education and Labor Committee of, 213, 214, 325; Foreign Affairs Committee of, 55, 62, 76; Government Operations Committee of, 62, 63, 440; and H.R. 6935 (truth in news broadcasting bill), 433, 434-35; Interior and Insular Affairs Committee of, 62; Interstate and Foreign Commerce Committee of, 61, 394, 406, 407; Judiciary Committee of, 62, 100, 448; Post Office and Civil Service Committee of, 62; Press Gallery of, 51, 54, 154, 166, 254, 379, 380; Radio-Television Gallery of, 51, 52, 53, 55, 70, 86, 379, 380; reforms needed in, 323-31; Rules Committee of, 324; Standing Rules in, 41, 43, 44, 45, 47-48, 216; and Subcommittee on Legislative Appropriations, 51; Un-American Activities Committee of, 67, 258, 301, 302, 303, 306, 307, 308; Ways and Means Committee of, 62, 189, 333; *see also* Congress; Congressional correspondents
House Out of Order (Bolling), 153
Howard, James J., 431
Hruska, Roman L., 363, 364, 365
Hudnut, William, 396
Hughes, Howard, 350, 393
Humphrey, Hubert, 68, 140, 141, 300, 355
Humphries, Harry, 161
Hungate, William L., 135, 146-49 ("Member Attitudes on News Media Role")
"Hunger in America" (CBS documentary), 421, 437
Hunt, William, 30, 32
Hunter, Marjorie, 49
Huntley, Chet, 148
Huston, Luther A., 40, 49-50 ("Access for the Underground Press")
Hutcheson, Maurice A., 464
Hutchinson, William K., 270

I Protest (Oxnam), 347
Ickes, Harold L., 59 and *n.*, 297
Inouye, Daniel K., 367, 368, 369
Institute of Pacific Relations, 290, 291

Interior Department, 388
Internal Security Act (1950), 130
International News Service, 347
Interpretive journalism, 196, 198, 265
Interstate and Foreign Commerce Committee, House, 61, 394, 406, 407
"Issues and Answers," 95, 117
ITT hearings, 201

Jackson, Henry M., 294, 295
Jackson, Robert, 311
Jackson, Robert H., 475
Jefferson, Thomas, 7, 105, 122
Jessup, Philip C., 290
Job of the Congressman, The (Tacheron and Udall), 370
Johnson, Alice, 292
Johnson, Lyndon B., 101, 105, 107-13 *passim*, 188, 239, 281, 316, 318, 320, 321, 354, 355, 356, 441, 443, 444, 445; Stewart Alsop on, 283-88
Johnson, Nicholas, 360, 366, 426
Johnson, Olin D., 319
Johnson, Richard M., 30, 34
Johnstone, J. W. C., 192 *n.*
Joint Atomic Energy Committee, 63
Joint Economic Committee, 63
Jolovitz, Herbert, 312
Jordan, Frank, 78, 79, 84-89 *passim*
Joseph Burstyn, Inc. v. *Wilson*, 415
Journal of Commerce, 32, 33
Journalism, interpretive, 196, 198, 265
Journalism Quarterly, 28, 40, 441 *n.*
Judiciary Committee, House, 62, 100, 448
Judiciary Committee, Senate, 62, 345, 357, 359-67 *passim*, 448, 458
Jump cut, defined, 433
Justice Department, 303, 307, 321, 454

Kastenmeier, Robert W., 448
Kefauver, Estes, 67, 258
Keifer, J. Warren, 42, 43, 44
Kelly, G. Milton, 270, 288, 289, 294
Kennan, George, 71, 75
Kennedy, Edward M., 211, 283, 363, 364, 365, 462
Kennedy, John F., 107, 109, 110, 112, 113, 208, 274, 275, 279, 283, 441, 444, 445
Kennedy, Robert F., 110, 208, 485
Kilpatrick, James J., 457
Kinescope, 82
Kingman, E., 30, 32
Kissinger, Henry, 395
Kleindienst, Richard, 211
Kluttz, Jerry, 303
Kneece, Jack, 334, 340
Knight, John S., 457
Knight Newspapers, 173

Knoll, 239, 315-22 ("The News Media and the Bobby Baker Case")
Kodachrome, 71
Korea, 374
Kosygin, Alexei, 352
Krock, Arthur, 260
Krulewitch v. *United States*, 475

Labor Press Association, 47, 48
LaFollette-Monroney Act (1946), 278
Laird, Melvin R., 71, 74
Lancaster Intelligencer, 31
Landau, Jack, 316, 317, 440, 447-55 ("The Federal Shield Law We Need")
Landmark Communications, 173
Lardner, George, Jr., 459, 460-64 ("The Battle of Watergate TV")
Larsen, Otto, 50
Latta, Delbert L., 75, 76, 77, 78, 82, 86, 87, 88
Lattimore, Owen, 290, 483
Lausche, Frank, 355
Lautier, Louis R., 45, 46
Lawrence (Kansas) *Journal*, 274
Leacacos, John, 312
Leamer, Laurence, 345, 356-67 ("The Sam Ervin Show"), 458, 459
Leggitt, Richard, 336, 340
Legislative Reorganization Act (1946), 59
Legislative Reorganization Act (1970), 58, 60, 61, 62, 67 n., 324 n.
Lenzner, Terry, 484, 485
Levy, Leonard, 401
Lewin, Nathan, 462
Lewis, Fulton, Jr., 66
Lewis, Jake, 211
Lewis, John L., 289, 297
Lewis, Sinclair, 358
Libel, 453
Liberty Magazine, 279
Liebling, A. J., 156
Life magazine, 163, 318, 425
Lightman, David, 454
Lincoln, Abraham, 280, 281
Lindsay, John J., 316
Lippmann, Walter, 159, 260, 360
Lisagor, Peter, 158
Lodge, Henry Cabot, Jr., 278, 279
London *Times*, 459, 482; on Watergate, and due process of law, 468-72, 480, 481
Long, Russell B., 212, 275
Los Angeles Herald-Examiner, 450
Los Angeles Times, 150, 172, 173, 182, 218, 219, 242, 271, 311, 320, 328
Lotto, Jack, 351
Louisville Courier-Journal, 42
Love, William C., 385
Lovett, Robert, 291

Lowenstein, Allard K., 323, 327
Luce, Robert B., 269, 300
Ludlow, Louis, 277
Lynch, John, 78, 79, 81, 82, 83, 85, 89

McAndrew, William, 66
MacArthur, Douglas, 290
MacArthur hearings, 347, 348
MacBride, William C., 42, 43
McCarran Committee, 290
McCarthy, Eugene, 276, 355
McCarthy, Joseph, 78, 129, 155, 256, 265, 296, 348, 350, 351, 483, 484, 485
McCarthy, Max, 202
McClatchy Newspapers of California, 173
McClellan, John, 157, 364 n., 485
McCord, James, 474, 475, 476
McCormack, John W., 67, 322, 323, 325, 326, 327, 330
McCormack, Medill, 277
McCormick, Colonel, 290, 292
McDade, Joseph M., 388, 397
McFall, John J., 326
McGee, Gale W., 200, 352
McGill, Ralph, 155, 273
McGovern, George, 141, 144, 145, 158, 247, 352, 387
McGraw-Hill News Bureau, 224 (table), 225 (table)
McGrory, Mary, 198, 274
Mackay, James A., 374
McKellar, Kenneth D., 264, 279, 280
McLaren, Richard, 454
McMillan, John, 340
McNamara, Robert S., 71, 75, 355
McNamee, Graham, 282
Madison, James, 105, 122, 414, 416
Magnuson, Warren G., 106, 294, 295
Magruder, Jeb Stuart, 460, 463, 466
Mahon, George, 394
Manchester Guardian, 159
Manelli, and Stanton, 432, 433
Mansfield, Mike, 76, 120, 121, 206, 394
Marbury, William L., 304
Marbut, Frederick B., 8, 28-38 ("The Letter-Writers in the Senate"), 40-48 ("The Standing Committee of Correspondents")
Marcy, Carl, 210
Marshall Plan, 278
Martin, Joe, Jr., 67
Mass Media and the Supreme Court (Devol), ix n.
Matthews, Chris, 396
Matthews, Donald R., 239, 253-69 ("'Covering' the Senate")
May, Buck, 281
Means, Marianna, 287

Medford Mail Tribune, 295, 296
Media, news, *see* News media
"Meet the Press," 95, 117, 179, 234 (table)
Melcher, John, 397
Member of the House (Miller), 160
Mencken, H. L., 329
Metcalf, Lee, xi
Metromedia Radio News, 176, 225 (table)
Meyer, Eugene, 289
Miller, Clem, 135, 160-64 ("A Newcomer's View of the Press"), 375 and *n.*
Miller, Harold O., 337, 342
Miller, Jack, 394
Millikin, Eugene, 272
Minneapolis Tribune, 311
Minow, Newton, 426
Minshall, William, 313, 314, 315, 432
Mitchell, James, 454
Mitchell, John N., 414, 454, 482, 484, 485
Mobile Daily Commercial Register and Patriot, 31, 33
Mobile office, Congressman's, 373
Mollenhoff, Clark, 311, 318, 394
Monroney, Mike, 277, 278
Montoya, Joseph M., 368, 475
Moody, Blair, 277
Moore, Irna, 333, 338, 339
Moore, Richard A., 484, 485
Moore, William Elwyn, 30
Moorhead, William S., 439, 440, 446
Moorhead Committee, 440, 443, 445, 446
Morgan, Edward P., 287
Morris, Thomas, 314
Morrison, Fred, 66
Morrison, Julian, 318
Morse, Wayne, 239, 264, 270, 271, 273, 353, 354; A. Robert Smith on, 288-300
Mortimer, John, 152
Morton, Thruston B., 188, 480
Moss, John E., 440, 442, 443, 444
Moss Committee, 401, 439, 440, 441, 443, 444, 445
Moynihan, Daniel P., 180
Muckraking, 196, 297, 315, 450
Mudd, Roger, 58, 67, 68, 69, 70, 73-78 *passim,* 171, 178, 217
"Mult box," 72, 73
Mundt, Karl E., 306, 353, 356, 387
Murnane, Tomas, 167
Murrow, Edward R., 78
Muskie, Edmund S., 208, 393
Muto, Al, 282
Muto, Frank, 282
Mutual Broadcasting System, 70, 176, 225 (table)

NAACP v. *Button,* 416
Nader, Ralph, 94, 344, 443
Nader Congress Project, 346, 387, 388, 390, 395
NASA, 397
Nation, 199, 396
National Association of Broadcasters, 449
National Broadcasting Company (NBC), 66, 70, 78, 85, 127, 176, 217, 225 (table), 234, (table), 282, 354, 355, 356, 366, 367, 418, 427, 449
National Catholic News Service, 224 (table)
National Commitments Resolution, 104
National Gazette, 7
National Intelligencer, 7, 8, 29, 34, 37
National Journal, 176, 225 (table), 233 (table), 234 (table), 235 (table)
National Newspaper Association, 441
National Press Club, 45, 246, 283
National Public Radio, 176, 225 (table)
Negro press, 45
New Deal, 294
New Left, 359
New Republic, 199
New Statesman and Nation (London), 318
New York Daily News, 173, 317, 318
New York Express, 29, 31, 32, 33, 36, 37, 38
New York Herald, 8, 28, 29, 32-37 *passim*
New York Herald Tribune, 68, 179, 256, 258, 260, 267, 278, 290, 304, 308, 309
New York Post, 150, 152, 153, 317, 318
New York Star, 290
New York Times, 42, 47, 49, 50, 149, 150, 152, 171-76 *passim,* 179, 182-85 *passim,* 188, 218, 219, 233 (table), 242, 244, 253, 256, 260, 265, 267, 292, 319, 363, 395, 408, 409, 449, 450, 469, 470, 476
New York Times v. *Sullivan,* 416
New York v. *Dillon,* 417
New York World, 42
New York World-Telegram, 291
New Yorker magazine, 159
Newhouse News Service, 173, 318
News from the Capital (Marbut), 40
News media: and Congress, as partners in propaganda (Bagdikian), 388-98; congressional perspectives on, 135-64 *passim;* elements of, 243-46; and Freedom of Information (FOI) Act, 402, 439, 440, 441, 442, 443; local, 244, 245; national, 244, 245, 246; public access to, theory of, 365; regional, 244, 245; and shield legislation, 440, 449-57; and survey of organizations, 223-26 (tables); *see also* Congressional cor-

News media (*Continued*)
respondents; Newspapers; Press; Radio; Reporters of Senate news Television
Newsletters, congressional, 335, 382-83, 385
Newspaper Guild, 449
Newspaper Preservation Act, 454
Newspapers, 223-24 (table); relied on by correspondents, 182, 183, 184, 185, 233 (table); specialized, 224 (table); *see also* Congressional correspondents; News media; Press; Reporters of Senate news
Newsweek, 183, 184, 218, 219, 225 (table), 233 (table), 287, 316, 396, 449
Nicodemus, Charles, 310
Niles, John M., 30, 31, 32, 33, 34
Nimmo, Dan, 444
Nixon, Richard M., 105, 107, 110, 111, 112, 113, 141, 150, 188, 198, 215, 239, 245, 246, 258, 279, 294, 339, 394, 414, 426, 441; and Hiss-Chambers case, 267, 300-09; and Watergate, 469, 470, 471, 475, 476, 480, 481, 482, 483, 485, 486, 487
Nokes, J. Richard, 293
North American Aviation, Inc., 311
North American Newspaper Alliance, 224 (table)
North Vietnam, 111, 245, 286, 352
Norvell, John, 30, 31
Novak, Bob, 273
Novak, Gertrude C., 316
Nuclear Test Ban Treaty, 107, 110, 112

Obey, David, 385, 386
Obscenity and Pornography Commission, 49, 50
Observer (London), 350
Office of International Information, 46
Office of War Information (OWI), 46
O'Hara, James G., 325, 419
Ohio Statesman, 31, 33
Ohio-Washington News Bureau, 173
Oil Daily, 175, 224 (table)
Oklahoma News, 277
O'Konski, Alvin, 384, 386
Oliver Wendell Holmes Bill of Rights Award (1964), 158
O'Mahoney, Joseph, 276
Opinion Makers, The (Rivers), 375 *n.*
Oregon Journal, 292, 293, 296, 297
Oregon Statesman, 295, 299
Oregonian, 293, 298
Orwant, Jack E., 167
Otis, James F., 30
Oxnam, G. Bromley, 347 *n.*

Pace, Charles F., 279
Packwood, Robert, 63
Paine, Tom, 409
Pappas, Paul, 408 *n.*, 447, 451
Parris, Stan, 331, 332, 334, 335, 336, 337, 340, 341
Pastore, John, 108, 109, 113, 115, 117, 118, 119, 120
Patman, Wright, 76, 211
Patton, George, 274, 369
Pearson, Drew, 148, 207, 264, 273, 297, 298, 321
Pecora hearings, 349
Peel, Robert, 153
Pelly, Thomas M., 421
Pendleton East Oregonian, 296
Pennington, Joseph, 454
Pentagon, 259, 291, 309, 312, 313, 314, 315, 355, 443
Pentagon Papers, 359, 395, 402, 406, 407, 408, 440, 453
People's Right to Know, The (Cross), 402 *n.*
Percy, Charles H., 188
Peress, Irving, 483
Periodical Gallery, 53, 54, 55, 166, 213, 380
Periodicals, 224-25 (table); relied on by correspondents, 233 (table)
Perry, William, 55, 56
Petrillo, Jimmy, 67
Philadelphia Daily News, 396
Philadelphia Press, 274
Phillips, Cebell, 149 *n.*, 320
Photographers, employed by House campaign committees, 380
Photographers' Gallery, 54, 56, 282
Pickle, J. J., 429
Pierson, W. Theodore, 123
Poage, William, 386
Poetics (Aristotle), 128
Polsby, Nelson W., 100, 131-34 ("Congress, Publicity and Public Policy")
Poore, Benjamin Perley, 35
Porter, Alexander, 29
Post-Newsweek Company, 118
Potter, Charles E., 67
Potter, Philip, 286
"Powers That Be, The" (NBC documentary), 427
Pravda, 48
President: as Commander-in-Chief, 104; news conferences by, 115, 116; policy initiated by, 133; powers of, 105; use of media by, 99, 100-03
President's Room, 239, 250; view from (Riedel), 269-83
Press: and Agnew, 139-46; blacks in, 150, 151, 152, 153; and Congress, 136-38,

240-49, 375-80; credibility problem of, among conservatives, 203; freedom of, 117, 357, 358, 360, 361, 363, 366, 367, 401, 403, 407, 409, 419, 421-25 *passim*, 431, 432, 435, 436, 456, 457, 458, 459; and House reform, failure to deal with, 324-31; methods of gaining coverage by, 246-47; national prestige, 172; Negro, 45; newcomer's view of (Miller), 160-64; oldtimer's view of (Bolling), 153-59; prestige, 172, 244; and protectionism for Congress, 252, 253; and pseudo-news, 156-57; regional prestige, 172; as source of senators' information, 259-60; Washington's suburban, 332, 334, 340-42; and Washington's suburban congressmen, 441-46 (Wolfson); *see also* Congressional correspondents; News media; Newspapers; Reporters of Senate news

Press assistant, 379
Press Galleries of Congress, 40-47 *passim*, 52, 53, 66, 154, 162, 166, 213, 227 (table), 246, 251, 254, 261, 277, 379, 380
Press release, 246, 248, 337, 379, 385, 390
Press secretary, 248, 379
Preston, William C., 33
Price, H. Douglas, 445
Price, Hank, 248
Printing Office, Government, 55
Progressive, 396
Provensen, Hurlif, 282
Proxmire, William, 312, 313, 314, 315, 480
Pseudo-news, 156-57
Public Broadcasting Corporation, 86
Public Officials and the Press (Dunn), 95 *n.*
Public Opinion Quarterly, 192 *n.*
Public Policy, 131
Pulitzer Prize, 162, 267, 273, 311
Pursley, Bill, 259, 360
Purtell, William A., 251

Questionnaires, congressman's use of, 383-84
Quill, The, 440

Racism, 149
Radio, 148, 149, 171, 179, 223 (table), 244, 246, 247, 282, 297, 335; and beeper, 246; and CHNS rates, 397; and Congress, 138, 139, 380, 381, 386; congressional hearings covered by, 72; relied on by correspondents, 184, 234 (tables); sanctions imposed on, 212; *see also* Broadcast groups
Radio Gallery, 66, 213, 282, 296

Radio News Bureau, 176
Radio-Television Galleries, 51, 52, 53, 55, 66, 70, 72, 86, 166, 227 (tables), 283, 379, 380
Radio-Television News Directors Association, 86
Randall, Samuel J., 42, 43, 44, 47
Randolph, Jennings, 211
Rankin, John, 302
Rarick, John R., 435
Rash, Bryson, 283
Rassadin, Gregorii, 48
Rather, Dan, 287
Rayburn, Sam, 45, 58, 67, 284, 387
Rayburn Rule, 67
Reader's Digest, 225 (table), 273, 279
Reardon, Paul C., 462, 463
Reardon Report, 462
Reasoner, Harry, 365
Red Lion decision, 361, 364, 410
Reed, Thomas B., 45
Reedy, George, 285
Reese, Bob, 388, 397
Register of Debates, 8
Reid, Ogden, 412
Reporters Committee for Freedom of the Press, 449
Reporters of Senate news, 250, 251, 252, 253-69; attacks upon, by senators, 264-65; in conflicts with senators, 265, 266, 267; and cooperation with senators, 267-68; exclusives for, 262, 263, 264, 266; friendship ploy by, 263-64; influence on sources for, 256-57; as informal advisors, 258, 260; and interviews, off-the-record, 262, 263; and intra-Senate conflict, 268-69; and leaks, 262, 263, 264, 265; limited sources for, 254-56; news defined by, 257-58, 260; and off-the-record interviews, 262, 263; political role of, 257; "pressuring" by, 259, 260; sanctions imposed on, 265; and two levels of reporting, 254; *see also* Congressional correspondents; News media; Newspapers; Press
Republican National Committee, 56, 105, 123, 347
Republican party, 41, 188, 215, 282, 290, 294, 299
Reston, James, 260, 267
Reynolds, Don B., 316, 320, 321
Reynolds, Frank, 287
Ribicoff, Abraham, 63, 209, 272
Richards, Myra, 274
Richardson, Elliot, 459
Ridder Publications, 173
Riedel, Richard L., 239, 269-83 ("A View from the President's Room")
Rivers, L. Mendel, 314, 326

Rivers, William L., 183, 375 *n.*
Roberts, Charles, 287
Robinson, Max, 333
Rogers, Paul G , 210
Rogers, William P., 71, 74, 199, 300
Roosevelt, Eleanor, 274
Roosevelt, Franklin D., 66, 105, 280, 282, 283, 285, 349
Roosevelt, Theodore, 286, 293
Roper survey, 140
Rosenbloom v. *Metromedia*, 414, 415, 426
Rosenfeld, Harry, 331, 332, 338, 339, 343
Rosten, Leo C., 183
Roth, William V., 63
Rourke, Francis E., 99, 100, 128-34 ("Congressional Use of Publicity"), 444, 446
Roush, J. Edward, 396
Royce, Dick, 211
Royster, Vermont, 457
Ruby, Jack, 462
Ruhl, Robert W., 296
Rusk, Dean, 71, 75, 354, 356
Russell, Richard B., 69, 114, 243, 270
Ruyle, Jane, 55

St. Louis Post-Dispatch, 152, 173, 218, 219, 253, 290, 292, 451
Salant, Richard, 69, 425
Salt Lake Tribune, 49
Saltonstall, Leverett, 276
San Antonio Express, 150
San Antonio News, 150
San Francisco Chronicle, 150, 393, 396
San Francisco Examiner, 393
Saturday Evening Post, 283, 284
Schechter, Barbara, 167
Scherer, Ray, 287
Schiebel Washington Bureau News, Kenneth M., 224 (table)
Schwartz, Louis B., 461
Science magazine, 159
Science Service, 224 (table)
Scott, Arthur, 282
Scott, Hugh, 107, 108, 118, 120, 121, 122, 123, 363, 364, 365
Scranton Tribune, 388
Scripps-Howard Newspaper Alliance, 49, 173
Seaton, William W., 8
Seattle Post-Intelligencer, 294, 295
Seattle Times, 292, 295
Secrecy and Publicity: Dilemmas of Democracy (Rourke), 128
Secrest, David, 54
Secret Diary of Harold L. Ickes, The, 59 *n.*
Sedition Act, 401

"Selling of the Pentagon, The" (CBS documentary), 404, 406, 412, 417, 418, 420, 421, 422, 425, 431, 432, 437, 451, 455
Seminar magazine, 180 *n.*
Senate, 7, 94, 95, 100, 106, 113, 131, 132, 133, 134, 174, 177, 198, 206, 207, 209, 239, 241, 245, 250, 252; Appropriations Committee of, 6, 214; Armed Services Committee of, 62, 210; Banking and Currency Committee of, 259, 319; Commerce Committee of, 62, 106; correspondents' coverage of, 227 (tables), 253-69 (*see also* Reporters of Senate news); Finance Committee of, 62, 108, 209, 272; Foreign Relations Committee of, 71, 75, 77, 88, 104, 118, 120, 210, 276, 354, 356; Interior and Insular Affairs Committee of, 62; Judiciary Committee of, 62, 345, 359-67 *passim*, 448, 458; Labor and Public Welfare Committee of, 62; letter-writers in (Marbut), 28-38; Periodical Gallery of, 55; Photographers' Gallery of, 54, 56, 282; press as source of information for, 259-60; Press Gallery of, 41, 46, 51, 54, 154, 166, 204, 251, 254, 261; Public Works Committee of, 211; publicity hounds in, 260-61, 264; as publicity machine, 132; Radio-Television Gallery of, 55, 70, 283; Select Committee of, on Presidential Campaign Activities, 345, 458, 459, 460, 466, 468, 469, 471, 473, 474, 475, 476, 477, 480, 481, 482, 483, 486, 487; *see also* Congress; Congressional correspondents; President's Room; Reporters of Senate news
Senate Majority Leader, 250
Sevareid, Eric, 273, 353, 354
Sevier, Ambrose H., 30
Sexism, 149
Shannon, Eileen, 395
Sheehan, John J., 298
Shield legislation, 440, 449-57
Sidey, Hugh, 287
Sigma Delta Chi, 50, 310, 441, 449
Sirhan, Sirhan, 462
Sirica, John J., 459, 461, 463, 464-68 ("Fair Trial and the Watergate Hearings")
Sisk, B. F., 73, 77, 78, 79, 81-89 *passim*
Sixth Amendment, 462
Slawski, Edward J., 192 *n.*
Small, William, 58, 66-70 ("Equality of Access for Broadcast Journalism"), 78, 79, 80, 81, 84, 86, 87, 88, 89, 345, 352-56 ("Congress, Television and War Protests")

Smith, A. Robert, 264 n., 288-300 ("Senator Wayne Morse: A Correspondent's View")
Smith, Carleton, 66
Smith, H. Alexander, 276
Smith, H. Allen, 79, 80, 81, 83, 87
Smith, Margaret Chase, 208
Smith, Merriman, 45, 287
Smith, Robert A., 239
Smith, Samuel Harrison, 7, 8, 15, 17, 18, 29
Smith, Scot, 340
Smyth, Jeannette, 346, 367-70 ("TV Lights, Invitations, Kisses and Phone Calls")
Southard, Samuel, 34, 35, 37, 38
Southern Caucus, 213
Southern Patriot, 31, 33
Soviet Union, 110, 158
Spain, 109
Sparkman, John J., 319
Speaker of the House, 250
Speaker's Lobby, 163, 209, 215
SST, 202, 387
Staggers, Harley O., 394, 405-12 passim, 426, 434, 438, 454
Standing Committee of Correspondents, 40-48, 52, 54, 57, 169, 215
Stanton, Frank, 354, 364, 365, 406, 407, 409, 410, 412, 413, 419, 421, 422, 428, 431, 432, 433, 434, 454
State Department, 46, 48, 168, 185, 255, 301, 303, 306
State of the Union messages, Johnson's, 101
States' Rights, 359 n.
Steele, Jack, 304
Steffens, Lincoln, 450
Stein, John, 212
Steinman, Clay, 396
Stennis, John, 73, 204, 205, 210, 213, 353, 354
Sterling, Don, Jr. 293
Stern, Laurence, 239, 310, 311, 315-22 ("The News Media and the Bobby Baker Case")
Stevenson, Adlai, 294, 299
Stevenson, Charles, 279
Stevenson, Francis Xavier, 279
Stone, I. F., 215
Stonehouse, M. F., 46
Stripling, Bob, 304, 305, 306, 307
Sulzberger, C. L., 287
Sunday Observer (London), 159
Superintendents (gallery), 55, 56-57; salaries of, 51
Superior Films v. Department of Education, 415

Superior Films v. Department of Education, 415
Supreme Court, 215, 309, 361, 401, 402, 407, 408, 410, 413, 414, 415, 416, 424, 425, 438, 440, 447, 456, 464
Supreme Court, and the News Media, The (Grey), ix n.
Susquehanna Broadcasting Company, 177, 225 (table)
Sutton, Robert, 35, 37

Tacheron, Donald G., 346, 370-84 ("Keeping in Touch with the People, Getting Along with the Press . . .")
Taft, Robert A., 267, 279, 292
Taft-Hartley bill, 293
Talbott, Harold, 259
Talmadge, Herman E., 215, 367, 368, 369, 370
Taylor, Davis, 448
Taylor, Telford, 349
Teamsters Union, 130
Teapot Dome scandals, 259
Telephony, 175, 225 (table)
Television, 106, 107, 108, 109, 114, 115, 116, 119, 122, 125, 126, 140, 148, 149, 171, 178, 179, 197, 209, 225 (table), 244, 245, 246, 247, 283, 345; access to, public, theory of, 365, 409; cable, 363, 391; and CHNS rates, 397; civil-rights filibuster covered by (1964), 67-70; and Congress, 138, 139, 380, 381, 386, 391, 392, 393; and coverage of Congress, question of adequacy of, 217, 218; educational, 86; and governmental control, freedom from, 358; House rejection of coverage by, 67, 325; and impact of presidential appearances, 109-13; as ordeal for witness in congressional hearing, 347; power of, 360, 363, 365, 366, 437; public access to, theory of, 365, 409; relied on by correspondents, 183, 184, 234 (table); sanctions imposed on, 212, 214; and Vietnam, 107, 111, 112, 352-56; in Watergate hearings, damaging presence of (Agnew), 476; see also Broadcast groups; Broadcast networks; Congressional Hearings; Radio-Television Galleries
Thomasson, Dan K., 49, 50
Thompson, Frank, 325
Thomson Newspapers, Inc., 173
Thornton, Harry, 454
Thurmond, Strom, 364 n.
Tiger in the Senate (Smith), 288
Time magazine, 183, 184, 218, 219, 225 (table), 233 (table), 252
Timmons News Service, 49

To Be a Congressman: The Promise and the Power (Groennings and Hawley, eds.), 240

To Kill a Messenger (Small), 66, 352

"Today," 95, 127

Tonkin resolution, 109, 113, 354

Traffic World, 175, 225 (table)

Tragedy of History, A (Bert and Peter Andrews), 300, 308

Transradio Press Service, 66

Trees, George, 341

Trohan, Walter, 290

Trout, Bob, 282

Truman, Harry S, 67, 259, 290, 291, 292, 297, 298, 463

Truth-in-Negotiations Act, 312, 314

Tufty News Bureau, 173

Tugman, and Morse, 291, 292, 293, 295

Tunney, John, 364 *n.*

TV Digest, 438

Twain, Mark, 329

Tydings, Millard, 351

Tyler, John, 34

Udall, Morris K., 325, 346, 370-84 ("Keeping in Touch with the People, Getting Along with the Press . . .")

Un-American Activities Committee, House, 67, 258, 301, 302, 303, 306, 307, 308

Underground Press Service, 40, 49

United Feature Syndicate, 224 (table)

United Nations, 279, 354

United Press International (UPI), 45, 49, 54, 70, 155, 160, 161, 167, 171, 172, 185, 216, 219, 223 (table), 253*n.*, 296

United States Information Agency, 46-47

U.S. Medicine, 175, 225 (table)

U.S. News and World Report, 66, 233 (table)

U.S. Senators and Their World (Matthews), 253

Vail, Thomas, 312, 313

Vandenberg, Arthur, 267, 277, 279

Vend magazine, 317

Vesco, Robert L., 484

Vietnam, 88, 110, 141, 188, 199, 200, 245, 279, 310, 322, 327, 345, 355, 443, 455; and television, 107, 111, 112, 352-56

"Vietnam Perspective" broadcasts, 353

Village Voice, 215

Von Hoffman, Nicholas, 50

Voting Rights Act (1965), 281

Waggoner, Joe, 204

Waldie, Jerome R., 322, 323, 324, 326

Wall Street Journal, 159, 173, 179, 184, 185, 218, 219, 233 (table), 286, 309, 333, 363

Wallace, George, 54, 245

Wallace, Henry, 294

Walters, Robert, 346 *n.*

Ward, Ray, 312, 313

Warner, Albert, 66

Warner, Mrs. Murray, 291

Warren, Ernie, 293

Washington, George, 122

Washington, L. Q., 42

Washington Daily News, 318, 396

Washington Freedom of Information Center, 325

Washington Globe, 8

Washington Monthly, 322

Washington Post, 50, 95 *n.*, 118, 149, 158, 172, 173, 174, 182, 183, 184, 185, 198, 218, 219, 233 (table), 240, 244, 251, 259, 303, 311, 316, 317, 320, 321, 331, 332, 333, 337, 338-39, 343, 367, 459, 469, 470, 479-82 ("Due Process and the President")

Washington press corps, 93, 156, 157, 158, 180, 221, 261, 309, 362, 381; *see also* Congressional correspondents; National Press Club

Washington Star-News, 149, 150, 183, 191, 218, 219, 233 (table), 240, 244, 273, 293, 319, 331, 332, 333, 337, 340, 343, 476

Washington Times-Herald, 251, 274, 275, 290

Washington Witch Hunt (Andrews), 301

Washingtonian magazine, 331

Water Pollution Control Act (1970), 338

Watergate, 100, 332, 338, 339, 340, 344, 389, 403, 452, 455, 459, 461, 462, 463, 464, 470

Watergate hearings, 346, 368, 369, 402, 403, 458, 459, 460; and due process of law, 468-72, 473, 479-82; and fair trial (Sirica), 464-68; Lardner on, 460-64; London *Times* on, 468-72, 480, 481; safeguards missing at (Agnew), 472-79; TV's damaging presence at (Agnew), 476; *Washington Post* on, 479-82; as witch hunt, 486-87; Witcover on, 459, 482-85

Watkins, Charles, 293

Watson, Murray, 386

Watzman, Sanford (Whitey), 309, 312, 313, 314, 315

Ways and Means Committee, House, 62, 189, 333

Wayward Pressman, The (Liebling), 156

WBNS-TV, 177, 226 (table)

WDEF-TV, 451

Weaver, Andrew, 289

Weicker, Lowell P., Jr., 248, 368, 370, 390, 482, 485, 486
Weiler, Joseph, 454
West, Benjamin, 54
Westerman, Sylvia, 353
Western Stamp Collector, 175, 225 (table)
Whalen, Charles W., 314, 424
Wheeler, William, 305, 306
Whig party, 34
Whipple, Robert B., 298
White, Byron R., 361, 402, 447, 448, 449, 450
White, Harry Dexter, 290
White, James, 5, 40, 50-57 ("Modern Accommodation: The New Patronage?")
White, Wendy, 167
White, William Allen, 329
White, William S., 47, 267, 273, 287
White House, 168, 185, 218, 220, 221, 239, 254, 255, 286, 388, 389
White House Correspondents' Association, 45, 50
White House News Photographers' Association, 82
Whitehead, Don, 298
Who Runs Congress? (Green et al.), 384
Who's Who, 188
Wicker, Tom, 409
Wiggins, J. Russell, 58, 59-63 ("Emigration of Power to the Little Legislatures"), 317
Wight, E. B., 42, 43

Wiley, Alexander, 276, 277
Wilkinson, Clyde, 282
Williams, John J., 114, 319
Williams Washington News Service, Jack, 71-72, 177, 225 (table)
Wills, Joseph E., 41, 54, 279
Wilson, Roger, 386
Wilson, Woodrow, 66, 128, 280
Witcover, Jules, 171, 459, 482-85 ("Trial by Publicity?")
Witman, William H., 30
Witness (Chambers), 308
WMAL AM-FM-TV, 87, 148, 226 (table), 282
Wolfson, Lewis W., 167, 240, 331-44 ("The Press and Washington's Own Suburban Five")
Women's Liberation, 359
Woodward, Bob, 459, 486-87 ("Nixon and His Aides Believe Hearing Is a Witchhunt")
WTOP News AM-FM, 87, 226 (table), 234 (table), 282

York Gazette and Daily, 294
Young, John, 81, 82
Young, Stephen, 312, 314

Zagoria, Sam, 251
Zengler, John Peter, 432
Zwick, David R., 384-87 (". . . And, Frankly, Getting Re-elected")
Zwicker, Ralph, 483, 484